{ CHAPTER OPENERS

1 Self-Management and *Slumdog Millionaire*

2 Learning Style and *Mr. Holland's Opus*

3 Individual Character and *The Blind Side*

4 Self-Confidence and *Red Eye*

5 Time Management and *27 Dresses*

6 Resiliency and *Forrest Gump*

7 Critical Thinking and *Tron: Legacy*

8 Empowerment and *Patch Adams*

9 Tolerance for Ambiguity and *The Terminal*

10 Professionalism and *Iron Man 2*

11 Integrity and *Love Happens*

12 Ambition and *The Social Network*

13 Engagement and *The Incredibles*

14 Team Contributions and *Lost*

15 Communication/Networking and *The Devil Wears Prada*

16 Diversity Maturity and *Finding Forrester*

17 Cultural Awareness and *The Amazing Race*

18 Risk Taking and *The Bourne Ultimatum*

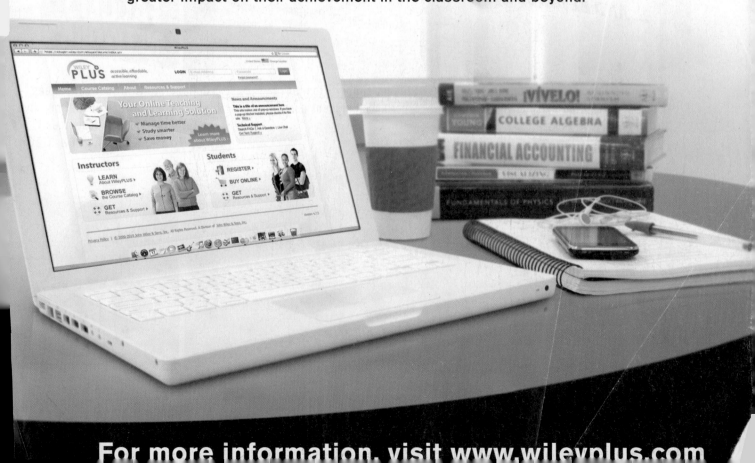

{ THIRD EDITION

Exploring Management

John R. Schermerhorn, Jr.

Ohio University

WILEY

John Wiley & Sons, Inc.

VICE PRESIDENT & EXECUTIVE PUBLISHER	George Hoffman
EXECUTIVE EDITOR	Lisé Johnson
DEVELOPMENTAL EDITOR	Susan McLaughlin
ASSOCIATE EDITOR	Sarah Vernon
PROJECT EDITOR	Brian Baker
ASSOCIATE DIRECTOR OF MARKETING	Amy Scholz
MARKETING MANAGER	Kelly Simmons
MARKETING ASSISTANT	Ashley Tomeck
DESIGN DIRECTOR	Harry Nolan
INTERIOR DESIGNER	Tom Nery
SENIOR CONTENT MANAGER	Dorothy Sinclair
SENIOR PRODUCTION EDITOR	Erin Bascom
EXECUTIVE MEDIA EDITOR	Allison Morris
MEDIA SPECIALISTS	Elena Santa Maria and Thomas Caruso
PHOTO DEPARTMENT MANAGER	Hilary Newman
PHOTO RESEARCHER	Teri Stratford
EDITORIAL ASSISTANT	Melissa Solarz
ILLUSTRATION EDITOR	Anna Melhorn
PRODUCTION MANAGEMENT SERVICES	Ingrao Associates
COVER DESIGNER	Wendy Lai
COVER PHOTO	© Kaitlyn Watson
UMBRELLA ICON	© Monti26/Shutterstock

This book was typeset in 10/12 Kepler Std Regular at Aptara®, Inc. and printed and bound by Courier/Kendallville. The cover was printed by Courier/Kendallville.

This book is printed on acid free paper. ∞

Founded in 1807, John Wiley & Sons, Inc. has been a valued source of knowledge and understanding for more than 200 years, helping people around the world meet their needs and fulfill their aspirations. Our company is built on a foundation of principles that include responsibility to the communities we serve and where we live and work. In 2008, we launched a Corporate Citizenship Initiative, a global effort to address the environmental, social, economic, and ethical challenges we face in our business. Among the issues we are addressing are carbon impact, paper specifications and procurement, ethical conduct within our business and among our vendors, and community and charitable support. For more information, please visit our website: www.wiley.com/go/citizenship.

Evaluation copies are provided to qualified academics and professionals for review purposes only, for use in their courses during the next academic year. These copies are licensed and may not be sold or transferred to a third party. Upon completion of the review period, please return the evaluation copy to Wiley. Return instructions and a free of charge return shipping label are available at www.wiley.com/go/returnlabel. If you have chosen to adopt this textbook for use in your course, please accept this book as your complimentary desk copy. Outside of the United States, please contact your local representative.

ISBN 13 978-0-470-87821-7
        978-1-118-2935-7

Printed in the United States of America.

10 9 8 7 6 5 4 3 2

■ *I once again dedicate this book to the person who lovingly helps me explore and appreciate life's wonders: My wife, Ann.*

■About the Author

DR. JOHN R. SCHERMERHORN JR. is the Charles G. O'Bleness Professor Emeritus of Management in the College of Business at Ohio University where he teaches undergraduate and MBA courses in management, organizational behavior, and Asian business. He earned a PhD degree in organizational behavior from Northwestern University, after receiving an MBA degree (with distinction) in management and international business from New York University, and a BS degree in business administration from the State University of New York at Buffalo.

Highly dedicated to instructional excellence and serving the needs of practicing managers, Dr. Schermerhorn focuses on bridging the gap between the theory and practice of management both in the classroom and in his textbooks. He has won awards for teaching excellence at Tulane University, The University of Vermont, and Ohio University, where he was named a *University Professor*, the university's leading campus-wide award for undergraduate teaching. He also received the excellence in leadership award for his service as Chair of the Management Education and Development Division of the Academy of Management.

Dr. Schermerhorn's international experience adds a unique global dimension to his teaching and textbooks. He holds an honorary doctorate from the University of Pécs in Hungary, awarded for his international scholarly contributions to management research and education. He has also served as a Visiting Professor of Management at the Chinese University of Hong Kong, as on-site Coordinator of the Ohio University MBA and Executive MBA programs in Malaysia, and as Kohei Miura visiting professor at the Chubu University of Japan. Presently he is Adjunct Professor at the National University of Ireland at Galway, a member of the graduate faculty at Bangkok University in Thailand, and Permanent Lecturer in the PhD program at the University of Pécs in Hungary.

An enthusiastic scholar, Dr. Schermerhorn is a member of the Academy of Management, where he served as chairperson of the Management Education and Development Division. Educators and students alike know him as author of *Management 11e* (Wiley, 2011) and senior co-author of *Organizational Behavior 12e* (Wiley, 2012). His many books are available in Chinese, Dutch, French, Indonesian, Portuguese, Russian, and Spanish language editions. Dr. Schermerhorn has also published numerous articles in publications such as the *Academy of Management Journal, Academy of Management Review, Academy of Management Executive, Organizational Dynamics, Journal of Management Education, and the Journal of Management Development.*

Dr. Schermerhorn is a popular guest speaker at colleges and universities. His recent student and faculty workshop topics include innovations in business education, teaching the millennial generation, global perspectives in management, and textbook writing and scholarly manuscript development.

{ DEAR READER:

Welcome to *Exploring Management, Third Edition.*

I hope you find it both interesting and useful as you prepare for future career success. My own career as a management educator has been a journey of wonderful exploration and personal growth. I have been continuously enriched by the opportunity to learn from my students and colleagues around the world.

I believe the study of management is also an exploration, a daily one, whether we are instructors or students. After all, management is part of our everyday lives—at work, at school, at home, and even at leisure. It is ever present as we sort through the challenges of multiple responsibilities, distant horizons, constantly changing opportunities, great potential, and the wonders of a diverse global community.

Perhaps these words from T. S. Eliot's poem *Little Gidding* best describe the quest we all share:

> *We shall not cease from exploration*
> *And the end of all our exploring*
> *Will be to arrive where we started*
> *And know the place for the first time.*

The study of management is an ongoing journey, one full of enrichment and exploration. But in the end we return to application, trying to use what we have learned through experience to better our lives and those of others. This is really what this book, *Exploring Management, Third Edition,* is all about.

Take a minute to look at the book's cover, browse through the book's overall design, and just flip through some of the pages. Does the art inspire you and the design attract you to consider not only what's ahead in the book and in your management course, but also in your own life? I hope so. Because after all, how well we manage our lives, careers, and organizations can make a big difference in our increasingly complex world.

Please join me in using *Exploring Management, Third Edition,* and your management course as great learning opportunities, ones that can have life-long career and personal benefits. I believe you'll find the experience rich with the potential for lasting personal and professional value.

Have a great course and a valuable learning experience.

Sincerely,

John Schermerhorn

▪ Preface

||| What makes *Exploring Management, Third Edition*, different?

Students tell me over and over again that they learn best when their courses and assignments fit well in the context of their everyday lives, career aspirations, and personal experiences. I have written *Exploring Management, Third Edition* to meet and engage the new generation of students in their personal spaces. It uses lots of examples, applications, visual highlights, and learning aids to convey the essentials of management. It also asks students lots of thought-provoking questions as they read. My hope is that this special approach and underlying pedagogy will help management educators work in many unique and innovative ways to enrich the learning experiences of their students.

▪ *Exploring Management* offers a flexible, topic-specific presentation.

The first thing you'll notice is that *Exploring Management* presents material in a way that meets student preferences for reading and studying "chunks" of material that can be digested in relatively short time periods. This is in direct response to my classroom experiences where I, and my students, find the typical book chapters increasingly cumbersome to handle. In *Exploring Management* students never read more than several pages before hitting a "Study Guide" section that asks and allows them to bring closure to what they have just read in a meaningful way. When students can read and achieve closure on a "chapter" of material, they tend to study it better, remember it better, and achieve better on tests and assignments dealing with it.

Topics in the book are easily assignable and sized just right for a class session or a class discussion. Although presented in the traditional planning, organizing, leading, and controlling framework, everything can be used in any order based on instructor preferences. There are many options available for courses of different types, lengths, and meeting schedules, including online and distance learning formats. It all depends on what fits best with your course design, learning approaches, and class session objectives.

▪ *Exploring Management* uses an integrated learning design.

Every chapter opens with a catchy subtitle and clear visual presentation that help students understand material right from the beginning. The opening **Management Live** vignette links chapter topics with popular culture examples from movies and television. Key learning objectives are listed in **Your Chapter Takeaways**, and **What's Inside** highlights five interesting and useful chapter features—Explore Yourself, Role Models, Ethics Check, Facts to Consider, and Manager's Library. Within the chapter, each major section begins with a visual overview that helps students frame their reading. The overview poses a **Takeaway** question with **Answers to Come**—a listing of answers to the takeaway question as found in the section subheadings. Each major section ends with a **Study Guide**—a one-page checkpoint for learning and test preparation allows students to pause, consolidate, and check learning before moving on to the next section. The study guide elements include

- *Rapid Review*—bullet-list summary of concepts and points,
- *Terms to Define*—glossary quiz for vocabulary development,
- *Be Sure You Can*—checkpoint of major learning outcomes for mastery,
- *Questions for Discussion*—questions to stimulate inquiry and prompt class discussions,
- *What Would You Do?*—asks students to apply section topics to a problem-solving situation.

||| How will *Exploring Management, Third Edition*, motivate students to learn about management?

Today's students continuously deal with a wide variety of conflicting demands and distractions. In working with them, I find that my teaching methods and instructional materials must constantly evolve. That's why I have taken special care to write *Exploring Management, Third Edition*, with a student-friendly writing style, emphasis on visual learning, inclusion of lots of timely features and examples, and an appealing design to the book's pages. I hope you'll agree that I am writing and presenting material in ways that come closer to meeting our students in their spaces—rich, varied, colorful, spontaneous, and digital.

■ *Exploring Management* relates concepts to students' experiences and interests.

To better connect with the student reader, *Exploring Management* includes a number of special features that present timely content in a visually appealing and meaningful way. The following features are not only interesting to the reader, they are also prompts and frames that can be used for class discussions and assignments.

- **Role Models**—introduces a real person's experience with the issues being discussed and asks students to answer What's the Lesson Here? Examples include Ursula Burns, CEO of Xerox and the first African American woman to head a *Fortune* 500 firm; Jeff Bezos, founder and CEO of Amazon; and Gary Hirshberg, social entrepreneur and Co-founder of Stonyfield Farms.
- **Ethics Check**—poses an ethical dilemma and asks students to answer "You Decide" examples including "Good and Bad News for Middle Managers," "Millennials May Need Special Handling," "Recession a Great Time for Prioritizing," and "Internet Censorship Spurs Cultural Debate."
- **Explore Yourself**—reminds students how chapter content relates to important personal skills and characteristics, and asks them to "Get to Know Yourself Better" by taking self-assessments and completing other active learning activities. Examples include self-management, learning style, integrity, self-confidence, diversity maturity, and cultural awareness.
- **Facts to Consider**—brief summary of data and facts that stimulate critical inquiry and offer fuel for class discussions and debates asks students "What Are Your Thoughts?" after considering the facts presented. Examples include "Diversity Contradictions in Employment Trends," "Office Romance Policies Vary Widely," and "Corruption and Bribes Haunt International Business."
- **Manager's Library**—brief review of a popular book that is on the reading list of many managers, and asks students to "Reflect and React" to what the book is all about. Examples include **Delivering Happiness** by Tony Hsieh, **Women Count** by Susan Bulkeley Butler, and **The Trophy Kids Grow Up** by Ron Alsop.

■ *Exploring Management* uses a conversational and interactive writing style.

The author's voice in *Exploring Management* breaks away from the textbook norm of communicating as the "sage on stage." So, I have tried to speak with students the way I do in the classroom—conversationally, interactively, and in a nondidactic fashion. User experiences with the second edition confirmed that this is the right approach.

Although it may seem unusual to have an author speaking directly to his audience, just as with this preface, my goal is to be a real person and to approach the student readers in the spirit of what Ellen Langer calls *mindful learning*.[1] She describes this as engaging students from a perspective of active inquiry rather than as consumers of facts and prescriptions. I view it as a way of trying to move textbook writing in the same direction we are moving our teaching—being less didactic and more interactive, trying to involve students in a dialog around meaningful topics, questions, examples, and even dilemmas.

In short, I want students to actively question and engage the world around them; I want them to be informed; I want them to take ownership of the principles and insights of our discipline. Don't you want the same, and more?

■ *Exploring Management* visually enhances the content presentation to appeal to visual learners.

Most students are very visual in their attention to information; this is a reflection of trends in popular culture. They watch movies, play video games, read and work online, chat, follow Facebook, and Tweet—often all at once! This has to make a difference in how they approach their courses, and it is why I visually enhance the presentation of text content in two significant ways.

First, in *major figures* that have some complexity the figure title or caption is posed as a question. I then answer that question both in the figure drawing and in a short narrative summary below the figure. I call these "talking figures" in that the narrative speaks to the reader as he or she visualizes the topic being discussed.

Second, I periodically supplement the running text presentation with visual highlights. Whether it is a *table* that briefly lists important points, a *boxed highlight* that summarizes a key point or theory, or a *mini-figure* that schematically summarizes a

---

[1]Ellen J. Langer, *The Power of Mindful Learning* (Reading, MA: Perseus, 1997).

concept under discussion, everything is designed to fit into and flow naturally with the text. These visual accents and reminders are designed as informative parts of a holistic reading experience, much as we engage when reading magazines, newspapers, and Internet content.

||| How will *Exploring Management, Third Edition*, ensure that students understand and apply management concepts and practices?

Good things, like the field of management itself, grow from strong foundations. As instructors we need to help our students not only gain those foundations, but also see the connections to the real world of management applications and practices. We need to help them develop intellectual capital that is supported by personal capacities for growth, continuous learning, and good old-fashioned hard work.

■ *Exploring Management* includes a carefully selected set of end-of-chapter learning activities.

Keeping in mind what often matters most to students—grades—my first priority is to help them prepare for quizzes and tests and to earn the best possible grades in their course. **Test Prep** asks students to answer multiple choice, short response, and integration and application questions to provide a good starting point for testing success. When coupled with the additional interactive test versions available on the *Exploring Management* student companion Web site, Test Prep becomes a substantial learning resource.

Once the Test Prep is complete, students are directed to additional active learning and personal development activities that fit chapter content. These activities are found in two end-of-book sections—the **Skill-Building Portfolio** and **Cases for Critical Thinking**.

- **Skill-Building Portfolio**—includes **Self-Assessments**, **Class Exercises**, and **Team Projects**. Each has been carefully chosen to be a good match for the recommended chapters, a sound way of engaging students in further reflection and skills development, and an enriching opportunity for individual or team assignments.
- **Cases for Critical Thinking**—offers **Chapter Cases** that engage students in critical thinking about timely situations and events involving real people in organizations. Written in magazine style, many with sidebars that become mini-cases in themselves, each case can be used for both class discussion and individual or team assignments.

Each chapter is accompanied by a chapter **Self-Assessment,** found in the end of the book, chosen to complement the subject matter. Examples include Learning Tendencies, Internal/External Locus of Control, and Managerial Assumptions. Students score and interpret the assessments to encourage greater self-reflection and personal exploration. A **Case Snapshot** introduces the recommended case study using a "tag line" and magazine format to interest the student reader and focus him or her on key issues and themes relevant to material being studied. Further, the **Online Interactive Learning Resources** section includes recommended active-learning activities (located online and in WileyPLUS). These include **More Self-Assessments**—to help students to further explore their managerial skills, tendencies, and personal characteristics; **Experiential Exercises**—for class activities and teamwork relating to the chapter content; and at least one **Team Project**—an active-learning group assignment that requires research, writing, and presentation on a current topic or issue.

■ Student and Instructor Resources

||| What additional special materials does *Exploring Management, Third Edition*, offer to both instructors and students?

When it comes to support packages, it's always helpful to have a lot of useful material available. With that in mind, I worked closely with Wiley and my colleagues in designing materials for instructors and students that extend the goals of this book. The next two pages are just a sampler of the additional resources that can enrich your course.

- **Companion Web Site** The Companion Web site for *Exploring Management* at http://www.wiley.com/college/schermerhorn, contains a myriad of tools and links to aid both teaching and learning, including nearly all of the resources described in this section.

- **Instructor's Resource Guide** Prepared by Susan Verhulst, Des Moines Area Community College, the Instructor's Resource Guide includes a Conversion Guide; Chapter Outlines; Chapter Objectives; Teaching Notes on how to integrate and assign special features; and suggested answers for all quiz and test questions found in the text. A series of Lecture Notes are included to help integrate the various resources available. The Instructor's Resource Guide also includes additional discussion questions and assignments that relate specifically to the cases, as well as case notes, self-assessments, and team exercises.

- **Test Bank** This Test Bank prepared by Amit Shah, Frostburg State University, consists of over 40 true/false, multiple-choice, and short-answer questions per chapter. It was specifically designed so that the questions vary in degree of difficulty, from straightforward recall to challenging, to offer instructors the most flexibility when designing their exams. Adding more flexibility is the *Computerized Test Bank*, which requires a PC running Windows. The Computerized Test Bank, which contains all the questions from the manual version, includes a test-generating program that allows instructors to customize their exams.

- **PowerPoint Slides** Prepared by Susan Verhulst, Des Moines Area Community College, this set of interactive PowerPoint slides includes lecture notes to accompany each slide. This resource provides another visual enhancement and learning aid for students, as well as additional talking points for instructors. Instructors can access the PowerPoint slides and lecture notes on the instructor portion of the book's Web site.

- **Personal Response System** PRS or "Clicker" content for each chapter will spark additional discussion and debate in the classroom. For more information on PRS, please contact your local Wiley sales representative.

- **Web Quizzes** This resource, prepared by Amit Shah, Frostburg State University, available on the student portion of the *Exploring Management* companion Web site, offers online quizzes, with questions varying in level of difficulty, designed to help students evaluate their individual progress through a chapter. Each chapter's quiz includes 10 questions. These review questions, developed by the Test Bank author, were created to provide the most effective and efficient testing system. Within this system, students have the opportunity to "practice" the type of knowledge they'll be expected to demonstrate on the exam.

- **New Management Weekly Updates** Keep you and your students updated and informed on the very latest in business news stories. Each week you will find links to 5 new articles, video clips, business news stories, and so much more with discussion questions to elaborate on the stories in the classroom. http://wileymanagementupdates.com

- **Management Calendar** Provides daily management tips for discussion.

- **Videos and Video Teaching Guide** were prepared by Jessica-April and Amit Shah, Frostburg State University. This set of short video clips provides an excellent starting point for lectures or for general classroom discussion.

- **Business Extra Select** Wiley has launched this online program, found at http://www.wiley.com/college/bxs, to provide instructors with millions of content resources, including an extensive database of cases, journals, periodicals, newspapers, and supplemental readings. This courseware system lends itself extremely well to integrating real-world content within the management course, thereby enabling instructors to convey the relevance of the course to their students.

■ WileyPLUS

WileyPLUS is an innovative, research-based, online environment for effective teaching and learning.

||| What do students receive with *WileyPLUS*?

A Research-based Design. *WileyPLUS* provides an online environment that integrates relevant resources, including the entire digital textbook, in an easy-to-navigate framework that helps students study more effectively.

- *WileyPLUS* adds structure by organizing textbook content into smaller, more manageable "chunks."
- Related media, examples, and sample practice items reinforce the learning objectives.
- Innovative features such as calendars, visual progress tracking, and self-evaluation tools improve time management and strengthen areas of weakness.

One-on-one Engagement. With *WileyPLUS* for *Exploring, 3rd Edition*, students receive 24/7 access to resources that promote positive learning outcomes. Students engage with related examples (in various media) and sample practice items, including:

- Animated Figures
- CBS/BBC videos
- Self-Assessments quizzes students can use to test themselves on topics such as emotional intelligence, diversity awareness, and intuitive ability.

- Management Calendar including Daily Management tips
- iPhone Applications for Download
- Flash Cards
- Hot Topic Modules
- Crossword Puzzles
- Self-Study Questions

Measurable Outcomes. Throughout each study session, students can assess their progress and gain immediate feedback. *WileyPLUS* provides precise reporting of strengths and weaknesses, as well as individualized quizzes, so that students are confident they are spending their time on the right things. With *WileyPLUS*, students always know the exact outcome of their efforts.

⫴ What do instructors receive with *WileyPLUS*?

WileyPLUS provides reliable, customizable resources that reinforce course goals inside and outside of the classroom as well as visibility into individual student progress. Pre-created materials and activities help instructors optimize their time:

Customizable Course Plan: *WileyPLUS* comes with a pre-created Course Plan designed by a subject matter expert uniquely for this course. Simple drag-and-drop tools make it easy to assign the course plan as-is or modify it to reflect your course syllabus.

Pre-created Activity Types Include:
- Questions
- Readings and resources
- Presentation
- Print Tests
- Concept Mastery
- Project

Course Materials and Assessment Content:
- Lecture Notes PowerPoint Slides
- Classroom Response System (Clicker) Questions
- Image Gallery
- Instructor's Manual
- Gradable Reading Assignment Questions (embedded with online text)
- Question Assignments: all end-of-chapter problems
- Testbank
- Pre- and Post-Lecture Quizzes
- Web Quizzes
- Video Teaching Notes—includes questions geared towards applying text concepts to current videos

Gradebook: *WileyPLUS* provides instant access to reports on trends in class performance, student use of course materials and progress towards learning objectives, helping inform decisions and drive classroom discussions.

WileyPLUS. Learn More. www.wileyplus.com.
Powered by proven technology and built on a foundation of cognitive research, *WileyPLUS* has enriched the education of millions of students, in over 20 countries around the world.

■ Acknowledgments

This isn't the typical "book" project that most publishers deal with, one developed from a neat proposal. Instead, *Exploring Management, Third Edition*, is a "concept" book, which began, grew, and found life and form in its first and second editions over the course of many telephone conversations, conference calls, e-mail exchanges, and face-to-face meetings. It has since matured and been refined in content, style, and direction as a third edition through the useful feedback provided by many satisfied users and reviewers. It has also benefited from the continued commitments and sharp eyes of a most professional staff at John Wiley & Sons.

As always, there wouldn't be an *Exploring Management* without the support, commitment, creativity, and dedication of the following members of the Wiley team. It's a team with which I am most proud to be associated. My thanks travel now to you all: Lisé Johnson, *Executive Editor*, who led the team with a helpful and steady hand, while always providing me what an author so often needs when struggling to accomplish seemingly elusive goals—friendship; George Hoffman, *Vice President and Publisher*; Sarah Vernon, *Assistant Editor*; Melissa Solarz, *Editorial Assistant*; Kelly Simmons, *Marketing Manager*; Sandra Dumas, *Senior Production Editor*; Harry Nolan, *Creative Director*; Hilary Newman, *Photo Manager*; Teri Stratford, *Photo Researcher*; and Anna Melhorn, *Illustration Editor*.

I am especially indebted to two of the Wiley team whose invaluable contributions were ever present through the many highs and lows of a very complex project—Susan McLaughlin, whose enthusiasm, initiative, and expertise provided the very best support as *Developmental Editor*, and Suzanne Ingrao, *Outside Production Service Manager* and head of Ingrao Associates, whose diligence and persistence led all of us through a demanding production cycle.

My special thanks go to Robert (Lenie) Holbrook of Ohio University for contributing the *Management Live* feature that introduces each chapter, the instructor's guide that shows instructors how to truly make this feature go "live" in their classrooms, and the creative supplement *Art Imitates Life* that more broadly describes how popular culture can be readily used to enhance student engagement and learning. The fine work of Brandon Warga of Kenyon College in creating a timely and compelling set of chapter cases is also appreciated.

Focus Group Participants:

Maria Aria, *Camden County College*
Ellen Benowitz, *Mercer County Community College*
John Brogan, *Monmouth University*
Lawrence J. Danks, *Camden County College*
Matthew DeLuca, *Baruch College*
David Fearon, *Central Connecticut State University*
Stuart Ferguson, *Northwood University*
Eugene Garaventa, *College of Staten Island*
Scott Geiger, *University of South Florida, St. Petersburg*

Larry Grant, *Bucks County Community College*
Fran Green, *Pennsylvania State University, Delaware County*
F. E. Hamilton, *Eckerd College*
Don Jenner, *Borough of Manhattan Community College*
John Podoshen, *Franklin and Marshall College*
Neuman Pollack, *Florida Atlantic University*
David Radosevich, *Montclair State University*
Moira Tolan, *Mount Saint Mary College*

Virtual Focus Group Participants:

George Alexakis, *Nova Southeastern University*
Steven Bradley, *Austin Community College*
Paula Brown, *Northern Illinois University*
Elnora Farmer, *Clayton State University*
Paul Gagnon, *Central Connecticut State University*
Eugene Garaventa, *College of Staten Island*
Larry Garner, *Tarleton State University*
Wayne Grossman, *Hofstra University*
Dee Guillory, *University of South Carolina, Beaufort*
Julie Hays, *University of St. Thomas*
Kathleen Jones, *University of North Dakota*
Marvin Karlins, *University of South Florida*

Al Laich, *University of Northern Virginia*
Vincent Lutheran, *University of North Carolina, Wiilmington*
Douglas L. Micklich, *Illinois State University*
David Oliver, *Edison College*
Jennifer Oyler, *University of Central Arkansas*
Kathleen Reddick, *College of Saint Elizabeth*
Terry L. Riddle, *Central Virginia Community College*
Roy L. Simerly, *East Carolina University*
Frank G. Titlow, *St. Petersburg College*
David Turnipseed, *Indiana University—Purdue University, Fort Wayne*
Michael Wakefield, *Colorado State University, Pueblo*
George A. (Bud) Wynn, *University of Tampa*

Reviewers:

M. David Albritton, *Northern Arizona University*
Mitchell Alegre, *Niagara University*
Karen R. Bangs, *California State Polytechnic University*
Heidi Barclay, *Metropolitan State University*
Patrick Bell, *Elon University*
Michael Bento, *Owens Community College*
William Berardi, *Bristol Community College*
Robert Blanchard, *Salem State University*
Peter Geoffrey Bowen, *University of Denver*
Ralph R. Braithwaite, *University of Hartford*
David Bright, *Wright State University-Dayton*
Kenneth G. Brown, *University of Iowa*
Diana Bullen, *Mesa Community College*
Beverly Bugay, *Tyler Junior College*
Robert Cass, *Virginia Wesleyan College*
Savannah Clay, *Central Piedmont Community College*
Suzanne Crampton, *Grand Valley State University*

Kathryn Dansky, *Pennsylvania State University*
Susan Davis, *Claflin University*
Jeanette Davy, *Wright State University*
Matt DeLuca, *Baruch College*
Karen Edwards, *Chemeketa Community College*
Valerie Evans, *Lincoln Memorial University*
Paul Ewell, *Bridgewater College*
Gary J. Falcone, *LaSalle University*
Elnora Farmer, *Clayton State University*
Gail E. Fraser, *Kean University*
Nancy Fredericks, *San Diego State University*
Larry Garner, *Tarleton State University*
Cindy Geppert, *Palm Beach State College*
Richard J. Gibson, *Embry-Riddle University*
Dee Guillory, *University of South Carolina, Beaufort*
Aaron Hines, *SUNY New Paltz*
Tammy Hunt, *University of North Carolina Wilmington*

Debra Hunter, *Troy University*
Kimberly Hurnes, *Washtenaw Community College*
Gary S. Insch, *West Virginia University*
Barcley Johnson, *Western Michigan University*
Louis Jourdan, *Clayton State University*
Edward Kass, *University of San Francisco*
Judith Kizzie, *Howard Community College*
Robert Klein, *Philadelphia University*
John Knutsen, *Everett Community College*
Al Laich, *University of Northern Virginia*
Susan Looney, *Delaware Technical & Community College*
Vincent Lutheran, *University of North Carolina, Wilmington*
Jim Maddox, *Friends University*
John Markert, *Wells College*
Marcia Marriott, *Monroe Community College*
Brenda McAleer, *Colby College*
Randy McCamery, *Tarleton State University*
Gerald McFry, *Coosa Valley Technical College*
Diane Minger, *Cedar Valley College*
Michael Monahan, *Frostburg State University*
Lam Nguyen, *Palm Beach State College*
Joelle Nisolle, *West Texas A&M University*

Penny Olivi, *York College of Pennsylvania*
Jennifer Oyler, *University of Central Arkansas*
Kathy Pederson, *Hennepin Technical College*
Nancy Ray-Mitchell, *McLennan Community College*
Catherine J. Ruggieri, *St. John's University*
Joseph C. Santora, *Essex County College*
Charles Seifert, *Siena College*
Sidney Siegel, *Drexel University*
Wendy Smith, *University of Delaware*
Howard Stanger, *Canisius College*
Henry A. Summers, *Stephen F. Austin State University*
Daryl J. Taylor, *Pasadena City College*
Jody Tolan, *University of Southern California, Marshall School of Business*
David Turnipseed, *Indiana University—Purdue University, Fort Wayne*
Robert Turrill, *University of Southern California*
Vickie Tusa, *Embry-Riddle University*
Michael Wakefield, *Colorado State University, Pueblo*
Charles D. White, *James Madison University*
Daniel Wubbena, *Western Iowa Tech Community College*
Alan Wright, *Henderson State University*

Student Focus Group Participants, Baruch College:

Farhana Alam, Laureen Attreed, Sarah Bohsali, Susanna Eng, Dino Genzano, Annie Gustave, Andrew Josefiak, Diana Pang, Vidushi Parmar, Dulari Ramkishun, Vicky Roginskaya, Jessica Scheiber, Ruta Skarbauskaite, Darren Smith, Anita Alickaj, Dana Fleischer, Mandie Gellis, Haider Mehmood, and Dina Shlafman

▪Brief Contents

{ Managers and Management

1   Managers and the Management Process: Everyone becomes a manager someday.   2

2   Management Learning: Great things grow from strong foundations.   30

3   Ethics and Social Responsibility: Character doesn't stay home when we go to work.   54

{ Planning and Controlling

4   Managers as Decision Makers: There is no substitute for a good decision.   84

5   Plans and Planning Techniques: Get there faster with objectives.   110

6   Controls and Control Systems: What gets measured happens.   132

7   Strategy and Strategic Management: Insight and hard work deliver results.   156

{ Organizing

8   Organization Structure and Design: It's all about working together.   178

9   Organizational Cultures, Innovation, and Change: Adaptability and values set the tone.   204

10   Human Resource Management: Nurturing turns potential into performance.   230

{ Leading

11   Leadership: A leader lives in each of us.   256

12   Individual Behavior: There's beauty in individual differences.   282

13   Motivation: Respect unlocks human potential.   306

14   Teams and Teamwork: Two heads really can be better than one.   330

15   Communication: Listening is the key to understanding.   358

{ Environment

16   Diversity and Global Cultures: There are new faces in the neighborhood.   382

17   Globalization and International Business: Going global isn't just for travelers.   402

18   Entrepreneurship and Small Business: Taking risks can make dreams come true.   422

Skill-Building Portfolio   SB-1

Cases for Critical Thinking   C-1

▪Detailed Contents

{1   **Managers and the Management Process**   2

1.1 What Does It Mean to Be a Manager?   4
- Organizations have different types and levels of managers.   4
- Accountability is a cornerstone of managerial performance.   6
- Effective managers help others achieve high performance and satisfaction.   6
- Managers must meet multiple changing expectations.   7

1.2 What Do Managers Do and What Skills Do They Use?   10
- Managerial work is often intense and demanding.   10
- Managers plan, organize, lead, and control.   11
- Managers enact informational, interpersonal, and decisional roles.   13
- Managers pursue action agendas and engage in networking.   14
- Managers use a variety of technical, human, and conceptual skills.   15
- Managers can and should learn from experience.   16

1.3 What Are Some Important Career Issues in the New Workplace?   19
- Globalization and job migration are changing the world of work.   19
- Failures of ethics and corporate governance are troublesome.   20
- Diversity and discrimination are continuing social priorities.   22
- Intellectual capital and self-management skills are essential for career success.   23

{2   **Management Learning**   30

2.1 What Are the Lessons of the Classical Management Approaches?   32
- Taylor's scientific management sought efficiency in job performance.   32
- Weber's bureaucratic organization is supposed to be efficient and fair.   34
- Fayol's administrative principles describe managerial duties and practices.   36

2.2 What Are the Contributions of the Behavioral Management Approaches?   38
- Follett viewed organizations as communities of cooperative action.   38
- The Hawthorne studies focused attention on the human side of organizations.   40
- Maslow described a hierarchy of human needs with self-actualization at the top.   41
- McGregor believed managerial assumptions create self-fulfilling prophecies.   42
- Argyris suggests that workers treated as adults will be more productive.   43

2.3 What Are the Foundations of Modern Management Thinking?   45
- Managers use quantitative analysis and tools to solve complex problems.   45
- Organizations are open systems that interact with their environments.   46
- Contingency thinking holds that there is no one best way to manage.   48
- Quality management focuses attention on continuous improvement.   49
- Evidence-based management seeks hard facts about what really works.   50

{3 Ethics and Social Responsibility 54

3.1 How Do Ethics and Ethical Behavior Play Out in the Workplace? 56
- Ethical behavior is values driven. 57
- What is considered ethical varies among moral reasoning approaches. 58
- What is considered ethical can vary across cultures. 60
- Ethical dilemmas arise as tests of personal ethics and values. 61
- People have tendencies to rationalize unethical behaviors. 63

3.2 How Can We Maintain High Standards of Ethical Conduct? 65
- Personal character and moral development influence ethical decision making. 65
- Training in ethical decision making can improve ethical conduct. 67
- Protection of whistleblowers can encourage ethical conduct. 68
- Managers as positive role models can inspire ethical conduct. 68
- Formal codes of ethics set standards for ethical conduct. 69

3.3 What Should We Know About the Social Responsibilities of Organizations? 72
- Social responsibility is an organization's obligation to best serve society. 73
- Scholars argue cases for and against corporate social responsibility. 74
- Social responsibility audits measure the social performance of organizations. 75
- Sustainability is an important social responsibility goal. 76
- Social business and social entrepreneurship point the way in social responsibility. 79

{4 Managers as Decision Makers 84

4.1 How Do Managers Use Information to Solve Problems? 86
- Managers deal with problems posing threats and offering opportunities. 86
- Managers can be problem avoiders, problem solvers, or problem seekers. 88
- Managers make programmed and nonprogrammed decisions when solving problems. 88
- Managers can use systematic and intuitive thinking. 89
- Managers use different cognitive styles to process information for decision making. 89
- Managers make decisions under conditions of certainty, risk, and uncertainty. 90

4.2 What Are Five Steps in the Decision-Making Process? 93
- Step 1 is to identify and define the problem. 94
- Step 2 is to generate and evaluate alternative courses of action. 94
- Step 3 is to decide on a preferred course of action. 95
- Step 4 is to implement the decision. 96
- Step 5 is to evaluate results. 97
- Ethical reasoning is important at all steps in decision making. 98

4.3 What Are Some Current Issues in Managerial Decision Making? 100
- Personal factors help drive creativity in decision making. 100
- Group decision making has both advantages and disadvantages. 102
- Judgmental heuristics and other biases and traps may cause decision-making errors. 103
- Managers must be prepared for crisis decision making. 104

{5 Plans and Planning Techniques 110

5.1 How and Why Do Managers Use the Planning Process? 112
- Planning is one of the four functions of management. 112
- Planning is the process of setting objectives and identifying how to achieve them. 113

- Planning improves focus and action orientation.   114
- Planning improves coordination and control.   115
- Planning improves time management.   115

5.2 What Types of Plans Do Managers Use?   118
- Managers use short-range and long-range plans.   118
- Managers use strategic and operational plans.   118
- Organizational policies and procedures are plans.   119
- Budgets are plans that commit resources to activities.   121

5.3 What Are Some Useful Planning Tools and Techniques?   123
- Forecasting tries to predict the future.   123
- Contingency planning creates backup plans for when things go wrong.   124
- Scenario planning crafts plans for alternative future conditions.   124
- Benchmarking identifies best practices used by others.   125
- Participatory planning improves implementation capacities.   126
- Goal setting helps align plans and activities throughout an organization.   127

{6   Controls and Control Systems   132

6.1 How and Why Do Managers Use the Control Process?   134
- Controlling is one of the four functions of management.   134
- Control begins with objectives and standards.   135
- Control measures actual performance.   136
- Control compares results with objectives and standards.   137
- Control takes corrective action as needed.   138

6.2 What Types of Controls Are Used by Managers?   140
- Managers use feedforward, concurrent, and feedback controls.   140
- Managers use both internal and external controls.   142
- Managing by objectives is a way to integrate planning and controlling.   143

6.3 What Are Some Useful Control Tools and Techniques?   146
- Quality control is a foundation of modern management.   146
- Gantt charts and CPM/PERT are used in project management and control.   147
- Inventory controls help save costs.   148
- Breakeven analysis shows where revenues will equal costs.   149
- Financial ratios measure key areas of financial performance.   149
- Balanced scorecards help top managers exercise strategic control.   150

{7   Strategy and Strategic Management   156

7.1 What Types of Strategies Are Used by Organizations?   158
- Strategy is a comprehensive plan for achieving competitive advantage.   158
- Organizations use corporate, business, and functional strategies.   159
- Growth strategies focus on expansion.   160
- Restructuring and divestiture strategies focus on consolidation.   161
- Global strategies focus on international business initiatives.   162
- Cooperative strategies focus on alliances and partnerships.   163
- E-business strategies focus on using the Internet for business success.   163

7.2 How Do Managers Formulate and Implement Strategies?   166
- The strategic management process formulates and implements strategies.   166
- Strategy formulation begins with the organization's mission and objectives.   167

- SWOT analysis identifies strengths, weaknesses, opportunities, and threats.   167
- Porter's five forces model examines industry attractiveness.   168
- Porter's competitive strategies model examines business and product strategies.   169
- Portfolio planning examines strategies across multiple businesses or products.   171
- Strategic leadership ensures strategy implementation and control.   172

{8   Organization Structure and Design   178

8.1 What Is Organizing as a Managerial Responsibility?   180
- Organizing is one of the management functions.   180
- Organization charts describe the formal structures of organizations.   181
- Organizations also operate with informal structures.   182
- Informal structures have good points and bad points.   183

8.2 What Are the Most Common Types of Organization Structures?   185
- Functional structures group together people using similar skills.   185
- Divisional structures group together people by products, customers, or locations.   187
- Matrix structures combine the functional and divisional structures.   188
- Team structures use many permanent and temporary teams.   189
- Network structures extensively use strategic alliances and outsourcing.   190

8.3 What Are the Trends in Organizational Design?   194
- Organizations are becoming flatter, with fewer levels of management.   194
- Organizations are increasing decentralization.   195
- Organizations are increasing delegation and empowerment.   196
- Organizations are becoming more horizontal and adaptive.   198
- Organizations are using more alternative work schedules.   199

{9   Organizational Cultures, Innovation, and Change   204

9.1 What Is the Nature of Organizational Culture?   206
- Organizational culture is the personality of the organization.   206
- Organizational culture shapes behavior and influences performance.   207
- The observable culture is what you see and hear as an employee or customer.   208
- The core culture is found in the underlying values of the organization.   209
- Value-based management supports a strong organizational culture.   210

9.2 How Do Organizations Support and Achieve Innovation?   213
- Organizations pursue process, product, and business model innovations.   213
- Green innovations pursue and support the goals of sustainability.   214
- Social innovations seek solutions to important societal problems.   214
- Commercializing innovation turns new ideas into salable products.   215
- Innovative organizations share many common characteristics.   216

9.3 How Do Managers Lead the Processes of Organizational Change?   219
- Organizations pursue both transformational and incremental changes.   219
- Three phases of planned change are unfreezing, changing, and refreezing.   220
- Managers use force-coercion, rational persuasion, and shared power change strategies.   222
- Change leaders identify and deal positively with resistance to change.   224

{10 Human Resource Management 230

10.1 What Are the Purpose and Legal Context of Human Resource Management? 232
- Human resource management attracts, develops, and maintains a talented workforce. 232
- Strategic human resource management aligns human capital with organizational strategies. 233
- Government legislation is supposed to protect workers against employment discrimination. 234
- Laws can't guarantee that employment discrimination will never happen. 235

10.2 What Are the Essential Human Resource Management Practices? 238
- Recruitment attracts qualified job applicants. 238
- Selection makes decisions to hire qualified job applicants. 240
- Socialization and orientation integrate new employees into the organization. 241
- Training continually develops employee skills and capabilities. 241
- Performance management appraises and rewards accomplishments. 242
- Retention and career development provide career paths. 244

10.3 What Are Current Issues in Human Resource Management? 247
- Today's lifestyles increase demands for flexibility and work-life balance. 247
- Organizations are using more independent contractors and part-time workers. 248
- Compensation plans influence employee recruitment and retention. 249
- Fringe benefits are an important part of employee compensation packages. 250
- Labor relations and collective bargaining are closely governed by law. 251

{11 Leadership 256

11.1 What Are the Foundations for Effective Leadership? 258
- Leadership is one of the four functions of management. 258
- Leaders use position power to achieve influence. 259
- Leaders use personal power to achieve influence. 260
- Leaders bring vision to leadership situations. 261
- Leaders display different traits in the quest for leadership effectiveness. 262
- Leaders display different styles in the quest for leadership effectiveness. 262

11.2 What Can We Learn from the Contingency Leadership Theories? 265
- Fiedler's contingency model matches leadership styles with situational differences. 265
- The Hersey-Blanchard situational leadership model matches leadership styles with the maturity of followers. 267
- House's path-goal theory matches leadership styles with task and follower characteristics. 267
- Leader-member exchange theory describes how leaders treat in-group and out-group followers. 268
- The Vroom-Jago model describes a leader's choice of alternative decision-making methods. 269

11.3 What Are Current Issues and Directions in Leadership Development? 272
- Transformational leadership inspires enthusiasm and great performance. 272
- Emotionally intelligent leadership handles emotions and relationships well. 273
- Interactive leadership emphasizes communication, listening, and participation. 274
- Moral leadership builds trust from a foundation of personal integrity. 275
- Servant leadership is follower centered and empowering. 277

{12 Individual Behavior 282

12.1 How Do Perceptions Influence Individual Behavior? 284
- Perceptual distortions can obscure individual differences. 285
- Perception can cause attribution errors as we explain events and problems. 287
- Impression management is a way of influencing how others perceive us. 287

12.2 How Do Personalities Influence Individual Behavior? 290
- The Big Five personality traits describe work-related individual differences. 290
- The Myers-Briggs Type Indicator is a popular approach to personality assessment. 291
- Self-monitoring and other personality traits influence work behavior. 292
- People with Type A personalities tend to stress themselves. 293
- Stress has consequences for work performance and personal health. 294

12.3 How Do Attitudes, Emotions, and Moods Influence Individual Behavior? 297
- Attitudes predispose people to act in certain ways. 297
- Job satisfaction is a positive attitude toward one's job and work experiences. 298
- Job satisfaction influences work behaviors. 299
- Job satisfaction has a complex relationship with job performance. 300
- Emotions and moods are positive and negative states of mind that influence behavior. 300

{13 Motivation 306

13.1 How Do Human Needs Influence Motivation to Work? 308
- Maslow described a hierarchy of needs topped by self-actualization. 308
- Alderfer's ERG theory deals with existence, relatedness, and growth needs. 309
- McClelland identified acquired needs for achievement, power, and affiliation. 310
- Herzberg's two-factor theory focuses on higher-order need satisfaction. 312
- The core characteristics model integrates motivation and job design. 313

13.2 How Do Thought Processes and Decisions Affect Motivation to Work? 316
- Equity theory explains how social comparisons motivate individual behavior. 316
- Expectancy theory considers Motivation = Expectancy × Instrumentality × Valence. 318
- Goal-setting theory shows that well-chosen and well-set goals can be motivating. 320

13.3 How Does Reinforcement Influence Motivation to Work? 323
- Operant conditioning influences behavior by controlling its consequences. 323
- Positive reinforcement connects desirable behavior with pleasant consequences. 325
- Punishment connects undesirable behavior with unpleasant consequences. 325

{14 Teams and Teamwork 330

14.1 Why Is It Important to Understand Teams and Teamwork? 332
- Teams offer synergy and other benefits to organizations and their members. 332
- Teams often suffer from common performance problems. 333
- Organizations are networks of formal teams and informal groups. 334
- Organizations use committees, task forces, and cross-functional teams. 335
- Virtual teams are increasingly common in organizations. 336
- Self-managing teams are a form of job enrichment for groups. 337

14.2 What Are the Building Blocks for Successful Teamwork? 339
- Teams need the right members and other inputs to be effective. 340
- Teams need the right processes to be effective. 342

- Teams move through different stages of development.   342
- Team performance is affected by norms and cohesiveness.   344
- Team performance is affected by task and maintenance roles.   345
- Team performance is affected by use of communication networks.   346

14.3 How Can Managers Create and Lead High-Performance Teams?   348
- Team building helps team members learn to better work together.   348
- Team performance is affected by use of decision-making methods.   349
- Team performance suffers when groupthink leads to bad decisions.   350
- Team performance benefits from good conflict management.   352

{ 15 Communication   358

15.1 What Is Communication and When Is It Effective?   360
- Communication is a process of sending and receiving messages with meanings attached.   361
- Communication is effective when the receiver understands the sender's messages.   361
- Communication is efficient when it is delivered at low cost to the sender.   362
- Communication is persuasive when the receiver acts as the sender intends.   363

15.2 What Are the Major Barriers to Effective Communication?   366
- Poor use of channels makes it hard to communicate effectively.   367
- Poor written or oral expression makes it hard to communicate effectively.   367
- Failure to spot nonverbal signals makes it hard to communicate effectively.   368
- Status differences make it hard to communicate effectively.   368
- Physical distractions make it hard to communicate effectively.   369

15.3 How Can We Improve Communication with People at Work?   371
- Active listening helps people say what they really mean.   371
- Constructive feedback is specific, timely, and relevant.   372
- Office spaces can be designed to encourage interaction and communication.   373
- Transparency and openness ensure that accurate and timely information is shared.   373
- Appropriate use of technology can facilitate more and better communication.   375
- Sensitivity and etiquette can improve cross-cultural communication.   376

{ 16 Diversity and Global Cultures   382

16.1 What Should We Know About Diversity in the Workplace?   384
- There is a business case for diversity.   384
- Inclusive organizational cultures value and support diversity.   385
- Organizational subcultures can create diversity challenges.   385
- Minorities and women suffer diversity bias in many situations.   387
- Managing diversity should be a top leadership priority.   388

16.2 What Should We Know About Diversity Among Global Cultures?   391
- Culture shock comes from discomfort in cross-cultural situations.   391
- Cultural intelligence is the capacity to adapt to foreign cultures.   392
- The "silent" languages of cultures include context, time, and space.   393
- Hofstede identifies five value differences among national cultures.   394
- Country clusters show cultural differences.   397

{**17 Globalization and International Business 402**

17.1 How Does Globalization Affect International Business? 404
- Globalization involves the growing interdependence of the world's economies. 405
- Globalization creates a variety of international business opportunities. 405
- International business is done by global sourcing, import/export, licensing, and franchising. 406
- International business is done by joint ventures and wholly owned subsidiaries. 408
- International business is complicated by different legal and political systems. 409

17.2 What Are Global Corporations and How Do They Work? 412
- Global corporations or MNCs do substantial business in many countries. 412
- The actions of global corporations can be controversial at home and abroad. 413
- Managers of global corporations face a variety of ethical challenges. 414
- Planning and controlling are complicated in global corporations. 414
- Organizing can be difficult in global corporations. 416
- Leading is challenging in global corporations. 416

{**18 Entrepreneurship and Small Business 422**

18.1 What Is Entrepreneurship and Who Are Entrepreneurs? 424
- Entrepreneurs are risk takers who spot and pursue opportunities. 425
- Entrepreneurs often share similar backgrounds and experiences. 426
- Entrepreneurs often share similar personality traits. 428
- Women and minority entrepreneurs are growing in numbers. 428
- Social entrepreneurs seek novel solutions to pressing social problems. 430

18.2 What Should We Know About Small Business and How to Start One? 433
- Small businesses are mainstays of the economy. 433
- Small businesses must master three life-cycle stages. 434
- Family-owned businesses can face unique challenges. 435
- Most small businesses fail within five years. 436
- Assistance is available to help small businesses get started. 437
- A small business should start with a sound business plan. 438
- There are different forms of small business ownership. 439
- There are different ways of financing a small business. 440

Skill-Building Portfolio SB-1

Self-Assessments
1. Personal Career Readiness
2. Managerial Assumptions
3. Terminal Values Survey
4. Intuitive Ability
5. Time Management Profile
6. Internal/External Control
7. Handling Facts and Inferences
8. Empowering Others
9. Tolerance for Ambiguity
10. Performance Appraisal Assumptions
11. Least-Preferred Co-Worker Scale

12. Stress Test
13. Two-Factor Profile
14. Team Leader Skills
15. Feedback and Assertiveness
16. Diversity Awareness
17. Global Intelligence
18. Entrepreneurship Orientation

Class Exercises
1. My Best Manager
2. Evidence-Based Management Quiz
3. Confronting Ethical Dilemmas
4. Lost at Sea
5. The Future Workplace
6. Stakeholder Maps
7. Strategic Scenarios
8. Organizational Metaphors
9. Force-Field Analysis
10. Upward Appraisal
11. Leading by Participation
12. Job Satisfaction Preferences
13. Why We Work
14. Understanding Team Dynamics
15. Communication and Teamwork Dilemmas
16. Alligator River Story
17. American Football
18. Entrepreneurs Among Us

Team Projects
1. Managing Millennials
2. Management in Popular Culture
3. Organizational Commitment to Sustainability
4. Crisis Management Realities
5. Personal Career Planning
6. After Meeting/Project Review
7. Contrasting Strategies
8. Network "U"
9. Organizational Culture Walk
10. The Future of Labor Unions
11. Leadership Believe-It-Or-Not
12. Difficult Personalities
13. CEO Pay
14. Superstars on the Team
15. How Words Count
16. Job Satisfaction Around the World
17. Globalization Pros and Cons
18. Community Entrepreneurs

Cases for Critical Thinking   C-1

Case 1: Trader Joe's: Keeping a Cool Edge
Case 2: Zara International: Fashion at the Speed of Light

Case 3: Patagonia: Leading a Green Revolution

Case 4: Amazon: One E-Store to Rule Them All/**Sidebar:** Barnes & Noble: Adapting to an Uncertain Future

Case 5: Nordstrom: Planning a Better Inventory/**Sidebar:** Zappos: How Zappos Did it

Case 6: Electronic Arts: Inside Fantasy Sports/**Sidebar:** Zynga: Building an Army of Social Games

Case 7: Dunkin' Donuts: Betting Dollars on Donuts

Case 8: Nike: Spreading Out to Stay Together

Case 9: Apple: People and Design Create the Future

Case 10: Netflix: Making Movie Magic/**Sidebar:** Redbox: Will Customers Wait for New Releases?

Case 11: SAS: Business Decisions at the Speed of Light/**Sidebar:** Sungard: Risky Business

Case 12: Facebook: Social Networking Is Big Business/**Sidebar:** LinkedIn: Social Networking's All Grown Up

Case 13: Panera Bread Company: Staying Ahead of Long-Term Trends/**Sidebar:** TOMS: Get One, Give One

Case 14: Pixar: Animated Geniuses/**Sidebar:** DreamWorks: DreamWorks Delights

Case 15: Twitter: Redefining Communications/**Sidebar:** Yammer: Microblogging Goes Corporate

Case 16: Toyota: Looking Far into the Future/**Sidebar:** Ford: The Assembly Line Goes Global

Case 17: Harley-Davidson: Style and Strategy Have Global Reach

Case 18: In-N-Out Burger: Building a Better Burger/**Sidebar:** Sprinkles: Leading a Sweet Trend

Test Prep Answers   AN-1

Glossary   G-1

Endnotes   EN-1

Photo Credits   PC-1

Name Index   NI-1

Subject Index   SI-1

Organization Index   OI-1

{THIRD EDITION

Exploring Management

Zappos CEO Tony Hsieh is into happiness. His goal is "to set up an environment where the personalities, creativities, and individuality of all different employees come out and shine."

Managers and the Management Process

Everyone Becomes a Manager Someday

Management Live

Self-Management and *Slumdog Millionaire*

*T*he *Times* of London called this movie an "exotic, edgy thriller," while *The New York Times* described it as a "gaudy, gorgeous rush of color, sound and motion." What's your take on this rags-to-riches story of an orphan growing up in Mumbai, India, and finding his way to a TV game show offering him the chance to be a "slumdog millionaire"?

When the disgruntled game-show host has the police chief rough up the main character Jamal (Dev Patel) the night before the big show, he asks: "What the hell can a slum boy possibly know?" Facing the chief and the prospect of more mistreatment, Jamal looks him in the eye and says in return: "The answers."

This movie is a study in discipline, confidence, and **self-management**—the capacity to act with a strong sense of self-awareness. As a career skill, this ability helps us stay confident, build on strengths, overcome weaknesses, and avoid viewing ourselves both more favorably or more negatively than is justified.

You have to admire the way Jamal held up under the police chief's torture. And, he didn't fall prey to the quiz master's repeated attempts to deceive and pressure him into not believing his own best answers. It's a classic case of self-management in action.

Even if you've already seen it, *Slumdog Millionaire* is worth another viewing. Watch for lessons on management and personal career development that you might explore with your friends and classmates.

YOUR CHAPTER 1 TAKEAWAYS

1. Understand what it means to be a manager.

2. Know what managers do and what skills they use.

3. Recognize important career issues in the new workplace.

WHAT'S INSIDE

Explore Yourself
More on self-management

Role Models
Ursula Burns leads Xerox with confidence and a strategic eye

Ethics Check
Coke's secret formula a tempting target

Facts to Consider
Employment contradictions in workforce diversity

Manager's Library
Delivering Happiness by Tony Hsieh

Takeaway 1.1
What Does It Mean to Be a Manager?

ANSWERS TO COME

- Organizations have different types and levels of managers.
- Accountability is a cornerstone of managerial performance.
- Effective managers help others achieve high performance and satisfaction.
- Managers must meet multiple and changing expectations.

YOU FIND THEM EVERYWHERE, IN SMALL AND LARGE BUSINESSES, VOLUNTARY associations, government agencies, schools, hospitals, and wherever people work together for a common cause. Even though the job titles vary from team leader to department head, project leader, president, administrator, and more, the people in these jobs all share a common responsibility—helping others do their best work. We call them **managers**—persons who directly supervise, support, and help activate work efforts to achieve the performance goals of individuals, teams, or even an organization as a whole. In this sense, I think you'll agree with the chapter subtitle: Everyone becomes a manager someday.

> A **manager** is a person who supports and is responsible for the work of others.

‖ Organizations have different types and levels of managers.

Look at Figure 1.1. It describes an organization as a series of layers, each of which represents different levels of work and managerial responsibilities.[1]

First-Line Managers and Team Leaders

"I've just never worked on anything that so visibly, so dramatically changes the quality of someone's life. Some days you wake up, and if you think about all the work you have to do it's so overwhelming, you could be paralyzed." These are the words of Justin Fritz as he described his experiences leading a 12-member team to launch a new product at Medtronic, a large medical products company. He is a **first-line manager**—someone who is formally in charge of a small work group composed of nonmanagerial workers. About the challenge of managerial work, Fritz says: "You just have to get it done."[2]

> **First-line managers** supervise people who perform nonmanagerial duties.

FIGURE 1.1

What Are the Typical Job Titles and Levels of Management in Organizations?
The traditional organization is structured as a pyramid. The top manager, typically a CEO, president, or executive director, reports to a board of directors in a business or to a board of trustees in a nonprofit organization. Middle managers report to top managers, and first-line managers or team leaders report to middle managers.

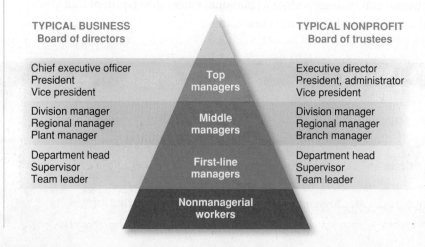

TYPICAL BUSINESS Board of directors		TYPICAL NONPROFIT Board of trustees
Chief executive officer President Vice president	Top managers	Executive director President, administrator Vice president
Division manager Regional manager Plant manager	Middle managers	Division manager Regional manager Branch manager
Department head Supervisor Team leader	First-line managers	Department head Supervisor Team leader
	Nonmanagerial workers	

A first job in management typically involves serving as a team leader or supervisor. Typical job titles for these first-line managers include department head, team leader, and unit manager. For example, the leader of an auditing team is considered a first-line manager, as is the head of an academic department in a university. Even though most people enter the workforce as technical specialists such as auditor, market researcher, or systems analyst, sooner or later they often advance to these positions of initial managerial responsibility. And they serve as essential building blocks for organizational performance.[3]

Middle Managers

Look again at Figure 1.1. This time consider where Justin may be headed in his career. At the next level above team leader we find **middle managers**—persons in charge of relatively large departments or divisions consisting of several smaller work units or teams.

Middle managers oversee the work of large departments or divisions.

Middle managers usually supervise several first-line managers. Examples include clinic directors in hospitals; deans in universities; and division managers, plant managers, and regional sales managers in businesses. Because of their position "in the middle," these managers must be able to work well with people from all parts of the organization—higher, lower, and side-to-side. As Justin moves up the career ladder to middle management, there will be more pressure and new challenges. But there should also be rewards and satisfaction.

Top Managers

Some middle managers advance still higher in the organization, earning job titles such as chief executive officer (CEO), chief operating officer (COO), chief financial officer (CFO), chief information officer (CIO), president, and vice president. These **top managers** are part of a senior management team that is responsible for the performance of an organization as a whole or for one of its larger parts. They must be alert to trends and developments in the external environment, recognize potential problems and opportunities, set strategy, and lead the organization to success.[4]

Top managers guide the performance of the organization as a whole or of one of its major parts.

Procter & Gamble's former CEO, A. G. Lafley, once said his job was to "link the external world with the internal organization . . . make sure the voice of the consumer is heard . . . shape values and standards."[5] The best top managers are future-oriented strategic thinkers in tune with their environments and able to make good decisions under competitive and uncertain conditions. As Lafley points out, they should be "balancing the need for performance in the short term with the need to invest for the longer term."[6]

As executive editor at *Business Week*, John A. Byrne enjoyed the rush of accomplishment from doing a challenging job well.[7] Even with extreme hours, he said, "rarely do I leave thinking I've wasted a day doing something that I didn't want to do." Byrne even joked that his job was sometimes like being in college and pulling all-nighters on major projects. And he claimed "More often than not I walk out feeling immensely proud of the people I work with and of the amazing things we have achieved together."

Boards of Directors

Both A. G. Lafley and John Byrne seem responsible and successful, but think about those top managers who are just the opposite. You have to admit that some don't live up to expectations and even take personal advantage of their positions, perhaps to the point of ethics failures and illegal acts. Who or what keeps CEOs and other senior managers focused and high performing?

If you look back at Figure 1.1 you'll see that even the CEO or president of an organization reports to a higher-level boss. In business corporations, this is a **board of directors**, whose members are elected by stockholders to represent their ownership interests. In nonprofit organizations, such as a hospital or university, top managers report to a *board of trustees*. These board members may be elected by local citizens, appointed by government bodies, or invited to serve by existing members.

In both business and the public sector, the basic responsibilities of a board are the same. Its members are supposed to oversee the affairs of the organization and the performance of its top management. In other words, they are supposed to make sure that the organization is always being run right. This is called **governance**, the oversight of top management by an organization's board of directors or board of trustees.

> Members of a **board of directors** are elected by stockholders to represent their ownership interests.

> **Governance** is oversight of top management by a board of directors or board of trustees.

⦀ Accountability is a cornerstone of managerial performance.

Throughout the workplace, not just at the top, the term **accountability** describes the requirement of one person to answer to a higher authority for performance achieved in his or her area of work responsibility. This notion of accountability is an important aspect of managerial performance. In the traditional organizational pyramid, accountability flows upward. Team members are accountable to a team leader, the team leader is accountable to a middle manager, the middle manager is accountable to a top manager, and the top manager is accountable to a board of directors.

Lets not forget that accountability in managerial performance is always accompanied by dependency. At the same time that any manager is being held accountable by a higher level for the performance results of her or his area of supervisory responsibility, the manager is dependent on others to do the required work. In fact, we might say that a large part of the study of management is all about learning how to best manage the dynamics of accountability and dependency as shown in the small figure.

> **Accountability** is the requirement to show performance results to a supervisor.

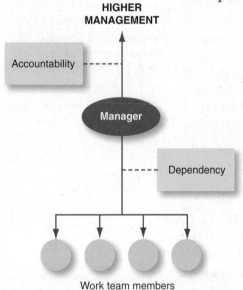

HIGHER MANAGEMENT

Accountability

Manager

Dependency

Work team members

⦀ Effective managers help others achieve high performance and satisfaction.

This discussion of performance accountability and related challenges may make you wonder: What exactly is an effective manager? Most people, perhaps you, would reply that an effective manager is someone who helps people and organizations perform. That's a fine starting point, but we should go a step further. I define an **effective manager** as someone who successfully helps others achieve both high performance and satisfaction in their work.

> An **effective manager** successfully helps others achieve high performance and satisfaction in their work.

Working Mother Looks for the Best

Great Employers Put Top Value on People

Working Mother magazine's annual listing of the "100 Best Companies for Working Mothers" has become an important management benchmark—both for employers who want to be among the best and for potential employees who want to work only for the best. The magazine, part of Working Mother Media, has a monthly readership of over 3 million and is well worth a look. Topics in *Working Mother* cover the full gamut from kids to health to personal motivation and more.

Self-described as helping women "integrate their professional lives, their family lives and their inner lives," *Working Mother* mainstreams coverage of work-life balance issues and needs for women. One issue reported on moms who "pushed for more family-friendly benefits and got them." The writer described how Kristina Marsh worked to get lactation support for nursing mothers as a formal benefit at Dow Corning, and how Beth Schiavo started a Working Moms Network in Ernst & Young's Atlanta offices and then got it approved as a corporate program nationwide.

A list of best employers for multicultural women includes Allstate, American Express, Deloitte, Ernst & Young, IBM, and General Mills. In terms of making the selections, *Working Mother* says: "All of our winning companies not only require manager training on diversity issues but also rate manager performance partly on diversity results, such as how many multicultural women advance."

FIND INSPIRATION

Pick up a copy of *Working Mother* magazine or browse the online version. It's a chance to learn more about the complexities of work-life balance, including the challenges faced by women blending motherhood with a career. It's also a place to learn which employers are truly great in respecting quality of work life issues.

The concern for not just work performance but also job satisfaction is a central theme in our society. It calls attention to **quality of work life** (QWL) issues—the overall quality of human experiences in the workplace. Have you experienced a "high QWL" environment? Most people would describe it as a place where they are respected and valued by their employer. They would talk about fair pay, safe work conditions, opportunities to learn and use new skills, room to grow and progress in a career, and protection of individual rights. They would say everyone takes pride in their work and the organization.

Quality of work life is the overall quality of human experiences in the workplace.

Are you willing to work anywhere other than in a high QWL setting? Would you, as a manager, be pleased with anything less than helping others achieve not just high performance but also job satisfaction?[8] Sadly, the real world doesn't always live up to these expectations. Talk to parents, relatives and friends who go to work every day. You might be surprised. Many people still labor in difficult, sometimes even hostile and unhealthy, conditions—ones we would consider low QWL for sure![9]

⦀ Managers must meet multiple and changing expectations.

As president and CEO of Cornerstone Research, Cindy Zollinger directly supervises 24 people. But she says: "I don't really manage them in a typical way; they largely run themselves. I help them in dealing with obstacles they face, or in making the most of opportunities they find."[10] As Cindy's comments suggest, we are in a time when the best managers are known more for "helping" and "supporting" than for "directing" and "order giving." The terms "coordinator," "coach," and "team leader" are heard as often as "supervisor" or "boss." The fact is that most organizations need more than managers who simply sit back and tell others what to do.

Take a moment to jot down a few notes on the behaviors and characteristics of the *best* managers you've ever had. My students describe theirs as leading by example, willing to do any job, treating others as equals and with respect, acting approachable, being enthusiastic, expecting outstanding performance, and helping others grow. They talk about managers who often work alongside those they supervise, spending most of their time providing advice and support so that others can perform to the best of their abilities and with satisfaction. How does this listing compare with your experiences?

Figure 1.2 uses the notion of an *upside-down pyramid* to describe a new mindset for managers—a real expression of what it means to act as a coach rather than an order-giver. The concept of the **upside-down pyramid** fits well with Cindy Zollinger's description of her job as a manager, and it should also be consistent with how you described your best manager.

Prominent at the top of the upside-down pyramid are nonmanagerial workers—people who interact directly with customers and clients or produce products and services for them. Managers are shown a level below. Their attention is concentrated on supporting these workers so they can best serve the organization's customers.

In the upside-down pyramid view, there is no doubt that the organization exists to serve its customers. And it is clear that managers are there to help and support the people whose work makes that possible. Doesn't that sound like the way things should be?

The **upside-down pyramid** view puts customers at the top of the organization being served by workers who are supported by managers below them.

FIGURE 1.2
How Do Mindsets Change When the Organization Is Viewed as an Upside-Down Pyramind?
If we turn the traditional organizational pyramid upside down, we get a valuable look at how managerial work is viewed today. Managers are at the bottom of the upside-down pyramid, and they are expected to support the operating workers above them. Their goal is to help these workers best serve the organization's customers at the top. The appropriate mindset of this supportive manager is more "coaching" and "helping" than "directing" and "order giving."

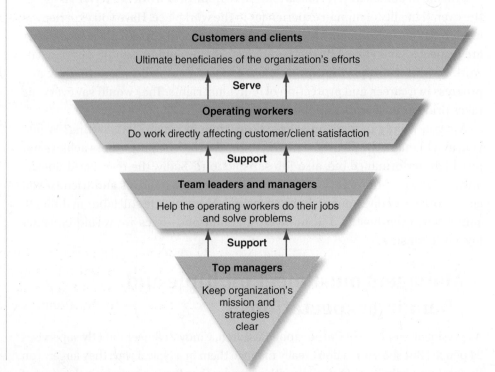

Customers and clients
Ultimate beneficiaries of the organization's efforts

Serve

Operating workers
Do work directly affecting customer/client satisfaction

Support

Team leaders and managers
Help the operating workers do their jobs and solve problems

Support

Top managers
Keep organization's mission and strategies clear

STUDY GUIDE

Takeaway 1.1
What Does It Mean to Be a Manager?

Terms to Define

Accountability

Board of directors

Effective manager

First-line manager

Governance

Manager

Middle managers

Quality of work life

Top managers

Upside-down pyramid

Rapid Review

• Managers support and facilitate the work efforts of other people in organizations.

• Top managers scan the environment and pursue long-term goals; middle managers coordinate activities among large departments or divisions; first-line managers, like team leaders, supervise and support nonmanagerial workers.

• Everyone in organizations is accountable to a higher-level manager for his or her performance accomplishments; at the highest level, top managers are held accountable by boards of directors or boards of trustees.

• Effective managers help others achieve both high performance and high levels of job satisfaction.

• New directions in managerial work emphasize "coaching" and "supporting," rather than "directing" and "order giving."

• In the upside-down pyramid view of organizations, the role of managers is to support nonmanagerial workers who serve the needs of customers at the top.

Questions for Discussion

1. Other than at work, in what situations do you expect to be a manager during your lifetime?
2. Why should a manager be concerned about the quality of work life in an organization?
3. In what ways does the upside-down pyramid view of organizations offer advantages over the traditional view of the top-down pyramid?

Be Sure You Can

• explain how managers contribute to organizations
• describe the activities of managers at different levels
• explain how accountability operates in organizations
• describe an effective manager
• list several ways the work of managers is changing from the past
• explain the role of managers in the upside-down pyramid

What Would You Do?

When people are promoted into positions of managerial responsibility they often end up supervising friends and colleagues. What is the best way for the newly appointed manager to deal with this situation, while earning the respect of others and building a smoothly functioning work team?

Takeaway 1.2
What Do Managers Do and What Skills Do They Use?

ANSWERS TO COME

- Managerial work is often intense and demanding.
- Managers plan, organize, lead, and control.
- Managers enact informational, interpersonal, and decisional roles.
- Managers pursue action agendas and engage in networking.
- Managers use a variety of technical, human, and conceptual skills.
- Managers can and should learn from experience.

THE MANAGERS WE HAVE BEEN DISCUSSING ARE INDISPENSABLE TO ORGANIZATIONS. Their efforts bring together resources, technology, and human talents to get things done. Some are fairly routine tasks that are repeated day after day. Many others, however, are challenging and novel, often appearing as unexpected problems and opportunities. But regardless of the task at hand, managers are expected to make things happen in ways that best serve the goals of the organization, the needs of its customers, and the interests of its employees or members.

Managerial work is often intense and demanding.

> The manager can never be free to forget the job, and never has the pleasure of knowing, even temporarily, that there is nothing else to do. . . . Managers always carry the nagging suspicion that they might be able to contribute just a little bit more. Hence they assume an unrelenting pace in their work.[11]

Although what managers do may seem straightforward, this quote from scholar and consultant Henry Mintzberg shows that putting it into practice can be much more complicated. In his classic book *The Nature of Managerial Work*, Mintzberg describes the daily work of corporate chief executives this way. "There was no break in the pace of activity during office hours. The mail...telephone calls...and meetings...accounted for almost every minute from the moment these executives entered their offices in the morning until they departed in the evenings."[12] Today, we might add the constant demands of our smartphones, ever-full e-mail and voice-mail inboxes, and constant streams of instant messages and social media alerts to Mintzberg's list of executive preoccupations.[13]

Can you imagine a day filled with managerial responsibilities? The managers Mintzberg observed had little free time because unexpected problems and continuing requests for meetings consumed almost all the time that was available. Their workdays were intense, hectic, and fast paced; the pressure for always improving performance was all-encompassing. Any manager, according to

Mintzberg, must be ready to work long hours on fragmented and varied tasks at an intense pace, while getting things done through communication and interpersonal relationships.

⫸ Managers plan, organize, lead, and control.

If you are ready to perform as a manager or to get better as one, a good starting point is Figure 1.3. It shows the four functions in the **management process**—planning, organizing, leading, and controlling. The belief is that all managers, regardless of title, level, and organizational setting, are responsible for doing each of them well.[14]

The **management process** is planning, organizing, leading, and controlling the use of resources to accomplish performance goals.

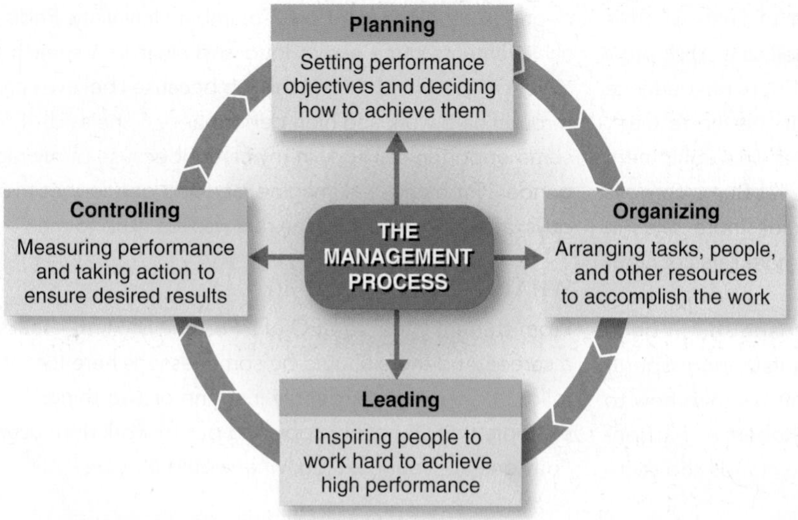

Planning
Setting performance objectives and deciding how to achieve them

Controlling
Measuring performance and taking action to ensure desired results

THE MANAGEMENT PROCESS

Organizing
Arranging tasks, people, and other resources to accomplish the work

Leading
Inspiring people to work hard to achieve high performance

FIGURE 1.3
What Four Functions Make Up the Management Process? The management process consists of four functions: planning, organizing, leading, and controlling. Planning sets the direction as performance objectives. Organizing arranges people and tasks to do the work. Leading inspires others to work hard. Controlling measures performance to make sure that plans and objectives are accomplished.

Planning

In management, **planning** is the process of setting performance objectives and determining what actions should be taken to accomplish them. When managers plan, they set goals and objectives, and select ways to achieve them.

Planning is the process of setting objectives and determining what should be done to accomplish them.

There was a time, for example, when Ernst & Young's top management grew concerned about the firm's retention rates for women.[15] Why? Turnover rates at the time were much higher among women than among men, running some 22% per year and costing the firm about 150 percent of each person's annual salary to hire and train a replacement. Then Chairman Philip A. Laskawy responded to the situation by setting a planning objective to reduce turnover rates for women.

Organizing

Even the best plans will fail without strong implementation. Success begins with **organizing**, the process of assigning tasks, allocating resources, and coordinating the activities of individuals and groups. When managers organize, they bring people and resources together to put plans into action.

Organizing is the process of assigning tasks, allocating resources, and coordinating work activities.

At Ernst & Young, Laskawy organized to meet his planning objective by convening and personally chairing a Diversity Task Force of partners. He also established a new Office of Retention and hired Deborah K. Holmes, now Global Director of Corporate Responsibility, to head it. As retention problems were identified

{ **"I'M IN THIS JOB BECAUSE I BELIEVE I EARNED IT THROUGH HARD WORK AND HIGH PERFORMANCE."**

Role Models

■ URSULA BURNS LEADS XEROX WITH CONFIDENCE AND A STRATEGIC EYE

"Frankness," "sharp humor," "willingness to take risks," "deep industry knowledge," "technical prowess." These are all phrases used to describe Ursula Burns, CEO of Xerox Corporation. Her career began as a Xerox intern and has led her to become the first African-American woman to head a *Fortune* 500 firm.

Burns took over the firm at the height of financial crisis and faced declining sales and profits, as well as a stock price that had lost half its value in a year's time. But her experience and leadership skills were well matched to the firm's many challenges—less paper being used in offices, less equipment being bought or leased, and falling prices. Yet Burns conveys confidence with a smile, intending to pursue more sales in emerging markets, better efficiencies, and more sales of high-margin services.

In her prior role as president, Burns made tough decisions on downsizing, closed Xerox manufacturing operations, and changed the product mix. She also knows how to work well with the firm's board. Director Robert A. McDonald of Procter & Gamble says. "She understands the tech-

nology and can communicate it in a way that a director can understand it."

Burns is a working mother and spouse with a teenage daughter and 20+-year-old stepson. She was raised by a single mom in New York City public housing and eventually earned a master's degree in engineering from Columbia University. Pride in her achievements came across loud and clear in a speech to the YWCA in Cleveland. "I'm in this job because I earned it through hard work and high performance," she said. "Did I get some opportunities early in my career because of my race and gender? Probably . . . I imagine race and gender got the hiring guys' attention. And then the rest was really up to me."

WHAT'S THE LESSON HERE?

From student intern to CEO of a *Fortune* 500 firm—that's quite a career. And there should be some lessons here for others to follow. If you were to identify just one or two things from this example that you could copy and put to work right now or on "day one" of your next job, what would they be?

---

in various parts of the firm, Holmes created special task forces to tackle them and recommend location-specific solutions.

Leading is the process of arousing enthusiasm and inspiring efforts to achieve goals.

Leading

The management function of **leading** is the process of arousing people's enthusiasm to work hard and inspiring their efforts to fulfill plans and accomplish objectives. When managers lead, they build commitments to plans and influence others to do their best work in implementing them. This is one of the most talked about managerial responsibilities, and it deserves lots of personal thought. Not every manager is a good leader, but every great manager is one for sure.

Deborah Holmes actively pursued her leadership responsibilities at Ernst & Young. She noticed that, in addition to the intense work at the firm, women often faced more stress because their spouses also worked. She became a champion of improved work-life balance and pursued it relentlessly. She started "call-free holidays" where professionals did not check voice mail or e-mail on weekends and holidays. She also started a "travel sanity" program that limited staffers' travel to four days a week so that they could get home for weekends. And she started a Woman's Access Program to provide mentoring and career development.

Controlling

Controlling is the process of measuring work performance, comparing results to objectives, and taking corrective action as needed. As you have surely experienced, things don't always go as planned. When managers control, they stay in contact with people as they work, gather and interpret information on performance results, and use this information to make adjustments.

At Ernst & Young, Laskawy and Holmes regularly measured retention rates for women at the firm and compared them to the rate that existed when their new programs were started. By comparing results with plans and objectives, they were able to track changes in work-life balance and retention rates, and pinpoint where they needed to make further adjustments in their programs. Over time, turnover rates for women were, and continue to be, reduced at all levels in the firm.[16]

> **Controlling** is the process of measuring performance and taking action to ensure desired results.

‖ Managers enact informational, interpersonal, and decisional roles.

When you consider the four management functions, don't be unrealistic. The functions aren't always performed one at a time or step-by-step. Remember the manager's workday as earlier described by Mintzberg—intense, fast-paced, and stressful. The reality is that managers must plan, organize, lead, and control continuously while dealing with the numerous events, situations, and problems of the day.

To describe how managers actually get things done, Mintzberg identified three sets of roles that he believed all good managers enact successfully.[17] These are the interpersonal, informational, and decisional roles shown in the small figure.

INTERPERSONAL ROLES	**INFORMATIONAL ROLES**	**DECISIONAL ROLES**
How a manager interacts with other people • Figurehead • Leader • Liaison	How a manager exchanges and processes information • Monitor • Disseminator • Spokesperson	How a manager uses information in decision making • Entrepreneur • Disturbance handler • Resource allocator • Negotiator

A manager's *informational roles* focus on the giving, receiving, and analyzing of information. The *interpersonal roles* reflect interactions with people inside and outside the work unit. The *decisional roles* involve using information to make decisions to solve problems or address opportunities.[18] It is through performing all of these roles, so to speak, that managers fulfill their planning, organizing, leading, and controlling responsibilities.

Speaking of roles, each chapter of this book has a Role Models feature that introduces you to successful managers and executives in a variety of settings. Ursula Burns of Xerox was just featured as our first role model, and her story is well worth a look.

‖ Managers pursue action agendas and engage in networking.

While we are discussing workday realities, consider this description of just one incident from the life of a general manager.[19]

> On the way to a scheduled meeting, a general manager met a staff member who did not report to him. They exchanged "hellos" and in a two-minute conversation the manager: (a) asked two questions and received helpful information; (b) reinforced his relationship with the staff member by sincerely complimenting her on recent work; and (c) enlisted the staff member's help on another project.

Can you see the pattern here? In just two short minutes, this general manager accomplished a lot. In fact, he demonstrated excellence with two activities that management consultant and scholar John Kotter considers critical to succeeding with the management process—agenda setting and networking.[20]

Agenda Setting

Agenda setting identifies important action priorities.

Through **agenda setting**, managers develop action priorities. These agendas may be incomplete and loosely connected in the beginning. But over time, as the manager utilizes information continually gleaned from many different sources, the agendas become more specific. Kotter believes that the best managers keep their agendas always in mind so they can quickly recognize and take advantage of opportunities to advance them. In the example above, what might have happened if the manager had simply nodded "hello" to the staff member and continued on to his meeting?

Networking

Networking involves building and maintaining positive relationships with other people.

Through **networking**, managers build and maintain positive relationships with other people, ideally those whose help might be useful someday. These networks create the opportunities through which priority agenda items can be fulfilled.

Social capital is the capacity to attract support and help from others in order to get things done.

Much of what managers need to get done is beyond their individual capabilities alone. The support and contributions of other people often make the difference between success and failure. Networking is a way of developing all-important **social capital**—the capacity to attract support and help from others in order to get things done. You can think of it as a capacity to get things done based on the people you know and how well you relate to them.

The manager in our example needed help from someone who did not report directly to him. Although he wasn't in a position to order the staff person to help him out, this wasn't a problem. Because of the working relationship they maintained through networking, she wanted to help when asked. Most managers maintain extensive networks with peers, members of their work teams, higher-level executives, and people at various points elsewhere in the organization at the very least. Many are expected to network even more broadly, such as with customers, suppliers, and community representatives.

⫼ Managers use a variety of technical, human, and conceptual skills.

The discussion of roles, agendas, and networking is but a starting point for inquiry into your personal portfolio of management skills. Another step forward is found in the work of Harvard scholar Robert L. Katz. He classified the essential skills of managers into three categories—technical, human, and conceptual. As shown in Figure 1.4, the relative importance of each skill varies by level of managerial responsibility.[21]

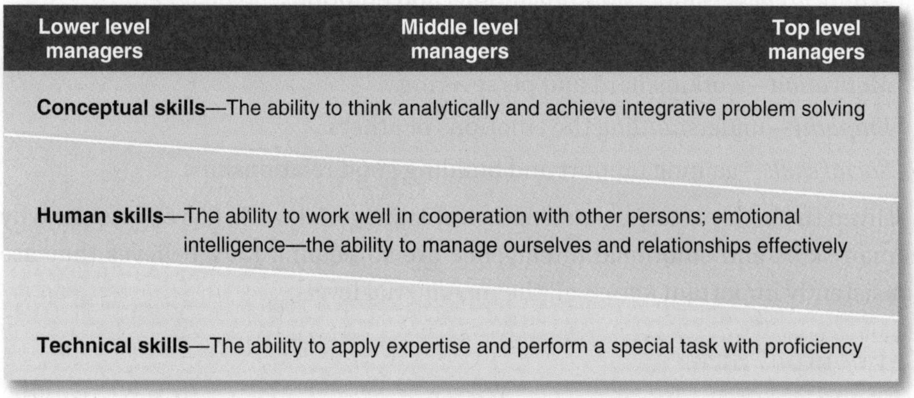

Lower level managers	Middle level managers	Top level managers

Conceptual skills—The ability to think analytically and achieve integrative problem solving

Human skills—The ability to work well in cooperation with other persons; emotional intelligence—the ability to manage ourselves and relationships effectively

Technical skills—The ability to apply expertise and perform a special task with proficiency

FIGURE 1.4   What Are Three Essential Managerial Skills and How Does Their Importance Vary Across Levels?
All managers need essential technical, human, and conceptual skills. At lower levels of management, the technical skills are more important than conceptual skills, but at higher levels of management, the conceptual skills become more important than technical skills. Because managerial work is so heavily interpersonal, human skills are equally important across all management levels.

Technical Skill

A **technical skill** is the ability to use a special proficiency or expertise to perform particular tasks. Accountants, engineers, market researchers, financial planners, and systems analysts, for example, possess obvious technical skills. Other baseline technical skills for any college graduate today include such things as written and oral communication, computer literacy, and math and numeracy.

In Katz's model, technical skills are very important at career entry levels. So how do you get them? Formal education is an initial source for learning these skills, but continued training and job experiences are important in further developing them. Why not take a moment to inventory your technical skills, the ones you have and the ones you still need to learn for your future career? Katz tells us that the technical skills are especially important at job entry and early career points. Surely, you want to be ready the next time a job interviewer asks the bottom-line question: "What can you really do for us?"

*A **technical skill** is the ability to use expertise to perform a task with proficiency.*

Human Skill

The ability to work well with others is a **human skill**, and it is a foundation for managerial success. How can we excel at networking, for example, without an

*A **human skill** is the ability to work well in cooperation with other people.*

ability and willingness to relate well with other people? How can we develop social capital without it? A manager with good human skills will have a high degree of self-awareness and a capacity to understand or empathize with the feelings of others. You would most likely observe this person working with others in a spirit of trust, enthusiasm, and genuine involvement.

A manager with good human skills is also likely to be high in **emotional intelligence**. Considered an important leadership attribute, EI is defined by scholar and consultant Daniel Goleman as the "ability to manage ourselves and our relationships effectively."[22] He believes that emotional intelligence is built upon the following five foundations.

1. *Self-awareness*—understanding moods and emotions
2. *Self-regulation*—thinking before acting; controlling disruptive impulses
3. *Motivation*—working hard and persevering
4. *Empathy*—understanding the emotions of others
5. *Social skills*—gaining rapport and building good relationships

> **Emotional intelligence** is the ability to manage ourselves and our relationships effectively.

Given the highly interpersonal nature of managerial work, it is easy to see why human skills and emotional intelligence are so helpful. Katz believes they are consistently important across all the managerial levels.

Conceptual Skill

The ability to think critically and analytically is a **conceptual skill**. It involves the capacity to break down problems into smaller parts, see the relations between the parts, and recognize the implications of any one problem for others.

> A **conceptual skill** is the ability to think analytically and solve complex problems.

As Figure 1.4 previously showed, Katz believes conceptual skills gain in relative importance as we move from lower to higher levels of management. This is because the problems faced at higher levels of responsibility are often ambiguous and unstructured, accompanied by many complications and interconnections, and full of longer-term consequences for people and organizations. In respect to personal development, the question to ask is: "Am I developing the strong critical thinking and problem solving capabilities I will need for sustained career success?" The Steps for Further Learning selections at the end of each chapter are good ways to test your conceptual skills in a management context.

‖ Managers can and should learn from experience.

Functions, roles, agendas, networks, skills! How can anyone develop and be consistently good at all of these things? How can the capacity to do them all well be developed and maintained for long-term career success?

This book can be a good starting point for career development, a foundation for the future. Take your time and give some thought to answering the questions that I ask as you read. Consider also how you might apply what you are learning to your current situations—school, work, and personal. And then ask what you can learn from these situations in turn. It is well recognized that successful managers do this all the time. We call it learning from experience.

> **Lifelong learning** is continuous learning from daily experiences.

The challenge for all of us is to be good at **lifelong learning**—the process of continuously learning from our daily experiences and opportunities. Consider the following point by State Farm CEO Edward B. Rust, Jr.[23]

I think the whole concept of lifelong learning is more relevant today than ever before. It's scary to realize that the skill sets we possess today are likely to be inadequate five years from now, just due to the normal pace of change. As more young people come into the workforce, they need a deeper, fundamental understanding of the basic skills—not just to get a job, but to grow with the job as their responsibilities change over their lifetimes.

Does Rust's assessment of lifelong learning sound daunting? Or is it a challenge you are confident in meeting? Do you agree that this is an accurate description of today's career environment? If you do, and I believe you should, you'll also have to admit that learning, learning, and more learning are top priorities in our lives. Why not use Table 1.1, *Six "Must Have" Managerial Skills*, as a preliminary checklist for assessing your managerial learning and career readiness? How do you stack up?

Table 1.1 Six "Must Have" Managerial Skills

Teamwork Able to work effectively as team member and leader; strong on team contributions, leadership, conflict management, negotiation, consensus building

Self-Management Able to evaluate self, modify behavior, and meet obligations; strong on ethical reasoning, personal flexibility, tolerance for ambiguity, performance responsibility

Leadership Able to influence and support others to perform complex and ambiguous tasks; strong on diversity awareness, project management, strategic action

Critical Thinking Able to gather and analyze information for problem solving; strong on information analysis and interpretation, creativity and innovation, judgment, and decision making

Professionalism Able to sustain a positive impression and instill confidence in others; strong on personal presence, initiative, and career management

Communication Able to express self well in communication with others; strong on writing, oral presentation, giving and receiving feedback, technology utilization

With the prior list as a starting point, the rest of this book should be even more meaningful for your personal development. And in this regard, another question is worth asking. Given all the hard work and challenges that it involves, why would anyone want to be a manager? Beyond the often-higher salaries, there is one very compelling answer—pride! As pointed out by management theorist Henry Mintzberg, being a manager is an important and socially responsible job[24]:

No job is more vital to our society than that of the manager. It is the manager who determines whether our social institutions serve us well or whether they squander our talents and resources. It is time to strip away the folklore about managerial work, and time to study it realistically so that we can begin the difficult task of making significant improvement in its performance.

STUDY GUIDE

Takeaway 1.2
What Do Managers Do and What Skills Do They Use?

Terms to Define

Agenda setting

Conceptual skill

Controlling

Emotional intelligence

Human skill

Leading

Lifelong learning

Management process

Networking

Organizing

Planning

Social capital

Technical skill

Rapid Review

- The daily work of managers is often intense and stressful, involving long hours and continuous performance pressures.
- In the management process, planning sets the direction, organizing assembles the human and material resources, leading provides the enthusiasm and direction, and controlling ensures results.
- Managers perform interpersonal, informational, and decision-making roles while pursuing high-priority agendas and engaging in successful networking.
- Managers rely on a combination of technical skills (ability to use special expertise), human skills (ability to work well with others), and conceptual skills (ability to analyze and solve complex problems).
- Everyday experience is an important source of continuous lifelong learning for managers.

Questions for Discussion

1. Is Mintzberg's view of the intense and demanding nature of managerial work realistic and, if so, why would you want to do it?
2. If Katz's model of how different levels of management use essential skills is accurate, what are its career implications for you?
3. Why is emotional intelligence an important component of one's human skills?

Be Sure You Can

- describe the intensity and pace of a typical workday for a manager
- give examples of each of the four management functions
- list the three managerial roles identified by Mintzberg
- explain how managers use agendas and networks in their work
- give examples of a manager's technical, human, and conceptual skills
- explain how these skills vary in importance across management levels
- explain the importance of experience as a source of managerial learning

What Would You Do?

It's time now to take a first interview for your "dream" job. The interviewer is sitting across the table from you. She smiles, looks you in the eye, and says: "You have a very nice academic record, and we're impressed with your extracurricular activities. Now tell me, exactly what can you do for us that will add value to the organization right from day one if you were to be offered this job?" How do you respond in a way that clearly shows you are "job ready" with strong technical, human, and conceptual skills?

Takeaway 1.3
What Are Some Important Career Issues in the New Workplace?

ANSWERS TO COME

- Globalization and job migration are changing the world of work.
- Failures of ethics and corporate governance are troublesome.
- Diversity and discrimination are continuing social priorities.
- Intellectual capital and self-management skills are essential for career success.

YOU MIGHT ALREADY HAVE NOTICED THAT THIS TEXT MAY DIFFER FROM OTHERS you've read. I'm going to ask you a lot of questions and expose you to different viewpoints and possibilities. This process of active inquiry begins with the recognition that we live and work in a time of great changes, ones that are not only socially troublesome and personally challenging, but also ones that are likely to increase, not decrease, in number, intensity, and complexity in the future. Are you ready for the challenges ahead? Are you informed about the issues and concerns that complicate our new workplace? Are you willing to admit that this is no time for complacency?

Globalization and job migration are changing the world of work.

Look around—there's hardly a person you know who hasn't been touched in some way or another by the recession. Many have lost jobs, savings, and even homes. Today's students wonder what the future holds for them after graduation; parents worry about how they can help pay for their childrens' college educations. And at the very time that our domestic economy is suffering, other countries are struggling as well. We're all interconnected now, and the fortunes and misfortunes of one country easily spill over to affect others.

Speaking of the global economy, do you know where your favorite athletic shoes or the parts for your computer and cell phone were manufactured? Can you go to the store and buy a toy or piece of apparel that is really "Made in America"? And whom do you speak with when calling a service center with computer problems, trying to track a missing package, or seeking information on how to change an airline ticket? More likely than not, the person serving you is on the phone from India, the Philippines, Ireland, or even Ghana.

Japanese management consultant Kenichi Ohmae calls this a "borderless world" where national boundaries have largely disappeared in world business.[25] Take the example of Hewlett-Packard.[26] It operates in 178 countries and most of its 304,000 employees work outside of the United States. It is the largest technology company in Europe, the Middle East, and Russia. Although headquartered in Palo Alto, California, one has to wonder: Is HP truly an American company anymore?

What we are talking about is **globalization**, the worldwide interdependence of resource flows, product markets, and business competition.[27] In the global

Globalization is the worldwide interdependence of resource flows, product markets, and business competition.

economy, businesses sell goods and services to customers around the world. They also search the world to buy the things they need wherever they can be found at the lowest price. This is **global sourcing**—hiring workers and contracting for supplies and services in other countries. The firms save money by manufacturing and getting jobs done in countries with lower costs of labor. When, for example, a shoe that costs $12 to make in the United States can be made in China for less than a dollar, doesn't it make business sense for Ohio-based Rocky Brands to shut down its American production line and outsource in China? Or is there more to the story?[28]

Global sourcing involves contracting for work that is performed in other countries.

One controversial side effect to global sourcing is **job migration**, the shifting of jobs from one country to another. At present, the U.S. economy is a net loser to such job migration. By contrast, countries such as China, India, and the Philippines are net gainers. And such countries aren't just sources of unskilled labor anymore. They are now able to offer highly trained workers—engineers, scientists, accountants, health professionals—for as little as one-fifth the cost of an equivalent U.S. worker.

Job migration occurs when global outsourcing shifts from one country to another.

Politicians and policymakers regularly debate how best to deal with the high costs of job migration, as local workers lose their jobs and their communities lose economic vitality. One side looks for new government policies to stop job migration by protecting the jobs of U.S. workers. The other side calls for patience, believing that the global economy will readjust in the long run and create new jobs for U.S. workers. Recent data suggest, in fact, that this is starting to happen as rising labor and transportation costs make manufacturing at home more attractive. Which side are you on—more regulation, or let markets take care of themselves?

‖ Failures of ethics and corporate governance are troublesome.

When Bernard Madoff was sentenced to 150 years in jail for crimes committed during the sensational collapse of his investment company and its $60+ billion fraudulent Ponzi scheme, the message was crystal clear.[29] There is no excuse for senior executives in any organization to act illegally and tolerate management systems that enrich the few while damaging the many.

The harm done by Madoff touched individuals who lost lifelong and retirement savings, charitable foundations that had invested monies with his firm, and the employees of his firm and others that went out of business as a result of the fraud. You could also argue that society at large paid a price when faith in the nation's business system was damaged by the scandal.[30] Worse yet, Madoff is not alone. All too often we learn about more scandals affecting banks and other financial institutions, as well as businesses and organizations of many other types. How would you recover if an employer bankruptcy or major business fraud affected you?

At the end of the day we depend on individual people, working at all levels of organizations, to act ethically. **Ethics** is a code of moral principles that sets standards of conduct for what is "good" and "right" as opposed to "bad" or "wrong."

Ethics set moral standards of what is "good" and "right" behavior in organizations and in our personal lives.

Given all the scandals, you might be cynical about ethical behavior in organizations. But even though ethics failures get most of the publicity, there is still a lot of good happening in the world of work. Look around. You'll also find stronger **corporate governance**, described earlier as the active oversight of management

Corporate governance is oversight of a company's management by a board of directors.

decisions, corporate strategy, and financial reporting by a company's board of directors.[31] Many people and organizations exemplify a new ethical reawakening, one that places high value on personal integrity and moral leadership.

In a book entitled *The Transparent Leader*, Herb Baum, former CEO of Dial Corporation, argues that integrity is a major key to ethics in leadership. He also tries to walk the talk—no reserved parking place, open door, honest communication, careful listening, and hiring good people. Believing that most CEOs are overpaid, he once gave his annual bonus to the firm's lowest-paid workers. He also tells the story of an ethical role model—a rival CEO, Reuben Mark of Colgate Palmolive. Mark called him one day to say that a newly hired executive had brought with him to Colgate a disk containing Dial's new marketing campaign. Rather than read it, he returned the disk to Baum—an act Baum called "the clearest case of leading with honor and transparency I've witnessed in my career."[32]

And as for you, why not make ethics a personal priority? Don't forget to read and consider the situations presented in Ethics Check for each chapter of this book.

{ THE YOUNG EXECUTIVE REALLY WANTS TO IMPRESS THE "BIG" BOSS.

Ethics Check

■ COKE'S SECRET FORMULA A TEMPTING TARGET

Scene: Corporate headquarters of PepsiCo. A young executive is gesturing excitedly, and three more obviously senior ones listen attentively. The CEO sits at her desk, swiveling occasionally in the chair while listening carefully to the conversation.

Young executive [*acting a bit proud to be there*]: It started with a telephone call. I agreed to meet with a former employee of Coca-Cola at his request. We met and, lo and behold, he offered me the "secret formula."

One of the senior executives [*cautiously*]: Let me be sure I understand. You received a call from someone who said they used to work at Coke, and that person was requesting a face-to-face meeting. Correct?

Young executive [*quickly and proudly*]: Right!

Senior executive [*with a bit of challenge*]: Why? Why would you meet with someone that said they just left Coke?

Young executive [*tentative now*]: Well . . . I . . . uh . . . It seemed like a great chance to get some competitive information and maybe even hire someone who really knows their strategies.

Second senior executive: So, what happened next?

Young executive [*excited again*]: Well, after just a minute or two conversing, he said that he had the formula!

Second senior executive: And . . .?

Young executive [*uncertain all of a sudden and now speaking softly*]: He said it was "for sale."

Third senior executive [*with a bit of edge in her voice*]: So what did you say?

Young executive [*looking down and shuffling slightly backward*]: I said that I'd take it "up the ladder." I'm supposed to call him back . . .

CEO [breaking into the conversation (*Note: As CEO speaks, other senior executives move over to stand behind her. Everyone looks in the direction of the young executive*)]: And we're glad you did "bring it up the ladder," as you say. But now that you have, what do you propose we do about this opportunity to buy Coke's most important secret?

YOU DECIDE

What do you think this junior executive will recommend? His or her career might rest on the answer. Better yet, how would you respond?

{ THE PAY GAP FOR WOMEN IN FINANCIAL
SERVICES IS THE LARGEST FOR ANY INDUSTRY.

Facts to Consider

■ EMPLOYMENT CONTRADICTIONS IN WORKFORCE DIVERSITY

The nonprofit research group Catalyst points out: "Now more than ever, as companies examine how to best weather an economy in crisis, we need talented business leaders, and many of these leaders, yet untapped, are women." But research studies and news reports show contradictions in workforce diversity.

- Women earn some 60% of college degrees, hold 50.6% of managerial jobs, and hold 15.7% of board seats at *Fortune* 500 companies; women of color hold 3.2% of board seats, and only 4% of firms have two women of color on their boards.
- The median compensation of female CEOs in North American firms is 85% that of males; in the largest firms it is 61%.
- For each $1 earned by male managers, female managers earn 79 cents; female managers in finance earn only 58.8 cents for each $1 earned by male managers.

- For each $1 earned by men, African-American women earn 64 cents and Hispanic women earn 52 cents.
- African Americans are 11.5% of the workforce and hold 8.3% of managerial and professional jobs.
- Asian Americans are 4.7% of the workforce and hold 6.3% of managerial and professional jobs.
- Hispanics are 11.1% of the workforce and hold 5% of managerial jobs.

YOUR THOUGHTS?

How can these data be explained? What are the implications for you and your career aspirations? What other contradictions in workforce diversity can you spot, and how can they be justified?

‖ Diversity and discrimination are continuing social priorities.

Workforce diversity describes differences among workers in gender, race, age, ethnicity, religion, sexual orientation, and able-bodiedness.

The term **workforce diversity** describes the composition of a workforce in terms of differences among people on gender, age, race, ethnicity, religion, sexual orientation, and physical ability.[33] The diversity trends of changing demographics are well recognized. Minorities now constitute more than one-third of the U.S. population and the proportion is growing. The U.S. Census Bureau predicts that by 2050 whites will be in the minority and the combined populations of African Americans, Native Americans, Asians, and Hispanics will be the new majority. Hispanics are now the largest minority group and the fastest growing—over 50 million and up 43% since 2000. By 2030, more than 20% of the population of the United States will be aged 65+ years. And, more seniors presently at work are deciding to postpone retirement.[34]

Even though our society is diverse, many diversity issues in employment remain as open challenges. Look at the diversity facts in the nearby box and ask how they can be explained. Consider also how to explain research in which résumés with white-sounding first names, like Brett, received 50% more responses from potential employers than those with black-sounding first names, such as Kareem.[35] The fact that these résumés were created with equal credentials suggests diversity bias.

U.S. laws strictly prohibit the use of demographic characteristics when human resource management decisions such as hiring, promotion, and firing are made. But laws are one thing, actions are yet another. Do you ever wonder why women and minorities hold few top jobs in large companies? One explanation is a subtle form of discrimination known as the **glass ceiling effect**. It occurs when an

The **glass ceiling effect** is an invisible barrier limiting career advancement of women and minorities.

invisible barrier, or "ceiling," prevents members of diverse populations from advancing to high levels of responsibility in organizations.[36]

There is little doubt that women and minorities still face special work and career challenges in our society at large.[37] Although progress is being made—for example more corporate board seats going to women—diversity bias still exists in too many of our work settings.[38] This bias begins with **prejudice**, the holding of negative, irrational attitudes regarding people who are different from us. It may surprise you, but an example is lingering prejudice against working mothers. The nonprofit Families and Work Institute reports that in 1977 only 49% of men and 71% of women believed that mothers could be good employees; in 2008 the figures had risen to 67% and 80% respectively.[39] Don't you wonder why the figures don't show 100% support of working mothers?

Prejudice becomes active **discrimination** when people in organizations treat minority members unfairly and deny them full membership benefits. Discrimination was evident in the résumés study described earlier. And prejudice also becomes discrimination when a male or female manager refuses to promote a working mother in the belief that "she has too many parenting responsibilities to do a good job at this level." Scholar Judith Rosener suggests that employment discrimination of any form comes at a high cost—not just to the individuals involved, but also to society. The organization's loss for any discriminatory practices, she says, is "undervalued and underutilized human capital."[40]

Many voices call diversity a "business imperative," meaning that today's increasingly diverse and multicultural workforce should be an asset that, if tapped, creates opportunities for performance gains. But even with such awareness existing, consultant R. Roosevelt Thomas says that too many employers still address diversity with the goal of "making their numbers."[41] A female vice president at Avon once described the challenges of truly valuing and managing diversity this way: "Consciously creating an environment where everyone has an equal shot at contributing, participating, and most of all advancing."[42]

⫼ Intellectual capital and self-management skills are essential for career success.

No matter how you look at it, the future poses a complex setting for career success. And if current trends continue, it will be more and more of a **free-agent economy**. Like professional athletes, many of us will be changing jobs more often and even working on flexible contracts with a shifting mix of employers over time.[43] British scholar and consultant Charles Handy uses the analogy of the **shamrock organization**, shown here, to describe the implications.[44] Each leaf in the shamrock organization represents a different group of workers.

The first leaf in Handy's shamrock organization is a core group of permanent, full-time employees with critical skills, who follow standard career paths. The second leaf consists of workers hired as freelancers and independent contractors. They provide organizations with specialized skills and talents for specific projects and then change employers when projects are completed. An increasing number of jobs in the new economy fall into this category. Some call this a time of *giganomics*, where even well-trained professionals

Prejudice is the display of negative, irrational attitudes toward women or minorities.

Discrimination actively denies women and minorities the full benefits of organizational membership.

In a **free-agent economy**, people change jobs more often, and many work on independent contracts with a shifting mix of employers.

A **shamrock organization** operates with a core group of full-time long-term workers supported by others who work on contracts and part time.

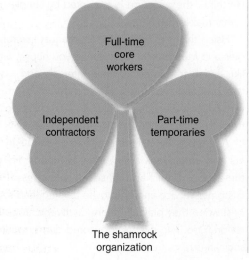

Full-time core workers

Independent contractors

Part-time temporaries

The shamrock organization

make their livings moving from one "gig" to the next, instead of holding a traditional full-time job.[45] The third leaf is a group of temporary part-timers. Their hours of work increase or decrease as the needs of the business rise or fall. They often work without benefits and are the first to lose their jobs when an employer runs into economic difficulties.

As you might guess, today's college graduates must be prepared to succeed in the second and third leaves of Handy's shamrock organization, not just the first. And to achieve success, Handy advises everyone to maintain a portfolio of skills that is always up-to-date and attractive to potential employers, regardless of where in the shamrock your goals may center.

You might begin by thinking seriously about your **intellectual capital**—what you can offer an employer in terms of brainpower, skills, and capabilities. Ideally, these will be things valued by the employer that also differentiate you a bit from others who might want the same job. A good way to address the issue is to use this intellectual capital equation:[46]

> **Intellectual capital** is the collective brainpower or shared knowledge of a workforce.

$$\text{Intellectual Capital} = \text{Competency} \times \text{Commitment}.$$

Competency represents our talents or job-relevant capabilities, while commitment represents our willingness to work hard in applying them to important tasks. Obviously, both are essential. One without the other is not enough to meet

Manager's Library

■ DELIVERING HAPPINESS: A PATH TO PROFITS, PASSION, AND PURPOSE

WHAT ARE YOU GOING TO BE WHEN YOU GROW-DOWN?

"What are you going to be when you grow up?" Those words echo through the mind starting in childhood and grow louder as adulthood approaches. The moment of truth finally arrives. Or has it? According to Tony Hsieh, author of the book *Delivering Happiness* (2010, Business Plus), 'being' something is more of a mindset than an occupation. He thinks the question is answered by simply asking yourself "what makes you happy?"

Hsieh thinks rules in business are just like rules about hobbies and friends—do what makes you happy with people you like. Hsieh translated youthful interests and associations into two profitable ventures. He founded two Internet start-ups with college friends—LinkExchange and Zappos.com—selling them for $256 million and $1.2 billion, respectively.

As Zappos' CEO, Hsieh cultivates a culture in which customers and employees are treated as friends. He considers this the Zappos brand and its secret to success. He emphasizes customer service and employee training, and says adults work best when they playfully share discoveries together, much like children do. Fun events sponsored during work hours enable social ties to cultivate.

Zappos welcomes customer calls and online chats as opportunities to create friendly bonds. They aren't timed, no script is used, and agents are guided by personal judgment. Zappos' mission is to 'Deliver WOW' and loyal customers receive surprise upgrades to overnight shipping.

Employees control career progression by choosing which company-designed courses to take and when to complete them. They receive incremental title and pay boosts rather than infrequent employer-driven reviews. This creates a pipeline of wide-ranging talent. Hsieh believes people must decide when and how to advance based on their happiness at each level.

Finding purpose in work comes with finding happiness; staying connected with others in common purpose beyond self-serving needs feels more like play than work. Hsieh reflects on his childhood worm farm and college pizza business as examples where work and friendship merged meaningfully. He stays busy having fun rather than growing up to be "something."

REFLECT AND REACT

Is Hsieh on to something here? How do you think the rules of work compare or contrast to the rules of play? Do you view play and work as individual pursuits or group undertakings? How are friends and coworkers similar or different? What are your pathways to happiness?

anyone's career needs or any organization's performance requirements. Max DePree, former CEO of Herman Miller, puts it this way: "We talk about the difference between being successful and being exceptional. Being successful is meeting goals in a good way—being exceptional is reaching your potential."[47]

When it comes to human potential, the workplace is well into the *information age* dominated by **knowledge workers**. These are persons whose minds, not just physical capabilities, are critical assets.[48] And things are not standing still. Futurist Daniel Pink says that we are already moving toward a *conceptual age* in which intellectual capital rests with people who are both "high concept"—creative and good with ideas, and "high touch"—joyful and good with relationships.[49] Pink believes the future will belong to those with "whole-mind" competencies, ones that combine left-brain analytical thinking with right-brain intuitive thinking.

> **Knowledge workers** use their minds and intellects as critical assets to employers.

There is no doubt that the free-agent economy places a premium on your capacity for **self-management**, realistically assessing yourself and actively managing your personal development. It means showing emotional intelligence, exercising initiative, accepting responsibility for accomplishments and failures, and continually seeking new learning opportunities and experiences. Take a look at the Explore Yourself feature. It's in each chapter and is designed to help you become better acquainted with your managerial skills and the implications for your career readiness. The first one is on self-management and the question you should be asking when reading it is: How well do I stack up?

> **Self-management** is the ability to understand oneself, exercise initiative, accept responsibility, and learn from experience.

The fact is that what happens from this point forward in your career is largely up to you. Would you agree that there is no better time than the present to start taking charge of what can be called your "personal brand"—a unique and timely package of skills and capabilities of real value to a potential employer? Management consultant Tom Peters advises that your brand should be "remarkable, measurable, distinguished, and distinctive" relative to the competition—others who want the same career opportunities that you do.[50]

Have you thought about what employers want? Are you clear and confident about the brand called "You"? Does your personal portfolio include new workplace survival skills?

{ SELF-MANAGEMENT HELPS US AVOID VIEWING OURSELVES MORE FAVORABLY THAN IS JUSTIFIED.

Explore Yourself

■ SELF-MANAGEMENT

When it comes to doing well as a student and in a career, a lot rests on how well you know yourself and what you do with this knowledge. **Self-management** involves acting with a strong sense of self-awareness, something that helps us build on strengths, overcome weaknesses, and avoid viewing ourselves more favorably than is justified. This capacity is an important career skill.

It can be easy to talk about self-management but much harder to master it. Why not use the many self-assessments in this book to get in better touch with this and other important career skills?

> Get to know yourself better by taking the self-assessment on **Personal Career Readiness** and completing the other activities in the *Exploring Management* **Skill-Building Portfolio**.

STUDY GUIDE

Takeaway 1.3
What Are Some Important Career Issues in the New Workplace?

Terms to Define

Corporate governance

Discrimination

Ethics

Free-agent economy

Glass ceiling effect

Global sourcing

Globalization

Intellectual capital

Job migration

Knowledge workers

Prejudice

Self-management

Shamrock organization

Workforce diversity

Rapid Review

- Globalization has brought increased use of global outsourcing by businesses and concern for the adverse effects of job migration.
- Society increasingly expects organizations and their members to perform with high ethical standards and in socially responsible ways.
- Organizations operate with diverse workforces, and each member should be respected for her or his talents and capabilities.
- Work in the new economy is increasingly knowledge-based, relying on people with valuable intellectual capital to drive high performance.
- Careers in the new economy are becoming more flexible, requiring personal initiative to build and maintain skill portfolios that are always up-to-date and valued by employers.

Questions for Discussion

1. How are current concerns about ethics in business, globalization, and changing careers addressed in your courses and curriculum?
2. Is it possible for members of minority groups to avoid being hurt by prejudice, discrimination, and the glass ceiling effect in their careers?
3. In what ways can the capacity for self-management help you to prosper in a free-agent economy?

Be Sure You Can

- describe how corporate governance influences ethics in organizations
- explain how globalization and job migration are changing the economy
- differentiate prejudice, discrimination, and the glass ceiling effect
- state the intellectual capital equation
- discuss career opportunities in the shamrock organization
- explain the importance of self-management to career success

What Would You Do?

One of the plus sides of globalization is that a growing number of locals are now working domestically for foreign employers that have established businesses in their local communities. How about you? Does it make any difference if you receive a job offer from a foreign employer such as Haier—a Chinese firm that makes popular home appliances—or a domestic employer? What are the "pluses and minuses" of working at home for a foreign employer? Do the pluses outweigh the minuses for you?

TestPrep 1

Multiple-Choice Questions

1. If a sales department supervisor is held accountable by a middle manager for the department's performance, on whom is the department supervisor dependent in making this performance possible?
   (a) board of directors
   (b) top management
   (c) customers or clients
   (d) department sales persons

2. The management function of _____ is being activated when a bookstore manager measures daily sales in the magazine section and compares them with daily sales targets.
   (a) planning
   (b) agenda setting
   (c) controlling
   (d) delegating

3. The process of building and maintaining good working relationships with others who may someday help a manager implement his or her work agendas is called _____.
   (a) governance
   (b) networking
   (c) emotional intelligence
   (d) entrepreneurship

4. According to Robert Katz, _____ skills are more likely to be emphasized by top managers than by first-line managers.
   (a) human   (b) conceptual
   (c) informational (d) technical

5. An effective manager is someone who helps others to achieve high levels of both _____ and _____.
   (a) pay; satisfaction
   (b) performance; satisfaction
   (c) performance; pay
   (d) pay; quality work life

6. _____ is the active oversight by boards of directors of top management decisions in such areas as corporate strategy and financial reporting.
   (a) Value chain analysis
   (b) Productivity
   (c) Outsourcing
   (d) Corporate governance

7. When a manager denies promotion to a qualified worker simply because of personally disliking her because she is Hispanic, this is an example of _____.
   (a) discrimination
   (b) workforce diversity
   (c) self-management
   (d) a free-agent economy

8. A company buys cloth in one country, has designs made in another country, has the garments sewn in another country, and sells the finished product in yet other countries. This firm is actively engaging in the practice of _____.
   (a) job migration
   (b) performance effectiveness
   (c) value creation
   (d) global sourcing

9. The intellectual capital equation states: Intellectual Capital = _____ × Commitment.
   (a) Diversity
   (b) Confidence
   (c) Competency
   (d) Communication

10. If the direction in managerial work today is away from command and control, what is it toward?
    (a) coaching and facilitating
    (b) telling and selling
    (c) pushing and pulling
    (d) carrot and stick

11. The manager's role in the "upside-down pyramid" view of organizations is best described as providing _____ so that operating workers can directly serve _____.
    (a) direction; top management
    (b) leadership; organizational goals
    (c) support; customers
    (d) agendas; networking

12. When a team leader clarifies desired work targets and deadlines for a work team, he or she is fulfilling the management function of _____.
    (a) planning
    (b) delegating
    (c) controlling
    (d) supervising

13. The research of Mintzberg and others concludes that most managers _____.
    (a) work at a leisurely pace
    (b) have blocks of private time for planning
    (c) always live with the pressures of performance responsibility
    (d) have the advantages of short workweeks

14. Emotional intelligence helps us to manage ourselves and our relationships effectively. Someone that is high in emotional intelligence will have the capacity to _____, an ability to think before acting and to control potentially disruptive emotions and actions.
    (a) set agendas
    (b) show motivation
    (c) self-regulate
    (d) act as a leader

15. Which of the following is a responsibility that is most associated with the work of a CEO, or chief executive officer, of a large company?
    (a) linking the company with the external environment
    (b) reviewing annual pay raises for all employees
    (c) monitoring short-term performance by task forces and committees
    (d) conducting hiring interviews for new college graduates

Short-Response Questions

16. What is the difference between prejudice and workplace discrimination?

17. How is the emergence of a free-agent economy changing career and work opportunities?

18. In what ways will the job of a top manager typically differ from that of a first-line manager?

19. How does planning differ from controlling in the management process?

Integration and Application Question

20. Suppose you have been hired as the new supervisor of an audit team for a national accounting firm. With four years of auditing experience, you feel technically well prepared. However, it is your first formal appointment as a manager. The team has 12 members of diverse demographic and cultural backgrounds, and varying work experience. The workload is intense, and there is a lot of performance pressure.

    Questions: In order to be considered *effective* as a manager, what goals will you set for yourself in the new job? What skills will be important to you, and why, as you seek success as the audit team supervisor?

Steps*for*FurtherLearning

Many learning resources are found at the end of the book and online within WileyPLUS.

Don't Miss These Selections from the **Skill-Building Portfolio**

■ **SELF-ASSESSMENT 1:** *Personal Career Readiness*

■ **CLASS EXERCISE 1:** *My Best Manager*

■ **TEAM PROJECT 1 :** *Managing Millennials*

Take advantage of this Selection from **Cases for Critical Thinking**

■ **CHAPTER 1 CASE**
Trader Joe's—Managing with a Cool Edge

Case Snapshot It's just an average day at Trader Joe's, the gourmet, specialty, and natural-foods store that offers staples such as milk and eggs along with curious, one-of-a-kind foods at below-average prices in almost thirty states. Foodies, hipsters, and recessionistas alike are attracted to the chain's charming blend of low prices, tasty treats, and laid-back but enthusiastic customer service.

Shopping at Trader Joe's is less a chore than it is immersion into another culture. In keeping with its whimsical faux-nautical theme, crew members and managers wear loud tropical-print shirts. Chalkboards around every corner unabashedly announce slogans such as, "You don't have to join a club, carry a card, or clip coupons to get a good deal." Take a walk down the aisle of Trader Joe's and learn how sharp attention to the fundamentals of retail management made this chain more than the average Joe.

Make notes here on what you've learned about yourself from this chapter.

■ **LEARNING JOURNAL 1**

Great management isn't new, and it isn't all high tech . . . it is part of our history.

Management Learning

2

Great Things Grow from Strong Foundations

Learning Style and *Mr. Holland's Opus*

Glenn Holland (Richard Dreyfus) is an aspiring musician who wants to compose. He takes a job as a high school music teacher to gain more time for composition. One day he has an epiphany—he realizes his students do not learn music the way he did.

Gertrude Lang (Alicia Witt) desperately wants to play the clarinet because everyone else in her family excels at something. As much as she practices, she never improves. Mr. Holland helps her understand that music is about heart and feeling and that she needs to trust herself in order to play effectively. So, she learns to play by imagining a song as a sunset.

Louis Russ (Terrence Howard) must learn to play the bass drum to remain eligible for sports. The way he learns is different; he needs action and a model to follow. Mr. Holland gets Russ to understand timing and rhythm by imitating his beat.

Each of us has a preferred **learning style**, a set of ways through which we like to learn by receiving, processing, and recalling new information. For Gertrude Lang, it was being able to create a mental image that allowed music to flow from her heart to her fingertips. Lou Russ's style involved physically feeling and duplicating the rhythm being tapped by his teacher. As in these examples, we can often learn better when our styles are understood. How about you? Are you in touch with your learning style?

YOUR CHAPTER 2 TAKEAWAYS

1. Understand the lessons of the classical management approaches.

2. Identify the contributions of the behavioral management approaches.

3. Recognize the foundations of modern management thinking.

WHAT'S INSIDE

Explore Yourself
More on learning styles

Role Models
Carol Bartz used executive experience to create change at Yahoo!

Ethics Check
Employment agreements can be tricky

Facts to Consider
Generations differ when rating their bosses

Manager's Library
Outliers by Malcolm Gladwell

Takeaway 2.1
What Are the Lessons of the Classical Management Approaches?

ANSWERS TO COME

- Taylor's scientific management sought efficiency in job performance.
- Weber's bureaucratic organization is supposed to be efficient and fair.
- Fayol's administrative principles describe managerial duties and practices.

HISTORIANS TRACE MANAGEMENT AS FAR BACK AS 5000 B.C., WHEN ANCIENT Sumerians used written records to assist in governmental and commercial activities.[1] Management contributed to the construction of the Egyptian pyramids, the rise of the Roman Empire, and the commercial success of 14th-century Venice. During the Industrial Revolution in the 1700s, great social changes helped to prompt a leap forward in the manufacture of basic staples and consumer goods. Adam Smith's ideas of efficient production through specialized tasks and the division of labor further accelerated industrial development.

By the turn of the 20th century, Henry Ford and others were making mass production a mainstay of the emerging economy.[2] What we now call the classical school was launching a path of rapid and continuing development in the science and practices of management.[3] Prominent representatives of this school and their major contributions to management thinking include Frederick Taylor—scientific management, Max Weber—bureaucracy, and Henri Fayol—administrative principles.

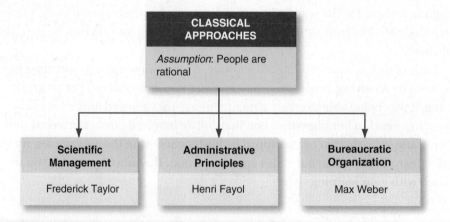

⦀ Taylor's scientific management sought efficiency in job performance.

In 1911, Frederick W. Taylor stated the following in his book *The Principles of Scientific Management:* "The principal object of management should be to secure maximum prosperity for the employer, coupled with the maximum prosperity for the employee."[4] Taylor had noticed that many workers did their jobs in their own way—perhaps haphazard—and without consistent supervision. And it seemed to him that a lack of clear and uniform methods caused workers to lose efficiency and perform below their true capacities. As a result, their organizations also underperformed.

To correct this problem, Taylor believed that jobs should be studied to identify their basic steps and motions as well as determine the most efficient ways of doing them. Once this job "science" was defined, workers could be trained to follow it, and supervisors could be trained to support and encourage workers to perform to the best of their abilities. This approach became known as **scientific management** and it included these four core principles.

1. Develop a "science" for each job—rules of motion, standard work tools, and proper work conditions.
2. Hire workers with the right abilities for the job.
3. Train and motivate workers to do their jobs according to the science.
4. Support workers by planning and assisting their work according to the science.

> **Scientific management** emphasizes careful selection and training of workers and supervisory support.

One of the most enduring legacies of the scientific management approach grew out of Taylor's first principle and involves **motion study**, the science of reducing a job or task to its basic physical motions. Two of Taylor's contemporaries, Frank and Lillian Gilbreth, pioneered the use of motion studies as a management tool.[5] In one famous case, they reduced the number of motions used by bricklayers and tripled their productivity.[6]

> **Motion study** is the science of reducing a job or task to its basic physical motions.

Are you clear about the principles of scientific management? Think about what happens when a top coach trains a group of soccer players. If the coach teaches players the techniques of their positions and how the positions fit into the overall team strategy, the team will probably do better in its games, right? In the same way, Taylor hoped to improve the productivity of workers and organizations. With a stopwatch and notebook in hand, he analyzed tasks and motions to describe the most efficient ways to perform them.[7] He then linked these requirements with job training, monetary incentives for performance success, and better direction and assistance from supervisors.

A ready example of how Taylor's ideas are still used is United Parcel Service. Sorters at regional centers are timed according to strict task requirements and are expected to load vans at a set number of packages per hour. GPS technology plots the shortest routes; delivery stops are studied and carefully timed; supervisors generally know within a few minutes how long a driver's pickups and deliveries will take. Industrial engineers also devise precise routines for drivers. The point in classic scientific management fashion is that savings of seconds on individual stops adds up to significant increases in productivity.

Tips to Remember

■ SCIENTIFIC MANAGEMENT LESSONS FOR TODAY'S MANAGERS

- Make results-based compensation a performance incentive.
- Carefully design jobs with efficient work methods.
- Carefully select workers with the abilities to do these jobs.
- Train workers to perform jobs to the best of their abilities.
- Train supervisors to support workers to best perform their jobs.

‖ Weber's bureaucratic organization is supposed to be efficient and fair.

> The purely bureaucratic type of administrative organization . . . is from a purely technical point of view capable of attaining the highest degree of efficiency. . . . It is superior to any other form in precision, in stability, in the stringency of its discipline, and in its reliability. It thus makes possible a particularly high degree of calculability of results for the heads of the organization and for those acting in relation to it. It is finally superior both in intensive efficiency and in the scope of its operations and is formally capable of application to all kinds of administrative tasks.
>
> Max Weber, *The Theory of Social Economic Organization*

Max Weber was a late-19th-century German intellectual whose insights have made a significant impact on the field of management and the sociology of organizations.[8] Like Taylor, his ideas developed somewhat in reaction to what he considered to be poor performance by the organizations of his day. He was especially concerned that people were in positions of authority not because of their job-related capabilities but because of their social standing or "privileged" status in German society.

Have you seen similar problems? Have you ever been upset that people rise to positions of major responsibility in organizations not because of their competencies, but because of whom they know or how well they play political games? Look around, talk to friends and relatives. Are Weber's concerns at all relevant today?

At the heart of Weber's proposal for correcting performance problems with organizations was a specific approach he called a **bureaucracy**.[9] When staffed and structured along the lines listed in Table 2.1, *Characteristics of an Ideal Bureaucracy,* he believed organizations could be both highly efficient and very fair in treating their members and clients. For Weber, an organization of this type—the bureaucracy—was ideal and rational. And in effect, he was recommending that this is how all organizations should be run.

A **bureaucracy** is a rational and efficient form of organization founded on logic, order, and legitimate authority.

Table 2.1 Characteristics of an Ideal Bureaucracy

Clear Division of Labor Jobs are well defined, and workers become highly skilled at performing them.

Clear Hierarchy of Authority Authority and responsibility are well defined, and each position reports to a higher-level one.

Formal Rules and Procedures Written guidelines describe expected behavior and decisions in jobs; written files are kept for the historical record.

Impersonality Rules and procedures are impartially and uniformly applied; no one gets preferential treatment.

Careers Based on Merit Workers are selected and promoted on ability and performance; managers are career employees of the organization.

A bureaucracy works well, in theory at least, because of its reliance on logic, order, and legitimate authority. It also works well because people are selected for their jobs because of competency and are only promoted to higher-level ones because of demonstrated performance. But if it is so good, why do we so often hear the terms "bureaucracy" and "bureaucrat" used negatively? That's because bureaucracies don't always live up to Weber's expectations.

Think of the last time you were a client of a traditional bureaucracy, perhaps a government agency or the registrar at your school. Would you agree that they are sometimes slow in handling problems, making changes, and adapting to new customer or client needs? As a customer, have you sometimes encountered employees who seem disconnected, hesitant to make a decision, resistant to change, and even apathetic in relating to you? When was the last time you were frustrated at the service you received and complained about an organization's excessive "red tape"?

These and other disadvantages of bureaucracy are most likely to limit performance and cause problems for organizations that must be flexible and quick in adapting to changing times—a common situation today. And they are irritants for demanding customers, perhaps like you, who want quick service and a quality customer experience.

The bureaucratic model isn't the best choice for all organizations. It works well sometimes, but not all of the time. In fact, a major challenge for research on organizational design is to identify when and under what conditions bureaucratic features work well and what the best alternatives are when they don't. Later in the module we'll call this "contingency thinking."

{ THE MILLENNIAL GENERATION IS MORE POSITIVE THAN BABY BOOMERS ABOUT BOSSES' PERFORMANCE.

Facts to Consider

■ GENERATIONS DIFFER WHEN RATING THEIR BOSSES

Would it surprise you that Millennials (born 1982–1996) have somewhat different views of their bosses than their Generation X and Baby Boomer co-workers? Check out these data from a Kenexa survey that asked 11,000 respondents to rate their managers' performance.

- Overall performance positive—Boomers 55%, Gen Xers 59%, Millennials 68%
- People management positive—Boomers 50%, Gen Xers 53%, Millennials 62%
- Work management positive—Boomers 52%, Gen Xers 55%, Millennials 63%
- Keeping commitments positive—Boomers 59%, Gen Xers 60%, Millennials 65%
- Outstanding leader—Boomers 39%, Gen Xers 43%, Millennials 51%

YOUR THOUGHTS?

A Kenexa researcher says that Millennials are "more willing to take direction and accept authority" while "as we grow older, our ideas become more concrete and less flexible." Does this seem like an accurate conclusion? How can these generational differences in evaluating managers be explained? And, by the way, what do these data suggest if you are managing people from these different generations?

Fayol's administrative principles describe managerial duties and practices.

Another branch in the classical approaches to management includes attempts to document and understand the experiences of successful managers. The most prominent writer in this realm is Henri Fayol.

In 1916, after a career in French industry, Henri Fayol published *Administration Industrielle et Générale*.[10] The book outlines his views on the proper management of organizations and the people within them. It identifies five "rules" or "duties" of management in respect to foresight, organization, command, coordination, and control:

- *Foresight*—complete a plan of action for the future.
- *Organization*—provide and mobilize resources to implement plan.
- *Command*—lead, select, and evaluate workers.
- *Coordination*—fit diverse efforts together, ensure information is shared and problems are solved.
- *Control*—make sure things happen according to plan, take necessary corrective action.

Look closely at Fayol's duties. Do you see how they resemble the four functions of management that we talk about today—planning, organizing, leading, and controlling? Importantly, Fayol believed that managers could be taught to put these functions into practice in the best ways. For example, he offered the following "principles" as guides to managerial action. You'll still hear them talked about in the vocabulary of everyday management. Fayol's **scalar chain principle** stated that there should be a clear and unbroken line of communication from the top to the bottom in the organization. His **unity of command principle** stated that each person in an organization should receive orders from only one boss. Would you say that these principles still make sense today?

The **scalar chain principle** states that organizations should operate with clear and unbroken lines of communication top to bottom.

The **unity of command principle** states that a worker should receive orders from only one boss.

{ SOME EMPLOYERS HAVE POLICIES THAT REQUIRE NEW HIRES TO SIGN "NO-COMPETE" AGREEMENTS.

Ethics Check

▪ EMPLOYMENT AGREEMENTS CAN BE TRICKY

Nelsonville, Ohio—Rocky Brands chief executive Mike Brooks filed a suit in Athens County Common Pleas Court against Joe P. Marciante, former regional vice president for sales. Marciante had resigned from Rocky, and Brooks believed he was going to work for a competitor. The suit claimed Marciante violated a "no-compete" agreement he had signed, which stipulated he would not go to work for a competitor for one year after leaving Rocky Brands. The court was asked to enforce the one-year waiting period and require that Marciante return all materials in his possession that contained inside information on Rocky Brands.

YOU DECIDE

No-compete clauses and nondisclosure agreements are increasingly common in employment contracts. Chances are that you will be asked to sign one someday. Is it ethical for a firm to ask a new hire to sign such an agreement? Is it ethical for someone leaving a firm to try to break such an agreement? Ask your friends, co-workers, and family for their views and even their personal experiences. What advice about employment agreements is available from the professionals and perhaps from your college or campus placement services?

STUDY GUIDE

Takeaway 2.1
What Are the Lessons of the Classical Management Approaches?

Terms to Define

Bureaucracy

Motion study

Scalar chain principle

Scientific management

Unity of command principle

Rapid Review

- Taylor's principles of scientific management focused on the need to carefully select, train, support, and reward workers in their jobs.
- Weber considered bureaucracy, with its clear hierarchy, formal rules, well-defined jobs, and competency-based staffing, to be a form of organization that is efficient and fair.
- Fayol suggested that managers learn and fulfill duties we now call the management functions of planning, organizing, leading, and controlling.

Questions for Discussion

1. How did Taylor and Weber differ in the approaches they took to improving the performance of organizations?
2. Should Weber's concept of the bureaucratic organization be scrapped, or does it still have potential value today?
3. What are the risks of accepting the "lessons of experience" offered by successful executives such as Fayol?

Be Sure You Can

- list the principles of Taylor's scientific management
- list key characteristics of bureaucracy
- explain why Weber considered bureaucracy an ideal form of organization
- list possible disadvantages of bureaucracy
- describe how Fayol's "duties" overlap with the four functions of management

What Would You Do?

It's summer job time and you've found something that just might work—handling customer service inquiries at a local Internet provider. The regular full-time employees are paid by the hour. Summer hires like you fill in when they go on vacation. You will be paid by the call, $1.25 for each customer that you handle. How will this pay plan affect your behavior as a customer service representative? Is this pay plan a good choice for the Internet provider to use for its summer hires?

Takeaway 2.2
What Are the Contributions of the Behavioral Management Approaches?

ANSWERS TO COME

- Follett viewed organizations as communities of cooperative action.
- The Hawthorne studies focused attention on the human side of organizations.
- Maslow described a hierarchy of human needs with self-actualization at the top.
- McGregor believed managerial assumptions create self-fulfilling prophecies.
- Argyris suggests that workers treated as adults will be more productive.

DURING THE 1920S, EMPHASIS ON THE HUMAN SIDE OF THE WORKPLACE INFLUENCED the emergence of behavioral management approaches. As shown in Figure 2.1, this new school of thought included Follett's notion of the organization as a community, the well-known Hawthorne studies, and Maslow's theory of human needs, as well as theories generated from the work of Douglas McGregor and Chris Argyris. The underlying assumptions are that people are social and self-actualizing, and that workers seek satisfying social relationships, respond to group pressures, and search for personal fulfillment. Does that sound like you?

FIGURE 2.1

Who Are the Major Contributors to the Behavioral or Human Resource Approaches to Management Thinking?

The human resource approaches shifted management thinking away from physical factors and work structures and toward the human side of organizations. The contributors shown here each focused on people as individuals and how their needs may influence their attitudes and behavior at work.

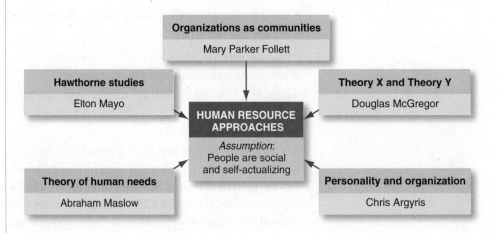

⦀ Follett viewed organizations as communities of cooperative action.

On her death in 1933, Mary Parker Follett was eulogized as "one of the most important women America has yet produced in the fields of civics and sociology."[11] She has been called a "prophet" of management, and her work is a reminder that good things really do grow from strong foundations.[12]

Even though Follett's ideas were expressed more than 80 years ago, many would consider them very farsighted indeed.[13] Her ideas still offer the wisdom of history. She advocated social responsibility, respect for workers, and better cooperation throughout organizations; she warned against the dangers of too

"Life Is Good" Means Business

Happiness May Be Your Guide to Career Building

Imagine! Yes, you can! Go for it! Life is good. Well, make that: Life is really good! These are thoughts that turn dreams into realities. They're also part and parcel of the $80 million company named Life Is Good. It began with two brothers, Bert and John Jacobs, making T-shirts for street sales and has grown into a 200+ employee company selling a variety of fun apparel and related products in 14 or more countries. *Inc.* magazine calls it a "fine small business that only wants to make me happy."

Bert, Chief Executive Optimist, and Jake, Chief Creative Optimist, built a company devoted to humor and humility. John says: "It's important that we're saying 'Life is good,' not 'Life is great' or 'Life is perfect,' there's a big difference. . . . Don't determine that you're going to be happy when you get the new car or the big promotion or meet that special person. You can decide that you're going to be happy today." And that's the message of the Life Is Good brand.

Bert and Jake have stuck to their values on this journey to business success. They live the brand, enjoying leisure pursuits such as kayaking and ultimate Frisbee; they support philanthropies such as Camp Sunshine for children with serious illnesses and Project Joy for traumatized children; and the company runs seasonal Life Is Good festivals to help raise money for charities.

Life is good.®

FIND INSPIRATION

Bert and John didn't start with business degrees or experience, but they had good instincts, creativity, and positive views on life. And they learned as they progressed. Each step forward was a chance to capture business and management experience, learn from it, and keep getting better. How about you? Can we say that you're a student of history and use past experiences to improve in the future?

much hierarchy and called for visionary leadership. Many of these themes are still central to management theory, even though we describe them by terms such as "empowerment," "involvement," "flexibility," "self-management," and "transformational leadership."

Follett suggested that making every employee an owner in the business would create feelings of collective responsibility. Today, we address the same issues as "employee ownership," "profit sharing," and "gain-sharing plans." Follet believed that business problems involve a wide variety of factors that must be considered in relationship to one another. Today, we talk about "systems" when describing the same phenomenon. Follett viewed businesses as services, organizations that should always consider making profits vis-á-vis the public good. Today, we pursue the same issues as "managerial ethics" and "corporate social responsibility."

And what can be said about executive success today?[14] I wonder what Follett would say? My guess is that Follett would agree that the successful 21st-century executive must be an *inspiring leader* who attracts talented people and motivates them in a setting where everyone can do his or her best work. She would argue that every manager, regardless of level, should be an *ethical role model*—always acting ethically, setting high ethical standards, and infusing ethics throughout the organization. And she would point out that anyone aspiring to managerial success must be an *active doer,* someone ready to make things happen, focus attention on the right things, and make sure that they really get done.

‖ The Hawthorne studies focused attention on the human side of organizations.

The **Hawthorne effect** is the tendency of persons singled out for special attention to perform as expected.

In 1924, the Western Electric Company commissioned a study of individual productivity at the Hawthorne Works of the firm's Chicago plant.[15] The initial "Hawthorne studies," with a research team headed by Elton Mayo of Harvard University, sought to determine how economic incentives and the physical conditions of the workplace affected the output of workers. But their results were perplexing. After failing to find that better lighting in the manufacturing facilities would improve productivity, they concluded that unforeseen "psychological factors" somehow interfered with their study. Yet similar results occurred when they conducted further tests.

After isolating six relay-assembly workers in a special room, Mayo and his team measured the effect on outputs of various rest pauses as well as lengths of workdays and workweeks. They found no direct relationship between changes in physical working conditions and performance; productivity increased regardless of the changes made. The researchers concluded that these results were caused by the new "social setting" in the test room. The six workers in the test room shared pleasant conversations with one another and received more attention from the researchers than they got from supervisors in their usual jobs. As a result, they tried to do what they thought the researchers wanted them to do—a good job.

This tendency to try to live up to expectations became known as the **Hawthorne effect**. One of its major implications is the possibility that people's performance will be affected by the way they are treated by their managers. Have you noticed that people given special attention will tend to perform as expected? Could the Hawthorne effect explain why some students, perhaps you, do better in smaller classes or for instructors who pay more attention to them in class?

The Hawthorne studies continued until the economic conditions of the Depression forced their termination. By then, interest in the human factor had broadened to include employee attitudes, interpersonal relations, and group relations. For example, over 21,000 employees were interviewed to learn what they liked and disliked about their work environment. "Complex" and "baffling" results led the researchers to conclude that the same things that satisfied some workers—such as work conditions or wages—led to dissatisfaction for others. And a "surprise" finding in a final study was that people would restrict their output in order to avoid the displeasure of the group, even if it meant sacrificing increased pay. Mayo and his team had recognized firsthand what most of us realize already: that groups can have strong negative, as well as positive, influences on the behaviors of their members.

Scholars have criticized the Hawthorne studies for poor research design, weak empirical support for the conclusions drawn, and overgeneralized findings.[16] And there is no doubt that management research has moved on with greater care in the use of scientific methods. But the Hawthorne studies were significant turning points in the evolution of management thought. They helped shift the attention of managers and researchers away from the technical and structural concerns of the classical approaches and toward social and human concerns as important keys to workplace productivity.

Maslow described a hierarchy of human needs with self-actualization at the top.

The work of psychologist Abraham Maslow in the area of human needs emerged as a key component of the new direction in management thinking.[17] He began with the notion of the human **need**, a physiological or psychological deficiency that a person feels compelled to satisfy. Why, you might ask, is this a significant concept for managers? The answer is because needs create tensions that can influence a person's work attitudes and behaviors.

What needs, for example, are important to you? How do they influence your behavior, the way you study and the way you work? You probably already know that Maslow described the five levels of human needs shown in **Figure 2.2**. They are grouped as lower-order needs—physiological, safety, and social, and higher-order needs—esteem and self-actualization.

A **need** is a physiological or psychological deficiency that a person wants to satisfy.

Self-actualization needs

Highest level: need for self-fulfillment; to grow and use abilities to fullest and most creative extent

Esteem needs

Need for esteem in eyes of others; need for respect, prestige, recognition and self-esteem, personal sense of competence, mastery

HIGHER-ORDER NEEDS

Social needs

Need for love, affection, sense of belongingness in one's relationships with other people

Safety needs

Need for security, protection, and stability in the events of day-to-day life

LOWER-ORDER NEEDS

Physiological needs

Most basic of all human needs: need for biological maintenance; food, water, and physical well-being

FIGURE 2.2

How Does Maslow's Hierarchy of Human Needs Operate?
In Abraham Maslow's theory, human needs are satisfied in a step-by-step progression. People first satisfy the lower-order needs: physiological, safety, and social. Once these are satisfied, they focus on the higher-order ego and self-actualization needs. A satisfied need no longer motivates behavior, except at the level of self-actualization. At this top level, the need grows stronger the more it is satisfied.

According to Maslow, people try to satisfy the five needs in sequence, moving step-by-step from the lowest to the highest. He called this the **progression principle**—a need only becomes activated after the next-lower-level need is satisfied. Once a need is activated, it dominates attention and

Maslow's **progression principle** is that a need at any level becomes activated only after the next-lower-level need is satisfied.

Maslow's **deficit principle** is that people act to satisfy needs for which a satisfaction deficit exists; a satisfied need doesn't motivate behavior.

determines behavior until it is satisfied. But then it no longer motivates behavior. Maslow called this the **deficit principle**—people act to satisfy deprived needs for which a satisfaction "deficit" exists. Only at the highest level of self-actualization do the deficit and progression principles cease to operate. The more this need is satisfied, the stronger it grows.

Maslow's theory can help us to better understand people's needs and help find ways to satisfy them through their work. Of course, this is easier said than done. If it were easy, we wouldn't have so many cases of workers going on strike against their employers, complaining about their jobs, or quitting to find better ones. Consider also the case of volunteers working for the local Red Cross, a community hospital, or a youth soccer league. Our society needs volunteers; most nonprofit organizations depend on them. But what needs move people to do volunteer work? How can one keep volunteers involved and committed in the absence of pay?

⫽ McGregor believed managerial assumptions create self-fulfilling prophecies.

Maslow's work, along with the Hawthorne studies, surely influenced another prominent management theorist, Douglas McGregor. His classic book, *The Human Side of Enterprise,* suggests that managers should pay more attention to the social and self-actualizing needs of people at work.[18] He framed his argument as a contrast between two opposing views of human nature: a set of negative assumptions he called "Theory X" and a set of positive ones he called "Theory Y."

Theory X assumes people dislike work, lack ambition, are irresponsible, and prefer to be led.

Managers holding **Theory X** assumptions expect people to generally dislike work, lack ambition, act irresponsibly, resist change, and prefer to follow rather than to lead. McGregor considered such thinking wrong, believing that **Theory Y** assumptions are more appropriate and consistent with human potential. Managers holding Theory Y assumptions expect people to be willing to work, capable of self-control and self-direction, responsible, and creative.

Theory Y assumes people are willing to work, accept responsibility, are self-directed, and are creative.

Can you spot differences in how you behave or react when treated in a Theory X way or a Theory Y way? McGregor strongly believed that these assumptions create **self-fulfilling prophecies.** That is, as with the Hawthorne effect, people end up behaving consistently with the assumptions. Managers holding Theory X assumptions are likely to act in directive "command-and-control" ways, often giving people little say over their work. This in turn often creates passive, dependent, and reluctant subordinates who do only what they are told to do. Have you ever encountered a manager or instructor with a Theory X viewpoint?

A **self-fulfilling prophecy** occurs when a person acts in ways that confirm another's expectations.

Managers with Theory Y assumptions behave quite differently. They are more "participative," likely giving others more control over their work. This creates opportunities to satisfy higher-order esteem and self-actualization needs. In response, the workers are more likely to act with initiative, responsibility, and high performance. The self-fulfilling prophecy occurs again, but this time it is a positive one. You should find Theory Y thinking reflected in a lot of the ideas and developments discussed in this book, such as valuing diversity, employee involvement, job enrichment, empowerment, and self-managing teams.[19]

Explore Yourself

■ LEARNING STYLE

Each of us has a preferred **learning style**, a set of ways through which we like to learn by receiving, processing, and recalling new information. Hopefully, you take advantage of this book to gain insights into your style and where and how it works best.

Given that learning is any change of behavior that results from experience, one of our most significant challenges is to always embrace experiences—at school, at work, and in everyday living—and try our best to learn from them. The same can be said about unlocking the wisdom of history. This chapter is a reminder about management history and how the achievements of the past can still provide insights that can help us deal with the present.

> Get to know yourself better by taking the self-assessment on **Managerial Assumptions** and completing the other activities in the *Exploring Management* **Skill-Building Portfolio**.

⦀ Argyris suggests that workers treated as adults will be more productive.

Ideas set forth by the well-regarded scholar and consultant Chris Argyris also reflect the positive views of human nature advanced by Maslow and McGregor. In his book *Personality and Organization,* Argyris contrasts the management practices found in traditional and hierarchical organizations with the needs and capabilities of mature adults.[20]

Argyris clearly believes that when problems such as employee absenteeism, turnover, apathy, alienation, and low morale plague organizations, they may be caused by a mismatch between management practices and the adult nature of their workforces. His basic point is that no one wants to be treated like a child, but that's just the way many organizations treat their workers. The result, he suggests, is a group of stifled and unhappy workers who perform below their potential.

Does Argyris seem to have a good point? For example, scientific management assumes that people will work more efficiently on better-defined tasks. Argyris would likely disagree, believing that simplified jobs limit opportunities for self-actualization in one's work. In a Weberian bureaucracy, typical of many of our government agencies, people work in a clear hierarchy of authority, with higher levels directing and controlling the work of lower levels.[21] This is supposed to be an efficient way of doing things. Argyris would worry that workers lose initiative and end up being less productive. Also, Fayol's administrative principles assume that efficiency will increase when supervisors plan and direct a person's work. Argyris might suggest that this sets up conditions for psychological failure; psychological success is more likely when people define their own goals.

STUDY GUIDE

Takeaway 2.2
What Are the Contributions of the Behavioral Management Approaches?

Terms to Define

Deficit principle

Hawthorne effect

Need

Progression principle

Self-fulfilling prophecies

Theory X

Theory Y

Rapid Review

- Follett's ideas on groups, human cooperation, and organizations that served social purposes foreshadowed current management themes.
- The Hawthorne studies suggested that social and psychological forces influence work behavior and that good human relations may lead to improved work performance.
- Maslow's hierarchy of human needs suggested the importance of self-actualization and the potential for people to satisfy important needs through their work.
- McGregor criticized negative Theory X assumptions about human nature and advocated positive Theory Y assumptions that view people as independent, responsible, and capable of self-direction in their work.
- Argyris pointed out that people in the workplace are mature adults who may react negatively when management practices treat them as if they were immature.

Questions for Discussion

1. How did insights from the Hawthorne studies redirect thinking from the classical management approaches and toward something quite different?
2. If Maslow's hierarchy of needs theory is correct, how can a manager use it to become more effective?
3. Where and how do McGregor's notions of Theory X and Theory Y overlap with Argyris's ideas regarding adult personalities?

Be Sure You Can

- explain why Follett's ideas were quite modern in concept
- summarize findings of the Hawthorne studies
- explain and illustrate the Hawthorne effect
- explain Maslow's deficit and progression principles
- distinguish between McGregor's Theory X and Theory Y assumptions
- explain the self-fulfilling prophecies created by Theory X and Theory Y
- explain Argyris's concern that traditional organizational practices are inconsistent with mature adult personalities

What Would You Do?

As a manager in a small local firm, you've been told that because of the poor economy workers can't be given any pay raises this year. You have some really hardworking and high-performing people on your team, and you were counting on giving them solid raises. Now what can you do? How can you use insights from Maslow's hierarchy of needs to solve this dilemma? Is it really possible to find suitable rewards other than pay for team members' high performance?

Takeaway 2.3
What Are the Foundations of Modern Management Thinking?

ANSWERS TO COME

- Managers use quantitative analysis and tools to solve complex problems.
- Organizations are open systems that interact with their environments.
- Contingency thinking holds that there is no one best way to manage.
- Quality management focuses attention on continuous improvement.
- Evidence-based management seeks hard facts about what really works.

THE NEXT STEP IN THE TIMELINE OF MANAGEMENT HISTORY SETS THE STAGE FOR a stream of new developments that are continuing to this day. Loosely called the modern management approaches, they share the assumption that people and organizations are complex, growing and changing over time in response to new problems and opportunities in their environments. The many building blocks of modern management include use of quantitative tools and techniques, recognition of the inherent complexity of organizations as systems, contingency thinking that rejects the search for universal management principles, attention to quality management, and the desire to ground management practice in solid scientific evidence.

⫼ Managers use quantitative analysis and tools to solve complex problems.

About the same time that some scholars were developing human resource approaches to management, others were investigating how quantitative techniques could improve managerial decision making. The foundation of these analytical decision sciences approaches is the assumption that mathematical techniques can be used for better problem solving. At Google, for example, a math formula has been developed to aid in retaining talent. It pools information from performance reviews and surveys, promotions, and pay histories to identify employees who might feel underutilized and be open to offers from other firms. Human resource management plans are then developed to try and retain them.[22]

In our world of vast computing power and the easy collection and storage of data, there is renewed emphasis on how to use available data to make better management decisions. This is an area of management practice known as **analytics**, the use of data to solve problems and make informed decisions using systematic analysis.[23] And in respect to analytics, scholars are very interested in learning how managers can use mathematical tools to conduct quantitative and statistical analyses.

The terms **management science** and **operations research** are often used interchangeably to describe the use of mathematical techniques to solve management problems. A typical quantitative approach proceeds as follows. A problem

Analytics is the systematic use and analysis of data to solve problems and make informed decisions.

Management science and **operations research** apply mathematical techniques to solve management problems.

is encountered, it is systematically analyzed, appropriate mathematical models and computations are applied, and an optimum solution is identified. Consider these examples.

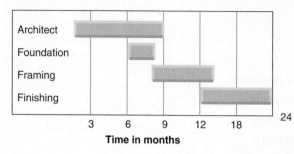

Time in months

Problem A real estate developer wants to control costs and finish building a new apartment complex on time. Quantitative approach: *Network models* like the Gantt chart pictured nearby break large tasks into smaller components to track completion of many different activities on the required timetables.

Problem An oil exploration company is worried about future petroleum reserves in various parts of the world. Quantitative approach: *Mathematical forecasting* helps make future projections for reserve sizes and depletion rates that are useful in the planning process.

Problem A big box retailer is trying to deal with pressures on profit margins by minimizing costs of inventories while never being "out of stock" for customers. Quantitative approach: *Inventory analysis* helps control inventories by mathematically determining how much to automatically order and when.

Problem A grocery store is getting complaints from customers that waiting times are too long for checkouts during certain times of the day. Quantitative approach: *Queuing theory* helps allocate service personnel and workstations based on alternative workload demands and in a way that minimizes both customer waiting times and costs of service workers.

Problem A manufacturer wants to maximize profits for producing three different products on three different machines, each of which can be used for different periods of times and at different costs. Quantitative approach: *Linear programming* is used to calculate how best to allocate production among different machines.

An important counterpart to these management science approaches is **operations management**, which focuses on how organizations produce goods and services efficiently and effectively. The emphasis is on the study and improvement of operations, the transformation process through which goods and services are actually created. The essentials of operations management include such things as business process analysis, workflow designs, facilities layouts and locations, work scheduling and project management, production planning, inventory management, and quality control.

Operations management is the study of how organizations produce goods and services.

Organizations are open systems that interact with their environments.

The concept of system is a key ingredient of modern management thinking. **Figure 2.3** shows that organizations are **open systems** that interact with their environments to obtain resources—people, technology, information, money, and supplies—that are transformed through work activities into goods and services for their customers and clients. All organizations, from IBM to the U.S. Postal Service to your college or university and the local bookstore, can be described this way.

An **open system** transforms resource inputs from the environment into product outputs.

FIGURE 2.3

How Do Organizations as Open Systems Interact with Their External Environments? As open systems, organizations continually interact with their external environments to obtain resource inputs, transform those inputs through work activities into goods and services, and deliver finished products to their customers. Feedback from customers indicates how well they are doing.

The open-systems concept helps explain why there is so much emphasis today on organizations being customer-driven. This means they try hard to focus their resources, energies, and goals on continually satisfying the needs of their customers and clients. Look again at Figure 2.3 and you should recognize the logic. Can you see how customers hold the keys to the long-term prosperity and survival of a business, such as an auto manufacturer? Their willingness to buy products or use services provides the revenues needed to obtain resources and keep the cycle in motion. And as soon as the customers balk or start to complain, someone should be listening. This feedback is a warning that the organization needs to change and do things better in the future.

Any organization also operates as a complex network of **subsystems**, or smaller components, whose activities individually and collectively support the work of the larger system.[24] **Figure 2.4** shows the importance of cooperation among organizational subsystems.[25] In the figure, for example, the operations and service management systems serve as a central point. They provide the integration among other subsystems, such as purchasing, accounting, sales, and information, all of which are essential to the work, and the success, of the organization. But the reality is that the cooperation is often imperfect and could be improved upon. Just how organizations achieve this, of course, is a major management challenge.

A **subsystem** is a smaller component of a larger system.

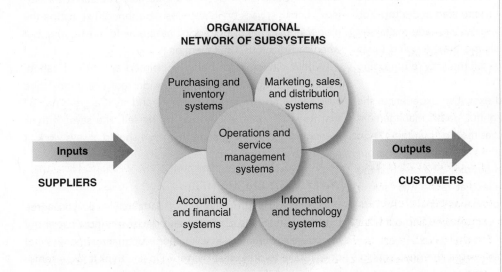

FIGURE 2.4

How Do Organizations Operate as Complex Networks of Subsystems? Externally, organizations interact with suppliers and customers in their environments. Internally, many different subsystems must interact and work well together so that high-quality inputs are transformed into products satisfying customers' needs. Common subsystems of a business include purchasing, information technology, operations management, marketing and sales, distribution, human resources, and accounting and finance.

||| Contingency thinking holds that there is no one best way to manage.

Contingency thinking tries to match management practices with situational demands.

Rather than try to find the one best way to manage in all circumstances, modern management adopts **contingency thinking**. That is, it recognizes organizational complexities and attempts to identify practices that best fit with the unique demands of different situations.

Consider again the concept of bureaucracy. Weber offered it as an ideal form of organization. But from a contingency perspective, the strict bureaucratic form is only one possible way of organizing things. What turns out to be the best structure in any given situation will depend on many factors, including environmental uncertainty, available technology, staff competencies, and more. Contingency thinking recognizes that the structure that works well for one organization may not work well for another in different circumstances. Also, what works well at one point in time may not work as well in the future if circumstances have changed.[26]

You should find a lot of contingency thinking in this book. Its implications extend to all of the management functions—from planning and controlling for diverse environmental conditions, to organizing for diverse workforces and multiple tasks, to leading in different performance situations. And this is a good reflection of everyday realities. Don't you use a lot of contingency thinking when solving problems and otherwise going about your personal affairs?

{ "I THINK MANAGING IS A REAL JOB, SOMETHING YOU SHOULD ALWAYS WORK AT AND TRY TO DO BETTER."

Role Models

■ CAROL BARTZ USED EXECUTIVE EXPERIENCE TO CREATE CHANGE AT YAHOO!

When Carol Bartz was interviewed by the *Wall Street Journal* regarding her leadership as the new CEO of Yahoo, Inc., she said: "Fair but tough. We all work hard, and work has to be an interesting, fun place. And that has to start at the top. You have to be willing to say, 'I don't know,' 'I made mistakes,' and change. When somebody tells me they're going to do something, I want them to do it or tell me they're not going to do it."

With plenty of technology and executive experience, she is known for being strong and insightful. Bartz's management style has been described by others as mixing "bluntness" and "humor." One of her former executives at Autodesk points out that "she could get the best out of people." She says that the first thing she did when taking the lead at Yahoo was "set up 45-minute sessions with as many people as I could." According to Bartz, "If you sit quiet long enough, you find out what people really think."

Throughout her career, Bartz has fought the glass ceiling, making no bones about what she considered discrimination from a business community ruled by men. She cites an incident that occurred in a meeting with U.S. Senators. One turned to Carol Bartz and said: "So, how are we going to start the meeting?" Looking back on it, she says: "He thought I must be the moderator. It's annoying. I don't have time for these guys, but when it's ridiculous, I call them on it."

Within six weeks of being appointed as CEO of Yahoo, Bartz was "preparing a company-wide reorganization." She calls Yahoo an "important property and such a great name" that needs "structure." And as for herself, she says, "I think managing is a real job, something you should always work at and try to do better."

WHAT'S THE LESSON HERE?

Whatever you might think about Bartz's style, do you agree that she certainly is confident and decisive? And what about her career experiences as a woman in top management? What does it take to do well at the top? Do you think it takes something "extra" if you are a woman?

▌ Quality management focuses attention on continuous improvement.

The work of W. Edwards Deming is a cornerstone of the quality movement in management.[27] His story began in 1951, when he was invited to Japan to explain quality control techniques that had been developed in the United States. "When Deming spoke," we might say, "the Japanese listened." The principles he taught the Japanese were straightforward, and they worked: Tally defects, analyze and trace them to the source, make corrections, and keep a record of what happens afterward. Deming's approach to quality emphasizes constant innovation, use of statistical methods, and commitment to training in the fundamentals of quality assurance.[28]

One outgrowth of Deming's work was the emergence of **total quality management**, or TQM. This process makes quality principles part of the organization's strategic objectives, applying them to all aspects of operations and striving to meet customers' needs by doing things right the first time. Most TQM approaches begin with an insistence that the total quality commitment applies to everyone in an organization, from resource acquisition and supply chain management, through production and into the distribution of finished goods and services, and ultimately to customer relationship management.

The search for and commitment to quality is now tied to the emphasis modern management gives to the notion of **continuous improvement**—always looking for new ways to improve on current performance.[29] The goal is that one can never be satisfied; something always can and should be improved upon.

> **Total quality management** is managing with an organization-wide commitment to continuous improvement, product quality, and customer needs.

> **Continuous improvement** involves always searching for new ways to improve work quality and performance.

{ ACHIEVEMENT-ORIENTED INDIVIDUALS POSSESS CAN-DO ATTITUDES AND PERSIST THROUGH DIFFICULTY WHEN OTHERS GIVE UP.

Manager's Library

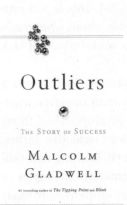

Outliers

THE STORY OF SUCCESS

MALCOLM GLADWELL

#1 bestselling author of The Tipping Point and Blink

■ *OUTLIERS* BY MALCOLM GLADWELL

WHAT IS YOUR PATH TO SUCCESS?

Studies of individual greatness lead many observers to the adage "great leaders are born, not made." But according to author Malcolm Gladwell in the book *Outliers* (2008, Little, Brown and Company), extraordinary people—or outliers—are made, not born. Ingredients like practice, social savvy, and positive attitude are needed along with opportunity to nurture these skills.

Gladwell insists that high IQ cannot predict success and instead a minimum threshold is necessary. Your environment provides more critical elements, and he cites the "10,000 hour rule" that defines the amount of work logged by eventual masters of various disciplines. Gladwell contends that you must practice to become great, not simply once you become great. He contends achievement-oriented individuals possess a can-do attitude, and persist through difficulty when others give up. He recommends you choose complex and meaningful interests that promote self-direction. By exerting and reflecting on your progress you can train yourself to become a master.

Gladwell argues that success is not an innate ability but something that most can achieve given the right chance. He laments that we select individuals with exceptional ability over those with threshold ability. Those born bright often fail to make themselves successful, while those born with modest intellect could flourish given the opportunity to make themselves great.

REFLECT AND REACT

Are you destined for greatness? How much time do you spend on your favorite activity? Are you entitled to good things in life and how do you assert yourself? When you do poorly on something do you give up or try until you do well? Is someone with a high GPA more likely to succeed than someone who leads a student organization and works twenty hours a week?

‖ Evidence-based management seeks hard facts about what really works.

Looking back on the historical foundations of management, one thing that stands out is criticism by today's scholars of the scientific rigor of some historical cornerstones, among them Taylor's scientific management approach and the Hawthorne studies. The worry is that we may be too quick in accepting as factual the results of studies that are based on weak or even shoddy empirical evidence. And if the studies are flawed, perhaps more care needs to be exercised when trying to apply their insights to improve management practices. This problem isn't limited to the distant past.[30]

A book by Jim Collins, *Good to Great,* achieved great acclaim and best-seller status for its depiction of highly successful organizations.[31] But Collins's methods and findings have since been criticized by researchers.[32] And after problems appeared at many firms previously considered by him to be "great," he wrote a follow-up book called *How the Mighty Fall.*[33] The point here is not to discredit what keen observers of management practice like Collins and others report. But it is meant to make you cautious and a bit skeptical when it comes to separating fads from facts and conjecture from informed insight.

Today's management scholars are trying to move beyond generalized impressions of excellence to understand more empirically the characteristics of **high-performance organizations**—ones that consistently achieve high-performance results while also creating high quality-of-work-life environments for their employees. Following this line of thinking, Jeffrey Pfeffer and Robert Sutton make the case for **evidence-based management**, or EBM. This is the process of making management decisions on "hard facts"—that is, about what really works—rather than on "dangerous half-truths"—things that sound good but lack empirical substantiation.[34]

Using data from a sample of some 1,000 firms, for example, Pfeffer and a colleague found that firms using a mix of well selected human resource management practices had more sales and higher profits per employee than those that didn't.[35] Those practices included employment security, selective hiring, self-managed teams, high wages based on performance merit, training and skill development, minimal status differences, and shared information. Examples of other EBM findings include challenging goals accepted by an employee are likely to result in high performance, and that unstructured employment interviews are unlikely to result in the best person being hired to fill a vacant position.[36]

Scholars pursue a variety of solid empirical studies using proven scientific methods in many areas of management research. Some carve out new and innovative territories, while others build upon and extend knowledge that has come down through the history of management thought. By staying abreast of such developments and findings, managers can have more confidence that they are approaching decisions from a solid foundation of evidence rather than mere speculation or hearsay.

A **high-performance organization** consistently achieves excellence while creating a high-quality work environment.

Evidence-based management involves making decisions based on hard facts about what really works.

Basic Scientific Methods

- A research question or problem is identified.
- Hypotheses, or possible explanations, are stated.
- A research design is created to systematically test the hypotheses.
- Data gathered in the research are analyzed and interpreted.
- Hypotheses are accepted or rejected based upon the evidence.

STUDY GUIDE

Takeaway 2.3
What Are the Foundations of Modern Management Thinking?

Terms to Define

Analytics

Contingency thinking

Continuous improvement

Evidence-based management

High-performance organization

Management science

Open system

Operations management

Operations research

Subsystem

Total quality management

Rapid Review

- Advanced quantitative techniques in decision sciences and operations management help managers solve complex problems.
- The systems view depicts organizations as complex networks of subsystems that must interact and cooperate with one another if the organization as a whole is to accomplish its goals.
- Contingency thinking avoids "one best way" arguments, recognizing instead that managers need to understand situational differences and respond appropriately to them.
- Quality management focuses on making continuous improvements in processes and systems.
- Evidence-based management uses findings from rigorous scientific research to identify management practices for high performance.

Questions for Discussion

1. Can you use the concepts of open system and subsystem to describe the operations of an organization in your community?
2. In addition to the choice of organization structures, in what other areas of management decision making do you think contingency thinking plays a role?
3. Does evidence-based management allow for managers to learn from their own experiences as well as the experiences of others?

Be Sure You Can

- discuss the importance of quantitative analysis in management decision making
- use the terms "open system" and "subsystem" to describe how an organization operates
- explain how contingency thinking might influence a manager's choices of organization structures
- describe the role of continuous improvement in total quality management
- give examples of workplace situations that can benefit from evidence-based management

What Would You Do?

You've just come up with a great idea for improving productivity and morale in a shop that silk-screens T-shirts for Life is Good (featured earlier in the chapter). You will allow workers to work four 10-hour days if they want instead of the normal five-day/40-hour week. With the added time off, you reason, they'll he happier and more productive while working. But your boss isn't so sure. "Show me some evidence," she says. Can you design a research study that can be done in the shop to show whether or not your proposal is a good one?

TestPrep 2

Multiple-Choice Questions

1. A management consultant who advises managers to carefully study jobs, train workers to do them with efficient motions, and tie pay to job performance is using ideas from _____.
   - √(a) scientific management
   - (b) contingency thinking
   - (c) Henri Fayol
   - (d) Theory Y

2. The Hawthorne studies were important in management history because they raised awareness about the influence of _____ on productivity.
   - (a) organization structures
   - (b) human factors
   - (c) physical work conditions
   - (d) pay and rewards

3. If Douglas McGregor heard an instructor complaining that her students were lazy and irresponsible, he would say these assumptions _____.
   - (a) violated scientific management ideas
   - (b) focused too much on needs
   - √(c) would create a negative self-fulfilling prophecy
   - (d) showed contingency thinking

4. If your local bank or credit union is a complex system, then the loan-processing department of the bank would be considered a _____.
   - √(a) subsystem
   - (b) closed system
   - (c) learning organization
   - (d) bureaucracy

5. When a manager puts Kwabena in a customer relations job because he has strong social needs and gives Sherrill lots of daily praise because she has strong ego needs, he is displaying _____.
   - (a) systems thinking
   - (b) Theory X
   - √(c) contingency thinking
   - (d) administrative principles

6. Which of the following is one of the characteristics of Weber's ideal bureaucracy?
   - (a) few rules and procedures
   - √(b) impersonality
   - (c) promotion by privilege not by merit
   - (d) ambiguous hierarchy of authority

7. Which principle states that a person should only receive orders from one boss in an organization?
   - (a) scalar
   - (b) contingency
   - (c) Hawthorne
   - √(d) unity of command

8. One of the conclusions from the Hawthorne studies was that _____.
   - (a) motion studies could improve performance
   - √(b) groups can sometimes restrict the productivity of their members
   - (c) people respond well to monetary incentives
   - (d) supervisors should avoid close relations with their subordinates

9. If an organization was performing poorly, what would Henri Fayol most likely advise as a way to improve things?
   - √(a) teach managers to better plan, organize, lead, and control
   - (b) give workers better technology
   - (c) promote only the best workers to management
   - (d) find ways to improve total quality management

10. When a worker has a family, makes car payments, and is active in local organizations, how might Argyris explain her poor work performance?
    - √(a) She isn't treated as an adult at work.
    - (b) Managers are using Theory Y assumptions.
    - (c) Organizational subsystems are inefficient.
    - (d) She doesn't have the right work skills.

11. _____ management assumes people are complex, with widely varying needs.
    - (a) Classical
    - (b) Neoclassical
    - √(c) Behavioral
    - (d) Modern

12. Conflict between the mature adult personality and a rigid organization was a major concern of _____.
    - √(a) Argyris
    - (b) Follett
    - (c) Gantt
    - (d) Fuller

13. The highest level in Maslow's hierarchy is
_____.

(a) safety   (b) esteem

✓(c) self-actualization   (d) physiological

14. If an organization is considered an open system, work activities that turn resources into outputs are part of the _____ process.

(a) input   ✓(b) transformation

(c) output   (d) feedback

15. When managers make decisions based on solid facts and information, this is known as
_____.

(a) continuous improvement

(b) evidence-based management

(c) Theory Y

(d) Theory X

Short-Response Questions

16. Give an example of how principles of scientific management can apply in organizations today.

17. How do the deficit and progression principles operate in Maslow's hierarchy?

18. Compare the Hawthorne effect with McGregor's notion of self-fulfilling prophecies.

19. Explain by example several ways a manager might use contingency thinking in the management process.

Integration and Application Question

20. Enrique Temoltzin is the new manager of a college bookstore. He wants to do a good job and decides to operate the store on Weber's concept of bureaucracy.   **Question:** Is bureaucracy the best approach here? What are its potential advantages and disadvantages? How could Enrique use contingency thinking in this situation?

StepsforFurtherLearning

Many learning resources are found at the end of the book and online within WileyPLUS.

Don't Miss These Selections from the **Skill-Building Portfolio**

■ **SELF-ASSESSMENT 2:** *Managerial Assumptions*

■ **CLASS EXERCISE 2:** *Evidence-Based Management Quiz*

■ **TEAM PROJECT 2:** *Management in Popular Culture*

Don't Miss This Selection from **Cases for Critical Thinking**

■ **CHAPTER 2 CASE**
Zara International: Fashion at the Speed of Light

Snapshot Shoppers in 77 countries are fans of Zara's knack for bringing the latest styles from sketchbook to clothing rack at lightning speed—and reasonable prices. Low prices and a rapid response to fashion trends give Zara a top ranking among global clothing vendors. The chain specializes in quick turnarounds of the latest designer trends at prices tailored to the young— about $27 an item. Louis Vuitton fashion director Daniel Piette described Zara as "possibly the most innovative and devastating retailer in the world."

"How do you excuse betraying thousands," said Bernard Madoff when sentenced to 150 years in jail for a multi-billion dollar financial fraud.

Ethics and Social Responsibility

3

Character Doesn't Stay Home When We Go to Work

Individual Character and *The Blind Side*

In *The Blind Side,* Academy Award winner Sandra Bullock plays Leigh Anne Tuohy, a strong-willed southern woman. She reaches out to help an African-American high school student with no stable home, a history of academic underachievement, and raw athletic talent.

The movie is based on real-life events. It shows how Tuohy first met Michael Oher on a cold, rainy night following a school play. The story quickly moves to the point where she persuaded her family to take him in and eventually become his legal guardians.

Oher thrives with Tuohy and her family, going on to become a standout high school and college football player. He was eventually picked in the first round of the National Football League draft by the Baltimore Ravens.

What Leigh Anne Tuohy showed in terms of individual character and integrity in the situation can be an inspiration for us all. Our **individual character** isn't something to think about only on occasion. Along with its foundation of personal integrity, individual character deserves constant attention.

Watch the movie, read this chapter on ethics and social responsibility, and think about the many ways you might help those around you.

YOUR CHAPTER 3 TAKEAWAYS

1. Understand how ethics and ethical behavior play out in the workplace.

2. Know how to maintain high standards of ethical conduct.

3. Identify when organizations are and are not acting in socially responsible ways.

WHAT'S INSIDE

Explore Yourself
More on individual character

Role Models
Gary Hirshberg goes for triple bottom line at Stonyfield Farm

Ethics Check
Committing to a green supply chain

Facts to Consider
Behavior of managers key to an ethical workplace

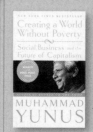

Manager's Library
Creating a World Without Poverty by Muhammad Yunus

Takeaway 3.1
How Do Ethics and Ethical Behavior Play Out in the Workplace?

ANSWERS TO COME

- Ethical behavior is values driven.
- What is considered ethical varies among moral reasoning approaches.
- What is considered ethical can vary across cultures.
- Ethical dilemmas arise as tests of personal ethics and values.
- People tend to rationalize unethical behaviors.

DOES LEARNING ABOUT BAD BUSINESS BEHAVIOR SHOCK AND DISMAY YOU? "MADOFF fraud bankrupts charities." "Madoff gets 150 years in prison." "Worldcom CEO sentenced to 25 years in prison." "Owner of peanut factory refuses to testify at congressional hearing into *Salmonella* deaths." Such headlines and their underlying scandals are all too frequent in the news. And the stories underlying them aren't ones of incompetence; they tell tales of personal failures and greed.[1] With bleak reports like these, it's understandable that some people, perhaps a lot of them, are left feeling cynical, pessimistic, and even helpless regarding the state of executive leadership in our society.[2]

So what can be done? For starters, would you say that it is time to get serious about the moral aspects and social implications of behavior in and by organizations? Can we agree here that in your career and for any manager the goal should always be to achieve performance objectives through ethical and socially responsible actions? As you think about these questions, keep in mind this advice from Desmond Tutu, archbishop of Capetown, South Africa, and winner of the Nobel Peace Prize.[3]

You are powerful people. You can make this world a better place where business decisions and methods take account of right and wrong as well as profitability. . . . You must take a stand on important issues: the environment and ecology, affirmative action, sexual harassment, racism and sexism, the arms race, poverty, the obligations of the affluent West to its less-well-off sisters and brothers elsewhere.

Ethics sets standards of good or bad, or right or wrong, in our conduct.

Ethical behavior is "right" or "good" in the context of a governing moral code.

It is tempting to say that any behavior that is legal can also be considered ethical. But this is too easy; the "letter of the law" does not always translate into what others would consider to be ethical actions.[4] U.S. laws once allowed slavery, permitted only men to vote, and allowed young children to work full-time jobs. Today we consider such actions unethical.

Ethics is defined as the code of moral principles that sets standards of good or bad, or right or wrong, in our conduct.[5] Personal ethics are guides for behavior, helping people make moral choices among alternative courses of action. Most typically, we use the term **ethical behavior** to describe what we accept as "good" and "right" as opposed to "bad" or "wrong."

‖ Ethical behavior is values driven.

It's one thing to look back and make ethical judgments; it is a bit harder to make them in real time. Is it truly ethical for an employee to take longer than necessary to do a job … to make personal telephone calls on company time … to call in sick and go on vacation instead? While not strictly illegal, many people would consider any one or more of these acts to be unethical. How about you? How often and in what ways have you committed or observed acts that could be considered unethical in your school or workplace?[6]

Many ethical problems arise at work when people are asked to do something that violates their personal beliefs. For some, if the act is legal, they proceed with confidence and consider their behavior ethical. For others, the ethical test goes beyond legality and extends to personal **values**—underlying beliefs and judgments regarding what is right or desirable and that influence individual attitudes and behaviors.

The psychologist Milton Rokeach distinguishes between "terminal" and "instrumental" values.[7] **Terminal values** focus on desired ends, such as the goal of lifelong learning. Examples of terminal values considered important by managers include self-respect, family security, freedom, inner harmony, and happiness. **Instrumental values** focus on the means for accomplishing these ends, such as the role of intellectual curiosity in lifelong learning. Instrumental values held important by managers include honesty, ambition, courage, imagination, and self-discipline.

Although terminal and instrumental values tend to be quite enduring for any one individual, they can vary considerably from one person to the next. A contrast of such values might help to explain why different people respond quite differently to the same situation. Although two people might share the terminal

> **Values** are broad beliefs about what is appropriate behavior.

> **Terminal values** are preferences about desired end states.

> **Instrumental values** are preferences regarding the means to desired ends.

{ THE MOST COMMON UNETHICAL ACTS BY MANAGERS INCLUDE VERBAL, SEXUAL, AND RACIAL HARASSMENT.

Facts to Consider

■ THE BEHAVIOR OF MANAGERS IS KEY TO AN ETHICAL WORKPLACE

Managers make a big difference in ethical behavior at work, according to a survey conducted for Deloitte & Touche USA. Some findings include:

- 42% of workers say the behavior of their managers is a major influence on an ethical workplace.
- The most common unethical acts by managers and supervisors include verbal, sexual, and racial harassment; misuse of company property; and giving preferential treatment.
- 91% of workers are more likely to behave ethically when they have work-life balance; 30% say they suffer from poor work-life balance.
- Top reasons for unethical behavior are lack of personal integrity (80%) and lack of job satisfaction (60%).

- Most workers consider it unacceptable to steal from an employer, cheat on expense reports, take credit for another's accomplishments, and lie on time sheets.
- Most workers consider it acceptable to ask a work colleague for a personal favor, take sick days when not ill, and use company technology for personal affairs.

YOUR THOUGHTS?

Are there any surprises in these data? Is this emphasis on manager and direct supervisor behavior justified as the key to an ethical workplace? Would you make any changes to what the workers in this survey report as acceptable and unacceptable work behaviors?

value of career success, they might disagree on how to balance the instrumental values of honesty and ambition in accomplishing it.

Talk with some of your friends or classmates about their terminal values (what you and they want to achieve) and instrumental values (how you and they are willing to do it). Don't be surprised to find values differences, and don't be surprised to find that these differences create conflicts. Some of them may rest on significant differences in what behaviors are and are not considered ethical.

Consider this situation. About 10% of an MBA class at Duke University was once caught cheating on a take-home final exam.[8] The "cheaters" averaged 29 years of age and six years of work experience; they were also big on music downloads, file sharing, open-source software, text messaging, and electronic collaboration. Some say what happened is a good example of "postmodern learning" where students are taught to collaborate, work in teams, and utilize the latest communication technologies. For others, there is no doubt—it was an individual exam and those students cheated.

What is considered ethical varies among moral reasoning approaches.

Figure 3.1 shows four different philosophical views of ethical behavior, with each representing an alternative approach to moral reasoning.[9] They are the utilitarian, individualism, justice, and moral rights views.

FIGURE 3.1
How Do Alternative Moral Reasoning Approaches View Ethical Behavior?
People often differ in the approaches they take toward moral reasoning, and they may use different approaches at different times and situations. Four ways to reason through the ethics of a course of action are utilitarianism, individualism, moral rights, and justice. Each approach can justify an action as ethical, but the reasoning will differ from that of the other views.

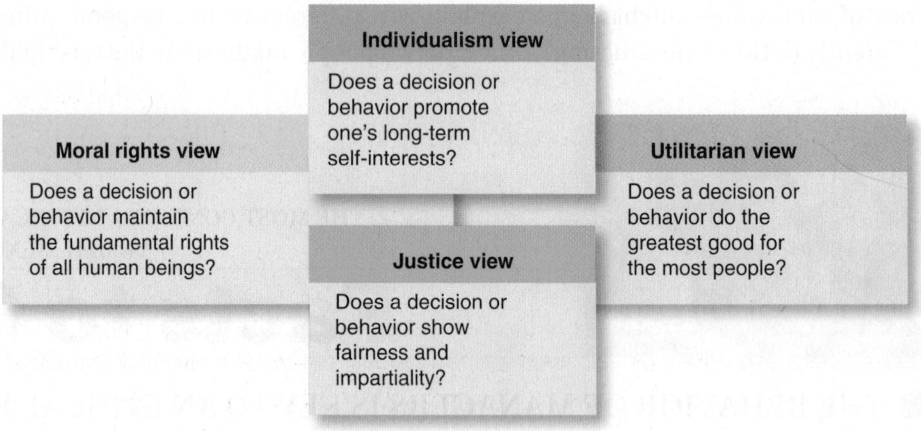

Individualism view
Does a decision or behavior promote one's long-term self-interests?

Moral rights view
Does a decision or behavior maintain the fundamental rights of all human beings?

Utilitarian view
Does a decision or behavior do the greatest good for the most people?

Justice view
Does a decision or behavior show fairness and impartiality?

In the **utilitarian view**, ethical behavior delivers the greatest good to the most people.

Utilitarian View

The **utilitarian view** considers ethical behavior to be that which delivers the greatest good to the greatest number of people. Founded in the work of 19th-century philosopher John Stuart Mill, this results-oriented view tries to assess the moral implications of our actions in terms of their consequences. Business executives, for example, might use profits, efficiency, and other performance criteria to judge what decision is best for the most people.

An example of the utilitarian view toward ethical behavior is the manager who decides to cut 30% of a plant's workforce in order to keep the plant profitable and save the remaining jobs, rather than lose them all to business failure. This decision seems defensible from a utilitarian perspective, but we also have to be careful. Utilitarian thinking relies on the assessment of future outcomes that are often difficult to predict and that are tough to measure accurately. What is the economic value of a human life when deciding how rigid safety regulations need to be on an offshore drilling rig, for example? Is it even appropriate to try to put an economic value on the potential loss of human life?

Individualism View

Whereas in the utilitarian view ethical behavior delivers the greatest good to the most people, the **individualism view** focuses on the long-term advancement of self-interests. The notion is people become self-regulating as they strive for individual advantage over time; ethics are maintained in the process. Suppose, for example, that you consider cheating on your next test. You also realize this quest for short-term gain might lead to a long-term loss if you get caught and expelled. This reasoning shows an individualism view toward ethical behavior and should cause you to quickly reject the original inclination to cheat on the exam.

Not everyone, as you might expect, agrees that decisions based on the individualism view will result in honesty and integrity. One complaint is that individualism in business practice too often results in a *pecuniary ethic*. This has been described by one executive as a tendency to "push the law to its outer limits" and "run roughshod over other individuals to achieve one's objectives."[10] The individualism view also presumes that individuals are self-regulating. But we know that not everyone has the same capacity or desire to control their behaviors. Even if only a few individuals take unethical advantage of the freedom allowed under this perspective, such instances can disrupt the degree of trust that exists within a business community and make it difficult to predict how others will act.

> In the **individualism view**, ethical behavior advances long-term self-interests.

Justice View

The **justice view** of moral reasoning considers a behavior ethical when people are treated impartially and fairly, according to legal rules and standards. It judges the ethical aspects of any decision on the basis of how equitable it is for everyone affected.[11] Today, researchers often speak about four types of workplace justice—procedural, distributive, interactional, and commutative.

Procedural justice involves the fair administration of policies and rules. For example, does a sexual harassment charge levied against a senior executive receive the same full hearing as one made against a first-level supervisor? **Distributive justice** involves the allocation of outcomes without respect to individual characteristics, such as those based on ethnicity, race, gender, or age. For example, does a woman with the same qualifications and experience as a man receive the same consideration for hiring or promotion?

Interactional justice focuses on treating everyone with dignity and respect. For example, does a bank loan officer take the time to fully explain to an applicant why he or she was turned down for a loan?[12] **Commutative justice** focuses on the fairness of exchanges or transactions. An exchange is deemed to be fair if all parties enter into it freely, have access to relevant and available information, and obtain some type of benefit from the transaction.[13]

You should notice that the justice view of ethical reasoning places an emphasis on fairness and equity. But which type of justice is paramount? Is it more important to ensure that everyone is treated exactly the same way—creating procedural justice, or to ensure that those from different backgrounds are adequately represented in terms of the final outcome—creating distributive justice?

> In the **justice view**, ethical behavior treats people impartially and fairly.

> **Procedural justice** focuses on the fair application of policies and rules.

> **Distributive justice** focuses on treating people the same regardless of personal characteristics.

> **Interactional justice** is the degree to which others are treated with dignity and respect.

> **Commutative justice** focuses on the fairness of exchanges or transactions.

Moral Rights View

*In the **moral rights view**, ethical behavior respects and protects fundamental rights.*

Finally, a **moral rights view** considers behavior to be ethical when it respects and protects the fundamental rights of people. Based on the teachings of John Locke and Thomas Jefferson, this view believes all people have rights to life, liberty, and fair treatment under the law. In organizations, this translates into protecting the rights of employees to privacy, due process, free speech, free consent, health and safety, and freedom of conscience.

The moral rights view of ethical reasoning protects individual rights, but it doesn't guarantee that the outcomes will be beneficial to broader society. What happens, for example, when someone's right to free speech conveys messages hurtful to others?

Compounding this problem is the fact that various nations have different laws and cultural expectations. As we grapple with the complexities of global society, human rights are often debated. Even though the United Nations stands by the Universal Declaration of Human Rights passed by the General Assembly in 1948, business executives, representatives of activist groups, and leaders of governments still argue and disagree over rights issues in various circumstances.[14] And without doubt, one of the areas where human rights can be most controversial is the arena of international business.

Excerpts from the Universal Declaration of Human Rights, United Nations

- **Article 1**—All human beings are born free and equal in dignity and right.
- **Article 18**—Everyone has the right to freedom of thought, conscience, and religion.
- **Article 19**—Everyone has the right to freedom of opinion and expression.
- **Article 23**—Everyone has the right to work, to free choice of employment, to just and favorable conditions of work.
- **Article 26**—Everyone has the right to education.

⦀ What is considered ethical can vary across cultures.

Situation: A 12-year-old boy is working in a garment factory in Bangladesh. He is the sole income earner for his family. He often works 12-hour days and was once burned quite badly by a hot iron. One day he is told he can't work. His employer was given an ultimatum by the firm's major American customer—"no child workers if you want to keep our contracts." The boy says: "I don't understand. I could do my job very well. My family needs the money."

"Should this child be allowed to work?" This question is but one example among the many ethics challenges faced in international business. Robert Haas, former Levi CEO, once said that an ethical problem "becomes even more difficult when you overlay the complexities of different cultures and values systems that exist throughout the world."[15] It would probably be hard to find a corporate leader or business person engaged in international business who would disagree. Put yourself in their positions. How would you deal with an issue such as child labor in a factory owned by one of your major suppliers?

Those who believe that behavior in foreign settings should be guided by the classic rule of "when in Rome, do as the Romans do" reflect an ethical position of cultural relativism.[16] This is the belief that there is no one right way to behave and that ethical behavior is always determined by its cultural context. An American international business executive guided by rules of cultural relativism, for example, would argue that the use of child labor is okay in another country as long as it is consistent with local laws and customs.

Figure 3.2 contrasts cultural relativism with the alternative of **moral absolutism**. This is a universalist ethical position suggesting that if a behavior or practice is not okay in one's home environment, it is not acceptable practice anywhere else. In other words, ethical standards are absolute and should apply universally across cultures and national boundaries. In the former example, the American executive would not do business in a setting where child labor was used, since it is unacceptable at home. Critics of the universal approach claim it is a form of **ethical imperialism**, or the attempt to externally impose one's ethical standards on others.

> **Cultural relativism** suggests there is no one right way to behave; cultural context determines ethical behavior.

> **Moral absolutism** suggests ethical standards apply universally across all cultures.

> **Ethical imperialism** is an attempt to impose one's ethical standards on other cultures.

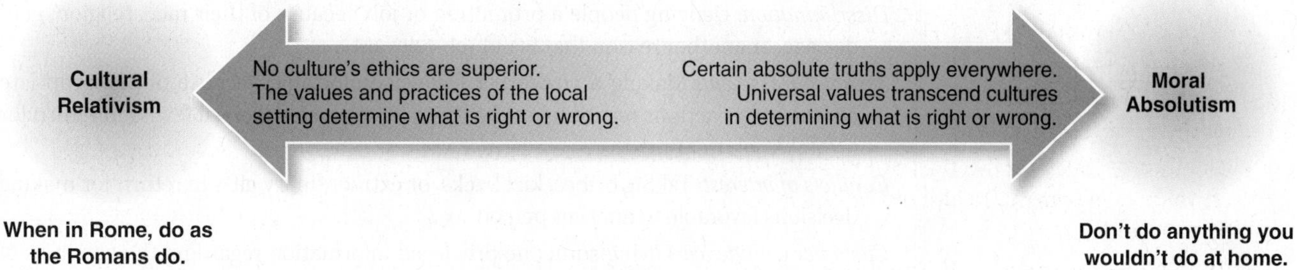

Cultural Relativism

No culture's ethics are superior. The values and practices of the local setting determine what is right or wrong.

Certain absolute truths apply everywhere. Universal values transcend cultures in determining what is right or wrong.

Moral Absolutism

When in Rome, do as the Romans do.

Don't do anything you wouldn't do at home.

FIGURE 3.2   How Do Cultural Relativism and Moral Absolutism Influence International Business Ethics?
The international business world is one of the most challenging settings in respect to ethical decision making. This figure identifies two diametrically opposed extremes. Cultural relativism justifies a decision if it conforms to local values, laws, and practices. Moral absolutism justifies a decision only if it conforms to the ways of the home country.
(*Source:* Developed from Thomas Donaldson, "Values in Tension: Ethics Away from Home," *Harvard Business Review,* vol. 74 (September/October 1996), pp. 48–62.)

Business ethicist Thomas Donaldson finds fault with both cultural relativism and moral absolutism. He argues instead that fundamental human rights and ethical standards can be preserved while values and traditions of a local culture are respected.[17] The core values or "hyper-norms" that must travel across cultural and national boundaries focus on human dignity, basic rights, and good citizenship. But once these core values have been met, Donaldson believes that international business behaviors can be tailored to local cultures. In the case of child labor, the American executive might ensure that any children employed in a factory under contract to his or her business work in safe conditions, and are provided regular schooling during scheduled work hours.[18]

‖ Ethical dilemmas arise as tests of personal ethics and values.

It's all well and good to discuss cases about ethical behavior in theory and in the safety of the college classroom. The tough personal test, however, occurs when we encounter a real-life situation that challenges our ethical beliefs and standards. Sooner or later, we all will. Often ambiguous and unexpected, these ethical challenges are inevitable. Think ahead to your next job search. Suppose you have accepted a job offer only to get a better one from another employer two weeks later. Should you come up with an excuse to back out of the first job so that you can accept the second one instead?

An **ethical dilemma** is a situation requiring a decision about a course of action that, although offering potential benefits, may be considered unethical. As a further complication, there may be no clear consensus on what is "right" and "wrong." In these circumstances, one's personal values are often the best indicators that something isn't right. An engineering manager speaking from experience sums it up this way: "I define an unethical situation as one in which I have to do something I don't feel good about."[19]

Take a look at Table 3.1—Common Examples of Unethical Behavior at Work.[20] Have you been exposed to anything like this? Are you ready to deal with these situations and any ethical dilemmas that they may create?

Table 3.1 Common Examples of Unethical Behavior at Work

Discrimination: Denying people a promotion or job because of their race, religion, gender, age, or another reason that is not job-relevant

Sexual harassment: Making a co-worker feel uncomfortable because of inappropriate comments or actions regarding sexuality, or by requesting sexual favors in return for favorable job treatment

Conflicts of interest: Taking bribes, kickbacks, or extraordinary gifts in return for making decisions favorable to another person

Customer confidence: Giving someone privileged information regarding the activities of a customer

Organizational resources: Using official stationery or a business e-mail account to communicate personal opinions or to make requests from community organizations

Managers responding to a *Harvard Business Review* survey reported that many of their ethical dilemmas arise out of conflicts with superiors, customers, and subordinates.[21] The most frequent issues involve dishonesty in advertising and in communications with top management, clients, and government agencies. Other ethics problems involve dealing with special gifts, entertainment expenses, and kickbacks.

Isn't it interesting that managers single out their bosses as frequent causes of ethical dilemmas? They complain about bosses who engage in various forms of harassment, misuse organizational resources, and give preferential treatment to certain persons.[22] They report feeling pressured at times to support incorrect viewpoints, sign false documents, overlook the boss's wrongdoings, and do business with the boss's friends. A surprising two-thirds of chief financial officers in a *Newsweek* survey, for example, said that they had been asked by their bosses to falsify financial records. Of them, 45% said they refused the directive, while 12% said they complied.[23]

Often at the top of lists of bad boss behaviors is holding people accountable for unrealistically high performance goals.[24] When individuals feel extreme performance pressures, they sometimes act incorrectly and engage in questionable practices in attempting to meet these expectations. As scholar Archie Carroll says: ". . . otherwise decent people start cutting corners on accuracy or quality, or start covering up incidents, lying or deceiving customers."[25] The management lesson is to be realistic and supportive in what you request of others. In Carroll's words again: "Good management means that one has to be sensitive to how pressure to perform might be perceived by those who want to please the boss."[26]

An **ethical dilemma** is a situation that, although offering potential benefit or gain, is also unethical.

||| People have tendencies to rationalize unethical behaviors.

What happens after someone commits an unethical act? Most of us generally view ourselves as "good" people. When we do something that is or might be "wrong," it leaves us doubtful, uncomfortable, and anxious. A common response is to rationalize the questionable behavior to make it seem acceptable in our minds. Although rationalizations might give us a false sense of justification, they come at a high cost.[27]

A rationalizer might say: *It's not really illegal.* This implies that the behavior is acceptable, especially in ambiguous situations. When dealing with shady or borderline situations, you may not be able to precisely determine right from wrong. In such cases, it is important to stop and reconsider things. When in doubt about the ethics of a decision, the best advice is: Don't do it.

A rationalizer might also say: *It's in everyone's best interests.* This response suggests that just because someone might benefit from the behavior, it is okay. To overcome this "ends justify the means" rationalization, we need to look beyond short-run results and carefully assess longer-term implications.

Sometimes a rationalizer uses a third excuse: *No one will ever know about it.* This implies that something we do is wrong only if it is discovered. Lack of accountability, unrealistic pressures to perform, and a boss who prefers "not to know" can all reinforce this tendency. But especially in today's world of great transparency, such thinking is risky and hard to accept.

Finally, a rationalizer might try to justify a questionable action on the belief that *the organization will stand behind me.* This is misperceived loyalty. The individual believes that the organization's best interests stand above all others, that top managers will protect the individual from harm. But if caught doing something wrong, would you want to count on the organization going to bat for you? And when you read about people who have done wrong and then try to excuse it by saying "I only did what I was ordered to do," how sympathetic are you?

{ WE HAVE TO KNOW OURSELVES AND OUR PERSONAL VALUES WELL ENOUGH TO MAKE PRINCIPLED DECISIONS.

Explore Yourself

■ INDIVIDUAL CHARACTER

Character is something that people tend to think more about during presidential election years or when famous people, such as professional athletes or politicians, commit unethical acts. But, the fact is that **individual character** can't be given only an occasional concern.

Along with its foundation of personal integrity, individual character deserves constant attention. Indeed, it is often tested by ethics and social responsibility situations in organizations today. Ethical dilemmas can arise unexpectedly. To deal with them we have to know ourselves and our personal values well enough to make principled decisions, ones that we can be proud of and that others will respect. After all, it's the character of people making key decisions that determines whether our organizations act in socially responsible or irresponsible ways.

Get to know yourself better by taking the self-assessment on **Terminal Values** and completing the other activities in the *Exploring Management* **Skill-Building Portfolio.**

STUDY GUIDE

Takeaway 3.1
How Do Ethics and Ethical Behavior Play Out in the Workplace?

Terms to Define

Commutative justice

Cultural relativism

Distributive justice

Ethical behavior

Ethical dilemmas

Ethical imperialism

Ethics

Individualism view

Instrumental values

Interactional justice

Justice view

Moral rights view

Procedural justice

Terminal values

Moral absolutism

Utilitarian view

Values

Rapid Review

- Ethical behavior is that which is accepted as "good" or "right" as opposed to "bad" or "wrong."
- The utilitarian, individualism, moral rights, and justice views offer different approaches to moral reasoning; each takes a different perspective of when and how a behavior becomes ethical.
- Cultural relativism argues that no culture is ethically superior to any other; moral absolutism believes there are clear rights and wrongs that apply universally, no matter where in the world one might be.
- An ethical dilemma occurs when one must decide whether to pursue a course of action that, although offering the potential for personal or organizational gain, may be unethical.
- Ethical dilemmas faced by managers often involve conflicts with superiors, customers, and subordinates over requests that involve some form of dishonesty.
- Common rationalizations for unethical behavior include believing the behavior is not illegal, is in everyone's best interests, will never be noticed, or will be supported by the organization.

Questions for Discussion

1. For a manager, is any one of the moral reasoning approaches better than the others?
2. Will a belief in cultural relativism create inevitable ethics problems for international business executives?
3. Are ethical dilemmas always problems, or can they be opportunities?

Be Sure You Can

- differentiate between legal behavior and ethical behavior
- differentiate between terminal and instrumental values, and give examples of each
- list and explain four approaches to moral reasoning
- illustrate distributive, procedural, interactive, and commutative justice in organizations
- explain the positions of cultural relativism and moral absolutism in international business ethics
- illustrate the types of ethical dilemmas common in the workplace
- explain how bad management can cause ethical dilemmas
- list four common rationalizations for unethical behavior

What Would You Do?

Perhaps you've been here before and perhaps not. You have just seen one of your classmates snap a cell phone photo of the essay question on the exam everyone is taking. The instructor has missed this, and you're not sure if anyone else observed what just happened. You know that the instructor is giving an exam to another section of the course starting next class period. Do you let this pass and pretend it isn't all that important? Or, do you take some action?

Takeaway 3.2
How Can We Maintain High Standards of Ethical Conduct?

ANSWERS TO COME

- Personal character and moral development influence ethical conduct.
- Training in ethical decision making can improve ethical conduct.
- Protection of whistleblowers can encourage ethical conduct.
- Managers as positive role models can inspire ethical conduct.
- Formal codes of ethics set standards for ethical conduct.

AS QUICK AS WE ARE TO RECOGNIZE THE BAD NEWS AND PROBLEMS ABOUT ETHICAL behavior in organizations, we shouldn't forget that there is a lot of good news, too. There are many organizations out there whose leaders and members set high ethical standards for themselves and others, and engage in a variety of methods to encourage consistent ethical behaviors. John Mackey, for example, built Whole Foods with a commitment to "whole food, whole people, and whole planet."[28]

Look around. You'll see many people and organizations operating in ethical and socially responsible ways. Some are quite well known, like Patagonia as featured in the recommended chapter case study. Others are less visible, but still performing every day with high ethical standards. Surely there are examples right in your local community of how "profits with principles" can be achieved. But even as you think about organizations that do good things, don't forget that the underlying foundations rest with the people who run them—individuals like you and me.

⦀ Personal character and moral development influence ethical decision making.

There are many possible influences on our personal ethics and how we apply them at work. One set traces to who we are as a person, what might be called our "character," as described in the Explore Yourself feature that ended the last section. Our character is reflected in how we behave and what we stand for. It is a product of family influences, religious beliefs, personal standards, personal values, and even past experiences.

As the chapter subtitle says: Character shouldn't stay home when we go to work. But we also know that it isn't always easy to stand up for what you believe. This problem grows when we are exposed to extreme pressures, when we get contradictory or just plain bad advice, and when our career is at stake. "Do this or lose your job!" is a terribly intimidating message. So it may be no surprise that 56% of U.S. workers in one survey reported feeling pressured to act unethically in their jobs.[29] Sadly, the same survey also revealed that 48% of respondents had themselves committed questionable acts within the past year.

Problems become more manageable when we have solid **ethical frameworks**, or well-thought-out personal rules and strategies for ethical decision making.

Ethical frameworks are well-thought-out personal rules and strategies for ethical decision making.

They can help us to act consistently and confidently. Ethical anchors that give high priority to such virtues as honesty, fairness, integrity, and self-respect can help us make correct decisions even under the most difficult conditions.

The many personal influences on ethical decision making come together in the three levels of moral development described by Lawrence Kohlberg and shown in Figure 3.3.[30] Kohlberg believes that we move step-by-step through the levels and their stages as we grow in maturity and education. Not everyone, in fact perhaps only a few of us, reaches the postconventional level.

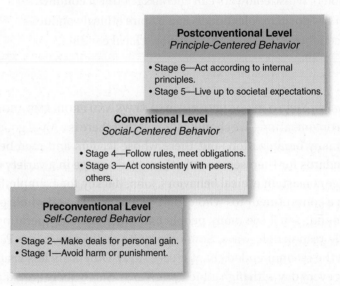

FIGURE 3.3   What Are the Stages in Kohlberg's Three Levels of Moral Development?
At the preconventional level of moral development, the individual focuses on self-interests, avoiding harm and making deals for gain. At the conventional level, attention becomes more social-centered, and the individual tries to be consistent and meet obligations to peers. At the postconventional level of moral development, principle-centered behavior results in the individual living up to societal expectations and personal principles.

In Kohlberg's *preconventional stage* of moral development the individual is self-centered. Moral thinking is largely limited to issues of punishment, obedience, and personal interest. Decisions made in the preconventional stage are likely to be directed toward personal gain and based on obedience to rules.

In the *conventional stage,* by contrast, attention broadens to include more social concerns. Decisions made in this stage are likely to be based on following social norms, meeting the expectations of others, and living up to agreed-upon obligations.

In the *postconventional stage* of moral development, also referred to as the principled stage, the individual is strongly driven by core principles and personal beliefs. A strong ethics framework is evident and the individual is willing to break with norms and conventions, even laws, to act consistent with personal principles. An example is the student who passes on an opportunity to cheat on a take-home examination because he or she believes it is wrong, even though the consequence will be a lower grade. Another example is someone who refuses to use pirated computer software, preferring to purchase it and show respect for intellectual property rights.

Training in ethical decision making can improve ethical conduct.

It would be nice if people had access through their employers to **ethics training** that helps them understand and best deal with ethical aspects of decision making. Although not all will have this opportunity, more and more are getting it, including college students. Most business schools, for example, now offer required and elective courses on ethics or integrate ethics into courses on other subjects.[31]

In college or in the workplace, however, we should keep ethics training in perspective. It won't work for everyone; it won't provide surefire answers to all ethical dilemmas; it won't guarantee ethical behavior for every person or throughout an organization. But it does help. An executive at Chemical Bank once put it this way: "We aren't teaching people right from wrong—we assume they know that. We aren't giving people moral courage to do what is right—they should be able to do that anyhow. We focus on dilemmas."[32]

One of the biggest differences between facing an ethical dilemma in a training seminar or as part of class discussions is pressure. Many times we must, or believe we must, move fast. Tips to Remember offers a reminder that it often helps to pause and double-check important decisions before taking action in uncomfortable circumstances. It presents a seven-step checklist that is used in some corporate training workshops.

Would you agree that the most powerful of the steps in the decision checklist is Step 6? This is what some call the test of the **spotlight questions**. You might think of it as highlighting the risk of public disclosure for your actions. Asking and answering the spotlight questions about how you would feel if family, friends, and role models learn of your actions is a powerful way to test whether a decision is consistent with your ethical standards.[33] By the way, never underestimate the risk of Internet exposure. Hardly a day goes by that we don't hear of someone, even public officials, who are publicly embarrassed to the point of career damage by something they said or photos they posted on the Web.

Ethics training seeks to help people understand the ethical aspects of decision making and to incorporate high ethical standards into their daily behavior.

Spotlight questions highlight the risks from public disclosure of one's actions.

{ "HOW WOULD I FEEL IF MY FAMILY FOUND OUT ABOUT MY DECISION?"

Tips to Remember

■ CHECKLIST FOR DEALING WITH ETHICAL DILEMMAS

Step 1. Recognize the ethical dilemma.
Step 2. Get the facts.
Step 3. Identify your options.
Step 4. Test each option: Is it legal? Is it right? Is it beneficial?
Step 5. Decide which option to follow.
Step 6. Ask *spotlight questions* to double-check your decision.
Step 7. Take action.

- *"How would I feel if my family found out about my decision?"*
- *"How would I feel if my decision is reported in the local newspaper or posted on the Internet?"*
- *"What would the person I know who has the strongest character and best ethical judgment say about my decision?"*

||| Protection of whistleblowers can encourage ethical conduct.

Agnes Connolly pressed her employer to report two toxic chemical accidents.

Dave Jones reported that his company was using unqualified suppliers in constructing a nuclear power plant.

Margaret Newsham revealed that her firm allowed workers to do personal business while on government contracts.

Herman Cohen charged that the ASPCA in New York was mistreating animals.

Barry Adams complained that his hospital followed unsafe practices.

Who are these people? They are **whistleblowers**, persons who expose organizational misdeeds in order to preserve ethical standards and protect against wasteful, harmful, or illegal acts.[34] They were also fired from their jobs.

Whistleblowers take significant career risks when they expose wrongdoing in organizations. Although there are federal and state laws that offer whistleblowers some defense against "retaliatory discharge," the protection is still inadequate overall. Laws vary from state to state, and the federal laws mainly protect government workers. Furthermore, even with legal protection, there are other reasons why potential whistleblowers might hesitate to act.

Have you ever encountered a student cheating on an exam or homework assignment? If so, did you blow the whistle by informing the instructor? A survey by the Ethics Resource Center reports that some 44% of U.S. workers fail to report the wrongdoings they observe at work. The top reasons for not reporting are "the belief that no corrective action would be taken, and the fear that reports would not be kept confidential."[35]

Another reason we don't hear about more whistleblowing is that the very nature of organizations as power structures creates potential barriers that discourage the practice. A *strict chain of command* can make it hard to bypass the boss if he or she is the one doing something wrong. *Strong work group identities* can discourage whistleblowing and encourage loyalty and self-censorship. And, working under conditions of *ambiguous priorities* can sometimes make it hard to distinguish right from wrong.[36]

||| Managers as positive role models can inspire ethical conduct.

While still a college student, Gabrielle Melchionda started Mad Gab's Inc., an all-natural skin-care business in Portland, Maine. After her sales had risen to over $300,000, an exporter offered to sell $2 million of her products abroad. She turned it down. Why? The exporter also sold weapons, something that contradicted her sense of ethical behavior. Melchionda's personal values guide all of her business decisions, from offering an employee profit-sharing plan to hiring disabled adults to using only packaging designs that minimize waste.[37]

The way business owners and top managers approach ethics can make a big difference in what happens in their organizations. They have a lot of power to shape an organization's policies and set its moral tone. Some of this power works through the attention given to policies that set high ethics standards—

Whistleblowers expose misconduct of organizations and their members.

and to their enforcement. Another and significantly large part of this power works through the personal examples those at the top set as role models. In order to have a positive impact on ethical conduct throughout an organization, they, like Gabrielle Melchionda, must walk the talk.

Of course, it's not just the owners and top managers who have the power to shape ethical behavior and the responsibility to use that power well. Managers at all levels have more power than they realize to influence the ethical behavior of others. Again, part of this power is walking the talk, setting the example, and acting as an ethical role model. Another part is just practicing good management day-by-day, keeping goals and performance expectations realistic and achievable for example. A *Fortune* survey reported that 34% of its respondents felt a company president can help to create an ethical climate by setting reasonable goals "so that subordinates are not pressured into unethical actions."[38]

As you think about managers as ethics role models, consider these ideas from management scholar Archie Carroll. He makes the distinction between amoral, immoral, and moral managers as shown here.[39]

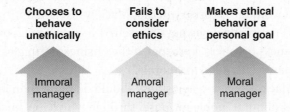

The **immoral manager** in Carroll's view chooses to behave unethically. He or she does something purely for personal gain and intentionally disregards the ethics of the action or situation. The **amoral manager** also disregards the ethics of an act or decision, but does so unintentionally. This manager simply fails to consider the ethical consequences of his or her actions.

In contrast to both prior types, the **moral manager** considers ethical behavior as a personal goal. He or she always makes decisions and acts in full consideration of ethical issues. We can say that this manager has a strong ethical framework and moral individual character. In Kohlberg's terms, this manager operates at the postconventional or principled stage of moral development.[40]

Although it may seem surprising, Carroll suggests that most of us act amorally as managers and in work roles. Although well intentioned, we remain mostly uninformed or undisciplined in considering the ethical aspects of our behavior. Should we just accept this as some natural human tendency? Or is Carroll's observation better considered a call to action—a challenge to seek the moral high ground at work and in our personal lives?

> An **immoral manager** chooses to behave unethically.

> An **amoral manager** fails to consider the ethics of her or his behavior.

> A **moral manager** makes ethical behavior a personal goal.

⫻ Formal codes of ethics set standards for ethical conduct.

At Gap Inc., global manufacturing is governed by a formal Code of Vendor Conduct.[41] You'll find statements like these in the code.

- *Discrimination*—"Factories shall employ workers on the basis of their ability to do the job, not on the basis of their personal characteristics or beliefs."
- *Forced labor*—"Factories shall not use any prison, indentured or forced labor."

Whole Foods Is a Natural

CEO Makes the Planet a Business Priority

From the day Whole Foods Market opened its doors in 1980 in Austin, Texas, it was an immediate success in the natural foods industry. Founder and CEO John Mackey still leads the firm with a commitment to nutrition, people, and the environment.

If you ask, Mackey will tell you he runs the company on three principles—"whole food, whole people, and whole planet." He also says "Whole Foods offers tasty, natural, and organic food within a decentralized and self-directed team culture to create a respectful workplace where employees are treated fairly and are highly motivated to succeed." That's a real mouthful, but it's classic Mackey.

Whole Foods is a regular on *Fortune* magazine's list of the "100 Best Companies to Work For." The company pays better than most retailers, offers good benefits, and shares financial data with employees. And would it surprise you that Mackey is a great critic of extremes in CEO pay? Indeed, he pays himself $1 a year. "I'm an owner . . . . If the business prospers, I prosper. If the business struggles, I struggle," he declares. "It's good for morale."

Mackey believes a business should do more than make money. He talks about a "noble purpose" through which any business or organization ultimately "serves society" through its day-to-day activities.

FIND INSPIRATION

What is it about Whole Foods as an organization and Mackey as a leader that might be inspiring to employees? Is it possible that organizations that serve a "noble purpose" will have highly motivated employees? Who are the best employers in your community and what do they do different from the "also-rans"?

A **code of ethics** is a formal statement of values and ethical standards.

- *Working conditions*—"Factories must treat all workers with respect and dignity and provide them with a safe and healthy environment."
- *Freedom of association*—"Factories must not interfere with workers who wish to lawfully and peacefully associate, organize or bargain collectively."

Many, if not most, organizations now operate with a **code of ethics** that formally states the values and ethical principles members are expected to display. Some employers even require new hires to sign and agree to their ethics code as a condition of employment. Don't be surprised if you are asked to do this someday. Ethics codes may be specific on how to behave in situations susceptible to ethical dilemmas—such as how sales representatives and purchasing agents should handle giving and receiving gifts. They might also specify consequences for unethical acts like taking bribes and kickbacks.

Ethics codes are common in the complicated world of international business. Global firms like the Gap rely on them where situations such as use of child labor and unfair or unsafe work conditions by contractors are possible and perplexing.[42] Now that corporate executives realize customers and society hold them accountable for the actions of their foreign suppliers, they are much stricter in using ethics codes and policing their international operations.[43]

But don't forget that you have to be careful in expecting too much of ethics codes. They set forth nice standards but they can't guarantee good conduct.[44] That, we might say, depends once again on employing people with the right moral character and putting them in a work environment where they are led by strong and positive ethics role models. Would you agree that inspiration can be found at Whole Foods?

STUDY GUIDE

Takeaway 3.2
How Can We Maintain High Standards of Ethical Conduct?

Terms to Define

Amoral manager

Code of ethics

Ethical frameworks

Ethics training

Immoral manager

Moral manager

Spotlight questions

Whistleblowers

Rapid Review

- Ethical behavior is influenced by an individual's character and represented by core values and beliefs.
- Kohlberg describes three levels of moral development—preconventional, conventional, and postconventional—with each of us moving step-by-step through the levels as we grow ethically over time.
- Ethics training can help people better understand how to make decisions when dealing with ethical dilemmas at work.
- Whistleblowers who expose the unethical acts of others have incomplete protection from the law and can face organizational penalties.
- All managers are responsible for acting as ethical role models for others.
- Immoral managers choose to behave unethically; amoral managers fail to consider ethics; moral managers make ethics a personal goal.
- Formal codes of conduct spell out the basic ethical expectations of employers regarding the behavior of employees and other contractors.

Questions for Discussion

1. Is it right for organizations to require ethics training of employees?

2. Should whistleblowers have complete protection under the law?

3. Should all managers be evaluated on how well they serve as ethical role models?

Be Sure You Can

- explain how ethical behavior is influenced by personal factors
- list and explain Kohlberg's three levels of moral development
- explain the term "whistleblower"
- list three organizational barriers to whistleblowing
- compare and contrast ethics training, ethics role models, and codes of conduct for their influence on ethics in the workplace
- state the spotlight questions for double-checking the ethics of a decision
- describe differences between the inclinations of amoral, immoral, and moral managers when facing difficult decisions

What Would You Do?

One of your first assignments as a summer intern for a corporate employer is to design an ethics training program for the firm's new hires. Your boss says that the program should familiarize the participants with the corporate code of ethics for sure. But it should go beyond this to provide each new employee with a foundation for handling ethical dilemmas in a confident and moral way. What would your proposed training program look like?

Takeaway 3.3
What Should We Know About the Social Responsibilities of Organizations?

ANSWERS TO COME

- Social responsibility is an organization's obligation to best serve society.
- Scholars argue cases for and against corporate social responsibility.
- Social responsibility audits measure the social performance of organizations.
- Sustainability is an important social responsibility goal.
- Social business and social entrepreneurs point the way in social responsibility.

Stakeholders are people and institutions most directly affected by an organization's performance.

THE ORGANIZATIONS, GROUPS, AND PERSONS WITH WHOM AN ORGANIZATION interacts and conducts business are known as its **stakeholders** because they have a direct "stake" or interest in its performance. They are affected in one way or another by what the organization does and how it performs. As Figure 3.4 shows, the stakeholders include customers, suppliers, competitors, regulators, investors/owners, employees, as well as future generations.

Importantly, an organization's stakeholders can have different interests. Customers typically want value prices and quality products; owners want profits as returns on their investments; suppliers want long-term business relationships; communities want good corporate citizenship and support for public services; employees want good wages, benefits, security, and satisfaction in their work.

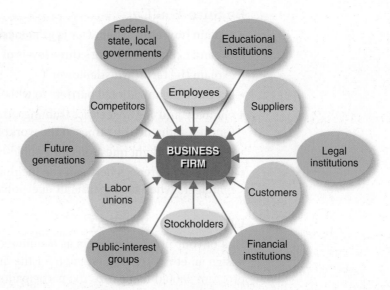

FIGURE 3.4　**Who Are the Stakeholders of Organizations?**
Stakeholders are the individuals, groups, and other organizations that have a direct interest in how well an organization performs. A basic list of stakeholders for any organization would begin with the employees and contractors who work for the organization, customers and clients who consume the goods and services, suppliers of needed resources, owners who invest capital, regulators in the form of government agencies, and special-interest groups such as community members and activists.

⫴ Social responsibility is an organization's obligation to best serve society.

The way organizations behave in relationship with their many stakeholders is a good indicator of their underlying ethical characters. When we talk about the "good" and the "bad" in business and societal relationships, **corporate social responsibility** is at issue. Often called CSR, it is defined as an obligation of the organization to act in ways that serve both its own interests and the interests of its stakeholders, representing society at large.

Even though corporate "irresponsibility" seems to get most of the media's attention, we can't forget that there is a lot of responsible behavior taking place as well. Increasingly this has become part of what is called the **triple bottom line**— how well an organization performs when measured not only on financial criteria but also on social and environmental ones. Some call this triple bottom line the **3 Ps of organizational performance**—profit, people, and planet.[45] The triple bottom line in business decision making is checked by asking these questions: Is the decision economically sound? Is the decision socially responsible? Is the decision environmentally sound?

Showing CSR and concerns for the triple bottom line is most likely the way you'd like your future employers to behave. "Students nowadays want to work for companies that help enhance the quality of life in their surrounding community," says an observer.[46] In one survey, 70% of students report that "a company's reputation and ethics" was "very important" when deciding whether or not to accept a job offer; in another survey, 79% of 13- to 25-year-olds say they "want to work for a company that cares about how it affects or contributes to society."[47]

> **Corporate social responsibility** is the obligation of an organization to serve its own interests and those of its stakeholders.

> The **triple bottom line** of organizational performance includes financial, social, and environmental criteria.

> The **3 Ps of organizational performance** are profit, people, and planet.

{ **"OFFER A PURE AND HEALTHY PRODUCT THAT TASTES GOOD AND EARN A PROFIT WITHOUT HARMING THE ENVIRONMENT."**

Role Models

■ GARY HIRSHBERG GOES FOR TRIPLE BOTTOM LINE AT STONYFIELD FARM

President, CEO, and co-founder of Stonyfield Farm, Gary Hirshberg, makes a career out of organic yogurt. He's also a firm believer that "business is the most powerful force in the world." Considered a social entrepreneur, Hirshberg has always been at the forefront of movements for environmental and social transformation. He studied climate change at Hampshire College, built energy-producing windmills, and worked at a nonprofit research center.

At Stonyfield Farm he's helping craft a clear mission: "Offer a pure and healthy product that tastes good and earn a profit without harming the environment." Indeed, Hirshberg says "we factor the planet into all of our decisions."

Stonyfield Farm focuses on the triple bottom line of being economically, socially, and environmentally responsible—what some call profit, people, and planet. "It's a simple strategy but a powerful one," says Hirshberg proudly. "Going green is not just the right thing to do, but a great way to build a successful business." His results speak for themselves. Stonyfield Farm is now the number-one maker of organic yogurt in the world.

WHAT'S THE LESSON HERE?

Granted, Stonyfield Farm has succeeded with Hirshberg's social business model and a commitment to the 3 Ps of profit, people, and planet. But can something like this be done only when starting a firm from scratch? Can an existing firm be turned in this direction? What does it take to lead organizations with a commitment to ethics and social responsibility?

⦀ Scholars argue cases for and against corporate social responsibility.

It may seem that corporate social responsibility, or CSR, is one of those concepts and goals that most everyone agrees upon. There are, however, two contrasting views that stimulate debate in academic and public-policy circles. The classical view takes a stand against making corporate social responsibility a business priority, while the socioeconomic view advocates for it.[48]

The **classical view of CSR** holds that management's only responsibility in running a business is to maximize profits and shareholder value. It puts the focus on the single bottom line of financial performance. In other words: "The business of business is business." This narrow stakeholder perspective is represented in the views of the late Milton Friedman, a respected economist and Nobel Laureate. He says: "Few trends could so thoroughly undermine the very foundations of our free society as the acceptance by corporate officials of social responsibility other than to make as much money for their stockholders as possible."[49]

The arguments against corporate social responsibility include fears that its pursuit will reduce business profits, raise business costs, dilute business purpose, and give business too much social power. Yet events such as the huge BP oil spill in the Gulf of Mexico seem to argue otherwise. Concerns for the natural environment are now high among societal values. The public was outraged about the oil spill, and BP's CEO was the target of lots of criticism for his company's actions. Demands were quickly made for stronger government oversight and control over corporate practices such as deep-water oil drilling that might put our natural world at risk.

The **socioeconomic view of CSR** holds that management of any organization should be concerned for the broader social welfare, not just corporate profits. This broad stakeholder perspective puts the focus on the expanded triple bottom line of not just financial performance, such as shareholder returns, but also social and environmental performance. It is supported by Paul Samuelson, another distinguished economist and also a Nobel Laureate.

Those in favor of corporate social responsibility argue that it will add long-run profits for businesses, improve their public images, and help them avoid government regulation. And because businesses often have vast resources with the potential for great social impact, business executives have ethical obligations to ensure that their firms act in socially responsible ways. The public at large seems to want businesses and other organizations to act with genuine social responsibility. And, many stakeholders are demanding that organizations integrate social responsibility into core values and daily activities.

What's your position on these alternative views of corporate social responsibility? At the very least, it is hard to argue that social responsibility will hurt the financial bottom line. A worst-case scenario seems to be that it has no adverse impact.[50] And, there is evidence for the existence of a **virtuous circle** where corporate social responsibility leads to improved financial performance that leads to more socially responsible actions in the future.[51] This is consistent with the notion of **shared value** as advocated by Michael Porter and Mark Kramer.[52] It basically means that business executives should make decisions that show full understanding that economic and social progress are fundamentally interconnected. An example might be the "cradle-to-grave" manufacturing approach featured in the nearby ethics check.

The **classical view of CSR** is that business should focus on the pursuit of profits.

The **socioeconomic view of CSR** is that business should focus on contributions to society, not just making profits.

A **virtuous circle** exists when corporate social responsibility leads to improved financial performance that leads to more social responsibility.

Shared value approaches business decisions with understanding that economic and social progress are interconnected.

{ AFTER INVESTING IN CRADLE-TO-GRAVE MANUFACTURING, THE FIRM
EXPERIENCED "SO MUCH INNOVATION THAT WE SAW A SWIFT PAY OUT."

Ethics Check

■ COMMITTING TO A GREEN SUPPLY CHAIN

It's called "cradle-to-grave manufacturing," and you might wonder why more companies aren't involved. The basic principle is that you must start with "nonhazardous" materials and then build products that are disassembled at the end of their lives to become biodegradable waste or new products. The approach was adopted by Stef Kranendijk, CEO of Desso, a carpet manufacturer, when he set new sustainability goals for his firm. He saw it as a potential stimulus to innovation and a way to differentiate his company from the competition. In his words: "We launched it as a design and quality initiative that would boost our innovation capability with positive effects on the environment and public health.

The pathways to cradle-to-grave manufacturing aren't easy. Shareholders and owners have to agree on the goals and benefits; suppliers have to join in the quest for sustainable materials; designs have to be created to meet the end of product life goals. But Kranendijk found that Desso's employees were highly supportive and reported increased satisfaction. He also said the firm experienced "so much innovation that we saw a swift pay out."

YOU DECIDE

Desso's commitment to cradle-to-grave manufacturing requires lots of investment, both monetary and otherwise, from the manufacturer and its supply chain members. But is it ethical for a business to turn its back on such possibilities? Should we as consumers push for these types of sustainability initiatives? Or, is it unethical to try to force businesses to pursue green goals before the market as a whole does it for us? And while you are thinking about the issues, is it ethical to claim social responsibility for pursuing environmentally friendly practices only to avoid government regulation or adverse publicity? In other words, does it make a difference if a firm does "good things" for selfish reasons?

‖ Social responsibility audits measure the social performance of organizations.

If we are to get serious about social responsibility, we need to get rigorous about measuring corporate social performance and holding business leaders accountable for the results. A **social responsibility audit** can be used at regular intervals to report on and systematically assess an organization's performance in various areas of corporate social responsibility.

The social performance of business firms varies along a continuum that ranges from *compliance*—acting to avoid adverse consequences, to *conviction*— acting to create positive impact.[53] As shown in the figure, an audit of corporate social performance might cover the organization's performance on four criteria for evaluating socially responsible practices: economic, legal, ethical, and discretionary.[54]

An organization is meeting its *economic responsibility* when it earns a profit through the provision of goods and services desired by customers. While it might seem unusual to focus on financial

> A **social responsibility audit** measures and reports on an organization's performance in various areas of corporate social responsibility.

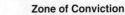

Zone of Compliance		Zone of Conviction	
Economic Responsibility: *Be Profitable*	Legal Responsibility: *Obey the Law*	Ethical Responsibility: *Do What Is Right*	Discretionary Responsibility: *Contribute to Community*

performance as a component of CSR, a firm's economic performance provides the foundation upon which all the other types of responsibility rest. If a firm is not financially viable, it will not be able to take care of its owners or employees or engage in any of the other aspects of CSR. *Legal responsibility* is fulfilled when an organization operates within the law and according to the requirements of various external regulations. An organization meets its *ethical responsibility* when its actions voluntarily conform not only to legal expectations but also to the broader values and moral expectations of society.

The highest level of social performance comes through the satisfaction of *discretionary responsibility*. At this level, the organization moves beyond basic economic, legal, and ethical expectations to provide leadership in advancing the well-being of individuals, communities, and society as a whole. An example is found at the Bellisio Foods plant in Jackson, Ohio. Ryan Wright is the manager in charge of utility and sustainability, and he's found a number of ways to "green up" a manufacturing facility. A large treatment plant digests food waste, using bioorganisms to create the methane that becomes fuel to run the factory's boilers. Wright believes the process cuts CO_2 output by 43,000 tons per year by saving on costs of natural gas and transporting waste to a landfill. Although the price of the system was $4.65 million, he says: "It's a great project; we're proud of it; it's the right thing to do."[55]

⫼ Sustainability is an important social responsibility goal.

The BP oil spill in the Gulf of Mexico and the nuclear power plant disaster in Fukushima, Japan, certainly made the link between organizations and our natural environment a front-page issue. These cases should cause you to wonder about the extent to which business practices pose risks, present and future, to humankind and the natural environment. And it should prompt you to be concerned about the extent to which we are abusing versus protecting, and consuming versus conserving, the world's resources.

United Nations Encourages Global Business Leaders on Sustainability Goals

The UN Global Leaders Compact brings together some corporate CEOs worldwide to discuss how responsible business behavior and investment can assist in global sustainability. At a recent conference the United Nations General Secretary Ban Ki-moon told the business leaders: "You are at the forefront of globalization. That means emphasizing sustainability across your operations and in your investment strategies." He further stated that "corporate sustainability is becoming a byword" and that "principles and profits are two sides of the same coin."

Sustainable Business

Think about the issues of our day—things like resource scarcity, climate change, carbon footprints, and alternative energy. Think about popular terms and slogans—ones like renew, recycle, conserve, and preserve. They all reflect the importance of **sustainability** as a priority of the times, affecting all of us and all institutions of our society. You can think of it as a goal, one that addresses the rights of both present and future generations as stakeholders of the world's natural resources—everything from the air that we breathe to the precious metals that give life to our many electronic devices.

Gavin Neath, vice president for Unilever, poses the sustainability issue this way. "With a global population at 6.5 billion," he says, "we are already consuming resources at a rate far in excess of nature's capacity to replenish them. Water is becoming scarce and global warming and climate change are accelerating."[56] Under such conditions, it is little wonder that 93% of CEOs in a recent survey admit that the future success of their firms depends in part on how well they meet sustainability challenges.[57] And as United Nations General Secretary Ban Ki-moon says, "It means thinking differently about how and where we invest, thinking differently about creating markets of the future, and creating opportunities for growth."[58]

These points and ideas introduce the notion of **sustainable business**, where firms operate in ways that both meet the needs of customers and protect or advance the well-being of our natural environment.[59] You can think of a sustainable business as one that operates in harmony with nature rather than by exploiting nature. Its actions produce minimum negative impact on the environment and help preserve it for future generations. The hallmarks of sustainable business practices include less waste, less toxic materials, more resource efficiency, more energy efficiency, and more renewable energy.

Sustainable Development

If sustainability is a goal for businesses and other organizations, just what is **sustainable development**? Most often, the term describes practices that make use of environmental resources to support societal needs today while also preserving and protecting the environment for future use. The World Business Council for Sustainable Development, whose membership includes the CEOs of global corporations, defines sustainable development as "forms of progress that meet the needs of the present without compromising the ability of future generations to meet their needs."[60]

The conversation about our planet and sustainable development stands at the interface between how people live and how organizations operate, and the capacity of the natural environment to support them. Simply put, we want prosperity, convenience, comfort, and luxury in our everyday lives. But we are also more aware that attention must be given to the "costs" of these aspirations and how those costs can be borne in a way that doesn't impair the future. At PepsiCo, for example, CEO Indra Nooyi has said that her firm's "real profit" should be assessed in the following way: Revenue less Cost of Goods Sold less Costs to Society. "All corporations operate with a license from society," says Nooyi. "It's critically important that we take that responsibility very, very seriously; we have to make sure that what corporations do doesn't add costs to society."[61]

An increasingly popular and useful term in conversations about sustainable development is **environmental capital** or **natural capital**. It refers to the available

Sustainability is a goal that addresses the rights of present and future generations as co-stakeholders of present day natural resources.

Sustainable business is where firms operate in ways that both meet the needs of customers and protect or advance the well-being of our natural environment.

Sustainable development is making use of natural resources to meet today's needs while also preserving and protecting the environment for use by future generations.

Environmental capital or **natural capital** is the storehouse of natural resources—atmosphere, land, water, and minerals—that we use to sustain life and produce goods and services for society.

Manager's Library

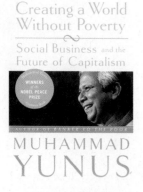

■ *CREATING A WORLD WITHOUT POVERTY* BY MUHAMMAD YUNUS

CAN BUSINESS LEND A HELPING HAND?

Some argue that businesses have an obligation to 'give back' to society. Their products and services improve consumers' lives and their well-paying jobs give employees means, but could businesses balance the pursuit of profit with genuine aims toward public goodwill? Corporate social responsibility today implies that businesses strive to overcome social ills such as pollution, poverty, and sickness, among others. Perhaps the social science of business in the 21st century will incorporate new methods to eliminate these social ills?

In the book *Creating a World Without Poverty* (2007, PublicAffairs), author Muhammad Yunus outlines a transformational business model designed to eliminate global poverty and solve other enduring social problems. Yunus creates a 'social business' model in which company products or services target and benefit only specific stakeholders who suffer from social ills. He started the world's first multinational social business, Grameen Danone, in collaboration with German yogurt maker Danone. It manufactures nutritional yogurt targeted and sold at cost to the poor in Bangladesh.

Yunus laments that current methods to address poverty and other social problems are flawed. Corporate initiatives, government actions, and private efforts may perpetuate rather than reduce these public burdens. Multinational companies exploit cheap labor globally. Governments provide handouts to the poor, reinforcing a form of reliance. And private philanthropies contribute in sporadic streams in critical times and economic downturns.

Yunus's social business model entails that businesses provide venture capital and know-how for new products or services targeting specific groups that suffer from social ills. Profits are then reinvested, not paid out as dividends. Businesses recover initial investments, but no more. Further profits go to cheaper and better goods and services or expanding access to more users. A second type of social business allows target groups to assume shareholder control from the venturing business and receiving paid dividends. Yunus's ventures have reduced poverty, homelessness, and sickness, and he has targeted pollution, disease, and crime in future aims.

REFLECT AND REACT

Does business have an obligation to 'give back' to society? Can business balance the pursuit of profit and public goodwill? Are corporate social responsibility efforts genuine or just for show? And by the way, do you agree that corporations, governments, and philanthropies perpetuate rather than eliminate social problems?

ISO 14001 is a global quality standard that certifies organizations that set environmental objectives and targets, account for the environmental impact of their activities, and continuously improve environmental performance.

storehouse of natural resources that exist in the atmosphere, land, water, and minerals that we use to sustain life and produce goods and services for society.[62] The importance of environmental capital is reflected in **ISO 14001**, a global quality standard that requires certified organizations to set environmental objectives and targets; account for the environmental impact of their activities, products, or services; and continuously improve environmental performance.[63]

Human Sustainability

The notion of sustainability and the pursuit of sustainable development goals can be made much broader than a focus on the natural environment alone. Scholar Jeffrey Pfeffer offers a strong case in favor of giving management attention not only to issues of ecological and environmental sustainability—traditional green management themes—but also to social and human sustainability. He says: "Just as there is concern for protecting natural resources, there could be a similar level of concern for protecting human resources. . . . Being a socially responsible business ought to encompass the effect of management practices on employee physical and psychological well-being."[64] You might think of Pfeffer's point this way: While valuing the "planet," don't forget that "people" are also part of the 3 Ps of organizational performance.

‖ Social business and social entrepreneurs point the way in social responsibility.

Take a good look at the example of Muhammad Yunus just featured in the Manager's Library. On one level, his work with the Grameen Bank was a business innovation—bringing microcredit lending into the forefront. But at another level it is a **social business** in that the underlying business model directly addresses a social problem—using microcredit lending to help fight poverty. And in the expanding domain of social business, Yunus's ideas and examples have set benchmarks. In fact, they earned him a Nobel Prize.[65]

Social businesses are profit driven. But, instead of the profits being returned to investors or owners, they are used to pay off initial start-up costs and then reinvested to expand the social business to serve more clients and customers. These businesses are developed by **social entrepreneurs**, people who take business risk with the goal of finding novel ways to solve pressing social problems at home and abroad.[66] Social entrepreneurs are like business entrepreneurs with one big difference: They are driven by a social mission, not financial gain.[67] They pursue original thinking and innovations to help solve social problems and make lives better for people who are disadvantaged.

You'll be hearing and reading a lot more about social businesses and social entrepreneurs. They are already being called the new "fourth sector" of our economy—joining private for-profit businesses, public government organizations, and nonprofits.[68] As the late management guru Peter Drucker once said: "Every single social and global issue of our day is a business opportunity in disguise."[69]

Housing and job training for the homeless . . . Bringing technology to poor families . . . Improving literacy among disadvantaged youth . . . Bringing expanded health-care to impoverished communities . . . and more. Think of all the possibilities. Could social business and social entrepreneurship be part of your future some day?

> A **social business** is one in which the underlying business model directly addresses a social problem.

> **Social entrepreneurs** take business risks to find novel ways to solve pressing social problems.

Social Entrepreneurs Need Support Too

And they can get it if they catch the attention of Vanessa Kirsch and the organization she founded—New Profit Inc. She developed the idea while traveling to interview social entrepreneurs around the world. After seeing so many great ideas struggle to achieve broad scale, but finding a bottle of Coke pretty much everywhere, Kirsch wondered: "What prevents social entrepreneurs from scaling their innovations at the same pace and quality as Coca-Cola?" That's now the ultimate goal of New Profit—to strengthen, connect, and amplify the potential of visionary leaders, removing obstacles to impact and building networks of excellence that multiply their efforts. Social entrepreneurs selected by New Profit receive multi-year growth capital grants and strategic support to help achieve new results and opportunities across the country.

STUDY GUIDE

Takeaway 3.3
What Should We Know About the Social Responsibilities of Organizations?

Terms to Define

3 Ps of organizational performance

Classical view of CSR

Corporate social responsibility

Environmental capital or natural capital

ISO 14001

Shared value

Social business

Social entrepreneurs

Social responsibility

Socioeconomic view of CSR

Stakeholders

Sustainability

Sustainable business

Sustainable development

Triple bottom line

Virtuous circle

Rapid Review

- Corporate social responsibility is an obligation of the organization to act in ways that serve both its own interests and the interests of its stakeholders.
- In assessing organizational performance today, the concept of the triple bottom line evaluates how well organizations are doing on economic, social, and environmental performance criteria.
- Criteria for evaluating corporate social performance include how well it meets economic, legal, ethical, and discretionary responsibilities.
- The argument against corporate social responsibility says that businesses should focus on making profits; the argument for corporate social responsibility says that businesses should use their resources to serve broader social concerns.
- The concept of sustainable development refers to making use of environmental resources to support societal needs today while also preserving and protecting the environment for use by future generations.
- Social businesses and social entrepreneurs pursue business models that help to directly address important social problems.

Questions for Discussion

1. Choose an organization in your community. What questions would you ask to complete an audit of its social responsibility practices?
2. Is the logic of the virtuous circle a convincing argument in favor of corporate social responsibility?
3. Should government play a stronger role in making sure organizations commit to sustainable development?

Be Sure You Can

- explain the concept of social responsibility
- summarize arguments for and against corporate social responsibility
- illustrate how the virtuous circle of corporate social responsibility might work
- explain the notion of social business

What Would You Do?

It's debate time and you've been given the task of defending corporate social responsibility, or CSR. Make a list of all possible arguments for making CSR an important goal for any organization. For each item on the list, find a good current example that confirms its importance based on real events. In what order of priority will you present your arguments in the debate? And, what arguments "against" CSR will you be prepared to defend against?

TestPrep 3

Multiple-Choice Questions

1. A business owner makes a decision to reduce a plant's workforce by 10% in order to cut costs and be able to save jobs for the other 90% of employees. This decision could be justified as ethical using the _____ approach to moral reasoning.
   - ✓(a) utilitarian
   - (b) individualism
   - (c) justice
   - (d) moral rights

2. If a manager fails to enforce a late-to-work policy for all workers—that is, by allowing some favored employees to arrive late without penalties—this would be considered a violation of _____.
   - (a) human rights
   - (b) personal values
   - ✓(c) distributive justice
   - (d) cultural relativism

3. According to research on ethics in the workplace, _____ is/are often a major and frequent source of pressures that create ethical dilemmas for people in their jobs.
   - (a) declining morals in society
   - (b) long work hours
   - (c) low pay
   - ✓(d) requests or demands from bosses

4. Someone who exposes the ethical misdeeds of others in an organization is usually called a/an _____.
   - ✓(a) whistleblower
   - (b) ethics advocate
   - (c) ombudsman
   - (d) stakeholder

5. Two employees are talking about ethics in their workplaces. Jay says that ethics training and codes of ethical conduct are worthless; Maura says they are the only ways to ensure ethical behavior by all employees. Who is right and why?
   - (a) Jay—no one really cares about ethics at work.
   - (b) Maura—only the organization can influence ethical behavior.
   - ✓(c) Neither Jay nor Maura—training and codes can encourage but never guarantee ethical behavior.
   - (d) Neither Jay nor Maura—only the threat of legal punishment will make people act ethically.

6. Which ethical position has been criticized as a source of "ethical imperialism"?
   - (a) individualism
   - ✓(b) absolutism
   - (c) utilitarianism
   - (d) relativism

7. If a manager takes a lot of time explaining to a subordinate why he did not get a promotion and sincerely listens to his concerns, this is an example of an attempt to act ethically according to _____ justice.
   - (a) utilitarian
   - (b) commutative
   - ✓(c) interactional
   - (d) universal

8. At what Kohlberg calls the _____ level of moral development, an individual can be expected to act consistent with peers, meet obligations, and follow rules of social conduct.
   - (a) postconventional
   - ✓(b) conventional
   - (c) preconventional
   - (d) nonconventional

9. In respect to the link between bad management and ethical behavior, research shows that _____.
   - ✓(a) managers who set unrealistic goals can cause unethical behavior
   - (b) most whistleblowers just want more pay
   - (c) only top managers really serve as ethics role models
   - (d) a good code of ethics makes up for any management deficiencies

10. A person's desires for a comfortable life and family security represent _____ values, while his or her desires to be honest and hard working represent _____ values.
   - ✓(a) terminal; instrumental
   - (b) instrumental; terminal
   - (c) universal; individual
   - (d) individual; universal

11. A proponent of the classical view of corporate social responsibility would most likely agree with which of these statements?

    (a) Social responsibility improves the public image of business.

    √ (b) The primary responsibility of business is to maximize profits.

    (c) By acting responsibly, businesses avoid government regulation.

    (d) Businesses should do good while they are doing business.

12. The triple bottom line of organizational performance would include measures of financial, social, and _____ performance.

    (a) philanthropic   √ (b) environmental

    (c) legal   (d) economic

13. An amoral manager _____.

    (a) always acts in consideration of ethical issues

    (b) chooses to behave unethically

    (c) makes ethics a personal goal

    √ (d) acts unethically but does so unintentionally

14. In a social responsibility audit of a business firm, positive behaviors meeting which of the following criteria would measure the highest level of commitment to socially responsible practices?

    (a) legal—obeying the law

    (b) economic—earning a profit

    √ (c) discretionary—contributing to community

    (d) ethical—doing what is right

15. What organizational stakeholder would get priority attention if a corporate board is having a serious discussion regarding how the firm could fulfill its obligations in respect to sustainable development?

    (a) owners or investors

    (b) customers

    (c) suppliers

    √ (d) future generations

Short-Response Questions

16. How does distributive justice differ from procedural justice?

17. What are the three Spotlight Questions that people can use for double-checking the ethics of a decision?

18. If someone commits an unethical act, how can he or she rationalize it to make it seem right?

19. What is the virtuous circle of corporate social responsibility?

Integration and Application Questions

20. A small outdoor clothing company in the U.S. has just received an attractive proposal from a business in Tanzania to manufacture the work gloves that it sells. Accepting the offer from the Tanzanian firm would allow for substantial cost savings compared to the current supplier. However, the American firm's manager has recently read reports that some businesses in Tanzania are forcing people to work in unsafe conditions in order to keep their costs down. The manager is now seeking your help in clarifying the ethical aspects of this opportunity.

    Questions: How would you describe to this manager his or her alternatives in terms of cultural relativism and moral absolutism? What would you identify as the major issues and concerns in terms of the cultural relativism position versus the absolutist position? Finally, what action would you recommend in this situation, and why?

StepsforFurtherLearning

Many learning resources are found at the end of the book and online within WileyPLUS.

Don't Miss These Selections from the **Skill-Building Portfolio**

■ **SELF-ASSESSMENT 3:** *Terminal Values*

■ **CLASS EXERCISE 3:** *Confronting Ethical Dilemmas*

■ **TEAM PROJECT 3 :** *Organizational Commitment to Sustainability*

Don't Miss This Selection from **Cases for Critical Thinking**

■ **CHAPTER 3 CASE**

Patagonia: Leading a Green Revolution

Case Snapshot   Patagonia has managed to stay both green and profitable at a time when the economy is down, consumers are tight for cash, and "doing the profitable thing" is not necessarily doing the right thing. How has Patagonia achieved its success without compromising their ideals?

With recent annual revenues of $314.5 million, Patagonia succeeds by staying true to Chouinard's vision.

"They've become the Rolls-Royce of their product category," says Marshal Cohen, chief industry analyst with market research firm NPD Group. "When people were stepping back, and the industry became copycat, Chouinard didn't sell out, lower prices, and dilute the brand. Sometimes, the less you do, the more provocative and true of a leader you are."

Make notes here on what you've learned about yourself from this chapter.

■ **LEARNING JOURNAL 3**

For 69 days shift leader Luis Urzúa kept the men trapped in the Chilean mine organized and hopeful. On the 70th day, he was the last man safely out.

Managers as Decision Makers

There Is No Substitute for a Good Decision

Management Live

Self-Confidence and *Red Eye*

In *Red Eye*, things get hectic at the Lux Atlantic Hotel when manager Lisa Reisert (Rachel McAdams) is away attending her grandmother's funeral. Her assistant Cynthia (Jayma Mays) is unable to handle a series of problems that arise. She calls Reisert, who is en route to the airport for a return flight to Miami. Reisert calmly talks Cynthia through the handling of a deleted reservation for frequent guests, identifies another issue as a nonproblem, and gives details for handling a high-security guest who is arriving 12 hours early.

Clearly, Reisert is confident in her abilities and can deal with multiple issues even under pressure. This confidence comes into play later in the movie when Reisert develops a strategy to defeat a terrorist who wants to use her to threaten the high-security guest.

How is it that some managers always seem to make the right moves while others cave in at the slightest sign of trouble? The difference may be **self-confidence**; they must believe in their decisions and the information foundations for them. Effective managers are good decision makers. This involves gathering and processing information, deciding, implementing, and then getting those involved to take action.

A good understanding of the many topics in this chapter can improve your decision-making skills. A better understanding of your personal style in gathering and processing information can also help build your self-confidence as a decision maker.

YOUR CHAPTER 4 TAKEAWAYS

1. Recognize how managers use information to solve problems.

2. Identify five steps in the decision-making process.

3. Understand current issues in managerial decision making.

WHAT'S INSIDE

Explore Yourself
More on self-confidence

Role Models
Indra Nooyi brings style and strategic vision to Pepsi

Ethics Check
Left to die on Mt. Everest

Facts to Consider
Greenhouse gas emissions as executive priorities

THE SHALLOWS
WHAT THE INTERNET IS DOING TO OUR BRAINS
Nicholas Carr

Manager's Library
The Shallows
by Nicholas Carr

Takeaway 4.1
How Do Managers Use Information to Solve Problems?

ANSWERS TO COME

- Managers deal with problems posing threats and offering opportunities.
- Managers can be problem avoiders, problem solvers, or problem seekers.
- Managers make programmed and nonprogrammed decisions when solving problems.
- Managers can use systematic and intuitive thinking.
- Managers use different cognitive styles to process information for decision making.
- Managers make decisions under conditions of certainty, risk, and uncertainty.

ON AUGUST 5, 2010, THE SAN JOSÉ COPPER AND GOLD MINE COLLAPSED IN CHILE; 32 miners, along with their shift leader Carlos Urzua, were trapped inside.[1] "The most difficult moment was when the air cleared and we saw the rock," said Urzua, "I had thought maybe it was going to be a day or two days, but not when I saw the rock . . ." In fact, the miners were trapped 2300 hundred feet below the surface for 69 days. Getting them out alive was a problem that caught the attention of the entire world. After the rescue shaft was completed, Urzua was the last man out. "The job was hard," he said, "they were days of great pain and sorrow." But the decisions Urzua made as shift leader—organizing the miners into work shifts, keeping them busy, studying mine diagrams, making escape plans, raising morale—all contributed to the successful rescue. After embracing Urzua when he arrived at the surface, Chile's President Sebastian Pinera said, "He was a shift boss who made us proud."

Most managers will never have to face such an extreme crisis, but decision making and problem solving are parts of every manager's job. Not all decisions are going to be easy ones; some will have to be made under tough conditions; and, not all decisions will turn out right. But as with the case of Urzua, the goal is to do the best you can under the circumstances.

||| Managers deal with problems posing threats and offering opportunities.

All of those case studies, experiential exercises, class discussions, and even essay exam questions are intended to engage students in the complexities of managerial decision making, the potential problems and pitfalls, and even the pressures of crisis situations. From the classroom forward, however, it's all up to you. Only you can determine whether you step ahead and make the best out of very difficult problems or collapse under pressure.

Problem solving is the process of identifying a discrepancy between an actual and a desired state of affairs, and then taking action to resolve it. The context for managerial problem solving is depicted in Figure 4.1. It shows

Problem solving involves identifying and taking action to resolve problems.

why managers fit the definition of **knowledge workers,** persons whose value to organizations rests with their intellectual, not physical, capabilities.[2] All managers continually solve problems as they gather, give, receive, and process information from many sources. In fact, one of your most critical skills might be described as **information competency**—the ability to locate, retrieve, evaluate, organize, and analyze information to make decisions that solve problems. This means not just getting information off the Internet; it means getting credible and valuable information, and then using it well.

Knowledge workers add value to organizations through their intellectual capabilities.

Information competency is the ability to gather and use information to solve problems.

FIGURE 4.1 In What Ways Do Managers Serve as Information Nerve Centers in Organizations?
Managers sit at the center of complex networks of information flows; they serve as information-processing hubs or nerve centers. Each of the management functions—planning, organizing, leading, and controlling—requires the gathering, use, and transferring of information in these networks. Managers must have the information competencies needed to perform well in these roles.

The most obvious problem-solving situation for managers, or anyone for that matter, is a **performance threat.** This occurs as an actual or potential performance deficiency. Something is wrong, or is likely to be wrong in the near future. Hurricane Katrina is an example worth remembering. There were lots of warnings about this storm, but many underestimated or were either ambivalent or overconfident in preparing for it. Too many people weren't ready when Katrina slammed New Orleans, and a high price was paid for their errors.

A **performance threat** is a situation where something is wrong or likely to be wrong.

Let's not forget, however, that problem solving often involves, or should involve, chances to deal with a **performance opportunity.** This is a situation that offers the possibility of a better future if the right steps are taken now. Suppose that a regional manager notices that sales at one retail store are unusually high. Does she just say "Great," and go on about her business? That's an opportunity missed. A really sharp manager says: "Wait a minute, there may be something happening here that I could learn from and possibly transfer to other stores. I had better find out what's going on." That's an opportunity gained.

A **performance opportunity** is a situation that offers the possibility of a better future if the right steps are taken.

Managers can be problem avoiders, problem solvers, or problem seekers.

What do you do when you receive a lower grade than expected on an exam or assignment? Do you get the grade, perhaps complain a bit to yourself or friends, and then forget it? Or do you get the grade, recognize that a problem exists, and try to learn from it so that you can do better in the future? Managers are just like you and me. They approach problem solving in different ways and realize different consequences.

Some managers are *problem avoiders*. They ignore information that would otherwise signal the presence of a performance threat or opportunity. They are not active in gathering information, and prefer not to make decisions or deal with problems.

Other managers are *problem solvers*. They make decisions and try to solve problems, but only when required. They are reactive, gathering information and responding to problems when they occur, but not before. These managers may deal reasonably well with performance threats, but they are likely to miss many performance opportunities.

Still other managers, the really better ones, are *problem seekers*. They are always looking for problems to solve or opportunities to explore. True problem seekers are proactive as information gatherers, and they are forward thinking. They anticipate threats and opportunities, and they are eager to take action to gain the advantage in dealing with them.

Managers make programmed and nonprogrammed decisions when solving problems.

So far in this discussion, we have used the word "decision" rather casually. From this point forward, though, let's agree that a **decision** is a choice among possible alternative courses of action. Let's also agree that decisions can be made in different ways, with some ways working better than others in various circumstances.

Some management problems are routine and repetitive. They can be addressed through **programmed decisions** that apply preplanned solutions based on the lessons of past experience. Such decisions work best for structured problems that are familiar, straightforward, and clear with respect to information needs. In human resource management, for example, decisions always have to be made on things such as vacations and holiday work schedules. Forward-looking managers can use past experience and plan ahead to make these decisions in programmed, not spontaneous, ways.

Other management problems, many in fact, arise as new or unusual situations full of ambiguities and information deficiencies. These unstructured problems require **nonprogrammed decisions** that craft novel solutions to meet the unique demands of a situation. In the recent financial crisis, for example, all eyes were on President Obama's choice of Treasury Secretary Timothy Geithner. His task was to solve the problems with billions in bad loans made by the nation's banks and restore stability to the financial markets. But it was

A **decision** is a choice among possible alternative courses of action.

A **programmed decision** applies a solution from past experience to a routine problem.

A **nonprogrammed decision** applies a specific solution that has been crafted to address a unique problem.

uncharted territory; no prepackaged solutions were readily available. Geithner and his team did what they believed was best. But in difficult and dynamic circumstances, only time would tell if the nonprogrammed decisions they made were the right ones.

Managers can use systematic and intuitive thinking.

Managers differ in their use of "systematic" and "intuitive" thinking. In **systematic thinking** a person approaches problems in a rational, step-by-step, and analytical fashion. You might recognize this when someone you are working with tries to break a complex problem into smaller components that can be addressed one by one. We might expect systematic managers to make a plan before taking action, and to search for information and proceed with problem solving in a fact-based and step-by-step fashion.

Someone using **intuitive thinking** is more flexible and spontaneous than the systematic thinker, and they may be quite creative.[3] You might observe this pattern in someone who always seems to come up with an imaginative response to a problem, often based on a quick and broad evaluation of the situation. Intuitive managers tend to deal with many aspects of a problem at once, jump quickly from one issue to another, and act on either hunches based on experience or on spontaneous ideas. Amazon.com's Jeff Bezos says that when it's not possible for the firm's top managers to make systematic fact-based decisions, "you have to rely on experienced executives who've honed their instincts" and are able to make good judgments.[4] In other words, there's a place for both systematic and intuitive decision making in management.

Systematic thinking approaches problems in a rational and analytical fashion.

Intuitive thinking approaches problems in a flexible and spontaneous fashion.

Managers use different cognitive styles to process information for decision making.

When US Airways Flight 1549 took off from LaGuardia airport on January 15, 2009, all was normal. It was normal, that is, until the plane hit a flock of birds and both engines failed; Flight 1549 was going to crash. Pilot Chesley Sullenberger quickly realized he couldn't get to an airport and decided to land in the Hudson River—a highly risky move. But he had both a clear head and a clear sense of what he had been trained to do. The landing was successful and no lives were lost. Called a "hero" for his efforts, Sullenberger described his thinking this way.[5]

I needed to touch down with the wings exactly level. I needed to touch down with the nose slightly up. I needed to touch down at . . . a descent rate that was survivable. And I needed to touch down just above our minimum flying speed but not below it. And I needed to make all these things happen simultaneously.

Cognitive style is the way an individual deals with information while making decisions.

The Flight 1549 example points us toward a discussion of **cognitive styles**, or the way individuals deal with information while making decisions. If you take the self-assessment "Intuitive Ability" at the end of the book, you can examine your cognitive style in problem solving. This involves a contrast of tendencies toward information gathering (sensation vs. intuition) and information evaluation (feeling vs. thinking). Pilot Sullenberger would most likely score high in both sensation and thinking, and that is probably an ideal type for his job. But as shown in the figure, this is only one of four master cognitive styles.[6]

	Thinking	Sensation Thinkers "STs"—like facts, goals	Intuitive Thinkers "ITs"—idealistic, theoretical
Information Evaluation	Feeling	Sensation Feelers "SFs"—like facts, feelings	Intuitive Feelers "IFs"—thoughtful, flexible
		Sensing	Intuition
		Information Processing	

- *Sensation thinkers*—STs tend to emphasize the impersonal rather than the personal and take a realistic approach to problem solving. They like hard "facts," clear goals, certainty, and situations of high control.

- *Intuitive thinkers*—ITs are comfortable with abstraction and unstructured situations. They tend to be idealistic, prone toward intellectual and theoretical positions; they are logical and impersonal but also avoid details.

- *Intuitive feelers*—IFs prefer broad and global issues. They are insightful and tend to avoid details, being comfortable with intangibles; they value flexibility and human relationships.

- *Sensation feelers*—SFs tend to emphasize both analysis and human relations. They tend to be realistic and prefer facts; they are open communicators and sensitive to feelings and values.

As the descriptions suggest, people with different cognitive styles may approach problems and make decisions in ways quite different from one another. It is important to understand our cognitive styles and tendencies, as well as those of others. In the social context of the workplace, lots of decisions are made by people working together in small groups and teams. The more diverse the cognitive styles, the more difficulty we might expect as they try to make decisions.

Managers make decisions under conditions of certainty, risk, and uncertainty.

It's not just personal styles that differ in problem solving; the environment counts, too. Figure 4.2 shows three different conditions or problem environments in which managers make decisions—certainty, risk, and uncertainty.

As you might expect, the levels of risk and uncertainty in problem environments tend to increase the higher one moves in management ranks. You might think about this each time you hear about Coca-Cola or Pepsi launching a new flavor or product or advertising campaign. Are the top executives making these decisions *certain* that the results will be successful? Or are they taking *risks* in market situations that are *uncertain* as to whether the new flavor or product or ad will be positively received by customers?

It would be nice if we could all make decisions and solve problems in the relative predictability of a **certain environment**. This is an ideal decision situation where factual information exists for the possible alternative courses of action and their consequences. All a decision maker needs to do is study the alternatives and choose the best solution. It isn't easy to find examples of decision situations with such

A **certain environment** offers complete information on possible action alternatives and their consequences.

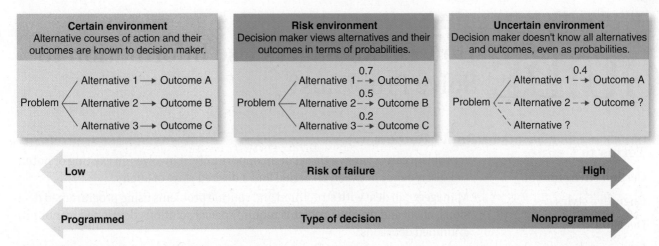

FIGURE 4.2 What Are the Differences Between Certain, Risk, and Uncertain Decision-Making Environments?
Managers rarely face a problem where they can know all the facts, identify all alternatives and their consequences, and chart a clear course of action. Such *certainty* is more often than not replaced by problem environments involving risk and uncertainty. *Risk* is where alternatives are known but their consequences can be described in terms of probabilities. *Uncertainty* is where all alternatives are not known and their consequences are highly speculative.

certain conditions. One possibility is a decision to take out a "fixed-rate" loan—say for college studies or a new car. At least you can make the decision knowing future interest costs and repayment timetables. But this situation changes significantly, doesn't it, if the lender is offering you a "variable-rate" loan? In this case the interest rate you have to pay will vary in the future according to what happens with market interest rates. How willing are you to take a loan while not knowing if interest rates will go down (to your gain) or up (to your loss) in the future?

Whereas absolute certainty is the best scenario for decision makers, the reality is that in our personal lives and in management we more often face **risk environments** where information and facts are incomplete. An example is the offer of a variable rate loan as just discussed. In risk conditions, alternative courses of action and their consequences can be analyzed only as *probabilities* (e.g., 4 chances out of 10). One way of dealing with risk is by gathering as much information as possible, perhaps in different ways. In the case of a new product, such as Coke Zero or even a college textbook like this, it is unlikely that marketing executives would make go-ahead decisions without lots of data gathering and analysis. Often this involves getting reports from multiple focus groups that test the new product in its sample stages.

When facts are few and information is so poor that managers have a hard time even assigning probabilities to things, an **uncertain environment** exists. This is the most difficult decision condition.[7] It's also more common than you might think. And the border line between risk and uncertainty isn't always clear. When the Japanese built a nuclear power plant at Fukushima—on the sea coast and in an earthquake zone, were decision makers just taking a calculated risk or were they acting in the face of absolute uncertainty? Decisions made in uncertain conditions depend greatly on intuition, judgment, informed guessing, and hunches—all of which leave considerable room for error. This is one situation where group decisions are often useful. When things are uncertain, the more information, perspectives, and creativity that can be brought to bear on the situation, the better. This increases chances for a good decision, or at least a better one than the individual alone might make.

A **risk environment** lacks complete information but offers probabilities of the likely outcomes for possible action alternatives.

An **uncertain environment** lacks so much information that it is difficult to assign probabilities to the likely outcomes of alternatives.

STUDY GUIDE

Takeaway 4.1
How Do Managers Use Information to Solve Problems?

Terms to Define

Certain environment

Cognitive styles

Decision

Information competency

Intuitive thinking

Knowledge workers

Nonprogrammed decision

Performance opportunity

Performance threat

Problem solving

Programmed decision

Risk environment

Systematic thinking

Uncertain environment

Rapid Review

- A problem can occur as a threat or an opportunity; it involves an existing or potential discrepancy between an actual and a desired state of affairs.
- Managers can deal with structured and routine problems using programmed decisions; novel and unique problems require special solutions developed by nonprogrammed decisions.
- Managers deal with problems in different ways, with some being problem avoiders, others being reactive problem solvers, and still others being proactive problem seekers.
- Managers using systematic thinking approach problems in a rational step-by-step fashion; managers using intuitive thinking approach them in a more flexible and spontaneous way.
- Managers display different cognitive styles when dealing with information for decision making—sensation thinkers, intuitive thinkers, intuitive feelers, and sensation feelers.
- The problems that managers face occur in environments of certainty, risk, and uncertainty.

Questions for Discussion

1. Can a manager be justified for acting as a problem avoider in certain situations?
2. Would an organization be better off with mostly systematic or mostly intuitive thinkers?
3. Is it possible to develop programmed decisions for use in conditions of risk and uncertainty?

Be Sure You Can

- explain the importance of information competency for successful problem solving
- differentiate programmed and nonprogrammed decisions
- describe different ways managers approach and deal with problems
- discuss the differences between systematic and intuitive thinking
- identify differences between the four cognitive styles used in decision making
- explain the challenges of decision making under conditions of certainty, risk, and uncertainty environments

What Would You Do?

Even though some problems in organizations seem to "pop up," many can be anticipated. Examples are an employee who calls in sick at the last minute, a customer who is unhappy with a product or service and wants a refund, and even a boss who asks you to do something that isn't job-relevant. How can such situations be best handled from a decision-making standpoint?

Takeaway 4.2
What Are Five Steps in the Decision-Making Process?

ANSWERS TO COME

- Step 1 is to identify and define the problem.
- Step 2 is to generate and evaluate alternative courses of action.
- Step 3 is to decide on a preferred course of action.
- Step 4 is to implement the decision.
- Step 5 is to evaluate results.
- Ethical reasoning is important at all steps in decision making.

THE **DECISION-MAKING PROCESS** INVOLVES A STRAIGHTFORWARD SERIES OF STEPS shown in Figure 4.3—Identify and define the problem, generate and evaluate alternative solutions, decide on a preferred course of action, implement the decision, and then evaluate results. An ethics double-check should be done at each step along the way.[8]

The **decision-making process** begins with identification of a problem and ends with evaluation of implemented solutions.

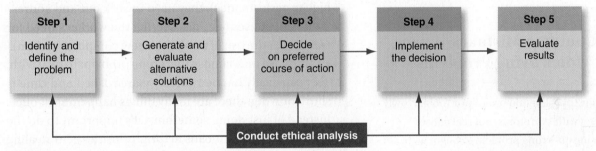

FIGURE 4.3 What Are Five Steps in the Decision-Making Process?
Decision making can be viewed as a series of steps—(1) find and define the problem, (2) generate and evaluate solutions, (3) choose a preferred alternative, (4) implement the decision, and (5) evaluate the results. It is important to conduct ethical analysis at all steps in the decision-making process—from initial problem identification all the way to the evaluation of results. When the ethics of a decision are questioned, it's time to stop and rethink the entire process. This helps the decision maker to be confident that all underlying moral problems have been identified and dealt with in the best possible ways.

Let's look at this process with a timely example. When General Motors announced it was closing nine plants in North America and cutting 30,000 jobs, it was a blow to workers, their families, and communities.[9] The following case isn't quite as sensational, but it's equally real. It helps show how the decision-making steps apply in real situations.

The Ajax case   On December 31, the Ajax Company decided to close down its Murphysboro plant. Market conditions and a recessionary economy were forcing layoffs, and the company hadn't been able to find a buyer for the plant. Of the 172 employees, some had been with the company as long as 18 years, others as little as 6 months. Ajax needed to terminate all of them. Under company policy, they would be given severance pay equal to one week's pay per year of service.

This opening to the Ajax case reflects how competition, changing times, and the forces of globalization can take their toll on organizations, the people that work for them, and the communities in which they operate. How would you feel—as one of the affected employees, as the mayor of this small town, or as an Ajax executive having to make tough decisions in this situation?

Step 1 is to identify and define the problem.

The first step in decision making is to identify and define the problem. This is a stage of information gathering, information processing, and deliberation. It is also where goals are clarified to specify exactly what a decision should accomplish. The more specific the goals, the easier it is to evaluate results after implementing the decision.

Three mistakes are common in this critical first step in decision making. First, we may define the problem too broadly or too narrowly. To take a classic example, instead of stating the problem as "Build a better mousetrap," we define it as "Get rid of the mice." Ideally, problems are defined in ways that give them the best possible range of problem-solving options.

Second, we may focus on symptoms instead of causes. Symptoms only indicate that problems may exist; they aren't the problems themselves. Of course, managers need to be good at spotting problem symptoms (e.g., a drop in performance). But instead of just treating symptoms (such as simply encouraging higher performance), they need to seek out and address their root causes (e.g., discovering the worker's need for training in the use of a complex new computer system).

Third, we may choose the wrong problem to deal with. This can easily happen when we are rushed and time is short, or when there are many things happening at once. Instead of just doing something, it's important to do the right things. This means setting priorities and dealing with the most important problems first.

Common Mistakes When Identifying Problems

1. Defining problem too broadly or too narrowly
2. Dealing with symptoms, not real causes
3. Focusing on wrong problem to begin with

Back to the Ajax case   Closing the plant will result in a loss of jobs for a substantial number of people from the small community of Murphysboro. The unemployment created will negatively impact these individuals, their families, and the community as a whole. The loss of the Ajax tax base will further hurt the community. Ajax management, therefore, defines the problem as how to minimize the adverse impact of the plant closing on the employees, their families, and the community.

Step 2 is to generate and evaluate alternative courses of action.

After the problem is defined, the next step in decision making is to gather the needed facts and information. Managers must be clear here on exactly what they know and what they need to know. Extensive information gathering should identify alternative courses of action as well as their anticipated consequences. Key stakeholders in the problem should be identified and the effects of each possible course of action on them should be considered. In the case of GM's plant closings and layoffs, for example, a union negotiator said: "While GM's continuing decline in market share isn't the fault of workers or our communities, it is these groups that will suffer."

Most managers use some form of **cost-benefit analysis** to evaluate alternatives. This compares what an alternative will cost with its expected benefits. At a minimum, benefits should exceed costs. In addition, an alternative should be timely, acceptable to as many stakeholders as possible, and ethically sound. And most often, the better the pool of alternatives and the better the analysis, the more likely it is that a good decision will result.

Cost-benefit analysis involves comparing the costs and benefits of each potential course of action.

Back to the Ajax case   Ajax will definitely close the plant; keeping it open is no longer an option. These alternatives are considered—close the plant on schedule and be done with it; delay the plant closing and try again to sell it to another firm; offer to sell the plant to the employees and/or local interests; close the plant and offer employees transfers to other Ajax plant locations; close the plant, offer transfers, and help the employees find new jobs in and around Murphysboro.

⦀ Step 3 is to decide on a preferred course of action.

Management theory recognizes two quite different ways that alternatives get explored and decisions get made: the classical and behavioral models shown in Figure 4.4. The **classical decision model** views the manager as acting rationally and in a fully informed manner. The problem is clearly defined, all possible action alternatives are known, and their consequences are clear. As a result, he or she makes an **optimizing decision** that gives the absolute best solution to the problem.

The **classical decision model** describes decision making with complete information.

An **optimizing decision** chooses the alternative providing the absolute best solution to a problem.

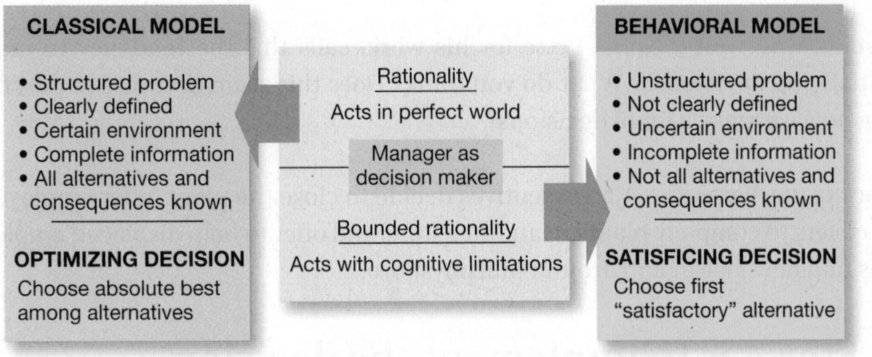

CLASSICAL MODEL
- Structured problem
- Clearly defined
- Certain environment
- Complete information
- All alternatives and consequences known

OPTIMIZING DECISION
Choose absolute best among alternatives

Rationality
Acts in perfect world

Manager as decision maker

Bounded rationality
Acts with cognitive limitations

BEHAVIORAL MODEL
- Unstructured problem
- Not clearly defined
- Uncertain environment
- Incomplete information
- Not all alternatives and consequences known

SATISFICING DECISION
Choose first "satisfactory" alternative

FIGURE 4.4

How Does the Classical Model of Managerial Decision Making Differ from the Behavioral Model?
The classical model views decision makers as having complete information and making optimum decisions that are the absolute best choices to resolve problems. The behavioral model views decision makers as having limited information-processing capabilities. They act with incomplete information and make satisficing decisions, choosing the first satisfactory alternative that comes to their attention.

Although the classical model sounds ideal, most of the time it's too good to be true. Because there are limits to our information-processing capabilities, something called *cognitive limitations*, it is hard to be fully informed and make perfectly rational decisions in all situations. Recognizing this, the premise of the **behavioral decision model** is that people act only in terms of their perceptions, which are frequently imperfect. Armed with only partial knowledge about the available action alternatives and their consequences, decision makers are likely to choose the first alternative that appears satisfactory to them. Herbert

The **behavioral decision model** describes decision making with limited information and bounded rationality.

Manager's Library

■ *THE SHALLOWS* BY NICHOLAS CARR

YOUR BRAIN ON THE INTERNET—MORE ENLIGHTENED OR LIGHTENED UP?

When the World Wide Web launched in 1991, human culture was forever altered. One profound impact has been that upon the human brain. It has evolved along with the tools that we use to communicate. While the Internet has enlightened us in various ways, it may also be lightening our thinking by replacing deep thought and reflection with shallow-minded pursuits.

In the book *The Shallows* (2010, W. W. Norton & Company), author Nicholas Carr discusses how human minds have changed along with communication technologies ranging from the spoken word to the written tablet, and the printing press to the Internet. Research shows that brains are "rewired" when using the Web as the "hypermedia" of links and audio-visual stimuli overwhelm its cognitive capacity. Studies show that brains cope with information overload by changing their neural networks of operation. "Linear" thought—deep thinking and slow reflection using long-term memory—is replaced by "non-linear" thought—temporary thinking and rapid scanning using short-term memory.

Carr says research shows book readers outperform "hypertext" readers in comprehension, memory, and learning.

Internet brains are distracted by abundant stimuli and grow their short-term memory circuits by converting and replacing long-term memory circuits. Permanent memory requires time and calm for ideas to pass into the unconscious mind, so he describes the Internet as a "technology of forgetfulness" and a "Web of distraction." Carr warns that critical mental skills are lost, and advises caution in Internet use. He thinks users should be purpose-driven, focus on fewer tasks simultaneously, and spend time away from the Web to read, ponder, and discuss ideas verbally.

He concedes that new skills are developed by Net use, like "power browsing" through titles, content pages, and abstracts to quickly obtain ideas. And "hunting and gathering" more efficiently for additional and varied facts. Carr speculates Web use may someday advance brains to multitask effectively, but those tasks may be less complex as humans' brains evolve to accommodate the shallow thinking demands of the Internet.

REFLECT AND REACT

Do you think the Internet makes you more, or less, smart? How can Internet distractions be managed? Do you think linear thinking may be developed within, or beyond, the Net? And by the way, do you agree that the Internet is a Web of distraction?

A **satisficing decision** chooses the first satisfactory alternative that presents itself.

Simon, who won a Nobel Prize for his work, calls this the tendency to make **satisficing decisions**.[10] What do you think? Does this seem accurate in describing how we make a lot of decisions?

Back to the Ajax case　Ajax executives decide to close the plant, offer employees transfers to company plants in another state, and offer to help displaced employees find new jobs in and around Murphysboro.

‖ Step 4 is to implement the decision.

Once a preferred course of action is chosen, managers must take action to fully implement it. Until they do, nothing new can or will happen to solve the problem. This not only requires the determination and creativity to arrive at a decision, it also requires the ability and personal willingness to act. Most likely it also requires the support of many other people. And more often than you might realize, it is lack of support that sabotages the implementation of many perfectly good decisions.

Lack-of-participation error is failure to include the right people in the decision-making process.

Managers fall prey to the **lack-of-participation error** when they don't include in the decision-making process those persons whose support is necessary for implementation. When managers use participation wisely, by contrast, they get

{ "WHATEVER ANYBODY SAYS OR DOES, ASSUME POSITIVE INTENT. YOU WILL BE AMAZED AT HOW YOUR WHOLE APPROACH TO A PERSON OR PROBLEM BECOMES VERY DIFFERENT."

Role Models

■ INDRA NOOYI BRINGS STYLE AND A STRATEGIC VISION TO PEPSI

The best advice she ever got, says Indra Nooyi, Pepsico's Chairman and CEO, was to always assume positive intent. The lesson came from her father: "Whatever anybody says or does, assume positive intent. You will be amazed at how your whole approach to a person or problem becomes very different. . . . You are trying to understand and listen because at your basic core you are saying, 'Maybe they are saying something to me that I am not hearing.'"

Her father's advice has carried Nooyi to the top ranks of global business, only the 12th woman to head a *Fortune* 500 firm. *Business Week* described her as a leader with "prescient business sense." Former CEO Roger Enrico says, "Indra can drive as deep and hard as anyone I've ever met, but she can do it with a sense of heart and fun." ABC news described her as a blend of "Indian culture mixed in with the traditional American working mom."

Nooyi is also a leader when it comes to corporate social responsibility. She has said that her firm's "real profit" should be assessed as Revenue less Cost of Goods Sold less Costs to Society.

WHAT'S THE LESSON HERE?

Indra Nooyi makes lots of decisions every day, many of them strategic and consequential for her firm. But as the last point about "real profit" indicates, she tries to make these decisions with a strong and confident sense of ethical direction. What things might provide her with the ability to always do so in this industry? And how about you? Do you have a solid ethics anchor point that helps you make consistently good decisions?

---

the right people involved from the beginning. This not only brings their inputs and insights to bear on the problem, it helps build commitments to take actions supporting the decision and make sure it all works as intended.

Back to the Ajax case   Ajax management ran an ad in the local and regional newspapers for several days. It announced to potential employers an "Ajax skill bank" composed of "qualified, dedicated, and well-motivated employees with a variety of skills and experiences." The ad urged interested employers to contact Ajax for further information.

⫼ Step 5 is to evaluate results.

A decision isn't much good if it doesn't achieve the desired outcomes or causes undesired side effects. This is why the decision-making process is not complete until results are evaluated. Doing so is a form of control, gathering data so that performance results can be measured against initial goals. If things aren't going well it means reassessing and perhaps redoing earlier steps in the decision-making process. If things are better than expected, it means trying to learn why, so these lessons can be used in the future.

Back to the Ajax case   How effective was Ajax's decision? Well, we don't know for sure. After Ajax ran the skill-bank advertisement for 15 days, the plant's industrial relations manager said: "I've been very pleased with the results." However, we really need a lot more information for a true evaluation. How many employees got new jobs locally? How many transferred to other Ajax plants? How did the local economy perform in the following months? Probably you can add evaluation questions of your own to this list.

⫼ Ethical reasoning is important at all steps in decision making.

If you look back to Figure 4.3, you'll see that each step in the decision-making process is linked with ethical reasoning.[11] Attention to ethical analysis helps identify any underlying moral problems. You can think of this as an ongoing "ethics double-check." It is accomplished by asking and answering two sets of questions.

The first set of ethics questions is based on four criteria described in the work of ethicist Gerald Cavanagh and his associates.[12]

1. *Utility*—Does the decision satisfy all constituents or stakeholders?
2. *Rights*—Does the decision respect the rights and duties of everyone?
3. *Justice*—Is the decision consistent with the canons of justice?
4. *Caring*—Is the decision consistent with my responsibilities to care?

The second set of ethics questions exposes a decision to public disclosure and the prospect of shame.[13] These so-called **spotlight questions**, discussed also in the last chapter, are especially powerful when the decision maker comes from a morally scrupulous family or social structure.

1. "How would I feel if my family found out about this decision?"
2. "How would I feel if this decision was published in the local newspaper or posted on the Internet?"
3. "What would the person I know who has the strongest character and best ethical judgment say about my decision?"

Spotlight questions highlight the risks of public disclosure of one's actions.

{ "HUMAN LIFE IS FAR MORE IMPORTANT THAN JUST GETTING TO THE TOP OF A MOUNTAIN."

Ethics Check

◼ LEFT TO DIE ON MT. EVEREST

Some 40 climbers are winding their ways to the top of Mt. Everest. About 1,000 feet below the summit sits a British mountain climber in trouble, collapsed in a shallow snow cave. Most of those on the way up just look while continuing their climbs. Sherpas from one passing team pause to give him oxygen before moving on. Within hours, David Sharp, 34, is dead of oxygen deficiency on the mountain.

A climber who passed by says: "At 28,000 feet it's hard to stay alive yourself . . . he was in very poor condition . . . , it was a very hard decision . . . he wasn't a member of our team."

Someone who made the summit in the past says: "If you're going to go to Everest . . . I think you have to accept responsibility that you may end up doing something that's not ethically nice . . . you have to realize that you're in a different world."

After hearing about this case, the late Sir Edmund Hillary, who reached the top in 1953, said: "Human life is far more important than just getting to the top of a mountain."

YOU DECIDE

Who's right and who's wrong here? And, by the way, in our personal affairs, daily lives, and careers, we are all, in our own ways, climbing Mt. Everest. What are the ethics of our climbs? How often do we notice others in trouble, struggling along the way? And, like the mountain climbers heading to the summit of Everest, how often do we pass them by to continue our own journeys? Can you identify examples—from business, school, career, sports, and so on—that pose similar ethical dilemmas?

Takeaway 4.2
What Are Five Steps in the Decision-Making Process?

Terms to Define

Behavioral decision model

Classical decision model

Cost-benefit analysis

Decision-making process

Lack-of-participation error

Optimizing decision

Satisficing decision

Spotlight questions

Rapid Review

- The steps in the decision-making process are: (1) identify and define the problem; (2) generate and evaluate alternatives; (3) decide on the preferred course of action; (4) implement the decision; (5) evaluate the results; conduct ethics double-check in all steps.
- A cost-benefit analysis compares the expected costs of a decision alternative with its expected results.
- In the classical model, an optimizing decision chooses the absolute best solution from a known set of alternatives.
- In the behavioral model, cognitive limitations lead to satisficing decisions that choose the first satisfactory alternative to come to attention.
- The ethics of a decision can be checked on the criteria of utility, rights, justice, and caring, as well as by asking the spotlight questions.

Questions for Discussion

1. Do the steps in the decision-making process have to be followed in order?
2. Do you see any problems or pitfalls for managers using the behavioral decision model?
3. Is use of the spotlight questions sufficient to ensure an ethical decision?

Be Sure You Can

- list the steps in the decision-making process
- apply these steps to a sample decision-making situation
- explain cost-benefit analysis
- compare and contrast the classical and behavioral decision models
- illustrate optimizing and satisficing in your personal decision-making experiences
- list and explain the criteria for evaluating the ethics of a decision
- list three questions for double-checking the ethics of a decision

What Would You Do?

Well, it has finally happened. You've done the ethics analysis and a decision you are about to make fails all three of the recommended spotlight questions. You are under a lot of pressure because the problem situation involves social loafing and poor performance by one of your team members. You have come up with a reason to remove her from the team. But, you feel very uneasy knowing that your intention fails the spotlight test. As team leader, what do you do now?

Takeaway 4.3
What Are Some Current Issues in Managerial Decision Making?

ANSWERS TO COME

- Personal factors help drive creativity in decision making.
- Group decision making has both advantages and disadvantages.
- Judgmental heuristics and other biases and traps may cause decision-making errors.
- Managers must be prepared for crisis decision making.

ONCE YOU ACCEPT THE FACT THAT EACH OF US IS LIKELY TO MAKE IMPERFECT decisions at least some of the time, it makes sense to probe even further into the how's and why's of decision making in organizations. In addition to the issues of ethical reasoning and analysis just discussed, other concerns are possible causes of decision bias and error, advantages and disadvantages of group decision making, and the challenges of decision making under crisis conditions.

Personal factors help drive creativity in decision making.

Lonnie Johnson is a former U.S. Air Force captain and a NASA engineer. You probably don't know him, but you may be familiar with something he invented—the Super Soaker water gun. Johnson didn't set out to invent the water gun; he was working in his basement on an idea for refrigeration systems that would use water rather than Freon. Something connected in his mind and the Super Soaker was born. Johnson says: "The Super Soaker changed my life." He now heads his own research and development company and, among other things, always has fun toys in development.[14]

We can think of **creativity** as the generation of a novel idea or unique approach to solving performance problems or exploiting performance opportunities.[15] Just imagine what we can accomplish with all the creative potential that exists in an organization's workforce. But how do you turn that potential into actual creativity in decision making—the Lonnie Johnson model, so to speak?

Creativity is one of our greatest personal assets, even though it may be too often unrecognized by us and by others. We exercise creativity every day in lots of ways—solving problems at home, building something for the kids, or even finding ways to pack too many things into too small a suitcase. But are we creative when it would really help in solving workplace problems?

One source of insight into personal creativity drivers is the three-component model of task expertise, task motivation, and creativity skills shown in the small figure on the next page.[16] From a management standpoint, the model is helpful because it points us in the direction of actions that can be taken to build creativity drivers into the work setting and encourage creativity in decision making.

Creative decisions are more likely to occur when the person or team has a lot of task expertise. As in the case of Lonnie Johnson, creativity is an

Creativity is the generation of a novel idea or unique approach that solves a problem or crafts an opportunity.

Explore Yourself

■ SELF-CONFIDENCE

Managers are decision makers. And if they are to make consistently good decisions, they must be skilled at gathering and processing information. Managers are also implementers. Once decisions are made, managers are expected to rally people and resources to put them into action. This is how problems get solved and opportunities get explored in organizations.

In order for all this to happen, managers must have the **self-confidence** to turn decisions into action accomplishments; they must believe in their decisions and the information foundations for them. A good understanding of the many topics in this chapter can improve your decision-making skills. A better understanding of your personal style in gathering and processing information can also go a long way toward building your self-confidence as a decision maker.

> Get to know yourself better by taking the self-assessment on **Cognitive Style** and completing the other activities in the *Exploring Management* **Skill-Building Portfolio**.

---

outgrowth of skill and typically extends in new directions something one is good at or knows about. Creativity is also more likely when the people making decisions are highly task motivated. It tends to occur in part because people work exceptionally hard to resolve a problem. In the course of old-fashioned hard work—Lonnie Johnson spending hours in his home basement, for example—something new and different is accomplished.

Creative decisions are more likely when the people involved have strong creativity skill sets. In popular conversations you might refer to this as the contrast between "right-brain" thinking—imagination, intuition, spontaneity, and emotion—and "left-brain" thinking—logic, order, method, and analysis. But just what are we talking about here? Is creativity something that is built into some of us and not built into others? Or is creativity something that one can work to develop along with other personal skills and competencies?

Researchers argue the prior points. But, they tend to agree both that the following characteristics often describe creative people and that most of us can develop these abilities into creativity skill sets. Why not use the list as a personal test—a self-check of potential strengths and weaknesses in creativity skills?[17]

- Ability to work with high energy
- Ability to hold one's ground in the face of criticism
- Ability to be resourceful even in difficult situations
- Ability to think "outside of the box"—divergent thinking
- Ability to use "lateral thinking"—looking at diverse ways to solve problems
- Ability to transfer learning from one setting to others
- Ability to "step back," be objective, and question assumptions

Personal Creativity Drivers

Task expertise

Task motivation

Creativity skills

CREATIVITY

||| Group decision making has both advantages and disadvantages.

Sometimes the most important decisions we make involve choosing whether to make them alone or with the help of others. And it really shouldn't be an either/or question. Effective managers and team leaders typically switch back and forth between individual and group decision making, trying to use the best methods for the problems at hand. To do this well, however, you need to understand the implications of Table 4.1—*Potential Advantages and Disadvantages of Group Decision Making.*[18]

Table 4.1 Potential Advantages and Disadvantages of Group Decision Making

Why group decisions are often good

More information—More information, expertise, and viewpoints are available to help solve problems.

More alternatives—More alternatives are generated and considered during decision making.

Increased understanding—There is increased understanding and a greater acceptance of the decision by group members.

Greater commitment—There is an increased commitment of group members to work hard and support the decision.

Why group decisions can be bad

Conformity with social pressures—Some members feel intimidated by others and give in to social pressures to conform.

Domination by a few members—A minority dominates; some members get railroaded by a small coalition of others.

Time delays—More time is required to make decisions when many people try to work together.

In respect to advantages, group decisions can be good because they bring greater amounts of information, knowledge, and expertise to bear on a problem. They often expand the number and even the creativity of action alternatives examined. And as noted earlier in our discussion of lack-of-participation error, participation helps group members gain a better understanding of any decisions reached. This increases the likelihood that they will both accept decisions made and work hard to help implement them.

In respect to disadvantages, we all know that it is sometimes difficult and time consuming for people to make group decisions. The more people involved, the longer it can take to reach a group decision, and the more likely that problems will arise. There may be social pressure to conform that leads to premature consensus and agreement in group situations. Some individuals may feel intimidated or compelled to go along with the apparent wishes of others who have authority, or who act aggressive and uncompromising. Minority domination might cause some members to feel forced or railroaded into a decision advocated by one vocal individual or a small coalition. And, lots of decisions get made quickly or at the last minute just because a group is running out of meeting time.

||| Judgmental heuristics and other biases and traps may cause decision-making errors.

Why do well-intentioned people sometimes make bad decisions? The reason often traces to simplifying strategies we use when making decisions with limited information, time, and even energy. These strategies, known as *heuristics,* can cause decision-making errors.[19]

The **availability heuristic** occurs when people use information "readily available" from memory as a basis for assessing a current event or situation. You may decide, for example, not to buy running shoes from a company if your last pair didn't last long. The potential bias is that the readily available information may be wrong or irrelevant. Even though your present running shoes are worn out, you may have purchased the wrong model for your needs or used them in the wrong conditions.

> The **availability heuristic** uses readily available information to assess a current situation.

The **representativeness heuristic** occurs when people assess the likelihood of something happening based on its similarity to a stereotyped set of past occurrences. An example is deciding to hire someone for a job vacancy simply because he or she graduated from the same school attended by your last and most successful new hire. Using the representative stereotype may mask the truly important factors relevant to the decision—the real abilities and career expectations of the new job candidate; the school attended may be beside the point.

> The **representativeness heuristic** assesses the likelihood of an occurrence using a stereotyped set of similar events.

The **anchoring and adjustment heuristic** involves making decisions based on adjustments to a previously existing value or starting point. For example, a manager may set a new salary level for a current employee by simply raising the prior year's salary by a percentage increment. The problem is that this increment is anchored in the existing salary level, one that may be much lower than the employee's true market value. Rather than being pleased with the raise, the employee may be unhappy and start looking elsewhere for another, higher-paying job.

> The **anchoring and adjustment heuristic** adjusts a previously existing value or starting point to make a decision.

{ WALMART WANTS TO CUT GREENHOUSE GAS EMISSIONS IN ITS SUPPLY CHAINS BY 20 MILLION METRIC TONS.

Facts to Consider

■ GREENHOUSE GAS EMISSIONS AS EXECUTIVE PRIORITIES

Walmart wants to cut its carbon footprint by 20% by 2012, and cut greenhouse gas emissions in its supply chains by 20 million metric tons by 2015. By its own measurements, it actions are falling short of goals, but good progress is being made. Business executives are taking notice as consumers become more informed about the carbon footprints of their favorite products.

- *Car:* Toyota Prius—97,000 pounds (from production through use and ultimate disposal)
- *Fleece jacket:* Patagonia Talus—66 pounds
- *Six-pack of beer:* Fat Tire Amber Ale—7 pounds
- *Half-gallon of milk:* Aurora Organic Dairy—7.2 pounds
- *Laundry detergent:* Tesco nonbiological liquid (1.5 liter)—31 pounds
- *Hiking boots:* Timberland Winter Park slip-ons—121 pounds

YOUR THOUGHTS?

When you look at these product numbers, is the glass "half full" or "half empty" when it comes to protection of our natural environment? How much do you worry about the carbon footprints of the products you consume? How high on the list of executive priorities should issues such as sustainability and carbon neutrality be? Should Walmart be praised for publicly setting carbon goals, or criticized for missing them?

Framing error is solving a problem in the context perceived.

In addition to heuristic biases, **framing error** is another potential decision trap. Framing occurs when managers evaluate and resolve a problem in the context in which they perceive it—either positive or negative. You might consider this as the "glass is half empty versus the glass is half full" dilemma. Suppose marketing data show that a new product has a 40% market share. What does this really mean? A negative frame says there's a problem because the product is missing 60% of the market. "What are we doing wrong?" is the likely follow-up question. But if the marketing team used a positive frame and considered the 40% share as a success story, the conversation might well be: "How can we do even better?" By the way, we are constantly exposed to framing in the world of politics; the word used to describe it is "spin."

Another of our tendencies is to try to find ways to justify a decision after making it. In the case of unethical acts, for example, we try to rationalize with statements like: "No one will ever find out" or "The boss will protect me." Such thinking causes a decision-making trap known as **confirmation error**. This means that we notice, accept, and even seek out only information that confirms or is consistent with a decision we have just made. Other and perhaps critical information is downplayed or denied. This is a form of selective perception. The error is that we neglect other points of view or disconfirming information that might lead us to a different decision.

Confirmation error is when we attend only to information that confirms a decision already made.

Yet another decision-making trap is **escalating commitment**. This is a tendency to increase effort and perhaps apply more resources to pursue a course of action that signals indicate is not working.[20] It is an inability or unwillingness to call it quits even when the facts suggest this is the best decision under the circumstances. Ego and the desire to avoid being associated with a mistake can play a big role in escalation.

Escalating commitment is the continuation of a course of action even though it is not working.

How about it? Are you disciplined enough to minimize the risk of escalating commitments to previously chosen, but erroneous, courses of action? Fortunately, researchers have provided some good ideas on how to avoid the escalation trap. They include:

- Setting advance limits on your involvement in and commitment to a particular course of action; stick with these limits.
- Making your own decisions; don't follow the lead of others, since they are also prone to escalation.
- Carefully determining just why you are continuing a course of action; if there are insufficient reasons to continue, don't.
- Reminding yourself of the costs of a course of action; consider saving these costs as a reason to discontinue.

||| Managers must be prepared for crisis decision making.

Think back to the example of shift leader Carlos Urzua and the Chilean mine disaster in the photo that opened this chapter. One of the most challenging of all decision situations is the **crisis**. This is an unexpected problem that can lead to disaster if not resolved quickly and appropriately. The ability to handle crises could well be the ultimate test of any manager's decision-making capabilities, and Urzua certainly fulfilled his responsibilities with flying colors. Not everyone

A **crisis** is an unexpected problem that can lead to disaster if not resolved quickly and appropriately.

does as well. In fact, as another recent example helps show, we sometimes react to crises by doing exactly the wrong things.

It caught most people by surprise when Toyota, the king of automobile quality, recalled over 5 million vehicles for quality defects—a real crisis for the automaker. But it wasn't just the size of the recall that caught our attention; the way Toyota's management handled the crisis was scrutinized as well.[21] One observer called the situation a "public relations nightmare for Toyota" and said that "crisis management does not get any more woeful than this." This poor crisis management was described as a fault of Toyota's insular corporate culture, one that discouraged early disclosure of quality problems and contributed to poor public relations when the crisis finally hit the news.

Even though Toyota's CEO Akio Toyoda eventually apologized in public and pledged a return to high standards of quality, by the time he did so customers and government regulators considered it too late and inadequate. Both he and the firm were criticized for "initially denying, minimizing and mitigating the problems." It even turns out that data on quality problems had been available within the system for a long time. But it wasn't acted upon. The top U.S. executive for the company said: "We did not hide it. But it was not properly shared."[22]

Managers err in crisis situations when they isolate themselves and try to solve the problem alone or in a small, closed group.[23] This denies them access to crucial information at the very time that they need it the most. It not only sets them up for poor decisions, it may create even more problems. This is why many organizations are developing formal crisis management programs. They train managers in crisis decision making (see Tips to Remember), assign people ahead of time to crisis management teams, and develop crisis management plans to deal with various contingencies.

Fire and police departments, the Red Cross, and community groups plan ahead and train to best handle civil and natural disasters; airline crews train for flight emergencies. So too can managers and work teams plan ahead and train to best deal with organizational crises.[24] This only makes sense, doesn't it?

{ THE ABILITY TO HANDLE CRISES COULD BE THE ULTIMATE TEST OF YOUR DECISION-MAKING CAPABILITIES.

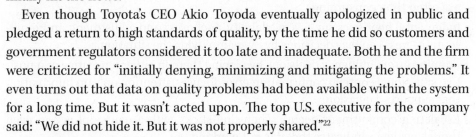

Tips to Remember

■ SIX RULES FOR CRISIS MANAGEMENT

1. *Figure out what is going on*—Dig in to thoroughly understand what's happening and the conditions under which the crisis must be resolved.

2. *Remember that speed matters*—Attack the crisis as quickly as possible, trying to catch it when it is small and before it gets overwhelmingly large.

3. *Remember that slow counts, too*—Know when to back off and wait for a better opportunity to make progress with the crisis.

4. *Respect the danger of the unfamiliar*—Understand the danger of entering all-new territory where you and others have never been before.

5. *Value the skeptic*—Don't look for and get too comfortable with early agreement; appreciate skeptics and let them help you see things differently in sorting out what to do.

6. *Be ready to "fight fire with fire"*—When things are going wrong and no one seems to care, you may have to fuel the crisis to get their attention.

STUDY GUIDE

Takeaway 4.3
What Are Some Current Issues in Managerial Decision Making?

Terms to Define

Anchoring and adjustment heuristic

Availability heuristic

Confirmation error

Crisis

Escalating commitment

Framing error

Representativeness heuristic

Rapid Review

- Creativity in decision making can be enhanced by the personal creativity drivers of individual creativity skills, task expertise, and motivation.
- Group decisions offer the potential advantages of more information, greater understanding, and expanded commitments; a major disadvantage is that they are often time consuming.
- Judgmental heuristics such as availability, anchoring and adjustment, and representativeness can bias decisions by oversimplifying the situation.
- Framing errors influence decisions by placing them in either a negative or a positive situational context; confirmation error focuses attention only on information that supports a decision.
- Escalating commitment occurs when one sticks with a course of action even though evidence indicates that it is not working.
- A crisis problem occurs unexpectedly and can lead to disaster if managers fail to handle it quickly and properly.

Questions for Discussion

1. How can you avoid being hurt by the anchoring and adjustment heuristic in your annual pay raises?
2. What are some real-world examples of how escalating commitment is affecting decision making in business, government, or people's personal affairs?
3. Is it really possible to turn a crisis into an opportunity, and, if so, how?

Be Sure You Can

- identify personal factors that can be developed or used to drive greater creativity in decision making
- list potential advantages and disadvantages of group decision making
- explain the availability, representativeness, and anchoring and adjustment heuristics
- illustrate framing error and continuation error in decision making
- explain and give an example of escalating commitment
- describe what managers can do to prepare for crisis decisions

What Would You Do?

You have finally caught the attention of senior management. Top executives asked you to chair a task force to develop a creative new product that can breathe new life into an existing product line. First, you need to select the members of the task force. What criteria will you use to choose members who are most likely to bring high levels of creativity to this team?

TestPrep 4

Multiple-Choice Questions

1. A manager who is reactive and works hard to address problems after they occur is described as a _____.

   (a) problem seeker
   (b) problem solver
   (c) rational thinker
   (d) strategic opportunist

2. A problem is a discrepancy between a/an _____ situation and a desired situation.

   (a) unexpected
   (b) risk
   (c) actual
   (d) uncertain

3. If a manager approaches problems in a rational and analytical way, trying to solve them in step-by-step fashion. He or she is well described as a/an _____.

   (a) systematic thinker
   (b) intuitive thinker
   (c) problem seeker
   (d) behavioral decision maker

4. The first step in the decision-making process is to _____.

   (a) generate a list of alternatives
   (b) assess the costs and benefits of each alternative
   (c) identify and define the problem
   (d) perform the ethics double-check

5. When the members of a special task force are asked to develop a proposal for increasing the international sales of a new product, this problem most likely requires _____ decisions.

   (a) routine   (b) programmed
   (c) crisis   (d) nonprogrammed

6. Costs, benefits, timeliness, and _____ are among the recommended criteria for evaluating alternative courses of action in the decision-making process.

   (a) ethical soundness
   (b) past history
   (c) availability
   (d) simplicity

7. The _____ decision model views managers as making optimizing decisions, whereas the _____ decision model views them as making satisficing decisions.

   (a) behavioral; judgmental heuristics
   (b) classical; behavioral
   (c) judgmental heuristics; ethical
   (d) crisis; routine

8. When a manager makes a decision about someone's annual pay raise only after looking at the person's current salary, the risk is that the decision will be biased because of _____.

   (a) a framing error
   (b) escalating commitment
   (c) anchoring and adjustment
   (d) strategic opportunism

9. One of the reasons why certainty is the most favorable environment for problem solving is that it can be addressed through _____ decisions.

   (a) satisficing
   (b) optimizing
   (c) programmed
   (d) intuitive

10. A common mistake by managers facing crisis situations is _____.

    (a) trying to get too much information before responding

    (b) relying too much on group decision making

    (c) isolating themselves to make the decision alone

    (d) forgetting to use their crisis management plan

11. In which decision environment does a manager deal with probabilities regarding possible courses of action and their consequences?

    (a) risk

    (b) certainty

    (c) uncertainty

    (d) optimal

12. A manager who decides against hiring a new employee that just graduated from Downstate University because the last person hired from there turned out to be a low performer is falling prey to _____ error.

    (a) availability   (b) adjustment

    (c) anchoring   (d) representativeness

13. Which decision-making error is most associated with the old adage: "If you don't succeed, try and try again"?

    (a) satisficing

    (b) escalating commitment

    (c) confirmation

    (d) too late to fail

14. Personal creativity drivers include creativity skills, task expertise, and _____.

    (a) strategic opportunism

    (b) management support

    (c) organizational culture

    (d) task motivation

15. The last step in the decision-making process is to _____.

    (a) choose a preferred alternative

    (b) evaluate results

    (c) find and define the problem

    (d) generate alternatives

Short-Response Questions

16. How does an optimizing decision differ from a satisficing decision?

17. What is the difference between a risk environment and an uncertain environment in decision making?

18. How can you tell from people's behavior if they tend to be systematic or intuitive in problem solving?

19. What is escalating commitment and how can it be avoided?

Integration and Application Question

20. With the goals of both expanding your resumé and gaining valuable experience, you have joined a new mentoring program between your university and a local high school. One of the first activities is for you and your teammates to offer "learning modules" to a class of sophomores. You have volunteered to give a presentation and engage them in some learning activities on the topic: "Individual versus group decision making: Is one better than the other?"

Question: What will you say and do, and why?

StepsforFurtherLearning

Many learning resources are found at the end of the book and online within WileyPLUS.

Don't Miss These Selections from the **Skill-Building Portfolio**

- **SELF-ASSESSMENT 4:** *Intuitive Ability*
- **CLASS EXERCISE 4:** *Lost at Sea*
- **TEAM PROJECT 4:** *Crisis Management Realities*

Don't Miss This Selection from **Cases for Critical Thinking**

- **CHAPTER 4 CASE**
  Amazon.com—One E-Store to Rule Them All

Snapshot Amazon.com has soared ahead of other online merchants. What the firm can't carry in its 29 world-wide warehouses, affiliated retailers distribute for it. Not content to rest on past laurels, CEO Jeff Bezos has introduced a number of Amazon products, including a set-top box and several versions of the Kindle.

In just over a decade, Amazon.com has grown from a one-man operation into a global giant of commerce. By forging alliances to ensure that he has what customers want and making astute purchases, Jeff Bezos has made Amazon the go-to brand for online shopping. But with its significant investments in new media and services, does the company risk spreading itself too thin? Will customers continue to flock to Amazon, the go-to company for their every need?

Make notes here on what you've learned about yourself from this chapter.

- **LEARNING JOURNAL 4**

"Considering the future of our children and young people ... we have no choice but to go ahead with the village-wide evacuation." Mayor Noro Kanno of Kawamata-cho town, after a 9.0 earthquake and monster tsunami wrecked nuclear power facilities in Fukushima, Japan.

Plans and Planning Techniques

Get There Faster with Objectives

Management Live

Time Management and *27 Dresses*

In *27 Dresses*, Jane Nichols (Katherine Heigl) works as a personal assistant for George (Edward Burns), the owner of Urban Everest. Jane has a penchant for detail and also lives a second life as "professional" bridesmaid and unofficial wedding planner.

The movie opens with Jane standing in for a bride as final alterations are made on the dress, then scurrying off to attend two weddings occurring almost simultaneously. We learn that Jane is a fastidious planner who keeps a "file of facts" and a tight schedule.

Time management is an essential planning skill in the fast-paced and complicated world of business and for new graduates entering the workforce. Time management involves more than making a good to-do list. Jane is an excellent example. Unlike some who are good at writing things down but then never get the really important work done, Jane has a flair for wrapping things up with style.

What about you? You probably juggle multiple responsibilities, such as school, a job, relationships, and extracurricular activities. Are you able to do it like Jane, consistently getting the right things done in the right ways? As you read the chapter, look for insights and tools to help improve your planning skills.

YOUR CHAPTER 5 TAKEAWAYS

1. Understand how and why managers use the planning process.
2. Identify the types of plans used by managers.
3. Describe useful planning tools and techniques.

WHAT'S INSIDE

Explore Yourself
More on time management

Role Models
Don Thompson's leadership keeps McDonald's on focus

Ethics Check
E-waste graveyards as easy way out

Facts to Consider
Policies on office romances vary widely

Manager's Library
Analytics at Work by Thomas Davenport et al.

Takeaway 5.1
How and Why Do Managers Use the Planning Process?

ANSWERS TO COME

- Planning is one of the four functions of management.
- Planning is the process of setting objectives and identifying how to achieve them.
- Planning improves focus and action orientation.
- Planning improves coordination and control.
- Planning improves time management.

IT CAN BE EASY TO GET SO ENGROSSED IN THE PRESENT THAT WE FORGET ABOUT the future. Yet a mad rush to the future can sometimes go off track without solid reference points in the past. The trick is to blend past experiences and lessons with future aspirations and goals, and to be willing to adjust as new circumstances arise. The management function of **planning** helps us do just that. It is a process of setting goals and objectives, and determining how to best accomplish them. Said a bit differently, planning involves looking ahead, identifying exactly what you want to accomplish, and deciding how best to go about it.

Planning is the process of setting performance objectives and determining how to accomplish them.

‖ Planning is one of the four functions of management.

Among the four management functions shown in Figure 5.1, planning comes first. When done well, it sets the stage for the others: organizing—allocating and arranging resources to accomplish tasks; leading—guiding the efforts of human resources to ensure high levels of task accomplishment; and controlling—monitoring task accomplishments and taking necessary corrective action.

In today's demanding organizational and career environments, effective planning is essential to staying one step ahead of the competition. An Eaton Corporation annual report, for example, once stated: "Planning at Eaton means taking the hard decisions before events force them upon you, and anticipating the future needs of the market before the demand asserts itself."[1]

You really should take these words to heart. But instead of a company, think about your personal situation. What hard decisions do you need to make? Where are the job markets going? Where do you want to be in your career and personal life in the next 5 or 10 years?

Planning
to set the direction
- Decide where you want to go.
- Decide how to best go about it.

Organizing
to create structures

MANAGEMENT PROCESS

Leading
to inspire effort

Controlling
to ensure results

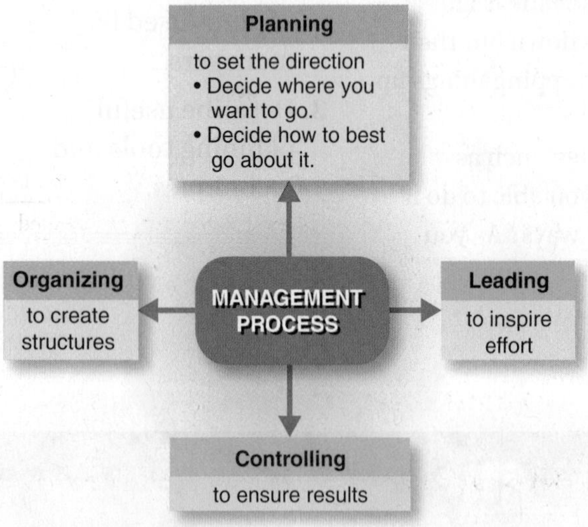

FIGURE 5.1 Why Does Planning Play a Central Role in the Management Process?
Planning is the first of the four management functions. It is the process of setting objectives—deciding where you want to go—and then identifying how to accomplish them—determining how to get there. When planning is done well, it provides a strong foundation for success with the other management functions.

Planning is the process of setting objectives and identifying how to achieve them.

From experience alone, you are probably familiar with planning and all that it involves. But it also helps to understand Table 5.1—*Steps in the Planning Process* and its action implications.

Table 5.1 Steps in the Planning Process

Step 1. Define your objectives Know where you want to go; be specific enough to know you have arrived when you get there and how far off you are along the way.

Step 2. Determine where you stand vis-à-vis objectives Know where you presently stand in reaching the objectives; identify strengths that work in your favor and weaknesses that can hold you back.

Step 3. Develop premises regarding future conditions Generate alternative scenarios for what may happen; identify for each scenario things that may help or hinder progress toward your objectives.

Step 4. Make a plan Choose the action alternative most likely to accomplish your objectives; describe what must be done to implement this course of action.

Step 5. Implement the plan and evaluate results Take action; measure progress toward objectives as implementation proceeds; take corrective actions and revise the plan as needed.

Step 1 in planning is to define your **objectives** and to identify the specific results or desired goals you hope to achieve. This step is important enough to stop and reflect a moment. Whether you call them goals or objectives, they are targets. They point us toward the future and provide a frame of reference for evaluating progress. With them, as the module subtitle suggests, you should get where you want to go and get there faster.

Step 2 in planning is to compare where you are at present with the objectives. This establishes a baseline for performance; the present becomes a standard against which future progress can be gauged. *Step 3* is to formulate premises about future conditions. It is where one looks ahead, trying to figure out what may happen. *Step 4* is to make an actual **plan.** This is a list of actions that must be taken in order to accomplish the objectives. *Step 5* is to implement the plan and evaluate results. This is where action takes place and measurement happens. Results are compared with objectives and, if needed, plans are modified to improve things in the future.

Have you thought about how well you plan and how you might do it better? Managers should be asking the same question. They rarely get to plan while working alone in quiet rooms free from distractions. Because of the fast pace and complications of the typical workday, managerial planning is ongoing. It takes place even as one deals with a constant flow of problems in a sometimes hectic and demanding work setting.[2] Yet it's all worth it: Planning offers many benefits to people and organizations.[3]

> **Objectives** are specific results that one wishes to achieve.

> A **plan** is a statement of intended means for accomplishing objectives.

Good Planning Makes Us . . .

- **Action oriented**—keeping a results-driven sense of direction
- **Priority oriented**—making sure the most important things get first attention
- **Advantage oriented**—ensuring that all resources are used to best advantage
- **Change oriented**—anticipating problems and opportunities so they can be best dealt with

Manager's Library

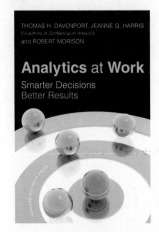

THOMAS H. DAVENPORT, JEANNE G. HARRIS
Co-authors of *Competing on Analytics*
and ROBERT MORISON

Analytics at Work
Smarter Decisions
Better Results

■ *ANALYTICS AT WORK* BY THOMAS DAVENPORT, JEANNE HARRIS, AND ROBERT MORISON

FACE THE FACTS, THOSE GUT FEELINGS COULD BE MISLEADING YOU

In the book *Analytics at Work* (2010, Harvard Business Press), authors Thomas Davenport, Jeanne Harris, and Robert Morison argue that organizations can improve their strategies by making better use of available information to guide decisions. A key point is that organizations have access to vast amounts of data but often fail to leverage it for competitive gain. Analytical approaches to decision making can yield smarter choices with improved results. Data sources include, among others, transactional records within ERP systems and databases, clickstream data from Web activity, scanner data, and information from customer loyalty programs.

The authors suggest that all aspects of organizations are ripe for analytic improvement. Customer relationships can be enhanced by segmenting types, understanding preferences, predicting desires, and identifying loyal or departing patrons. Supply chains can be streamlined by optimizing inventory levels, delivery routes, and production schedules. Human resources can be improved by hiring those likely to stay and predicting those prone to depart.

Analytics are great tools and we need to get better at using them. The authors say organizations are more intelligent when managers use facts, and not feelings, to guide decisions.

REFLECT AND REACT

Identify a business and describe the analytics it might use to plan improvements in a process such as customer relationship management. For example, how might it determine which products are most popular, most profitable, or trending toward less popular? How might it optimize inventory levels or hire better workers? And by the way, do you agree that better analytics can help in personal planning as well?

⦀ Planning improves focus and action orientation.

Planning can help sharpen focus and increase flexibility, both of which improve performance. An organization with focus knows what it does best and what it needs to do. Individuals with focus know where they want to go in a career or situation, and they keep the focus even when difficulties arise. An organization with flexibility is willing and able to change and adapt to shifting circumstances. An individual with flexibility adjusts career plans to fit new and developing opportunities.

Planning helps us avoid the **complacency trap** of being lulled into inaction by successes or failures of the moment. Instead of being caught in the present, planning keeps us looking toward the future. Management consultant Stephen R. Covey describes this as an action orientation with a clear set of priorities.[4] He says the most successful executives "zero in on what they do that adds value to an organization." They know what is important, and they work first on the things that really count. They don't waste time by working on too many things at once.

Would a friend or relative describe you as focused on priorities, or as always jumping from one thing to another? Could you achieve more by getting your priorities straight and working hard on things that really count?

The **complacency trap** is being lulled into inaction by current successes or failures.

Planning improves coordination and control.

Organizations consist of many people and subsystems doing many different things at the same time. But even as they pursue the various tasks, their accomplishments must add together meaningfully if the organization is to succeed. Good planning facilitates coordination by linking people and subsystems together in a **hierarchy of objectives**. This is a means–ends chain in which lower-level objectives (the means) lead to the accomplishment of higher-level objectives (the ends). An example is the total quality management program shown in Figure 5.2.

In a **hierarchy of objectives**, lower-level objectives help to accomplish higher-level ones.

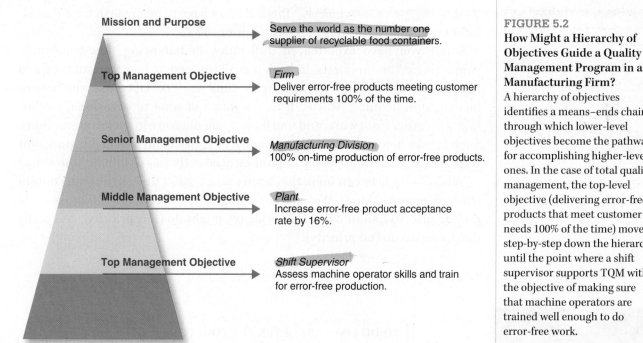

Mission and Purpose — Serve the world as the number one supplier of recyclable food containers.

Top Management Objective — *Firm* Deliver error-free products meeting customer requirements 100% of the time.

Senior Management Objective — *Manufacturing Division* 100% on-time production of error-free products.

Middle Management Objective — *Plant* Increase error-free product acceptance rate by 16%.

Top Management Objective — *Shift Supervisor* Assess machine operator skills and train for error-free production.

FIGURE 5.2
How Might a Hierarchy of Objectives Guide a Quality Management Program in a Manufacturing Firm?
A hierarchy of objectives identifies a means–ends chain through which lower-level objectives become the pathways for accomplishing higher-level ones. In the case of total quality management, the top-level objective (delivering error-free products that meet customer needs 100% of the time) moves step-by-step down the hierarchy until the point where a shift supervisor supports TQM with the objective of making sure that machine operators are trained well enough to do error-free work.

Good planning also sets the stage for controlling in the management process. It's hard to exercise control if you haven't set objectives. Without control, plans may fail because of a lack of follow-through. With both, it's a lot easier to see when things aren't going well and make the necessary adjustments. Two years after launching a costly information technology upgrade, for example, the CEO of McDonald's realized that the system couldn't deliver on its promises. He stopped the project, took a loss of $170 million, and refocused the firm's resources on projects with more direct impact on customers.[5]

Planning improves time management.

When Daniel Vasella was CEO of Novartis AG and its 98,000 employees spread across 140 countries, he was calendar bound—"locked in by meetings, travel and other constraints." To stay on track he would list priorities of things to do. As CEO of ING US Wealth Management, Kathleen Murphy was also calendar bound, with conferences and travel booked a year ahead. She scheduled meetings at half-hour intervals, worked 12-hour days, and spent 60% of her time traveling. She also

You *Can* Manage Your Time Better

- Set priorities for what really needs to get done.
- Work on the most important things first.
- Leave details for later, or delegate them to others.
- Say "No!" to requests that divert attention from your priorities.
- Take charge of your schedule; don't let others control what you do and when.
- Stick with your choices; not everything deserves immediate attention.

made good use of her time on planes, where, she says, "no one can reach me by phone and I can get reading and thinking done."[6]

These are common executive stories—tight schedules, little time alone, lots of meetings and phone calls, and not much room for spontaneity. And the keys to success in these classic management scenarios rest, in part at least, on another benefit of good planning—time management. It is an important management skill and competency, and a lot of time management comes down to discipline and priorities. Lewis Platt, former chairman of Hewlett-Packard, once said: "Basically, the whole day is a series of choices."[7] These choices have to be made in ways that allocate your time to the most important priorities.

Surely you have experienced difficulties in balancing time-consuming commitments and requests. Indeed, it is all too easy to lose track of time and fall prey to what consultants identify as "time wasters." Of course, you have to be careful in defining "waste." It isn't a waste of time to occasionally relax, take a breather from work, and find humor and pleasure in social interactions. Such breaks help us gather and replenish energies to do well in our work. But it is a waste to let other people or nonessential activities dominate your time.[8]

While to-do lists can help, they aren't much good unless the lists contain the high-priority things. We need to distinguish between things that we must do (top priority), should do (high priority), might do (low priority), and really don't need to do (no priority).

{ TO-DO LISTS ARE OFTEN PUT TOGETHER WITH BEST INTENTIONS BUT FAIL TO DELIVER RESULTS AT THE END OF THE DAY.

Explore Yourself

■ TIME MANAGEMENT

One of the most consistently top rated "must-have" skills for new graduates entering fast-paced and complicated careers in business and management is **time management**. Many, perhaps most, of us keep to-do lists. But it's the rare person who is consistently successful in living up to one.

Time management is a form of planning, and planning can easily suffer the same fate as the to-do lists—put together with the best of intentions, but with little or nothing to show in terms of results at the end of the day. There are a lot of good ideas in this chapter on how to plan, both in

management and in our personal lives. Now is a good time to get in touch with your time management skills and to start improving your capabilities to excel with planning as a basic management function.

> Get to know yourself better by taking the **Time Management Profile** self-assessment and completing the other activities in the *Exploring Management* **Skill-Building Portfolio**.

Takeaway 5.1
How and Why Do Managers Use the Planning Process?

Terms to Define

Complacency trap

Hierarchy of objectives

Objectives

Plan

Planning

Rapid Review

- Planning is the process of setting performance objectives and determining how to accomplish them.
- A plan is a set of intended actions for accomplishing important objectives.
- The steps in the planning process are: (1) define your objectives; (2) determine where you stand vis-à-vis objectives; (3) develop premises regarding future conditions; (4) make a plan to best accomplish objectives; (5) implement the plan, and evaluate results.
- The benefits of planning include better focus and action orientation, better coordination and control, and better time management.
- Planning improves time management by setting priorities and avoiding time wasters.

Questions for Discussion

1. Should all employees plan, or just managers?

2. Which step in the planning process do you think is the hardest to accomplish?

3. How could better planning help in your personal career development?

Be Sure You Can

- explain the importance of planning as the first of four management functions
- list the steps in the formal planning process
- explain the important link between planning and controlling as management functions
- illustrate the benefits of planning for a business or an organization familiar to you
- illustrate the benefits of planning for your personal career development
- list at least three things you can do now to improve your time management

What Would You Do?

Take a step forward in time management. Make a list of all the things you plan to do tomorrow. Note down which ones are (A) *most important*—top priority, (B) *important*—not top priority, and (C) *least important*—low priority. Double-check your Bs; should any really be As or Cs? Check your As; should any really be Bs or Cs? Now, proceed with your day tomorrow and see how things turn out. Does an exercise like this help you take charge of your time and get the really important things done first?

Takeaway 5.2
What Types of Plans Do Managers Use?

ANSWERS TO COME

- Managers use short-range and long-range plans.
- Managers use strategic and operational plans.
- Organizational policies and procedures are plans.
- Budgets are plans that commit resources to activities.

MANAGERS FACE DIFFERENT PLANNING CHALLENGES IN THE FLOW AND PACE OF activities in organizations. In some cases, the planning environment is stable and predictable. In others, it is more dynamic and uncertain. To meet these different needs, managers rely on a variety of plans.

‖ Managers use short-range and long-range plans.

We live and work in a fast-paced world where planning horizons are becoming compressed. We now talk about planning in Internet time, where businesses are continually changing and updating plans. Even most top managers would likely agree that *long*-range planning is becoming shorter and shorter. A reasonable rule of thumb in this context is that **short-range plans** cover a year or less, whereas **long-range plans** look ahead three or more years into the future.[9]

Quite frankly, the advent of Internet time and shorter planning horizons might be an advantage for many of us. Management researcher Elliot Jaques found that very few people have the capacity to think long term.[10] As shown in the figure, he believes that most of us work comfortably with only three-month time spans; some can think about a year into the future; only about one person in several million can handle a 20-year time frame.

Do Jaques's conclusions match your experience? And if we accept his findings, what are their implications for managers and career development? Although a team leader's planning challenges may rest mainly in the weekly or monthly range, a chief executive needs to have a vision extending at least some years into the future. Career progress to higher management levels still requires the conceptual skills to work well with longer-range time frames.[11]

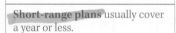

Short-range plans usually cover a year or less.

Long-range plans usually cover three years or more.

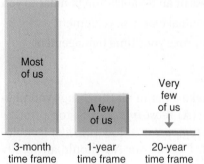

Most of us — 3-month time frame

A few of us — 1-year time frame

Very few of us ↓ — 20-year time frame

‖ Managers use strategic and operational plans.

A **strategic plan** identifies long-term directions for the organization.

A **vision** clarifies the purpose of the organization and expresses what it hopes to be in the future.

When planning for the organization as a whole or a major component, the focus is on **strategic plans**. These longer-term plans set broad and comprehensive directions for an organization. Well crafted strategic plans create a framework for allocating resources for best long-term performance impact. They take a **vision** that clarifies the purpose of the organization and what it hopes to be in the future, and set out the ways to turn that vision into reality.

Gaming Entrepreneurs Also Play the Strategy Game

Zynga is the brainchild of Marc Pincus, self-described as having one part the DNA of an entrepreneur and a second part the DNA of a competitive gamer. His company's mission is to connect the world through games like its wildly popular FarmVille, ranked number one as a Facebook application. But when Zynga was ready to launch CitiVille, expected to be the next blockbuster in the firm's strategy, Pincus decided to delay. He was worried the game wasn't ready and, above all else, he wanted it perfect right from the start. When finally launched, CitiVille was every bit the success he hoped for.

When a sports team enters a game, it typically does so with a "strategy." Most often this strategy is set by the head coach in conjunction with assistants. The goal is clear—win the game. But as the game unfolds, a variety of situations arise that require adjustments and responses to solve problems or exploit opportunities. They call for "tactics" that deal with the situation at hand while advancing the overall strategy for winning against the competition. These tactics are often decided upon by assistant coaches, perhaps in consultation with the head coach.

The same logic holds true for organizations. **Operational plans**, also called **tactical plans**, are developed to implement strategic plans. They are shorter term and step-by-step means for putting the strategies into action. In the sports context, you might think of tactical plans as involving the use of "special teams" plans or as "special plays" designed to meet a particular threat or opportunity. In business, tactical plans often take the form of **functional plans** that indicate how different parts of the enterprise will contribute to the overall strategy. Such functional plans might include the following:

An **operational plan** or **tactical plan** sets out ways to implement a strategic plan.

- *Financial plans* deal with the money required to support various operations.
- *Facilities plans* deal with facilities development and work layouts.
- *Marketing plans* deal with the requirements of selling and distributing goods or services.

A **functional plan** identifies how different parts of an enterprise will contribute to accomplishing strategic plans.

- *Human resource plans* deal with the recruitment, selection, and placement of people into various jobs.
- *Production plans* deal with the methods and technology needed by people in their work.

⦀ Organizational policies and procedures are plans.

In addition to strategic and operational plans, organizations also need plans that provide members with day-to-day guidance on such things as attendance, hiring practices, ethical behavior, privacy, trade secrets, and more. This is often provided in the form of organizational policies and procedures.

A **policy** communicates broad guidelines for making decisions and taking action in specific circumstances. Common human resource policies address

A **policy** is a standing plan that communicates broad guidelines for decisions and action.

{ "HE HAS THE ABILITY TO LISTEN, BLEND IN, ANALYZE, AND COMMUNICATE. PEOPLE FEEL AT EASE WITH HIM."

Role Models

■ DON THOMPSON'S LEADERSHIP KEEPS McDONALD'S ON FOCUS

Some call Don Thompson, President and COO of McDonald's, the accidental executive. He's not only one of the youngest top managers in the *Fortune* 500, he also may have followed the most unusual career path. After graduating from Purdue with a degree in electrical engineering, Johnson went to work for Northrop Grumman, a leading global security company. One day he received a call from a head-hunter. Thompson listened, thinking the job being offered was at McDonnell Douglas Company, a firm in which engineering is central. After finding out it was at McDonald's, he almost turned the opportunity down. But, after some encouragement he took the interview. His career and McDonald's haven't been the same since.

Thompson hit the ground running at McDonald's and did well, but he became frustrated after failing to win the annual McDonald's President's Award. On the recommendation of the firm's diversity officer, he spoke with Raymond Mines, at the time the firm's highest-ranking African-American executive. When Thompson confided that he "wanted to have an impact on decisions," Mines told him to move out of engineering and into the operations side of the business. Thompson did. His work not only excelled, it got him the attention he needed to advance to ever-higher responsibilities that spanned restaurant operations, franchisee relations, and strategic management.

From his childhood on Chicago's South Side to his position as the head of the world's largest fast-food hamburger chain, Don Thompson rose quickly in his career. He works from a corner office that has no door, and the building is configured with an open floor plan. All that fits well with Thompson's style and personality. His former mentor Raymond Mines says: "He has the ability to listen, blend in, analyze, and communicate. People feel at ease with him. A lot of corporate executives have little time for those below them. Don makes everyone a part of the process." As for Thompson, he says "I want to make sure others achieve their goals, just as I have."

WHAT'S THE LESSON HERE?

Don Thompson has done very well in his career. How much of his success traces to strong motivation and clear goals? How about the choices he made regarding jobs to seek? Is his resiliency when things didn't always go according to plan a strength that many others might lack? Could it have been a career maker for him?

A **procedure** or rule precisely describes actions to take in specific situations.

such matters as employee hiring, termination, performance appraisals, pay increases, promotions, discipline, and civility. Consider the issue of sexual harassment. How should individual behavior be guided? A sample sexual harassment policy states: "Sexual harassment is specifically prohibited by this organization. Any employee found to have violated the policy against sexual harassment will be subject to immediate and appropriate disciplinary action including but not limited to possible suspension or termination."

Procedures, or *rules*, describe exactly what actions to take in specific situations. They are often found in employee handbooks or manuals as SOPs (standard operating procedures). Whereas a policy sets broad guidelines, procedures define specific actions to be taken. A sexual harassment policy, for example, should be backed up with procedures that spell out how to file a sexual harassment complaint, as well as the steps through which any complaint will be handled.[12] When Judith Nitsch started her engineering consulting business, for example, she defined a sexual harassment policy, established clear procedures for its enforcement, and designated both a male and a female employee for others to talk with about sexual harassment concerns.[13]

Facts to Consider

■ POLICIES ON OFFICE ROMANCES VARY WIDELY

A former CEO of Boeing was asked to resign by the firm's board after his relationship with a female executive became public. But, employer policies on office relationships vary.

- 24%—prohibit relationships among persons in the same department.
- 13%—prohibit relationships among persons who have the same supervisor.
- 80%—prohibit relationships between supervisors and subordinates.
- 5%—have no restrictions on office romances.

- New trend—"love contracts," where employees pledge that their romantic relationships in the office won't interfere with their work.

YOUR THOUGHTS?

Do you know anyone who has been involved in an office relationship? What are your thoughts? Is this an area that employers should be regulating, or should office romance be left to the best judgments of those involved?

‖ Budgets are plans that commit resources to activities.

A **budget** is a plan that commits resources to activities, programs, or projects. It is a powerful tool that allocates scarce resources among multiple and often competing uses. Managers typically negotiate with their bosses to obtain budgets that support the needs of their work units or teams. They are also expected to achieve performance objectives while keeping within their budgets.

Managers deal with and use various types of budgets. *Financial budgets* project cash flows and expenditures. *Operating budgets* plot anticipated sales or revenues against expenses. *Nonmonetary* budgets allocate resources such as labor, equipment, and space. A *fixed budget* allocates a fixed amount of resources for a specific purpose, such as $50,000 for equipment purchases in a given year. A *flexible budget* allows resources to vary in proportion with various levels of activity, such as monies to hire temporary workers when workloads exceed certain levels.

All budgets play important roles in organizations by linking planned activities with the resources needed to accomplish them. But budgets can also get out of control. Sometimes, perhaps much too often, they creep higher and higher without getting enough critical scrutiny. If in doubt, just tune in to the latest debates over local and national government budgets. One of the most common problems is that resource allocations get rolled over from one time period to the next without any real performance review. A **zero-based budget** deals with this problem by approaching each budget period as if it were brand new. No guarantee exists for renewing any past funding. Instead, all proposals compete with a fresh start for available resources. This helps eliminate waste by making sure scarce resources are not spent on unproductive, outdated, or low priority activities.

A **budget** is a plan that commits resources to projects or activities.

A **zero-based budget** allocates resources as if each budget was brand new.

STUDY GUIDE

Takeaway 5.2
What Types of Plans Do Managers Use?

Terms to Define

Budget

Functional plan

Long-range plan

Operational (tactical) plan

Policy

Procedures

Short-range plan

Strategic plan

Vision

Zero-based budget

Rapid Review

- Short-range plans tend to cover a year or less, whereas long-range plans extend out to three years or more.
- Strategic plans set critical long-range directions; operational plans are designed to support and help implement strategic plans.
- Policies, such as a sexual harassment policy, are plans that set guidelines for the behavior of organizational members.
- Procedures are plans that describe actions to take in specific situations, such as how to report a sexual harassment complaint.
- Budgets are plans that allocate resources to activities or projects.
- A zero-based budget allocates resources as if each new budget period is brand new; no "rollover" resource allocations are allowed without new justifications.

Questions for Discussion

1. Is there any need for long-range plans in today's fast-moving environment?
2. What types of policies do you believe are essential for any organization?
3. Are there any possible disadvantages to zero-based budgeting?

Be Sure You Can

- differentiate short-range and long-range plans
- differentiate strategic and operational plans
- explain how strategic and operational plans complement one another
- differentiate policies and procedures, and give examples of each
- explain the benefits of a zero-based budget

What Would You Do?

One of the persons under your supervision has a "possible" sexual harassment complaint about the behavior of a co-worker. She says that she understands the sexual harassment policy of the organization, but the procedures are not clear. You're not clear either and take the matter to your boss. She tells you to draft a set of procedures that can be taken to top management for approval. What procedures will you recommend so that sexual harassment complaints like this one can be dealt with in a fair manner?

Takeaway 5.3
What Are Some Useful Planning Tools and Techniques?

ANSWERS TO COME

- Forecasting tries to predict the future
- Contingency planning creates backup plans for when things go wrong
- Scenario planning crafts plans for alternative future conditions
- Benchmarking identifies best practices used by others
- Participatory planning improves implementation capacities
- Goal setting helps align plans and activities throughout an organization

THE BENEFITS OF PLANNING ARE BEST REALIZED WHEN PLANS ARE BUILT FROM strong foundations. Useful planning tools and techniques include forecasting, contingency planning, scenarios, benchmarking, participatory planning, and use of goal setting.

⫶ Forecasting tries to predict the future.

Who would have predicted on New Year's Eve 2008 that General Motors and Chrysler would soon declare bankruptcy; that Italy's Fiat would buy Chrysler; that GM's Pontiac and Saturn brands would be discontinued? Who would have predicted even a few years ago that Chinese firms would now own Volvo and Hummer or that China would now be the largest car market in the world? Would you believe that by the year 2025 (at the latest) China is expected to have more cars on the roads than the United States has today?

What are top executives at the world's automakers thinking about as they make plans for the future? Are they on top of the right trends? At least one corporate CEO, GE's Jeffery Immelt, is frank about his failure to plan well for the recent economic and financial crisis before it actually hit. "I should have done more to anticipate the radical changes that occurred" he says. Immelt is now restructuring GE around a model he believes is more consistent with new economic realities.[14]

Forecasting is the process of predicting what will happen in the future.[15] Periodicals such as *Business Week, Fortune*, and *The Economist* regularly report forecasts of industry conditions, interest rates, unemployment trends, and national economies, among other issues.[16] Some rely on **qualitative** forecasting which uses expert opinions to predict the future. Others involve **quantitative** forecasting which uses mathematical models and statistical analysis of historical data and surveys.

Most plans involve forecasts of some sort. But, any forecast should be used with caution. Forecasts are planning aids, not planning substitutes. It is said that a music agent once told Elvis Presley: "You ought to go back to driving a truck because you ain't going nowhere." That's the problem with forecasts. They always rely on human judgment, and that judgment can be wrong.

Forecasting attempts to predict the future.

‖ Contingency planning creates backup plans for when things go wrong.

Of course things often go wrong. It is highly unlikely that any plan will ever be perfect. But picture this scene. A golfer is striding down the golf course with an iron in each hand. The one in her right hand is "the plan"; the one in her left is the "backup plan." Which club she uses will depend on how the ball lies on the fairway. One of any professional golfer's greatest strengths is being able to adjust to the situation by putting the right club to work in the circumstances at hand.

Planning in our work and personal affairs is often like that of the golfer. By definition, planning involves thinking ahead. But the more uncertain the environment, the more likely one's original assumptions, forecasts, and intentions may prove inadequate or wrong. And when they do, the best managers and organizations have alternative plans ready to go.

Contingency planning identifies alternative courses of action that can be implemented to meet the needs of changing circumstances. A really good contingency plan will contain "trigger points" for activating preselected alternatives. This is really an indispensable planning tool. But, it's surprising how many organizations lack good contingency plans to deal with unexpected events.

Poor contingency planning was very much in the news when debates raged over how BP managed the disastrous Deepwater Horizon oil spill in the Gulf of Mexico. Everyone from the public at large to U.S. lawmakers to oil industry experts criticized BP not only for failing to contain the spill quickly, but also for failing to anticipate and have contingency plans in place to handle such a crisis.

A BP spokesperson initially said—"You have here an unprecedented event . . . the unthinkable has become thinkable and the whole industry will be asking questions of itself."

An oil industry expert responded—"There should be a technology that is pre-existing and ready to deploy at the drop of a hat . . . it shouldn't have to be designed and fabricated now, from scratch."

Former BP CEO Tony Hayward finally admitted—"There are some capabilities that we could have available to deploy instantly, rather than creating as we go."[17]

The lesson here is hard-earned but very clear. Contingency planning can't prevent crises from occurring. But when things do go wrong, there's nothing better to have in place than good contingency plans.

‖ Scenario planning crafts plans for alternative future conditions.

A long-term version of contingency planning, called **scenario planning**, identifies several alternative future scenarios. Managers then make plans to deal with each, so they will be better prepared for whatever occurs.[18] In this sense, scenario planning forces them to really think far ahead.

This approach was developed years ago at Royal Dutch/Shell when top managers asked themselves a perplexing question: "What would Shell do after its oil supplies ran out?" Although recognizing that scenario planning can never be inclusive of all future possibilities, a Shell executive once said that it helps "condition the organization to think" and better prepare for "future shocks."

Contingency planning identifies alternative courses of action to take when things go wrong.

Scenario planning identifies alternative future scenarios and makes plans to deal with each.

Shell uses scenario planning to tackle such issues as climate change, sustainable development, fossil-fuel alternatives, human rights, and biodiversity. Most typically it involves descriptions of "worst cases" and "best cases." In respect to oil supplies, for example, a worst case scenario might be—global conflict and devastating effects on the natural environment occur as nations jockey with one another to secure increasingly scarce supplies of oil and other natural resources. A best cases scenario might be—governments work together to find pathways that take care of everyone's resource needs while supporting the sustainability of global resources. It's anyone's guess which scenario will materialize or if something else altogether will happen. But these words of former Shell CEO Jeroen van der Veer highlight the value of the scenario planning process: "This will require hard work and time is short."[19]

‖ Benchmarking identifies best practices used by others.

All too often managers become too comfortable with the ways things are going. They fall into the complacency trap discussed earlier, and let habits and overconfidence trick them into believing the past is a good indicator of the future. Planning helps us deal with such tendencies by challenging the status quo and reminding us not to always accept things as they are. One way to do this is through **benchmarking**, a planning technique that makes use of external comparisons to better evaluate current performance.[20]

Benchmarking uses external comparisons to gain insights for planning.

{ OUR UNWANTED ELECTRICAL PRODUCTS OFTEN END UP IN OFFSHORE E-WASTE GRAVEYARDS.

Ethics Check

■ E-WASTE GRAVEYARDS AS EASY WAY OUT

"Give me a plan," says the boss. "We need to get rid of our electronic waste."

This isn't an uncommon problem. Just think about all those old stereo components, out-of-date cell phones, used computers and displays, and so on. Did you know that they often end up in e-waste graveyards in countries like Ghana, China, and Vietnam? The waste arrives by sea container or barge and ends up in huge dumps. Local laborers, perhaps including children, disassemble the waste products to salvage valuable metals. They often burn the plastic and mother boards to release sought-after scraps.

It can be expensive to properly dispose of electronic waste. That's the hidden problem behind the boss's directive here. But what are the adverse environmental and health effects of taking the low-cost option of using offshore e-waste graveyards?

What harm to people and planet is done? It isn't a stretch to say that the workers often inhale toxic fumes; nearby streams can get polluted with runoff waste; and even the streets and living areas of the workers get cluttered with electronic debris.

YOU DECIDE

As some countries become hosts for e-waste products, their governments may look the other way when it comes to the environmental and human costs. Whose responsibility is it to deal with the adverse consequences of e-waste disposal? Is it just a local matter? Do the originating country and consumer have obligations to reduce waste creation and assist with safe waste disposal? If the "plan" that is given to the boss in this case simply involves "ship it to Ghana," is that acceptable business practice?

Managers use benchmarking to discover what other people and organizations are doing well and plan how to incorporate these ideas into their own operations. They search for **best practices** inside and outside of the organization, and among competitors and noncompetitors alike. These are things that others are doing and that help them to achieve superior performance. As a planning tool, benchmarking is basically a way of learning from the successes of others. There's little doubt that sports stars benchmark one another; scientists and scholars do it; executives and managers do it. Could you be doing it, too?

Many top firms make good use of best practices benchmarks. Xerox, for example, has benchmarked L. L. Bean's warehousing and distribution methods, Ford's plant layouts, and American Express's billing and collections. In building its "world car," the Fiesta, Ford benchmarked BMW's 3 series. James D. Farley, Ford's global marketing head says: "The ubiquity of the 3 series engenders trust in every part of the world, and its design always has a strong point of view . . ."[21] And in the fast-moving apparel industry, the Spanish retailer Zara has exploded on the world scene and become a benchmark for both worried competitors and others outside the industry.[22] Zara is praised for excellence in affordable "fast-fashion." The firm's design and manufacturing systems allow it to get new fashions from design to stores in two weeks, while competitors may take months. Zara produces only in small batches that sell out and create impressions of scarcity. Shoppers at Zara know they have to buy now because an item will not be replaced. At competitors, shoppers often have to wait for sales and inventory clearance bargains.

Best practices are methods that lead to superior performance.

Participatory planning includes the persons who will be affected by plans and/or who will be asked to implement them.

||| Participatory planning improves implementation capacities.

When it comes to implementation, participation can be a very important word in planning. **Participatory planning**, as shown in **Figure 5.3**, includes in all steps of the process those people whose ideas and inputs can benefit the plans and whose support is needed for implementation. It has all the advantages of group decision making discussed in Chapter 4.

Participatory planning can increase the creativity and information available, it can increase understanding and acceptance of plans, and it can build stronger commitments to a plan's success. When 7-Eleven executives planned for new upscale products and services, such as selling fancy meals-to-go, they learned this lesson the hard way. Although their ideas sounded good at the top, franchise owners and managers disagreed. Their resistance taught the executives the value of taking time to involve lower levels in planning new directions for the stores.[23]

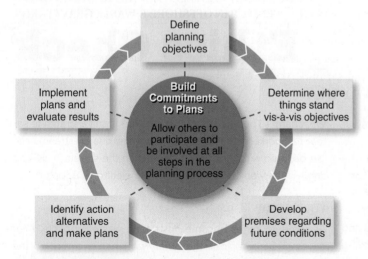

FIGURES 5.3 How Do Participation and Involvement Help Build Commitments to Plans?
Any plan needs the efforts and support of many people to make it work. It is easier and more likely to get this commitment when the people responsible for implementation have had the opportunity to participate in developing the plans in the first place. When managers use participatory planning and allow others to become involved in the planning process, it leads to better plans, a deeper understanding of the plans, and a strengthened commitment to fully implementing the plans.

⫶ Goal setting helps align plans and activities throughout an organization.

In the dynamic and highly competitive technology industry, CEO T. J. Rodgers of Cypress Semiconductor Corp. has earned a reputation for valuing both performance goals and accountability. He supports a planning system where employees work with clear and quantified work goals that they help set. He believes the system helps people find problems before they interfere with performance. Says Rodgers: "Managers monitor the goals, look for problems, and expect people who fall behind to ask for help before they lose control of or damage a major project.[24]

Although Rodgers makes us aware of the importance of goal setting in management, he may make it look too easy. Actually, the way goals are set can make a major difference in how well they work in pointing people in the right directions and making sure plans are well implemented. To have the desired effects, goals and objectives have to be good ones; they should push you to achieve substantial, not trivial, things. Jack Welch, former CEO of GE, believed in **stretch goals**—performance targets that we have to work extra hard and really stretch to reach.[25] Would you agree that stretch goals can add real strength to the planning process, for organizations and for individuals?

> **Stretch goals** are performance targets that we have to work extra hard and stretch to reach.

The following guidelines are starting points in moving from "no goals" and even just everyday run-of-the-mill "average goals" to having really "great goals"—ones that result in plans being successfully implemented. Great goals are:

1. *Specific*—clearly target key results and outcomes to be accomplished.
2. *Timely*—linked to specific timetables and "due dates."
3. *Measurable*—described so results can be measured without ambiguity.
4. *Challenging*—include a stretch factor that moves toward real gains.
5. *Attainable*—although challenging, realistic and possible to achieve.

Even when individual goals are well set as part of a plan, managers must still make sure that the goals and plan for one person or work unit help accomplish the goals of the organization as a whole. It's always important to align goals from one level to the next so that the right things happen at the right times throughout an organization. Goals set anywhere in the organization should ideally help advance its overall mission or purpose. Strategic goals set by top management should cascade down the organization to become goals and objectives for lower levels. Ideally, goals link together across levels in a consistent "means–end" fashion as suggested earlier in Figure 5.2. When a hierarchy of goals and objectives is well defined through good planning, this helps improve coordination among the multiple tasks, components, and levels of work in organizations.

STUDY GUIDE

Takeaway 5.3
What Are Some Useful Planning Tools and Techniques?

Terms to Define

Benchmarking

Best practices

Contingency planning

Forecasting

Participatory planning

Scenario planning

Stretch goals

Rapid Review

- Forecasting, which attempts to predict what might happen in the future, is a planning aid but not a planning substitute.
- Contingency planning identifies alternative courses of action to implement if and when circumstances change and an existing plan fails.
- Scenario planning analyzes the implications of alternative versions of the future.
- Benchmarking utilizes external comparisons to identify best practices that could become planning targets.
- Participation and involvement open the planning process to valuable inputs from people whose efforts are essential to the effective implementation of plans.

Questions for Discussion

1. If forecasting is going to be imperfect, why bother with it?
2. Shouldn't all planning provide for contingency plans?
3. Are stretch goals a good fit for today's generation of college students when they enter the workplace?

Be Sure You Can

- differentiate among forecasting, contingency planning, scenario planning, and benchmarking
- explain the importance of contingency planning
- describe the benefits of participatory planning as a special case of group decision making

What Would You Do?

A consulting firm has been hired to help write a strategic plan for your organization. The plan would be helpful, but you are worried about getting "buy-in" from all members, not just those at the top. What conditions can you set for the consultants so that they not only provide a solid strategic plan, but also create strong commitments to implementing it from members of your organization?

TestPrep 5

Multiple-Choice Questions

1. Planning is best described as the process of _____ and _____.
   - (a) developing premises about the future; evaluating them
   - (b) measuring results; taking corrective action
   - (c) measuring past performance; targeting future performance
   - (d) setting objectives; deciding how to accomplish them

2. The benefits of planning should include _____.
   - (a) improved focus
   - (b) less need for controlling
   - (c) more accurate forecasts
   - (d) increased business profits

3. The first step in the planning process is to _____.
   - (a) decide how to get where you want to go
   - (b) define your objectives
   - (c) identify possible future conditions or scenarios
   - (d) act quickly to take advantage of opportunities

4. In order to help implement her firm's strategic plans, the CEO of a business firm would most likely want marketing, manufacturing, and finance executives to develop _____.
   - (a) means–ends chains
   - (b) operational plans
   - (c) flexible budgets
   - (d) project management

5. _____ planning identifies alternative courses of action that can be taken if problems occur with the original plan.
   - (a) Benchmark
   - (b) Participatory
   - (c) Staff
   - (d) Contingency

6. A "no smoking" rule and a sexual harassment policy are examples of _____ that are types of _____ in organizations.
   - (a) long-range plans; policies
   - (b) single-use plans; means–ends chains
   - (c) policies; standing-use plans
   - (d) operational plans; short-range plans

7. When a manager is asked to justify a new budget proposal on the basis of projected activities rather than as an incremental adjustment to the prior year's budget, this is an example of _____.
   - (a) zero-based budgeting
   - (b) strategic planning
   - (c) operational planning
   - (d) contingency planning

8. One of the expected benefits of participatory planning is _____.
   - (a) faster planning
   - (b) less need for forecasting
   - (c) greater attention to contingencies
   - (d) more commitment to implementation

9. When managers use benchmarking in the planning process, they usually try to _____.
   - (a) set up flexible budgets
   - (b) identify best practices used by others
   - (c) find the most accurate forecasts that are available
   - (d) use expert staff planners to set objectives

10. In a hierarchy of objectives, plans at lower levels are supposed to act as _____ for accomplishing higher-level plans.
    - (a) means
    - (b) ends
    - (c) scenarios
    - (d) benchmarks

11. In addition to providing better focus, good planning offers the benefits of _____.

    (a) guaranteed performance success

    (b) eliminating the need to change

    (c) improved action orientation

    (d) less emphasis on coordination and control

12. From a time management perspective, which manager is likely to be in best control of his or her time? One who _____.

    (a) tries to never say "no" to requests from others

    (b) works on the most important things first

    (c) immediately responds to instant messages

    (d) always has "an open office door"

13. A marketing plan in a business firm would most likely deal with _____.

    (a) production methods and technologies

    (b) money and capital investments

    (c) facilities and workforce recruiting

    (d) sales and product distribution

14. The best goals or objectives for planning purposes would have which of the following characteristics?

    (a) Easy enough so that no one fails to reach them

    (b) Realistic and possible to achieve, while still challenging

    (c) Open ended, with no clear end point identified

    (d) No set timetable or due dates

15. The planning process isn't complete until _____.

    (a) future conditions have been identified

    (b) stretch goals have been set

    (c) plans are implemented and results evaluated

    (d) budgets commit resources to plans

Short-Response Questions

16. List the five steps in the planning process, and give examples of each.

17. How does planning facilitate controlling?

18. What is the difference between contingency planning and scenario planning?

19. Why is participation good for the planning process?

Integration and Application Question

20. My friends Curt and Rich own a local bookstore. They are very interested in making plans for improving the store and better dealing with competition from the other bookstores that serve college students in our town. I once heard Curt saying to Rich: "We should be benchmarking what some of the successful coffee shops, restaurants, and novelty stores are doing." Rich replied: "I don't see why; we should only be interested in bookstores. Why don't we study the local competition and even look at what the best bookstores are doing in the big cities?"

    Questions: Who is right, Curt or Rich? If you were hired as a planning consultant to them, what would you suggest as the best way to utilize benchmarking as a planning technique to improve their bookstore? And, how would you use the planning process to help Curt and Rich come to a point of agreement on the best way forward for their bookstore?

SFL StepsforFurtherLearning

Many learning resources are found at the end of the book and online within WileyPLUS.

Don't Miss These Selections from the **Skill-Building Portfolio**

- **SELF-ASSESSMENT 5:** *Time Management Profile*
- **CLASS EXERCISE 5:** *The Future Workplace*
- **TEAM PROJECT 5:** *Personal Career Planning*

Don't Miss This Selection from **Cases for Critical Thinking**

■ CHAPTER 5 CASE
Nordstrom: Planning a Better Inventory

Snapshot How has Nordstrom managed to stay profitable heads and tails above the competition? It brought time-honored retail practices—keeping customers happy and managing inventory tightly—into a new era. Nordstrom hopes to inspire customer loyalty with its recent $150+ million investment in an ultramodern inventory management system.

The upgrade, spearheaded by the fourth generation of Nordstrom family members in corporate leadership, accomplished two key goals: correlate purchasing with demand to keep inventory as lean as possible, and present both customers and sales associates with a comprehensive view of Nordstrom's entire inventory, including every store and warehouse.

Make notes here on what you've learned about yourself from this chapter.

■ LEARNING JOURNAL 5

Toyota president Akio Toyoda meets the press to apologize for his firm's quality problems. He says, "I am deeply sorry for any accidents Toyota drivers have experienced."

Controls and Control Systems

What Gets Measured Happens

6

Management Live

Resiliency and *Forrest Gump*

Growing up in the Deep South, Forrest Gump (Tom Hanks) is no stranger to adversity. Despite bullying about his learning disability and close relationship with his mother, Gump develops as a runner and parlays this into an opportunity to play football at the University of Alabama.

During the Vietnam War, Gump is wounded while saving soldiers, including his dying friend Bubba. He receives the Medal of Honor from President Kennedy.

Instead of retiring after the war on a military pension, Gump capitalizes on another opportunity. He learns how to play ping pong during his recovery and gets to take part in a sports exchange to improve diplomatic relations with China. Following his world tour, he returns to the United States to make good on a promise to start the Bubba Gump Shrimp Company—named for his war-time friend.

Gump's positive outlook, often stated using the phrase "life is like a box of chocolates," and actions demonstrate **resiliency**, the ability to call upon inner strength and keep moving forward even when things are tough.

How well do you respond to adversity? Watch *Forrest Gump*. It's a feel-good story with plenty of emotion. Ask yourself whether you would be able to bounce back as often as Gump does. As you review the chapter, think about ways you can develop internal control mechanisms and make yourself more resilient.

YOUR CHAPTER TAKEAWAYS

1. Understand how and why managers use the control process.

2. Identify types of controls used by managers.

3. Describe useful control tools and techniques.

WHAT'S INSIDE

Explore Yourself
More on resiliency

Role Models
Patricia Karter shows how values help control growth

Ethics Check
Privacy and censorship worries

Facts to Consider
Beware of corporate thieves

Manager's Library
The Facebook Effect by David Kirkpatrick

Takeaway 6.1
How and Why Do Managers Use the Control Process?

ANSWERS TO COME

- Controlling is one of the four functions of management.
- Control begins with objectives and standards.
- Control measures actual performance.
- Control compares results with objectives and standards.
- Control takes corrective action as needed.

"KEEPING IN TOUCH" . . . "STAYING INFORMED" . . . "BEING IN CONTROL." THESE ARE important responsibilities for every manager. Yet "control" is a word like "power." If you aren't careful when and how the word is used, it leaves a negative connotation. But control plays a positive and necessary role in the management process. To have things "under control" is good; for things to be "out of control" is generally bad.

So, you might ask: What happened at Toyota?[1] Something certainly went wrong with quality control when the global giant had to recall more than 6 million vehicles to fix throttle problems and shut down production of models with defects until corrections could be made. It was a major blow to a firm previously praised for its quality vehicles. Reputation, sales, and profits were lost immediately. In "An Open Letter to Toyota Customers," Toyota North America's president and COO Jim Lentz said: "I am truly sorry for the concern our recalls have caused, and want you to know we're doing everything we can—as fast as we can—to make things right. . . . We'll continue to do everything we can to meet—and exceed—your expectations and justify your continued trust in Toyota."[2]

How did this company known for its product quality lose control? Was it a management lapse, a technology breakdown, or simply the aftermath of growing too fast in too many locations around the world?

||| Controlling is one of the four functions of management.

Controlling is the process of measuring performance and taking action to ensure desired results.

Managers understand **controlling** as a process of measuring performance and taking action to ensure desired results. Its purpose is straightforward—to make sure that plans are achieved and that actual performance meets or surpasses objectives. Like any aspect of decision making, the foundation of control is information. Henry Schacht, former CEO of Cummins Engine Company, once discussed control in terms of what he called "friendly facts." "Facts that reinforce what you are doing . . . are nice," he said, "because they help in terms of psychic reward. Facts that raise alarms are equally friendly, because they give you clues about how to respond, how to change, where to spend the resources."[3]

Just how does control fit in with the other management functions? Planning sets the directions. Organizing arranges people and resources for work.

Leading inspires people toward their best efforts. And as shown in **Figure 6.1**, controlling sees to it that the right things happen, in the right way, and at the right time. If things go wrong, control helps get things back on track.

Effective control offers the great opportunity of learning from experience. Consider, for example, the program of **after-action review** pioneered by the U.S. Army and now utilized in many corporate settings. This is a structured review of lessons learned and results accomplished through a completed project, task force assignment, or special operation. Participants answer questions like: "What was the intent?" "What actually happened?" "What did we learn?"[4] The after-action review encourages everyone involved to take responsibility for his or her performance efforts and accomplishments.

Even though improving performance through learning is one of the great opportunities offered by the control process, the potential benefits are realized only when learning is translated into corrective actions. After setting up Diversity Network Groups (DNGs) worldwide, for example, IBM executives learned that male attitudes were major barriers to the success of female managers. They addressed this finding by making male senior executives report annually on the progress of women managers in their divisions. This action is credited with substantially increasing the percentage of women in IBM's senior management ranks.[5]

FIGURE 6.1   Why Is Controlling So Important in the Management Process?
Controlling is one of the four management functions. It is the process of measuring performance—finding out how well you are doing, and taking action to ensure desired results—making sure results meet expectations. When controlling is done well, it sets a strong foundation for performance. As the old adage says: What gets measured happens.

After-action review is a structured review of lessons learned and results accomplished through a completed project, task force assignment, or special operation.

Control begins with objectives and standards.

The control process consists of the four steps shown in **Figure 6.2**. The process begins with setting performance objectives and standards for measuring them. It can't start any other way. This is the planning part: setting the performance objectives against which results can eventually be compared. Measurement standards are important, too. It isn't always easy to set them, but they are essential.

We often hear about earnings per share, sales growth, and market shares as standards for measuring business performance. Others include quantity and quality of production, costs incurred, service or delivery time, and error rates. But how about other types of organizations, such as a symphony orchestra? When the Cleveland Orchestra wrestled with performance standards, the members weren't willing to rely on vague generalities like "we played well," "the audience seemed happy," "not too many mistakes were made." Rather, they decided to track standing ovations, invitations to perform in other countries, and how often other orchestras copied their performance styles.[6]

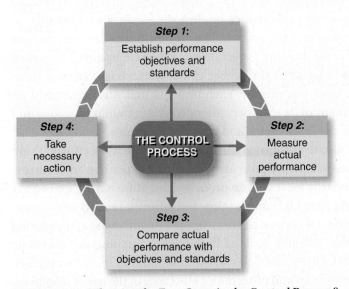

FIGURE 6.2   What Are the Four Steps in the Control Process?
The control process is straightforward: (1) set performance objectives and standards, (2) measure actual performance, (3) compare actual performance with objectives and standards, (4) take corrective action as needed. Although essential to management, these steps apply equally well to personal careers. Without career objectives, how do you know where you really want to go? How can you allocate time and other resources to take best advantage of opportunities? Without measurement, how can you assess how well you are doing and make adjustments to do better in the future?

{ MAJORITY OF FIRMS PLANNING TO SPEND MORE
TO DEFEND INTELLECTUAL PROPERTY.

Facts to Consider

■ BEWARE OF CORPORATE THIEVES

There's a lot of crime in the corporate world, and a bad economy tends to bring out the worst in some of us. Consider these survey results.

- 20% say worker theft is a "moderate to very big problem."
- 18% report an increase in money crimes such as stolen cash or fraudulent transactions.
- 24% report an increase in thefts of office supplies and company products.
- 17% have tightened security to prevent employee theft.
- In global business, 48% of firms report fear of fraud, keeping them from investing in places like China and Africa.

- 27% of companies report data fraud problems.
- 50% of firms plan to spend more defending intellectual property.

YOUR THOUGHTS?

Do these data tell the real story: Is employee theft mainly a "bad economy" problem? Is it a smaller or larger problem than indicated here? Have you witnessed such theft and, if so, what did you do about it? And have you been a participant in such bad employee behavior?

> An **output standard** measures performance results in terms of quantity, quality, cost, or time.

Things like earnings per share for a business and standing ovations for a symphony are examples of **output standards**. They measure actual outcomes or work results. When Allstate Corporation launched a new diversity initiative, it created a "diversity index" to quantify performance on diversity issues. The standards included how well employees met the goals of bias-free customer service and how well managers met the firm's diversity expectations.[7] When GE became concerned about managing ethics in its 320,000-member global workforce, it created measurement standards to track compliance. Each business unit was required to report quarterly on how many of its members attended ethics training sessions and what percentage signed the firm's "Spirit and Letter" ethics guide.[8]

> An **input standard** measures work efforts that go into a performance task.

The control process also uses **input standards** to measure work efforts. These are helpful in situations where outputs are difficult or expensive to measure. Examples of input standards for a college professor might be having an orderly course syllabus, showing up at all class sessions, and returning exams and assignments in a timely fashion. Of course, as this example might suggest, measuring inputs doesn't mean that outputs, such as high-quality teaching and learning, are necessarily achieved. Other examples of input standards in the workplace include conformance with rules and procedures, efficiency in the use of resources, and work attendance or punctuality.

‖ Control measures actual performance.

The second step in the control process is to measure actual performance using agreed-upon standards. Accurate and timely measurement is essential in order to spot differences between what is really taking place and what was originally planned. Unless we are willing to measure, very little control is possible. And as the module subtitle indicates, willingness to measure has its rewards. What gets measured tends to happen.

The "what gets measured happens" lesson can go a long way in nurturing a career. Linda Sanford, senior vice president for IBM, grew up on a family farm, where she developed an appreciation for measuring results. "At the end of the day, you saw what you did, knew how many rows of strawberries you picked." This experience carried over into her work at IBM. She earned a reputation for walking around the factory just to see "at the end of the day how many machines were going out of the back dock."[9]

‖ Control compares results with objectives and standards.

The third step in the control process is to compare actual results with objectives and standards. You might remember its implications by this **control equation**:

$$\text{Need for Action} = \text{Desired Performance} - \text{Actual Performance}$$

{ "WE HAVE HAD FAILURES AS WELL—AND SURVIVED THEM WITH A SENSE OF HUMOR."

Role Models

■ PATRICIA KARTER SHOWS HOW VALUES HELP CONTROL GROWTH

A sweet treat is what one gets when digging into one of Dancing Deer Baking's Cherry Almond Ginger Chew cookies. The company, founded by Patricia Karter, sells about $8 million worth of them and other confectionary concoctions every year. Each product is made with all-natural ingredients, packaged in recycled materials, and produced in inner-city Boston.

Dancing Deer began with a $20,000 investment and two ovens in a former pizza shop. It may not have been the original plan, but growth came quickly as the bakery prospered. Customer demand led to expansion; an acquisition led to further expansion; being recognized on national TV as having the "best cake in the nation" fueled growth further.

It isn't easy to stay on course and in control while changing structures, adding people, and building brands for competitive advantage. But for Karter the anchor point has always been clear: Let core values be the guide. Dancing Deer's employees get stock options and free lunches; 35% of profits from the firm's Sweet Home cakes are donated to help the homeless find accommodations and jobs. When offered a chance to make a large cookie sale to Williams-Sonoma, Karter declined because the contract would have required use of preservatives. Williams-Sonoma was so impressed that it contracted to sell her bakery mixes. Instead of lost opportunity, the firm gained more sales.

"There's more to life than selling cookies," says Dancing Deer's Web site, "but it's not a bad way to make a living." And Karter hopes controlled growth will make Dancing Deer "big enough to make an impact, to be a social economic force." The firm sums up its story to date this way: "It has been an interesting journey. Our successes are due to luck, a tremendous amount of dedication and hard work, and a commitment to having fun while being true to our principles. We have had failures as well—and survived them with a sense of humor."

WHAT'S THE LESSON HERE?

Whether it's moving ahead in our career or growing a work unit or organization, our aspirations can sometimes get the better of us. Patricia Karter seems to be nicely in control—of herself and of her firm. How important are personal values when it comes to staying on course and staying ethical in times of challenge, change, and performance pressures?

The control equation is a valuable tool. Identifying the need for action can point you in two possible directions. It can point toward the need to deal with a performance threat or deficiency (when actual is less than desired), or to explore a performance opportunity (when actual is more than desired).

Of course, the question of what constitutes desired performance plays an important role in the control equation and its implications. This is ideally clarified when original objectives and standards are set, such as in the earlier example of ethics at GE. But other approaches are available.

Some organizations use *engineering comparisons* to identify desired performance. An example is UPS. The firm carefully measures the routes and routines of its drivers to establish the times expected for each delivery. When a delivery manifest is scanned as completed, the driver's time is registered in an electronic performance log that is closely monitored by supervisors. Some make use *of historical comparisons*. These use past experience as a basis for evaluating current performance. And, *relative comparisons* are also common. They benchmark performance against that being achieved by other people, work units, or organizations.

⫿ Control takes corrective action as needed.

The final step in the control process occurs when action is taken to address gaps between desired and actual performance. You might hear the term **management by exception** used in this regard. It is the practice of giving attention to high-priority situations that show the greatest need for action.

Management by exception basically adds discipline to our use of the control equation by focusing attention not just on needs for action but also on the highest-priority needs for action. In this way it can save valuable time, energy, and other resources that might be spent correcting things of lesser importance while those of greater importance get missed or delayed.

Management by exception focuses attention on differences between actual and desired performance.

{ WE NEED THE COURAGE TO ADMIT
WHEN THINGS ARE GOING WRONG.

Explore Yourself

■ RESILIENCY

The control process is one of the ways through which managers help organizations best use their resources and systems to achieve productivity. In many ways our daily lives are similar quests for productivity, and the control process counts there, too. But how well we do depends a lot on our capacity for **resiliency**—the ability to call upon inner strength and keep moving forward even when things are tough. We need the courage and confidence to admit when things are going wrong, to change ways that aren't working well, and to hold on and keep things moving forward even in the face of adversity.

Get to know yourself better by taking the self-assessment on **Internal/External Control** and completing the other activities in the *Exploring Management* **Skill-Building Portfolio**.

STUDY GUIDE

Takeaway 6.1
How and Why Do Managers Use the Control Process?

Terms to Define

After-action review

Controlling

Input standards

Management by exception

Output standards

Rapid Review

- Controlling is the process of measuring performance and taking corrective action as needed.
- The control process begins when performance objectives and standards are set; both input standards for work efforts and output standards for work results can be used.
- The second step in control is to measure actual performance in the control process.
- The third step compares results with objectives and standards to determine the need for corrective action.
- The final step in the control process involves taking action to resolve problems and improve things in the future.
- The control equation states: Need for action = Desired performance − Actual performance.
- Management by exception focuses attention on the greatest need for action.

Questions for Discussion

1. What performance standards should guide a hospital emergency room or fire department?
2. Can one control performance equally well with input standards and output standards?
3. What are the possible downsides to management by exception?

Be Sure You Can

- explain the role of controlling in the management process
- list the steps in the control process
- explain how planning and controlling should work together in management
- differentiate output standards and input standards
- state the control equation
- explain management by exception

What Would You Do?

A work colleague comes to you and confides that she feels "adrift in her career" and "just can't get enthused about what she's doing anymore." How can you respond helpfully by pointing out that this might be a problem of self-management and personal control? What can you suggest for using the steps in the management control process to better understand and correct her situation?

Takeaway 6.2
What Types of Controls Are Used by Managers?

ANSWERS TO COME

- Managers use feedforward, concurrent, and feedback controls.
- Managers use both internal and external controls.
- Managing by objects is a way to integrate planning and controlling.

‖ Managers use feedforward, concurrent, and feedback controls.

You should recall discussions in earlier modules of how organizations operate as open systems that interact with their environments in an input-throughput-output cycle. Figure 6.3 now shows how three types of managerial controls—feedforward, concurrent, and feedback—apply to each phase.[10]

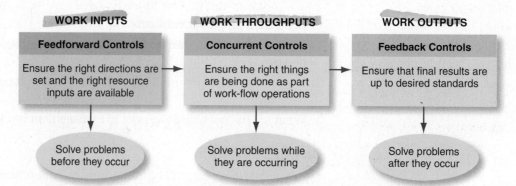

WORK INPUTS	**WORK THROUGHPUTS**	**WORK OUTPUTS**
Feedforward Controls	**Concurrent Controls**	**Feedback Controls**
Ensure the right directions are set and the right resource inputs are available	Ensure the right things are being done as part of work-flow operations	Ensure that final results are up to desired standards
Solve problems before they occur	Solve problems while they are occurring	Solve problems after they occur

FIGURE 6.3   **What Are the Differences Between Feedforward, Concurrent, and Feedback Controls?**
Organizations are input-throughput-output systems, and each point in the cycle offers its own opportunities for control over performance. Feedforward controls try to solve problems before they occur, by making sure the production systems have high-quality inputs. Concurrent controls try to solve problems as they occur, by monitoring and correcting problems during the work process. Feedback controls try to correct problems after they have occurred and inform the system so that similar mistakes can be avoided in the future.

Feedforward control ensures clear directions and needed resources before the work begins.

Feedforward controls, also called *preliminary controls*, take place before work begins. Their goal is to prevent problems before they occur. This is a forward-thinking and proactive approach to control, one that we should all try to follow whenever we can. At McDonald's, for example, preliminary control of food in-gredients plays an important role in the firm's quality program. Suppliers of its hamburger buns produce them to exact specifications, covering everything from texture to uniformity of color. Even in overseas markets, the firm works hard to develop local suppliers of dependable quality.[11]

Digging into Chick-fil-A

Performance Leaves No Room for Complacency

You can get a tasty sandwich at Chick-fil-A, but don't plan on stopping in on a Sunday. All of the chain's stores are closed. It is a tradition started by founder Truett Cathy, who believes employees deserve a day of rest.

Someone who places "people before profits," Truett has built a successful, and fast-growing, franchise known for consistent quality and great customer service. The president of the national Restaurant Association Educational Foundation says this about Chick-fil-A: "I don't think there's any chain that creates such a wonderful culture around the way they treat their people and the respect they have for their employees."

Current President Dan T. Cathy believes the Sunday day of rest is a statement about that culture. He says: "If we take care of our team members and operators behind the counter, then they are going to do a better job on Monday. In fact, I say our food tastes better on Monday because we are closed on Sunday."

Truett believes in "continuous improvement" to upgrade menus and stores even after years of increasing sales. Woody Faulk, vice president of brand development, says: "It would be very easy for us to pause after a successful year, but in doing that, we would be in jeopardy of falling into a trap of complacency." He adds: "Change in the quick-service industry is much like that of the fashion industry. Customer needs are constantly fluctuating, and we have to be intentional about staying ahead of and remaining relevant to those changes."

Concurrent controls focus on what happens during the work process; they take place while people are doing their jobs. The goal is to solve problems as they occur. Sometimes called *steering controls*, they make sure that things are always going according to plan. The ever-present shift leaders at McDonald's restaurants are a good example of how this happens through direct supervision. They constantly observe what is taking place, even while helping out with the work. They are trained to correct things on the spot. The question continually asked is: "What can we do to improve things right now?"

Feedback controls, or *post-action controls*, take place after a job or project is completed. Think about your experiences as a student. Most course evaluation systems ask "Was this a good learning experience?" only when the class is almost over. Think also about your experiences as a restaurant customer. Very often we're asked "was everything alright?" when it's time to pay the bill. And think of the electronic devices you buy. Probably the last question a cell phone maker asks before your device is shipped from the factory floor is "Does it work?" Although the prior questions are good ones most often asked in good faith, feedback controls focus on the quality of finished products. Although this type of control may prevent you from receiving a defective cell phone, it may not help you much while taking a poorly organized college course or after eating a bad meal.

FIND INSPIRATION

Truett Cathy's success with Chick-fil-A probably traces in part to his management philosophy: A well-treated staff delivers consistent results. In other words, people will do the right things more often than not if you respect and support them. This puts the focus on self-control and trusts workers to exercise it. Why don't more employers get this message?

Concurrent control focuses on what happens during the work process.

Feedback control takes place after completing an action.

Manager's Library

■ *THE FACEBOOK EFFECT* BY DAVID KIRKPATRICK

ONLINE PRIVACY—ARE YOU AN OPEN BOOK, OR DO YOU FEAR LOSING FACE?

As online networking grows, so does the tension between desires for social interaction and control of personal privacy. People offer different versions of themselves to others online, just as they do offline. But the Web lacks constraints of time and space, and digital data is proliferating and remains permanent. Online privacy can be controlled, but is it practical or even necessary?

In the book *The Facebook Effect* (2010, Simon & Schuster), author David Kirkpatrick says Facebook.com exists on the idea of "radical transparency"—the concept that everyone knows everything about anyone. Privacy controls are available, but the belief is that users want less control as a more open society evolves.

Kirkpatrick says Facebook is shifting society's attitude toward privacy. A vast majority of users register their true identities. They are given "granular" controls—they can choose exact users who may view precise postings—and may specify collections of data to be shared with various 'groups' such as family, friends, or coworkers. However, Facebook's default settings are for 'everyone' to view all personal data.

Facebook's approach has challenged users' comfort levels, but ultimately they are embracing standard of openness. Kirkpatrick thinks Facebook will never remove users' ability to control privacy, only their desire to do so. Managing privacy may prove too strenuous in an open society that tolerates people for who they truly are.

REFLECT AND REACT

What personal information do you want to keep private on Facebook, if any? Are you in control of your online persona? List the basic groups that users might create and identify different information shared with these groups. And by the way, do you agree that society will become more open with time and adopt Facebook's notion of "radical transparency"?

‖ Managers use both internal and external controls.

Internal control, or self-control, occurs as people exercise self-discipline in fulfilling job expectations.

We all exercise self-control in our daily lives; we do so in respect to managing our money, our relationships, our work-life balance, and more.[12] Managers can take advantage of this human capacity by unlocking and setting up conditions that support **internal control, or self-control,** in the workplace. According to Douglas McGregor's Theory Y perspective, discussed in Chapter 2, people are ready and willing to exercise self-control in their work.[13] This potential is increased when capable people have a clear sense of organizational mission, know their goals, and have the resources necessary to do their jobs well.

External control occurs through direct supervision or administrative systems.

In addition to encouraging and allowing internal control, managers also set up and use various forms of **external control** to structure situation so that things happen as planned.[14] The alternatives include bureaucratic or administrative control, clan control, and market control.

Bureaucratic control influences behavior through authority, policies, procedures, job descriptions, budgets, and day-to-day supervision.

The logic of **bureaucratic control** is that authority, policies, procedures, job descriptions, budgets, and day-to-day supervision help make sure that people behave in ways consistent with organizational interests. As discussed in the previous chapter on planning, for example, organizations typically have policies and procedures regarding sexual harassment. They are designed to make sure people behave toward one another respectfully and without sexual pressures or improprieties.

Whereas bureaucratic control emphasizes hierarchy and authority, **clan control** influences behavior through social norms and peer expectations. This is the power of collective identity; persons who share values and identify strongly with each other tend to behave in ways that are consistent with one another's expectations. Just look around the typical college classroom and campus. You'll see clan control reflected in dress, language, and behavior as students tend to act consistent with the expectations of those peers and groups they identify with. The same holds true in organizations where close-knit employees display common behavior patterns.

Market control is essentially the influence of market competition on the behavior of organizations and their members. Business firms adjust products, pricing, promotions, and other practices in response to customer feedback and competitor moves. An example is the growing emphasis on "green" products and practices. When a firm such as Wal-Mart starts to get good publicity from its expressed commitment to eventually power all of its stores with renewable energy, the effect is felt by its competitors.[15] They have to adjust practices to avoid giving up this public relations advantage to Wal-Mart. In this sense, the time-worn phrase "keeping up with the competition" is really another way of expressing the dynamics of market controls in action.

> **Clan control** influences behavior through social norms and peer expectations.

> **Market control** is essentially the influence of market competition on the behavior of organizations and their members.

Managing by objectives is a way to integrate planning and controlling.

A useful technique for integrating planning and controlling is **managing by objectives**. Often called MBO, it is a structured process of regular communication in which a supervisor or team leader and a subordinate or team member jointly set performance objectives and review accomplished results.[16] As **Figure 6.4** shows, the process creates an agreement between the two parties regarding performance

> **Managing by objectives** is a process of joint objective setting between a superior and a subordinate.

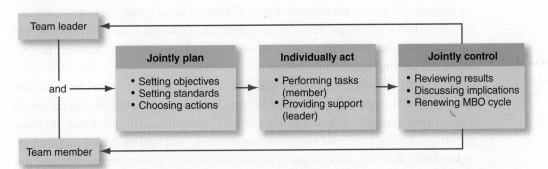

FIGURE 6.4　How Does Managing by Objectives Help to Integrate Planning and Controlling?
Managing by objectives is a structured process of communication between a supervisor and a subordinate, or team leader and team members. Planning is accomplished when both parties communicate to identify the subordinate's performance objectives. This is a form of participatory planning, and the goal is agreement. Informed by the objectives, the supervisor provides support for the subordinate as work progresses. Controlling is accomplished when the two parties meet at scheduled times to jointly discuss progress and results, and make new plans setting future performance objectives.

Tips to Remember

■ HOW TO WRITE A GOOD PERFORMANCE OBJECTIVE

- *Clarify the target*—be specific; clearly describe the key result to be accomplished.
- *Make it measurable*—state how the key result will be measured and documented.
- *Define the timetable*—identify a date by which the key result will be accomplished.

- *Avoid the impossible*—be realistic; don't promise what cannot be accomplished.
- *Add challenge*—be optimistic; build in "stretch" to make the accomplishment significant.
- *Don't overcomplicate*—stick to the essentials; write to fit a Post-It note reminder.

Improvement objectives document intentions to improve performance in a specific way.

Personal development objectives document intentions to accomplish personal growth, such as expanded job knowledge or skills.

objectives for a given time period, plans for accomplishing them, standards for measuring them, and procedures for reviewing them.

In the previous chapter on planning, we talked about "great goals." You can think of them in the present context as objectives that have real meaning in terms of significant performance consequences. When a team leader and team member are working together in a managing by objectives approach, for example, it is helpful to consider two types of objectives that can have an element of "greatness" to them. **Improvement objectives** document intentions for improving performance in a specific way. An example is "to reduce quality rejects by 10%." **Personal development objectives** focus on expanding job knowledge or skills. An example is "to learn the latest version of a computer spreadsheet package."

Whether we are talking about improvement or personal objectives, it's always important to remember that the best objectives are specific, time defined, challenging, and measurable. And, to make objectives measurable they must be specified as clearly as possible. Ideally, this involves agreement on a *measurable end product*, for example, "to reduce housekeeping supply costs by 5% by the end of the fiscal year." But this can be hard to do in some cases. Instead, performance objectives can be stated as *verifiable work activities*. For example, a team leader can commit to holding weekly team meetings as a means for achieving better communications.

You might already be wondering if managing by objectives can become too complicated a process.[17] The answer is "yes." Critics note that problems can arise when objectives are linked too closely with pay, focused too much on easy accomplishments, involve excessive paperwork, and end up being dictated by supervisors. But, the advantages of making objectives a clear part of the ongoing conversation between managers and those reporting to them are also clear.[18] It keeps workers focused on the most important tasks and priorities, and keeps supervisors focused on the best ways to help them meet agreed-upon objectives. Because the process requires direct communication, furthermore, it helps build good interpersonal relationships. And by increasing employees' participation in decisions that affect their work, it encourages self-management.[19]

STUDY GUIDE

Takeaway 6.2
What Types of Controls Are Used by Managers?

Terms to Define

Bureaucratic control

Clan control

Concurrent control

External control

Feedback control

Feedforward control

Improvement objectives

Internal control (self-control)

Managing by objectives

Market control

Personal development objectives

Rapid Review

- Feedforward controls try to make sure things are set up right before work begins; concurrent controls make sure that things are being done correctly; feedback controls assess results after an action is completed.

- Internal control is self-control that occurs as people take personal responsibility for their work.

- External control is accomplished by use of bureaucratic, clan, and market control systems.

- Management by objectives is a process through which team leaders work with team members to "jointly" set performance objectives and "jointly" review performance results.

Questions for Discussion

1. How does bureaucratic control differ from clan control?
2. What is Douglas McGregor's main point regarding internal control?
3. Can MBO work when there are problems in the relationship between a team leader and a team member?

Be Sure You Can

- illustrate the use of feedforward, concurrent, and feedback controls
- explain the nature of internal control or self-control
- differentiate among bureaucratic, clan, and market controls
- list the steps in the MBO process as it might operate between a team leader and a team member

What Would You Do?

You have a highly talented work team whose past performance has been outstanding. Recently, though, team members are starting to act like the workday is mainly a social occasion. Getting the work done seems less important than having a good time, and performance is on the decline. How can you use external controls in a positive way to restore performance to high levels in this team?

Takeaway 6.3
What Are Some Useful Control Tools and Techniques?

ANSWERS TO COME

- Quality control is a foundation of modern management.
- Gantt charts and CPM/PERT are used in project management and control.
- Inventory controls help save costs.
- Breakeven analysis shows where revenues will equal costs.
- Financial ratios measure key areas of financial performance.
- Balanced scorecards help top managers exercise strategic control.

MOST ORGANIZATIONS USE A VARIETY OF COMPREHENSIVE AND SYSTEM-WIDE controls. You should be familiar with quality control, purchasing and inventory controls, and breakeven analysis, as well as the use of key financial controls and balanced scorecards.

▌ Quality control is a foundation of modern management.

If managing for high performance is a theme of the day, *quality control* is one of its most important watchwords. As pointed out in Chapter 2, the term **total quality management (TQM)** is quite common in modern management. It is used to describe operations that make quality an everyday performance objective and strive to always do things right the first time.[20] A foundation of TQM is the quest for **continuous improvement**, meaning that one is always looking for new ways to improve on current performance.[21] The notion is that you can never be satisfied, that something always can and should be improved upon.[22]

The basic cornerstone of quality control in any organization is measurement. If you want quality, you have to tally defects, analyze and trace them to the sources, make corrections, and keep records of what happens afterwards.[23] A quality tool often used in manufacturing, for example, is the **control chart** shown below.

Total quality management (TQM) commits to quality objectives, continuous improvement, and doing things right the first time.

Continuous improvement involves always searching for new ways to improve work quality and performance.

Control charts are graphical ways of displaying trends so that exceptions to quality standards can be identified.

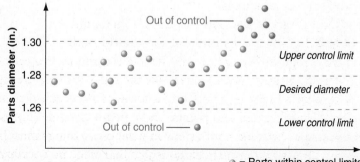

Control charts are graphical ways of displaying trends so that exceptions to quality standards can be identified for special attention. In the prior figure, for example, an upper control limit and a lower control limit specify the allowable tolerances for measurements of a machine part. As long as the manufacturing process produces parts that fall within these limits, things are "in control." However, as soon as parts start to fall outside the limits, it is clear that something is going wrong that is affecting quality. The process can then be investigated, even shut down, to identify the source of the errors and correct them.

The use of statistics adds power to sampling as a basis for decision making and quality management. Many manufacturers now use a **Six Sigma** program, meaning that statistically the firm's quality performance will tolerate no more than 3.4 defects per million units of goods produced or services completed. This translates to a perfection rate of 99.9997%. As tough as it sounds, Six Sigma is a common quality standard for many, if not most, major competitors in our demanding global marketplace.

Six Sigma is a quality standard of 3.4 defects or less per million products or service deliveries.

▥ Gantt charts and CPM/PERT are used in project management and control.

It might be something personal such as planning an anniversary party for one's parents, preparing for a renovation to your home, or watching the completion of a new student activities building on a campus. What these examples and others like them share in common is that they are relatively complicated tasks. Multiple components must be completed in a certain sequence, within budget, and by a specified date. In management we call them **projects**.

Projects are one-time activities with many component tasks that must be completed in proper order and according to budget.

Project management is responsibility for the overall planning, supervision, and control of projects. Basically, a project manager's job is to ensure that a project is well planned and then completed according to plan—on time, within budget, and consistent with objectives. In practice, this is often assisted by two control techniques known as Gantt charts and CPM/PERT.

Project management makes sure that activities required to complete a project are planned well and accomplished on time.

A **Gantt chart** graphically displays the scheduling of tasks that go into completing a project. As developed in the early twentieth century by Henry Gantt, an industrial engineer, this tool has become a mainstay of project management. Use of the visual overview of what needs to be done on a project allows for progress checks to be made at different time intervals. It helps with event or activity sequencing to make sure that things get accomplished in time for later work to build upon them. One of the biggest problems with projects, for example, is when delays in early activities create problems for later ones.

A **Gantt chart** graphically displays the scheduling of tasks required to complete a project.

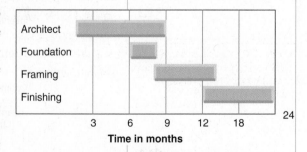

A more advanced use of the Gantt chart is a technique known as **CPM/PERT**—a combination of the critical path method and the program evaluation and review technique. Project planning based on CPM/PERT uses a network chart like the one shown at the top of the next page. Such charts break a project into a series of small sub-activities that each have clear beginning and end points. These points become "nodes" in the charts, and the arrows between nodes show in what order things must be done. The full diagram shows all the interrelationships that must be coordinated for the entire project to be successfully completed.

CPM/PERT is a combination of the critical path method and the program evaluation and review technique.

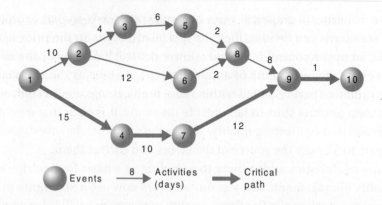

Use of CPM/PERT techniques helps project managers track activities to make sure they happen in the right sequence and on time. If you look at the network in the figure, you should notice that the time required for each activity can be easily computed and tracked. The pathway from start to conclusion that involves the longest completion times is called the **critical path**. It represents the quickest time in which the entire project can be finished, assuming everything goes according to schedule and plans. In the example, the critical path is 38 days.

⦀ Inventory controls help save costs.

Cost control ranks right up there with quality control as an important performance concern. And a very good place to start is with inventory. The goal of **inventory control** is to make sure that any inventory is only big enough to meet one's immediate performance needs.

The **economic order quantity** form of inventory control, shown in the figure, automatically orders a fixed number of items every time an inventory level falls to a predetermined point. The order sizes are mathematically calculated to minimize costs of inventory. A good example is your local supermarket. It routinely makes hundreds of daily orders on an economic order quantity basis.

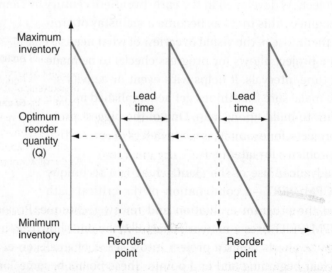

Another and very popular approach to inventory control is **just-in-time scheduling (JIT)**. First made popular by the Japanese, these systems reduce costs and improve workflow by scheduling materials to arrive at a workstation or facility

The **critical path** is the pathway from project start to conclusion that involves activities with the longest completion times.

Inventory control ensures that inventory is only big enough to meet immediate needs.

The **economic order quantity** method places new orders when inventory levels fall to predetermined points.

Just-in-time scheduling (JIT) routes materials to workstations just in time for use.

just in time for use. Because JIT nearly eliminates the carrying costs of inventories, it is an important business productivity tool. But, the recent tsunami and nuclear disaster in Japan also showed some of the risks of JIT. Many global companies, among them Boeing and Dell, faced product delays when just-in-time shipments were disrupted as Japanese firms in their supply chains were closed or their operations scaled back due to the disaster.[24]

⫴ Breakeven analysis shows where revenues will equal costs.

When business executives are deliberating new products or projects, a frequent control question is: "What is the **breakeven point?**" Figure 6.5 shows that breakeven occurs at the point where revenues just equal costs. You can also think of it as the point where losses end and profit begins. A breakeven point is computed using this formula.

The **breakeven point** occurs where revenues just equal costs.

$$\text{Breakeven Point} = \text{Fixed Costs} \div (\text{Price} - \text{Variable Costs})$$

Managers rely on **breakeven analysis** to perform what-if calculations under different projected cost and revenue conditions. Suppose, for example, the proposed target price for a new product is $8 per unit, fixed costs are $10,000, and variable costs are $4 per unit. What sales volume is required to break even? (*Answer:* Breakeven at 2500 units.) What happens if you are good at cost control and can keep variable costs to $3 per unit? (*Answer:* Breakeven at 2000 units.) Now, suppose you can only produce 1000 units in the beginning and at the original costs. At what price must you sell them to break even? (*Answer:* $14.) Business executives perform these types of cost control analyses every day.

Breakeven analysis performs what-if calculations under different revenue and cost conditions.

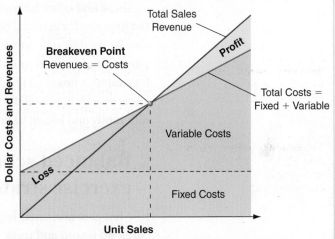

FIGURE 6.5   How Do Managers Use Breakeven Analysis to Make Informed What-If Decisions?

A common question asked by managers when considering a new product or service investment is: "What is the breakeven point?" A breakeven point is computed using this formula: Breakeven Point = Fixed Costs ÷ (Price − Variable Costs). As shown in this figure, breakeven occurs at the point where revenues just equal costs. You can also think of it as the point where losses end and profit begins. This approach helps managers perform what-if calculations under different projected cost and revenue conditions.

⫴ Financial ratios measure key areas of financial performance.

The pressure is always on for organizations to use their financial resources well to achieve high performance. And, the analysis of an organization's financial performance is an important aspect of managerial control.

At a minimum, business managers should be able to understand these financial performance measures: (1) *liquidity*—ability to generate cash to pay bills; (2) *leverage*—ability to earn more in returns than the cost of debt; (3) *asset management*—ability to use resources efficiently and operate at minimum cost; and (4) *profitability*—ability to earn revenues greater than costs. All of these measures can be assessed using financial ratios such as those listed next.

Liquidity—measures ability to meet short-term obligations.

- *Current Ratio* = Current Assets ÷ Current Liabilities
- *Quick Ratio* = (Current Assets − Inventory) ÷ Current Liabilities
- ↑ Higher is better: You want more assets and fewer liabilities.

Leverage—measures use of debt.

- *Debt Ratio* = Total Debts ÷ Total Assets
- ↓ Lower is better: You want fewer debts and more assets.

Asset Management—measures asset and inventory efficiency.

- *Asset Turnover* = Sales ÷ Total Assets
- *Inventory Turnover* = Sales ÷ Average Inventory
- ↑ Higher is better: You want more sales and fewer assets or lower inventory.

Profitability—measures profit generation.

- *Net Margin* = Net Income ÷ Sales
- *Return on Assets* (ROA) = Net Income ÷ Total Assets
- *Return on Equity* (ROE) = Net Income ÷ Owner's Equity
- ↑ Higher is better: You want as much net income or profit as possible for sales, assets, and equity.

These and other financial ratios can be used for historical comparisons within the firm and for external benchmarking relative to industry performance. They can also be used to set company-level financial targets or goals to be shared with employees and tracked to indicate success or failure. At Civco Medical Instruments, for example, financial results are distributed monthly to all employees. They always know exactly how well the firm is doing. This helps them focus on what they can do differently and better, to help improve the firm's bottom line.[25]

⫼ Balanced scorecards help top managers exercise strategic control.

If "what gets measured happens," then managers should take advantage of "scorecards" to record and track performance results. When an instructor takes class attendance and assigns grades based on it, students tend to come to class. When an employer tracks the number of customers each employee serves per day, employees tend to serve more customers. Do the same principles hold for organizations?

Strategic management consultants Robert S. Kaplan and David P. Norton think so. They advocate using what is called the **balanced scorecard** in respect to management control.[26] It gives top managers, as they say, "a fast but comprehensive view of the business." The basic principle is that to do well and to win, you have to keep score. And like sports teams, organizations perform better when all members know the score.

Developing a balanced scorecard for any organization begins with a clarification of the organization's mission and vision—what it wants to be and how it wants to be perceived by its key stakeholders. Next, the following questions are asked and answered to develop balanced scorecard goals and performance measures.

- *Financial Performance*—"How well do our actions directly contribute to improved financial performance?" To improve financially, how should we appear to our shareholders? Sample goals: survive, succeed, and prosper. Sample

A **balanced scorecard** measures performance on financial, customer service, internal process, and innovation and learning goals.

measures: cash flow, sales growth and operating income, increased market share, and return on equity.

- *Customer Satisfaction*—"How well do we serve our customers and clients?" To achieve our vision, how should we appear to our customers? Sample goals: new products, responsive supply. Sample measures: percentage sales from new products, percentage on-time deliveries.

- *Internal Process Improvement*—"How well do our activities and processes directly increase value provided to our customers and clients?" To satisfy our customers and shareholders, at what internal business processes should we excel? Sample goals: manufacturing productivity, design excellence, new product introduction. Sample measures: cycle times, engineering efficiency, new product time.

- *Innovation and Learning*—"How well are we learning, changing, and improving things over time?" To achieve our vision, how will we sustain our ability to change and improve? Sample goals: technology leadership, time to market. Sample measures: time to develop new technologies, new product introduction time versus competition.

When balanced scorecard measures are taken, recorded, shared, and critically reviewed, Kaplan and Norton expect organizations to perform better in those areas. Their point is one we've made before: What gets measured happens.

Think about the possibilities here. How can the balanced scorecard approach be used by the following organizations: an elementary school, a hospital, a community library, a mayor's office, a fast-food restaurant? How do the performance dimensions and indicators vary among these different types of organizations? And if balanced scorecards make sense, why is it that more organizations don't use them?

{ WHO WINS (AND LOSES) WHEN GLOBAL INTERNET FIRMS
AND LOCAL GOVERNMENTS BATTLE FOR CONTROL?

Ethics Check

■ PRIVACY AND CENSORSHIP WORRIES

London—Amnesty International claims that Yahoo!, Microsoft, and Google violated human rights in China by complying with government requests for censorship. Amnesty says that "corporate values and policies" are compromised in the quest for profits. A spokesperson for Yahoo's China business, Alibaba.com, says: "By creating opportunities for entrepreneurs and connecting China's exporters to buyers around the world, Alibaba.com and Yahoo! China are having an overwhelmingly positive impact on the lives of average people in China."

Beijing—Skype is told by the Chinese government that its software must filter words that the Chinese leadership considers offensive from text messages. If the company doesn't, it can't do business in the country. After refusing at first, company

executives finally agree: phrases such as "Falun Gong" and "Dalai Lama" no longer appear in text messages delivered through Skype's Chinese joint venture partner, Tom Online.

YOU DECIDE

Skype cofounder Niklas Zennstrom says: "I may like or not like the laws and regulations to operate businesses in the UK or Germany or the U.S., but if I do business there I choose to comply." What do you think? Do company executives have any choice but to comply with the requests of governments? Are there times when profits should be sacrificed for principles? When should business executives stand up and challenge laws and regulations used to deny customers the privacy they expect?

STUDY GUIDE

Takeaway 6.3
What Are Some Useful Control Tools and Techniques?

Terms to Define

Balanced scorecard

Breakeven analysis

Breakeven point

Continuous improvement

Control chart

Critical path

CPM/PERT

Economic order quantity

Gantt chart

Inventory control

Just-in-time scheduling (JIT)

Project

Project management

Six Sigma

Total quality management (TQM)

Rapid Review

- Total quality management tries to meet customers' needs and do things right on time, the first time, and all the time.
- Organizations use control charts and statistical techniques such as the Six Sigma system to measure the quality of work samples for quality control purposes.
- Economic order quantities and just-in-time deliveries are common approaches to inventory cost control.
- The breakeven equation is: Breakeven Point = Fixed Costs ÷ (Price − Variable Costs).
- Breakeven analysis identifies the points where revenues will equal costs under different pricing and cost conditions.
- Financial control of business performance is facilitated by use of financial ratios, such as those dealing with liquidity, leverage, assets, and profitability.
- The balanced scorecard measures overall organizational performance in respect to four areas: financial, customers, internal processes, innovation.

Questions for Discussion

1. Can a firm such as Wal-Mart ever go too far in controlling its inventory costs?
2. Is the concept of total quality management out of date?
3. Does the "balanced scorecard" as described in this chapter measure the right things?

Be Sure You Can

- explain the role of continuous improvement in TQM
- explain how Gantt charts and CPM/PERT helps organizations with project management
- explain two common approaches to inventory cost control
- state the equation to calculate a breakeven point and its use in explaining breakeven analysis
- state the common financial ratios used in organizational control
- identify the balanced scorecard components and control questions

What Would You Do?

You've had three years of solid work experience after earning your undergraduate degree. A lot of your friends are talking about going to graduate school, and the likely target for you would be an MBA degree. Given all the potential costs and benefits of getting an MBA, how can breakeven analysis help you make the decision to (1) go or not go, (2) go full time or part time, and (3) even where to go?

TestPrep 6

Multiple-Choice Questions

1. After objectives and standards are set, what step comes next in the control process?

(a) Measure results.

(b) Take corrective action.

(c) Compare results with objectives.

(d) Modify standards to fit circumstances.

2. When a soccer coach tells her players at the end of a losing game, "You did good in staying with the game plan," she is using a/an _____ as a measure of performance.

(a) input standard

(b) output standard

(c) historical comparison

(d) relative comparison

3. When an automobile manufacturer is careful to purchase only the highest-quality components for use in production, this is an example of an attempt to ensure high performance through _____ control.

(a) concurrent

(b) statistical

(c) inventory

(d) feedforward

4. Management by exception means _____.

(a) managing only when necessary

(b) focusing attention where the need for action is greatest

(c) the same thing as concurrent control

(d) the same thing as just-in-time delivery

5. A total quality management program is most likely to be associated with _____.

(a) EOQ

(b) continuous improvement

(c) return on equity

(d) breakeven analysis

6. The _____ chart graphically displays the scheduling of tasks required to complete the project.

(a) exception

(b) Taylor

(c) Gantt

(d) after-action

7. When MBO is done right, who does the review of a team member's performance accomplishments?

(a) the team member

(b) the team leader

(c) both the team member and team leader

(d) the team leader, the team member, and a lawyer

8. A good performance objective is written in such a way that it _____.

(a) has a flexible timetable

(b) is general and not too specific

(c) is impossible to accomplish

(d) can be easily measured

9. A manager is not living up to the concept of MBO if he or she _____.

(a) sets performance objectives for subordinates

(b) stays in touch and tries to support subordinates in their work

(c) jointly reviews performance results with subordinates

(d) keeps a written record of subordinates' performance objectives

10. If an organization's top management establishes a target of increasing new hires of minority and female candidates by 15% in the next six months, this is an example of a/an _____ standard for control purposes.

(a) input

(b) output

(c) management by exception

(d) concurrent

11. When a supervisor working alongside of an employee corrects him or her when a mistake is made, this is an example of _____ control.
    (a) feedforward
    (b) external
    (c) concurrent
    (d) preliminary

12. In CPM/PERT, "CPM" stands for _____.
    (a) critical path method
    (b) control planning management
    (c) control plan map
    (d) current planning matrix

13. In a CPM/PERT analysis, the focus is on _____ and the event _____ that link them together with the finished project.
    (a) costs; budgets
    (b) activities; sequences
    (c) timetables; budgets
    (d) goals; costs

14. When one team member advises another team member that "your behavior is crossing the line in terms of our expectations for workplace civility," she is exercising a form of _____ control over the other's inappropriate behaviors
    (a) clan
    (b) market
    (c) internal
    (d) preliminary

15. Among the financial ratios often used for control purposes, Current Assets/Current Liabilities is known as the _____.
    (a) debt ratio
    (b) net margin
    (c) current ratio
    (d) inventory turnover ratio

Short-Response Questions

16. What type of control is being exercised in the U.S. Army's after-action review?

17. How could clan control be used in a TQM program?

18. How can a just-in-time system reduce inventory costs?

19. What four questions could be used to set up a balanced scorecard for a small business?

Integration and Application Question

20. Put yourself in the position of a management consultant who specializes in MBO. The local Small Business Enterprise Association has asked you to be the speaker for its luncheon next week. The president of the association says that the group would like to learn more about the topic: "How to Use Management by Objectives for Better Planning and Control."

    Questions: Your speech will last 15 to 20 minutes. What is the outline for your speech? How will you explain the potential benefits of MBO to this group of small business owners?

Steps*for*FurtherLearning

Many learning resources are available at the end of the book and online within WileyPLUS.

Don't Miss These Selections from the **Skill-Building Portfolio**

- **SELF-ASSESSMENT 6:** *Internal/External Control*
- **CLASS EXERCISE 6:** *Stakeholder Maps*
- **TEAM PROJECT 6:** *After Meeting/Project Review*

Don't Miss This Selection from **Cases for Critical Thinking**

- **CHAPTER 6 CASE**
  Electronic Arts: Inside Fantasy Sports

Snapshot Electronic Arts is one of the largest and most profitable third-party video game makers. Exclusive contracts with professional sports teams have enabled it to dominate the sports gaming market. But as gaming has shifted from consoles to laptops, phones, and tablets, it is struggling to stay relevant. Can EA regain the pole position in a crowded and contentious market?

Until recently, EA's devotion to sports games was a winning asset—it dominated the market as the world's largest video-game publisher. But over the course of a few short years, the gaming market radically changed. Now EA finds itself in third place behind two strong competitors whose successes represent areas in which EA needs to double down to stay in the game.

Make notes here on what you've learned about yourself from this chapter.

- **LEARNING JOURNAL 6**

Chinese factories run by Foxconn Technology Group supply electronic components for global brands. To help prevent suicides, Foxconn has installed nets on employee dormitories.

Strategy and Strategic Management

Insight and Hard Work Deliver Results

Management Live

Critical Thinking and *Tron: Legacy*

Acting on a mysterious pager message sent to a family confidant, Sam Flynn (Garrett Hedlund) finds himself in a virtual world known as The Grid. Sam is captured and designated as a game player, with his only instruction being to "survive." That is the plot for the sci-fi movie *Tron: Legacy*. Sam knows nothing about this virtual world. He is left to anticipate what will happen and use his instincts to stay alive. Through observation, he quickly learns how to use his disc and a light cycle to defeat other players. Sam is eventually reunited with his father, Kevin Flynn (Jeff Bridges) and uses his intuition to save Quorra (Olivia Wilde).

Pretty heady stuff that you only see in the movies, right? Not so. The complexity and uncertainty of the business world forces managers to respond in similar ways. Strategic management requires a set of skills for monitoring the competitive environment and developing organizational strategy. Foremost among these skills is **critical thinking**, the ability to perceive situations, gather and interpret relevant information, and make decisions.

Case studies and other problem-based methods of learning can help develop your critical thinking skills. Just remember, though, that case studies are neat and tidy while the real world can be much more complex and unstructured. The more practice you get now with critical thinking, the better prepared you will be when you encounter uncertainties.

YOUR CHAPTER 7 TAKEAWAYS

1. Identify the types of strategies used by organizations.

2. Understand how managers formulate and implement strategies.

WHAT'S INSIDE

Explore Yourself
More on critical thinking

Role Models
Roger W. Ferguson Jr. provides strategic leadership at TIAA-CREF

Ethics Check
Life and death at an outsourcing factory

Facts to Consider
CEO pay is heading high again

Manager's Library
Behind the Cloud by Marc Benioff and Carlye Adler

Takeaway 7.1
What Types of Strategies Are Used by Organizations?

ANSWERS TO COME

- Strategy is a comprehensive plan for achieving competitive advantage.
- Organizations use corporate, business, and functional strategies.
- Growth strategies focus on expansion.
- Restructuring and divestiture strategies focus on consolidation.
- Global strategies focus on international business initiatives.
- Cooperative strategies focus on alliances and partnerships.
- E-business strategies focus on using the Internet for business success.

RECENT CHANGES IN THE AUTOMOBILE INDUSTRY HAVE BEEN FAST, DRAMATIC, and, hopefully, strategically well done. It wasn't always that way. There was a time when the automakers were quite literally in the driver's seat. Henry Ford once said of his Model T's: "The customer can have any color he wants as long as it's black." Not so in our era of high gasoline prices, tight credit, and lots full of unsold cars. We've seen a great shift in ways businesses make plans and appeal to customers. When Stephen Haeckel was director of strategic studies at IBM's Advanced Business Institute, he described the shift as "a difference between a bus, which follows a set route, and a taxi, which goes where customers tell it to go."[1]

The bus-taxi analogy can also be applied to your career strategy. Will you be acting like the bus following the set route, or the taxi following opportunities? Don't be afraid to move back and forth between the worlds of business strategy and personal strategy as our discussions in this chapter develop. The applications go both ways.

Success in the business world requires leaders with the abilities to move their organizations forward strategically. "If you want to make a difference as a leader," says *Fast Company* magazine, "you've got to make time for strategy."[2] The same holds true for your career.

||| Strategy is a comprehensive plan for achieving competitive advantage.

A **strategy** is a comprehensive action plan that identifies long-term direction for an organization and guides resource utilization to accomplish its goals. Strategy focuses leadership attention on the competitive environment. It represents a "best guess" about what to do to be successful in the face of rivalry and changing conditions.

A good strategy provides leaders with a plan for allocating and using resources with consistent **strategic intent**. Think of this as having all organizational energies directed toward a unifying and compelling target or goal.[3] Coca-Cola, for example, describes its strategic intent as "To put a Coke within 'arm's reach' of every consumer in the world."

A **strategy** is a comprehensive plan guiding resource allocation to achieve long-term organization goals.

Strategic intent focuses organizational energies on achieving a compelling goal.

Ultimately, a good strategy helps an organization achieve **competitive advantage**. This means that it is able to outperform rivals. In fact, the best strategies provide **sustainable competitive advantage**. This means that they operate in successful ways that are hard for competitors to imitate.[4] When you think sustainable competitive advantage, think about Apple and its iPad. It was first to market with an innovative product linking design, technology, and customer appeal. And, all backed by a super efficient supply chain. And it kept the ball rolling, so to speak. One analyst observed: "Apple moved the goal posts before most of their competitors even took the field."[5]

Organizations use corporate, business, and functional strategies.

You can identify strategies at three levels in most organizations. At the top level, **corporate strategy** provides direction and guides resource allocation for the organization as a whole. The *strategic question* at the corporate strategy level is: In what industries and markets should we compete? In large, complex organizations, such as PepsiCo, IBM, and General Electric, decisions on corporate strategy identify how the firm intends to compete across multiple industries, businesses, and markets.

Business strategy focuses on the strategic intent for a single business unit or product line. The *strategic question* at the business strategy level is: How are we going to compete for customers within this industry and in this market? Typical

A **competitive advantage** is an ability to outperform rivals.

A **sustainable competitive advantage** is achieved in ways that are difficult to imitate.

A **corporate strategy** sets long-term direction for the total enterprise.

A **business strategy** identifies how a division or strategic business unit will compete in its product or service domain.

{ *BLACK ENTERPRISE* CALLED HIM ONE OF THE "100 MOST POWERFUL AFRICAN AMERICANS IN CORPORATE AMERICA."

Role Models

■ ROGER W. FERGUSON JR. PROVIDES STRATEGIC LEADERSHIP AT TIAA-CREF

Leading a huge financial institution with over $70 billion under its management is a big challenge. But Roger W. Ferguson Jr. is well prepared for the job. *Black Enterprise* magazine listed him as one of the "100 most powerful African Americans in corporate America."

His experience and capabilities seem well up to the strategic leadership task. With a PhD in economics, he has prior experience as vice chairman of the Board of Governors of the Federal Reserve System and chairman of Swiss Re America Holding Corp. And when U.S. President Barack Obama set up a new Economic Advisory Board and charged its members "to meet regularly so that I can hear different ideas and sharpen my own, and seek counsel that is candid and informed by the wider world," Roger W. Ferguson Jr. was chosen as a member. Ferguson leads a firm that proudly proclaims "Diversify isn't

just smart financial advice. It's a sound hiring policy as well." The firm includes "promoting diversity" in its mission and states the belief that "all benefit from a work environment that fosters respect, integrity and opportunity for people from a wide variety of backgrounds."

WHAT'S THE LESSON HERE?

When TIAA-CREF appointed Ferguson, it made him one of only six other African American executives serving as CEOs of *Fortune* 500 companies. He brought a range of experience and personal capabilities to the position and is one of the most respected financial executives in America. What does it take to achieve this level of professional success? Are we talking luck, career strategy, something else, or all of these things?

business strategy decisions include choices about product and service mix, facilities locations, new technologies, and the like. For smaller, single-business enterprises, business strategy is the corporate strategy.

A functional strategy guides activities within one specific area of operations.

Functional strategy guides activities to implement higher-level business and corporate strategies. This level of strategy unfolds within a specific functional area such as marketing, manufacturing, finance, and human resources. The *strategic question* for functional strategies is: How can we best utilize resources within the function to support implementation of the business strategy? Answers to this question involve a wide variety of practices and initiatives to improve things such as operating efficiency, product quality, customer service, or innovativeness.

Growth strategies focus on expansion.

A growth strategy involves expansion of the organization's current operations.

You often read and hear about organizations trying to get bigger. They are pursuing **growth strategies** to increase the size and scope of current operations. Many executives view growth as necessary for long-run profitability. But you should probably question this assumption and probe deeper right from the start. Is growth always the best path? And if the strategic choice is to grow, how should it be accomplished?

Growth through concentration means expansion within an existing business area.

A strategy of growth through **concentration** seeks expansion within an existing business area, one in which the firm has experience and presumably expertise. You don't see McDonald's trying to grow by buying bookstores or gasoline stations; it keeps opening more restaurants at home and abroad. You don't see Walmart trying to grow by buying a high-end department store chain or a cell-phone company; it keeps opening more Walmart stores. These are classic growth by concentration strategies.

Growth through diversification means expansion by entering related or new business areas.

Growth can also take place through **diversification**, where expansion occurs by entering new business areas. As you might expect, diversification involves risk because the firm may be moving outside existing areas of competency. One way to moderate the risk is to pursue *related diversification*, expanding into similar or complementary new business areas. PepsiCo did this when it purchased Tropicana. Although Tropicana's fruit juices were new to Pepsi, the business is related to its expertise in the beverages industry.

Some firms get involved in *unrelated diversification* that pursues growth in entirely new business areas. Did you know, for example, that Exxon once owned Izod? Does that make sense? Can you see the risk here and why growth through unrelated diversification might cause problems? Research, in fact, is quite clear that business performance may decline for firms that get into too much unrelated diversification.[6]

Growth through vertical integration occurs by acquiring suppliers or distributors.

Diversification can also take the form of **vertical integration**. This is where a business acquires its suppliers *(backward vertical integration)* or its distributors *(forward vertical integration)*. Backward vertical integration has been a historical pattern in the automobile industry as firms purchased parts suppliers, although recent trends are to reverse this. It's now evident at Apple Computer, where the firm has bought chip manufacturers to give it more privacy and sophistication in developing microprocessors for products like the iPad. In beverages, both Coca-Cola and PepsiCo have pursued forward vertical integration by purchasing some of their major bottlers.

Restructuring and divestiture strategies focus on consolidation.

When organizations run into performance difficulties, perhaps because of too much growth and diversification, these problems have to be solved. A **retrenchment strategy** seeks to correct weaknesses by making radical changes to current ways of operating.

The most extreme form of retrenchment is **liquidation,** where a business closes down and sells its assets to pay creditors. A less extreme and more common form of retrenchment is **restructuring.** This involves making major changes to cut costs, gain short-term efficiencies, and buy time to try new strategies to improve future success.

When a firm is in desperate financial condition and unable to pay its bills, a situation faced by Chrysler and General Motors during the financial crisis, restructuring by **Chapter 11 bankruptcy** is an option under U.S. law. This protects the firm from creditors while management reorganizes things in an attempt to restore solvency. The goal is to emerge from bankruptcy as a stronger and profitable business, something achieved by both GM and Chrysler.

Downsizing is a restructuring approach that often makes the news. It cuts the size of operations and reduces the workforce.[7] When you learn of organizations downsizing by across-the-board cuts, however, you might be a bit skeptical. Research shows that downsizing is most successful when cutbacks are done selectively and focused on key performance objectives.[8]

Finally, restructuring by **divestiture** involves selling parts of the organization to refocus on core competencies, cut costs, and improve operating efficiency. This type of retrenchment often occurs when organizations have become overdiversified. An example is eBay's purchase for $3.1 billion of the Internet telephone

A **retrenchment strategy** changes operations to correct weaknesses.

Liquidation occurs when a business closes and sells its assets to pay creditors.

Restructuring reduces the scale or mix of operations.

Chapter 11 bankruptcy protects an insolvent firm from creditors during a period of reorganization to restore profitability.

Downsizing decreases the size of operations.

Divestiture involves selling off parts of the organization to refocus attention on core business areas.

{ MANAGERS RARELY HAVE THE LUXURY OF FULL INFORMATION BOXED UP FOR ANALYSIS IN A NICE NEAT CASE FORMAT.

Explore Yourself

■ CRITICAL THINKING

Strategic management requires managers to deal with a complex array of forces and uncertainties. All must be analyzed to craft a strategy that moves an organization forward with success.

Critical thinking is a "must have" for success in strategic management. It is what enables you to perceive problems, hone in on their more essential aspects, gather and interpret useful information, and make good decisions in complex conditions.

The same critical thinking that is part of a case study in your course is what helps managers create winning strategies. But with all the uncertainties that exist today, managers

rarely have the luxury of full information boxed up for analysis in a nice neat case format. Critical thinking in the real world must be multidimensional, and embrace both the systematic and intuitive aspects of decision making.

Get to know yourself better by taking the self-assessment on **Handling Facts and Inferences** and completing the other activities in the *Exploring Management* **Skill-Building Portfolio.**

service Skype. The expected synergies between Skype and eBay's online auction business never developed, and Skype was later sold to private investors.[9]

Global strategies focus on international business initiatives.

International business offers a variety of growth opportunities. Many large U.S. firms—including McDonald's, Intel, and Colgate-Palmolive, now get the majority of their revenues internationally. But, along with the growth opportunities of international business also come many challenges. And, firms strategically engage them in different ways.[10]

A **globalization strategy** adopts standardized products and advertising for use worldwide.

Firms pursuing a **globalization strategy** tend to view the world as one large market. They try to advertise and sell standard products for use everywhere. For example, Gillette sells and advertises its latest razors around the world; you get the same product in Italy or South Africa as in America.

Firms pursuing a *multidomestic strategy* customize products and advertising to fit local cultures and needs. Bristol Myers, Procter & Gamble, and Unilever all vary their products to match consumer preferences in different countries and cultures.[11]

A **transnational firm** tries to operate globally without having a strong national identity.

A third approach is the *transnational strategy*, where firms seek a balance between efficiencies in global operations and responsiveness to local markets. A **transnational firm** tries to operate without a strong national identity, hoping instead to blend with the global economy. Firms using a transnational strategy try to fully utilize business resources and tap customer markets worldwide. Ford, for example, draws on design, manufacturing, and distribution expertise all over the world to build car platforms. These are then modified within regions to build cars that meet local tastes.

{ THE WORK IS MEANINGLESS, NO CONVERSATION IS ALLOWED ON THE PRODUCTION LINES, AND BATHROOM BREAKS ARE LIMITED.

Ethics Check

■ LIFE AND DEATH AT AN OUTSOURCING FACTORY

A major outsourcing firm in China, Foxconn makes products for Apple, Dell, and Hewlett-Packard, among others. Over 250,000 people work in a huge complex stretching over 1 square mile in Shenzen, China. It's full of dormitories and includes restaurants and a hospital in addition to the factory spaces. And, the firm has experienced problems with employee suicides. Netting draped from the dormitories is designed to prevent suicidal employees from jumping to their death from the roofs.

One worker complains that the work is meaningless, no conversation is allowed on the production lines, and bathroom breaks are limited. Another says: "I do the same thing every day. I have no future." A supervisor points out that the firm

provides counseling services since most workers are young and this is the first time they have been away from their homes. "Without their families," says the supervisor, "they're left without direction. We try to provide them with direction and help."

YOU DECIDE

What ethical responsibilities do firms have when they contract for outsourcing in foreign plants? Whose responsibility is it to make sure workers are well treated? And as consumers, should we support bad practices by buying products from firms whose outsourcing partners are known to treat workers poorly?

Cooperative strategies focus on alliances and partnerships.

The trend today is toward more cooperation among organizations, often in **strategic alliances** where two or more organizations join together in partnership to pursue an area of mutual interest. A common form involves *outsourcing alliances*, contracting to purchase specialized services from another organization. Many organizations today, for example, are outsourcing their IT function to firms such as EDS, Infosys, and IBM. The belief is that these services are better provided by a firm with special expertise in this area.

Cooperation in the supply chain also takes the form of *supplier alliances*, which guarantee a smooth and timely flow of quality supplies among alliance partners. Another approach is cooperation in *distribution alliances*, in which firms join together to accomplish product or services sales and distribution.

Some cooperation strategies even involve strategic alliances with competitors. Known as **co-opetition**, it has been called a "revolution mindset" that business competitors can be cooperating partners.[12] United and Lufthansa are international competitors, but they cooperate in the Star Alliance network that allows customers to book each other's flights and share frequent flyer programs. Likewise, luxury car competitors Daimler and BMW are cooperating to co-develop new motors and components for hybrid cars.[13]

In a **strategic alliance,** organizations join together in partnership to pursue an area of mutual interest.

Co-opetition is the strategy of working with rivals on projects of mutual benefit.

E-business strategies focus on using the Internet for business success.

Without a doubt, most business executives today have been asked: "What is your **e-business strategy**?" This is the strategic use of the Internet to gain competitive advantage.[14] Table 7.1—*Web-Based Business Models*—lists some of the most common ways for doing this.

An **e-business strategy** strategically uses the Internet to gain competitive advantage.

Table 7.1 Web-Based Business Models

Advertising model: Providing free information or services and then generating revenues from paid advertising to viewers (e.g., Yahoo!, Google)

Brokerage model: Bringing buyers and sellers together for online business transactions and taking a percentage from the sales (e.g., eBay, Priceline)

Community model: Providing a meeting point sold by subscription or supported by advertising (e.g., eHarmony, Facebook)

Freemium model: Offering a free service and encouraging users to buy extras (e.g., Skype, Zynga)

Infomediary model: Providing free service in exchange for collecting information on users and selling it to other businesses (e.g., Epinions, Yelp)

Merchant model: E-tailing, or selling products direct to customers through the Web (e.g., Amazon, Apple, iTunes Store)

Referral model: Providing free listings and getting referral fees from online merchants for directing potential customers to them (e.g., Shopzilla, PriceGrabber)

Subscription model: Selling access to high-value content through a subscription Web site (e.g., Wall Street Journal Interactive, Netflix)

A **B2B business strategy** uses IT and Web portals to link organizations vertically in supply chains.

B2C business strategy uses IT and Web portals to link businesses with customers.

A **social media strategy** uses social media to better engage with an organization's customers, clients, and external audiences in general.

Crowdsourcing is strategic use of the Internet to engage customers and potential customers in providing opinions and suggestions on products and their designs.

B2B business strategies are business-to-business. They use the Web to vertically link organizations with members of their supply chains. For example, Dell Computer sets up special website services that allow its major corporate customers to manage their accounts online. Walmart links its suppliers to the firm's information systems so they can electronically manage inventories for their own products. **B2C business strategies** are business-to-customer. They use the Web to link businesses with customers. Whenever you buy a music download from Apple's iTunes Store, order a book from Amazon.com, or shop Patagonia.com for the latest outdoor gear, you are the "C" in a B2C strategy.

A lot of buzz today is on an organization's **social media strategy**. You can think of this as using social media such as Facebook or Twitter to better engage with an organization's customers, clients, and external audiences. How often do you hear or read "find us on Facebook"? That's what Procter & Gamble says. If you go to Facebook, you'll find a P&G page dedicated to Pampers. It's used to sell the product, host a forum for users to discuss the product, and encourage people to perform "Miracle Missions" that qualify them to enter free Pampers sweepstakes.

Crowdsourcing is a special type of social media strategy. It uses the Internet to engage customers and potential customers to make suggestions and express opinions on products and their designs. An example is Threadless.com. The firm's website allows online visitors to submit designs for tee shirts. The designs are voted on by other viewers—the "crowd," and top rated ones get selected for production and sale to customers.[15]

Manager's Library

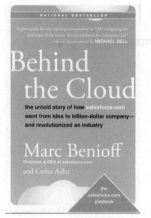

■ *BEHIND THE CLOUD* BY MARC BENIOFF AND CARLYE ADLER

WHICH NUMBERED KEY OPENS THE DOOR TO SUCCESS?

When Marc Benioff took time off from his executive software position to travel through India, he didn't realize his journey would transform not only him, but also the software industry and existing business paradigms. His chance meeting with a "hugging saint" yielded the first of several keys he later used to achieve personal and professional success.

In his book *Behind the Cloud* (2009, Jossey-Bass), Benioff records 111 management strategies he used to create and build Salesforce.com, the first SaaS (Software as a Service) business model. Before SaaS, software companies created huge and expensive programs to install on costly and problematic corporate systems. He pioneered "cloud computing," known as ASP (application service provisioning) in which software programs could be delivered by the Internet using remote hardware systems.

His book is written in the form of a playbook. The first tip is "Allow Yourself Time to Recharge" and the second is "Have a Big Dream." Others are "Define Your Values and Culture Up Front," "Create a Persona," and "Differentiate." "Differentiate" was achieved using "No Software" logos with a red circle and backslash, and print ads showing a jet fighter shooting down a biplane.

Sales insights include "Sell to the End User," not executives, "Don't Dis Your Product with a Discount" since they carry perceived risks, and "Sales Is a Numbers Game" so hire more salespeople to increase revenue. For corporate philanthropy he says "Make Your Foundation Part of Your Business Model," so he founded a 501(c)(3) and adopted a 1-1-1 model, donating 1% of Salesforce time, products, and equity.

REFLECT AND REACT

What was unique in the way Marc Benioff used the Internet to craft a unique business strategy? Does his "playbook" seem to offer insights valuable to others that might like to follow in his footsteps? How "sustainable" is the competitive advantage Salesforce.com now gets from cloud computing?

STUDY GUIDE

Takeaway 7.1
What Types of Strategies Are Used by Organizations?

Terms to Define

B2B business strategy

B2C business strategy

Business strategy

Chapter 11 bankruptcy

Competitive advantage

Concentration

Co-opetition

Corporate strategy

Crowdsourcing

Diversification

Divestiture

Downsizing

E-business strategy

Functional strategy

Globalization strategy

Growth strategy

Liquidation

Restructuring

Retrenchment strategy

Social media strategy

Strategic alliance

Strategic intent

Strategy

Sustainable competitive advantage

Transnational firm

Vertical integration

Rapid Review

- A strategy is a comprehensive plan that sets long-term direction for an organization and guides resource allocations to achieve competitive advantage, operating in ways that outperform the competition.
- Corporate strategy sets the direction for an entire organization; business strategy sets the direction for a large business unit or product division; functional strategy sets the direction within business functions.
- Growth strategies seek to expand existing business areas through concentration or add new ones by related or unrelated diversification.
- Retrenchment strategies try to streamline or consolidate organizations for better performance through restructuring and divestiture.
- Global strategies pursue international business opportunities.
- Cooperative strategies make business use of alliances and partnerships.
- E-business strategies use the Internet to pursue competitive advantage.

Questions for Discussion

1. With things changing so fast today, is it really possible for a business to achieve "sustainable" competitive advantage?
2. Why is growth such a popular business strategy?
3. Is it good news or bad news for investors when a business announces that it is restructuring?

Be Sure You Can

- differentiate strategy, strategic intent, and competitive advantage
- differentiate corporate, business, and functional levels of strategy
- list and explain major types of growth and diversification strategies
- list and explain restructuring and divestiture strategies
- explain alternative global strategies
- differentiate B2B and B2C as e-business strategies

What Would You Do?

A neighborhood business association has this set of members: coffee shop, bookstore, drugstore, dress shop, hardware store, and bicycle shop. The owners of these businesses are interested in how they might "cooperate" for better success. As a business consultant to the association, what would you propose as possible strategic alliances that would join sets of these businesses together for mutual gain?

Takeaway 7.2
How Do Managers Formulate and Implement Strategies?

ANSWERS TO COME

- The strategic management process formulates and implements strategies.
- Strategy formulation begins with the organization's mission and objectives.
- SWOT analysis identifies strengths, weaknesses, opportunities, and threats.
- Porter's five forces model examines industry attractiveness.
- Porter's competitive strategies model examines business or product strategies.
- Portfolio planning examines strategies across multiple businesses or products.
- Strategic leadership ensures strategy implementation and control.

THE LATE AND GREAT MANAGEMENT GURU PETER DRUCKER ONCE SAID: "THE future will not just happen if one wishes hard enough. It requires decision—now. It imposes risk—now. It requires action—now. It demands allocation of resources, and above all, of human resources—now. It requires work—now."[16] Drucker's views fit squarely with the chapter subtitle: Insight and hard work deliver results. Now's the time to talk more about the hard work of strategic management.

The strategic management process formulates and implements strategies.

Strategic management is the process of formulating and implementing strategies.

Strategic formulation is the process of creating strategies.

Figure 7.1 shows **strategic management** as the process of formulating and implementing strategies to accomplish long-term goals and sustain competitive advantage. **Strategy formulation** is the process of crafting strategy. It reviews current mission, objectives, and strategies, assesses the organization

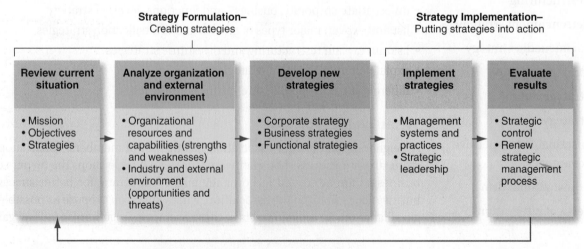

Strategy Formulation– Creating strategies

Strategy Implementation– Putting strategies into action

Review current situation	Analyze organization and external environment	Develop new strategies	Implement strategies	Evaluate results
• Mission • Objectives • Strategies	• Organizational resources and capabilities (strengths and weaknesses) • Industry and external environment (opportunities and threats)	• Corporate strategy • Business strategies • Functional strategies	• Management systems and practices • Strategic leadership	• Strategic control • Renew strategic management process

FIGURE 7.1 What Are the Steps in the Strategic Management Process?
The strategic management process involves responsibilities for both formulating and implementing organizational strategies. The process begins with review of existing mission, objectives, and strategies to set a baseline for further action. Next, organizational strengths and weaknesses as well as environmental opportunities and threats are analyzed. Strategies are then crafted at corporate, business, and functional levels. Finally, the strategies are put into action. This requires strategic leadership and control to ensure that all organizational resources and systems fully support strategy implementation.

and environment, and develops new strategies to deliver future competitive advantage. **Strategy implementation** is the process of putting strategies into action. It leads and activates the entire organization to put strategies to work.

Can you see that both activities are necessary, that success is only possible when strategies are both well formulated and well implemented? Competitive advantage in business or in a career doesn't just happen. It is created when great strategies are implemented to full advantage.

Strategy formulation begins with the organization's mission and objectives.

Strategy formulation begins with review of the organizational mission and current strategies objectives.[17] You should remember that the **mission** describes the purpose of an organization, its reason for existence in society.[18] The best organizations have clear missions that communicate a sense of direction and motivate members to work hard in their behalf.[19] They also link these missions with well-chosen **operating objectives** that serve as short-term guides to performance.[20] A sampling of typical business operating objectives includes: profitability, cost efficiency, market share, product quality, innovation, and social responsibility.

When mission and objectives are clear, a planning baseline is established. The next step in strategy formulation is to understand how well the organization is currently positioned to achieve competitive advantage.

SWOT analysis identifies strengths, weaknesses, opportunities, and threats.

A **SWOT** analysis involves a detailed examination of organizational *strengths* and *weaknesses* as well as environmental *opportunities* and *threats*. As **Figure 7.2** shows, the results of this examination can be portrayed in a straightforward and very useful planning matrix.

Strategy implementation is the process of putting strategies into action.

The **mission** is the organization's reason for existence in society.

Operating objectives are specific results that organizations try to accomplish.

A **SWOT analysis** examines organizational strengths and weaknesses, as well as environmental opportunities and threats.

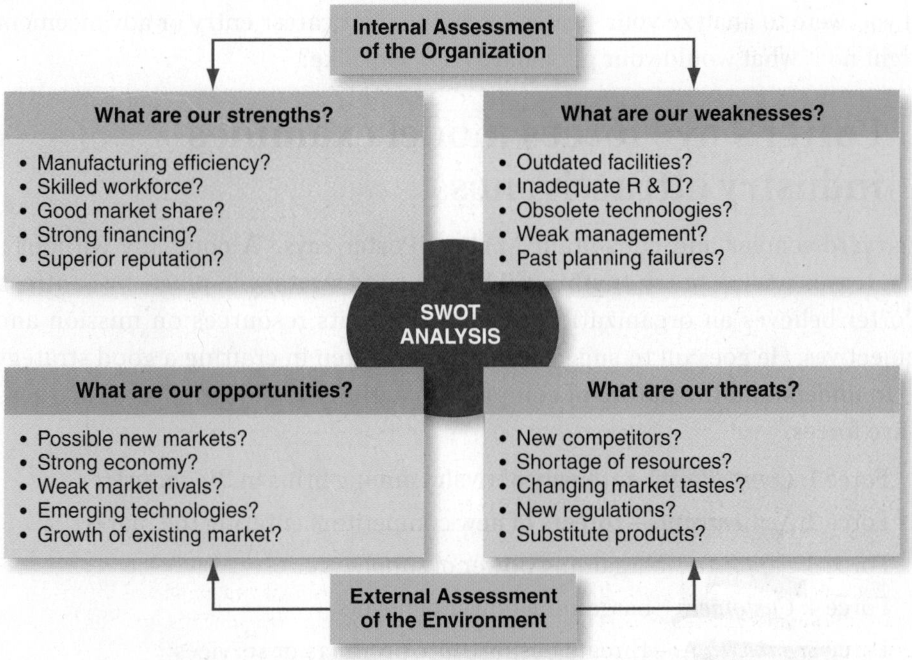

FIGURE 7.2
What Does a SWOT Analysis Try to Discover?
The SWOT analysis is a way of identifying organizational strengths and weaknesses as well as environmental opportunities and threats. It forces strategists to discover key facts and conditions with potential consequences for strategic performance. It also organizes this information in a structured manner that is useful for making strategy decisions. Managers using a SWOT analysis should be looking for organizational strengths that can be leveraged as core competencies to make future gains, as well as environmental opportunities that can be exploited.

{ OPERATING OBJECTIVES LINK MISSION AND ORGANIZATIONAL PERFORMANCE.

Tips to Remember

■ HOW TO ASSESS KEY OPERATING OBJECTIVES

When executives meet to discuss how well an organization is doing, these operating objectives are often under scrutiny:

- *Profits*—operating with revenues greater than costs
- *Cost efficiency*—operating with low costs; finding ways to lower costs
- *Market share*—having a solid and sustainable pool of customers
- *Product quality*—producing goods and services that satisfy customers

- *Talented workforce*—attracting and retaining high-quality employees
- *Innovation*—using new ideas to improve operations and products
- *Social responsibility*—earning the respect of multiple stake-holders
- *Sustainability*—developing sustainable processes, products, and supply chains

---

> A **core competency** is a special strength that gives an organization a competitive advantage.

When looking at the organization's strengths, one goal is to identify **core competencies**. These are special strengths that the organization has or does exceptionally well in comparison with its competitors. When an organization's core competencies are unique and costly for others to imitate, they become potential sources of competitive advantage.[21] Organizational weaknesses are the flip side of the picture. They must also be investigated and understood to develop a realistic perspective on the organization's capabilities.

The same discipline holds when examining conditions in the environment. It's not only the opportunities that count—such as new markets, a strong economy, weak competitors, and emerging technologies. The threats must also be considered—perhaps the emergence of new competitors, resource scarcities, changing customer tastes, and new government regulations.

By the way, don't forget the career planning implications of this discussion. If you were to analyze your strategic readiness for career entry or advancement right now, what would your personal SWOT look like?

‖ Porter's five forces model examines industry attractiveness.

Harvard scholar and consultant Michael Porter says, "A company without a strategy is willing to try anything."[22] With a good strategy in place, by contrast, Porter believes an organization can best focus its resources on mission and objectives. He goes on to suggest that the first step in crafting a good strategy is to understand the nature of competition within the industry based on these "five forces."

Force 1: *Competitors*—intensity of rivalry among firms in the industry

Force 2: *New entrants*—threats of new competitors entering the market

Force 3: *Suppliers*—bargaining power of suppliers

Force 4: *Customers*—bargaining power of buyers

Force 5: *Substitutes*—threats of substitute products or services[23]

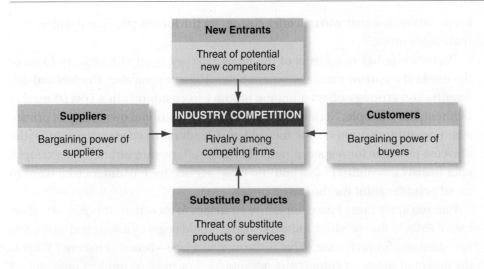

FIGURE 7.3
What Is Porter's Five Forces Model of Industry Attractiveness?
Strategic management is very challenging in an *unattractive industry* that has intense competitive rivalries, substantial threats in the form of possible new entrants and substitute products, and powerful suppliers and buyers who dominate any bargaining with the firm. Strategy management is less of a problem in an *attractive industry* that has little existing competition, few threats from new entrants or substitutes, and low bargaining power among suppliers and buyers.

Porter's five forces model of industry attractiveness is shown in Figure 7.3. An unattractive industry will have intense competitive rivalries, substantial threats in the form of possible new entrants and substitute products, and powerful suppliers and buyers who dominate any bargaining with the firm. As you might expect, this is a very challenging environment for strategy formulation.

A very attractive industry will have little existing competition, few threats from new entrants or substitutes, and low bargaining power among suppliers and buyers. These are much more favorable conditions for strategy formulation.

Porter's competitive strategies model examines business or product strategies.

Once industry forces are understood, attention shifts to how a business or its products can be strategically positioned relative to competitors. Porter believes that competitive strategies can be built around differentiation, cost leadership, and focus.

A **differentiation strategy** seeks competitive advantage through uniqueness. This means developing goods and services that are clearly different from the competition. The strategic objective is to attract customers who stay loyal to the firm's products and lose interest in those of its competitors.

Success with a differentiation strategy depends on customer perceptions of product quality and uniqueness. This requires organizational strengths in marketing, research and development, and creativity. An example is Polo Ralph Lauren, retailer of upscale classic fashions and accessories. In Ralph Lauren's words, "Polo redefined how American style and quality is perceived. Polo has always been about selling quality products by creating worlds and inviting our customers to be part of our dream."[24] If you've seen any Polo ads in magazines or on television, you'll know that the company aggressively markets this perception.

A **cost leadership strategy** seeks competitive advantage by operating with lower costs than competitors. This allows organizations to make profits while selling products or services at low prices their competitors can't profitably match. The objective is to continuously improve operating efficiencies in purchasing, production, distribution, and other organizational systems.

Success with the cost leadership strategy requires tight cost and managerial controls, as well as products or services that are easy to create and distribute. This is what might be called the "Walmart" strategy—do everything you can to

A **differentiation strategy** offers products that are unique and different from those of the competition.

A **cost leadership strategy** seeks to operate with lower costs than competitors.

keep costs so low that you can offer customers the lowest prices and still make a reasonable profit.[25]

Porter describes two forms of the focus strategy, both of which try to serve the needs of a narrow market segment better than anyone else. The **focused differentiation strategy** offers a unique product to customers in a special market segment. For example, NetJets offers air travel by fractional ownership of private jets to wealthy customers. The **focused cost leadership strategy** tries to be the low-cost provider for a special market segment. Low-fare airlines, for example, offer heavily discounted fares and "no frills" service for customers who want to travel point-to-point for the lowest prices.

Can you apply these four competitive strategies to an actual situation, say, alternative sodas in the soft-drink industry? Porter would begin by asking and answering two questions for each soda: What is the market scope—broad or narrow? What is the potential source of competitive advantage—low price or product uniqueness? Figure 7.4 shows how answers to these questions might strategically position some soft drinks with which you might be familiar.

The makers of Coke and Pepsi follow a differentiation strategy. They spend billions on advertising to convince consumers that their products are of high quality and uniquely desirable. Bubba Cola, a Save-A-Lot Brand, Go2 Cola, a Safeway Brand, sell as cheaper alternatives. In order to make a profit at the lower selling price, these stores must follow a cost leadership strategy.

What about a can of A & W Root Beer or a can of Mountain Dew? In Porter's model they represent a strategy of focused differentiation—products with unique tastes for customers wanting quality brands. This is quite different from the strategy behind Giant store's Quist or Stop & Shop's Sun Pop. These are classic cases of focused cost leadership—a product with a unique taste for customers who want a low price.

> A **focused differentiation strategy** offers a unique product to a special market segment.

> A **focused cost leadership strategy** seeks the lowest costs of operations within a special market segment.

Porter's Competitive Strategies

- *Differentiation*—make products that are unique and different.
- *Cost leadership*—produce at lower cost and sell at lower price.
- *Focused differentiation*—use differentiation and target needs of a special market.
- *Focused cost leadership*—use cost leadership and target needs of a special market.

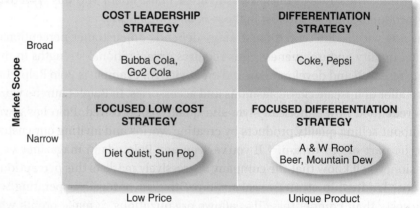

FIGURE 7.4 What Are the Strategic Options in Porter's Competitive Strategies Model? Porter's competitive strategies model asks two basic questions to identify alternative business and product strategies. First, what is the market scope—broad or narrow? Second, what is the expected source of competitive advantage—lower price or product uniqueness? The four possible combinations of answers result in differentiation, cost leadership, focused differentiation, and focused cost leadership strategies. The figure uses examples from the soft-drink industry to show how these strategies can be used for different products.

Portfolio planning examines strategies across multiple businesses or products.

As you might expect, strategic management gets quite complicated for companies that operate multiple businesses selling many different products and services. A good example is the global conglomerate General Electric. The firm owns a portfolio of diverse businesses ranging from jet engines, to capital services, to medical systems, to power systems, and even more. CEO Jeffrey Immelt faces a difficult strategic question all the time: How should GE's resources be allocated across this mix, or portfolio, of businesses?[26] These portfolio-planning questions are better made systematically than haphazardly.[27]

The Boston Consulting Group recommends a portfolio planning approach summarized in Figure 7.5 and known as the **BCG Matrix**. This strategic framework asks managers to analyze business and product strategies based on market growth rate and market share.[28]

Stars in the BCG Matrix have high market shares in high-growth markets. They produce large profits through substantial penetration of expanding markets. The preferred strategy for stars is growth. The BCG Matrix recommends making further resource investments in them. Stars are not only high performers in the present, they offer future potential to do the same or even more so.

Cash cows have high market shares in low-growth markets. They produce large profits and a strong cash flow, but with little upside potential. Because the markets offer little growth opportunity, the preferred strategy for cash cows is stability or modest growth. Like real dairy cows, the BCG Matrix advises firms to "milk" these businesses to generate cash for investing in other more promising areas.

Question marks have low market shares in high-growth markets. Although they may not generate much profit at the moment, the upside potential is there because of the growing markets. Question marks make for difficult strategic decision making. The BCG Matrix recommends targeting only the most promising question marks for growth, while retrenching those that are less promising.

Dogs have low market shares in low-growth markets. They produce little if any profit, and they have low potential for future improvement. The preferred strategy for dogs is straightforward: retrenchment by divestiture.

The **BCG Matrix** analyzes business opportunities according to market growth rate and market share.

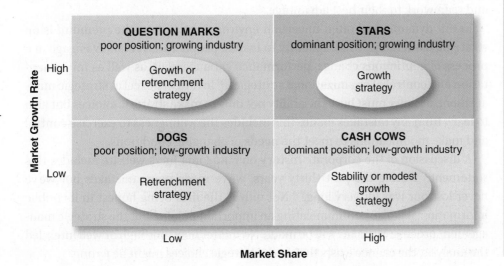

FIGURE 7.5

Why Is the BCG Matrix Useful in Strategic Planning?

The BCG Matrix is useful in situations where managers must make strategic decisions that allocate scarce organizational resources among multiple and competing uses. This is a typical situation for organizations that have a range of businesses or products. The BCG Matrix sorts businesses or products into four strategic types (dogs, stars, question marks, and cash cows), based on market shares held and market growth rates. Specific master strategies are recommended for each strategic type.

Climbing High with Patagonia, Inc.

Passion and Values Make for Strategic Success

Headquartered in Ventura, California, Patagonia sells top quality and high priced outdoor clothing and gear. That may seem like nothing special perhaps, but the company is noteworthy. It is known for a commitment to sustainability and respect for the natural environment.

Talk about unique. Patagonia's earnings are consistently above the industry average. Its workforce is loyal and inspired. And you are as likely to find its founder, Yvon Chouinard, climbing a mountain in Yosemite or the Himalayas as working in the office.

Most analysts would call Patagonia a strategic success story anchored to its clear mission: "Build the best product, cause no unnecessary harm, use business to inspire and implement solutions to the environmental crisis." There's no doubt Chouinard leads Patagonia with a personal commitment to sustainability and expects the firm to live up to its responsibilities as a steward of the natural environment. He says: "Most people want to do good things but don't. At Patagonia it's an essential part of your life."

FIND INSPIRATION

Yvon Chouinard believes in talent and self-control. "I have an M.B.A. theory of management," he says, "Management by Absence. I take off for weeks at a time and never call in. We hire the best people we can and then leave them to do their jobs." Can inspiring leadership be this easy?

Strategic leadership inspires people to implement organizational strategies.

Strategic leadership ensures strategy implementation and control.

The rest of *Exploring Management 3/e* is really all about strategy implementation. In order to successfully put strategies into action, the entire organization and all of its resources and systems must be mobilized in support of them. This, in effect, involves the complete management process—from planning and controlling through organizing and leading. No matter how well or elegantly planned, a strategy requires supporting structures, a good allocation of tasks and work-flow designs, and the right people to staff all aspects of operations. The strategy needs to be enthusiastically supported by leaders who are capable of motivating everyone, building individual performance commitments, and utilizing teams and teamwork to their best advantage.

In our dynamic and often-uncertain environment, in fact, the premium is on **strategic leadership**—the capability to inspire people to successfully engage in a process of continuous change, performance enhancement, as well as implementation and control of organizational strategies.[29] In order to excel at strategic management, a leader must have the ability not only to make strategic choices but also to learn from any mistakes made. This includes the willingness to exercise control and make modifications to meet the needs of changing conditions.

A discussion of the corporate history on Patagonia Inc.'s website includes this statement: "During the past thirty years, we've made many mistakes but we've never lost our way for very long."[30] Not only is the firm being honest in its public information, it is also communicating an important point about the strategic management process: Mistakes will be made. No matter how thorough or well intended the analysis, the chance exists that one's strategic choices might be wrong.

Facts to Consider

■ CEO PAY IS HEADING HIGH AGAIN

- Top paid CEOs for 2010 include: Philippe P. Daumon of Viacom—$84.3 million; Lawrence J. Ellison of Oracle—$68.6 million; Leslie Moonves of CBS—$53.9 million, and Michael White of DirecTV—$32.6 million.
- CEOs at S&P 500 firms earned average pay of $9 million. If the combined pay of the top 299 CEOs was used to hire workers earning the median wage, 102,325 of them could be employed.
- CEO and top executive compensation often includes a combination of salary, bonuses, long-term incentives, and stock grants.

- The Dodd-Frank Wall Street Reform and Consumer Protection Act of 2010 gives non-binding "say-on-pay" rights to shareholders of publicly traded companies, allowing them to voice opinions and concerns regarding executive compensation.

YOUR THOUGHTS?

Where do you stand on the issues of CEO pay? Is it too high across the board compared to what's happening to everyday workers? Or, is such high pay justified by the strategic leadership responsibilities these executives bear? How would you feel earning $55,000 per year at a firm whose CEO makes millions?

One of the big lessons learned in studying how business firms fared in the recent economic crisis is that a strategic leader has to maintain **strategic control**. This means that the CEO and other top managers should always be in touch with the strategy, know whether it is generating performance success or failure, and recognize when the strategy needs to be tweaked or changed.

Michael Porter, whose five forces and competitive strategy models for strategic management were discussed earlier, places a great emphasis on the role of CEO as chief strategist. He describes the task in the following ways.[31]

- *A strategic leader has to be the guardian of trade-offs*. It is the leader's job to make sure that the organization's resources are allocated in ways consistent with the strategy. This requires the discipline to sort through many competing ideas and alternatives to stay on course and not get sidetracked.

- *A strategic leader needs to create a sense of urgency*. The leader must not allow the organization and its members to grow slow and complacent. Even when doing well, the leader keeps the focus on getting better and being alert to conditions that require adjustments to the strategy.

- *A strategic leader must make sure that everyone understands the strategy*. Unless strategies are understood, the daily tasks and contributions of people lose context and purpose. Everyone might work very hard, but unless efforts are aligned with strategy, the impact is dispersed and fails to advance common goals.

- *A strategic leader must be a teacher*. It is the leader's job to teach the strategy and make it a "cause," says Porter. In order for strategy to work, it must become an ever-present commitment throughout the organization. This means that a strategic leader must be a great communicator. Everyone must understand the strategy and how it makes the organization different from others.

> **Strategic control** makes sure strategies are well implemented and that poor strategies are scrapped or changed.

STUDY GUIDE

Takeaway 7.2
How Do Managers Formulate and Implement Strategies?

Terms to Define

BCG Matrix

Core competencies

Cost leadership strategy

Differentiation strategy

Focused cost
leadership strategy

Focused differentiation
strategy

Mission

Operating objectives

Strategic control

Strategic leadership

Strategic management

Strategy formulation

Strategy
implementation

SWOT analysis

Rapid Review

- Strategic management is the process of formulating and implementing strategies to achieve a sustainable competitive environment.
- A SWOT analysis sets a foundation for strategy formulation by systematically assessing organizational strengths and weaknesses as well as environmental opportunities and threats.
- Porter's five forces model analyzes industry attractiveness in terms of competitors, threat of new entrants, substitute products, and the bargaining powers of suppliers and buyers.
- Porter's competitive strategies describes business and product strategies based on differentiation (distinguishing one's products from the competition), cost leadership (minimizing costs relative to the competition), and focus (concentrating on a special market segment).
- The BCG Matrix is a portfolio-planning approach that describes strategies for businesses classified as stars, cash cows, question marks, or dogs.
- Strategic leadership is the responsibility for activating people, organizational resources, and management systems to continually pursue and fully accomplish strategy implementation.

Questions for Discussion

1. Can an organization have a good strategy but a poor sense of mission?
2. Would a monopoly receive a perfect score for industry attractiveness in Porter's five forces model?
3. Does the BCG Matrix oversimplify a complex strategic management problem?

Be Sure You Can

- describe the strategic management process
- explain Porter's five forces model
- explain Porter's competitive strategies model
- describe the purpose and use of the BCG Matrix
- explain the responsibilities of strategic leadership

What Would You Do?

For some years now, you've owned a small specialty bookshop in a college town. You sell some textbooks but mainly cater to a broader customer base. The store always has the latest fiction, nonfiction, and children's books in stock. Recently, you've experienced a steep decline in overall sales, even for those books that would normally be considered best sellers. You suspect this is because of the growing popularity of e-books and e-readers such as the Amazon Kindle and Barnes & Noble Nook. Some of your friends say it's time to close up because your market is dying. Is it hopeless or is there a business strategy that might save you?

TestPrep 7

Multiple-Choice Questions

1. Which is the best question to ask when starting the strategic management process?
   - (a) "What is our mission?"
   - (b) "How well are we currently doing?"
   - (c) "How can we get where we want to be?"
   - (d) "Why aren't we doing better?"

2. The ability of a firm to consistently outperform its rivals is called _____.
   - (a) vertical integration
   - (b) competitive advantage
   - (c) strategic intent
   - (d) core competency

3. General Electric is a complex conglomerate that owns many firms operating in very different industries. The strategies pursued for each of these units within GE would best be called _____-level strategies.
   - (a) corporate
   - (b) business
   - (c) functional
   - (d) transnational

4. An organization that is downsizing by cutting staff to reduce costs can be described as pursuing a _____ strategy.
   - (a) liquidation
   - (b) divestiture
   - (c) retrenchment
   - (d) stability

5. When you buy music downloads online, the firm selling them to you is engaging in which type of e-business strategy?
   - (a) B2C
   - (b) B2B
   - (c) infomediary
   - (d) crowdsourcing

6. A _____ in the BCG Matrix would have a high market share in a low-growth market.
   - (a) dog
   - (b) cash cow
   - (c) question mark
   - (d) star

7. In Porter's five forces model, which of the following conditions is most favorable from the standpoint of industry attractiveness?
   - (a) many competitive rivals
   - (b) many substitute products
   - (c) low bargaining power of suppliers
   - (d) few barriers to entry

8. If Google's top management were to announce that the firm was going to buy Federal Express, this would indicate a growth strategy of _____.
   - (a) diversification
   - (b) concentration
   - (c) horizontal integration
   - (d) vertical integration

9. The alliances that link together firms in supply chain management relationships are examples of how businesses try to use _____ strategies.
   - (a) B2C
   - (b) growth
   - (c) cooperation
   - (d) concentration

10. Among the global strategies that international businesses might pursue, the _____ strategy most directly tries to tailor products to fit local needs and cultures in different countries.
    - (a) concentration
    - (b) globalization
    - (c) transnational
    - (d) multidomestic

11. When Coke and Pepsi spend millions on ads trying to convince customers that their products are unique, they are pursuing a _____ strategy.
    (a) transnational
    (b) concentration
    (c) diversification
    (d) differentiation

12. Porter's model of competitive strategies suggests a firm that wants to compete with its rivals in a broad market by selling a very-low-priced product would need to successfully implement a _____ strategy.
    (a) retrenchment
    (b) differentiation
    (c) cost leadership
    (d) diversification

13. _____ are special strengths that an organization has or does exceptionally well and that help it outperform competitors.
    (a) Core competencies
    (b) Strategies
    (c) Alliances
    (d) Operating objectives

14. The two questions asked by Porter to identify the correct competitive strategy for a business or product line are: 1—What is the market scope? 2—What is the _____?
    (a) market share
    (b) source of competitive advantage
    (c) core competency
    (d) industry attractiveness

15. Which is an example of a cooperative strategy?
    (a) retrenchment
    (b) strategic alliance
    (c) bankruptcy
    (d) vertical integration

Short-Response Questions

16. What is the difference between corporate strategy and functional strategy?

17. Why is a cost leadership strategy so important when one wants to sell products at lower prices than competitors?

18. What strategy should be pursued for a "question mark" in the BCG Matrix, and why?

19. What is strategic leadership?

Integration and Application Question

20. Kim Harris owns and operates a small retail store, selling the outdoor clothing of an American manufacturer to a predominantly college-student market. Lately, a large department store outside of town has started selling similar but lower-priced clothing manufactured in China, Thailand, and Bangladesh. Kim is starting to lose business to this store. She has asked your instructor to have a student team analyze the situation and propose some strategic alternatives to best deal with this threat. You are on the team.

    Questions: Why would a SWOT analysis be helpful in addressing Kim's strategic management problem? How could Porter's competitive strategies model be helpful as well?

StepsforFurtherLearning

Many learning resources are available at the end of the book and online within WileyPLUS.

Don't Miss These Selections from the **Skill-Building Portfolio**

■ **SELF-ASSESSMENT 7:** *Handling Facts and Inferences*

■ **CLASS EXERCISE 7:** *Strategic Scenarios*

■ **TEAM PROJECT 7:** *Contrasting Strategies*

Don't Miss This Selection from **Cases for Critical Thinking**

■ **CHAPTER 7 CASE**
Dunkin' Donuts: Betting Dollars on Donuts

Snapshot Once a niche company operating in the northeast, Dunkin' Donuts is opening hundreds of stores and entering new markets. At the same time, the java giant is expanding both its food and coffee menus to ride the wave of fresh trends, appealing to a new generation of customers. But is the rest of the world ready for Dunkin' Donuts? And can the company keep up with its own rapid growth?

The company is banking on mutually beneficial partnerships to help it achieve widespread marketplace prominence. If Dunkin' Donuts can find the sweet spot by being within most consumers' reach while falling just short of a Big Brother-like omnipresence, the company's strategy of expansion may well reward it very handsomely.

Make notes here on what you've learned about yourself from this chapter.

■ **LEARNING JOURNAL 7**

When Carol Bartz took over as Yahoo's CEO, she said the firm's organization chart was "odd" and "looked like a Dilbert cartoon."

Organization Structure and Design

It's All About Working Together

Management Live

Empowerment and *Patch Adams*

The movie *Patch Adams* is based on the true-life story of Hunter "Patch" Adams. In the movie, Adams (Robin Williams) becomes increasingly disillusioned with medical bureaucracy. After a heart-wrenching incident at the hospital where he volunteers, Adams is inspired to create a new kind of hospital—one free from the usual constraints. The idea involves unconventional methods of treatment. Doctors and patients work side-by-side; patients take responsibility for their own care. Adams believed medical treatment would be more effective when patients had control.

This is how **empowerment** works in any setting. It frees people to make decisions about how they work. It recognizes their full potential. While structures and processes are necessary, they only carry an organization so far. People are the real difference.

Think back to a time when you had a problem with a product or service. How was the situation resolved? Was the person with whom you dealt able to use discretion and make a decision on how to best resolve your problem?

As you read about organizational structures and designs, try to imagine the advantages and disadvantages of each. One thing is certain—organizations are only as good as the people who work within them. Too many managers fail to properly empower their employees and end up wondering why their organizations underperform.

YOUR CHAPTER 8 TAKEAWAYS

1. Understand organizing as a managerial responsibility.

2. Identify common types of organizational structures.

3. Recognize current trends in organizational design.

WHAT'S INSIDE

Explore Yourself
More on empowerment

Role Models
Alan Mulally makes mark by restructuring Ford

Ethics Check
Flattened into exhaustion

Facts to Consider
Bosses may be overestimating their managing skills

Manager's Library
The Truth About Middle Managers
by Paul Osterman

Takeaway 8.1
What Is Organizing as a Managerial Responsibility?

ANSWERS TO COME

- Organizing is one of the management functions.
- Organization charts describe the formal structures of organizations.
- Organizations also operate with informal structures.
- Informal structures have good points and bad points.

FIGURE 8.1   **What Is the Importance of Organizing in the Management Process?**
Organizing is one of the four management functions. It is the process of arranging people and resources to create structures so that they work well together in accomplishing goals. Key organizing decisions made by managers include those that divide up the work to be done, staff jobs with talented people, position resources for best utilization, and coordinate activities.

Organizing arranges people and resources to work toward a goal.

LIKE MOST THINGS, IT IS MUCH EASIER TO TALK ABOUT high-performing organizations than to actually create them. In true contingency fashion, there is no one best way to do things; no one organizational form meets the needs of all circumstances. And what works well at one moment in time can quickly become outdated, even dysfunctional, in another. This is why you often read and hear about organizations making changes and reorganizing in an attempt to improve their performance.

Nothing is constant in most organizations, at least not for long. This is a major reason why management scholar Henry Mintzberg points out that people often have problems.[1] Whenever job assignments and reporting relationships change, whenever the organization grows or shrinks, whenever old ways of doing things are reconfigured, people naturally struggle to understand the new ways of working. And perhaps even more importantly, they will worry about the implications for their jobs and careers.

Organizing is one of the management functions.

Most of us like to be organized—at home, at work, when playing games. We tend to get uncomfortable and anxious when things are disorganized. It shouldn't surprise you, therefore, that people in organizations need answers to such questions as: "Where do I fit in?" "How does my work relate to that of others?" "Who runs things?"[2] People need these answers when they first join an organization, when they take new jobs, and whenever things are substantially changed.

This is where and why **organizing** comes into play as one of the four functions of management shown in Figure 8.1. It is the process of arranging people and resources to work together to accomplish goals. Planning sets the goals; through organizing, managers begin to carry them out.[3]

Organization charts describe the formal structures of organizations.

When managers organize things, they arrange people and jobs into meaningful working relationships. They clarify who is to do what, who is in charge of whom, and how different people and work units are supposed to cooperate. This creates what we call the **organization structure**, a formal arrangement that links the various parts of an organization to one another.

You probably know the concept of structure best in terms of an **organization chart**. This is a diagram, like the one in the nearby figure, of positions and reporting relationships within an organization.[4] A typical organization chart identifies major job titles and shows the hierarchy of authority and communication that links them together. It describes the organization's **division of labor**—people and groups performing different jobs, ideally ones for which they are well skilled.

Check out Table 8.1—*What You Can Learn from an Organization Chart*. And indeed you can learn quite a bit from an organization chart, but only in respect to the **formal structure**. This is the "official" structure, or the way things are supposed to operate. It aligns positions, people, and responsibilities in the best ways. But as things change over time, managers find themselves tinkering with the formal structure to get the alignment right. And sometimes, the current structure doesn't make sense. When Carol Bartz asked to see Yahoo's organization chart before taking over as CEO, for example, she said: "It was like a Dilbert cartoon. It was very odd." Her response was: "You need management here."[5]

Problems with the organization structure were evident during recent performance failures in large companies such as General Motors, AIG, and Citibank. Some blame the failures on structures that allowed the same person to be both chairman of the board and CEO. What happens to corporate governance in such cases where the CEO essentially reports to himself or herself? How does this structure provide for critical oversight of top management? As you might expect, many firms are now changing their organization charts to separate the job of board chairman from that of CEO. The goal is to strengthen governance by not allowing the same person to fill both positions.[6]

Organization structure is a system of tasks, reporting relationships, and communication linkages.

An **organization chart** describes the arrangement of work positions within an organization.

The **division of labor** means that people and groups perform different jobs.

Formal structure is the official structure of the organization.

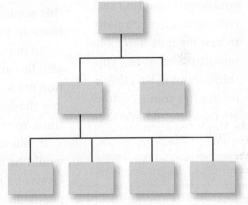

Table 8.1 What You Can Learn from an Organization Chart

Division of work—Positions and titles show work responsibilities.

Supervisory relationships—Lines between positions show who reports to whom in the chain of command.

Span of control—The number of persons reporting to a supervisor.

Communication channels—Lines between positions show routes for formal communication flows.

Major subunits—How jobs are grouped together in work units, departments, or divisions.

Staff positions—Staff specialists who support other positions and parts of the organization.

Levels of management—The number of management layers from top to bottom.

Lots to Learn at Build-A-Bear

Organizing Is Like Creating a Work of Art

Maxine Clark started Build-A-Bear Workshop Inc. with a simple concept: Pick out a bear or bunny or turtle that you like, add stuffing, and then personalize your own pet with clothing, shoes, and accessories. Each pet is unique—soccer player, teacher, doctor . . . you name it—and tailored to the user's tastes and interests.

Each Build-A-Bear store is arranged in a streamlined production process. Guest Bear Builders move along the Bear Pathway from the Choose Me workstation on to Stuff Me and finally to Name Me as their personal creation takes shape. Sounds a lot like organizations, doesn't it? Until you get to the "making it personal" part. That's where organizations often struggle—how to bring together hundreds, thousands, even hundreds of thousands of people in arrangements that make sense and allow personal talents to shine through.

FIND INSPIRATION

More expansion continues to be in the cards for Build-A-Bear. Clark's current challenge is to manage the growth by continually adapting and redesigning her company to best meet its new global opportunities. When you think about it, isn't this a lot like her young customers who love to build their own bears?

The **informal structure** is the set of unofficial relationships among an organization's members.

Social network analysis identifies the informal structures and their embedded social relationships that are active in an organization.

‖ Organizations also operate with informal structures.

Picture this scene: A worker his office cubicle overhears a conversation taking place in the next cubicle. Words such as "project being terminated" and "job cuts will be necessary" are used. At lunch he shares this with friends; word quickly spreads that their employer is going to announce layoffs. What's happening in this scenario falls outside of the formal structure of the organization; it takes place in the "shadows."

An important fact of organizational life is that behind every formal structure also lies an **informal structure**. You might think of this as a shadow organization made up of unofficial relationships between organizational members. Like any shadow, the shape of the informal structure will be blurry and change with time. You may have to work hard to understand its full complexities.

If you could draw the informal structure for your organization—and this would be an interesting exercise—you would find relationships cutting across levels and moving from side to side. Some would be work-related, reflecting how people have found the best ways to get their jobs done. Many others would be personal, reflecting who meets for coffee, stops in for office chats, meets together in exercise groups, and spends time together as friends, not just co-workers.[7]

A tool known as **social network analysis** is one way of identifying the informal structures and their embedded social relationships that are active in an organization. It asks people to identify others whom they turn to for help most often, whom they communicate with regularly, and who energizes and de-energizes them.[8] The results of a social network analysis are often described as a map with lines running from person to person according to frequency of communication and type of relationship maintained. The map shows who is linked with whom and how a lot of work really gets done in organizations, in contrast to the formal arrangements shown on the organization chart. This information can be used to redesign the formal structure for better performance, and identify who the key people are for possible leadership and mentoring roles.[9]

Informal structures have good points and bad points.

Lots happens in the emergent and spontaneous relationships of informal structures, as depicted in the small figure. One of the first things you probably learned in college was that knowing secretaries and departmental assistants is a very good way to get into classes that are "closed" or find out about new courses that will be offered. Think about all the different ways you use informal structures to get things done. Most people in most organizations do the same.

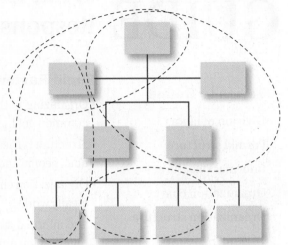

Let's start with the good points of informal structures and social networks. As just pointed out, they can be very helpful in getting work accomplished. Indeed, they may be essential in many ways to organizational success.

The relationships available in the informal structure are often important in helping people learn their jobs and solve problems while doing them. This occurs as people assist one another not because the structure requires it, but because they know and like one another. Informal relationships also provide a lot of social and emotional support. They give people access to friendships, conversations, and advice that can help make the normal workday pleasant and a bad workday less troublesome.

Informal structures can be especially helpful during times of change, when out-of-date formal structures just don't deal well with new or unusual situations. Because it takes time to change or modify formal structures, the informal structure helps fill the void. For these reasons and possibly more, it can be argued that informal structures are essential for any organization to succeed. They fill gaps missing in the formal structure and help compensate for its inadequacies.

Now let's consider the potential bad points of informal structures. Because they exist outside the formal system, things that happen in informal structures may work against the best interests of the organization as a whole. These shadow structures can be susceptible to rumor, carry inaccurate information, breed resistance to change, and even distract members from their work. And if you happen to end up as an "outsider" rather than an "insider in the informal networks," you may feel less a part of things. Some American managers in Japanese firms, for example, have complained about being excluded from what they call the "shadow cabinet"—an informal group of Japanese executives who hold the real power and sometimes act to the exclusion of others.[10]

The Society for Human Resource Management reported that after the economy suffered a round of massive layoffs, human resource (HR) professionals observed in their firms a 23% increase in workplace eavesdropping and a 54% increase in "gossip and rumors about downsizings and layoffs." Cafeterias are hotspots for gossip, and one HR director says she even notices people trying to hang out in hallways and sit as close as possible to executives in cafeterias in attempts to overhear conversations. A manager says he does his own eavesdropping to try to learn what he can from employee conversations; he calls this "alert listening."[11]

STUDY GUIDE

Takeaway 8.1
What Is Organizing as a Managerial Responsibility?

Terms to Define

Division of labor

Formal structure

Informal structure

Organization chart

Organization structure

Organizing

Social network analysis

Rapid Review

- Organizing is the process of arranging people and resources to work toward a common goal.
- Structure is the system of tasks, reporting relationships, and communication that links people and positions within an organization.
- Organization charts describe the formal structure and how an organization should ideally work.
- The informal structure of an organization consists of the unofficial relationships that develop among its members.
- Informal structures create helpful relationships for social support and task assistance, but they can be susceptible to rumors.

Questions for Discussion

1. Why is organizing such an important management function?
2. If organization charts are imperfect, why bother with them?
3. Could an organization consistently perform well without the help of its informal structure?

Be Sure You Can

- explain what you can learn from an organization chart
- differentiate formal and informal structures
- discuss potential good and bad points about informal structures

What Would You Do?

As the new manager of a branch bank location, you will be supervising 22 employees, most of whom have worked together for a number of years. How will you identify the informal structure of the branch? And, how will you try to use this structure to your advantage while establishing yourself as an effective manager in the new situation?

Takeaway 8.2
What Are the Most Common Types of Organization Structures?

ANSWERS TO COME

- Functional structures group together people using similar skills.
- Divisional structures group together people by products, customers, or locations.
- Matrix structures combine the functional and divisional structures.
- Team structures use many permanent and temporary teams.
- Network structures extensively use strategic alliances and outsourcing.

A TRADITIONAL PRINCIPLE OF ORGANIZING IS THAT HIGH PERFORMANCE DEPENDS on having a good division of labor whose parts are well coordinated. The process of arranging people by tasks and work groups is called **departmentalization**.[12] The most basic forms are the functional, divisional, matrix, team, and network structures. As you read about each, don't forget that organizations rarely use only one type of structure. Most often they will use a mixture, with different parts and levels having different structures because of their unique needs.

> **Departmentalization** is the process of grouping together people and jobs into work units.

⦀ Functional structures group together people using similar skills.

Take a look at Figure 8.2 on the next page. What organizing logic do you see? These are **functional structures** where people having similar skills and performing similar tasks are grouped together into formal work units. The assumption is that if the functions are well chosen and each acts properly, the organization should operate successfully. In business, for example, typical functions include marketing, finance, accounting, production, management information systems, and human resources. But functional structures are not limited to businesses. The figure also shows how other organizations such as banks and hospitals may use them.

> A **functional structure** groups together people with similar skills who perform similar tasks.

Functional structures work well for small organizations that produce only one or a few products or services. They also tend to work best for organizations, or parts of organizations, that have relatively stable environments where the problems are predictable and demands for change are limited. And they offer benefits to individuals. Within a given function—say, marketing—people share technical expertise, interests, and responsibilities. They can also advance in responsibilities and pursue career paths within the function.

Although functional structures have a clear logic, there are some potential downsides as well. When an organization is divided into functions it can be hard to pinpoint responsibilities for things such as cost containment, product or service quality, and innovation. And with everyone focused on meeting

Potential Advantages of Functional Structures

- Economies of scale make efficient use of human resources.
- Functional experts are good at solving technical problems.
- Training within functions promotes skill development.
- Career paths are available within each function.

FIGURE 8.2
What Does a Typical Functional Organization Structure Look Like?
Functional structures are common in organizations of all types and sizes. In a typical business you might have vice presidents or senior managers heading the traditional functions of accounting, human resources, finance, manufacturing, marketing, and sales. In a bank, they may head such functions as loans, investments, and trusts. In a hospital, managers or administrators are usually in charge of functions such as nursing, clinics, and patient services.

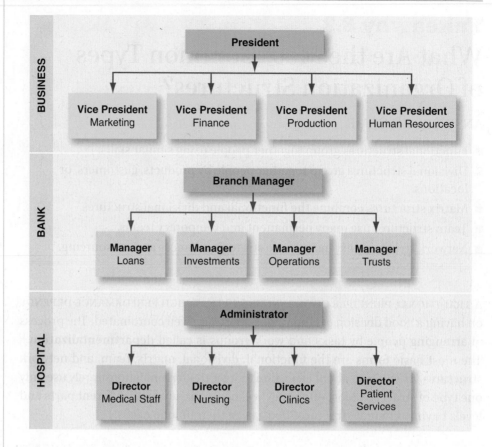

The **functional chimneys** or **functional silos problem** is a lack of communication and coordination across functions.

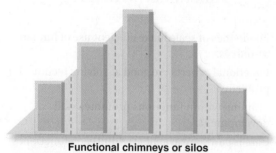

Functional chimneys or silos
- Too little communication across functions
- Too many problems referred upward for solution

functional goals, the sense of working for the good of the organization as a whole may get lost. People may also find that they get trapped in functional career niches that are hard to break out of in order to gain career-broadening experiences in other areas.

Another concern is something that you might hear called the **functional chimneys** or **functional silos problem**. Shown in the small figure, this problem occurs as a lack of communication, coordination, and problem solving across functions. Instead of cooperating with one another, members of functional units sometimes end up either competing or selfishly focusing on functional goals rather than broader organizational objectives. CEO Carol Bartz described a functional silo problem she discovered at Yahoo this way: "The home page people didn't want to drive traffic to the finance page because they wanted to keep them on the home page."[13] Such problems of poor cooperation and even just plain lack of helpfulness across functions can be very persistent. It often takes alert and strong managers such as Bartz to get things resolved.

Mars Inc. is the world's largest candy company and, like most firms of its size, it also suffers from the functional chimneys problem. When Paul Michaels took over as CEO, he says "the top team was siloed and replete with unspoken agendas. Members did not see the benefit of working together as a team; they were only concerned about success in their own region." Michaels's solution was to break the habits of functional thinking by realigning people and mindsets around teams and teamwork.[14]

Divisional structures group together people by products, customers, or locations.

A second organizational alternative is the **divisional structure** shown in Figure 8.3. It groups together people who work on the same product, serve similar customers, and/or are located in the same area or geographical region.[15]

The basic idea is to overcome the disadvantages of a functional structure, such as the functional chimneys problem. Toyota, for example, shifted to a divisional structure in its North American operations during the recent economic crisis. Engineering, manufacturing, and sales were brought together under a common boss, instead of each function reporting to its own top executive. One analyst said the problem was that "every silo reported back to someone different" and "they need someone in charge of the whole choir."[16]

A **divisional structure** groups together people working on the same product, in the same area, or with similar customers.

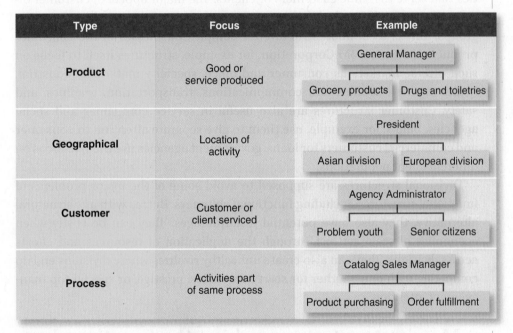

Type	Focus	Example
Product	Good or service produced	General Manager — Grocery products / Drugs and toiletries
Geographical	Location of activity	President — Asian division / European division
Customer	Customer or client serviced	Agency Administrator — Problem youth / Senior citizens
Process	Activities part of same process	Catalog Sales Manager — Product purchasing / Order fulfillment

FIGURE 8.3   What Are Some Ways Organizations Use Divisional Structures? In products structures, divisions are based on the product or service provided, such as consumer products and industrial products. In geographic structures, divisions are based on geography or territories, such as an Asia–Pacific division and a North American division. In customer structures, divisions are based on customers or clients served, such as graduate students and undergraduate students in a university.

Product structures group together jobs and activities devoted to a single product or service. They identify a common point of managerial responsibility for costs, profits, problems, and successes in a defined market area. An expected benefit is that the product division will be able to respond quickly and effectively to changing market demands and customer tastes. When Fiat took over Chrysler after it emerged from bankruptcy, CEO Sergio Marchionne said he wanted a new structure to "speed decision making and improve communication flow." He reorganized into product divisions for the firm's three brands—Chrysler, Jeep, and Dodge. Each was given its own chief executive and assigned responsibility for its own profits and losses.[17] The "new" General Motors took the same approach

A **product structure** groups together people and jobs working on a single product or service.

Potential Advantages of Divisional Structures

- Expertise is focused on special products, customers, or regions.
- Better coordination exists across functions within divisions.
- There is better accountability for product or service delivery.
- It is easier to grow or shrink in size as conditions change.

A **geographical structure** brings together people and jobs performed in the same location.

A **customer structure** groups together people and jobs that serve the same customers or clients.

A **matrix structure** combines functional and divisional approaches to emphasize project or program teams.

A **cross-functional team** brings together members from different functional departments.

---

and reorganized around four product divisions—Buick, Cadillac, Chevrolet, and GMC.[18]

Geographical structures, or *area structures,* group together jobs and activities in the same location or geographical region. Companies use geographical divisions when they need to focus attention on the unique product tastes or operating requirements of particular regions. As UPS operations expanded worldwide, for example, the company announced a change from a product to a geographical organizational structure. The company created two geographical divisions—the Americas and Europe/Asia—with each area responsible for its own logistics, sales, and other business functions.

Customer structures group together jobs and activities that serve the same customers or clients. The major appeal of customer divisions is the ability to best serve the special needs of the different customer groups. This is a common structure for complex businesses in the consumer products industries. 3M Corporation, for example, structures itself to focus on such diverse markets as consumer and office, specialty materials, industrial, health care, electronics and communications, transportation, graphics, and safety. Customer structures are also useful in service companies and social agencies. Banks, for example, use them to give separate attention to consumer and commercial customers for loans; government agencies use them to focus on different client populations.

Divisional structures are supposed to avoid some of the major problems of functional structures, including functional chimneys. But, as with any structural alternative, they also have potential disadvantages. They can be costly when economies of scale get lost through the duplication of resources and efforts across divisions. They can also create unhealthy rivalries where divisions end up competing with one another for scarce resources, prestige, or special top management attention.

‖ Matrix structures combine the functional and divisional structures.

The **matrix structure,** often called the *matrix organization,* combines the functional and divisional structures to try to gain the advantages of each. This is accomplished by setting up permanent teams that operate across functions to support specific products, projects, or programs.[19] Workers in a typical matrix structure, like **Figure 8.4,** belong to at least two formal groups at the same time—a functional group and a product, program, or project team. They also report to two bosses—one within the function and the other within the team.

The use of permanent **cross-functional teams** in matrix structures creates several potential advantages. These are teams whose members come together from different functional departments to work on a common task. Everyone, regardless of his or her departmental affiliation, is required to work closely with others and focus on team goals—no functional chimneys thinking is allowed. Expertise and information is shared to solve problems at the team level and make sure that things get accomplished in the best ways possible.

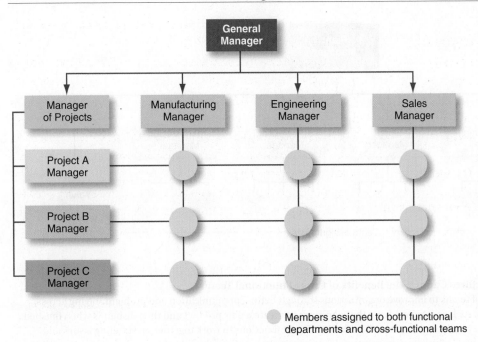

How Does a Matrix Structure Combine Functional and Divisional Structures?
A matrix structure is designed to combine the best of the functional and divisional forms. In a typical matrix, the normal functions create a traditional vertical structure, with heads of marketing and manufacturing, and so on. Then a new horizontal structure is added to create cross-functional integration. This is done using teams that are staffed by members from the functions.

Still, matrix structures aren't perfect; they can't overcome all the disadvantages of their functional and divisional parents. The two-boss system of the matrix can lead to power struggles if functional supervisors and team leaders make confusing or conflicting demands on team members. Matrix structures can be costly because they require a whole new set of managers to lead the cross-functional teams.[20] And as you might guess, team meetings in the matrix can be time consuming.

The matrix structure has gained a strong foothold in the workplace. Applications are found in such diverse settings as manufacturing (e.g., aerospace, electronics, pharmaceuticals), service industries (e.g., banking, brokerage, retailing), professional fields (e.g., accounting, advertising, law), and the nonprofit sector (e.g., government agencies, hospitals, universities).

Potential Advantages of Matrix Structures

- Performance accountability rests with program, product, or project managers.
- Better communication exists across functions.
- Teams solve problems at their levels.
- Top managers spend more time on strategy.

⦀ Team structures use many permanent and temporary teams.

Some organizations are adopting **team structures** that extensively use permanent and temporary teams to solve problems, complete special projects, and accomplish day-to-day tasks.[21] As **Figure 8.5** on the next page shows, these teams are often formed across functions and staffed with members whose talents match team tasks.[22] The goals are to reduce the functional chimneys problem, tap the full benefits of group decision making, and gain as much creativity in problem solving as possible. At Polaroid Corporation a research team developed a new medical imaging system in three years, when most had predicted it would take six. As one Polaroid executive noted, "Our researchers are not any smarter, but by working together they get the value of each other's intelligence almost instantaneously."[23]

A **team structure** uses permanent and temporary cross-functional teams to improve lateral relations.

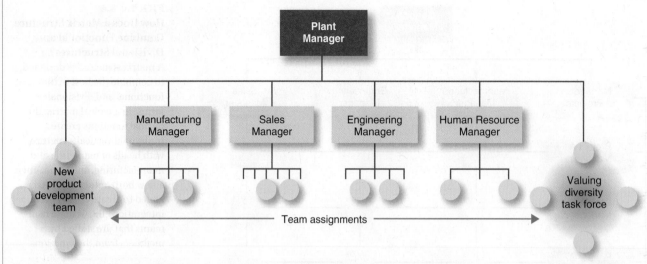

FIGURE 8.5   How Do Team Structures Capture the Benefits of Cross-Functional Teams?
Team structures make extensive use of teams to improve organizations through better communication and problem solving across functions. Some teams are temporary, such as a project team that convenes to create a new product and then disbands when finished. Other teams are more permanent. They bring together members from different functions to work together on standing issues and common problems, such as quality control, diversity management, labor-management relations, or health care benefits.

Potential Advantages of Team Structures

- Team assignments improve communication, cooperation, and decision making.
- Team members get to know each other as persons, not just job titles.
- Team memberships boost morale and increase enthusiasm and task involvement.

Things don't always work this well in team structures, however, since the complexities of teams and teamwork can create other problems. As with the matrix, team members sometimes have to deal with conflicting loyalties between their team and functional assignments. Teamwork always takes time. And as in any team situation, the quality of results often depends on how well the team is managed and how well team members gel as a group. This is why you'll most likely find that organizations with team structures invest heavily in team building and team training.

‖ Network structures extensively use strategic alliances and outsourcing.

A **network structure** uses IT to link with networks of outside suppliers and service contractors.

Another development in organizational structures uses strategic alliances and outsourcing to dramatically reduce the need for full-time staff. Shown in Figure 8.6, a **network structure** links a central core of full-time employees with "networks" of relationships to outside contractors and partners that supply essential services. Because the central core is relatively small and the surrounding networks can be expanded or shrunk as needed, the potential advantages are lower costs, more speed, and greater flexibility in dealing with changing environments.[24]

The example in Figure 8.6 shows a network structure for a company that sells lawn and deck furniture over the Internet and by mail order. The firm employs only a few full-time "core" employees. Other business requirements are met through a network of alliances and outsourcing relationships. A consultant creates product designs, while suppliers produce them at low-cost sites around the world. A supply chain management firm gets products shipped to and distributed

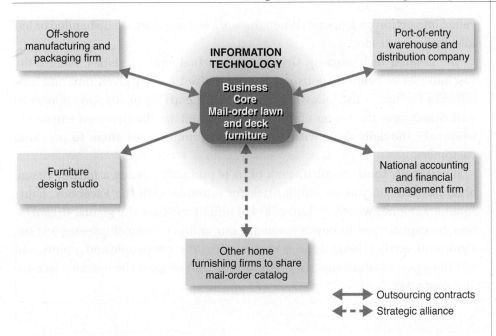

FIGURE 8.6

How Do Network Structures Take Advantage of Strategic Alliances and Outsourcing? Organizations using network structures replace some full-time positions and functions with services provided by alliance partners and outsourcing contractors. In these structures, "core" employees perform essential operations at the center of a "network" that links them with a shifting mix of outside partners and contractors. The example in this figure shows that a small group of people can run a mail-order business in this manner. A lot of network activities are made easy and cost efficient by using the latest information technologies.

from an outsourced warehouse. A quarterly catalog is mailed as part of a strategic alliance with two other firms that sell different home furnishings. Accounting services are outsourced. Even the company Web site that supports customer and network relationships is maintained by an outside contractor.

This may sound a bit radical, but it isn't. It is an increasingly common arrangement that raises lots of entrepreneurial opportunities. Could the growing popularity of network organization concepts make it easier for you to start your own business someday?

If network structures are highly streamlined, efficient, and adaptable, don't you wonder why even more organizations aren't adopting them? Part of the answer may lie in inertia, simply being caught up in old ways and finding it very hard to change. Another reason is the management complication of having to deal with a vast and sometimes shifting network of contracts and alliances.

When one part of the network breaks down or fails to deliver, the entire system may suffer the consequences. The recent Japanese tsunami and nuclear disaster is a good case in point. Many global firms suffered when their Japanese contractors and partners had to shut down or scale back operations. Too much reliance on outsourcing might also have hidden costs. Not too long ago, for example, Delta Air announced that it was shutting down its call-center operations in India because so many customers complained about communication difficulties with service providers.[25]

As information technology continues to evolve, a variation of the network structure is appearing. Called the **virtual organization**, it uses information technologies to operate a constantly shifting network of alliances.[26] The goal is to use virtual networks to eliminate boundaries that traditionally separate a firm from its suppliers and customers, and its internal departments and divisions from one another. The intense use of IT allows virtual relationships to be

Potential Advantages of Network Structures

- Lower costs due to fewer full-time employees.
- Better access to expertise through specialized alliance partners and contractors.
- Easy to grow or shrink with market conditions.

A **virtual organization** uses information technologies to operate as a shifting network of alliances.

called into action on demand. When the work is done, they are disbanded or left idle until next needed.

The popular tech start-up Groupon has virtual characteristics. Picture the vast number of coupon sponsors that are actived on any given day, and how different the mix is the following day. Picture the arrays of coupon clippers as well. Standing at the center of this virtual network are the Groupon employees who make the daily deals with retailers and communicate them to potential customers.

If you really think about it, each of us is probably already a part of virtual organizations. Do you see similarities, for example, with the Facebook, Foursquare, Tumblr, Twitter, or LinkedIn communities? Isn't the virtual organization concept similar to how we manage our online relationships—signing on, signing off, getting things done as needed with different people and groups, and all taking place instantaneously, temporarily, and without the need for face-to-face contacts?

Manager's Library

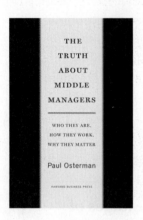

THE
TRUTH
ABOUT
MIDDLE
MANAGERS

WHO THEY ARE,
HOW THEY WORK,
WHY THEY MATTER

Paul Osterman

HARVARD BUSINESS PRESS

■ *THE TRUTH ABOUT MIDDLE MANAGERS* BY PAUL OSTERMAN

HEROES, VILLAINS, AND THE REINVENTION OF MIDDLE MANAGEMENT

Modern organizations still rely largely on hierarchical efficiencies. A few top executives determine hourly work for many below, while managers in-between align those decisions and actions. Expectations of middle managers shift as organizations adapt to swings in the economy and they are revealed as heroes, or cast as villains.

Now middle managers have undergone a makeover as organizations restructure. They've reinvented their roles to match new organizational demands.

In the book *The Truth About Middle Managers* (2008, Harvard Business School Publishing Corporation), Paul Osterman describes the changing landscape for managers nestled between levels of top management and hourly workers. Restructuring trends—fewer levels of management between top management and hourly workers, and fewer employees overall—require middle managers to assume broader duties and work longer hours. They have less autonomy since top managers are closer in the hierarchy, and less control as information technology allows monitoring and feedback, anytime, anywhere.

Osterman finds middle managers have increased job insecurity due to restructuring. Job tenure, or length of time spent with one employer, is decreasing and they are more likely to job hop. Stress has increased due to new realities, and they are less loyal to employers. They see top management as greedy, self-serving, and distant, and are frustrated by executive hires outside the organization. Many lose ambition since flat hierarchies mean fewer paths to the top.

Despite the challenges, Osterman believes middle managers are highly committed to their work. They enjoy their jobs as craft and thrive on skill execution. Restructuring has pushed high level duties upon many, and they welcome new strategic roles. They make key decisions involving resource allocations and negotiations with varied interests. They spend more time in informal interaction and unplanned activities, and experience more variety and complexity in assignments.

REFLECT AND REACT

Organizations now have fewer management levels and employees, so how would you describe middle management jobs and skills? Middle managers view work not only as a means to an end—money or promotion, but an end in itself—craftwork and fulfillment. Why is this? And by the way, what is the future likely to hold for middle managers as more organizations take on team, network, and virtual characteristics?

STUDY GUIDE

Takeway 8.2
What Are the Most Common Types of Organization Structures?

Terms to Define

Cross-functional teams

Customer structure

Departmentalization

Divisional structure

Functional chimneys, or functional silos, problem

Functional structure

Geographic structure

Matrix structure

Network structure

Product structure

Team structure

Virtual organization

Rapid Review

- Functional structures group together people using similar skills to perform similar activities.
- Divisional structures group together people who work on a similar product, work in the same geographical region, or serve the same customers.
- A matrix structure uses permanent cross-functional teams to try to gain the advantages of both the functional and divisional approaches.
- Team structures make extensive use of permanent and temporary teams, often cross-functional ones, to improve communication, cooperation, and problem solving.
- Network structures maintain a staff of core full-time employees and use contracted services and strategic alliances to accomplish many business needs.

Questions for Discussion

1. Why use functional structures if they are prone to functional chimneys problems?
2. Could a matrix structure improve performance for an organization familiar to you?
3. How can the disadvantages of group decision making hurt team structures?

Be Sure You Can

- compare the functional, divisional, and matrix structures
- draw charts to show how each structure might be used in a business
- list advantages and disadvantages of each structure
- explain the functional chimneys problem
- describe how cross-functional and project teams operate in team structures
- illustrate how an organization familiar to you might operate as a network structure
- list advantages and disadvantages of the network approach to organizing

What Would You Do?

The typical business school in a university is organized on a functional basis, with departments such as accounting, finance, information systems, management, and marketing all reporting to a dean. How would you redesign things to increase communication and collaboration across departments, as well as improve curriculum integration across all areas of study?

Takeaway 8.3
What Are the Trends in Organizational Design?

ANSWERS TO COME

- Organizations are becoming flatter, with fewer levels of management
- Organizations are increasing decentralization
- Organizations are increasing delegation and empowerment
- Organizations are becoming more horizontal and adaptive
- Organizations are using more alternative work schedules

JUST AS ORGANIZATIONS VARY IN SIZE AND TYPE, SO, TOO, DO THE VARIETY OF problems and opportunities they face.[27] This is why they use different ways of organizing—from the functional, divisional, and matrix structures to the team and network approaches reviewed in the previous modules. Now it's time to probe further. There is still more to the story of how managers try to align their organizations with the unique situations they face.

This process of alignment is called **organizational design**. It deals with the choices managers make to configure their organizations to best meet the problems and opportunities posed by their environments.[28] And because every organization faces unique challenges, there is no "one fits all" best design. Organizational design is a problem-solving activity where managers strive to get the best configuration to meet situational demands.

Organizational design is the process of configuring organizations to meet environmental challenges.

||| Organizations are becoming flatter, with fewer levels of management.

When organizations grow in size, they tend to get taller by adding more and more levels of management. This raises costs. It also increases the distance between top management and lower levels, making it harder for the levels to communicate with one another. Even with the benefits of new technologies, this increases the risks of slow and poorly informed decisions.

Taller organizations are generally viewed as less efficient, less flexible, and less customer-sensitive.[29] You shouldn't be surprised that the trend is for organizations to get flatter. One of the first announcements by Robert McDonald when taking over as Procter & Gamble's CEO was that he would "create a simpler, flatter and more agile organization . . . because simplification reduces cost, improves productivity and enhances employee satisfaction." His plan cut management levels from nine to seven.[30]

When organizations get flatter, one of the things often affected is **span of control**—the number of persons directly reporting to a manager. When span of control is narrow, as shown in the small figure, a manager supervises only a few people. Taller organizations have many levels of management and narrow spans of control. A manager with a wide span of control supervises many people. Flatter organizations with fewer levels of management have wider spans of control.

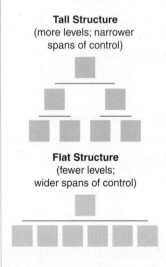

Tall Structure
(more levels; narrower spans of control)

Flat Structure
(fewer levels; wider spans of control)

Span of control is the number of persons directly reporting to a manager.

Ethics Check

■ FLATTENED INTO EXHAUSTION

Dear Stress Doctor:

My boss has come up with this great idea of cutting some supervisor positions, assigning more workers to those of us who remain, and calling us "coaches" instead of supervisors. She says this is all part of a new management approach to operate with a flatter structure and more empowerment.

For me this means a lot more work coordinating the activities of 17 operators instead of the 6 that I previously supervised. I can't get everything cleaned up on my desk most days, and I end up taking a lot of paperwork home.

As my organization "restructures" and cuts back staff, it puts a greater burden on those of us that remain. We get exhausted, and our families get short-changed and even angry. I even feel guilty now taking time to watch my daughter play soccer on Saturday mornings. Sure, there's some decent pay involved, but that doesn't make up for the heavy price I'm paying in terms of lost family times.

But you know what? My boss doesn't get it. I never hear her ask: "Henry, are you working too much; don't you think it's time to get back on a reasonable schedule?" No! What I often hear instead is "Look at Andy; he handles our new management model really well, and he's a real go-getter. I don't think he's been out of here one night this week before 8 p.m." What am I to do, just keep it up until everything falls apart one day? Is a flatter structure with fewer managers always best? Am I missing something in regard to this "new management"?

Sincerely,
Overworked in Cincinnati

YOU DECIDE

Is it ethical to restructure, cut management levels, and expect the remaining managers to do more work? Or is it simply the case that managers used to the "old" ways of doing things need extra training and care while learning "new" management approaches? And what about this person's boss—is she on track with her management skills? Aren't managers supposed to help people understand their jobs, set priorities, and fulfill them, while still maintaining a reasonable work-life balance?

⫼ Organizations are increasing decentralization.

While we are talking about levels of management, the next question becomes: Should top management make the decisions and the lower levels just carry them out? The answer is "No," at least not for all decisions. When top management keeps the power to make most decisions, the setup is called **centralization**. When top management allows lower levels to make decisions on matters where they are best prepared or informed, the setup is called **decentralization**.

If you had to choose right now, wouldn't you go for decentralization? Well, you wouldn't be wrong given the trends.[31] But you wouldn't be exactly right either. Do you really want lower levels making major decisions and changing things whenever they see fit?

The reality is that there is no need for a trade-off; an organization can have both. One of the unique opportunities of today's high-tech world is that top management can decentralize and still maintain centralized control. Computer technology and information systems allow top managers to easily stay informed about day-to-day performance results throughout an organization. This makes it easier for them to operate in more decentralized ways.[32]

> With **centralization**, top management keeps the power to make most decisions.

> With **decentralization**, top management allows lower levels to help make many decisions.

Role Models

■ ALAN MULALLY MAKES MARK BY RESTRUCTURING FORD

Why is it that a CEO brought in from outside the industry fared the best as the Big Three automakers went into crisis mode during the economic downturn? That's a question that Ford Motor Company's chairman, William Clay Ford Jr., is happy to answer. And the person he's talking about is Alan Mulally, a former Boeing executive Ford hired to retool the firm and put it back on a competitive track.

Many wondered if an "airplane guy" could run an auto company. It isn't easy to come in from outside an industry and successfully lead a huge firm. But Mulally's management experience and insights are proving well up to the task. One consultant remarked: "The speed with which Mulally has transformed Ford into a more nimble and healthy operation has been one of the more impressive jobs I've seen." He went on to say that without Mulally's impact, Ford might well have gone out of business.

In addition to many changes to modernize plants and streamline operations, Mulally has tackled the bureaucratic problems common to many extremely large organizations—particularly those dealing with functional chimneys and a lack of open communication. William Ford says that the firm had a culture that "loved to meet" and in which managers got together to discuss the message they wanted to communicate to the top executives. But Mulally

changed all that. He began with a focus on transparency and data-based decision making. He pushed for greater cooperation between Ford's divisions. And he pursued a more centralized approach to global operations, one that focused on building vehicles to sell in many markets. When some of the senior executives balked and tried to go directly to Ford with their complaints, he refused: "I didn't permit it," he says, thus reinforcing Mulally's authority to run the firm his way.

As for Mulally's success, only time will tell how the firm does in extremely difficult circumstances. For now, however, Ford is performing well and Mulally has gained lots of respect for his executive prowess. One of his senior managers says: "I'm going into my fourth year on the job. I've never had such consistency of purpose before."

WHAT'S THE LESSON HERE?

It takes a lot of confidence to come in from outside an industry and lead an organization with vision and a clear strategy. Mulally seems to be doing a good job of blending a strong central authority with decentralized action. He's got support from the board and has built his own top management team. How will you act when taking over a new position someday?

||| Organizations are increasing delegation and empowerment.

Decentralization brings with it another trend that is good for organizations and their members: increased delegation and empowerment. **Delegation** is the process of entrusting work to others by giving them the right to make decisions and take action.

You can think of delegation as the foundation for decentralization. Its three steps are:

(1) *Assign responsibility*—explain tasks and expectations to others.
(2) *Grant authority*—allow others to act as needed to complete tasks.
(3) *Create accountability*—require others to report back on the completed tasks.

Explore Yourself

■ EMPOWERMENT

Structures help bring order to organizational complexity. They put people together in ways that, on paper at least, make good sense in terms of getting tasks accomplished. But although there are many structural alternatives, as described in this chapter, they all struggle for success at times.

Things can change so fast that you might think of today's organization structures as solutions to yesterday's problems. This puts a great burden on people to fill in the gaps and deal spontaneously with things that the formal structures don't or can't cover at any point in time.

Empowerment is a way of unlocking talent and motivation so that people can act in ways that make a performance difference. It gives them freedom to make decisions about how they work. But, many managers fail when it comes to empowerment. And when they do, their organizations often underperform.

Are you willing, and able, to embrace empowerment as you work with others?

> Get to know yourself better by taking the self-assessment on **Empowering Others** and completing the other activities in the *Exploring Management* **Skill-Building Portfolio**.

Every manager really needs to know how and when to delegate. Even if you are already good at it, there are probably ways to get even better. On those days when you complain "I just can't get everything done," the real problem may be that you are trying to do everything yourself. Delegation involves deciding what work to do yourself and what you should allow others to accomplish. It sounds easy, but there is skill in doing delegation right.[33]

A classical management principle states that authority should equal responsibility when a supervisor delegates work to a subordinate. In other words, managers shouldn't delegate without giving the subordinate sufficient authority to perform. Can you think of a time when you were asked to get something done but didn't have the authority to do it? This was probably frustrating, and it may have even caused you to lose respect for the manager.

Some managers mistakenly go even one step further; they fail to delegate at all. Whether because they are unwilling or unable to trust others or are too inflexible in how they want things done, the failure to delegate is more common than you might think. And it creates problems. A failure to delegate not only makes it hard for people to do their jobs, it overloads the manager with work that really should be done by others.

Let's remember that the trend is toward more, not less, delegation. And let's not forget that when delegation is done well it leads to **empowerment**. This is the process of giving people the freedom to contribute ideas, make decisions, show initiative, and do their jobs in the best possible ways. Empowerment unlocks the full power of talent, experience, and intellect that people bring to their jobs. It is the engine that powers decentralization. And when it becomes part of the organizational culture, it helps everyone act faster and be more flexible when dealing with today's dynamic environments.

Empowerment gives people freedom to do their jobs as they think best.

Organizations are becoming more horizontal and adaptive.

A **bureaucracy** emphasizes formal authority, rules, order, fairness, and efficiency.

You should remember the concept of **bureaucracy** from earlier discussion in this book. Its distinguishing features are clear-cut division of labor, strict hierarchy of authority, formal rules and procedures, and promotion based on competency. According to Max Weber, bureaucracies should be orderly, fair, and highly efficient.[34] Yet chances are that your image of a bureaucracy is an organization bogged down with "red tape," which acts cumbersome and impersonal and is sometimes overcome to the point of inadequacy by rules and procedures.

Where, you might ask, are the decentralization, delegation, and empowerment that we have just been talking about? Well, researchers have looked into the question and arrived at some interesting answers. When Tom Burns and George Stalker investigated 20 manufacturing firms in England, they found that two quite different organizational forms could be successful.[35] The key was the "fit" between the form and challenges in the external environment.

Mechanistic designs are bureaucratic, using a centralized and vertical structure.

A more bureaucratic form of organization, which Burns and Stalker called the **mechanistic design**, thrived in stable environments. It was good at doing routine things in predictable situations. But in rapidly changing and uncertain situations, a much less bureaucratic form, called the **organic design**, performed best. It was adaptable and better suited to handle change and less predictable situations.

Organic designs are adaptive, using a decentralized and horizontal structure.

Figure 8.7 portrays these two approaches as opposite extremes on a continuum of organizational design alternatives. You can see that organizations with mechanistic designs typically operate as "tight" structures of the traditional vertical and bureaucratic form.[36] They are good for production efficiency. A ready example is your local fast-food restaurant. But what about a company like the software giant Microsoft?

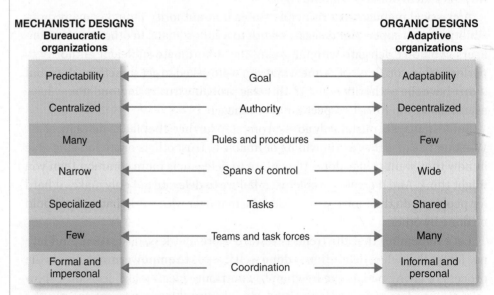

FIGURE 8.7   What Are the Major Differences Between Mechanistic and Organic Organizations Designs?
Some indicators of a more organic design are decentralization, few rules and procedures, wider spans of control, sharing of tasks, use of teams and task forces, and informal or personal approaches to coordination. This organic design is most associated with success in dynamic and changing environments. The more mechanistic design has mainly bureaucratic features and is more likely to have difficulty in change environments but to be successful in more stable ones.

Facts to Consider

■ BOSSES MAY BE OVERESTIMATING THEIR MANAGING SKILLS

A survey by Development Dimensions International, Inc., finds that managers may be overestimating their managing skills. "It doesn't matter what industry you're in. People have blind spots about where they are weak," says DDI vice president Scott Erker. These results are from a sample of 1,100 first-year managers:

- 72% never question their ability to lead others.
- 58% claim planning and organizing skills as strengths.
- 53% say they are strong in decision making.
- 50% say they are strong in communication.

- 32% claim proficiency in delegating.
- Skills rated as needing most development were delegating, gaining commitment, and coaching.

YOUR THOUGHTS?

Would you, like managers in this survey, probably overestimate your strengths in management skills? What might explain such tendencies toward overconfidence? And among the skills needing work, why would delegating be the one about which even very confident managers still feel some inadequacy?

Business Week has claimed that Microsoft suffers from "bureaucratic red tape" and endless meetings that bog employees down and limit their abilities to be creative and on top of market demands.[37] The *Wall Street Journal* has suggested it should be broken into smaller pieces to free the firm from the "bureaucracy that's stifling entrepreneurial spirits."[38] The idea is that the new and smaller components would be faster and more innovative in our changing world of technology. In other words, over time and with increasing size Microsoft may have become too mechanistic for its own good.

The organic organizational design is more horizontal and less vertical than its mechanistic counterpart. It emphasizes empowerment and teamwork, and gets a lot of work done through informal structures and interpersonal networks.[39] The result is an organization that is adaptive and flexible, and whose employees are allowed to be more spontaneous in dealing with changing markets and environments.[40] This design is good for creativity and innovation. Doesn't it sound like just the type of organization most likely to succeed in the technology industry today?[41]

‖ Organizations are using more alternative work schedules.

There's yet another organizing trend that's quite likely to become very important to you someday, if it isn't already—the use of alternative work schedules. The fact is that just because it was normal to work 40 hours each week in the past doesn't make this the only or best way to schedule work time.[42] Here are some possibilities.

A **compressed workweek** allows a worker to complete a full-time job in less than the standard five days of 8-hour shifts.[43] Its most common form is the "4–40," that is, accomplishing 40 hours of work in four 10-hour days. It's well used at USAA, a diversified financial services company that ranks among the 100 best companies to work for in America. A large part of the firm's San Antonio workforce is on

A **compressed workweek** allows a worker to complete a full-time job in less than five days.

a four-day schedule, with some working Monday through Thursday and others working Tuesday through Friday.[44] Although compressed workweeks can cause scheduling problems, possible customer complaints, and even union objections, the benefits are there as well. USAA reports improved morale, lower overtime costs, less absenteeism, and decreased use of sick leave.

The term **flexible working hours**, also called *flextime*, describes any work schedule that gives employees some choice in daily work hours. A typical flextime schedule offers choices of starting and ending times, while still putting in a full workday. Some may start earlier and leave earlier, while others do the opposite. The flexibility provides opportunities to attend to personal affairs such as parenting, elder care, medical appointments, and home emergencies. All top 100 companies in *Working Mother* magazine's list of best employers for working moms offer flexible scheduling. They find it reduces stress and unwanted job turnover.[45]

More and more people now do some form of **telecommuting**.[46] They spend at least a portion of scheduled work hours outside the office linked with co-workers, customers, and bosses by a variety of information technologies. And it's popular.[47] When asked what they like, telecommuters report increased productivity, fewer distractions, the freedom to be their own boss, and the benefit of having more time for themselves. On the negative side, some telecommuters report working too much, having less time to themselves, difficulty separating work and personal life, and having less time for family.[48] "You have to have self-discipline and pride in what you do," says one, "but you also have to have a boss that trusts you enough to get out of the way."[49]

A recent development in telecommuting is the *co-working center*, essentially a place where telecommuters go to share an office environment outside of the home and join the company of others. One marketing agency telecommuter says: "we have two kids, so the ability to work from home—it just got worse and worse. I found myself saying. 'If daddy could just have two hours....'" Now he has started his own co-working center to cater to his needs and those of others. One of those using his center says: "What you're paying for is not the desk, it's access to networking creativity and community."

Yet another alternative is **job sharing**, where two or more persons split one full-time job. This often involves each person working one-half day, but it can also be done via weekly or monthly sharing arrangements. Both the employees and the organizations benefit when talented people who cannot work full days or weeks are kept in or brought back into the workforce.

Flexible working hours give employees some choice in daily work hours.

Telecommuting involves using IT to work at home or outside the office.

Job sharing splits one job between two people.

Flexibility in work scheduling helps employers beat the "mommy drain."

It's well known that attracting and retaining talented workers has to be one of the top priorities for any organization. But what happens with new Moms? How do you get them onboard when you want to hire them? How do you keep them onboard when you already have them? The "Mommy drain," loss of mothers from the workforce, is real (there's a "Daddy drain" too). Flexibility is the rule for dealing with it. Things like extended pay and time off for maternity and parental leaves along with jobs that allow flexible hours, work-at-home time, and job sharing are essential. In-house career networks that support working parents are helpful too.

STUDY GUIDE

Takeaway 8.3
What Are the Current Trends in Organizational Design?

Terms to Define

Bureaucracy

Centralization

Compressed workweek

Decentralization

Delegation

Empowerment

Flexible working hours

Job sharing

Mechanistic design

Organic design

Organizational design

Span of control

Telecommuting

Rapid Review

- Organizations are becoming flatter—having fewer management levels, combining decentralization with centralization, and using more delegation and empowerment.
- Mechanistic organizational designs are vertical and bureaucratic; they perform best in stable environments with mostly routine and predictable tasks.
- Organic organizational designs are horizontal and adaptive; they perform best in change environments requiring adaptation and flexibility.
- Organizations are using alternative work schedules such as the compressed workweek, flexible working hours, and job sharing.

Questions for Discussion

1. Is "empowerment" just a buzzword, or is it something that can really make a difference in organizations today?
2. Knowing your personality, will you fit in better with an organization that has a mechanistic or an organic design?
3. How can alternative work schedules work to the benefit of both organizations and their members?

Be Sure You Can

- illustrate the link between tall or flat organizations and spans of control
- explain how decentralization and centralization can work together
- list the three steps in delegation
- differentiate mechanistic and organic organizational designs
- differentiate compressed workweek, flexible working hours, and job sharing
- list advantages and disadvantages of telecommuting

What Would You Do?

As the owner of a small computer repair and services business, you would like to allow employees more flexibility in their work schedules. But you also need consistency of coverage to handle drop-in customers as well as at-home service calls. Also, there are many times when customers need what they consider to be "emergency" help outside of normal 8 a.m. to 5 p.m. office times. A meeting with the employees is scheduled for next week. How can you work with them to develop a staffing plan? What will you present as "flexible work schedule" options that meet their needs as well as yours?

TestPrep 8

Multiple-Choice Questions

1. The main purpose of organizing as a management function is to _____.
   (a) make sure that results match plans
   (b) arrange people and resources to accomplish work
   (c) create enthusiasm for the needed work
   (d) link strategies with operational plans

2. An organization chart is most useful for _____.
   (a) mapping informal structures
   (b) eliminating functional chimneys
   (c) showing designated supervisory relationships
   (d) describing the shadow organization

3. Rumors and resistance to change are potential disadvantages often associated with _____.
   (a) virtual organizations
   (b) informal structures
   (c) functional chimneys
   (d) cross-functional teams

4. When an organization chart shows that vice presidents of marketing, finance, manufacturing, and purchasing all report to the president, top management is using a _____ structure.
   (a) functional   (b) matrix
   (c) network   (d) product

5. The "two-boss" system of reporting relationships is both a potential source of problems and one of the key aspects of _____ structures.
   (a) functional   (b) matrix
   (c) network   (d) product

6. A manufacturing business with a functional structure has recently acquired two other businesses with very different product lines. The president of the combined company might consider using a _____ structure to allow a better focus on the unique needs of each product area.
   (a) virtual   (b) team
   (c) divisional   (d) network

7. An organization using a _____ structure should expect that more problems will be solved at lower levels and that top managers will have more time free to engage in strategic thinking.
   (a) virtual   (b) matrix
   (c) functional   (d) product

8. The functional chimneys problem occurs when people in different functions _____.
   (a) fail to communicate with one another
   (b) try to help each other work with customers
   (c) spend too much time coordinating decisions
   (d) focus on products rather than functions

9. An organization that employs just a few "core" or essential full-time employees and outsources a lot of the remaining work shows signs of using a _____ structure.
   (a) functional   (b) divisional
   (c) network   (d) team

10. A "tall" organization will likely have _____ spans of control than a "flat" organization with the same number of members.
    (a) wider   (b) narrower
    (c) more ambiguous   (d) less centralized

11. If a student in one of your course groups volunteers to gather information for a case analysis and the other members tell him to go ahead and choose the information sources he believes are most important, the group is giving this student _____ to fulfill the agreed-upon task.
    (a) responsibility   (b) accountability
    (c) authority   (d) values

12. The bureaucratic organization described by Max Weber is similar to the _____ organization described by Burns and Stalker.
    (a) adaptive   (b) mechanistic
    (c) organic   (d) horizontal

13. Which organization would likely be a good fit for a dynamic and changing external environment?
    (a) vertical   (b) centralized
    (c) organic   (d) mechanistic

14. Workers following a compressed workweek schedule most often work 40 hours in _____ days.
(a) 3½　　(b) 4
(c) 5　　(d) a flexible schedule of

15. Which alternative work schedule is identified by *Working Mother* magazine as being used by all companies on its list of "100 Best Employers for Working Moms"?
(a) telecommuting　　(b) job sharing
(c) flexible hours　　(d) part-time

Short-Response Questions

16. Why should an organization chart be trusted "only so far"?

17. In what ways can informal structures be good for organizations?

18. How does a matrix structure combine functional and divisional forms?

19. Why is an organic design likely to be quicker and more flexible in adapting to changes than a mechanistic design?

Integration and Application Question

20. Imagine you are a consultant to your university or college president. The assignment is: Make this organization more efficient without sacrificing its educational goals. Although the president doesn't realize it, you are a specialist in network structures. You are going to suggest building a network organization, and your ideas are going to be radical and provocative. **Questions:** What would be the core of the network—is it the faculty members, who teach the various courses, or is it the administration, which provides the infrastructure that students and faculty use in the learning experience? What might be outsourced—grounds and facilities maintenance, food services, security, recreation programs, even registration? What types of alliances might prove beneficial—student recruiting, faculty, even facilities?

Steps*for*FurtherLearning

Many learning resources are found at the end of the book and online within WileyPLUS.

Don't Miss These Selections from the **Skill-Building Portfolio**

■ **SELF-ASSESSMENT 8:** *Empowering Others*

■ **TEAM PROJECT 8:** *Network "U"*

■ **CLASS EXERCISE 8:** *Organizational Metaphors*

Don't Miss This Selection from **Cases for Critical Thinking**

■ **CHAPTER 8 CASE**
Nike—Spreading Out to Stay Together

Snapshot　Nike is indisputably a giant in the athletics industry. But the Portland, Oregon, company has grown large precisely because it knows how to stay small. By focusing on its core competencies—and outsourcing all others—Nike has managed to become a sharply focused industry leader.

Banking on the star power of its Swoosh, Nike has successfully branded apparel, sporting goods, sunglasses, and even an MP3 player made by Philips. Like many large companies who have found themselves at odds with the possible limitations of their brands, Nike realized that it would have to master the one-two punch: identifying new needs and supplying creative and desirable products to fill those needs.

Salinee Tavaranan leads a team that installs solar panels in remote refugee camps on the Thai-Myanmar border. "The more people learn to harness natural energy," she says, "the better their lives become."

Organizational Cultures, Innovation, and Change

9

Adaptability and Values Set the Tone

Management Live

Tolerance for Ambiguity and *The Terminal*

In *The Terminal,* Viktor Navorski (Tom Hanks) travels from his native Krakozhia to New York City to get an autograph for his father from jazz musician Benny Golson. While he is in transit, Krakozhian soldiers overthrow their government and the United States no longer recognizes passports from Krakozhia. Navorski is refused entry, but he can't go home because Krakozhian airspace is closed.

Confined to the international transit lounge, Navorski at first doesn't know where to sleep, how to find food, or how to maintain personal hygiene. But he figures out how to do all of this. In addition, he earns money, first by rounding up unreturned baggage carts and then by getting an airport construction job.

The movie is loosely based on the true story of Mehran Nasseri, a dispossessed Iranian who spent 18 years living in Charles de Gaulle Airport. It seems unimaginable that anyone could live for more than a few days in these conditions. When they do, it reflects incredible **tolerance for ambiguity**, an ability to deal with uncertainty even when events are beyond personal control.

What about you? We live and work in changing, often uncertain, times. Do you find that you are able to deal effectively with circumstances that are unpredictable? How do you respond when something unexpected comes your way?

YOUR CHAPTER 9 TAKEAWAYS

1. Understand the nature of organizational culture.
2. Recognize how organizations support and achieve innovation.
3. Describe how managers lead the process of organizational change.

WHAT'S INSIDE

Explore Yourself
More on tolerance for ambiguity

Role Models
Tom Szaky puts eco-capitalism to work at Terra Cycle

Ethics Check
Facebook follies

Facts to Consider
Organization cultures face up to work-life trends

CHANGE BY DESIGN
TIM BROWN

Manager's Library
Change by Design
by Tim Brown

Takeaway 9.1
What Is the Nature of Organizational Culture?

ANSWERS TO COME

- Organizational culture is the personality of the organization.
- Organizational culture shapes behavior and influences performance.
- The observable culture is what you see and hear as an employee or customer.
- The core culture is found in the underlying values of the organization.
- Value-based management supports a strong organizational culture.

YOU PROBABLY HEAR THE WORD "CULTURE" A LOT THESE DAYS. IN TODAY'S GLOBAL economy, how can we fail to appreciate the cultural differences between people or nations? However, there's another type of culture that can be just as important: the cultures of organizations. Just as nations, ethnic groups, and families have cultures, organizations do too. These cultures help distinguish them from one another and give members a sense of collective identity.

Organizational culture is the personality of the organization.

Think of the stores that you shop in, the restaurants that you patronize, the place where you work. What is the "atmosphere" like? Do you notice how major retailers like Anthropologie, Hollister, and Abercrombie & Fitch have websites and store climates that seem to fit their brands and customer identities?[1] Such aspects of the internal environments of organizations are important in management. The term used to describe them is **organizational culture, the system of shared beliefs and values that develops within an organization and guides the behavior of its members.**[2]

Whenever someone speaks of "the way we do things here," he or she is talking about the organization's culture. You can think of this as the personality of the organization, the atmosphere within which people work. Sometimes called the *corporate culture*, it can have a strong impact on an organization's performance and the quality of work experiences of its members.

One firm now considered a benchmark for its special culture is Zappos. com, a popular e-tailer of shoes, clothing, and accessories. CEO Tony Hsieh has built a fun, creative, and customer-centered culture. Amazon CEO Jeff Bezos liked Zappos so much he bought the company, and the Girl Scouts sent executives to study Zappos and bring back ideas for improving its own culture. Hsieh says that "the original idea was to add a little fun" and things moved to the point where everyone shared in the idea that "we can do it better." Now the notion of an unhappy Zappos customer is almost unthinkable: "They may only call once in their life," says Hsieh, "but that is our chance to wow them."[3]

Organizational culture is a system of shared beliefs and values guiding behavior.

Netflix Runs a Fast Stream

New Thinking Thrives in the Right Culture

If you ask friends and neighbors to identify the most exciting Internet download they've received lately, it may well turn out to be a delivery from Netflix. CEO Reed Hastings—a *Fortune* magazine businessperson of the year—says that it's a commitment to customer service that keeps the company strong and growing.

Wired magazine describes Hastings as "a quiet disrupter, sabotaging business models silently and irretrievably" . . . "a quiet, hands-off leader . . . [who] sets the tone and objectives and lets his employees figure out how to execute them." The Netflix corporate culture fits its founder—unique and oriented toward high performance. Employees get to choose how much of their salary is paid in cash and how much in stock options; they get as much time off as they want for vacation; and day-to-day work rules are kept to a minimum so as to maximize individual freedom on the job.

FIND INSPIRATION

Think about Netflix, its culture and CEO Hastings' view of management the next time you watch a movie. Too many executives and organizations forget that culture counts, or they neglect to learn and change over time. What does the Netflix story tell us about leading organizations in today's day and age?

Organizational culture shapes behavior and influences performance.

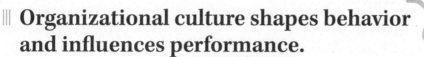

Zappos's Tony Hsieh says: "If we get the culture right, most of the other stuff, like brand and the customer service, will just happen."[4] And he's mostly right. Although culture isn't the only determinant of what happens in organizations, it does influence what they accomplish. Organizational culture helps to shape attitudes, reinforce beliefs, direct behavior, and establish performance expectations and the motivation to fulfill them. It helps set the organization's performance tone.[5] Meg Whitman, former eBay CEO, describes organization culture as "the set of values and principles by which you run a company" and create its "character." She says it becomes the "moral center" that helps every member understand what is right and what is wrong in terms of personal behavior.[6]

Groupon is an organization in the news these days, and it's been described as having a "noncorporate culture."[7] The firm has blossomed with a culture that allows for lots of fun and individualism while still focusing attention on high performance and bottom-line business accomplishments. One employee says: "I tell my friends that the atmosphere is like being in the library in college where everyone is working, but we're all working on a project for the same class, and it's everyone's favorite class."[8] Wouldn't you like to work this way?

Organizations like Zappos, Netflix, and Groupon have **strong cultures that are clear, well defined, performance driven, and widely shared by members.** These cultures fit the nature of the business and the talents of the employees, while keeping a clear performance vision front and center for all to rally around. They discourage dysfunctional behaviors and encourage positive ones, helping commit members to do things for and with one another that are good for the organization.[9]

Strong and positive cultures don't happen by chance. They are created through **socialization.**[10] This is the process of helping new members learn the culture and values of the organization, as well as the behaviors and attitudes that are shared among its members.[11]

Strong cultures are clear, well defined, and widely shared among members.

Socialization is the process through which new members learn the culture of an organization.

Career socialization often begins in an anticipatory sense with one's education, such as the importance of professional appearance and interpersonal skills. It then continues with an employer's orientation and training programs, which, when well done, can be strongly influential on new members. Each new Disney employee, for example, attends a program called "traditions." It educates them on the company mission, history, language, lore, traditions, and expectations. This commitment to socialization and a strong culture began with the founder, Walt Disney. He once said: "You can dream, create, design and build the most wonderful place in the world, but it requires people to make the dream a reality."[12]

The observable culture is what you see and hear as an employee or customer.

One way that you can try to understand organizational culture is through the two levels shown in **Figure 9.1**—the outermost or "observable" culture and the inner or "core" culture.[13] You might think of this in the sense of an iceberg. What lies below the surface and is harder to see is the core culture. What stands out above the surface and is more visible to the discerning eye is the observable culture.

FIGURE 9.1

What Are the Main Components of Organizational Culture?
With a bit of effort, one can easily identify the organizational culture. The most visible part is the observable culture. It is shown in the stories, rituals, heroes, and symbols that are part of the everyday life of the organization. The deeper, below-the-surface part is the core culture. It consists of the values that influence the beliefs, attitudes, and work practices among organizational members.

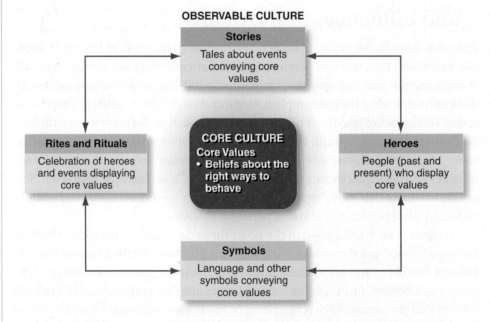

The **observable culture** is what you see and hear when walking around an organization.

The **observable culture** is what you see in people's behaviors and hear in their conversations. It is reflected in how people dress at work, arrange their offices, speak to and behave toward one another, and talk about and treat their customers. You'll notice it not only as an employee but also as a customer or client. Test this out the next time you go into a store, restaurant, or service establishment. How do people look, act, and behave? How do they treat one another? How do they treat customers? What's in their conversations? Are they enjoying themselves? When you answer these questions, you are starting to describe the observable culture of the organization.

The observable culture is also found in the stories, heroes, rituals, and symbols that are part of daily organizational life. In the university, it includes the pageantry of graduation and honors ceremonies; in sports teams, it's the pre-game rally, sidelines pep talk, and all the "thumping and bumping" that takes place after a good play. In workplaces it can be spontaneous celebrations of a work accomplishment or personal milestone such as a co-worker's birthday or wedding. And in organizations like Apple, Hewlett-Packard, Zappos, Google, and Amazon, it's in the stories told about the founders and the firm's history.

The presence or absence of such things, and the ways they are practiced, can say a lot about an organization's culture. They represent, communicate, and carry the culture over time, keeping it visible and clear in all members' eyes. New members learn the organization's culture through them, while all members keep the culture alive by sharing and joining in them.

⫴ The core culture is found in the underlying values of the organization.

A second and deeper level of organizational culture is called the **core culture**. It consists of the **core values**, or underlying assumptions and beliefs, that shape and guide people's behaviors. Values in some of the best companies, for example, often emphasize performance excellence, innovation, social responsibility, integrity, worker involvement, customer service, and teamwork.[14]

Values statements are typically found on websites, in mission statements, and in executive speeches. Here are some examples. Merck—"highest level of scientific excellence." Whole Foods—"Creating ongoing win-win partnerships with our suppliers." Fedex—"We are honest, ethical and do the right thing." Zynga—"Build games you & your friends love to play." Under Armour—"Innovation, Inspiration, Reliability and Integrity." Mozilla—"use the Mozilla assets (intellectual property such as copyrights and trademarks, infrastructure, funds, and reputation) to keep the Internet an open platform."[15]

> The **core culture** is found in the underlying values of the organization.

> **Core values** are beliefs and values shared by organization members.

{ BOTH BABY BOOMERS AND GEN YS RATE
FLEXIBLE WORK AS IMPORTANT.

Facts to Consider

■ ORGANIZATION CULTURES FACE UP TO WORK-LIFE TRENDS

If you have any doubts at all regarding the importance of work-life issues and their implications for organizational cultures and management practices, consider these facts:

- 78% of American couples are dual-wage earners.
- 63% believe they don't have enough time for their spouses or partners.
- 74% believe they don't have enough time for their children.
- 35% are spending time caring for elderly relatives.
- Both Baby Boomers (87%) and Gen Ys (89%) rate flexible work as important.

- Both Baby Boomers (63%) and Gen Ys (69%) want opportunities to work remotely at least part of the time.

YOUR THOUGHTS?

What organizational culture issues are raised by these facts? What should employers do to best respond to the situation described here? And when it comes to you, are you prepared to succeed in a work setting that doesn't respect these facts? Or, are you preparing right now to always find and be attractive to employers that do?

When trying to read or understand an organization's culture, don't be fooled by values statements alone. It's easy to write a set of values, post them on the Web, and talk about them. It's a lot harder to live up to them. If an organization's stated values are to have any positive effects, everyone in the organization from top to bottom must know the values and live up to them in day-to-day actions. That is characteristic of successful strong culture organizations. And in this sense, managers have a special responsibility to "walk the values talk" and make the expressed values real. After all, how might you react if you found out senior executives in your organization talked up values such as honesty and ethical behavior, but were also known to spend company funds on lavish private parties and vacations?

⫿ Value-based management supports a strong organizational culture.

Value-based management actively develops, communicates, and enacts shared values.

When managers practice the core values, model them for others, and communicate and reinforce them in all that they do, this is called **value-based management**. It is managing with a commitment to actively help develop, communicate, and represent shared values within an organization.

An incident at Tom's of Maine provides an example of value-based management.[16] After a big investment in a new deodorant, founder Tom Chappell was dismayed when he learned that customers were very dissatisfied with it. But having founded the company on values that include fairness and honesty in all matters, he decided to reimburse customers and pull the product from the market. Even though it cost the company more than $400,000, Tom did what he believed was the right thing. He was living up to the full spirit of the company's values and also setting a very positive example for others in the firm to follow.

A **symbolic leader** uses language and symbols and actions to establish and maintain a desired organizational culture.

Tom Chappell's actions in this incident show value-based management in action. They also show his strengths as a **symbolic leader**, someone who uses language and symbols well to communicate core values, and whose actions model the desired organizational culture.[17] Symbolic managers and leaders both act and talk the "language" of the organization. They are always careful to behave in ways that live up to the espoused core values. They are ever-present role models for others to emulate and follow.

Tips to Remember

■ SCORES—HOW TO READ AN ORGANIZATION'S CULTURE

S—How tight or loose is the *structure*?

C—Are decisions *change* oriented or driven by the status quo?

O—What *outcomes* or results are most highly valued?

R—What is the climate for *risk taking*, innovation?

E—How widespread is *empowerment*, worker involvement?

S—What is the competitive *style*, internal and external?

One thing you'll notice is that successful symbolic leaders continually highlight and even dramatize core values and the observable culture. They are careful to use spoken and written words to describe people, events, and even the competition in ways that reinforce and communicate core values. They tell key stories over and over again, and they encourage others to tell them. They may refer to the "founding story" about the entrepreneur whose personal values set a key tone for the enterprise. They remind everyone about organizational heroes, past and present, whose behaviors exemplify core values.

Language metaphors—the use of positive examples from another context—are very powerful in symbolic leadership. For example, newly hired workers at Disney are counseled to always think of themselves not as employees but as key "members of the cast" that work "on stage." After all, they are told Disney isn't just any business; it is an "entertainment" business.

Along these same lines, it is now popular to discuss something called **workplace spirituality**. Although the first tendency might be to associate the term "spirituality" with religion, it is used in management to reflect practices that try to nourish people's inner lives by bringing meaning to work and engaging each other with a sense of shared community.[18] The core values in a culture of workplace spirituality will have strong ethical foundations, recognize the value of individuals and respect their diversity, and focus on creating meaningful jobs that offer real value to society. When someone works in a culture of workplace spirituality, in other words, the person should derive personal pleasure from knowing that what is being accomplished is personally meaningful, created through community, and valued by others.

Workplace spirituality involves practices that create meaning and shared community among organizational members.

{ BE CAREFUL, OR YOUR FACEBOOK STATUS
MAY CHANGE TO "JUST GOT FIRED!"

Ethics Check

■ FACEBOOK FOLLIES

Facebook is fun, but don't post before checking your organizational culture. If you put the wrong things on your Facebook page—the wrong photo, a snide comment, or complaints about your boss—you might have to change your status to "Just got fired!"

Bed-surfing banker— After a Swiss bank employee called in sick with the excuse that she "needed to lie in the dark," company officials observed her surfing Facebook. She was fired and the bank's statement said it "had lost trust in the employee."

Angry mascot—The Pittsburgh Pirates fired their mascot after he posted criticisms of team management on his Facebook page. A Twitter campaign by supporters helped him get hired back.

Short-changed server—A server at a North Carolina pizza parlor used Facebook to call her customers "cheap" for not giving good tips. After finding out about the posting, her bosses fired her for breaking company policy.

YOU DECIDE

You may know of other similar cases where employees ended up being penalized for things they put on their Facebook pages. But where do you draw the line? Isn't a person's Facebook page separate from one's work? Shouldn't people be able to speak freely about their jobs, co-workers, and even bosses when outside the workplace? Or is there an ethical boundary that travels from work into one's public communications that needs to be respected? What are the ethics here—on the employee and the employer sides?

STUDY GUIDE

Takeaway 9.1
What Is the Nature of Organizational Culture?

Terms to Define

Core culture

Core values

Observable culture

Organizational culture

Socialization

Strong cultures

Symbolic leader

Value-based management

Workplace spirituality

Rapid Review

- Organizational culture is a climate of shared values and beliefs that guides the behavior of members; it creates the character and personality of the organization, and sets its performance tone.
- The observable culture is found in the everyday rites, rituals, stories, heroes, and symbols of the organization.
- The core culture consists of the core values and fundamental beliefs on which the organization is based.
- Value-based management communicates, models, and reinforces core values throughout the organization.
- Symbolic leadership uses words, symbols, and actions to communicate the organizational culture.

Questions for Discussion

1. Can an organization achieve success with a good organizational design but a weak organizational culture?
2. When you are in your local bank or any other retail establishment as a customer, what do you see and hear around you that identifies its observable culture?
3. What core values would you choose if you were creating a new organization and wanted to establish a strong performance-oriented culture?

Be Sure You Can

- explain organizational culture as the personality of an organization
- describe how strong cultures influence organizations
- define and explain the process of socialization
- distinguish between the observable and the core cultures
- explain value-based management
- explain symbolic leadership

What Would You Do?

You have two really nice job offers and will soon have to choose between them. They are both in the same industry, but you wonder which employer would be the "best fit" for you. What aspects of the cultures of these organizations would you investigate to help you make your choice? Why are these aspects of organizational culture most relevant to you as a person?

Takeaway 9.2
How Do Organizations Support and Achieve Innovation?

ANSWERS TO COME

- Organizations pursue process, product, and business model innovations.
- Green innovations pursue and support the goals of sustainability.
- Social innovations seek solutions to important societal problems.
- Commercializing innovation turns new ideas into salable products.
- Innovative organizations share many common characteristics.

THE IPAD, SUPER-SOAKER WATER GUN, KINDLE E-READER, POST-IT NOTES, as well as ATM machines, self-checkouts at the supermarkets, streaming movie rentals, overnight package deliveries and more—name your favorites! What we are discussing here are examples of **innovation**, the process of developing new ideas and putting them into practice.[19] The late management consultant Peter Drucker called innovation "an effort to create purposeful, focused change in an enterprise's economic or social potential."[20] Said a bit differently, it is the act of turning new ideas into usable applications.

> **Innovation** is the process of taking a new idea and putting it into practice.

Organizations pursue process, product, and business model innovations.

Innovation in and by organizations is often discussed in three forms. **Process innovations** result in better ways of doing things. **Product innovations** result in the creation of new or improved goods and services. **Business model innovations** result in new ways of making money for the firm.[21] Consider these examples.[22]

> **Process innovations** result in better ways of doing things.

> **Product innovations** result in new or improved goods or services.

> **Business model innovations** result in ways for firms to make money.

- *Process innovation*—Southwest Airlines keeps streamlining operations to fit its low-cost business strategy; IKEA sells furniture and fixtures in assemble-yourself kits; Amazon.com makes online shopping easy; Nike allows online customers to design their own sneakers.

- *Product innovation*—Groupon put coupons on the Web; Apple introduced the iPod, iPhone, and iPad, and made the "app" a must-have for smartphones and tablets; Amazon brought us the Kindle e-book reader; Facebook and Twitter made social media a part of everyday life.

- *Business model innovation*—Netflix turned movie rental into a subscription business; eBay earns revenues from users of its online marketplace; Google thrives on advertising revenues driven by ever-expanding Web technologies; Zynga made paying for "extras" profitable with free online games; Salesforce.com sells cloud-based software not as a product but as a service.

Green innovations pursue and support the goals of sustainability.

Today we can add **green innovation**, or **sustainable innovation**, to the list of innovation types. Green innovations support sustainability by reducing the carbon footprint of an organization or its products. These innovations are emerging quite frequently now as businesses strive to create new products and production methods that have minimal impact on the natural environment.

Sustainable innovations are found in areas like energy use, water use, packaging, waste management, and transportation practices, as well as in product development. The possibilities abound. Replacing air travel with videoconferencing eliminated 13,500 flights by Vodafone employees and cut some 5,000 tons of carbon emissions. Sierra Nevada Brewing Company fuels its generators with a blend of purchased natural gas and biogas from a water treatment plant. Adding in solar energy, the firm generates 80% of its own power, cutting electricity costs while also reducing air pollution. Patagonia buys used garments, breaks them down, and reweaves the fibers for clothing sold in its Common Threads line. The firm says savings in energy costs and carbon emissions are over 70%.[23]

The chapter opening photo showed Salinee Tavaranan, who is part of the Border Green Energy Team that brings green and sustainable innovations to rural and marginalized communities in Thailand.[24] BGET aims to improve lives by helping people access and learn to use renewable energy sources and sustainable technologies. This includes initiatives to expand use of solar electricity, solar cooking, bio-digesters to create cooking gas from animal and agricultural waste, UV water purification methods, and the hydro-ram pump which automatically pumps water without the use of electricity.

Social innovations seek solutions to important societal problems.

Although the tendency is to view innovation in a purely economic or business context, it's important to remember that it applies equally well to the world's social problems—poverty, famine, literacy, diseases, and the general conditions for social development. As Dipak C. Jain, the former dean of Northwestern's Kellogg School of Management, says: "Our primary goal should be producing leaders of real substance who put their knowledge to work in ways that make the world a better place."[25]

Social innovation can be described as innovation driven by a social conscience. It stems from creativity in **social entrepreneurship**, first discussed in Chapter 3 on ethics and social responsibility.[26] This is a unique form of entrepreneurship that pursues innovative ways to solve pressing social problems. Social entrepreneurs really try to make the world a better place.

What do you do, for example, about the chronic hunger that is the leading cause of death among African children? Sympathy wasn't enough for Andrew Youn. He's a social entrepreneur whose efforts have made a world of difference for many African families.[27] After returning from a Northwestern University internship in Africa, Youn attacked the problem of chronic child hunger with an innovative program—the One Acre Fund. It provides small loans to Kenya's poor families, enabling them to work their land with high-quality seed, fertilizer, equipment, and training. The goal is to help farmers "grow their way out of poverty" by finding ways to increase crop yields and avoid the devastating effects of Kenya's three-month "hunger season." The One Acre Fund won the SC Johnson Award for Socially Responsible Entrepreneurship and has expanded into Rwanda. Says Youn: "The mothers are absolutely inspiring. The things they do out of necessity are heroic."

Commercializing innovation is the process of turning new ideas into salable products.

Commercializing innovation turns new ideas into salable products.

The management of innovation requires encouragement and support for both *invention*, the act of discovery, and *application*, the act of use.[28] In business it is the process of **commercializing innovation** that turns new ideas—the inventions, into actual products, services, or processes—the applications, that generate profits through more sales or lower costs.[29] 3M Corporation, for example, owes its success to the imagination of employees such as Art Fry. He's the person whose creativity turned an adhesive that "wasn't sticky enough" into the blockbuster product known worldwide today as Post-It Notes®.

It's tempting to believe that commercializing an innovation such as the Post-It Note is easy. You might even consider it a "no brainer." But it isn't necessarily so. Art Fry and his colleagues had to actively "sell" the Post-It idea to 3M's marketing group and senior management before getting the financial support they needed to turn their invention into a salable product. Figure 9.2 shows how new product ideas such as Post-It might move through the typical steps of commercializing innovation.

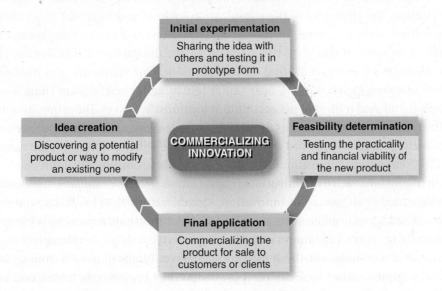

Initial experimentation
Sharing the idea with others and testing it in prototype form

Idea creation
Discovering a potential product or way to modify an existing one

COMMERCIALIZING INNOVATION

Feasibility determination
Testing the practicality and financial viability of the new product

Final application
Commercializing the product for sale to customers or clients

FIGURE 9.2

How Do Organizations Commercialize Innovation? In business it is the process of commercializing innovation that turns new ideas into actual products, services, or processes that can increase profits through greater sales or reduced costs. This requires management encouragement and support for idea creation (invention and the act of discovery), experimentation and feasibility determination, and final application (actually putting the tested idea into use).

One of the newer developments in commercializing innovation is called **reverse innovation**. Sometimes called *trickle-up innovation*, the concept got its start in the world of global business.[30] Firms have shifted away from only viewing innovation as something done "at home" and then transferred to "foreign or emerging markets." Instead, reverse innovation takes products and services developed in emerging markets, often subject to pricing constraints, and finds

Reverse innovation recognizes the potential for valuable innovations to be launched from lower organizational levels and diverse locations, including emerging markets.

ways to use them elsewhere. In fact, management scholar C. K. Prahalad goes so far as to call emerging market settings "laboratories for radical innovation."[31] And GE is a major believer. The firm has found expanded markets for hand-held and portable electrocardiogram and ultrasound machines that sell for a fraction of the price of larger units. The smaller units were developed in India and China and then moved through reverse innovation into the United States. Their mobility and lower prices have made them popular with emergency units.

Innovative organizations share many common characteristics.

How do you view Microsoft? Do you see a firm whose strategy and culture drive an innovation powerhouse? Or do you see what *PC World* once described as "a stodgy old corporation churning out boring software"? There are quite a few critics who believe Microsoft meets the latter description, not the former.[32] If you were Microsoft's current CEO, wouldn't you be thinking a lot about how to recapture some of the firm's past innovation glory?

Truly innovative organizations such as 3M, Google, and Apple have built enduring organizational capacities to innovate. And most of them share common features like these.[33]

HIGHLY INNOVATIVE ORGANIZATIONS				
Strategy includes innovation	Culture values innovation	Structures support innovation	Management supports innovation	Staffing for creativity and innovation

In highly innovative organizations the *corporate strategy and culture support innovation*. The strategies of the organization include and highlight innovation; the culture of the organization, as reflected in visions and values, emphasizes an innovation spirit. If you go to the Web site for the design firm IDEO, featured in the Manager's Library, you'll find this description: "Our values are part mad scientist (curious, experimental), bear-tamer (gutsy, agile), *reiki* master (hands-on, empathetic), and midnight tax accountant (optimistic, savvy). These qualities are reflected in the smallest details to the biggest endeavors, composing the medium in which great ideas are born and flourish."[34] There's little doubt that core values at IDEO encourage innovation and allow new ideas to continually flourish.

In highly innovative organizations, *organization structures support innovation*. Bureaucracy is an enemy of innovation. Organizations that break its confines take advantage of organic designs and team structures that empower people and eliminate functional chimneys and silos. *BusinessWeek* describes them this way: "Instead of assembly line, think swarming beehive. Teams of people from different disciplines gather to focus on a problem. They brainstorm, tinker and toy with different approaches."[35] The term **skunkworks** is often used to describe special units set free from the normal structure and given separate locations, special resources, and their own managers, all with the purpose of achieving innovation. Yahoo!, for example, has the "Brickhouse," an idea incubator in a separate facility where Yahoo staffers, some in bean bag chairs and playing with Nerf balls, work on ideas submitted from all over the company.[36] In other words, Brickhouse exists so that good ideas don't get lost in Yahoo's bureaucracy.

Skunkworks are special creative units set free from the normal structure for the purpose of innovation.

In highly innovative organizations, *staffing supports innovation*. Step one in meeting this goal is to make creativity an important criterion when hiring and moving people into positions of responsibility. Step two is allowing their creative talents to fully operate by inspiring and empowering them by the practices just discussed—strategy, culture, structure, and leadership.

In highly innovative organizations, *top management supports innovation*. Google's former CEO Eric Schmidt is a good example. Considered a master at fueling innovation, he gave the firm's engineers freedom to spend 20% of their time on projects of their own choosing.[37] But the best top managers go further. They not only encourage new ideas, they tolerate criticism and differences of opinion. They know that success doesn't always come in a straight line and admit that mistakes are often part of the innovation process. Johnson & Johnson's former CEO James Burke once said: "I try to give people the feeling that it's okay to fail, that it's important to fail."[38] And when talking about the firm's innovative electronic reader, the Kindle, Amazon's CEO Jeff Bezos said: "Our willingness to be misunderstood, our long-term orientation and our willingness to repeatedly fail are the three parts of our culture that make doing this kind of thing possible."[39]

Manager's Library

■ *CHANGE BY DESIGN*, BY TIM BROWN

BE CREATIVE AND IMPROVE BY NOT THINKING STRAIGHT

Some people like strong coffee and a quiet space to dream up new ideas, while other people prefer crowded social settings and hands-on activities to get their creative juices flowing. Either approach helps since creative thinking seems to be non-routine. But perhaps innovation is really that simple. Just avoid an ordinary mindset and try not to think straight!

In the book *Change By Design* (2009, HarperCollins), author Tim Brown discusses methods that people and organizations can use to change their regular approach and advance innovation. He says "design thinking" implies that people of all functions are innovators, not just artists, engineers, and marketers. Those near "externalities"—technology, consumers, and market forces outside the organization—are best placed and motivated to innovate.

Brown thinks human-centered ideas, not technology-centered ones, capture sustainable gains. New ideas should consider and alter human experiences—those of customers, employees, or business partners—and avoid use of existing resources to improve functionality for incremental but predictable gains. Services are particularly ripe and he urges construction of ideas with emotional benefits, saying a shift to an "experience economy" means consumers are actively seeking emotive experiences in products and services and avoiding basic feature improvements.

Brown provides anecdotes from a prolific career as a design consultant. He advocates building prototypes early in the design phase—ones that are rough and cheap. The goal is not to have working models, but to generate tangible results from abstract thought and realize their strengths and weaknesses. Prototyping "slows down the process to speed it up." In a sense, not thinking straight yields innovation since the road to success is less cluttered. Perhaps creative thought requires less effort than most people think?

REFLECT AND REACT

Describe products or services that provide you with an emotional experience rather than a functional utility. How can these feelings be evoked in other products or services? Describe circumstances where members of your organization interact with externalities—customers, technologies, broader society, etc. How can their observations yield innovations? And by the way, do you agree slowing down to speed up enables creative thinking?

STUDY GUIDE

Takeaway 9.2
How Do Organizations Support and Achieve Innovation?

Terms to Define

Business model innovation

Commercializing innovation

Green innovation

Innovation

Process innovations

Product innovations

Reverse innovation

Skunkworks

Social business innovation

Social entrepreneurship

Sustainable innovation

Rapid Review

- Innovation is a process that turns creative ideas into products or processes that benefit organizations and their customers.
- Organizations pursue process, product, and business model innovations.
- Organizations pursue green innovations that support sustainability.
- Organizations pursue social business innovations to tackle important societal problems.
- The process of commercializing innovation turns new ideas into useful applications.
- Highly innovative organizations tend to have supportive cultures, strategies, structures, staffing, and top management.

Questions for Discussion

1. Are there any potential downsides to making organizational commitments to green innovation?
2. What are the biggest trouble points in a large organization that might prevent a great idea from becoming a commercialized innovation?
3. What difference does a leader make in terms of how innovative an organization becomes?

Be Sure You Can

- discuss differences among process, product, and business model innovations
- explain green innovation and social business innovation
- list five steps in the process of commercializing innovation
- list and explain four characteristics of innovative organizations

What Would You Do?

Take a look around your present organization, be it a school or workplace. What three ideas can you come up with right away that would be possible sustainable or green innovations? How would your ideas, if implemented, benefit both the organization and society at large? What are the potential obstacles to putting your "green" ideas into practice? What could you really do as a "champion" to make your ideas really work?

Takeaway 9.3
How Do Managers Lead the Processes of Organizational Change?

ANSWERS TO COME

- Organizations pursue both transformational and incremental changes
- Three phases of planned change are unfreezing, changing, and refreezing
- Managers use force-coercion, rational persuasion, and shared power change strategies
- Change leaders identify and deal positively with resistance to change

WHAT IF THE EXISTING CULTURE OF THE ORGANIZATION DOESN'T SUPPORT HIGH performance and innovation? Just "change it," you might say. And the tendency may be to think of change as almost a matter of routine, something readily accepted by everyone involved. But the realities of trying to change organizations and the behaviors of people within them can be quite different. Former British Airways CEO Sir Rod Eddington once said, for example, that "altering an airline's culture is like trying to perform an engine change in flight."[40] Look at what is taking place in industry. You'll always find firms that are struggling, and it's not always because they don't have the right ideas—it's because they have difficulty adapting to new circumstances. In other words, they have difficulty creating organizational change.

Like many other new CEOs, when Angel Martinez became head of Rockport Company, he wanted to change traditional ways of doing things and increase the company's future competitiveness. But instead of embracing the changes, employees resisted. Martinez said they "gave lip service to my ideas and hoped I'd go away."[41] He was trying, but had trouble succeeding, to be a **change leader**. These are managers who act as *change agents*, who take leadership responsibility for changing the existing pattern of behavior of another person or social system.[42]

A **change leader** tries to change the behavior of another person or social system.

In theory, every manager should act as a change leader. But the reality described in the small figure is that people in organizations show major tendencies toward the status quo—accepting things as they are and not wanting to change. And it's the status quo that creates lots of difficulties as organizations strive to innovate and managers try to lead the processes of change.

Change leaders	Status quo managers
• Confident of ability • Willing to take risks • Seize opportunity • Expect surprise • Make things happen	• Threatened by change • Bothered by uncertainty • Prefer predictability • Support the status quo • Wait for things to happen

‖ Organizations pursue both transformational and incremental changes.

Many, if not most, people believe that only major, frame-breaking, radical change can save the large legacy companies hammered by the global financial crisis—big automakers, big airlines, big banks, and more. They are talking about the need for **transformational change** that results in a major and comprehensive redirection of the organization—new vision, new strategy, new culture, new structure, and even new people.[43]

Transformational change results in a major and comprehensive redirection of the organization.

As you might expect, transformational change is intense, highly stressful, and very complex to achieve. Reports are that as many as 70% or more of large-scale change efforts actually fail.[44] And, the main reason for failure is bad implementation. One of the most common mistakes is failure by top management to build commitments within the workforce so that everyone accepts and works hard to accomplish change goals.[45] See the nearby box for advice to would-be leaders of large-scale changes.[46]

Let's not forget that there is another more modest, frame-bending side to organizational change. This is **incremental change**. It tweaks and nudges people, systems, and practices to better align them with emerging problems and opportunities. The intent isn't to break and remake the system, but to move it forward through continuous improvements. Leadership of incremental change focuses on building on existing ways of doing things with the goal of doing them better in the future. Common incremental changes in organizations involve new products, new processes, new technologies, and new work systems.

One shouldn't get the idea, by the way, that incremental change is somehow inferior to transformational change. Think of it this way: incremental changes keep things tuned up (like the engine on a car) in between transformations (when the old car is replaced with a new one). Putting the two together probably offers organizations the best of both worlds.

When GE's former CEO Jack Welch first took the top job, for example, he was concerned about the firm's performance. So he began a large-scale restructuring of major workforce cuts and business realignment. Once the transformation was underway, however, he created a pathway for incremental change driven by employee involvement. He called the program Work-Out.[47] In GE's Work-Out sessions, employees confronted their managers in a "town meeting" format. The manager sat or stood in front listening to suggestions for everything from removing performance obstacles to improving operations. Welch expected the managers to respond immediately to the suggestions and to try to implement as many of them as possible.

Incremental change bends and adjusts existing ways to improve performance.

Guidelines for Leading Large-Scale Transformational Change

- Establish a sense of urgency for change.
- Form a powerful coalition to lead the change.
- Create and communicate a change vision.
- Empower others to move change forward.
- Celebrate short-term wins and recognize those who help.
- Build on success; align people and systems with new ways.
- Stay with it; keep the message consistent; champion the vision.

‖ Three phases of planned change are unfreezing, changing, and refreezing.

Managers seeking to lead change in organizations can benefit from a simple but helpful model developed by the psychologist Kurt Lewin. He describes how change situations can be analyzed and addressed in three phases: *unfreezing*—preparing a system for change; *changing*—making actual changes in the system; and *refreezing*—stabilizing the system after change.[48]

Unfreezing is the stage in which managers help others to develop, experience, and feel a real need for change. The goal here is to get people to view change as a way of solving a problem or taking advantage of an opportunity. Some might call this the "burning bridge" phase, arguing that in order to get people to jump off a bridge, you might just have to set it on fire. Managers can simulate the burning

Unfreezing is the phase during which a situation is prepared for change.

bridge by engaging people with facts and information that communicate the need for change—environmental pressures, declining performance, and examples of alternative approaches. And as you have probably experienced, conflict can help people to break old habits and recognize new ways of thinking about or doing things.

The **changing** phase is where actual change takes place. Ideally these changes are planned in ways that give them the best opportunities for success, having maximum appeal and posing minimum difficulties for those being asked to make them. Although this phase should follow unfreezing in Lewin's model, he believes it is often started too early. When change takes place before people and systems are ready for it, the likelihood of resistance and change failure is much greater. In this sense Lewin might liken the change process to building a house: You need to put a good foundation in place before you begin the framing.

As shown in Figure 9.3, the final stage in the planned change process is **refreezing**. Here, the focus is on stabilizing the change to make it as long lasting as needed. Linking change with rewards, positive reinforcement, and resource support all help with refreezing. Of course, in today's dynamic environments there may not be a lot of time for refreezing before things are ready to change again. You may well find that refreezing in Lewin's sense probably gives way quite often to another phase of evaluating and reassessing. In other words, we begin preparing for or undertaking more change even while trying to take full advantage of the present one.

> **Changing** is the phase where a planned change actually takes place.

> **Refreezing** is the phase at which change is stabilized.

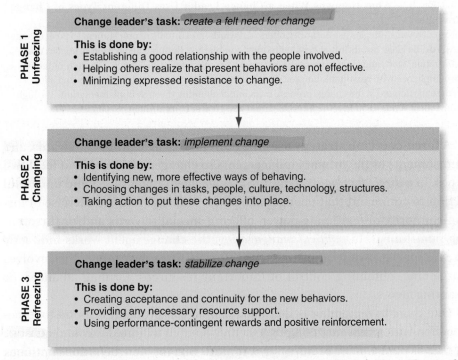

FIGURE 9.3 What Are the Change Leader's Responsibilities in Lewin's Three Phases of Planned Change?

Kurt Lewin identified three phases of the planned change process. The first is unfreezing, the phase where people open up and become receptive to the possibility of change. The second is changing, where the actual change happens and the new ways of doing things are put into place. Third is refreezing, the phase where changes are stabilized to become part of ongoing routines. Lewin believed that change agents often neglect unfreezing and move too quickly into the changing phase, thus setting the stage for change failures. They may also neglect refreezing, with the result that any achieved change has only temporary effects.

Managers use force-coercion, rational persuasion, and shared power change strategies.

When it comes to a manager actually being able to move people and systems toward change, the issue boils down to change strategy. Figure 9.4 summarizes three common change strategies—force-coercion, rational persuasion, and shared power. Each should be understood and most likely used by all change leaders.[49]

Change Strategy	Power Bases	Managerial Behavior	Likely Results
Force–Coercion Using position power to create change by decree and formal authority	Legitimacy Rewards Punishments	*Direct forcing and unilateral action* *Political maneuvering and indirect action*	Faster, but low commitment and only temporary compliance
Rational Persuasion Creating change through rational persuasion and empirical argument	Expertise	*Informational efforts using credible knowledge, demonstrated facts, and logical argument*	
Shared Power Developing support for change through personal values and commitments	Reference	*Participative efforts to share power and involve others in planning and implementing change*	Slower, but high commitment and longer term internalization

FIGURE 9.4 **What Happens When a Change Leader Uses Different Types of Change Strategies?**
Force-coercion strategies use authority, offers of rewards, and threats of punishment to push change forward. The likely results are, at best, temporary compliance. Rational persuasion strategies use information, facts, and logic to present a persuasive case in support of change. The likely outcomes are compliance with reasonable commitment. Shared power strategies engage others and allow them to participate in the change process, from initial planning through implementation. The high involvement tends to build more internalization and greater commitments to change.

A **force-coercion strategy** pursues change through formal authority and/or the use of rewards or punishments.

A **force-coercion strategy** uses the power bases of legitimacy, rewards, and punishments as the primary inducements to change.[50] It comes in at least two types. In a *direct forcing* strategy, the change agent takes direct and unilateral action to command that change take place. This involves the exercise of formal authority or legitimate power, offering special rewards and/or threatening punishment. In *political maneuvering*, the change agent works indirectly to gain special advantage over other persons to force the change. This involves bargaining, obtaining control of important resources, forming alliances, or granting favors.

One thing to remember is that most people will probably respond to force-coercion with temporary compliance. They'll act in a limited way and only out of fear of punishment or hope for a reward. But the new behavior continues only so long as the possibilities for rewards and punishments exist. This is why force-coercion may be most useful as an unfreezing strategy. It can help to break people from old habits and try new ones that eventually prove valuable enough to be self-sustaining. An example is General Electric's Work-Out program, discussed earlier.[51] Jack Welch started Work-Out to create a forum for active employee empowerment. But he made participation mandatory from the start; he used his authority to force employees to participate. And he was confident in doing so because he believed that, once started, the program would prove valuable enough to survive and prosper on its own. It did.

An alternative to force-coercion is the **rational persuasion strategy**, attempting to bring about change through persuasion backed by special knowledge, information, facts, and rational argument. The likely outcome of rational persuasion is compliance with reasonable commitment. This is actually the strategy that you learn and practice so much in school when writing reports and making formal presentations on group projects. You'll do a lot of rational persuasion in the real world as well. But as you probably realize, success with the strategy depends on having very good facts and information—the rational part, and then being able to communicate them well—the persuasion part.

The rational persuasion strategy works best when the change agent has credibility as an expert. This credibility can come from possessing special information or having a repution as an expert. It can also be gained from bringing in external consultants or experts, showing case examples or benchmarks, and conducting demonstration projects. Ford, for example, has sent managers to Disney World to

> A **rational persuasion strategy** pursues change through empirical data and rational argument.

{ IF A RETAILER BITES, WE ARE IN FULL PRODUCTION IN A MATTER OF WEEKS.

Role Models

■ TOM SZAKY PUTS ECO-CAPITALISM TO WORK AT TERRACYCLE

Decisions . . . hunches . . . achievements? It's all about being tuned into the environment. That's a message that seems well learned by Tom Szaky. He's ridden the roller coaster of all roller coasters, taking ideas for "sustainability," "green," and "recycling" from dorm room banter to the shelves of Walmart. If you read Tom Szaky's book *Revolution in a Bottle*, you enter the world of "upcycling"—the art, if you will, of turning waste that isn't recyclable into reusable packaging.

Szaky is what many call an "eco-capitalist," someone who brings environmentalism into the world of business and consumers. While a freshman at Princeton University, he ordered a million red worms with the goal of learning how to use them to recycle campus garbage. In conversations with classmate Jon Beyer, the original idea of eco-friendly waste management became one of creating and selling liquid fertilizer made from worm excrement. But they couldn't afford the expensive plastic bottles for packaging. More conversations, this time with entrepreneur Robin Tator, led to a new firm called TerraCycle with a mission to "find a meaningful use for waste materials."

Szaky's original liquid fertilizer became TerraCycle Plant Food. Now the firm *upcycles* a variety of waste products like cookie wrappers, drink containers, and discarded juice packs into usable products ranging from tote bags to containers of various sorts to pencil cases. And, yes, lots of them are found on Walmart's shelves. Szaky says: "Unlike most companies, which spend years in product development and testing, TerraCycle moves through these stages very quickly. First we identify a waste stream, then we figure out what we can make from that material. This is our strength—creatively solving the "what the hell do we make from it" issue. If a retailer bites, we are in full production in a matter of weeks."

WHAT'S THE LESSON HERE?

Tom Szaky made many decisions as he moved into the entrepreneurial world of eco-capitalism. It could have ended when the experiment with red worms and campus recycling proved more difficult than expected. But Szaky and his friends didn't stop there; learning from the experience, they persevered and made changes—more than once. We all talk about the planet, sustainability, and social values. But how often do we turn decisions into positive actions? Is there a bit of Tom Szaky in you?

learn about customer loyalty, hoping to stimulate them to lead customer service initiatives of their own. A Ford vice president says, "Disney's track record is one of the best in the country as far as dealing with customers."[52] In this sense the power of rational persuasion is straightforward: If it works for Disney, why can't it work for Ford?

A **shared power strategy** engages people in a collaborative process of identifying values, assumptions, and goals from which support for change will naturally emerge. Although slow, the process is likely to yield high commitment. Sometimes called a *normative re-educative strategy*, this approach relies on empowerment and participation. The change leader engages others as a team to develop the consensus needed to support change. This requires being comfortable and confident in allowing others to influence decisions that affect the planned change and its implementation. And because it entails a high level of involvement, this strategy is often quite time consuming. But shared power can deliver major benefits in terms of longer-lasting and internalized change.

The great strength of the shared power strategy lies with unlocking the creativity and experience of people within the system. Still, many managers hesitate to use it for fear of losing control or of having to compromise on important organizational goals. Harvard scholar Teresa M. Amabile points out, however, that managers and change leaders can share power regarding choice of means and processes, even if they can't debate the goals. "People will be more creative," she says, "if you give them freedom to decide how to climb particular mountains. You needn't let them choose which mountains to climb."[53]

> **A shared power strategy**
> pursues change by participation in assessing change needs, values, and goals.

||| Change leaders identify and deal positively with resistance to change.

You may have heard the adage that "change can be your best friend." At this point, however, we should probably add: "but only if you deal with resistance in the right ways." When people resist change, they are most often defending something important to them and that now appears threatened.

It is tempting to view resistance to change as something that must be overcome or defeated. But this mindset can easily cause problems. Perhaps a better way is to view resistance as feedback, as a source of information about how people view the change and its impact on them. A change leader can learn a lot by listening to resistance and then using it to develop ideas for improving the change and change process.[54]

The list in Table 9.1—*Why People May Resist Change*—probably contains some familiar items. Surely you've seen some or all of these types of change resistance in your own experience. And honestly now, haven't you also been a resister at times? When you were, how did the change leader or manager respond? How do you think they should have responded?

Researchers have found that once resistance appears in organizations, managers try to deal with it in various ways, and some of their choices are better than others.[55] *Education and communication* use discussions, presentations, and demonstrations to educate people about a change before it happens. *Participation and involvement* allows others to contribute ideas and help design and implement the change. *Facilitation and support* provide encouragement and training, channels for communicating problems and complaints, and ways of helping to

Table 9.1 **Why People May Resist Change**

Fear of the unknown—not understanding what is happening or what comes next

Disrupted habits—feeling upset to see the end of the old ways of doing things

Loss of confidence—feeling incapable of performing well under the new ways of doing things

Loss of control—feeling that things are being done "to" you rather than "by" or "with" you

Poor timing—feeling overwhelmed by the situation or feeling that things are moving too fast

Work overload—not having the physical or psychic energy to commit to the change

Loss of face—feeling inadequate or humiliated because it appears that the old ways weren't good ways

Lack of purpose—not seeing a reason for the change and/or not understanding its benefits

overcome performance pressures. *Negotiation and agreement* offer incentives to those who are actively resisting or ready to resist, trying to make trade-offs in exchange for cooperation.

Although very different, each of the prior strategies for dealing with resistance to change has a role to play in organizations. Two other approaches, also found in management practice, are considerably more risky and prone to negative side effects. Change leaders who use *manipulation and cooptation* try to covertly influence resisters by providing information selectively and structuring events in favor of the desired change. Those using *explicit and implicit coercion* try to force resisters to accept change by threatening them with a variety of undesirable consequences if they don't go along as asked. Would you agree that most people don't like to be on the receiving end of these strategies?

{ YOUR TOLERANCE FOR AMBIGUITY IS A GOOD INDICATOR OF HOW YOU DEAL WITH CHANGE.

Explore Yourself

■ TOLERANCE FOR AMBIGUITY

The next time you are driving somewhere and following a familiar route only to find a "detour" sign ahead, test your **tolerance for ambiguity**. Is the detour no big deal and you go forward without any further thought? Or is it a bit of a deal, perhaps causing anxiety or anger and demonstrating your tendencies to resist change in your normal routines?

Your tolerance for ambiguity is a good predictor of how you like to work and deal with change. Some organizations are structured and directive, while others are the opposite. Some of us embrace change, while others resist it. But remember, people today are being asked to be ever more creative and innovative in their work; organizations are, too.

Change, we often hear said, is now a given. And in so many ways it is. At work we are expected to support change initiatives launched from the top; we are also expected to be change leaders in our own teams and work units. This is a good time to check your readiness to meet the challenges of change in organizations and in personal affairs.

Get to know yourself better by taking the self-assessment on **Tolerance for Ambiguity** and completing the other activities in the *Exploring Management* **Skill-Building Portfolio**.

STUDY GUIDE

Takeaway 9.3
How Do Managers Lead the Processes of Organizational Change?

Terms to Define

Change leader

Changing

Force-coercion strategy

Incremental change

Rational persuasion strategy

Refreezing

Shared power strategy

Transformational change

Unfreezing

Rapid Review

- Transformational change makes radical changes in organizational directions; incremental change makes continuing adjustments to existing ways and practices.
- Change leaders are change agents who take responsibility for helping to change the behavior of people and organizational systems.
- Lewin's three phases of planned change are unfreezing (preparing a system for change), changing (making a change), and refreezing (stabilizing the system with a new change in place).
- Successful change agents understand the force-coercion, rational persuasion, and shared power change strategies, and the likely outcomes of each.
- People resist change for a variety of reasons, including fear of the unknown and force of habit; this resistance can be a source of feedback that can help improve the change process.
- Change agents deal with resistance to change in a variety of ways, including education, participation, facilitation, negotiation, manipulation, and coercion.

Questions for Discussion

1. When is it better to pursue incremental rather than transformational change?
2. Can the refreezing phase of planned change ever be completed in today's dynamic environment?
3. Should managers avoid the force-coercion change strategy altogether?

Be Sure You Can

- differentiate transformational and incremental change
- discuss a change leader's responsibilities for each phase of Lewin's change process
- explain the force-coercion, rational persuasion, and shared power change strategies
- list reasons why people resist change
- identify strategies for dealing with resistance to change

What Would You Do?

Times are tough at your organization, and, as the director of human resources, you have a problem. The company's senior executives have decided that 10% of the payroll has to be cut immediately. Instead of laying off about 30 people, you would like to have everyone cut back their work hours by 10%. This way the payroll would be cut but everyone would get to keep their jobs. But you've heard that this idea isn't popular with all the workers. Some are already grumbling that it's a "bad idea" and the company is just looking for excuses "to cut wages." How can you best handle this situation as a change leader?

TestPrep 9

Multiple-Choice Questions

1. Stories told about an organization's past accomplishments and heroes such as company founders are all part of what is called the _____ culture.
   - (a) observable
   - (b) underground
   - (c) functional
   - (d) core

2. Planned and spontaneous ceremonies and celebrations of work achievements illustrate how the use of _____ helps build strong corporate cultures.
   - (a) rewards
   - (b) structures
   - (c) rites and rituals
   - (d) core values

3. An organization with a strong culture is most likely to have _____.
   - (a) a tight, bureaucratic structure
   - (b) a loose, flexible design
   - (c) a small staff size
   - (d) clearly communicated mission

4. Honesty, social responsibility, and customer service are examples of _____ that can become foundations for an organization's core culture.
   - (a) rites and rituals
   - (b) values
   - (c) subsystems
   - (d) ideas

5. Product innovations create new goods or services for customers, while _____ innovations create new ways of doing things in the organization.
   - (a) content
   - (b) process
   - (c) quality
   - (d) task

6. The Kindle e-reader by Amazon and the iPad by Apple are examples of _____ innovations.
   - (a) business model
   - (b) social
   - (c) product
   - (d) process

7. Movie downloads by subscription (Netflix) and advertising revenues from Internet searches (Google) are examples of _____ innovations.
   - (a) business model
   - (b) social
   - (c) product
   - (d) process

8. Green innovation is most associated with the concept of _____.
   - (a) observable culture
   - (b) core culture
   - (c) sustainability
   - (d) skunkworks

9. The innovation process isn't really successful in an organization until a new idea is _____.
   - (a) tested as a prototype
   - (b) proven to be financially feasible
   - (c) put into practice
   - (d) discovered or invented

10. The basic role of a skunkworks is to _____.
    - (a) add more bureaucratic structure to the innovation process
    - (b) provide special free space in which people work together to achieve innovation
    - (c) make sure that any innovation occurs according to preset plans
    - (d) give people free time in their jobs to be personally creative

11. _____ change results in a major change of direction for an organization, while _____ makes small adjustments to current ways of doing things.
   (a) Frame breaking; radical
   (b) Frame bending; incremental
   (c) Transformational; frame breaking
   (d) Transformational; incremental

12. A manager using a force-coercion strategy is most likely relying on the power of _____ to bring about planned change.
   (a) expertise
   (b) reference
   (c) legitimacy
   (d) information

13. The most participative of the planned change strategies is _____.
   (a) negotiation and agreement
   (b) rational persuasion
   (c) shared power
   (d) education and communication

14. When a change leader tries to deal with resistance by trying to covertly influence others, offering only selective information and/or structuring events in favor of the desired change, this is an example of _____.
   (a) rational persuasion
   (b) manipulation and cooptation
   (c) negotiation
   (d) facilitation

15. The responses most likely to be associated with use of a force-coercion change strategy are best described as _____.
   (a) internalized commitment
   (b) temporary compliance
   (c) passive cooptation
   (d) active resistance

Short-Response Questions

16. What core values might be found in high-performance organizational cultures?

17. What is the difference between process, product, and business model innovation?

18. How do a manager's responsibilities for change leadership vary among Lewin's three phases of planned change?

19. What are the possible differences in outcomes for managers using force-coercion and shared power change strategies?

Integration and Application Question

20. One of the common experiences of new college graduates in their first jobs is that they often "spot things that need to be changed." They are full of new ideas, and they are ready and quick to challenge existing ways of doing things. They are enthusiastic and well intentioned. But more often than most probably expect, their new bosses turn out to be skeptical, not too interested, or even irritated; co-workers who have been in place for some time may feel and act the same.

Questions: What is the new employee to do? One option is to just forget it and take an "I'll just do my job" approach. Let's reject that. So then, how can you be an effective change leader in your next new job? How can you use change strategies and deal with resistance from your boss and co-workers in a manner that builds your reputation as someone with good ideas for positive change?

Human Resource Management

Nurturing Turns Potential into Performance

Management Live

Professionalism and *Iron Man 2*

Tony Stark (Robert Downey Jr.) is the rich, playboy owner of Stark Industries, a military weapons company started by his father. Tony was a child prodigy in technology and when his father dies, the company becomes his. The problem is that Tony doesn't know how to run a business. So, he turns it over to his faithful assistant Pepper Potts (Gwyneth Paltrow). Potts is the consummate professional, always willing to do whatever it takes to keep her boss on schedule and to keep the company running effectively. When Potts becomes CEO and Tony comes to the office acting in typical arrogant and self-centered fashion, she dismisses him.

Professionalism involves more than expertise. It means behaving with internalized commitments to special standards. Those standards may be determined by personal values, academic degrees, professional affiliations, and, most certainly, company culture and practices. Managers need to be thoroughly professional in all areas of work responsibility, including how they interact with and make decisions affecting human resources.

After reading the chapter, make an assessment of your professionalism. Where do you stand? Take advantage of opportunities to test your professional commitment. They're all around. Chances are your school has a student branch of the Society for Human Resource Management or some other professional organization. Consider getting involved to develop your professional skills.

YOUR CHAPTER 10 TAKEAWAYS

1. Understand the purpose and legal context of human resource management.

2. Identify essential human resource management practices.

3. Recognize current issues in human resource management.

WHAT'S INSIDE

Explore Yourself
More on professionalism

Role Models
Jim Goodnight makes people a top priority at SAS

Ethics Check
Help Wanted: Saleswomen

Facts to Consider
Human resource executives worry about performance measurement

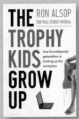

Manager's Library
The Trophy Kids Grow Up by Ron Alsop

Takeaway 10.1
What Are the Purpose and Legal Context of Human Resource Management?

ANSWERS TO COME

- Human resource management attracts, develops, and maintains a talented workforce.
- Strategic human resource management aligns human capital with organizational strategies.
- Government legislation protects against employment discrimination.
- Laws can't guarantee that employment discrimination will never happen.

> The key to managing people in ways that lead to profit, productivity, innovation, and real organizational learning ultimately lies in how you think about your organization and its people . . . . When you look at your people, do you see costs to be reduced? . . . Or, when you look at your people do you see intelligent, motivated, trustworthy individuals—the most critical and valuable strategic assets your organization can have?

THESE COMMENTS ARE FROM JEFFREY PFEFFER'S BOOK, *THE HUMAN EQUATION: Building Profits by Putting People First.*[1] What is your experience? Do you find employers treating people as costs or as assets? And what difference does this seem to make? Pfeffer and his colleague, John F. Veiga, believe it makes a performance difference, a potentially big one. They conclude: "There is a substantial and rapidly expanding body of evidence . . . that speaks to the strong connection between how firms manage their people and the economic results achieved."[2]

The core argument being advanced here is that organizations will perform better when they treat their members better.[3] And when it comes to how people are treated at work, we enter the territory of human resource management.

‖ Human resource management attracts, develops, and maintains a talented workforce.

A marketing manager at IDEO, the Palo Alto–based design firm, once said: "If you hire the right people . . . if you've got the right fit . . . then everything will take care of itself."[4] It really isn't quite that simple, but getting the right people on board is certainly a great starting point for success. The process of **human resource management (HRM)** is supposed to do just that—attract, develop, and maintain

Human resource management (HRM) is the process of attracting, developing, and maintaining a high-quality workforce.

a talented and energetic workforce. Its purpose is to ensure that an organization is always staffed with the best people so that all jobs get done in the best possible ways. You might think of the goal of HRM this way—to build organizational performance capacity through people.

The three major responsibilities of human resource management are typically described as:

1. *Attracting a quality workforce*—employee recruitment and selection
2. *Developing a quality workforce*—employee orientation, training and development, and performance management
3. *Maintaining a quality workforce*—career development, work-life balance, compensation and benefits, retention and turnover, and labor-management relations

‖ Strategic human resource management aligns human capital with organizational strategies.

High-performing organizations thrive on strong foundations of **human capital**, the economic value of people's abilities, knowledge, experience, ideas, energies, and commitments. When Sheryl Sandberg left her senior management post with Google to become Facebook's chief operating officer, she made human capital her top priority. She strengthened the firm's human resource management systems with updated approaches for employee performance reviews, innovative recruiting methods, and new management training.[5] These initiatives are consistent with the concept of **strategic human resource management**—mobilizing human capital through the HRM process to best implement organizational strategies.[6]

One indicator that the HRM process is truly strategic to an organization is when it is headed by a senior executive reporting directly to the chief executive officer. When former Home Depot executive Denis Donovan became the firm's first vice president for human resources, he said: "CEOs and boards of directors are learning that human resources can be one of your biggest game-changers in terms of competitive advantage."[7] The strategic importance of HRM has also been raised in respect to corporate ethics scandals. "It was a failure of people and that isn't lost on those in the executive suite," says Susan Meisinger, past president of the Society for Human Resource Development.[8]

There are many career opportunities in human resource management. HRM departments are common in most organizations. And HRM specialists are increasingly important in an environment complicated by legal issues, labor shortages, economic turmoil, changing corporate strategies, changing social values, and more. A growing number of firms provide specialized HRM services such as recruiting, compensation, outplacement, and the like. The Society for Human Resource Management, or SHRM, is a professional organization dedicated to keeping its membership up to date in all aspects of HRM and its complex legal environment.

Human capital is the economic value of people with job-relevant abilities, knowledge, ideas, energies, and commitments.

Strategic human resource management mobilizes human capital to implement organizational strategies.

Government legislation protects against employment discrimination.

Job discrimination occurs when someone is denied a job or job assignment for non-job-relevant reasons.

"Why didn't I get invited for a job interview? Is it because my first name is Omar?" "Why didn't I get that promotion? Is it because I'm so visibly pregnant?" If valuing people is at the heart of human resource management, **job discrimination** should be its enemy. It occurs when an organization denies someone employment or a job assignment or an advancement opportunity for reasons that are not performance relevant.[9]

An important cornerstone of U.S. laws designed to protect workers from job discrimination is *Title VII of the Civil Rights Act of 1964*, amended by the *Equal Employment Opportunity Act of 1972* and the *Civil Rights Act (EEOA) of 1991*. These acts provide for **equal employment opportunity (EEO)**, giving everyone the right to employment without regard to sex, race, color, national origin, or religion. It is illegal under Title VII to use any of these as criteria when making decisions about hiring, promoting, compensating, terminating, or otherwise changing someone's terms of employment.

Equal employment opportunity (EEO) is the right to employment and advancement without regard to race, sex, religion, color, or national origin.

When the U. S. Supreme Court ruled 5–4 in favor of Walmart in *Wal-mart v. Dukes*, it set off a flurry of controversy.[10] The case was a class-action lawsuit filed on behalf of some 1.5 million women who claimed Walmart violated Title VII of the Civil Rights Act by favoring men in pay and promotions. The ruling did not say that individual women had not been discriminated against; it said the "class" action did not show a policy of company-wide discriminatory practices. A corporate press release stated: "Walmart has had strong policies against discrimination for many years . . . the plaintiffs' claims were worlds away from showing a companywide discriminatory pay and promotion policy." Writing for the minority, Justice Ruth Bader Ginsburg said: "Managers, like all humankind, may be prey to biases of which they are unaware. The risk of discrimination is heightened when those managers are predominantly of one sex, and are steeped in a corporate culture that perpetuates gender stereotypes."

The intent of Title VII and equal employment opportunity is to ensure everyone the right to gain and keep employment based only on their ability and job performance. The Equal Employment Opportunity Commission (EEOC) enforces the legislation through its federal power to file civil lawsuits against organizations that do not provide timely resolution of any discrimination charges lodged against them. These laws generally apply to all public and private organizations that employ 15 or more people.

Affirmative action is an effort to give preference in employment to women and minority group members.

Title VII also requires organizations to show **affirmative action** in their efforts to ensure equal employment opportunity for members of *protected groups*, those historically underrepresented in the workforce. Employers are expected to analyze existing workforce demographics, compare them with those in the relevant labor markets, and set goals for correcting any underrepresentation that might exist. These goals are supported by *affirmative action plans* that are designed to ensure that an organization's workforce represents women and minorities in proportion to their labor market availability.[11]

You are likely to hear debates over the pros and cons of affirmative action. Critics tend to focus on the use of group membership, female or minority status, as a criterion in employment decisions.[12] The issues raised include claims of *reverse discrimination* by members of majority populations. White males, for example, may claim that preferential treatment given to minorities in a particular situation interferes with their individual rights.

As a general rule, the legal protections of EEO do not restrict an employer's right to establish **bona fide occupational qualifications**. These are criteria for employment that an organization can clearly justify as relating to a person's capacity to perform a job. However, EEO bars the use of employment qualifications based on race and color under any circumstances; those based on sex, religion, and age are very difficult to support.[13]

Table 10.1 is a reminder that legal protection against employment discrimination is quite extensive. But we must still be realistic. Laws help, but this doesn't mean you will never be affected by employment discrimination.[14]

Bona fide occupational qualifications are employment criteria justified by capacity to perform a job.

Table 10.1 A Sample of U.S. Laws Against Employment Discrimination

- *Pay*—The *Equal Pay Act of 1963* requires equal pay for women and men doing equal work. It describes equal work in terms of skills, responsibilities, and working conditions.
- *Age*—The *Age Discrimination in Employment Act of 1967 as amended in 1978 and 1986* protects workers against mandatory retirement ages. Age discrimination occurs when a qualified individual is adversely affected by a job action that replaces him or her with a younger worker.
- *Pregnancy*—The *Pregnancy Discrimination Act of 1978* protects female workers from discrimination because of pregnancy. A pregnant employee is protected against termination or adverse job action because of the pregnancy and is entitled to reasonable time off work.
- *Disabilities*—The *Americans with Disabilities Act of 1990 as amended in 2008* prevents discrimination against people with disabilities. The law requires employment decisions be based on a person's abilities and what he or she can do.
- *Family matters*—The *Family and Medical Leave Act of 1993* protects workers who take unpaid leaves for family matters from losing their jobs or employment status. Workers are allowed up to 12 weeks of leave for childbirth, adoption, personal illness, or illness of a family member.

Laws can't guarantee that employment discrimination will never happen.

Not too long ago, a woman wrote to the *Wall Street Journal* with this question: "I was interviewing for a sales job and the manager asked me what child care arrangements I had made . . . . Was his question legal?" The answer, according to an employment attorney, is that the manager's question is "a perfect example of what not to ask a job applicant" and "could be considered direct evidence of gender bias against women based on negative stereotypes."[15] Other examples of discriminatory practices can easily be found.

Employee privacy is the right to privacy on and off the job.

One of the emerging areas of controversy in employment discrimination involves issues of social media use and **employee privacy**—the rights of employees to privacy on and off the job.[16] Technology allows most employers to monitor telephone calls, e-mails, social media usage, and Internet searches to track your activities while on the job. The best advice on workplace privacy is to assume you have none and act accordingly. But beyond that, we don't always have privacy *outside* of work either. While vacationing in Europe, a Florida teacher posted to her "private setting" Facebook pages photos that showed her drinking alcoholic beverages. After it came to the attention of school administrators, she was asked to resign. And she did. Since, however, she has filed a lawsuit stating her resignation was forced.[17] The resolutions of a growing number of such social media lawsuits may help clear up just what is and is not against the law in the non-work zone of employee privacy.

Pay discrimination occurs when men and women are paid differently for doing equal work.

Pay discrimination is against the law. So when Lilly Ledbetter was about to retire from Goodyear and realized that male coworkers were being paid more, she sued. She initially lost the case because the Supreme Court said she had delayed too long in filing the claim. But she was smiling when the Lilly Ledbetter Fair Pay Act became the very first bill signed by President Barack Obama. It expanded workers' rights to sue employers on equal pay issues. Obama said he signed it in honor not only of Lilly but also of his own grandmother "who worked in a bank all her life, and even after she hit that glass ceiling, kept getting up again." When he signed the Lilly Ledbetter Fair Pay Act, President Obama said "making our economy work means making sure it works for everybody."[18]

Pregnancy discrimination penalizes a woman in a job or as a job applicant for being pregnant.

How about **pregnancy discrimination**? It's also against the law, but pregnancy bias complaints filed with the U.S. Equal Employment Opportunity Commission are still common. A spokesperson for the National Partnership of Women & Families said that problems of pregnancy discrimination are "escalating" and require "national attention."[19] And recent research paints a bleak picture as well. Actors played roles of visibly pregnant and nonpregnant applicants for jobs as corporate attorneys and college professors. Results showed that interviewers were more negative toward the "pregnant" females, making comments such as "she'll try to get out of doing work" and "she would be too moody."[20]

Age discrimination penalizes an employee in a job or as a job applicant for being over the age of 40.

Age discrimination, too, is against the law. But the EEOC is reporting an increased number of age bias complaints. Federal age discrimination laws protect employees aged 40 and up, and the proportion of workers in this age group is increasing with what some call the "graying" of the American workforce. When an older worker is laid off or loses his or her job, the possibility of age discrimination exists. However, it's hard to prove. "There's always the fine line between what discrimination is and what is a legitimate business decision," says one attorney. About 20% of age discrimination suits result in some financial settlement in favor of the person filing the claim, but this doesn't always include getting the job back. And there is no doubt that older workers face tough job searches. Data indicate that unemployment for workers over 50 lasts 27 more weeks than for younger ones.[21]

STUDY GUIDE

Takeaway 10.1
What Are the Purpose and Legal Context of Human Resource Management?

Terms to Define

Affirmative action

Age discrimination

Bona fide occupational qualifications

Comparable worth

Employee privacy

Equal employment opportunity (EEO)

Human capital

Human resource management (HRM)

Independent contractors

Job discrimination

Pay discrimination

Pregnancy discrimination

Strategic human resource management

Rapid Review

- The human resource management process involves attracting, developing, and maintaining a quality workforce.
- Job discrimination occurs when someone is denied an employment opportunity for reasons that are not job relevant.
- Equal employment opportunity legislation guarantees people the right to employment and advancement without discrimination.
- Current legal issues in the work environment deal with workplace privacy, pay, pregnancy, and age, among other matters.

Questions for Discussion

1. How might the forces of globalization affect human resource management in the future?
2. Are current laws protecting American workers against discrimination in employment sufficient, or do we need additional ones?
3. What employee-rights issues and concerns would you add to those discussed here?

Be Sure You Can

- explain the purpose of human resource management
- differentiate job discrimination, equal employment opportunity, and affirmative action
- identify major U. S. laws protecting against employment discrimination
- explain the issues of workplace privacy that today's college graduates should be prepared to face

What Would You Do?

If you were on a student committee appointed to investigate gender equity in sports on your campus, what areas would you look at? Based on your understanding of campus affairs, what changes would you suggest in athletic funding and administration to improve gender equity?

Takeaway 10.2
What Are the Essential Human Resource Management Practices?

ANSWERS TO COME

- Recruitment attracts qualified job applicants.
- Selection makes decisions to hire qualified job applicants.
- Socialization and orientation integrate new hires into an organization.
- Training continually develops employee skills and capabilities.
- Performance management appraises and rewards accomplishments.
- Retention and career development provide career paths.

Person-job fit is the match of individual skills, interests, and personal characteristics with the job.

Person-organization fit is the match of individual values, interests, and behavior with the organizational culture.

Recruitment is a set of activities designed to attract a qualified pool of job applicants.

A KEY GOAL OF HRM IS "FIT." **PERSON-JOB FIT** IS THE EXTENT TO WHICH AN individual's skills, interests, and personal characteristics are consistent with the requirements of the job. **Person-organization fit** is the extent to which an individual's values, interests, and behavior are consistent with the culture of the organization.

It makes sense that the first responsibility of human resource management is to attract and retain the right people to an organization's workforce. To do this, one must first know exactly what type of people to look for. This requires a clear understanding of the jobs to be done and the talents people need to do them well. And it requires having the right systems in place so that jobs are always filled with enthusiastic and high-performing workers.

Tony Hsieh, CEO of Zappos, takes the notion of fit to the extreme. If a new employee is unhappy with the firm after going through initial training, Zappos pays them to quit. Yes, believe it or not, the "bye-bye bounty" is $3,000. Some 2–3% of new hires take it each year.[22]

‖ Recruitment attracts qualified job applicants.

Recruitment is what organizations do to attract a qualified pool of applicants to an organization. The word "qualified" is especially important here. Recruiting should bring employment opportunities to the attention of people whose skills and abilities meet job requirements. Recruiting is basically a process of advertising the job, collecting a pool of applicants, and selecting from that pool those who are most promising in terms of potential employability.

More and more recruiters are turning to the Web and social media sites to disseminate job openings and search for qualified applicants. Monster.com and LinkedIn.com are two examples of the online career sites frequently used by job hunters and employers. U.S. Cellular, for example, reports that it saved $1 million in just one year by using LinkedIn to find job candidates rather than hiring through head-hunter firms.[23]

When you use online sites to disseminate your résumé, be sure to fill your online profile with key words that both display your skills and match employer interests. Many employers use special software to scan online profiles for indicators of real job skills and experiences that fit their needs. Also, don't forget that technology can also work to your disadvantage unless you maintain a truly professional Web presence. A CareerBuilder.com survey reports that some 45% of executives in one sample said they visited social network sites of job candidates, and about one-third of them found information that caused them to not hire the person.[24]

It's more common now that an early screening check after reviewing a résumé takes place over the telephone. This can be a make-or-break moment and shouldn't be taken lightly. Check out the Tips to Remember for ideas on how to succeed in telephone interviews.[25] Are you ready? The typical telephone interview can last an hour or more and get into lots of specifics that traditionally have been covered in face-to-face conversation. After being asked to describe her major past accomplishments, one job candidate said, "I was taken aback by how specific the interviewer was getting."[26]

And when it comes to the interview itself, be sure to look and press for a **realistic job preview.** It gives you both the good points and the bad points of the job and organization.[27] You might be easily misled by an interviewer that adopts a more traditional "tell-and-sell" approach, perhaps trying to hide or gloss over the potential negatives. It's far better to get a realistic and full picture of the situation before, not after, you decide to accept offer. Instead of "selling" only positive features, a realistic job preview tries to be open and balanced in describing the job and organization. Both favorable and unfavorable aspects are covered.

Realistic job previews provide job candidates with all pertinent information about a job and organization.

{ BE PREPARED TO ANSWER QUESTIONS ABOUT YOUR ONLINE PRESENCE.

Tips to Remember

■ STEPS TO SUCCESS IN TELEPHONE INTERVIEWS

- *Prepare ahead*—Learn everything you can about the organization; with this employer in mind, list your relevant strengths and capabilities.
- *Practice answers to common questions*—What value can you add to our organization on day one? Why do you want this job? What are your career goals?
- *Take the call in private*—Be in a quiet room, with privacy, without interruptions; set aside enough time to talk as long as the interviewer wants.
- *Dress professionally*—Don't be casual; dressing right increases confidence and helps set your interview tone.

- *Practice your interview voice*—What you say and how you sound affects the first impression you make; it often helps to stand up while talking; use correct telephone etiquette and don't answer other calls.
- *Have your questions ready*—Don't be caught hesitating; intersperse your best questions throughout the interview; don't be "smart" or "pushy," but show insight and interest.
- *Check your social persona*—Review your social media postings. Be prepared to answer questions about your online presence.
- *Ask what happens next*—Ask how to follow up and what additional information you can provide.

How can you tell if you are getting a realistic job preview? The interviewer might use phrases such as "Of course, there are some downsides . . . " "Things don't always go the way we hope . . . " "Something that you will want to be prepared for is . . . " "We have found that some new hires had difficulty with . . . " If you don't hear these phrases, ask the tough questions yourself. The answers you get will help establish realistic job expectations and better prepare you for the inevitable ups and downs of a new job. And the recruiter benefits too from higher levels of early job satisfaction and less inclination of new hires to quit prematurely.

‖ Selection makes decisions to hire qualified job applicants.

Selection is choosing whom to hire from a pool of qualified job applicants.

Once a good set of job candidates is identified, the next step is to decide whom to hire. **Selection** involves choosing to hire applicants who offer the greatest performance potential. This is really an exercise in prediction—trying to anticipate whether the candidate will perform well once on the job. The typical sequence involves in-depth interviewing, some form of testing, perhaps a real-time assessment of how well the candidate works on actual or simulated job tasks, and background checks that may include Web searches and reviews of personal postings on social media sites such as a Facebook profile.

Reliability means that a selection device gives consistent results over repeated measures.

Validity means that scores on a selection device have demonstrated links with future job performance.

It's quite common for job candidates to be asked to take employment tests. Some test job-specific knowledge and skills; others focus more on intelligence, aptitudes, personality, or general interests. Regardless of the intent, however, any employment test should be both reliable and valid. **Reliability** means that the test provides a consistent measurement, returning the same results time after time. **Validity** means that the test score is a good predictor of future job performance, with a high score associated with high job performance and vice versa.

An **assessment center** examines how job candidates handle simulated work situations.

Work sampling evaluates applicants as they perform actual work tasks.

One of the popular developments in employment testing is the use of **assessment centers**. They allow recruiters to evaluate a person's job potential by observing his or her performance in experiential activities designed to simulate daily work. A related approach is **work sampling**, which asks candidates to work on actual job tasks while observers grade their performance. Google uses a form of this called "Code Jams." These are essentially contests that the firm runs to find the most brilliant software coders. Winners get financial prizes and job offers. Code Jams are held worldwide and a company spokesperson says: "Wherever the best talent is, Google wants them."[28]

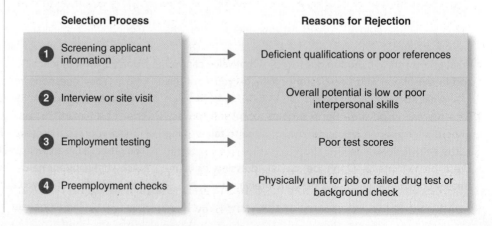

Selection Process		Reasons for Rejection
1 Screening applicant information	→	Deficient qualifications or poor references
2 Interview or site visit	→	Overall potential is low or poor interpersonal skills
3 Employment testing	→	Poor test scores
4 Preemployment checks	→	Physically unfit for job or failed drug test or background check

Socialization and orientation integrate new employees into the organization.

Once hired, a new member of any organization has to "learn the ropes" and become familiar with "the way things are done." **Socialization** is the process of influencing the expectations, behavior, and attitudes of a new hire in a desirable way. It begins with the human resource management practice of **orientation**—a set of activities designed to familiarize new employees with their jobs, co-workers, and key values, policies, and other aspects of the organization as a whole.

For years, Disney has been considered a master at this. During orientation at its Disney World Resort in Buena Vista, Florida, new employees learn the corporate culture. They also learn that the company places a premium on personality and expects all employees—from entertainers to ticket sellers to groundskeepers—"to make the customer happy." A Disney HRM specialist says: "We can train for skills. We want people who are enthusiastic, who have pride in their work, who can take charge of a situation without supervision."[29]

> **Socialization** systematically influences the expectations, behavior, and attitudes of new employees.

> **Orientation** familiarizes new employees with jobs, co-workers, and organizational policies and services.

Training continually develops employee skills and capabilities.

At this point, you should probably be keeping a list of things to look for in your next employer. Here's a big one: a willingness to invest in training so that you are continuously learning and updating your job skills. Training is so important at Procter & Gamble that managers are rated on how well they train and develop those reporting to them. And, those that develop reputations as great trainers usually get the promotions.[30]

We all need training. But it's especially critical today because new knowledge and technologies quickly make so many of our existing skills obsolete. A great employer won't let this happen. Instead of trying to avoid training and save costs, it willingly spends on training and views it as an investment in human resources.[31] This is a classic case of valuing employees as assets. In fact, you should probably ask questions about training opportunities in any job interview. And if the interviewer struggles for answers or evades the questions, you're getting a pretty good indication that the organization isn't likely to pass the "great employer" test.

A convenient and powerful training approach that you should be inquiring about is **coaching**. This is where an experienced person provides performance advice to someone else. Ideally, a new employee is assigned a coach who can model desired work behaviors and otherwise help him or her to learn and make progress. Sometimes, the best coach is the manager. At other times, it may be a co-worker. Always, the key is for the coach to be willing and able to show a newcomer by example how things should be done.

> **Coaching** occurs as an experienced person offers performance advice to a less experienced person.

You should also be interested in **mentoring**. This is where a new or early-career employee is assigned as a protégé to someone senior in his or her area of expertise, perhaps a high-level manager. Good mentoring programs can be a great boost to a newcomer's career. Mentors are supposed to take an interest in the junior person, provide guidance and advice on skills and career progress, and otherwise inform him or her about how one gets ahead careerwise in the organization. At Cisco Systems, for example, pre-retirement Baby Boomers serve as mentors for

> **Mentoring** assigns early-career employees as protégés to more senior ones.

Manager's Library

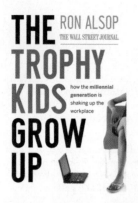

RON ALSOP
THE WALL STREET JOURNAL
THE TROPHY KIDS GROW UP

how the millennial generation is shaking up the workplace

■ *THE TROPHY KIDS GROW UP*, BY RON ALSOP

CEO—ARE WE THERE YET?

The Millennial generation—born 1980 to 2001—enters today's workplace trailing generations that possess different attitudes about work life. The Baby Boomers—born 1946 to 1964—lead most organizations, and Generation Xers—born 1965 to 1979—are likely to supervise. Millennials have been nurtured to be confident and reliant on technology, yet co-workers may be cautious of their need for advancement and advice. Baby Boomers toiled for years to attain leadership and expect patience from others, while Gen Xers were raised to be self-directed and not expect lots of guidance. Today's workplace will change as each generation adjusts to the others' capabilities.

In the book *The Trophy Kids Grow Up* (2008, Jossey-Bass), author Ron Alsop urges Millennials to make distinctions between their childhood treatments and adult work life. He suggests that in formative years everyone in this generation received participation trophies—rewarded for effort not performance. They chatted in shorthand text and Internet forums that were free from adults, and emphasized friends and interests as much as schoolwork. Their standard attire included jeans, flip-flops, and iPods. Though Millennials anointed themselves as the greatest generation and feel entitled to success, Alsop cautions they may need to rationalize how fantasy and past experience meets reality as they emerge from adolescence into the adult workplace.

Alsop believes Millennials expect more direction and feedback at work than Gen X or Baby Boomer bosses are used to providing. Young workers want checklists for direction and prefer teamwork. They possess a soft work ethic and casual approach to work structure. They limit work time to pursue outside interests, dress casually, loathe meetings, and have trouble with the 9 to 5 timetable at an office. But, there's a reality to face. Alsop advises Millennials that employers expect personal sacrifices to advance and that formal attire is necessary to respect others. Office interaction is essential to success and creates outcomes impossible through electronic means.

REFLECT AND REACT.

Will you expect your supervisor to counsel you the same way that your parents advise you? Is time commitment to a job more or less important than spending time with friends or hobbies? Are you prone to replacing face-to-face interactions with electronic ones? Have you posted material on the Web that might embarrass you if your employer viewed it? And by the way, do you agree that Millennials have a sense of entitlement?

Gen Ys just starting out with the firm. Executives believe this has helped in recruiting a new generation of employees.

Some enlightened employers are using **reverse mentoring** where younger employees mentor seniors. A good example is technology-savvy Gen Ys tutoring their seniors on how to use social media in their jobs. Reverse mentoring programs are not only informative for senior managers, they also provide younger employees with an important sense of buy-in and contribution. One human resource management consultant says: "It's exactly the kind of thing that's needed today because Gen-Yrs really want to be involved."[32]

> In **reverse mentoring**, younger and newly hired employees mentor senior executives, often on latest developments with digital technologies.

||| Performance management appraises and rewards accomplishments.

> **Performance appraisal** is the process of formally evaluating performance and providing feedback to a job holder.

Once a person is hired and on the job, one of the important functions of HRM is performance management. This involves using various techniques of **performance appraisal** to formally assess and give feedback on someone's work accomplishments.[33] The purposes of performance appraisal are twofold. First, it measures and documents performance for the record. Second, it initiates a process of development that can improve performance in the future.[34]

In order for an appraisal method to serve these two purposes with credibility, it must satisfy the same reliability and validity criteria as do employment tests.[35] Any manager who hires, fires, or promotes based on performance appraisals, must be able to confidently explain and discuss them with the persons involved even when disagreement is voiced. Managers may even need to defend such actions in discrimination-based lawsuits. It is hard to have a good performance review conversation or mount a legal case if the performance appraisal method can be faulted because of reliability or validity problems.

One of the most basic performance appraisal methods is a **graphic rating scale**. It is a checklist or scorecard for rating an employee on criteria such as work quality, attendance, and punctuality. Although simple, quick, and commonly used, graphic rating scales have questionable reliability and validity. At best they should probably be used only along with additional appraisal tools.

> A **graphic rating scale** uses a checklist of traits or characteristics to evaluate performance.

A more advanced approach to performance appraisal uses a **behaviorally anchored rating scale (BARS)**. This describes actual behaviors that exemplify various levels of performance achievement in a job. The example in Figure 10.1 shows a BARS for a customer service representative. "Extremely poor" performance is described with the behavioral anchor "treats a customer rudely and with disrespect." Because the BARS relates performance assessments to specific descriptions of work behavior, it is more reliable and valid than the graphic rating scale. The behavioral anchors can also be used for training in job skills and objectives.

> A **behaviorally anchored rating scale (BARS)** uses specific descriptions of actual behaviors to rate various levels of performance.

Outstanding performance

5 ← If a customer has defective merchandise that is not the responsibility of the store, you can expect this representative to help the customer arrange for the needed repairs elsewhere.

4 ← You can expect this representative to help a customer by sharing complete information on the store's policies on returns.

3 ← After finishing with a request, you can expect this representative pleasantly to encourage a customer to "shop again" in the store.

2 ← You can expect this representative to delay a customer without explanation while working on other things.

1 ← You can expect this representative to treat a customer rudely and with disrespect.

Unsatisfactory performance

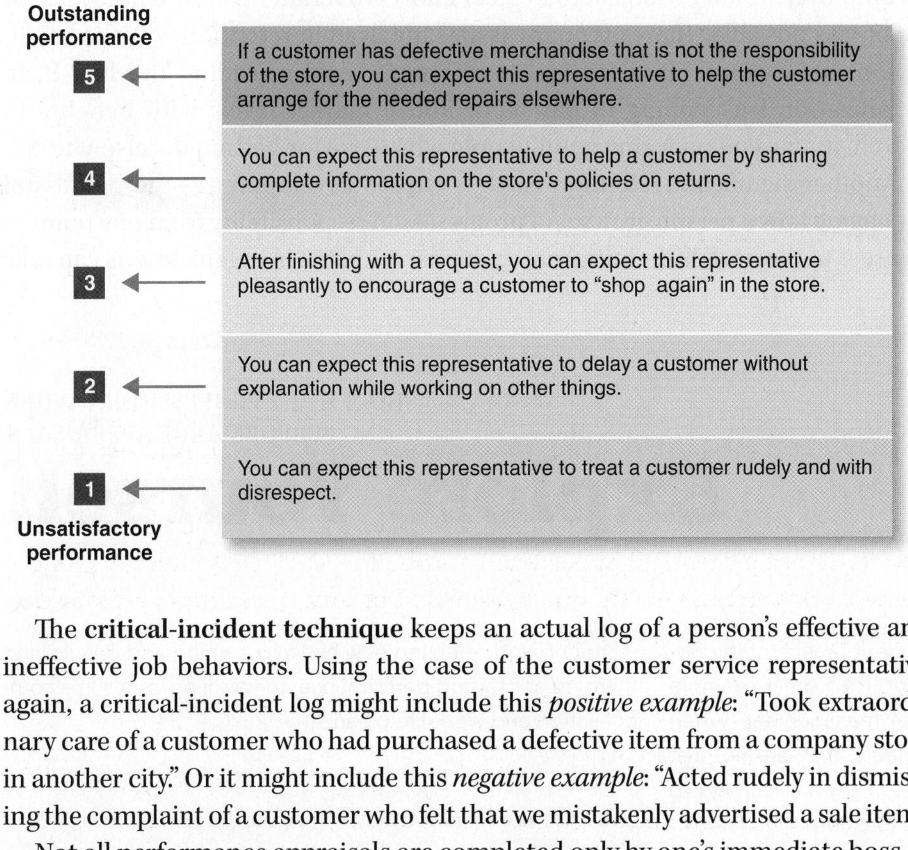

FIGURE 10.1
What Does a Behaviorally Anchored Rating Scale Look Like?
A behaviorally anchored rating scale (BARS) uses actual descriptions of positive and negative job behaviors to anchor rating points. In this example of how a customer service representative handles a merchandise return, various alternative behaviors are clearly identified. Consistent and documented rude or disrespectful behavior toward customers by a salesperson would earn a rating of "extremely poor." This specificity makes the BARS more reliable and valid.

The **critical-incident technique** keeps an actual log of a person's effective and ineffective job behaviors. Using the case of the customer service representative again, a critical-incident log might include this *positive example*: "Took extraordinary care of a customer who had purchased a defective item from a company store in another city." Or it might include this *negative example*: "Acted rudely in dismissing the complaint of a customer who felt that we mistakenly advertised a sale item."

> The **critical-incident technique** keeps a log of someone's effective and ineffective job behaviors.

Not all performance appraisals are completed only by one's immediate boss. It is increasingly popular to include self-appraisal, peer appraisals, and even upward appraisals from subordinates. This is called **360° feedback**, where superiors, subordinates, peers, and even internal and external customers are involved in the appraisal of a job holder's performance.[36] New technologies even allow

> **360° feedback** includes superiors, subordinates, peers, and even customers in the appraisal process.

360° feedback to be continuous rather than periodic. Accenture uses a computer program called Performance Multiplier that allows users to post projects, goals, and status updates for review by others. And a Toronto-based start-up company offers a program called Rypple. Users post questions in 140 characters or less; for example: "What did you think of my presentation?" or "How could I have run that meeting better?" Anonymous responses are compiled by the program and the 360°-type feedback is then sent to the person posting the query.[37]

A multiperson comparison compares one person's performance with that of others.

Finally, some performance appraisals use **multiperson comparisons** to avoid the problem of everyone being rated "about the same." Instead, they make managers rate and rank people relative to one another. These multiperson comparisons can be done by *rank-ordering* people from top to bottom in order of performance achievement, with no ties allowed. They can be done by *paired comparisons* that first evaluate each person against every other, and then create a summary ranking based on the number of superior scores. Or they can be done by a *forced distribution* that places each person into a frequency distribution with fixed performance classifications—such as top 10%, next 40%, next 40%, and bottom 10%.

‖ Retention and career development provide career paths.

After investing in recruitment, selection, orientation, training, and appraisal, an employer would be foolish to neglect efforts to retain the best employees for as long as possible. There are many issues involved in retention, with compensation and benefits as discussed in the next section leading the list. If an organization isn't willing to pay at or above market levels with benefits to match, it may end up losing good people who leave for better jobs elsewhere.

Career development is the process of managing how a person grows and progresses in a career.

Another significant retention issue is **career development**—the process of managing how a person grows and progresses in responsibility from one point in a career to the next. After initial entry, our career paths in organizations can take

{ MANAGERS SHOULD ACT PROFESSIONAL WHEN
DOING PERFORMANCE APPRAISALS.

Explore Yourself

■ PROFESSIONALISM

Chances are that your school has a student branch of the Society for Human Resource Management. It's a great example of how **professionalism** plays a role in management. When students work together on SHRM projects, they are not just learning HRM techniques and practices. They are learning to behave with internalized commitments to external standards.

All managers should show professionalism in their own areas of expertise and work responsibility. And, of course, they should be thoroughly professional in all aspects of human resource management discussed in this chapter—from recruiting and selecting new hires, to training and developing them, to appraising performance, to handling issues like compensation and work-life balance.

Get to know yourself better by taking the self-assessment on **Performance Appraisal Assumptions** and completing the other activities in the *Exploring Management* **Skill-Building Portfolio**.

off in many directions. Lots of choices will have to be made dealing with promotions, transfers, overseas assignments, mentors, higher degrees, even alternative employers and retirement.

Ideally, the employer and the individual work closely together in making career development choices. At Procter & Gamble, global human resources officer Moheet Nagrath says career tracks are built to match individual goals and company needs. If someone wants to become a top manager someday, for example, the company will plot moves through various brands as well as domestic and international assignments. "If you train people to work in different countries and businesses," he says, "you develop a deep bench."[38]

With people changing jobs frequently today and many working as independent contractors and freelancers, career development is becoming more and more a personal responsibility. This means that we each have to be diligent in **career planning,** the process of systematically matching career goals and individual capabilities with opportunities for their fulfillment. It involves answering such questions as "Who am I?" "What can I do?" "Where do I want to go?" and "How do I get there?"

Some suggest that we should view a career as something to be rationally planned and pursued in a logical step-by-step fashion. Others argue for flexibility, allowing our career to unfold in a somewhat random fashion as we respond to unexpected opportunities. But think about it. A well-managed career will probably include elements of each. A carefully thought-out career plan points you in a general direction; an eye for opportunity helps fill in the details as you proceed along the way. Are you ready?

> **Career planning** is the process of matching career goals and individual capabilities with opportunities for their fulfillment.

Ethics Check

■ HELP WANTED: SALESWOMEN

Are you successful working in sales at mall fashion clothing and retail shops? If so, a new and higher-paying option may be right for you. A local car dealership selling luxury vehicles wants outgoing, helpful women for client sales positions. Applicants should be honest and money-motivated, with high initiative and excellent communication skills. Pay based on wages, commissions, and bonuses can reach $80,000 per year. Watch for our recruiters at your mall this weekend.

This ad isn't real; you're unlikely to see anything like it in your local paper. But it is reflective of a trend in automobile sales—trying to hire more women and trying to recruit them in nontraditional settings. Marketing surveys show that women influence some 80% of car purchases and that many men prefer dealing with a female salesperson.

At a St. Louis dealership, the female owner claims that women are better organized and better at building a client base than are men; she wants to hire more. A law professor at Washington University in St. Louis says that it's okay to try to hire more women if the dealers aren't getting enough applicants.

YOU DECIDE

Suppose you're a qualified man, working in sales at a mall fashion store. You're also honest, self-starting, a good communicator, motivated by money, and in love with cars. Where does this ad leave you? Is it ethical for the car dealer to interview only women for this position?

STUDY GUIDE

Takeaway 10.2
What Are the Essential Human Resource Management Practices?

Terms to Define

Assessment center

Behaviorally anchored rating scale (BARS)

Career development

Career planning

Coaching

Critical-incident technique

Graphic rating scale

Mentoring

Multiperson comparison

Orientation

Performance appraisal

Person-job fit

Person-organization fit

Realistic job preview

Recruitment

Reliability

Reverse mentoring

Selection

Socialization

360° feedback

Validity

Work sampling

Rapid Review

- Recruitment is the process of attracting qualified job candidates to fill vacant positions; realistic job previews try to provide candidates with accurate information on the job and organization.
- Assessment centers and work sampling that mimic real job situations are increasingly common selection techniques.
- Orientation is the process of formally introducing new employees to their jobs and socializing them to the culture and performance expectations.
- Training keeps workers' skills up to date and job relevant; important training approaches include coaching and mentoring.
- Performance appraisal methods include graphic rating scales, behaviorally anchored rating scales, the critical-incidents technique, 360° feedback, and multiperson comparisons.
- Employee retention programs try to keep skilled workers in jobs and on career paths satisfying to them and beneficial to the employer.

Questions for Discussion

1. Is it realistic to expect that you can get a realistic job preview during the interview process?
2. If a new employer doesn't formally assign someone to be your coach or mentor, what should you do?
3. What are some of the possible downsides to receiving 360° feedback?

Be Sure You Can

- list steps in the recruitment process
- explain realistic job previews
- illustrate reliability and validity in employment testing
- illustrate how an assessment center might work
- explain the importance of socialization and orientation
- describe coaching and mentoring as training approaches
- discuss strengths and weaknesses of alternative performance appraisal methods

What Would You Do?

As the new head of retail merchandising at a local department store, you are disappointed to find that the sales clerks are evaluated on a graphic rating scale that uses a simple list of traits to gauge their performance. You want to propose an alternative and better approach for performance appraisal. Exactly what will you present as your proposal, and how will you present it to both the sales clerks and the boss?

Takeaway 10.3
What Are Current Issues in Human Resource Management?

ANSWERS TO COME

- Today's lifestyles increase demands for flexibility and work-life balance.
- Organizations use more independent contractors and part-time workers.
- Compensation plans influence employee recruitment and retention.
- Fringe benefits are an important part of employee compensation packages.
- Labor relations and collective bargaining are closely governed by law.

"HIRING GOOD PEOPLE IS TOUGH," STARTS AN ARTICLE IN THE *HARVARD BUSINESS Review*. The sentence finishes with "keeping them can be even tougher."[39] The point is that it isn't enough to hire and train workers to meet an organization's immediate needs. They must also be successfully nurtured, supported, and retained. When the Society for Human Resource Management surveyed employers, it learned that popular tools for maintaining a quality workforce included flexible work schedules and personal time off, as well as competitive salaries and good benefits—especially health insurance.[40]

‖ Today's lifestyles increase demands for flexibility and work-life balance.

Did you know that 78% of American couples are dual-wage earners, that 63% of workers believe they don't have enough time for spouses and partners, and that 74% say they don't have enough time for their children?[41] Today's fast-paced and complicated lifestyles have raised concerns for **work-life balance**, how people balance the demands of careers with their personal and family needs.[42] Not surprisingly, the "family-friendliness" of an employer is now frequently used as a screening criterion by job candidates. It is also used in "best employer" rankings by magazines such as *Business Week*, *Working Mother*, and *Fortune*.[43]

Work-life balance involves balancing career demands with personal and family needs.

Work-life balance is enhanced when workers have flexibility in scheduling work hours, work locations, and even such things as vacations and personal time off. Flexibility allows people to more easily manage their personal affairs and work responsibilities, and it has been shown that workers who have flexibility, at least with start and stop times, are less likely to leave their jobs.[44] Job designs that include flexible work hours and other alternative work schedules discussed in Chapter 8 are an increasingly popular starting point.[45] At Abbott Labs in Columbus, Ohio, for example, Wednesday is the only day employees have to be in the office; other days are open to flexible scheduling.[46]

More and more employers create flexibility by directly helping workers handle family matters through such things as on-site day care and elder care. Some have moved into innovative programs that include work sabbaticals—Schwab offers four weeks after five years employment; unlimited vacation days—a Dublin,

Ohio, advertising agency lets workers take as many vacation days as they want; purchased vacation time—Xerox allows workers to buy vacation days using payroll deductions; and on-call doctors—Microsoft sends doctors to employees' homes to keep them out of emergency rooms.[47] The accounting firm KPMG even keeps a "wellness scorecard" on employees to see if they are missing vacations or working too hard; if so, they are contacted by supervisors to discuss work patterns and ways to slow down.[48]

Independent contractors are hired on temporary contracts and are not part of the organization's permanent workforce.

⫼ Organizations are using more independent contractors and part-time workers.

Don't be surprised if you are asked some day to work only "as needed," as a "freelancer," or as an **independent contractor**. This would mean that you are expected to work for an agreed-upon period or for an agreed-upon task and without becoming part of the permanent workforce.

If there is one trend that has been reinforced by our tight economy, it's the use of more temporary and part-time workers. Gerry Grabowski of Pittsburgh knows the downside and the upside firsthand; he turned a temporary job in real estate into a full-time one. Says Grabowski: "A lot of people say it's a raw deal, and I guess it can be. But if I were an entrepreneur, I would never do a straight hire. I would use a contractor or temp first."[49] If you wonder why, *BusinessWeek* describes them as: "easy to lay off, no severance; no company funded retirement plan; pay own health insurance; get zero sick days and no vacation."[50]

{ "MY CHIEF ASSETS WALK OUT THE DOOR EVERY DAY. MY JOB IS TO MAKE SURE THEY COME BACK."

Role Models

▇ JIM GOODNIGHT MAKES PEOPLE A TOP PRIORITY AT SAS

After being voted as one of *Fortune* magazine's "Best Companies to Work for" 13 years in a row, this privately owned software firm in North Carolina has earned a top reputation as an employer. Here's a glimpse of what it's like to be one of Goodnight's 4000+ employees.

The typical workweek is 35 hours; no one monitors what time you show up; two in-house day-care centers are available; you can get dry cleaning, car washes and haircuts on site; and work-life or wellness centers provide everything from workout rooms to special programs in weight management to counseling on family issues.

Goodnight is the brains behind SAS's unique culture. He believes in treating employees well, giving them freedom and support, and trusting them to act as responsible adults. "My chief assets walk out the door every day," he says. "My job is to make sure they come back."

And come back they do. The turnover rate at SAS is 2%, compared to 22% for the industry as a whole; over 100 résumés are received for each job opening. And when it comes to performance, employee Bev Brown says: "Some may think that because SAS is family friendly and has great benefits that we don't work hard, but people do work hard here because they're motivated to care for company that takes care of them."

WHAT'S THE LESSON HERE?

Jim Goodnight says that "contented cows give more milk." Is that the lesson we should all be listening to? Is it possible that organizations that really do put people first and treat them as adults have a highly motivated workforce?

Part-time and temporary workers represent some 26% of the U.S. workforce, and the number keeps growing. We call them **contingency workers** because they supplement the full-time workforce by working as-needed and part-time, often on a long-term basis. Tammy DePew is one; she works from home as a contract employee of LiveOps, a contract call-center firm. Tammy gets paid by minutes of customer contact time and is glad to have steady and flexible work. "LiveOps was a lifesaver for me." She says: "Contracting and working from home may not be for everyone, but is empowering and I like it."[51]

Because contingency workers can be easily hired, contracted with, and terminated in response to changing needs, many employers like the flexibility they offer in controlling labor costs and dealing with cyclical demand. On the cost side, an employer can save up to 30% by hiring a contingency versus full-time worker.[52] On the other hand, some worry that temporary workers lack the commitment of permanent workers and may lower productivity. Perhaps the most controversial issues of part-time workers is that they may be paid less than their full-time counterparts, they may experience significant stress and anxiety from their part-time job status, and many do not receive important benefits such as health care, life insurance, pension plans, and paid vacations.

> **Contingency workers** work as needed and part-time, often on a longer-term basis.

‖ Compensation plans influence employee recruitment and retention.

Pay! It may be that no other work issue receives as much attention. And, the trend in compensation today is largely toward "pay-for-performance."[53]

If you are part of a **merit pay** system, your pay increases will be based on some assessment of how well you perform. The notion is that a good merit raise sends a positive signal to high performers and a low one sends a negative signal to poor performers, encouraging both to work hard in the future.

> **Merit pay** awards pay increases in proportion to performance contributions.

{ ONLY 3% OF HRM EXECUTIVES GIVE "A" GRADES TO THEIR FIRMS' PERFORMANCE MEASUREMENT SYSTEMS.

Facts to Consider

■ HUMAN RESOURCE EXECUTIVES WORRY ABOUT PERFORMANCE MEASUREMENT

A survey of human resource executives published in the *Wall Street Journal* says that they aren't pleased with the way managers in their organizations do performance reviews. Some are so concerned that they suggest dropping them altogether. Some survey findings were:

- Only 30% of the HR executives believed that employees trust their employer's performance measurement system.
- 40% rated their performance review systems as B, and only 3% rated them as A.
- Many HR executives were concerned that managers aren't willing to face employees and give constructive feedback.

- HR executives also complained that employees don't have a clear enough understanding of what rates as good and bad performance.

YOUR THOUGHTS?

Performance measurement is often a hot topic these days as things like "merit pay" and "performance accountability" are discussed in many job settings. Based on your experience, what should be done about it? Is it really possible to have a performance measurement system that is respected by all—employers and workers alike?

Although the pay-for-performance logic makes sense, merit systems are not problem-free. In many ways they are only as good as the performance appraisal methods used to measure performance. And this is a problem. A survey reported by the *Wall Street Journal* found that only 23% of employees believed they understood their companies' systems.[54] Typical questions are: Who assesses performance? Suppose the employee doesn't agree with the assessment? Is the system fair and equitable to everyone involved? Is there enough money available to make the merit increases meaningful for those who receive them?

In order for a merit pay system to work, it must be based on a solid foundation of agreed-upon and well-defined performance measures that can handle the prior questions and more. For example, at the restaurant chain Applebee's International Inc., managers know that part of their merit pay will be determined by the percentage of their best workers who are retained. In an industry known for high turnover, Applebee's makes retention of high performers a high-priority goal for managers.[55] But this system can still break down if Applebee's managers don't perceive that it is administered in a fair, consistent, and credible fashion.

There's more to the Applebee's story. If you are one of the employees that managers want to retain, you might be on the receiving end of "Applebucks"—small cash awards that are given to reward performance and raise loyalty to the firm.[56] This is an example of **bonus pay**—one-time or lump-sum payments to employees based on the accomplishment of specific performance targets or some other extraordinary contribution, such as an idea for a work improvement. How would you like to someday receive a letter like this one, once sent to two top executives by Amazon.com's chairman Jeff Bezos? "In recognition and appreciation of your contributions," his letter read, "Amazon.com will pay you a special bonus in the amount of $1,000,000."[57]

In contrast to straight bonuses, **profit sharing** distributes to employees a proportion of net profits earned by the organization in a performance period. **Gain sharing** extends the profit-sharing concept by allowing groups of employees to share in any savings or "gains" realized when their efforts result in measurable cost reductions or productivity increases.[58]

Yet another merit pay approach is to grant employees **stock options** linked to their performance.[59] Stock options give the owner the right to buy shares of stock at a future date at a fixed price. Stock owners gain financially the more the stock price rises above the original option price; they lose if the stock price moves lower. Some companies "restrict" the stock options so that they come due only after designated periods of employment. This practice is meant to tie high performers to the employer and is often called the *golden handcuff*. You'll find that many of the most admired U.S. companies are also ones that offer stock options to a greater proportion of their workforces.

Fringe benefits are an important part of employee compensation packages.

Benefits! They rank right up there with pay as a way of helping to attract and retain workers. How many times does a graduating college student hear, "Be sure to get a job with benefits!"?[60]

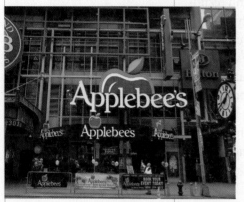

Bonus pay plans provide one-time payments based on performance accomplishments.

Profit sharing distributes to employees a proportion of net profits earned by the organization.

Gain sharing allows employees to share in cost savings or productivity gains realized by their efforts.

Stock options give the right to purchase shares at a fixed price in the future.

Any mention of **fringe benefits** directs attention toward nonmonetary forms of compensation such as health insurance and retirement plans. And they can be a hot button in conversations about work today. Benefits can add as much as 20% or more to a typical worker's earnings, and, at times, the cost of benefits increases faster than the cost of wages and salaries.

Fringe benefit costs, especially medical insurance and retirement, are a major worry for employers. Many are attempting to gain control over health care expenses by shifting more of the insurance costs to the employee and by restricting options in choosing health care providers. Many are also offering wellness programs and encouraging healthy lifestyles as a way of decreasing health insurance claims.

The growing significance of work-life balance is reflected in **family-friendly benefits** that help employees to better balance work and nonwork responsibilities. These include child care, elder care, flexible schedules, parental leave, and part-time employment options, among others. Also popular are **flexible benefits** programs that let the employee choose a personalized set of benefits within a certain dollar amount, and **employee assistance programs** that help with troublesome personal problems. Such EAP programs may include assistance in dealing with stress, counseling on alcohol and substance abuse, referrals for domestic violence and sexual abuse, family and marital counseling, and advice on community resources.

You'll probably hear a lot about fringe benefits in conversations with family and friends. A quick check of online discussions, for example, uncovered this question: "If I don't get the raise I was hoping for, what are some of the possible fringe benefits other than medical insurance that I might ask for to make up the difference?" Here's a list of the suggestions the questioner received: 401(k) or 403(b) options, life and disability insurance, lower premiums on health insurance, vision insurance, free fitness center membership, extra vacation time, more flexible hours, the option to work from home or the car, longer lunch periods, use of a company car, and new office furniture. If you're looking for a new job or getting ready to negotiate for a pay raise, what might be on your list of desired fringe benefits?

⫴ Labor relations and collective bargaining are closely governed by law.

Labor unions are organizations to which workers belong and that deal with employers on the workers' behalf. They act as a collective "voice" for their members, one that wouldn't be available to them as individuals. Historically, this voice of the unions has played an important role in American society. And even though unions are often associated with wage and benefit concerns, workers also join unions because of things like poor relationships with supervisors, favoritism or lack of respect by supervisors, little or no influence with employers, and failure of employers to provide a mechanism for grievance and dispute resolution.[61]

The average percentage of workers in the United States who belong to unions has been on the decline. Recent figures show that 11.0% of workers overall now belong to unions versus 14.9% in 1996. But the percentage of public sector workers who belong to unions—teachers, police, firefighters, and local government employees, is increasing. It nows stands at 36.2% of workers versus 6.9% in the private sector.[62] What do you think? Does the decline in private sector union membership mean that workers have pretty much decided they don't need union

---

Fringe benefits are nonmonetary forms of compensation such as health insurance and retirement plans.

Family-friendly benefits help employees achieve better work-life balance.

Flexible benefits programs allow choice to personalize benefits within a set dollar allowance.

Employee assistance programs help employees cope with personal stresses and problems.

A **labor union** is an organization that deals with employers on the workers' collective behalf.

A **labor contract** is a formal agreement between a union and an employer about the terms of work for union members.

Collective bargaining is the process of negotiating, administering, and interpreting a labor contract.

Two-tier wage systems pay new hires less than workers already doing the same jobs with more seniority.

representation anymore? Or do other factors explain these trends? Why is union membership increasing in the public sector?

Unions negotiate legal contracts affecting many aspects of the employment relationship for their members. These **labor contracts** typically specify the rights and obligations of employees and management with respect to wages, work hours, work rules, seniority, hiring, grievances, and other conditions of work. The front line in labor-management relationship is **collective bargaining**, the process that brings management and union representatives together in negotiating, administering, and interpreting labor contracts. During a collective bargaining session, these parties exchange a variety of demands, proposals, and counterproposals. Several rounds of bargaining may take place before a contract is reached or a dispute resolved. Sometimes the process breaks down, and one or both parties walk away. The impasse can be short or lengthy, in some cases leading to labor actions that can last months and even years before agreements are reached.

One of the areas where unions and employers can find themselves on different sides of the bargaining issue relates to so-called **two-tier wage systems**. These are systems that pay new hires less than workers already doing the same jobs with more seniority. Agreeing to a two-tier system in collective bargaining isn't likely to be the preference of union negotiators. At a Goodyear factory in Alabama where a two-tiered system is in place, one of the high-seniority workers says: "If I was doing the same job, working just as hard and earning what they make, I'd be resentful."[63] But the management side offers at least one strong argument in its favor. Getting a two-tier agreement in the labor contract can help keep the firm profitable and retain jobs in America that would otherwise be lost to foreign outsourcing. Such agreements are now in place at all the big U.S. automakers.[64]

When labor-management relations take on the adversarial character shown in Figure 10.2, the conflict can be prolonged and costly for both sides. That's not good for anyone, and there is quite a bit of pressure these days for more cooperative union-management relationships. Wouldn't it be nice if unions and management would work together in partnership, trying to address the concerns of both parties in ways that best meet the great challenges and competitive pressures of a global economy?

FIGURE 10.2 **What Happens When Labor-Management Relations Become Adversarial?**
When union and management representatives meet in collective bargaining, it would be nice if things were always cooperative. Unfortunately, they sometimes turn adversarial, and each side has weapons at its disposal to make things hard for the other. Unions can resort to strikes, boycotts, and picketing. Management can use lockouts, strike-breakers, and court injunctions to force strikers back to work. Although each side can find justifications in defense of using such tactics, they can also come with high price tags in terms of lost worker earnings and company profits.

STUDY GUIDE

Takeaway 10.3
What Are Current Issues in Human Resource Management?

Terms to Define

Bonus pay

Collective bargaining

Contingency workers

Employee assistance program

Flexible benefits

Family-friendly benefits

Fringe benefits

Gain sharing

Independent contractors

Labor contract

Labor union

Merit pay

Profit sharing

Stock options

Two-tier wage systems

Work-life balance

Rapid Review

- Complex job demands and family responsibilities have made work-life balance programs increasingly important in human resource management.
- Compensation and benefits packages must be attractive so that an organization stays competitive in labor markets.
- Labor unions are organizations to which workers belong and that deal with employers on the employees' behalf.
- Collective bargaining is the process of negotiating, administering, and interpreting a labor contract.
- Labor relations and collective bargaining are closely governed by law and can be cooperative or adversarial in nature.

Questions for Discussion

1. Are we giving too much attention these days to issues of work-life balance?
2. Can a good argument be made that merit pay just doesn't work?
3. Given economic trends, is it likely that unions will gain in future popularity?

Be Sure You Can

- define work-life balance and discuss its significance for the human resource management process
- explain why compensation and benefits are important in human resource management
- differentiate bonuses and profit sharing as forms of performance-based pay
- define the terms "labor union," "labor contract," and "collective bargaining"
- compare the adversarial and cooperative approaches to labor-management relations

What Would You Do?

As a student, you have become aware of a drive to organize the faculty of your institution and have them represented by a union. The student leaders on campus are holding a forum to gather opinions on the pros and cons of a unionized faculty. Because you represent a student organization in your college, you are asked to participate in the forum. What will you say and why?

Multiple-Choice Questions

1. Human resource management is the process of _____, developing, and maintaining a high-quality workforce.

(a) attracting   (b) compensating

(c) appraising   (d) selecting

2. A _____ is a criterion that organizations can legally justify for use in screening job candidates.

(a) job description

(b) bona fide occupational qualification

(c) realistic job preview

(d) BARS

3. _____ programs are designed to ensure equal employment opportunities for groups historically underrepresented in the workforce.

(a) Realistic recruiting   (b) Mentoring

(c) Affirmative action   (d) Coaching

4. An employment test that yields different results over time when taken by the same person lacks _____.

(a) validity   (b) reliability

(c) realism   (d) behavioral anchors

5. The assessment center approach to employee selection relies heavily on _____ to evaluate a candidate's job skills.

(a) intelligence tests

(b) simulations and experiential exercises

(c) 360° feedback

(d) formal one-on-one interviews

6. In the legal context of human resource management, which of the following is most likely a safe question for an interviewer to ask a job candidate during a telephone interview?

(a) Are you pregnant or planning to soon start a family?

(b) What skills do you have that would help you do this job really well?

(c) Will you be able to work at least ten years before hitting the retirement age?

(d) Do you get financial support from a spouse or companion who is also a wage earner?

7. Socialization of newcomers occurs during the _____ step of the staffing process.

(a) orientation   (b) recruiting

(c) selection   (d) advertising

8. Which phrase is most consistent with a recruiter offering a job candidate a realistic job preview?

(a) "There are just no downsides to this job."

(b) "No organization is as good as this one."

(c) "There just aren't any negatives."

(d) "Let me tell you what you might not like once you start work."

9. When a job candidate is asked to actually perform on-the-job for a period of time while being observed by a recruiter, this is a selection technique known as _____.

(a) mentoring   (b) work sampling

(c) job coaching   (d) critical incident testing

10. The _____ purpose of performance appraisal is being addressed when a manager describes training options that might help an employee improve future performance.

(a) development   (b) evaluation

(c) judgmental   (d) legal

11. When a team leader must rate 10% of team members as "superior," 80% as "good," and 10% as "unacceptable," this is an example of the _____ approach to performance appraisal.

(a) graphic

(b) critical-incident

(c) behaviorally anchored rating scale

(d) forced distribution

12. What is one of the reasons why employers are hiring more part-time or contingency workers?

(a) It's hard to get people to work full-time anymore.

(b) Part-timers are known to work much harder than full-timers.

(c) Full-time employees don't have up-to-date job skills.

(d) It's easy to hire part-timers when you need them, and let them go when you don't.

13. Whereas bonus plans pay employees for special accomplishments, gain-sharing plans reward them for _____.

    (a) helping to increase social responsibility

    (b) regular attendance

    (c) positive work attitudes

    (d) suggestions that lead to cost reductions

14. An employee with family problems that are starting to interfere with work would be pleased to learn that his employer had a(n) _____ plan.

    (a) employee assistance   (b) cafeteria benefits

    (c) comparable worth   (d) collective bargaining

15. When representatives of management and a labor union meet and negotiate the terms of a new labor contract, this process is known as _____.

    (a) boycotting   (b) collective bargaining

    (c) picketing   (d) wage negotiating

Short-Response Questions

16. Why is orientation important in the HRM process?

17. How does mentoring work as an on-the-job training approach?

18. When is an employment test or a performance appraisal method reliable?

19. How do the graphic rating scale and the BARS differ as performance appraisal methods?

Integration and Application Question

20. Sy Smith is not doing well in his job. The problems began to appear shortly after Sy's job changed from a manual to a computer-based operation. He has tried hard but is just not doing well in learning how to use the computer to meet performance expectations. He is 45 years old and has been with the company for 18 years. Sy has been a great worker in the past and is both popular and influential among his peers. Along with his performance problems, you have also noticed that Sy is starting to sometimes "badmouth" the firm. **Questions:** As Sy's manager, what options would you consider in terms of dealing with the issue of his retention in the job and in the company? What could you do by way of career development for Sy, and why?

Steps*for*FurtherLearning

Many learning resources are found at the end of the book and online within WileyPLUS.

Don't Miss These Selections from the **Skill-Building Portfolio**

■ **SELF-ASSESSMENT 10:** *Performance Appraisal Assumptions*

■ **CLASS EXERCISE 10:** *Upward Appraisal*

■ **TEAM PROJECT 10 :** *The Future of Labor Unions*

Don't Miss This Selection from **Cases for Critical Thinking**

■ **CHAPTER 10 CASE**

   Netflix—Making Movie Magic

Snapshot How can the most successful video-delivery company beat its already unbelievable one-day turnaround time? By making a growing portion of its immense catalog available for instant download. Netflix leverages emerging technologies, superior customer service, and an ever-growing subscriber base to transform the traditional video-rental model into a 21st-century on-demand concept.

"I have a dream," said Martin Luther King, Jr, and his voice traveled across generations. Visionary leaders communicate shared dreams and inspire others to pursue lofty goals.

Leadership

A Leader Lives in Each of Us

Integrity and *Love Happens*

Burke Ryan (Aaron Eckhardt) is a successful self-help guru. He travels around the country promoting his book and hosting workshops to help people overcome tragedies and move on in their lives. The only problem is that Ryan has not dealt effectively with his own tragedy—the death of his wife in a car accident.

While hosting a week-long seminar in Seattle, his former home, he meets eclectic florist Eloise Chandler (Jennifer Anniston). He also comes face-to-face with his father-in-law (Martin Sheen) for the first time since the tragedy. These forces help Ryan realize he can no longer live the lie. On the last day of the workshop, he makes a painful public admission that the accident was his fault and he has never forgiven himself. The audience erupts in a standing ovation as Ryan receives a tearful embrace of forgiveness from his father-in-law.

This movie helps remind us about the importance of **integrity**—being honest, credible, and consistent while living up to personal values. And it moves us to think more about leadership. Real leaders have lots of integrity. It helps them as they try to help others achieve their full potential. Real leaders are also humble, willing to serve others more than be in the spotlight.

How often do you think about integrity when it comes to leadership? When news media cover leaders, do their reports indicate integrity or its absence? What does this say about the status of leadership integrity in our society?

YOUR CHAPTER 11 TAKEAWAYS

1. Understand the foundations for effective leadership.

2. Identify insights of the contingency leadership theories.

3. Discuss current issues and directions in leadership development.

WHAT'S INSIDE

Explore Yourself
More on integrity

Role Models
Lorraine Monroe's leadership turns vision into inspiration

Ethics Check
When the boss asks too much

Facts to Consider
Workers report shortcomings of leaders and top managers

Manager's Library
Power by Jeffrey Pfeffer

Takeaway 11.1
What Are the Foundations for Effective Leadership?

ANSWERS TO COME

- Leadership is one of the four functions of management.
- Leaders use position power to achieve influence.
- Leaders use personal power to achieve influence.
- Leaders bring vision to leadership situations.
- Leaders display different traits in the quest for leadership effectiveness.
- Leaders display different styles in the quest for leadership effectiveness.

Leadership is the process of inspiring others to work hard to accomplish important tasks.

A GLANCE AT THE SHELVES IN YOUR LOCAL BOOKSTORE WILL QUICKLY CONFIRM that **leadership, the process of inspiring others to work hard to accomplish important tasks,** is one of the most popular management topics.[1] Consultant and author Tom Peters says that the leader is "rarely—possibly never—the best performer."[2] They don't have to be; leaders thrive through and by the successes of others. But not all managers live up to these expectations. Warren Bennis, a respected scholar and consultant, claims that too many U.S. corporations are "over-managed and under-led." The late Grace Hopper, the first female admiral in the U.S. Navy, advised that "you manage things; you lead people."[3] The bottom line is that leaders become great by bringing out the best in people.

FIGURE 11.1 Why Is Leading So Important in the Management Process?
Leading is one of the four management functions. It is the process of inspiring others to work hard to accomplish important tasks. Managers who are effective leaders act in ways that create high levels of enthusiasm among people to use their talents fully to accomplish tasks and pursue important plans and goals.

Leadership is one of the four functions of management.

Leadership is one of the four functions that make up the management process shown in Figure 11.1. *Planning* sets the direction and objectives; *organizing* brings together the resources to turn plans into action; *leading* builds the commitment and enthusiasm that allow people to apply their talents to help accomplish plans; and *controlling* makes sure things turn out right.

Where do you stand on leadership skills and capabilities? If, as the chapter subtitle states, "A leader lives in each of us," what leader resides in you?

Of course, managers sometimes face daunting challenges in their quest to succeed as leaders. The time frames for getting things accomplished are becoming shorter. Second chances are sometimes few and far between. The problems to be resolved through leadership are often complex, ambiguous, and multidimensional. And, leaders are expected to stay focused on long-term goals even while dealing with problems and pressures in the short term.[4] Anyone aspiring to career success in leadership must rise to these challenges and more. They must become good at using all the interpersonal skills discussed in this part of *Exploring Management 3/e*—power and influence, communication, motivation, teamwork, conflict, and negotiation.

‖ Leaders use position power to achieve influence.

Are you surprised that our discussion of leadership starts with power? Harvard professor Rossabeth Moss Kanter once called it "America's last great dirty word."[5] She worries that too many managers are uncomfortable with the concept and don't realize it is indispensable to leadership.

Power is the ability to get someone else to do something you want done, the ability to make things happen the way you want them to. Isn't that a large part of management, being able to influence other people? So, where and how do managers get power?

Most often we talk about two sources of managerial power that you might remember by this equation[6]:

Managerial Power = Position Power + Personal Power.

First is the power of the position, being "the manager." This power includes rewards, coercion, and legitimacy. Second is the power of the person, who you are and what your presence means in a situation. This power includes expertise and reference. Of course, some of us do far better than others at mobilizing and using the different types of power.[7]

If you look at the small figure, you'll see that **reward power** is the capability to offer something of value as a means of achieving influence. To use reward power, a manager says, in effect: "If you do what I ask, I'll give you a reward." Common rewards are things like pay raises, bonuses, promotions, special assignments, and compliments. As you might expect, reward power can work well as long as people want the reward and the manager or leader makes it continuously available. But take the value of the reward or the reward itself away, and the power is quickly lost.

Coercive power is the capability to punish or withhold positive outcomes as a way of influencing others. To mobilize coercive power, a manager is really saying: "If you don't do what I want, I'll punish you." Managers have access to lots of possible punishments, including reprimands, pay penalties, bad job assignments, and even termination. But how do you feel when on the receiving end of such threats? If you're like me, you'll most likely resent both the threat and the person making it. You might act as requested or at least go through the motions, but you're unlikely to continue doing so once the threat no longer exists.

Legitimate power is the capacity to influence through formal authority. It is the right of the manager, or person in charge, to exercise control over persons in subordinate positions. To use legitimate power, a manager is basically saying: "I am the boss; therefore, you are supposed to do as I ask." When an instructor assigns homework, exams, and group projects, don't you most often do what is requested? Why? You do it because the requests seem legitimate to the course. But if the instructor moves outside course boundaries, perhaps asking you to attend a sports event, the legitimacy is lost and your compliance is less likely.

Power is the ability to get someone else to do something you want done.

Power of the POSITION:
Based on things managers can offer to others

Rewards: "If you do what I ask, I'll give you a reward."

Coercion: "If you don't do what I ask, I'll punish you."

Legitimacy: "Because I am the boss, you *must* do as I ask."

Reward power achieves influence by offering something of value.

Coercive power achieves influence by punishment.

Legitimate power achieves influence by formal authority.

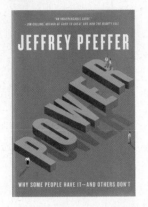

{ A PERSON'S ORGANIZATIONAL POWER CORRELATES
POSITIVELY WITH CAREER SUCCESS AND SALARY.

Manager's Library

■ *POWER* BY JEFFREY PFEFFER

DO YOURSELF SOME GOOD AND SCHEDULE A POWER TRIP—YOUR CAREER DEPENDS UPON IT!

People who believe good work in life gets noticed and leads to just rewards should take pause. Research shows the most critical factor for success is having power—authority and control over work environments, resources, and decisions.

In the book *Power* (2010, HarperCollins), author Jeffrey Pfeffer says research shows a person's organizational power correlates positively with career success, job performance, salary, and even one's lifespan. He urges people to use political savvy to rise within hierarchies to control more resources and decisions and build power, status, and influence.

Pfeffer says research links political savvy to career success. Effective leaders who are critical of others are seen as intelligent, while less effective leaders who are nice to others are viewed as weak.

Many people face obstacles and fail to gain power. They believe the world is just—rewards for good deeds and punishments for bad ones—and fail to learn from situations, both good and bad, and from people, even those they dislike. They fear failure so they avoid trying to preserve their self-image.

Pfeffer believes that attaining power requires will and skill, so personal qualities of ambition, energy, and focus are needed. Ambition keeps attention on achieving influence over others, especially those higher up. Energy fuels hard work and effort; it is contagious and signals commitment to others. Focus limits activities and skills to areas that will lead to more power, status, and influence.

REFLECT AND REACT

Think about the formal or informal hierarchies that you belong to. How are members selected and dismissed, and, how are members' tasks assigned? How are resources selected and used? How are decisions made and by whom? Are those in power perceived positively, negatively, intelligent, or weak? Do you agree that some people fail to gain power since they fear failure and avoid trying?

‖ Leaders use personal power to achieve influence.

After all is said and done, we need to admit that position power alone isn't going to be sufficient for any manager. In fact, how much personal power you can mobilize through expertise and reference may well make the difference someday between success and failure in a leadership situation—and even in a career.

As shown in the small figure, **expert power** is the ability to influence the behavior of others because of special knowledge and skills. When a manager uses expert power, the implied message is: "You should do what I want because of my special expertise or information."

Expert power achieves influence by special knowledge.

Power of the PERSON:
Based on how managers are viewed by others
Expertise —as a source of special knowledge and information
Reference —as a person with whom others like to identify

A leader's expertise may come from technical understanding or access to information relevant to the issue at hand. It can be acquired through formal education and evidenced by degrees and credentials. It is also acquired on the job, through experience, and by gaining a reputation as someone who is a high performer and really understands the work. Building expertise in these ways, in fact, may be one of your biggest early career challenges.

There's still more to personal power. Think of all the television commercials that show high-visibility athletes and personalities advertising consumer products. What's really going on here? The intent is to attract customers

{ "THE JOB OF A GOOD LEADER IS TO UPLIFT HER PEOPLE . . .
AS INDIVIDUALS OF INFINITE WORTH IN THEIR OWN RIGHT."

Role Models

■ LORRAINE MONROE'S LEADERSHIP TURNS VISION INTO INSPIRATION

Dr. Lorraine Monroe's career in the New York City Schools began as a teacher. She went on to serve as assistant principal, principal, and vice chancellor for curriculum and instruction. But her career really took off when she founded the Frederick Douglass Academy, a public school in Harlem, where she grew up. Under her leadership as principal, the school became highly respected for educational excellence. The academy's namesake was an escaped slave who later became a prominent abolitionist and civil rights leader.

Monroe sees leadership as vision driven and follower centered. She believes leaders must always start at the "heart of the matter" and that "the job of a good leader is to articulate a vision that others are inspired to follow." She believes in making sure all workers know that they are valued and that their advice is welcome. She also believes that workers and managers should always try to help and support one another. "I have never undertaken any project," she says, "without first imagining on paper what it would ultimately look like . . . all the doers who would be responsible for carrying out my imaginings have to be informed and let in on the dream."

As a consultant on public leadership Monroe states: "We can reform society only if every place we live—every school, workplace, church, and family—becomes a site of reform." She also runs the Lorraine Monroe Leadership Institute. Its goal is to train educational leaders in visionary leadership and help them go forth to build schools that transform children's lives.

Lorraine Monroe's many leadership ideas are summarized in what is called the "Monroe Doctrine." It begins with this advice: "The job of the leader is to uplift her people—not just as members of and contributors to the organization, but as individuals of infinite worth in their own right."

WHAT'S THE LESSON HERE?

Follower-centered leadership is high on Lorraine Monroe's list of priorities. And she's made a fine career by putting its principles to work. What is there in the Monroe Doctrine that can help you succeed as a leader? Do you have what it takes to truly value people who look up to you for leadership?

---

to the products through identification with the athletes and personalities. The same holds true in leadership. **Referent power** is the ability to influence the behavior of others because they admire and want to identify positively with you. When a manager uses referent power, the implied message is: "You should do what I want in order to maintain a positive self-defined relationship with me."

If referent power is so valuable, do you know how to get it? It comes in large part from good interpersonal relationships, ones that create admiration and respect for us in the eyes of others. My wife sums this up very simply by saying: "It's a lot easier to get people to do what you want when they like you than when they dislike you." Doesn't this make sense? This is good advice for how to approach your job and the people with whom you work every day.

> **Referent power** achieves influence by personal identification.

‖ Leaders bring vision to leadership situations.

"Great leaders," it is said, "get extraordinary things done in organizations by inspiring and motivating others toward a common purpose."[8] In other words, they use their power exceptionally well. And frequently today, successful leadership is associated with **vision**—a future that one hopes to create or achieve in order to improve upon the present state of affairs. According to the late John Wooden,

> A **vision** is a clear sense of the future.

a standout men's basketball coach at UCLA for 27 years: "Effective leadership means having a lot of people working toward a common goal. And when you have that with no one caring who gets the credit, you're going to accomplish a lot."[9]

The term **visionary leadership** describes a leader who brings to the situation a clear and compelling sense of the future, as well as an understanding of the actions needed to get there successfully.[10] But simply having the vision of a desirable future is not enough. Truly great leaders are extraordinarily good at turning their visions into accomplishments. This means being good at communicating the vision and getting people motivated and inspired to pursue the vision in their daily work. You can think of it this way. Visionary leadership brings meaning to people's work; it makes what they do seem worthy and valuable.

> **Visionary leadership** brings to the situation a clear sense of the future and an understanding of how to get there.

||| Leaders display different traits in the quest for leadership effectiveness.

For centuries, people have recognized that some persons use power well and perform successfully as leaders, whereas others do not. You've certainly seen this yourself. How can such differences in leadership effectiveness be explained?

An early direction in leadership research tried to answer this question by identifying traits and personal characteristics shared by well-regarded leaders.[11] Not surprisingly, results showed that physical characteristics such as height, weight, and physique make no difference. But a study of over 3,400 managers found that followers rather consistently admired leaders who were honest, competent, forward-looking, inspiring, and credible.[12] Another comprehensive review is summarized in Table 11.1—*Traits Often Shared by Effective Leaders.*[13] You might use this list as a quick check of your leadership potential.

Table 11.1 Traits Often Shared by Effective Leaders

Drive—Successful leaders have high energy, display initiative, and are tenacious.
Self-confidence—Successful leaders trust themselves and have confidence in their abilities.
Creativity—Successful leaders are creative and original in their thinking.
Cognitive ability—Successful leaders have the intelligence to integrate and interpret information.
Business knowledge—Successful leaders know their industry and its technical foundations.
Motivation—Successful leaders enjoy influencing others to achieve shared goals.
Flexibility—Successful leaders adapt to fit the needs of followers and the demands of situations.
Honesty and integrity—Successful leaders are trustworthy; they are honest, predictable, and dependable.

||| Leaders display different styles in the quest for leadership effectiveness.

In addition to leadership traits, researchers have also studied how successful and unsuccessful leaders behave when working with followers. Most of this research focused on two sets of behaviors: task-oriented behaviors and people-oriented behaviors. A leader high in concern for task plans and defines work goals, assigns task responsibilities, sets clear work standards, urges task completion, and monitors performance results. A leader high in concern for people acts warm

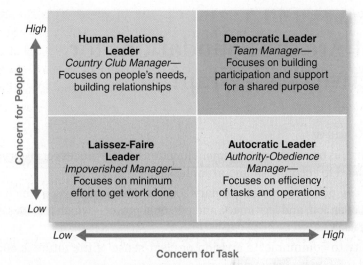

High

Human Relations Leader
Country Club Manager—
Focuses on people's needs, building relationships

Democratic Leader
Team Manager—
Focuses on building participation and support for a shared purpose

Concern for People

Laissez-Faire Leader
Impoverished Manager—
Focuses on minimum effort to get work done

Autocratic Leader
Authority-Obedience Manager—
Focuses on efficiency of tasks and operations

Low

Low   High

Concern for Task

FIGURE 11.2 What Are the Classic Leadership Styles?
It is common to describe leaders in terms of how their day-to-day styles show concern for people and concern for task. In this figure the leader low in concern for both people and task is described as "laissez-faire" and very ineffective. The leader high in concern for task but low in concern for people is "autocratic" and focused on performance. The leader high in concern for people and low in concern for task has a "human relations" style that focuses mainly on people and relationships. The "democratic" leader is high in concern for both people and task. This person is often highly successful as a true team manager who is able to engage people to accomplish common goals.

and supportive toward followers, maintains good relations with them, respects their feelings, shows sensitivity to their needs, and displays trust in them.

Leaders who show different combinations of task and people behaviors are often described as having unique **leadership styles**, such as you have probably observed in your own experiences. A popular summary of classic leadership styles used by managers is shown in Figure 11.2.[14]

Someone who emphasizes task over people is often described as an **autocratic leader**. This manager focuses on authority and obedience, delegates little, keeps information to himself or herself, and tends to act in a unilateral command-and-control fashion. Have you ever worked for someone fitting this description? How would you score his or her leadership effectiveness?

A leader who emphasizes people over task is often referred to as a **human relations leader**. This leader is interpersonally engaging, cares about others, is sensitive to feelings and emotions, and tends to act in ways that emphasize harmony and good working relationships.

Interestingly, researchers at first believed that the human relations style was the most effective for a leader. However, after pressing further, the conclusion emerged that the most effective leaders were strong in concerns for both people and task.[15] Sometimes called a **democratic leader**, a manager with this style shares decisions with followers, encourages participation, and supports the teamwork needed for high levels of task accomplishment.

One result of this research on leader behaviors was the emergence of training programs designed to help people become better leaders by learning how to be good at both task-oriented and people-oriented behaviors. How about you? Where do you fit on the above leadership diagram? What leadership training would be best for you? Hopefully you're not starting out as an "impoverished" manager with a **laissez-faire leader**, low on both task and people concerns.

Leadership style is the recurring pattern of behaviors exhibited by a leader.

An **autocratic leader** acts in unilateral command-and-control fashion.

A **human relations** leader emphasizes people over tasks.

A **democratic leader** encourages participation with an emphasis on task and people.

A **laissez-faire leader** is disengaged, showing low task and people concerns.

STUDY GUIDE

Takeaway 11.1
What Are the Foundations for Effective Leadership?

Terms to Define

Autocratic leader

Coercive power

Democratic leader

Expert power

Human relations leader

Laissez-faire leader

Leadership

Leadership style

Legitimate power

Power

Referent power

Reward power

Vision

Visionary leadership

Rapid Review

- Leadership, as one of the management functions, is the process of inspiring others to work hard to accomplish important tasks.
- Leaders use power from two primary sources: position power—which includes rewards, coercion, and legitimacy, and personal power—which includes expertise and reference.
- The ability to communicate a vision or clear sense of the future is considered essential to effective leadership.
- Personal characteristics associated with leadership success include honesty, competency, drive, integrity, and self-confidence.
- Research on leader behaviors focused attention on concerns for task and concerns for people, with the leader high on both and using a democratic style considered most effective.

Questions for Discussion

1. When, if ever, is a leader justified in using coercive power?
2. How can a young college graduate gain personal power when moving into a new job as team leader?
3. Why might a leader with a human relations style have difficulty getting things done in an organization?

Be Sure You Can

- illustrate how managers use position and personal power
- define vision and give an example of visionary leadership
- list five traits of successful leaders
- describe alternative leadership styles based on concern for task and concern for people

What Would You Do?

Some might say it was bad luck. Others will tell you it's life and you'd better get used to it. You've just gotten a new boss, and within the first week it was clear to everyone that she is as "autocratic" as can be. The previous boss was very "democratic," and so is the next-higher-level manager, with whom you've always had a good working relationship. Is there anything you and your co-workers can do to remedy this situation without causing anyone, including the new boss, to lose their jobs?

Takeaway 11.2
What Can We Learn from the Contingency Leadership Theories?

ANSWERS TO COME

■ Fiedler's contingency model matches leadership styles with situational differences.

■ The Hersey-Blanchard situational leadership model matches leadership styles with the maturity of followers.

■ House's path-goal theory matches leadership styles with task and follower characteristics.

■ Leader-member exchange theory describes how leaders treat in-group and out-group followers.

■ The Vroom-Jago model describes a leader's choice of alternative decision-making methods.

EVEN AS YOU CONSIDER YOUR LEADERSHIP STYLE AND TENDENCIES, YOU SHOULD know that researchers eventually concluded that no one style always works best. Not even the democratic, or "high-high," leader is successful all of the time. This finding led scholars to explore a **contingency leadership perspective**, one that recognizes that what is successful as a leadership style varies according to the nature of the situation and people involved.

The **contingency leadership perspective** suggests that what is successful as a leadership style varies according to the situation and the people involved.

⦀ Fiedler's contingency model matches leadership styles with situational differences.

One of the first contingency models of leadership was put forth by Fred Fiedler. He proposed that leadership success depends on achieving a proper match between your leadership style and situational demands.[16] He also believed that each of us has a predominant leadership style that is strongly rooted in our personalities. This is important because it suggests that a person's leadership style, yours or mine, is going to be enduring and hard to change.

Fiedler uses an instrument called the *least-preferred co-worker scale (LPC)* to classify our leadership styles as either task motivated or relationship motivated. The LPC scale is available in the end of book *Skill-Building Portfolio*. Why not complete it now and see how Fiedler would describe your style?

Leadership situations are analyzed in Fiedler's model according to three contingency variables—leader-member relations, task structure, and position power. These variables can exist in eight different combinations, with each representing a different leadership challenge. The most favorable situation provides high control for the leader. It has good leader–member relations, high task structure, and strong position power. The least favorable situation puts the leader in a low control setting. Leader–member relations are poor, task structure is low, and position power is weak.

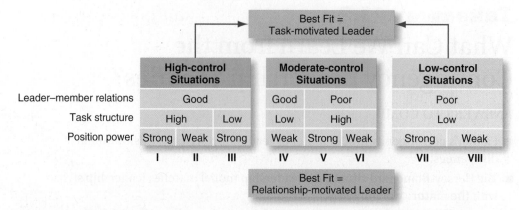

FIGURE 11.3 **What Are the Best Matches of Leadership Style and Situation According to Fiedler's Contingency Model?**
Fiedler believes that leadership success requires the right style-situation match. He classifies leadership styles as either task motivated or relationship motivated, and views them as strongly rooted in our individual personalities. He describes situations according to the leader's position power, quality of leader-member relations, and amount of task structure. In situations that are most favorable and unfavorable for leaders, his research shows the task-motivated style as the best fit. In more intermediate situations, the relationship-motivated style provides the best fit.

Fiedler's research revealed an interesting pattern when he studied the effectiveness of different styles in different leadership situations. As shown in Figure 11.3, a task-motivated leader is most successful in either very favorable (high-control) or very unfavorable (low-control) situations. In contrast, a relationship-motivated leader is more successful in situations of moderate control.

Don't let the apparent complexity of the figure fool you. Fiedler's logic is quite straightforward and, if on track, has some interesting career implications. It suggests that you must know yourself well enough to recognize your predominant leadership style. You should seek out or create leadership situations for which this style is a good match. And, you should avoid situations for which your style is a bad match.

Let's do some quick examples. First, assume that you are the leader of a team of bank tellers. The tellers seem highly supportive of you, and their job is clearly defined. You have the authority to evaluate their performance and to make pay and promotion recommendations. This is a high-control situation consisting of good leader–member relations, high task structure, and high position power. By checking Figure 11.3, you can see that a task-motivated leader is recommended.

Now suppose you are chairperson of a committee asked to improve labor-management relations in a manufacturing plant. Although the goal is clear, no one knows exactly how to accomplish it—task structure is low. Further, not everyone believes that a committee is even the right way to approach the situation—poor leader–member relations are likely. Finally, committee members are free to quit any time they want—you have little position power. Figure 11.3 shows that in this low-control situation, a task-motivated leader should be most effective.

Finally, assume that you are the new head of a fashion section in a large department store. Because you won the job over one of the popular sales clerks you now supervise, leader–member relations are poor. Task structure is high since the clerk's job is well defined. Your position power is low because clerks work under a seniority system, with a fixed wage schedule. Figure 11.3 shows that this moderate-control situation requires a relationship-motivated leader.

The Hersey-Blanchard situational leadership model matches leadership styles with the maturity of followers.

In contrast to Fiedler's notion that leadership style is hard to change, the Hersey-Blanchard situational leadership model suggests that successful leaders do adjust their styles. They do so contingently and based on the maturity of followers, as indicated by their readiness to perform in a given situation.[17] "Readiness," in this sense, is based on how able and willing or confident followers are to perform required tasks. As shown in Figure 11.4, the possible combinations of task and relationship behaviors result in four leadership styles.

- *Delegating*—allowing the group to take responsibility for task decisions; a low-task, low-relationship style
- *Participating*—emphasizing shared ideas and participative decisions on task directions; a low-task, high-relationship style
- *Selling*—explaining task directions in a supportive and persuasive way; a high-task, high-relationship style
- *Telling*—giving specific task directions and closely supervising work; a high-task, low-relationship style

The delegating style works best in high-readiness situations with able and willing or confident followers. The telling style works best at the other extreme of low readiness, where followers are unable and unwilling or insecure. The participating style is recommended for low-to-moderate readiness (followers able but unwilling or insecure); the selling style works best for moderate-to-high readiness (followers unable but willing or confident).

Hersey and Blanchard further believe that leadership styles should be adjusted as followers change over time. The model also implies that if the correct styles are used in lower-readiness situations, followers will "mature" and grow in ability, willingness, and confidence. This allows the leader to become less directive as followers mature. Although this situational leadership model is intuitively appealing, limited research has been accomplished on it to date.[18]

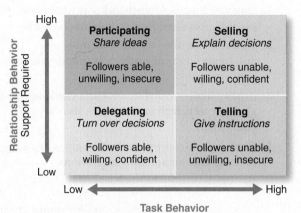

FIGURE 11.4 What Are the Leadership Implications of the Hersey-Blanchard Situational Leadership Model? The Hersey-Blanchard situational leadership model suggests that successful leaders adjust their styles based on the maturity of followers or how willing and able they are to perform in a given situation. The four style-follower matches are: delegating style for able and willing followers; participating style for able but unwilling followers; selling style for unable but willing followers; and telling style for unable and unwilling followers.

House's path-goal theory matches leadership styles with task and follower characteristics.

Another contingency leadership approach is the path-goal theory advanced by Robert House.[19] This theory suggests that leaders are effective when they help followers move along paths through which they can achieve both work goals and personal goals. The best leaders create positive path-goal linkages, raising motivation by removing barriers and rewarding progress.

Like Fiedler's approach, House's path-goal theory seeks the right fit between leadership and situation. But unlike Fiedler, House believes that a leader can move back and forth among the four leadership styles: directive, supportive, achievement-oriented, and participative.

Four Leadership Styles in House's Path-Goal Theory

1. *Directive leader*—lets others know what is expected; gives directions, maintains standards
2. *Supportive leader*—makes work more pleasant; treats others as equals acts friendly, shows concern
3. *Achievement-oriented leader*—sets challenging goals; expects high performance, shows confidence
4. *Participative leader*—involves others in decision making; asks for and uses suggestions

Substitutes for leadership are factors in the work setting that direct work efforts without the involvement of a leader.

When choosing among the different styles, House suggests that the leader's job is to "add value" to a situation. This means acting in ways that contribute things that are missing and not doing things that can otherwise take care of themselves. If you are the leader of a team whose members are expert and competent at their tasks, for example, why would you need to be directive? Members have the know-how to provide their own direction. More likely, the value you can add to this situation would be found in a participative leadership style that helps unlock the expertise of team members and apply it fully to the tasks at hand.

Path-goal theory provides a variety of research-based guidance of this sort to help leaders contingently match their styles with situational characteristics.[20] When job assignments are unclear, *directive leadership* helps to clarify task objectives and expected rewards. When worker self-confidence is low, *supportive leadership* can increase confidence by emphasizing individual abilities and offering needed assistance. When task challenge is insufficient in a job, *achievement-oriented leadership* helps to set goals and raise performance aspirations. When performance incentives are poor, *participative leadership* might clarify individual needs and identify appropriate rewards.

This contingency thinking has contributed to the recognition of what are called **substitutes for leadership**.[21] These are aspects of the work setting and the people involved that can reduce the need for a leader's personal involvement. In effect, they make leadership from the "outside" unnecessary because leadership is already provided from within the situation.

Possible substitutes for leadership include subordinate characteristics such as ability, experience, and independence; task characteristics such as how routine it is and the availability of feedback; and organizational characteristics such as clarity of plans and formalization of rules and procedures. When these substitutes are present, managers are advised to avoid duplicating them. Instead, they should concentrate on doing other and more important things.

‖ Leader-member exchange theory describes how leaders treat in-group and out-group followers.

One of the things you may have noticed in your work and study groups is the tendency of leaders to develop "special" relationships with some team members. This notion is central to leader–member exchange theory, or LMX theory as it is often called.[22] The theory is highlighted in the nearby figure and recognizes that in most, or at least many, leadership situations, not everyone is treated the same. People fall into "in-groups" and "out-groups," and the group you are in can have quite a significant influence on your experience with the leader.

The premise underlying leader–member exchange theory is that as a leader and follower interact over time, their exchanges end up defining the follower's role.[23] Those in a leader's in-group are often considered the best performers. They enjoy special and trusted high-exchange relationships with the leader that can translate into special assignments, privileges, and access to information. Those in the out-group are often excluded from these benefits due to low-exchange relationships with the leader.

For the follower in a high-LMX relationship, being part of the leader's inner circle or in-group can be a real positive. It's often motivating and satisfying to be on the inside of things in terms of getting rewards and favorable treatments. Being in the out-group because of a low-LMX relationship, however, can be a real negative, bringing fewer rewards and less favorable treatment. As to the leader, it is nice to be able to call on and depend upon the loyal support of those in the in-group. But the leader may also be missing out on opportunities that might come from working more closely with out-group members.

Research on leader–member exchange theory places most value on its usefulness in describing leader–member interactions. The notions of high-LMX and low-LMX relationships seem to make sense and correspond to working realities experienced by many people. Look around and you're likely to see examples of this in classroom situations between instructors and certain students, and in work situations between bosses and certain subordinates. In such settings, research finds that members of in-groups get more positive performance evaluations, report higher levels of satisfaction, and are less prone to turnover than are members of out-groups.[24]

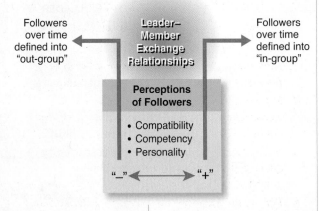

The Vroom-Jago model describes a leader's choice of alternative decision-making methods.

Yet another contingency leadership theory focuses on how managers lead through their use of decision-making methods. The Vroom-Jago leader-participation model views a manager as having three decision options, and in true contingency fashion, no one option is always superior to the others.[25]

1. **Authority decision**—The manager makes an individual decision about how to solve the problem and then communicates the decision to the group.
2. **Consultative decision**—The manager makes the decision after sharing the problem with and getting suggestions from individual group members or the group as a whole.
3. **Group decision**—The manager convenes the group, shares the problem, and then either facilitates a group decision or delegates the decision to the group.

Leadership success results when the manager's choice of decision-making method best matches the nature of the problem to be solved.[26] The rules for making the choice involve three criteria: (1) *decision quality*—based on who has

An **authority decision** is made by the leader and then communicated to the group.

A **consultative decision** is made by a leader after receiving information, advice, or opinions from group members.

A **group decision** is made by group members themselves.

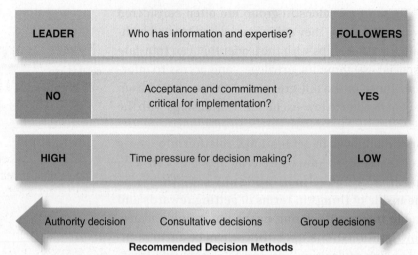

LEADER	Who has information and expertise?	FOLLOWERS
NO	Acceptance and commitment critical for implementation?	YES
HIGH	Time pressure for decision making?	LOW

Authority decision   Consultative decisions   Group decisions

Recommended Decision Methods

FIGURE 11.5 What Are the Leadership Implications of the Vroom-Jago Leader-Participation Model?

The leader-participation model suggests that leaders are effective when they use the appropriate decision method to solve a problem situation. Three criteria govern the choice among possible authority, consultative, and team or group decisions: (1) *decision quality*—based on who has the information needed for problem solving; (2) *decision acceptance*—based on the importance of follower acceptance of the decision to its eventual implementation; and (3) *decision time*—based on the time available to make and implement the decision.

the information needed for problem solving; (2) *decision acceptance*—based on the importance of follower acceptance of the decision to its eventual implementation; and (3) *decision time*—based on the time available to make and implement the decision. These rules are shown in Figure 11.5.

In true contingency fashion each of the decision methods is appropriate in certain situations, and each has its advantages and disadvantages.[27] Authority decisions work best when leaders have the expertise needed to solve the problem, are confident and capable of acting alone, others are likely to accept and implement the decision they make, and little time is available for discussion. By contrast, consultative and group decisions are recommended when:

- The leader lacks sufficient expertise and information to solve this problem alone.
- The problem is unclear and help is needed to clarify the situation.
- Acceptance of the decision and commitment by others are necessary for implementation.
- Adequate time is available to allow for true participation.

Using consultative and group decisions offers important leadership benefits.[28] Participation helps improve decision quality by bringing more information to bear on the problem. It helps improve decision acceptance as others gain understanding and become committed to the process. It also contributes to leadership development by allowing others to gain experience in the problem-solving process. However, a potential cost of participation is lost efficiency. Participation often adds to the time required for decision making, and leaders don't always have extra time available. When problems must be resolved immediately, the authority decision may be the only option.[29]

STUDY GUIDE

Takeaway 11.2
What Can We Learn from the Contingency Leadership Theories?

Terms to Define

Authority decision

Consultative decision

Contingency leadership perspective

Group decision

Substitutes for leadership

Rapid Review

- Fiedler's contingency model describes how situational differences in task structure, position power, and leader–member relations may influence the success of task-motivated and relationship-motivated leaders.
- The Hersey-Blanchard situational model recommends using task-oriented and people-oriented behaviors, depending on the "maturity" levels of followers.
- House's path-goal theory describes how leaders add value to situations by using supportive, directive, achievement-oriented, and/or participative styles as needed.
- Leader–member exchange theory recognizes that leaders respond differently to followers in their in-groups and out-groups.
- The Vroom-Jago leader-participation theory advises leaders to choose decision-making methods—authority, consultative, group—that best fit the problems to be solved.

Questions for Discussion

1. What are the potential career development lessons of Fiedler's contingency leadership model?

2. What are the implications of follower maturity for leaders trying to follow the Hersey-Blanchard situational leadership model?

3. Is it wrong for a team leader to allow the formation of in-groups and out-groups in his or her relationships with team members?

Be Sure You Can

- explain Fiedler's contingency model for matching leadership style and situation
- identify the three variables used to assess situational favorableness in Fiedler's model
- identify the four leadership styles in the Hersey-Blanchard situational leadership model
- explain the importance of follower "maturity" in the Hersey-Blanchard model
- describe the best use of directive, supportive, achievement-oriented, and participative leadership styles in House's path-goal theory
- explain how leader–member exchange theory deals with in-groups and out-groups among a leader's followers

What Would You Do?

You've just been hired as a visual effects artist by a top movie studio. But the team you are joining has already been together for about two months. There's obviously an in-group when it comes to team leader and team member relationships. This job is important to you; the movie is going to be great résumé material. But you're worried about the leadership dynamics and your role as a newcomer to the team. What can you do to get on board as soon as possible and be valued as a team member?

Takeaway 11.3
What Are Current Issues and Directions in Leadership Development?

ANSWERS TO COME

- Transformational leadership inspires enthusiasm and great performance
- Emotionally intelligent leadership handles emotions and relationships well
- Interactive leadership emphasizes communication and participation
- Moral leadership builds trust from a foundation of personal integrity
- Servant leadership is follower centered and empowering

YOU SHOULD NOW BE THINKING SERIOUSLY ABOUT YOUR LEADERSHIP QUALITIES, tendencies, styles, and effectiveness. You should also be thinking about your personal development as a leader. And, in fact, if you look at what people say about leaders in their workplaces, you should be admitting that most of us have considerable room to grow in this regard.[30]

‖ Transformational leadership inspires enthusiasm and great performance.

A charismatic leader develops special leader-follower relationships and inspires followers in extraordinary ways.

Transactional leadership directs the efforts of others through tasks, rewards, and structures.

Transformational leadership is inspirational and arouses extraordinary effort and performance.

It is popular to talk about "superleaders," persons whose visions and strong personalities have an extraordinary impact on others.[31] Martin Luther King, in his famous "I have a dream" speech delivered in August 1963 on the Washington Mall, serves as a good example. Some call people like King **charismatic leaders** because of their ability to inspire others in exceptional ways. We used to think charisma was limited to only a few lucky persons. Today, it is considered one of several personal qualities—including honesty, credibility, and competence, that we should be able to develop with foresight and practice.

Leadership scholars James MacGregor Burns and Bernard Bass have pursued this theme. They begin by describing the traditional leadership approaches we have discussed so far as **transactional leadership**.[32] You might picture the transactional leader engaging followers in a somewhat mechanical fashion, "transacting" with them by using power, employing behaviors and styles that seem to be the best choices at the moment for getting things done.

What is missing in the transactional approach, say Burns and Bass, is attention to things typically linked with superleaders—enthusiasm and inspiration, for example. These are among the charismatic qualities that they associate with something called **transformational leadership**.[33]

Transformational leaders use their personalities to inspire followers and get them so highly excited about their jobs and organizational goals that they strive for truly extraordinary performance accomplishments. Indeed, the easiest way to spot a truly transformational leader is through his or her followers. They are likely to be enthusiastic about the leader and loyal and devoted to his or her ideas, and to work exceptionally hard together to support them.

The goal of achieving excellence in transformational leadership is a stiff personal development challenge. It is not enough to possess leadership traits, know the leadership behaviors, and understand leadership contingencies. One must also be prepared to lead in an inspirational way and with a compelling personality. Transformational leaders raise the confidence, aspirations, and performance of followers through these special qualities.[34]

- *Vision*—has ideas and a clear sense of direction; communicates them to others; develops excitement about accomplishing shared "dreams"
- *Charisma*—uses the power of personal reference and emotion to arouse others' enthusiasm, faith, loyalty, pride, and trust in themselves
- *Symbolism*—identifies "heroes" and holds spontaneous and planned ceremonies to celebrate excellence and high achievement
- *Empowerment*—helps others grow and develop by removing performance obstacles, sharing responsibilities, and delegating truly challenging work
- *Intellectual stimulation*—gains the involvement of others by creating awareness of problems and stirring their imaginations
- *Integrity*—is honest and credible; acts consistently and out of personal conviction; follows through on commitments

⫼ Emotionally intelligent leadership handles emotions and relationships well.

The role of personality in transformational leadership raises another area of inquiry in leadership development—**emotional intelligence**. Popularized by the work of Daniel Goleman, emotional intelligence, or EI for short, is an ability to understand emotions in yourself and others, and use this understanding to handle one's social relationships effectively.[35] "Great leaders move us," say Goleman and his colleagues. "Great leadership works through emotions."[36]

Emotional intelligence is an important influence on leadership success, especially in more senior management positions. In Goleman's words: "The higher the rank of the person considered to be a star performer, the more emotional intelligence capabilities showed up as the reason for his or her effectiveness."[37] This is a pretty strong endorsement for making EI one of your leadership assets.[38]

Consider the four primary emotional intelligence competencies shown in the small figure. *Self-awareness* is the ability to understand our own moods and emotions, and to understand their impact on our work and on others. *Social awareness* is the ability to empathize, to understand the emotions of others, and to use this understanding to better deal with them. *Self-management,* or self-regulation, is the ability to think before acting and to be in control of otherwise disruptive impulses. *Relationship management* is the ability to establish rapport with others in ways that build good relationships and influence their emotions in positive ways.

Emotional intelligence (EI) is the ability to manage our emotions in leadership and social relationships.

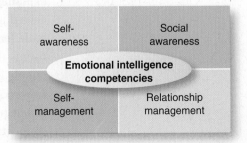

Kraft Foods Feeds Its Sweet Tooth

FIND INSPIRATION

This example of Irene Rosenfeld is designed to get you thinking about your leadership qualities and looking at the leadership models that abound in your experiences. Just who is the leader in you? What can you do to keep that leader growing and confident in the days and years ahead?

The **gender similarities hypothesis** holds that males and females have similar psychological makeups.

Leaders Provide the Roadmaps

When Kraft Foods was bidding to buy Cadbury, Irene Rosenfeld was often in the news. She was leading a dramatic attempt to capture the British candymaker against its wishes. It was all part of Rosenfeld's desire to transform Kraft—a firm she described as "not living up to our potential." Her roadmap to making Kraft a global powerhouse in snacks and confectionery, was one of growth. This included making the Cadbury acquisition against all odds. And she succeeded.

Rosenfeld is described as a risk taker who leads by pushing decision authority down the hierarchy. She lets managers of Kraft's major brands have control of their budgets and operations. She focuses on top management teamwork to bring perspectives in from all parts of the company. And she urges top managers to focus resources on what they do best in their customer markets. Keeping her turnaround strategy on track is always top priority. To create change, Rosenfeld says you need to "get the right people on the bus," "give them a roadmap," and "communicate frequently, consistently and honestly."

⫶ Interactive leadership emphasizes communication, listening, and participation.

When Sara Levinson was President of NFL Properties Inc., she once asked the all-male members of her management team: "Is my leadership style different from a man's?"[39] Would you be surprised to learn that they answered "Yes," telling her that just by asking the question she was providing evidence of the difference? They described her as a leader who emphasized communication, always gathering ideas and opinions from others. And when Levinson probed further by asking "Is this a distinctly 'female' trait?" they again said "yes" it was.

Are there gender differences in leadership? Before you jump in with your own answer, let's be clear on three things. First, research largely supports the **gender similarities hypothesis** that males and females are very similar to one another in terms of psychological properties.[40] Second, research leaves no doubt that both women and men can be effective leaders.[41] Third, what research does show is that men and women are sometimes perceived as using different styles, perhaps arriving at leadership success from different angles.[42]

A recent study employing 3,608 assessments found that women were rated more highly than men in all but one area of leadership—visioning.[43] A possible explanation is that women aren't considered as visionaries because they are perceived as acting less directive as leaders. And indeed, some studies report that male leaders are viewed as directive and assertive, using position power to get things done in traditional command-and-control ways.[44] Other studies report female leaders acting more participative than men. They are also rated by peers, subordinates, and supervisors as strong on motivating others, emotional intelligence, persuading, fostering communication, listening to others, mentoring, and supporting high-quality work.[45]

Facts to Consider

■ WORKERS REPORT SHORTCOMINGS OF LEADERS AND TOP MANAGERS

Harris Interactive periodically conducts surveys of workers' attitudes toward their jobs and employers. The results for "leaders" and "top managers" reveal lots of shortcomings:

- 37% believe their top managers display integrity and morality.
- 39% believe leaders most often act in the best interest of organization.
- 22% see leaders as ready to admit mistakes.
- 46% believe their organizations give them freedom to do their jobs.

- 25% of women and 16% of men believe their organizations pick the best people for leadership.
- 33% of managers are perceived by followers as "strong leaders."

YOUR THOUGHTS?

How do the leaders you have experienced stack up—"strong or weak," "moral or immoral"? What makes the most difference in the ways leaders are viewed in the eyes of followers?

This pattern of behaviors associated with female leaders has been called **interactive leadership**.[46] Interactive leaders are democratic, participative, and inclusive, often approaching problems and decisions through teamwork.[47] They focus on building consensus and good interpersonal relations through emotional intelligence, communication, and involvement. They tend to get things done with personal power, seeking influence over others through support and interpersonal relationships.

Rosabeth Moss Kanter says that in many ways "Women get high ratings on exactly those skills required to succeed in the Global Information Age, where teamwork and partnering are so important."[48] Her observations are backed up by data that show firms having more female directors and executives outperform others.[49] But let's be careful. One of the risks here is placing individual men and women into boxes in which they don't necessarily belong.[50] Perhaps we should focus instead on the notion of interactive leadership. The likelihood is that this style is a very good fit with the needs of today's organizations and workers.[51] And isn't there every reason to believe that both men and women can do interactive leadership equally well? What do you think?

> **Interactive leadership** is strong on communicating, participation, and dealing with problems by teamwork.

||| Moral leadership builds trust from a foundation of personal integrity.

As discussed many times in this book, society expects organizations to be run with **moral leadership**. This is leadership by ethical standards that clearly meet the test of being "good" and "correct."[52] We should expect anyone in a leadership position to practice high ethical standards of behavior and help others to also behave ethically in their work. But the facts don't always support this aspiration.

> **Moral leadership** has integrity and appears to others as "good" or "right" by ethical standards.

Ethics Check

■ WHEN THE BOSS ASKS TOO MUCH

Management scholars like to talk about the "zone of indifference" in leadership. It basically identifies the range of requests that a follower is willing to comply with just because someone is his or her boss.

But some bosses take things into ambiguous territory. They may ask us to do things that are not really within the job description and/or that don't really benefit the employing organization. Sure we're getting paid to do these things, but is it only the boss that benefits?

What if your boss wants to pay you overtime to make a set of presentation PowerPoints for a speech he is giving at a conference for his volunteer organization? Suppose the boss asks you to write a technology blog for the firm, but to do so during your free time on the weekend? Or what about a boss who views you as her personal assistant and consistently expects you to run personal errands—pick up dry cleaning, take the pet to the vet, make weekend dinner reservations, arrange her vacation travel?

YOU DECIDE

By helping the boss with these and similar requests, you may benefit directly from pay and privileges. You may also benefit indirectly through ingratiating yourself and gaining a positive leader-follower relationship. And the boss gains as well. But when there is little or no benefit to the organization that is paying the bill, what is the ethical response on your part? Do you say "Yes"? Do you say "No"? Just where do you draw the line on your zone of indifference?

Integrity in leadership is honesty, credibility, and consistency in putting values into action.

Are you surprised by the Harris Poll reported in the previous Facts to Consider? Why are so few people willing to describe their top managers as acting with "integrity and morality"?[53] Based on that result, it may not surprise you that a *Business Week* survey found that just 13% of top executives at large U.S. firms rated "having strong ethical values" as a top leadership characteristic.[54]

In contrast to the findings described in these surveys, is there any doubt that society today is demanding more ethical leadership in our organizations? Even if they don't always do so, we still want leaders to act ethically and maintain an ethical organizational culture. We want leaders to both help and require others to behave ethically in their work.[55] Hopefully this theme has been well communicated throughout this book. Hopefully too, you will agree that long-term success in work, and in life, can be built only on a foundation of solid ethical behavior.[56]

But where do we start when facing up to the challenge of building personal capacities for ethical leadership? A good answer is **integrity**.[57] You must start with honest, credible, and consistent behavior that puts your values into action. Words like "principled" and "fair" and "authentic" should come immediately to mind.

When a leader has integrity, he or she earns the trust of followers. And when followers believe that their leaders are trustworthy, they are more willing to try to live up to the leader's expectations. Southwest Airlines CEO Gary Kelly seems to have gotten the message. He says: "Being a leader is about character . . . being straightforward and honest, having integrity, and treating people right." And there's a payoff. One of his co-workers says this about Kelly's leadership impact: "People are willing to run through walls for him."[58]

Servant leadership is follower centered and empowering.

A classic and valuable observation about great leaders is that they view leadership as a responsibility, not a rank.[59] This view is consistent with the concept of **servant leadership.** It is based on a commitment to serving others and to helping people use their talents to full potential while working together in organizations that benefit society.[60]

You might think of servant leadership by asking this question: Who is most important in leadership, the leader or the followers? For those who believe in servant leadership, there is no doubt about the correct answer: the followers.

Servant leadership is "other centered," not "self-centered." And once one shifts the focus away from the self and toward others, what does that generate in terms of leadership opportunities? **Empowerment,** for one thing. This is the process of giving people job freedom and helping them gain power to achieve influence within the organization.[61]

Max DePree, former CEO of Herman Miller and a noted leadership author, praises leaders who "permit others to share ownership of problems—to take possession of the situation."[62] Lorraine Monroe of the School Leadership Academy says: "The real leader is a servant of the people she leads . . . a really great boss is not afraid to hire smart people. You want people who are smart about things you are not smart about."[63] Robert Greenleaf, who is credited with coining the term "servant leadership," says: "Institutions function better when the idea, the dream, is to the fore, and the person, the leader, is seen as servant to the dream."[64]

Think about these ideas and then reach back and take a good look in the mirror. Is the leader in you capable of being a servant?

> **Servant leadership** means serving others and helping them use their talents to help organizations best serve society.

> **Empowerment** gives people job freedom and power to influence affairs in the organization.

{ LEADERS WITH INTEGRITY ARE HONEST, CREDIBLE, HUMBLE, AND CONSISTENT.

Explore Yourself

■ INTEGRITY

Even though we can get overly enamored with the notion of the "great" or "transformational" leader, it is just one among many leadership fundamentals that are enduring and important. This chapter covers a range of theories and models useful for leadership development. Each is best supported by a base of personal **integrity**.

Leaders with integrity are honest, credible, humble, and consistent in all that they do. They walk the talk by living up to personal values in all their actions. Transformational leadership operates on a foundation of integrity. The very concept of moral leadership is centered on integrity. And, servant leadership represents integrity in action. Why is it, then, that in the news and in everyday experiences we so often end up wondering where leadership integrity has gone?

> Get to know yourself better by taking the self-assessment on **Least Preferred Co-Worker Scale** and completing the other activities in the *Exploring Management* **Skill-Building Portfolio.**

STUDY GUIDE

Takeaway 11.3
What Are Current Issues and Directions in Leadership Development?

Terms to Define

Charismatic leader

Emotional intelligence (EI)

Empowerment

Gender similarities hypothesis

Integrity

Interactive leadership

Moral leadership

Servant leadership

Transactional leadership

Transformational leadership

Rapid Review

- Transformational leaders use charisma and emotion to inspire others toward extraordinary efforts to achieve performance excellence.
- Emotional intelligence, the ability to manage our emotions and relationships effectively, is an important leadership capability.
- The interactive leadership style, sometimes associated with women, emphasizes communication, involvement, and interpersonal respect.
- Moral or ethical leadership is built from a foundation of personal integrity, creating a basis for trust and respect between leaders and followers.
- A servant leader is follower-centered, not self-centered, and empowers others to unlock their personal talents in the quest for goals and accomplishments that help society.

Questions for Discussion

1. Should all managers be expected to excel at transformational leadership?
2. Do women lead differently than men?
3. Is servant leadership inevitably moral leadership?

Be Sure You Can

- differentiate transformational and transactional leadership
- list the personal qualities of transformational leaders
- explain how emotional intelligence contributes to leadership success
- discuss research findings on interactive leadership
- explain the role of integrity as a foundation for moral leadership
- explain the concept of servant leadership

What Would You Do?

Okay, so it's important to be "interactive" in leadership. By personality, though, you tend to be a bit withdrawn. In fact, if you could do things by yourself, that's the way you would behave. Yet here you are taking over as a manager as the first upward career step in your present place of employment. How do you master the challenge of succeeding with interactive leadership in the new role?

TestPrep 11

Multiple-Choice Questions

1. When managers use offers of rewards and threats of punishments to try to get others to do what they want them to do, they are using which type of power?
   (a) formal authority
   (b) position
   (c) referent
   (d) personal

2. When a manager says, "Because I am the boss, you must do what I ask," what power base is being put into play?
   (a) reward
   (b) legitimate
   (c) moral
   (d) referent

3. The personal traits that are now considered important for managerial success include _____.
   (a) self-confidence
   (b) gender
   (c) age
   (d) personality

4. In the research on leader behaviors, which style of leadership describes the preferred "high-high" combination?
   (a) transformational
   (b) transactional
   (c) laissez-faire
   (d) democratic

5. In Fiedler's contingency model, both highly favorable and highly unfavorable leadership situations are best dealt with by a _____ -motivated leadership style.
   (a) task
   (b) vision
   (c) ethics
   (d) relationship

6. Which leadership theorist argues that one's leadership style is strongly anchored in personality and therefore very difficult to change?
   (a) Daniel Goleman
   (b) Peter Drucker
   (c) Fred Fiedler
   (d) Robert House

7. Vision, charisma, integrity, and symbolism are all attributes typically associated with _____ leaders.
   (a) people-oriented
   (b) democratic
   (c) transformational
   (d) transactional

8. In terms of leadership behaviors, someone who focuses on doing a very good job of planning work tasks, setting performance standards, and monitoring results would be described as _____.
   (a) task oriented
   (b) servant oriented
   (c) achievement oriented
   (d) transformational

9. In the discussion of gender and leadership, it was pointed out that some perceive women as having tendencies toward _____, a style that seems a good fit with developments in the new workplace.
   (a) interactive leadership
   (b) use of position power
   (c) command-and-control
   (d) transactional leadership

10. In House's path-goal theory, a leader who sets challenging goals for others would be described as using the _____ leadership style.
   (a) autocratic
   (b) achievement-oriented
   (c) transformational
   (d) directive

11. Someone who communicates a clear sense of the future and the actions needed to get there is considered a _____ leader.

(a) task-oriented

(b) people-oriented

(c) transactional

(d) visionary

12. Managerial Power = _____ Power × _____ Power.

(a) Reward; Punishment

(b) Reward; Expert

(c) Legitimate; Position

(d) Position; Personal

13. The interactive leadership style is characterized by _____.

(a) inclusion and information sharing

(b) use of rewards and punishments

(c) command-and-control behavior

(d) emphasis on position power

14. A leader whose actions indicate an attitude of "do as you want and don't bother me" would be described as having a(n) _____ leadership style.

(a) autocratic

(b) country club

(c) democratic

(d) laissez-faire

15. The critical contingency variable in the Hersey-Blanchard situational model of leadership is _____.

(a) follower maturity

(b) LPC

(c) task structure

(d) emotional intelligence

Short-Response Questions

16. Why are both position power and personal power essential in management?

17. Use Fiedler's terms to list the characteristics of situations that would be extremely favorable and extremely unfavorable to a leader.

18. Describe the situations in which House's path-goal theory would expect (a) a participative leadership style and (b) a directive leadership style to work best.

19. How do you sum up in two or three sentences the notion of servant leadership?

Integration and Application Question

20. When Marcel Henry took over as leader of a new product development team, he was both excited and apprehensive. "I wonder," he said to himself on the first day in his new assignment, "if I can meet the challenges of leadership." Later that day, Marcel shares this concern with you during a coffee break.

Question: How would you describe to Marcel the personal implications of current thinking on transformational and moral leadership and how they might be applied to his handling of this team setting?

Steps*for*FurtherLearning

Many learning resources are found at the end of the book and online within WileyPLUS.

Don't Miss These Selections from the **Skill-Building Portfolio**

■ **SELF-ASSESSMENT 11:** *Least Preferred Co-Worker Scale*

■ **CLASS EXERCISE 11:** *Leading by Participation*

■ **TEAM PROJECT 11:** *Leadership Believe-It-Or-Not*

Don't Miss This Selection from **Cases for Critical Thinking**

■ **CHAPTER 11 CASE**

SAS: Business Decisions at the Speed of Information

Snapshot Short for *Statistical Analysis System*, SAS is a set of integrated software tools that help decision makers cope with unwieldy amounts of unrelated data. It's the primary product of North Carolina-based SAS Institute, self-described as the "leader in business analytics software." While SAS is its primary product, the company has developed a peripheral business around supporting and training SAS users. One user describes its value as "empowering people with data to make efficient, effective decisions earlier." With Jim Goodnight at the helm, it's gained an impressive roster of clients: 92 of the top 100 Fortune Global 500 companies, more than 45,000 businesses, universities, and government agencies, with customers in 121 different countries. If you look below the surface, you'll find that Goodnight's special approach to leadership is as great as the firm's software.

Make notes here on what you've learned about yourself from this chapter.

■ **LEARNING JOURNAL 11**

You don't have to look in a mirror to gain more self-awareness. What does your smartphone screen say about your personality?

Individual Behavior

There's Beauty in Individual Differences

Management Live

Ambition and *The Social Network*

Appearing at a time when social media seem to rule the online world, Sony's movie *The Social Network* made $23 million on opening weekend. It's based on Facebook's visionary and controversial founder Mark Zuckerberg (Jesse Eisenberg).

Although Zuckerberg calls it pure "fiction," the movie raises ethical questions about his actions while developing the initial website, refining it, and eventually turning it into a global company valued at over $50 billion. Two former Harvard classmates, Cameron and Tyler Winklevoss, sued him, claiming the original idea was theirs. Another early collaborator and co-founder, Eduardo Saverin, was initially left out of the new firm's financial gains.

Entertainment Weekly asks: "Why did Zuckerberg betray these people? Or, in fact, did he really?"

One thing that cannot be denied is Zuckerberg's **ambition,** the desire to succeed and reach for high goals. He's the youngest self-made billionaire in business history. As the movie shows, ambition is one of those personality traits that can certainly have a big impact on individual behavior—both for the good and for the bad.

Why don't you watch *The Social Network* and discuss with your friends and classmates how different personalities and talents played out in creating the Facebook revolution? What can you learn that might help you deal with the ethics and intricacies of human behavior in work situations?

YOUR CHAPTER 12 TAKEAWAYS

1. Understand how perceptions influence individual behavior.

2. Understand how personalities influence individual behavior.

3. Understand how attitudes, emotions, and moods influence individual behavior.

WHAT'S INSIDE

Explore Yourself
More on ambition.

Role Models
Richard Branson leads with personality and flamboyance

Ethics Check
Personality test required

Facts to Consider
Trends show job satisfaction drifting lower

Manager's Library
Women Count by Susan Bulkeley Butler

Takeaway 12.1
How Do Perceptions Influence Individual Behavior?

ANSWERS TO COME

■ Perceptual distortions can obscure individual differences.

■ Perception can cause attribution errors as we explain events and problems.

■ Impression management is a way of influencing how others perceive us.

SOME YEARS AGO, KAREN NUSSBAUM FOUNDED AN ORGANIZATION CALLED 9 TO 5, devoted to improving women's salaries and promotion opportunities in the workplace. She had just left her job as a secretary at Harvard University. Describing what she calls "the incident that put her over the edge," Nussbaum says: "One day I was sitting at my desk at lunchtime, when most of the professors were out. A student walked into the office and looked me dead in the eye and said, 'Isn't anyone here'?" Nussbaum started 9 to 5 with a commitment to "remake the system so that it does not produce these individuals."[1]

When people communicate with one another, everything passes through two silent but influential shields: the "perceptions" of the sender and the receiver. **Perception** is the process through which people receive and interpret information from the environment. It is the way we form impressions about ourselves, other people, and daily life experiences.

As suggested in Figure 12.1, you might think of perception as a bubble that surrounds us and significantly influences the way we receive, interpret, and process information received from our environments.[2] And because our individual idiosyncrasies, backgrounds, values, and experiences influence our perceptions, this means that people can and do view the same things quite differently. These differences in perceptions influence how we communicate and behave in relationship to one another.

> **Perception** is the process through which people receive and interpret information from the environment.

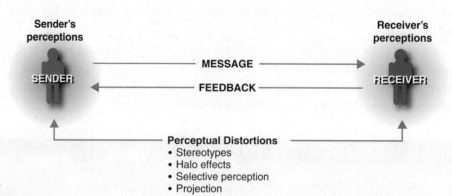

FIGURE 12.1   How Does Perception Influence Communication?
Perception is the process of receiving and interpreting information from our environment. It acts as a screen or filter through which we interpret messages in the communication process. And perceptions influence how we behave in response to information received. Because people often perceive the same things quite differently, perception is an important issue in respect to individual behavior at work. Perceptual distortions in the form of stereotypes, halo effects, projection, and selective perception can lead to inaccurate assumptions regarding other people and events.

Perceptual distortions can obscure individual differences.

Given the complexity of the stimuli constantly flowing toward us from our environments, human beings use various means of simplifying and organizing their perceptions. One of the most common is the **stereotype**. This occurs when you identify someone with a group or category, and then use the attributes associated with the group or category to describe the individual. Although this makes things easier by reducing the need to deal with unique individual characteristics, it is an oversimplification. By relying on the stereotype, we end up missing the real individual.

A **stereotype** assigns attributes commonly associated with a group to an individual.

As the 9 to 5 example showed, how we perceive and relate to one another often leaves room for improvement. Some of the stereotypes used in the workplace, and in life in general, relate to such factors as gender, age, race, and physical ability.

Consider how gender stereotyping might cause managers to misconstrue work behavior. If they see men in a discussion, they might think they are discussing a new deal; if it's a group of women, they might perceive them as gossiping. And how does gender stereotyping influence opportunity? Only a small portion of U.S. managers sent on international assignments are women. Do you wonder why? A Catalyst study of women in global business blames gender stereotypes that place women at a disadvantage to men for these jobs. The perception seems to be that women lack the abilities or willingness for working abroad.[3]

> ## Common Perceptual Distortions
>
> - *Stereotypes*—put people into categories and then use attributes of the category to describe the individual. Example: He's close to retirement; too old to learn the new technology.
> - *Halo Effects*—use one characteristic of a person or situation to form an overall impression. Example: She's always at work early; she's a great performer.
> - *Selective Perception*—focuses attention on things consistent with existing beliefs, needs, and actions. Example: Sales are down; I knew the new product design was flawed.
> - *Projection*—assumes others are just like us and assigns our attributes to them. Example: I'll schedule planning meetings for 7:30 am; it feels good to get an early start.

A **halo effect** occurs when we use one characteristic of a person or situation to form an overall impression. You probably do this quite often, as do I. When meeting someone new, for example, receiving a positive smile might create a halo effect that results in a positive impression. By contrast, the halo effect of an unfamiliar hairstyle or manner of dressing may create a negative impression.

A **halo effect** uses one attribute to develop an overall impression of a person or situation.

Halo effects cause the same problems as stereotypes. They obscure individual differences. The person who smiles might have a very negative work attitude; the person with the unique hairstyle might be a top performer. Halo effects are especially significant in performance evaluations where one factor, such as a person's punctuality or lack of it, may become the halo that inaccurately determines the overall performance rating.

Selective perception is the tendency to focus attention on those aspects of a situation or person that reinforce or appear consistent with one's existing beliefs, needs, or actions.[4] We screen out the rest. This often happens in organizations when people from different departments or functions—such as marketing or information systems, for example—tend to see things only from their own point of view.

Selective perception focuses attention on things consistent with existing beliefs, needs, or actions.

Like the other perceptual distortions, selective perception can bias our views of situations and individuals. One of the great benefits of teamwork and consultative decision making is the pooling of ideas and perceptions of many people, thus making it harder for selective perception to create problems.

Projection assigns personal attributes to other individuals.

Projection occurs when we assign our personal attributes to other individuals. Some call this the "similar-to-me" error. An example is to assume that other persons share our needs, desires, and values. Suppose that you enjoy a lot of responsibility and challenge in your work as a team leader. You might try to increase responsibilities and challenges for team members, wanting them to experience the same satisfactions as you. But this involves projection. Instead of designing jobs to best fit their needs, you have designed their jobs to fit yours. An individual team member may be quite satisfied and productive doing his or her current job, one that seems routine to you. We can control projection errors through self-awareness and a willingness to communicate and empathize with other persons, that is, to try to see things through their eyes.

Manager's Library

■ *WOMEN COUNT* BY SUSAN BULKELEY BUTLER

A WOMAN'S WORK IS NOT YET DONE

Although women compose half of the workforce, they account for only 3% of Fortune 500 CEOs. Seventy percent of women with children work, and forty percent are their family's primary breadwinner, yet women earn 78 cents for every dollar men earn.

Haven't women shown that these numbers are simply unacceptable?

In the book *Women Count* (2010, Purdue University Press), author Susan Bulkeley Butler urges women to stop accepting statistics that underrepresent their leadership value and, instead, take action. She says women can shift their paradigm of success and stop thinking about others first. Butler advises women to start by first helping themselves, which may require rebalancing roles in their work, home, and personal life. She states that women can't master these roles separately and suffer from obligation guilt. They must redefine the roles with the help of employers.

An example is the attorney who relocated so her children's grandparents could assist with childcare. The firm assigned her cases she could work on from home and the flexibility in rebalancing her work, family, and personal roles was essential to her success.

In this book, Butler cites research that women are good for performance. Companies with the most women, either on their Board of Directors or in top management positions, outperform those with the least women by 53% or 35%, respectively, measured by return on equity. She asserts that this is because women possess behavioral advantages over men—things like being more compassionate, less ego-driven, listening better, taking fewer risks, and tending to be consensus-builders. Butler believes organizations should increase female leadership to improve performance. This can be done by appointing at least two women to the board, having women report directly to the CEO, and by creating mentoring programs for female leaders.

Policies allowing women to rebalance life roles must also be commonplace. Butler herself mentors female executives and provides organizational resources through her Institute for the Development of Women Leaders.

The bottom line is that action is needed to insure the succession of more women into leadership roles. It may be that a woman's work is not done until the numbers reflect that women do really count.

REFLECT AND REACT

Why don't more women lead more companies? How can work, family, and personal roles of women conflict? How might organizations better accommodate professional females? What can a woman really do to "balance" multiple role expectations? And by the way, do you agree that women have behavioral advantages over men?

Perception can cause attribution errors as we explain events and problems.

One of the ways in which perception exerts its influence on behavior is through **attribution**. This is the process of developing explanations for events and their perceived causes. It is natural for people to try to explain what they observe and the things that happen to them. Suppose you perceive that someone else in a job or student group isn't performing up to expectations? How do you explain this? And, depending on the explanation, what do you do to try to correct things?

When considering so-called "poor" performance by someone else, we are likely to commit something called **fundamental attribution error**. This is a tendency to blame other people when things go wrong, whether or not this is really true. If I perceive that a student is doing poorly in my course, for example, this error pops up as a tendency to criticize the student's lack of ability or unwillingness to study hard enough. But that perception may not be accurate, as you may well agree. Perhaps there's something about the course design, its delivery, or my actions as an instructor that are contributing to the problem—a deficiency in the learning environment, not the individual.

Consider another case. This time it's you having a performance problem—at school, at work, wherever. How do you explain it? Again, the likelihood of attribution error is high, this time it is called **self-serving bias**. It's the tendency for people to blame personal failures or problems on external causes rather than accept personal responsibility. This is the "It's not my fault!" error. The flip side is to claim personal responsibility for any successes—"It was me; I did it!"

Attribution is the process of creating explanations for events.

The **fundamental attribution error** overestimates internal factors and underestimates external factors as influences on someone's behavior.

Self-serving bias underestimates internal factors and overestimates external factors as influences on someone's behavior.

Fundamental Attribution Error *"It's their fault."*	←	**They are performing poorly**	**I am performing poorly**	→	**Self-Serving Bias** *"It's not my fault."*

The significance of these attribution errors can be quite substantial. When we perceive things incorrectly we are likely to take the wrong actions and miss solving a lot of problems in the process. Think about self-serving bias the next time you hear someone blaming your instructor for a poor course grade. And think about the fundamental attribution error the next time you jump on a group member who didn't perform according to your standards. Our perceptions aren't always wrong, but they should always be double-checked and tested for accuracy. There are no safe assumptions when it comes to the power of attributions.

Impression management is a way of influencing how others perceive us.

Richard Branson, CEO of the Virgin Group, may be one of the richest and most famous executives in the world. One of his early business accomplishments was the successful start-up of Virgin Airlines, now a major competitor of British Airways (BA). In a memoir, the former head of BA, Lord King, said: "If Richard Branson had worn a shirt and tie instead of a goatee and jumper, I would not have underestimated him."[5] This is an example of how much our impressions count—both positive and negative. Knowing this, scholars now emphasize the importance of **impression management**, the systematic attempt to influence how others perceive us.[6]

Impression management tries to create desired perceptions in the eyes of others.

You might notice that we often do bits and pieces of impression management as a matter of routine in everyday life. This is especially evident when we enter new situations—perhaps a college classroom or new work team, what we post on Facebook or Twitter, and as we prepare to meet people for the first time, such as going out with a new friend for a social occasion or heading off to a job interview. In these and other situations we tend to dress, talk, act, and surround ourselves with things that help convey a desirable self-image to other persons.

Impression management that is well done can help us advance in jobs and careers, form relationships with people we admire, and even create pathways to desired social memberships. Some basic tactics are worth remembering: knowing when to dress up and when to dress down to convey positive appeal in certain situations, using words to flatter other people in ways that generate positive feelings toward you, making eye contact and smiling when engaged in conversations to create a personal bond, and displaying a high level of energy that indicates work commitment and initiative.[7]

{ **"YOU CAN'T BE A GOOD LEADER UNLESS YOU GENERALLY LIKE PEOPLE."**

Role Models

■ RICHARD BRANSON LEADS WITH PERSONALITY AND FLAMBOYANCE

Could you imagine starting an airline? Richard Branson decided he would and called it Virgin Atlantic. His career began in his native England with a student literary magazine and small mail-order record business. Since then he's built Virgin into one of the world's most recognized brand names.

Virgin Group is a business conglomerate employing some 25,000 people around the globe. It holds over 200 companies, including Virgin Mobile and the space venture Virgin Galactic. It's all very creative and ambitious—but that's Branson. "I love to learn things I know little about" and "before I do anything I first get tons of feedback," he says.

But if you bump into Branson on the street, you might be surprised. He's casual, he's smiling, and he's fun; he's also brilliant when it comes to business and leadership. Branson has been listed among the 25 most influential business leaders. His goal is to build Virgin into "the most respected brand in the world." And as the man behind the brand, he's described as "flamboyant," something he doesn't deny and also considers a major business advantage that keeps him and his ventures in the public eye.

About leadership Branson says: "Having a personality of caring about people is important. . . . You can't be a good leader unless you generally like people. That is how you bring out the best in them." His own style, he claims, was shaped by his family and childhood. At age 10 his mother put him on a 300-mile bike ride to build character and endurance. At 16, he started a student magazine. By the age of 22, he was launching Virgin record stores. And by the time he was 30, Virgin Group was running at high speed.

Now known as Sir Richard after being knighted in 1999, he enjoys Virgin today "as a way of life." But he adds: "In the next stage of my life I want to use our business skills to tackle social issues around the world. . . . Malaria in Africa kills four million people a year. AIDS kills even more. . . . I don't want to waste this fabulous situation in which I've found myself."

WHAT'S THE LESSON HERE?

Do actions speak louder than impressions? Richard Branson succeeded while staying true to himself. But then again, he's been a star right from the beginning and basically "runs his own shows." If you aren't at the top, should you be more worried about the impression you give and how it might affect your career?

STUDY GUIDE

Takeaway 12.1
How Do Perceptions Influence Individual Behavior?

Terms to Define

Attribution

Fundamental
attribution error

Halo effect

Impression
management

Perception

Projection

Selective perception

Self-serving bias

Stereotype

Rapid Review

- Perception acts as a filter through which all communication passes as it travels from one person to the next.
- Different people may perceive the same things differently.
- Stereotypes, projections, halo effects, and selective perception can distort perceptions and reduce communication effectiveness.
- Fundamental attribution error occurs when we blame others for their performance problems, without considering possible external causes.
- Self-serving bias occurs when, in judging our own performance, we take personal credit for successes and blame failures on external factors.
- Through impression management, we influence the way that others perceive us.

Questions for Discussion

1. How do advertising firms use stereotypes to influence consumer behavior?
2. Are there times when a self-serving bias is actually helpful?
3. Does the notion of impression management contradict the idea of personal integrity?

Be Sure You Can

- describe how perception influences behavior
- explain how stereotypes, halo effects, selective perceptions, and projection might operate in the workplace
- explain the concepts of attribution error and self-serving bias
- illustrate how someone might use impression management during a job interview

What Would You Do?

While standing in line at the office coffee machine, you overhear the person in front of you saying this to his friend: "I'm really tired of having to deal with the old-timers here. It's time for them to call it quits. There's no way they can keep up the pace and handle all the new technology we're getting these days." You can listen and forget, or you can listen and act. What would you do or say here, and why?

Takeaway 12.2
How Do Personalities Influence Individual Behavior?

ANSWERS TO COME

- The Big Five personality traits describe work-related individual differences.
- The Myers-Briggs Type Indicator is a popular approach to personality assessment.
- Self-monitoring and other personality traits influence work behavior.
- People with Type A personalities tend to stress themselves.
- Stress has consequences for work performance and personal health.

THINK OF HOW MANY TIMES YOU'VE COMPLAINED ABOUT SOMEONE'S "BAD personality" or told a friend how much you like someone else because they had such a "nice personality." Well, the same holds true at work. Perhaps you have been part of or the subject of conversations like these: "I can't give him that job. He's a bad fit; with a personality like that, there's no way he can work with customers." Or "Put Erika on the project; her personality is perfect for the intensity that we expect from the team."

Personality is the profile of characteristics making a person unique from others.

In management we use the term **personality** to describe the combination or overall profile of enduring characteristics that make each of us unique. And as the prior examples suggest, this uniqueness can have consequences for how we behave and how that behavior is regarded by others.

⦀ The Big Five personality traits describe work-related individual differences.

We all know that variations among personalities are both real and consequential in our relationships with everyone from family to friends to co-workers. Although there are many personality traits, scholars have identified a short list of five that are especially significant. Known as the Big Five, these personality traits are extraversion, agreeableness, conscientiousness, emotional stability, and openness to experience.[8]

Take a look at the descriptions in Table 12.1—*How to Identify the Big Five Personality Traits*. You can probably spot them pretty easily in people with whom you work, study, and socialize, as well as in yourself. And while you're at it, why not use the table as a quick check of your personality? Ask: What are the implications for my interpersonal and working relationships?

A considerable body of research links the Big Five personality traits with work and career outcomes. The expectation is that people with more extraverted, agreeable, conscientious, emotionally stable, and open personalities will have more positive relationships and experiences in organizations.[9] Conscientious persons tend to be highly motivated and high-performing in their work, while emotionally stable persons tend to handle change situations well. It's also likely that Big Five traits are implicit criteria used by managers when making judgments

Table 12.1 How to Identify the Big Five Personality Traits

Extraversion An extravert is talkative, comfortable, and confident in interpersonal relationships; an introvert is more private, withdrawn, and reserved.

Agreeableness An agreeable person is trusting, courteous, and helpful, getting along well with others; a disagreeable person is self-serving, skeptical, and tough, creating discomfort for others.

Conscientiousness A conscientious person is dependable, organized, and focused on getting things done; a person who lacks conscientiousness is careless, impulsive, and not achievement oriented.

Emotional stability A person who is emotionally stable is secure, calm, steady, and self-confident; a person lacking emotional stability is excitable, anxious, nervous, and tense.

Openness to experience A person open to experience is broad-minded, imaginative, and open to new ideas; and person who lacks openness is narrow-minded, has few interests, and resists change.

about people at work, handing out job assignments, building teams, and more. Psychologists even use the Big Five to steer people in the direction of career choices that may provide the best personality-job fits. Extraversion, for example, is a good predictor of success in management and sales positions.

The Myers-Briggs Type Indicator is a popular approach to personality assessment.

Another popular approach to personality assessment is the Myers-Briggs Type Indicator, a sophisticated questionnaire that probes into how people act or feel in various situations. Called the MBTI for short, it was developed by Katherine Briggs and her daughter Isabel Briggs-Myers from foundations set forth in the work of psychologist Carl Jung.[10]

Jung's model of personality differences included three main distinctions. First, extraversion and introversion, as just discussed, were used to describe personality differences in ways people relate with others. Second, Jung described how people vary in the way they gather information—by sensation (emphasizing details, facts, and routine) or by intuition (looking for the "big picture" and being willing to deal with various possibilities). Third, he described how they vary in ways of evaluating information—by thinking (using reason and analysis) or by feeling (responding to the feelings and desires of others). To the personality distinctions in Jung's original model, Briggs and Briggs-Myers added a fourth dimension—judging or perceiving. It describes how people vary in the ways they relate to the outside world.

The four dimensions of the Myers-Briggs Type Indicator follow.[11]

- *Extraversion vs. introversion (E or I)*—whether a person tends toward being outgoing and sociable or shy and quiet
- *Sensing vs. intuitive (S or N)*—whether a person tends to focus on details or on the big picture in dealing with problems
- *Thinking vs. feeling (T or F)*—whether a person tends to rely on logic or emotions in dealing with problems

Sample Myers-Briggs Types

- ESTJ (extraverted, sensing, thinking, judging)—practical, decisive, logical, and quick to dig in; common among managers
- ENTJ (extraverted, intuitive, thinking, judging)—analytical, strategic, forceful, quick to take charge; common for leaders
- ISFJ (introverted, sensing, feeling, judging)—conscientious, considerate, and helpful; common among team players
- INTJ (introverted, intuitive, thinking, judging)—insightful, free thinking, determined; common for visionaries

- *Judging vs. perceiving (J or P)*—whether a person prefers order and control or acts with flexibility and spontaneity

Based on MBTI scores, an individual is classified into one of the 16 possible personality types that result from combinations of these four dimensions. A sample is shown in the small box. The neat and understandable nature of the classification has made the MBTI very popular in management training and development, although it receives mixed reviews from researchers.[12] Employers and trainers tend to like it because once a person is "typed" on the Myers-Briggs, for example as an ESTJ or ISFJ, they can be trained to both understand their own styles and to learn how to better work with people having different styles.

Self-monitoring and other personality traits influence work behavior.

In addition to the Big Five dimensions and the Myers-Briggs Type Indicator, other personality traits can influence how people behave and work together.[13]

= Big Five

Those shown in the nearby figure include self-monitoring, locus of control, authoritarianism, Machiavellianism, and Type A orientation.

Scholars have a strong interest in **locus of control**, noting that some people believe they control their destinies while others believe what happens is beyond their control.[14] "Internals" are more self-confident and accept responsibility for their own actions; "externals" are prone to blaming others and outside forces when bad things happen. Interestingly, research suggests that internals tend to be more satisfied and less alienated from their work.

Authoritarianism is the degree to which a person defers to authority and accepts status differences.[15] Someone with an authoritarian personality might act rigid and control-oriented as a leader. Yet, this same person is often subservient as a follower. People with an authoritarian personality tend to obey orders. Of course, this can create problems when their supervisors ask them to do unethical or even illegal things.

In his 16th-century book *The Prince*, Niccolo Machiavelli gained lasting fame for his advice on how to use power to achieve personal goals.[16] Today we use the term **Machiavellianism** to describe someone who acts manipulatively and emotionally detached when using power. We usually view a "high-Mach" personality as exploitative and unconcerned about others, seemingly guided only by a belief that the end justifies the means. Those with "low-Mach" personalities, by contrast, allow others to exert power over them.

Finally, **self-monitoring** reflects the degree to which someone is able to adjust and modify behavior in new situations.[17] Persons high in self-monitoring tend to be

Locus of control is the extent to which one believes what happens is within one's control.

Authoritarianism is the degree to which a person defers to authority and accepts status differences.

Machiavellianism is the degree to which someone uses power manipulatively.

Self-monitoring is the degree to which someone is able to adjust behavior in response to external factors.

Spanx Has Lots of Snap

Real People and Personalities Make Things Happen

The headline reads: "Spanx queen leads from the bottom line." The story goes: Woman unhappy with the way she looks in white pants cuts feet off panty hose, puts them on, and attends party. The result is: Sara Blakely founds a $250+ million business called Spanx.

"I knew this could open up so many women's wardrobes," Blakely says. "All women have that clothing in the back of the closet that they don't wear because they don't like the way it looks." With this notion, $5,500 of her own money, and the idea for "body shaping" underwear, she set out to start a business. Her unique blend of skills and personality made it all work.

When her first attempts to convince manufacturers to make product samples met with resistance—with one calling it "a stupid idea"—Blakely persisted until one agreed. She aspired to place Spanx in high-end department stores. But again, department stores kept turning her down. Still, Blakely kept at it and finally persuaded a buyer at Neiman Marcus to give Spanx its first big chance. Blakely sent Oprah Winfrey samples, and sales took off after Oprah voted Spanx "one of her favorite things."

It was about this time that Blakely recognized her limits and realized additional skills were needed to handle the firm's fast-paced growth. "I was eager to delegate my weaknesses," she said after turning day-to-day operations over to a chief executive officer. This left her free to pursue creativity, new products, and brand development, as well as work with the Sara Blakely Foundation and its goal of "supporting and empowering women around the world."

Creative, outgoing, passionate, driven, persistent, and ambitious—these adjectives and more describe Sara Blakely and her personality. They can also go a long way in explaining how and why she was successful with Spanx. Any manager needs to understand people, both others and themselves. When you look in the mirror, what and whom do you see?

learners, comfortable with feedback, and both willing and able to change. Because they are flexible, however, others may perceive them as constantly shifting gears and hard to read. A person low in self-monitoring is predictable and tends to act consistently. But this consistency may not fit the unique needs of differing circumstances.

‖ People with Type A personalities tend to stress themselves.

Stress is a state of tension experienced by individuals facing extraordinary demands, constraints, or opportunities.[18] As you consider stress in your life and in your work, you might think about how your personality deals with it. Researchers describe the **Type A personality**, also shown among the personality traits in the last figure, as someone who is high in achievement orientation, impatience, and perfectionism. Type A's are likely to bring stress on themselves, even in circumstances that others find relatively stress-free.[19]

The work environment has enough potential *stressors*, or sources of stress, without this added burden of a stress-prone personality. Some 34% of workers in one survey actually said that their jobs were so stressful that they were thinking of quitting.[20] The stress they were talking about comes from long hours of work, excessive e-mails, unrealistic work deadlines, difficult bosses or co-workers, unwelcome or unfamiliar work, and unrelenting change.[21]

Stress is a state of tension experienced by individuals facing extraordinary demands, constraints, or opportunities.

A **Type A personality** is oriented toward extreme achievement, impatience, and perfectionism.

{ TYPE A PERSONALITIES BRING
STRESS ON THEMSELVES.

Tips to Remember

■ HOW TO SPOT TYPE A PERSONALITIES

1. Always moving, walking, and eating rapidly
2. Impatient, unhappy about waiting
3. Doing or trying to do several things at once
4. Feeling guilty when relaxing

5. Trying to schedule more in less time
6. Using nervous gestures such as clenched fists
7. Hurrying or interrupting the speech of others
8. Never satisfied with performance

As if work stress isn't enough for Type A's to deal with, there's the added kicker of stress in our personal lives. Things such as family events (e.g., the birth of a new child), economics (e.g., a sudden loss of extra income), and personal issues (e.g., a preoccupation with a bad relationship) are all sources of potential emotional strain. These and other personal stressors can spill over to negatively affect our behavior at work. Of course, the effects also hold in reverse; work stressors can have spillover impact on our personal lives.

‖ Stress has consequences for work performance and personal health.

How does all of this add up as an influence on your work and life? It's tempting to view stress all in the negative. But don't forget that stress can have its positive side as well.[22] Take the analogy of a violin.[23] When a violin string is too loose, the sound produced by even the most skilled player is weak and raspy. When the string is too tight, the sound gets shrill and the string might even snap. But when the tension on the string is just right, it creates a beautiful sound. Just enough stress, in other words, may optimize performance.

Constructive stress is energizing and performance enhancing.[24] You've probably felt this as a student. Don't you sometimes do better work "when the pressure is on," as we like to say? Moderate but not overwhelming stress can help us by encouraging effort, stimulating creativity, and enhancing diligence.

Just like tuning a violin string, however, achieving the right balance of stress for each person and situation is difficult. **Destructive stress** is dysfunctional because it is or seems to be so intense or long-lasting that it overloads and breaks down a person's physical and mental systems. One of its outcomes is **job burnout**. This is a sense of physical and mental exhaustion that drains our energies both personally and professionally. Another is **workplace rage**—overly aggressive behavior toward co-workers, bosses, or customers.[25] An extreme example is the "bossnapping" that made the news in France, where workers at a Caterpillar plant took their plant manager hostage and held him for 24 hours in protest of layoffs. A local sociologist said: "Kidnapping your boss is not legal. But it's a way workers have found to make their voices heard."[26]

Medical research also indicates that too much stress can reduce resistance to disease and increase the likelihood of physical and/or mental illness. It may contribute to health problems such as hypertension, ulcers, substance abuse, overeating, depression, and muscle aches.[27]

Constructive stress is a positive influence on effort, creativity, and diligence in work.

Destructive stress is a negative influence on one's performance.

Job burnout is physical and mental exhaustion from work stress.

Workplace rage is aggressive behavior toward co-workers or the work setting.

So what can we do about stress—how can it be managed? The best strategy is to prevent it from reaching excessive levels in the first place. If we can identify our stressors, whether work-related or personal, we can often take action to avoid or minimize their negative consequences. And as managers, we can take steps to help others who are showing stress symptoms. Things like temporary changes in work schedules, reduced performance expectations, long deadlines, and even reminders to take time off can all help.

When it comes to taking time off, the latest advice is that you can work better by working less. A Society for Human Resource Management Survey reports that some 70% of people suffer from self-imposed pressures and often work late or on weekends. But a study by the Boston Consulting Group also reports that requiring people to take time off from their work—by not skipping vacations or working too much overtime, for example, can be beneficial in terms of greater job satisfaction and better work-life balance. The professional services firm KPMG, for example, follows this advice almost to the letter. Its managers now use "wellness scorecards" to track and discuss with employees how well they are doing in taking their vacation days and not working excessive overtime.[28]

Finally, there is really no substitute for **personal wellness**. In management we use this term to describe the pursuit of a personal health-promotion program.[29] It begins by taking personal responsibility for your physical and mental health. It means getting rest, getting plenty of exercise, and eating a balanced diet. It means dealing with addictions to cigarettes, alcohol, or drugs. It means committing to a healthy lifestyle, one that helps you deal with stress and the demands of life and work.

> **Personal wellness** is the pursuit of a personal health-promotion program.

{ WHEN IS PERSONALITY TESTING AN
INVASION OF PERSONAL PRIVACY?

Ethics Check

■ IS PERSONALITY TESTING IN YOUR FUTURE?

Dear [your name goes here]:

I am very pleased to invite you to a second round of screening interviews with XYZ Corporation. Your on-campus session with our representative went very well, and we would like to consider you further for a full-time position. Please contact me to arrange a visit date. We will need a full day. The schedule will include several meetings with executives and your potential team members, as well as a round of personality tests.

Thank you again for your interest in XYZ Corp. I look forward to meeting you during the next step in our recruiting process.

Sincerely,
[signed]
Human Resource Director

Getting a letter like this is great news. It's a nice confirmation of your hard work and performance in college. You obviously made a good first impression. But have you thought about this "personality test" thing? What do you know about them and how they are used for employment screening?

A report in the *Wall Street Journal* advises that lawsuits can result when employers use personality tests that aren't specifically designed for hiring decisions. Some people might even consider their use an invasion of privacy.

YOU DECIDE

What are the ethical issues associated with the use of personality testing? In which situations might the use of personality tests be an invasion of privacy? Also, suppose that the specific personality test being used is not predictive of employee performance on the job. Could its use be termed unethical?

STUDY GUIDE

Takeaway 12.2
How Do Personalities Influence Individual Behavior?

Terms to Define

Agreeableness

Authoritarianism

Conscientiousness

Constructive stress

Destructive stress

Emotional stability

Extraversion

Job burnout

Locus of control

Machiavellianism

Openness

Personal wellness

Personality

Self-monitoring

Stress

Type A personality

Workplace rage

Rapid Review

- The Big Five personality factors are extraversion, agreeableness, conscientiousness, emotional stability, and openness.
- The Myers-Briggs Type Indicator (MBTI) identifies personality types based on extraversion-introversion, sensing-intuitive, thinking-feeling, and judging–perceiving.
- Additional personality dimensions of work significance are locus of control, authoritarianism, Machiavellianism, self-monitoring, and Type A orientation.
- Stress is a state of tension that accompanies extraordinary demands, constraints, or opportunities.
- For some people, having a Type A personality creates stress as a result of continual feelings of impatience and pressure.
- Stress can be destructive or constructive; a moderate level of stress can have a positive impact on performance.

Questions for Discussion

1. Which personality trait would you add to the Big Five to make it the Big "Six"?
2. What are the advantages and disadvantages of having people of different MBTI types working on the same team?
3. Can you be an effective manager and not have a Type A personality?

Be Sure You Can

- list the Big Five personality traits and give work-related examples of each
- list five more personality traits and give work-related examples for each
- list and explain the four dimensions used to create personality types in the MBTI
- identify common stressors in work and personal life
- describe the Type A personality
- differentiate constructive and destructive stress
- explain personal wellness as a stress management strategy

What Would You Do?

You've noticed that one of your co-workers is always rushing, always uptight, and constantly criticizing herself while on the job. She never takes time for coffee when the rest of you do, and even at lunch it's hard to get her to stay and just talk for awhile. Your guess is that she's fighting stress from some source or sources other than the nature of the job itself. How can you help her out?

Takeaway 12.3
How Do Attitudes, Emotions, and Moods Influence Individual Behavior?

ANSWERS TO COME

- Attitudes predispose people to act in certain ways.
- Job satisfaction is a positive attitude toward one's job and work experiences.
- Job satisfaction influences work behavior.
- Job satisfaction has a complex relationship with job performance.
- Emotions and moods are positive and negative states of mind that influence behavior.

AT ONE TIME, CHALLIS M. LOWE WAS ONE OF ONLY TWO AFRICAN-AMERICAN women among the five highest-paid executives in over 400 U.S. corporations.[30] She attained this success after a 25-year career that included several changes of employers and lots of stressors—working-mother guilt, a failed marriage, gender bias on the job, and an MBA degree earned part-time. Through it all, she says: "I've never let being scared stop me from doing something. Just because you haven't done it before doesn't mean you shouldn't try." Would you agree that Lowe has what we often call a "can-do" attitude?

Attitudes predispose people to act in certain ways.

An **attitude** is a predisposition to act in a certain way toward people and environmental factors.[31] Challis Lowe seemed disposed to take risks and embrace challenges. This positive attitude influenced her behavior when dealing with the inevitable problems, choices, and opportunities of work and career.

To fully understand attitudes, positive or negative, it's important recognize the three components shown in the small figure. First is the *cognitive component*, which reflects a belief or value. You might believe, for example, that your management course is very interesting. Second is the *affective* or *emotional component*, which reflects a specific feeling. For example, you might feel very good about being a management major. Third is the *behavioral component*, which reflects an intention to behave consistent with the belief and feeling. Using the same example again, you might say to yourself: "I am going to work hard and try to get As in all my management courses."

Have you noticed, however, that attitudes don't always predictor behavior? Despite pledging to work hard as a student, you might not. Despite wanting a more challenging job, you might keep the current one because of family or other nonwork reasons. In such cases we fail to live up to our own expectations. Usually it's not a good feeling.

> An **attitude** is a predisposition to act in a certain way.

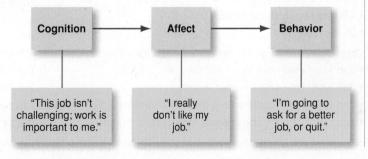

Cognitive dissonance is discomfort felt when attitude and behavior are inconsistent.

The psychological concept of **cognitive dissonance** describes the discomfort we feel in situations where our attitude is inconsistent with our behavior.[32] Most of us manage this dissonance by modifying our attitude to better fit the behavior ("Oh well, work isn't really that important, anyway"), changing future behavior to fit the attitude (not putting extra time in at work; focusing more attention on leisure and personal hobbies), or rationalizing in ways that make the attitude and behavior seem compatible ("I'm in no hurry; there will be a lot of opportunities for better jobs in the future").

‖ Job satisfaction is a positive attitude toward one's job and work experiences.

Job satisfaction is the degree to which an individual feels positive about a job and work experience.

People hold attitudes about many things in the workplace—bosses, each other, tasks, organizational policies, performance goals, paychecks, and more. A comprehensive or catch-all work attitude is **job satisfaction**, the degree to which an individual feels positive or negative about various aspects of his or her job and work experiences.[33]

When researchers study and people talk about job satisfaction, several things are usually at issue. Job satisfaction typically reflects attitudes toward these aspects of the work and social context:

- *The job itself*—responsibility, interest, challenge.
- *Quality of supervision*—task help, social support.
- *Co-workers*—harmony, respect, friendliness.
- *Opportunities*—promotion, learning, growth.
- *Pay*—actual and comparative.
- *Work conditions*—comfort, safety, support.
- *Security*—job and employment.

{ JOB SATISFACTION CORRELATES WITH OVERALL LIFE SATISFACTION.

Facts to Consider

■ TRENDS SHOW JOB SATISFACTION DRIFTING LOWER

When reporters from *Fortune* asked a sample of American workers about their job satisfaction, they found:
- 37% completely satisfied
- 47% somewhat satisfied
- 10% somewhat dissatisfied
- 4% completely dissatisfied
- 2% not sure

Ongoing research on job satisfaction indicates these trends:
- Job satisfaction has been declining since 1995.
- Job satisfaction runs higher in smaller firms.
- Job satisfaction correlates with overall life satisfaction
- Job satisfaction is about equal for men and women

- Most people who are dissatisfied aren't making plans to leave their current jobs.

YOUR THOUGHTS?

Do these data seem consistent with your work experiences and those of your friends and family? How do you think the many job layoffs of the recent economic crisis have affected job satisfaction? Are people with jobs going to be "satisfied" just for having them, or will the uncertainty over keeping their jobs make them "less satisfied" in general? What can a concerned employer do to create conditions for high job satisfaction?

If you watch or read the news, you'll regularly find reports on job satisfaction. You'll also find lots of job satisfaction studies in the academic literature. Interestingly, the majority of people tend to report being at least somewhat satisfied with their jobs. But the trend is down.[34] The least satisfying things about people's jobs often relate to feeling underpaid, not having good career advancement opportunities, and being trapped in the current job. And in respect to things that create job satisfaction, a global study finds pay, contrary to what you might expect, is less important than things like opportunities to do interesting work, recognition for performance, work-life balance, chances for advancement, and job security.[35]

‖ Job satisfaction influences work behavior.

At the beginning of this book, we identified two primary goals or concerns of an effective manager—to help others achieve both high performance and job satisfaction. Are you ready to agree that job satisfaction is important on quality-of-work-life grounds alone? Don't people deserve satisfying work experiences? Of course they do. But an important question remains: Is job satisfaction important in other than a "feel-good" sense?

Researchers tell us that there is a strong relationship between job satisfaction and the **withdrawal behaviors** of *absenteeism*—not showing up for work, and *turnover*—quitting one's job. In respect to absenteeism, workers who are more satisfied with their jobs are absent less often than those who are dissatisfied. In respect to turnover, satisfied workers are more likely to stay and dissatisfied workers are more likely to quit their jobs. The consequences of these withdrawal behaviors can be significant. Both absenteeism and excessive turnover are expensive for employers. In fact, one study found that changing retention rates—up or down—results in similar changes to corporate earnings.[36]

Researchers also identify a relationship between job satisfaction and **organizational citizenship behaviors**.[37] These behaviors show up as a willingness to "go beyond the call of duty" or "go the extra mile" in one's work.[38] A person who is a good organizational citizen does things that, although not required, help advance the performance of the organization. You might observe this as a service worker who goes to extraordinary lengths to take care of a customer, a team member who is always willing to take on extra tasks, or a friend who is always working extra hours without pay just to make sure things are done right for his employer.

Job satisfaction is also tied with **employee engagement**. You can recognize this in yourself and in others as a strong sense of belonging or connection with one's job and employer. It shows up both in high involvement—being willing to help others and always trying to do something extra to improve performance, and in high commitment—feeling and speaking positively about the organization. A survey of 55,000 American workers by the Gallup Organization suggests that more engaged workforces generate higher profits for employers.[39] Things that counted most toward employee engagement in the Gallup research were believing one has the opportunity to do one's best every day, believing one's opinions are valued, believing fellow workers are committed to quality, and believing there is a direct connection between one's work and the company's mission.

Withdrawal behaviors include absenteeism (not showing up for work) and turnover (quitting one's job).

Organizational citizenship behaviors are things people do to go the extras mile in their work.

Employee engagement is a strong sense of belonging and connection with one's work and employer.

||| Job satisfaction has a complex relationship with job performance.

Job satisfaction influences withdrawal, citizenship, and engagement. But, does it influence performance? The data on the job satisfaction and performance relationship are, as you might expect, somewhat complicated.[40] Consider a sign that once hung in a tavern near a Ford plant in Michigan: "I spend 40 hours a week here, am I supposed to work too?"

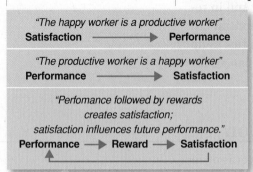

"The happy worker is a productive worker"
Satisfaction ⟶ Performance

"The productive worker is a happy worker"
Performance ⟶ Satisfaction

"Perfomance followed by rewards creates satisfaction; satisfaction influences future performance."
Performance ⟶ Reward ⟶ Satisfaction

Three different arguments on the satisfaction and performance relationship are shown in the small figure. One is that job satisfaction causes performance. The second is that performance causes job satisfaction. The third is that job satisfaction and performance are intertwined, influencing one another and mutually linked with other factors such as available rewards. Can you make a case for each argument based on your personal experiences?

Recent conclusions are that there is probably a modest link between job satisfaction and performance.[41] But emphasize the word "modest" in the last sentence. We need to be careful before rushing to conclude that making people happy is a surefire way to improve their job performance. The reality is that some people will like their jobs, be very satisfied, and still not perform very well. That's part of the complexity of individual behavior.

The link between performance and satisfaction holds pretty much to the same pattern. High-performing workers are likely to feel satisfied. But again, not everyone is likely to fit this model. Some people may get their work done and even meet high performance expectations while still not experiencing high job satisfaction. Can you think of a time where this was the case for you?

Finally, it is quite likely that job satisfaction and job performance influence each other. But the relationship, the subject of a lot of research, is most likely to hold under certain conditions. The role of rewards is especially important. In general, high performance followed by rewards that are valued and perceived as fair will create job satisfaction. This satisfaction, in turn, will likely increase motivation to work hard to achieve high performance in the future.

||| Emotions and moods are positive and negative states of mind that influence behavior.

Emotional intelligence is an ability to understand emotions and manage relationships effectively.

In Chapter 1 we first discussed **emotional intelligence** as an important human skill for managers and an important leadership capability. Daniel Goleman defines EI as an ability to understand emotions in ourselves and in others and to use this understanding to manage relationships effectively.[42] But what is an "emotion?" And, how does it influence our behavior—positively and negatively?

Emotions are strong feelings directed toward someone or something.

An **emotion** is a strong feeling directed toward someone or something. For example, you might feel positive emotion or elation when an instructor congratulates you on a fine class presentation; you might feel negative emotion or anger when an instructor criticizes you in front of the class. In both cases the object of your emotion is the instructor, but in each case the impact of the instructor's behavior on your feelings is quite different. And your behavior in response to the aroused emotions is likely to differ as well—perhaps breaking into a wide smile with the compliment or making a nasty side comment in response to criticism.

Goleman's point about emotional intelligence is that we perform better in work and social situations when we are good at recognizing and dealing with emotions in ourselves and others. In other words, EI allows us to avoid having our emotions "get the better of us."

Whereas emotions tend to be short-term and clearly targeted, **moods** are generalized positive and negative feelings or states of mind that may persist for some time. Everyone seems to have occasional moods, and we each know the full range of possibilities they represent. How often do you wake up in the morning and feel excited, refreshed, and just happy? Or, wake up feeling low, depressed, and generally unhappy? What are the consequences of these different moods for your behavior with friends and family, and at work or school?

When it comes to moods and the workplace, a *Business Week* article claims that it pays to be likable.[43] Harsh is now out and caring is in. Some CEOs are even hiring executive coaches to help them manage emotions and moods so as to come across as more personable and friendly in relationships with others. There's a bit of impression management to consider here. If a CEO, for example, goes to a meeting in a good mood and gets described as "cheerful," "charming," "humorous," "friendly," and "candid," she or he may be viewed as on the upswing. But if the CEO is in a bad mood and comes away perceived as "prickly," "impatient," "remote," "tough," "acrimonious," or even "ruthless," she or he may be seen as on the downhill slope.

Researchers are also increasingly interested in **mood contagion**, the spillover effects of one's mood onto others.[44] Findings indicate that positive emotions of leaders can be "contagious," causing followers to display more positive moods and also be both more attracted to the leaders and willing to rate the leaders more highly. As you might expect, mood contagion can also have positive and negative effects on the moods of co-workers and teammates, as well as family and friends.[45]

> **Moods** are generalized positive and negative feelings or states of mind.

> **Mood contagion** is the spillover of one's positive or negative moods onto others.

{ AMBITION SHOWS UP IN PERSONALITY AS COMPETITIVENESS AND A DESIRE TO BE THE BEST.

Explore Yourself

■ AMBITION

People are different; our styles vary in the way we work, relate to others, and even in how we view ourselves. One of the differences you might observe when interacting with other people is in **ambition**, or the desire to succeed and reach for high goals.

Ambition is one of those traits that can certainly have a big impact on individual behavior. It is evident in how we act and what we try to achieve at work, at home, and in leisure pursuits. It comes out in personality as competitiveness and desire to be the best at something. The more we understand ambition in our lives, and the more we understand how personality traits influence our behavior, the more successful we're likely to be in accomplishing our goals and helping others do the same.

> Get to know yourself better by taking the **Stress Test** self-assessment and completing the other activities in the *Exploring Management* **Skill-Building Portfolio.**

STUDY GUIDE

Takeaway 12.3
How Do Attitudes, Emotions, and Moods Influence Individual Behavior?

Terms to Define

Attitude

Cognitive dissonance

Emotion

Emotional intelligence

Employee engagement

Job satisfaction

Mood

Mood contagion

Organizational citizenship behaviors

Withdrawal behaviors

Rapid Review

- An attitude is a predisposition to respond in a certain way to people and things.
- Cognitive dissonance occurs when a person's attitude and behavior are inconsistent.
- Job satisfaction is an important work attitude, reflecting a person's evaluation of the job, co-workers, and other aspects of the work setting.
- Job satisfaction influences withdrawal behaviors of absenteeism and turnover, and organizational citizenship behaviors.
- Job satisfaction has a complex and reciprocal relationship with job performance.
- Emotions are strong feelings that are directed at someone or something; they influence behavior, often with intensity and for short periods of time.
- Moods are generalized positive or negative states of mind that can be persistent influences on one's behavior.

Questions for Discussion

1. Is cognitive dissonance a good or bad influence on us?
2. How can a manager deal with someone who has high job satisfaction but is a low performer?
3. What are the lessons of mood contagion for how a new team leader should behave?

Be Sure You Can

- identify the three components of an attitude
- explain cognitive dissonance
- describe possible measures of job satisfaction
- explain the consequences of job satisfaction for absenteeism and turnover
- explain the link between job satisfaction, organizational citizenship, and employee engagement
- list and describe three alternative explanations in the job satisfaction–performance relationship
- explain how emotions and moods influence work behavior

What Would You Do?

Your team leader has just told you that some of your teammates have complained to him that you have been in a really bad mood lately and it is rubbing off on the others. They like you and point out that this isn't characteristic of you at all. They don't know what to do about it. What can you do? Is their anything your team leader might do to help?

TestPrep 12

Multiple-Choice Questions

1. Among the Big Five personality traits, _____ indicates someone who tends to be responsible, dependable, and careful in respect to tasks.

    (a) authoritarian

    (b) agreeable

    (c) conscientious

    (d) emotionally stable

2. A person with a/an _____ personality would most likely act unemotional and manipulative when trying to influence others to achieve personal goals.

    (a) extroverted

    (b) sensation-thinking

    (c) self-monitoring

    (d) Machiavellian

3. When a person tends to believe that he or she has little influence over things that happen in life, this indicates a/an _____ personality.

    (a) low emotional stability

    (b) external locus of control

    (c) high self-monitoring

    (d) intuitive-thinker

4. How is a person with an authoritarian personality expected to act?

    (a) Strong tendency to obey orders.

    (b) Challenges the authority of others.

    (c) Tries to play down status differences.

    (d) Always flexible in personal behavior.

5. A new team leader who designs jobs for persons on her work team mainly "because I would prefer to work the new way rather than the old," is committing a perceptual error known as _____.

    (a) the halo effect

    (b) stereotyping

    (c) impression management

    (d) projection

6. If a manager allows one characteristic of a person—say, a pleasant personality—to bias performance ratings of that individual overall, the manager is falling prey to a perceptual distortion known as _____.

    (a) the halo effect   (b) impression management

    (c) stereotyping   (d) projection

7. Use of special dress, manners, gestures, and vocabulary words when meeting a prospective employer in a job interview are all examples of how people use _____ in daily life.

    (a) the halo effect

    (b) impression management

    (c) introversion

    (d) mood contagion

8. _____ is a form of attribution error that involves blaming the environment for problems that we may have caused ourselves.

    (a) Self-serving bias

    (b) Fundamental attribution error

    (c) Projection

    (d) Self-monitoring

9. _____ is a form of attribution error that involves blaming others for problems that they may not have caused for themselves.

    (a) Self-serving bias

    (b) Fundamental attribution error

    (c) Projection

    (d) Self-monitoring

10. The _____ component of an attitude is what indicates a person's belief about something, while the _____ component indicates a specific positive or negative feeling about it.

    (a) cognitive; affective

    (b) emotional; affective

    (c) cognitive; attributional

    (d) behavioral; attributional

11. The term for the discomfort someone feels when his or her behavior is inconsistent with a previously expressed attitude is _____.

   (a) alienation

   (b) cognitive dissonance

   (c) job dissatisfaction

   (d) job burnout

12. Job satisfaction is known from research to be a strong predictor of _____.

   (a) job performance   (b) job burnout

   (c) conscientiousness   (d) absenteeism

13. A person who is always willing to volunteer for extra work or to help someone else with his or her work is acting consistent with strong _____.

   (a) job performance

   (b) self-serving bias

   (c) emotional intelligence

   (d) organizational citizenship

14. A/an _____ represents a rather intense but short-lived feeling about a person or a situation, whereas a/an _____ describes a more generalized positive or negative state of mind.

   (a) stressor; role ambiguity

   (b) external locus of control; internal locus of control

   (c) self-serving bias; halo effect

   (d) emotion; mood

15. Which statement about the job satisfaction–job performance relationship is most true based on research?

   (a) A happy worker will be a productive worker.

   (b) A productive worker will be a happy worker.

   (c) A productive worker well rewarded for performance will be a happy worker.

   (d) There is no relationship between being happy and being productive in a job.

Short-Response Questions

16. What is the most positive profile of Big Five personality traits in terms of positive impact on work behavior?

17. What is the relationship between personality and stress?

18. How does the halo effect differ from selective perception?

19. If you were going to develop a job satisfaction survey, exactly what would you try to measure?

Integration and Application Question

20. When Scott Tweedy picked up a magazine article on "How to Manage Health Care Workers," he was pleased to find some apparent advice. Scott was concerned about poor performance by several of the respiratory therapists in his clinic. The author of the article said that the "best way to improve performance is to make your workers happy." Well, Scott was happy upon reading this and made a pledge to himself to start doing a much better job of "making the therapists happy in the future."

   Questions: Is Scott on the right track? Should he charge ahead as planned, or should he be concerned about this advice? What do we know about the relationship between job satisfaction and performance, and how can this understanding be used by Scott in this situation?

 Steps*for*FurtherLearning

Many learning resources are found at the end of the book and online within WileyPLUS.

Don't Miss These Selections from the **Skill-Building Portfolio**

- **SELF-ASSESSMENT 12:** *Stress Test*
- **CLASS EXERCISE 12:** *Job Satisfaction Preferences*
- **TEAM PROJECT 12:** *Difficult Personalities*

Don't Miss These Selections from **Cases for Critical Thinking**

- **CHAPTER 12 CASE**
  Facebook: Social Networking is Big Business

Snapshot Social networking websites are a dime a dozen these days, so how does Facebook stay at the top? By expanding its user base and working with developers and advertisers to create fresh content that keeps users at the site for hours on end. But can Facebook keep up the growth while deflecting concerns about its leadership?

Despite all of its successes, the management team of Facebook knows that they have serious work ahead in order to change the perception of advertisers, developers, and even some users regarding their ability to lead Facebook successfully and profitably into the future of social networking. Will adding experienced management alter advertisers' stereotypes about youthful Silicon Valley CEOs? Can Facebook overcome the bad impression being communicated about its privacy gaffes?

Make notes here on what you've learned about yourself from this chapter.

- **LEARNING JOURNAL 12**

When J. K. Rowling finished the first of her Harry Potter *books, she was a single mother living on just over $100 a week. "You sort of start thinking anything's possible," she once said, "if you've got enough nerve."*

Motivation

Respect Unlocks Human Potential

Management Live

Engagement and *The Incredibles*

Mr. Incredible (voiced by Craig T. Nelson) is no longer allowed to be a superhero. In his new life, he is Bob Parr, an ordinary claims adjuster for Insuricare. He works in a cubicle in a massive office complex. Parr hates his job because it is monotonous and because it doesn't use his special skills. And, because his boss prohibits him from helping truly needy customers. When Gilbert Huph (voiced by Wallace Shawn) calls Parr into his office for a lecture and threatens to fire him, it pushes Parr to the breaking point.

What is the difference between someone who dislikes her or his job and one who does not? A lot comes down to **engagement**—aspects of the work experience that create a sense of connection to the job and organization.

Workers who are engaged generally have positive attitudes toward their jobs, co-workers, and the organization. Disengaged workers, like Bob Parr, experience negative emotions and attitudes. They become largely unmotivated to work hard.

The content, process, and reinforcement theories discussed in the chapter offer a variety of ways to motivate employees and keep them engaged. Yet these theories are not limited to employees. What about your classmates? Do they act engaged in academics? If you were working on a team project with them, is there anything you could do to increase their engagement and increase the chances of high performance by the team?

YOUR CHAPTER 13 TAKEAWAYS

1. Describe how human needs influence motivation to work.

2. Identify how thoughts and decisions affect motivation to work.

3. Understand how reinforcement influences motivation to work.

WHAT'S INSIDE

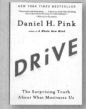

Explore Yourself
More on engagement

Role Models
Charlie Butcher shared his wealth with employees

Ethics Check
Information goldmine is an equity dilemma

Facts to Consider
Europe turning to quotas to increase female board members

Manager's Library
Drive by Daniel Pink

Takeaway 13.1
How Do Human Needs Influence Motivation to Work?

ANSWERS TO COME

- Maslow described a hierarchy of needs topped by self-actualization.
- Alderfer's ERG theory deals with existence, relatedness, and growth needs.
- McClelland identified acquired needs for achievement, power, and affiliation.
- Herzberg's two-factor theory focuses on higher-order need satisfaction.
- The core characteristics model integrates motivation and job design.

DID YOU KNOW THAT J. K. ROWLING'S FIRST *HARRY POTTER* BOOK WAS REJECTED by 12 publishers?[1] Thank goodness she didn't give up. In management we use the term **motivation** to describe forces within the individual that account for the level, direction, and persistence of effort expended at work. Simply put, a highly motivated person works hard at a job; an unmotivated person does not. A manager who leads through motivation creates conditions that consistently inspire other people to work hard.

A highly motivated workforce is obviously indispensable. So how do we get there? Why do some people work enthusiastically, persevering in the face of difficulty and often doing more than required to turn out an extraordinary performance? Why do others hold back, quit at the first negative feedback, and do the minimum needed to avoid reprimand or termination?

⫼ Maslow described a hierarchy of needs topped by self-actualization.

One of the best starting points in exploring the issue of motivation are theories from psychology that deal with differences in individual **needs**—unfulfilled desires that stimulate people to behave in ways that will satisfy them. And as you might expect, there are different theories about human needs and how they may affect people at work.

Abraham Maslow's theory of human needs is an important foundation in the history of management thought. He described a hierarchy built on a foundation of **lower-order needs** (physiological, safety, and social concerns) and moving up to **higher-order needs** (esteem and self-actualization).[2] Whereas lower-order needs focus on physical well-being and companionship, the higher-order needs reflect psychological development and growth.

A key part of Maslow's thinking relies on two principles. The *deficit principle* states that a satisfied need is not a motivator of behavior. People act in ways that satisfy deprived needs, ones for which a "deficit" exists. We eat because we are hungry; we call a friend when we are lonely; we seek approval from others when we are feeling insecure. The *progression principle* states that people try to satisfy lower-level needs first and then move step-by-step up the hierarchy. This happens until the level of self-actualization is reached. The more these needs

---

Motivation accounts for the level, direction, and persistence of effort expended at work.

A **need** is an unfulfilled physiological or psychological desire.

Lower-order needs are physiological, safety, and social needs in Maslow's hierarchy.

Higher-order needs are esteem and self-actualization needs in Maslow's hierarchy.

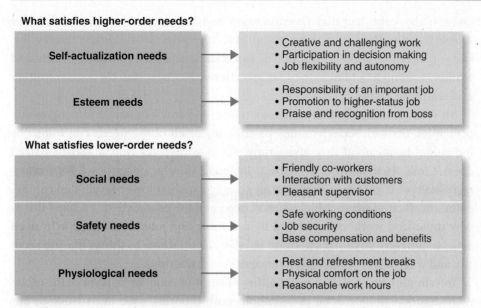

What satisfies higher-order needs?

| Self-actualization needs | → | • Creative and challenging work
• Participation in decision making
• Job flexibility and autonomy |
| Esteem needs | → | • Responsibility of an important job
• Promotion to higher-status job
• Praise and recognition from boss |

What satisfies lower-order needs?

Social needs	→	• Friendly co-workers • Interaction with customers • Pleasant supervisor
Safety needs	→	• Safe working conditions • Job security • Base compensation and benefits
Physiological needs	→	• Rest and refreshment breaks • Physical comfort on the job • Reasonable work hours

FIGURE 13.1 What Are the Opportunities for Need Satisfaction in Maslow's Hierarchy? For higher-order need satisfaction, people realize self-actualization by doing creative and challenging work and participating in important decisions; they boost self-esteem through promotions and praise, and by having responsibility for an important job. For lower-order need satisfaction, people meet social needs through positive relationships with co-workers, supervisors, and customers; they achieve safety needs in healthy working conditions and a secure job with good pay and benefits; and they realize physiological needs by having reasonable work hours and comfortable work spaces.

are satisfied, the stronger they will grow. Maslow believes opportunities for self-fulfillment should continue to motivate a person as long as the other needs remain satisfied.

Maslow's theory is a good starting point for examining human needs and their potential influence on motivation. It seems to make sense, for example, that managers should try to understand the needs of people working with and for them. And isn't it a manager's job to help others find ways of satisfying their needs through work? Figure 13.1 gives some suggestions along these lines.

Alderfer's ERG theory deals with existence, relatedness, and growth needs.

A well-regarded alternative to Maslow's work is the ERG theory proposed by Clayton Alderfer.[3] His theory collapses Maslow's five needs into three. **Existence needs** are desires for physiological and material well-being. **Relatedness needs** are desires for satisfying interpersonal relationships. **Growth needs** are desires for continued psychological growth and development.

Growth needs are essentially the higher-order needs in Maslow's hierarchy. And they are important. Consider this example.[4] During the recent recession, Laine Seator lost her management job and started volunteering. She now puts in 35-hour weeks working for five different organizations. She's finding that her time helping others is well spent; she's gaining new skills in grant writing and strategic planning that should help with future job hunting. "In a regular job," she says, "you'd need to be a director or management staff to be able to do these types of things, but on a volunteer basis they welcome the help." And at a United Way in

Existence needs are desires for physiological and material well-being.

Relatedness needs are desires for satisfying interpersonal relationships.

Growth needs are desires for continued psychological growth and development.

Boise, Idaho, volunteer Rick Overton says: "It's hard to describe how much better it feels to get to the end of the day and, even if you haven't made any money, feel like you did some good for the world." Don't Laine and Rick sound like motivated workers finding lots of higher-order growth need satisfaction through volunteer and nonprofit work?

It's worth noting that ERG theory rejects Maslow's deficit and progression principles. Instead, Alderfer suggests that any or all of the needs can influence individual behavior at any given time. He also believes that a satisfied need doesn't lose its motivational impact. Instead, Alderfer describes a *frustration-regression principle* through which an already-satisfied lower-level need can become reactivated when a higher-level need cannot be satisfied. Perhaps this is why unionized workers frustrated by assembly-line jobs (lacking growth need satisfaction) give so much attention in labor negotiations to things like job security and wage levels (offering existence need satisfaction).

You shouldn't be quick to reject either Maslow or Alderfer in favor of the other. Although questions can be raised about both theories, each adds value to our understanding of how individual needs can influence motivation.[5] And you should notice that Maslow's higher-order needs match up with Alderfer's growth needs.

McClelland identified acquired needs for achievement, power, and affiliation.

In the late 1940s, David McClelland and his colleagues began experimenting with the Thematic Apperception Test (TAT) of human psychology.[6] The TAT asks people to view pictures and write stories about what they see. Researchers then analyze the stories, looking for themes that display individual needs.

From this research McClelland identified three acquired needs that he considers central to understanding human motivation. The **need for achievement** is the desire to do something better or more efficiently, to solve problems, or to master complex tasks. The **need for power** is the desire to control other people, to influence their behavior, or to be responsible for them. The **need for affiliation** is the desire to have friendly and warm relations with other people.

McClelland encourages managers to learn how to recognize the strength of these needs in themselves and in other people. Because each need can be associated with a distinct set of work preferences, his insights offer helpful ideas for designing jobs and creating work environments that are rich in potential motivation.

Consider someone high in the need for achievement. Do you, for example, like to put your competencies to work, take moderate risks in competitive situations, and often prefer to work alone? Need achievers are like this, and their work preferences usually follow a pattern. Persons high in need for achievement like work that offers challenging but achievable goals, feedback on performance, and individual responsibility. If you take one or more of these away, they are likely to become frustrated and their performance may suffer. As a manager, these preferences offer pretty straightforward insights for dealing with a high need achiever. And if you are high in need for achievement, these are things you should be talking about with your manager.

Need for achievement is the desire to do something better, to solve problems, or to master complex tasks.

Need for power is the desire to control, influence, or be responsible for other people.

Need for affiliation is the desire to establish and maintain good relations with people.

Work Preferences of High Need Achievers

- Individual responsibilities
- Challenging but achievable goals
- Performance feedback

HopeLab Fights Disease with Fun

There Are Many Pathways to Motivation

While many teens play video games just for fun, teens with cancer can now play ones that can help them beat the disease. Picture a teenager who has a tough time keeping up with cancer medication schedules. Now imagine him playing the video game called Re-Mission and maneuvering a nanobot called Roxxi through the body of a cancer patient to destroy cancer cells. And, then think about an article in the medical journal *Pediatrics* that says teen patients who play the game at least one hour a week do a better job sticking to their medication schedules.

What's going on here is the brainchild of HopeLab, founded by Pam Omidyar, an immunology researcher and gaming enthusiast who saw the possible link between games and fighting disease. The nonprofit's mission is combining "rigorous research with innovative solutions to improve the health and quality of life of young people with chronic illness."

HopeLab is led by president and CEO Pat Christen. She came to the position after 20 years of nonprofit management experience, including president and executive director of the San Francisco AIDS Foundation and president of the Pangaea Global AIDS Foundation. Her career began in Kenya, East Africa, where she served as a Peace Corps volunteer. Christen now focuses her talents on helping HopeLab find innovative ways to improve the lives of young people fighting illnesses.

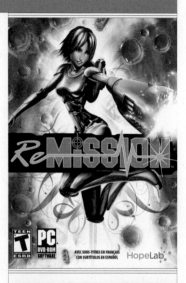

FIND INSPIRATION

Re-Mission is one positive step in the war against childhood cancer. With the founding vision of Pam Omidyar and the strategic leadership of Pat Christen, HopeLab received the Social Enterprise Award of the Year from *Fast Company* magazine. One of its current priorities is to unleash the power of video gaming to help in the fight against childhood obesity. Think about how creative approaches to motivation can improve lives and empower people.

McClelland's theory offers good insights about the other needs as well. People high in the need for affiliation prefer jobs offering companionship, social approval, and satisfying interpersonal relationships. People high in the need for power are motivated to behave in ways that have a clear impact on other people and events; they enjoy being in positions of control.

Importantly, McClelland distinguishes between two forms of the power need.[7] The need for *personal power* is exploitative and involves manipulation purely for the sake of personal gratification. As you might imagine, this type of power need is not respected in management. By contrast, the *need for social power* is the positive face of power. It involves the use of power in a socially responsible way, one that is directed toward group or organizational objectives rather than personal ones. This need for social power is essential to managerial leadership.

One interesting extension of McClelland's research found that successful senior executives tended to have high needs for social power that, in turn, were higher than otherwise strong needs for affiliation. Can you explain these results? It may be that managers high in the need for affiliation alone may let their desires for social approval interfere with business decisions. But with a higher need for power, they may be more willing to sometimes act in ways that other persons may disagree with. In other words, they'll do what is best for the organization even if it makes some people unhappy. Does this make sense?

Herzberg's two-factor theory focuses on higher-order need satisfaction.

Frederick Herzberg's work on human needs took a slightly different route. He began with extensive interviews of people at work and then content-analyzed their answers. The result is known as the two-factor theory.[8]

When questioned about what "turned them on," Herzberg found that workers mainly talked about the nature of the job itself— such things as a sense of achievement, feelings of recognition, a sense of responsibility, the opportunity for advancement, and feelings of personal growth. In other words, they told him about what they did. Herzberg called these **satisfier factors**, or *motivator factors*, and described them as part of *job content*. They are consistent with the higher-order needs of Maslow, growth needs of Alderfer, and achievement and power needs of McClelland.

When questioned about what "turned them off," Herzberg found that his respondents talked about quite different things—working conditions, interpersonal relations, organizational policies and administration, technical quality of supervision, and base wage or salary. They were telling him about where they worked, not about what they did. Herzberg called these **hygiene factors** and described them as part of *job context*. They seem most associated with Maslow's lower-order needs, Alderfer's existence and relatedness needs, and McClelland's affiliation need.

Herzberg's two-factor theory is shown in Figure 13.2. Hygiene factors influence job dissatisfaction, while satisfier factors influence job satisfaction. The distinction is important. Herzberg is saying that you can't increase job satisfaction by improving the hygiene factors. You will only get less dissatisfaction. Although minimizing dissatisfaction is a worthy goal, you can't expect much by way of increased motivation. At least that's his theory.

A **satisfier factor** is found in job content, such as a sense of achievement, recognition, responsibility, advancement, or personal growth.

A **hygiene factor** is found in the job context, such as working conditions, interpersonal relations, organizational policies, and salary.

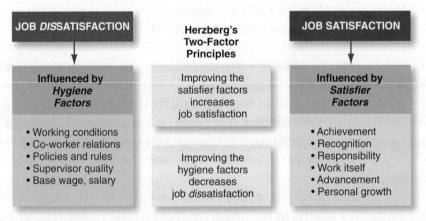

FIGURE 13.2 What Are the Motivational Implications of Job Content and Job Context in Herzberg's Two-Factor Theory?
Scholars criticize this theory because of its research foundations. However, Herzberg makes an interesting and useful distinction between the motivational implications of job content and job context. He believes that you can't increase job satisfaction and motivation by improving hygiene factors in the job context, for example, by increasing wages. This only reduces levels of dissatisfaction. Instead, he argues in favor of improving satisfier factors in the job content, things like responsibility and recognition. In the two-factor theory, such changes are pathways to higher job satisfaction and motivation.

Although scholars have criticized Herzberg's research as method-bound and difficult to replicate, the two-factor theory makes us think about both job content and job context.[9] It cautions managers not to expect too much by way of motivational gains from investments in things like pleasant work spaces and even high base salaries. Instead, it focuses our attention on building jobs to provide opportunities for responsibility, growth, and other sources of higher-order need satisfactions. And to create these high-content jobs, Herzberg suggests allowing people to manage themselves and exercise self-control over their work.

The core characteristics model integrates motivation and job design.

If you really think about it, you should see that for a job to be highly motivational there has to be a good fit between the needs and talents of the individual and tasks to be performed. And as you might expect, just what constitutes a good fit is going to vary from one individual and situation to the next. **Job design** is the allocation of specific work tasks to individuals and groups.[10] It's goal is a good person-job fit.

Herzberg, known for the two-factor theory just discussed, poses the job design challenge this way: "If you want people to do a good job, give them a good job to do."[11] He goes on to argue that this is best done through **job enrichment**, the practice of designing jobs rich in content that offers opportunities for higher-order need satisfaction. For him, an enriched job allows the individual to perform planning and controlling duties normally done by supervisors. In other words, job enrichment involves a lot of self-management.

Modern management theory values job enrichment and its motivating potential. However, in true contingency fashion, it recognizes that not everyone may have needs consistent with enriched jobs. The core characteristics model developed by J. Richard Hackman and his associates helps managers design jobs that best fit the needs of different people.[12]

Figure 13.3 shows that the core characteristics model approaches job design with a focus on five "core" job characteristics: skill variety, task identity, task

> **Job design** is the allocation of specific work tasks to individuals and groups.

> **Job enrichment** increases job content by adding work planning and evaluating duties normally performed by the supervisor.

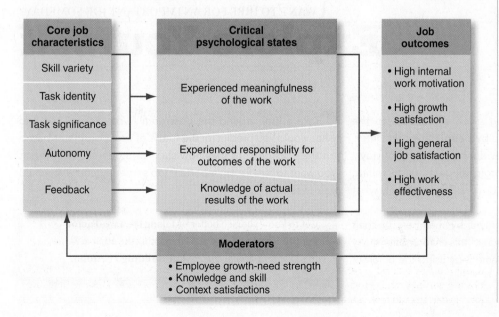

FIGURE 13.3

How Do Core Characteristics Influence Motivation Through Job Design?
This model shows how jobs can be designed according to five core characteristics—skill variety, task identity, task significance, autonomy, and feedback. Jobs that are high in these characteristics provide job holders with experienced meaningfulness and responsibility as well as knowledge of results. Under the right contingency conditions—high growth need strength and satisfaction with job context—these critical psychological states are motivational and set the stage for positive job outcomes.

significance, autonomy, and job feedback. Can you think of specific jobs that might score high and low on these characteristics? Here's a bit more detail on them.

1. *Skill variety*—the degree to which a job requires a variety of different activities to carry out the work and involves the use of a number of different skills and talents of the individual

2. *Task identity*—the degree to which the job requires completion of a "whole" and identifiable piece of work, one that involves doing a job from beginning to end with a visible outcome

3. *Task significance*—the degree to which the job has a substantial impact on the lives or work of other people elsewhere in the organization or in the external environment

4. *Autonomy*—the degree to which the job gives the individual freedom, independence, and discretion in scheduling work and in choosing procedures for carrying it out

5. *Feedback from the job itself*—the degree to which work activities required by the job result in the individual obtaining direct and clear information on his or her performance

The higher a job scores on the five core characteristics, the more enriched it is. But as you consider this model, don't forget the contingency logic. It recognizes that not everyone will be a good fit for a highly enriched job. Whether they do fit or not depends on the presence of three "moderators" also shown Figure 13.3. People are expected to respond most favorably to job enrichment when they have strong growth needs, have appropriate job knowledge and skills, and are otherwise satisfied with the job context. When these conditions are weak or absent, the fit between the individual and an enriched job may turn out less favorably than expected.

{ LOOK AROUND THE CLASSROOM; WHO WOULD YOU
WANT TO HIRE FOR AN IMPORTANT JOB SOMEDAY?

Explore Yourself

■ ENGAGEMENT

There's a lot of attention being given these days to the levels of **engagement** displayed by people at work. Differences in job engagement are evident in a variety of ways: Is someone enthusiastic or lethargic, diligent or lazy, willing to do more than expected or at best willing to do only what is expected?

Managers want high engagement by members of their work units and teams, and the ideas of this chapter offer many insights on how to create engagement by using the different theories of motivation.

Take a look around the classroom. What do you see and what would you predict for the future of your classmates based on the engagement they now show as students? Who might you want to hire for an important job someday, and who would you pass on?

> Get to know yourself better by taking the **Two-Factor Profile** self-assessment and completing the other activities in the *Exploring Management* **Skill-Building Portfolio.**

Takeaway 13.1
How Do Human Needs Influence Motivation to Work?

Terms to Define

Existence needs

Growth needs

Higher-order needs

Hygiene factors

Job design

Job enrichment

Lower-order needs

Motivation

Need

Need for achievement

Need for affiliation

Need for power

Relatedness needs

Satisfier factors

Rapid Review

- Motivation involves the level, direction, and persistence of effort expended at work; a highly motivated person can be expected to work hard.
- Maslow's hierarchy of human needs is moves from lower-order physiological, safety, and social needs up to higher-order ego and self-actualization needs.
- Alderfer's ERG theory identifies existence, relatedness, and growth needs.
- McClelland's acquired needs theory identifies the needs for achievement, affiliation, and power, all of which may influence what a person desires from work.
- Herzberg's two-factor theory identifies satisfier factors in job content as influences on job satisfaction; hygiene factors in job context are viewed as influences on job dissatisfaction.
- The core characteristics model of job design focuses on skill variety, task identity, task significance, autonomy, and feedback.

Questions for Discussion

1. Was Maslow right in suggesting we each have tendencies toward self-actualization?
2. Is high need for achievement always good for managers?
3. Why can't job enrichment work for everyone?

Be Sure You Can

- describe work practices that can satisfy higher-order needs in Maslow's hierarchy
- contrast Maslow's hierarchy with ERG theory
- explain needs for achievement, affiliation, and power in McClelland's theory
- differentiate the needs for personal and social power
- describe work preferences for a person with a high need for achievement
- describe differences in hygiene and satisfier factors in Herzberg's theory
- explain how a person's growth needs and job skills might affect his or her responses to job enrichment

What Would You Do?

At a campus recreation center that you manage, two student workers are being considered for promotions. One works really well with people and seems to thrive on teamwork and social interaction. The other tackles tough jobs with enthusiasm and always want to do her best, while preferring to do things alone rather than with others. Fortunately for you, the center's staff is expanding and you can design jobs to best fit each student. What jobs would you create for them?

Takeaway 13.2
How Do Thought Processes and Decisions Affect Motivation to Work?

ANSWERS TO COME

- Equity theory explains how social comparisons motivate individual behavior.
- Expectancy theory considers Motivation = Expectancy $\times$ Instrumentality $\times$ Valence.
- Goal-setting theory shows that well-chosen and well-set goals can be motivating.

HAVE YOU EVER RECEIVED AN EXAM OR PROJECT GRADE AND FELT GOOD ABOUT IT, only to get discouraged when you hear about someone who didn't work as hard getting the same or better grade? Or have you ever suffered a loss of motivation when the goal set by your boss or instructor seems so high that you don't see any chance at all of succeeding?

My guess is that most of us have had these types of experiences, and perhaps fairly often. They raise the question of exactly what influences decisions regarding whether to work hard or not in various situations? The equity, expectancy, and goal-setting theories of motivation all offer possible answers.

‖ Equity theory explains how social comparisons motivate individual behavior.

The equity theory of motivation is best known in management through the work of J. Stacy Adams.[13] Based on the logic of social comparisons, it pictures us continually checking our rewards for work accomplished against those of others. Any perceived inequities in these comparisons are uncomfortable. This makes us motivated to act in ways that restore a sense of equity to the situation. Think of it this way.

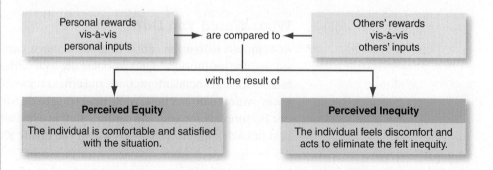

Check these equity dynamics against your own experiences. How have you reacted when your grade seems unfair compared with others? Did you reduce your efforts in the future . . . drop the course . . . rationalize that you really didn't work that hard . . . complain to the instructor and request a higher grade? All of these are ways to reduce the perceived grading inequity. And they are the same types of behaviors that perceived inequity can motivate people to engage in at work. Only instead of grades, the sources of inequity are more likely to be pay raises, job assignments, work schedules, office "perks," and the like. Pay, of course, is the really big one!

Research on equity theory has largely occurred in the laboratory. It is most conclusive with respect to **perceived negative inequity**—feeling uncomfortable at being unfairly treated. People who feel underpaid, for example, may experience disappointment or even a sense of anger. They will be motivated to try to restore perceived equity to the situation. This might be done by reducing work efforts to compensate for the missing rewards, asking for more rewards or better treatment, or even by quitting the job.[14]

Interestingly, there is also some evidence for an equity dynamic among people who feel overpaid. This **perceived positive inequity** is associated with a sense of guilt. It is discomfort felt over benefitting from unfair treatment. The individual is motivated to restore perceived equity by doing such things as increasing the quantity or quality of work, taking on more difficult assignments, or working overtime. Do you think this really happens? What if one of your instructors decides to inflate the grades of students on early assignments, thinking that perceived positive inequities will motivate them to study harder for the rest of the course? Would you work harder or perhaps work less?

> **Perceived negative inequity** is discomfort felt over being harmed by unfair treatment.

> **Perceived positive inequity** is discomfort felt over benefitting from unfair treatment.

{ "SHOULD I PASS THIS INFORMATION AROUND ANONYMOUSLY SO THAT EVERYONE KNOWS WHAT'S GOING ON?"

Ethics Check

■ INFORMATION GOLDMINE IS AN EQUITY DILEMMA

A worker opens the top of the office photocopier and finds a document someone has left behind. It's a list of performance evaluations, pay, and bonuses for 80 co-workers. She reads the document. Lo and behold, someone she considers a "non-starter" is getting paid more than others regarded as "super workers." New hires are also being brought in at much higher pay and bonuses than those of existing staff. And to make matters worse, she's in the middle of the list and not near the top where she would have expected to be. The fact is she makes a lot less money than many others.

Looking at the data, she begins to question why she is spending extra hours working on her laptop evenings and weekends at home, trying to do a really great job for the firm. She wonders to herself: "Should I pass this information around anonymously so that everyone knows what's going on? Or should I quit and find another employer who fully values me for my talents and hard work?"

In the end she decided to quit, saying: "I just couldn't stand the inequity." She also decided not to distribute the information to others in the office because "it would make them depressed, like it made me depressed."

YOU DECIDE

What would you do? Obviously, you are going to be concerned, and perhaps upset. Would you hit "print," make about 80 copies, and put them in everyone's mailboxes—or even just leave them stacked in a couple of convenient locations? That would get the information out into the gossip chains pretty quickly. But is this ethical? If you don't send out the information, is it ethical to let other workers go about their days with inaccurate assumptions about the firm's pay practices? By quitting and not sharing the information, did this worker commit an ethics mistake?

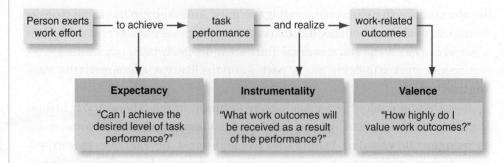

Although there are no clear answers available in equity theory, there are some very good insights. The theory is a reminder that rewards perceived as equitable should positively affect satisfaction and performance; those perceived as inequitable may create dissatisfaction and cause performance problems.[15] Probably the best advice is to anticipate potential equity problems whenever rewards of any type are being allocated.

We should also recognize that people may compare themselves not only with co-workers but with others elsewhere in the organization, including senior executives, and even persons employed by other organizations. And we should remember that people behave according to their perceptions. If someone perceives inequity, it is likely to affect his or her behavior whether the manager sees the situation the same way or not.

⦀ Expectancy theory considers Motivation = Expectancy × Instrumentality × Valence.

Victor Vroom offers another approach to understanding motivation. His expectancy theory asks: What determines the willingness of an individual to work hard at tasks important to the organization?[16] Vroom answers this question with an equation:

$$\text{Motivation} = \text{Expectancy} \times \text{Instrumentality} \times \text{Valence}$$

The terms in this expectancy equation are defined as follows. **Expectancy** is a person's belief that working hard will result in achieving a desired level of task performance (sometimes called *effort-performance expectancy*). **Instrumentality** is a person's belief that successful performance will lead to rewards and other potential outcomes (sometimes called *performance-outcome expectancy*). **Valence** is the value a person assigns to the possible rewards and other work-related outcomes. Think of them this way.

The use of multiplication signs in the expectancy equation ($M = E \times I \times V$) has important implications. Mathematically speaking, a zero at any location on the right side of the equation will result in zero motivation. This means that we cannot neglect any of the three factors—expectancy, instrumentality, or valence. In order for motivation to be high, all three must be positive.

Are you ready to test this theory? Most of us assume that people will work hard to get promoted. But is this necessarily true? Expectancy theory predicts that motivation to work hard for a promotion will be low if any one or more of three conditions apply. If *expectancy is low*, motivation suffers. The person feels that he or she cannot achieve the performance level necessary to get promoted.

Expectancy is a person's belief that working hard will result in high task performance.

Instrumentality is a person's belief that various outcomes will occur as a result of task performance.

Valence is the value a person assigns to work-related outcomes.

So why try? If *instrumentality is low*, motivation suffers. The person lacks confidence that high performance will actually result in being promoted. So why try? If *valence is low*, motivation suffers. The person doesn't want a promotion, preferring less responsibility in the present job. So, if it isn't a valued outcome, why work hard to get it?

Figure 13.4 summarizes the management implications of expectancy theory. It is a reminder that different people are likely to come up with different answers to the question: Why should I work hard today? Knowing that their answers will differ, Vroom's point is that each person must be respected as an individual with unique work needs, preferences, and concerns. His theory identifies the following ways to do this while creating work environments that are high in motivating potential.

To have high expectancies, people must believe in their abilities; they must believe that if they try hard to do something, they can perform well at it. Managers can help build these expectancies by selecting workers with the right abilities for the jobs to be done, providing them with the best training and development, and supporting them with resources so that the jobs can be done very well. All of these factors stimulate motivation based on something called **self-efficacy**, a person's belief that they are capable of performing a task.

To have high instrumentalities, people must perceive that their performance accomplishments will be followed by desired work outcomes. In others words, they believe that performance will lead to valued rewards. Managers can create positive instrumentalities by taking care to clarify the rewards to be gained by high performance. They must also continually confirm this "promise," so to speak,

Self-efficacy is a person's belief that they are capable of performing a task.

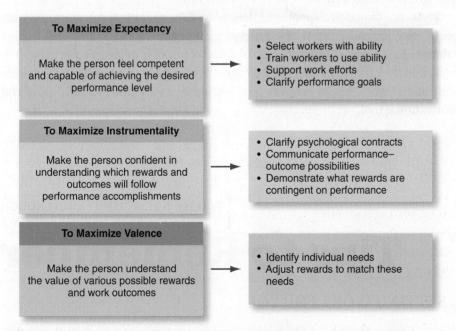

FIGURE 13.4 How Can Managers Use the Insights of the Expectancy Theory of Motivation?
Managers should act in ways that maximize expectancies, instrumentalities, and valences for others. To maximize expectancy, they need to hire capable workers, train and develop them continuously, and communicate goals and confidence in their skills. To maximize instrumentality, managers must clarify and stand by performance-reward linkages. Finally, to maximize valence, they need to understand individual needs and try to tie work outcomes to important sources of need satisfaction.

by actually delivering the expected results. Any disconfirmation or failure to deliver will diminish the instrumentality.

To have high and positive valences, people must value the outcomes associated with high performance. This means that the reward being offered is what they really want. Of course, this is a major source of individual differences. But managers should be able to use insights of the content theories—Maslow, Alderfer, McClelland, for example—to best match important individual needs with the rewards and outcomes that can be earned through high performance.

Goal-setting theory shows that well-chosen and well-set goals can be motivating.

When Steven A. Davis was a child, he got a lot of encouragement from his parents: "They never said that because you are an African American you can only go this far or do only this or that," he says, "they just said 'go for it.'" Davis also says that when he graduated from college, he set goals—to be corporate vice president in 10 years and a president in 20. He made it; Davis rose through a variety of management jobs to become president of Long John Silver's, part of Yum! Brands, Inc. He is now CEO of Bob Evans Farms in Columbus, Ohio.[17]

Victor Vroom would point out that Davis's parents increased his motivation by creating high positive expectancy during his school years. Edwin Locke would add that Davis found lots of motivation through the goals he set as a college graduate. His goal-setting theory recognizes the motivational influence of task goals.[18] The basic premise is that task goals can be highly motivating, but only *if* they are the right goals and *if* they are set in the right ways.[19]

Goals give direction to people in their work. Goals clarify the performance expectations between leaders and followers, among co-workers, and even across subunits in an organization. Goals establish a frame of reference for task feedback, and they provide a foundation for control and self-management.[20] In these and related ways, Locke believes goal setting is a very practical and powerful motivational tool.

{ "DO YOUR BEST" ISN'T GOOD ENOUGH WHEN IT COMES TO GOAL SETTING.

Tips to Remember

■ HOW TO MAKE GOAL SETTING WORK FOR YOU

- *Set specific goals*—avoid more generally stated ones, such as "Do your best."
- *Set challenging goals*—when realistic and attainable, they motivate better than easy ones.
- *Build commitments*—people work harder for goals they accept and believe in.

- *Clarify priorities*—expectations should be clear on which goals to pursue first.
- *Provide good feedback*—people need to know how well they are doing.
- *Reward results*—give reinforcement; don't let accomplishments pass unnoticed.

Facts to Consider

■ EUROPE TURNING TO QUOTAS TO INCREASE FEMALE BOARD MEMBERS

It's no secret that females are underrepresented relative to men on corporate boards. In Europe the data are being scrutinized and quotas are being discussed as possible ways to resolve the disparity. Diane Segalen, senior executive at a Paris-based executive search company, says: "Some men over 60 think suitable females don't exist because they have never had women as their peers. They think women can't take the pressure involved in serving on a board."

- An official British study questioned why the proportion of nonexecutive board seats filled by females at FTSE 100 firms was stalled at 12.5%.
- British headhunter firms are under threat of facing mandatory quotas for female board candidates unless the figures rise to 25% by 2015.
- France has already adopted a mandatory quota of 40% female board members by 2015 for firms with over 500 employees and $72 million in sales.

- With the quota in place, the proportion of board seats filled by women at French firms is expected to move from 7% to 20% within a year.

YOUR THOUGHTS?

When it comes to getting women their fair shares of board seats, is current underrepresentation a "pipeline" problem—just not enough qualified women available for these senior positions at this point in time? Or, is it a "discrimination" problem—men at the top of headhunting firms and corporations still aren't ready to open the doors to female candidates? And when it comes to correcting the problem, is it enough to keep the data in front of the decision makers and hope for change? Or, are quotas like the one used in France the way to go?

But what is a motivational goal? Research by Locke and his associates indicates that managers and team leaders should focus on how specific and difficult goals are, and how likely it is that others will accept and commit to them.[21] As you might suspect, this is a tall order. It is no easy task for managers to work with others to set the right goals in the right ways. And as Tips to Remember recommends, an important key to the goal-setting process is participation. Goals are most motivating when the individual has participated in setting them.

Although all this sounds ideal and good, we have to be realistic. We can't always choose our own goals; there are many times in work when goals come to us from above and we are expected to help accomplish them. Does this mean that the motivational properties of goal setting are lost? Not necessarily; even though the goals are set, there may be opportunities to participate in how to best pursue them. Locke's research also suggests that workers will respond positively to externally imposed goals if they trust the supervisors assigning them and they believe the supervisors will adequately support them.

The practice of management by objectives, discussed in Chapter 6 as an integrative approach to planning and controlling, can be a good example. When done well, MBO brings together team leaders and team members in a participative process of goal setting and performance review. Consistent with goal-setting theory, the positive impact of MBO is most likely when specific and difficult goals are set in ways that create mutual understanding and increase acceptance and commitment.

STUDY GUIDE

Takeaway 13.2
How Do Thought Processes and Decisions Affect Motivation to Work?

Terms to Define

Expectancy

Instrumentality

Perceived negative inequity

Perceived positive inequity

Self-efficacy

Valence

Rapid Review

- Adams's equity theory recognizes that social comparisons take place when rewards are distributed in the workplace.
- In equity theory, any sense of perceived inequity is considered a motivating state that causes a person to behave in ways that restore equity to the situation.
- Vroom's expectancy theory states that Motivation = Expectancy × Instrumentality × Valence.
- Managers using expectancy theory are advised to make sure rewards are achievable (maximizing expectancies), predictable (maximizing instrumentalities), and individually valued (maximizing valence).
- Locke's goal-setting theory emphasizes the motivational power of goals that are specific and challenging as well as set through participatory means.

Questions for Discussion

1. Is it against human nature to work harder as a result of perceived positive inequity?
2. Can a person with low expectancy ever be motivated to work hard at a task?
3. Will goal-setting theory work if the goals are fixed and only the means for achieving them are open for discussion?

Be Sure You Can

- explain the role of social comparison in Adams's equity theory
- list possible ways people with felt negative inequity may behave
- differentiate the terms "expectancy," "instrumentality," and "valence"
- explain the reason for "×" signs in Vroom's expectancy equation, $M = E \times I \times V$
- explain Locke's goal-setting theory
- describe the link between goal-setting theory and MBO

What Would You Do?

It's apparent that Kate isn't happy. Because of her great performance as a Web designer, you just promoted her to team leader for Web Design Services. But you notice that she appears anxious, stressed, and generally unhappy in the new assignment. This is quite a contrast from the highly motivated and happy Kate you knew in her old job. What might be wrong here and what can you, as her supervisor, do to fix it?

Takeaway 13.3
How Does Reinforcement Influence Motivation to Work?

ANSWERS TO COME

- Operant conditioning influences behavior by controlling its consequences.
- Positive reinforcement connects desirable behavior with pleasant consequences.
- Punishment connects undesirable behavior with unpleasant consequences.

THE THEORIES DISCUSSED SO FAR FOCUS ON PEOPLE SATISFYING NEEDS, RESOLVING felt inequities, and/or pursuing positive expectancies and task goals. Instead of looking within the individual to explain motivation in these ways, reinforcement theory takes a different approach. It views human behavior as determined by its environmental consequences.

⫴ Operant conditioning influences behavior by controlling its consequences.

The premises of reinforcement theory rely on what E. L. Thorndike called the **law of effect:** People repeat behavior that results in a pleasant outcome and avoid behavior that results in an unpleasant outcome.[22] Psychologist B. F. Skinner used this notion to popularize the concept of **operant conditioning**. This is the process of influencing behavior by manipulating its consequences.[23] You may think of operant conditioning as learning by reinforcement, and Figure 13.5 shows how managers stimulate it through four reinforcement strategies.[24]

The **law of effect** states that behavior followed by pleasant consequences is likely to be repeated; behavior followed by unpleasant consequences is not.

Operant conditioning is the control of behavior by manipulating its consequences.

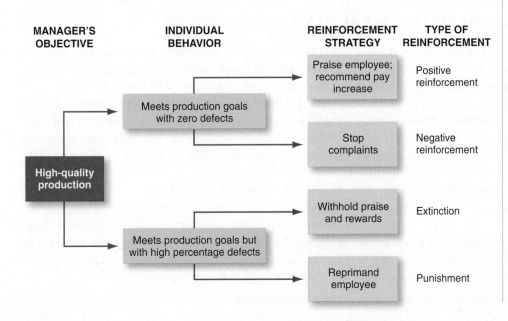

MANAGER'S OBJECTIVE	INDIVIDUAL BEHAVIOR	REINFORCEMENT STRATEGY	TYPE OF REINFORCEMENT
High-quality production	Meets production goals with zero defects	Praise employee; recommend pay increase	Positive reinforcement
		Stop complaints	Negative reinforcement
	Meets production goals but with high percentage defects	Withhold praise and rewards	Extinction
		Reprimand employee	Punishment

FIGURE 13.5
How Can Managers Use Reinforcement Strategies to Influence Work Behavior?
To strengthen quality work, a supervisor might use positive reinforcement by praising the individual or negative reinforcement by no longer complaining to him about poor-quality work. To discourage poor-quality work, a supervisor might use extinction (withholding things that are positively reinforcing, such as outcomes) or punishment (associating the poor-quality work with unpleasant results for the individual).

Positive reinforcement strengthens a behavior by making a desirable consequence contingent on its occurrence.

Negative reinforcement strengthens a behavior by making the avoidance of an undesirable consequence contingent on its occurrence.

Punishment discourages a behavior by making an unpleasant consequence contingent on its occurrence.

Extinction discourages a behavior by making the removal of a desirable consequence contingent on its occurrence.

Positive reinforcement strengthens or increases the frequency of desirable behavior by making a pleasant consequence contingent on its occurrence. *Example:* A manager nods to express approval to someone who makes a useful comment during a staff meeting. **Negative reinforcement** increases the frequency of or strengthens desirable behavior by making the avoidance of an unpleasant consequence contingent on its occurrence. *Example:* A manager who has nagged a worker every day about tardiness does not nag when the worker comes to work on time.

Punishment decreases the frequency of or eliminates an undesirable behavior by making an unpleasant consequence contingent on its occurrence. *Example:* A manager issues a written reprimand to an employee whose careless work creates quality problems. **Extinction** decreases the frequency of or eliminates an undesirable behavior by making the removal of a pleasant consequence contingent on its occurrence. *Example:* After observing that co-workers are providing social approval to a disruptive employee, a manager counsels co-workers to stop giving this approval.

If you look again at the case described in Figure 13.5, you'll see that the supervisor's goal is to improve work quality by an individual performer as part of a total quality management program. This goal can be reached if she can get the individual to show more positive quality behaviors and stop engaging in ones that harm or disregard quality goals. Notice that both the positive and negative reinforcement strategies are used to strengthen desirable behavior when it occurs. The punishment and extinction strategies are used to weaken or eliminate undesirable behaviors.

{ "CHARLIE REALLY WANTED TO TAKE CARE OF THE HOURLY FOLKS AND PEOPLE WHO PUT IN A LOT OF YEARS."

Role Models

■ CHARLIE BUTCHER SHARED HIS WEALTH WITH EMPLOYEES

At the age of 83, Charlie Butcher sold his family firm. It was a good deal for Charlie and family—$18 million! But there's more to this story than personal gain. Charlie shared the $18 million with the firm's employees!

He handed out checks the day after the sale, written to an average of $55,000 per person. President Paul P. McClaughlin said the employees "just filled up with tears. They would just throw their arms around Charlie and give him a hug." Butcher's administrative assistant, Lynne Ouellette, summed it up this way: "Charlie really wanted to take care of the hourly folks and people who put in a lot of years."

If you knew Charlie, they say, this wouldn't be a surprise. He always believed in people. This was just another chance to confirm the theory that he'd been practicing for years—treat talented people well and they'll create business success. "When people are happy in their jobs," said Charlie, "they are at least twice as productive."

And he meant it. Charlie once told an interviewer that it was the employees that made his business successful. In his words, "When the opportunity came to put my money where my mouth was, that's exactly what I did."

WHAT'S THE LESSON HERE?

Charlie's gone now, but his obituary called him a businessman "known for his generosity and passion for knowledge and justice." He was the model loyal employer. But you don't have to be the owner of a business to do good things for other people. Isn't that the goal for any manager?

⦀ Positive reinforcement connects desirable behavior with pleasant consequences.

Among the reinforcement strategies, positive reinforcement deserves special attention. It should be part of any manager's motivational strategy. In fact, it should be part of our personal life strategies as well—as parents working with children, for example. One of the ways to mobilize the power of positive reinforcement is through **shaping**. This is the creation of a new behavior by the positive reinforcement of successive approximations to it.

Sir Richard Branson, well-known founder of Virgin Group, is a believer in positive reinforcement. "For the people who work for you or with you, you must lavish praise on them at all times," he says. "If a flower is watered, it flourishes. If not, it shrivels up and dies."[25] David Novak, CEO of Yum! Brands, Inc., is another believer. He claims "you can never underestimate the power of telling someone he's doing a good job."[26]

Whether we are talking about verbal praise, a pay raise, or any other forms of positive reinforcement, two laws govern the process. The **law of contingent reinforcement** states: For a reward to have maximum reinforcing value, it must be delivered only if the desired behavior is exhibited. The **law of immediate reinforcement** states: The more immediate the delivery of a reward after the occurrence of a desirable behavior, the greater the reinforcing value of the reward. Table 13.1—*Guidelines for Positive Reinforcement and Punishment*—presents several useful guidelines for using these two laws.

> **Shaping** is positive reinforcement of successive approximations to the desired behavior.

> **Law of contingent reinforcement**—deliver the reward only when desired behavior occurs.

> **Law of immediate reinforcement**—deliver the reward as soon as possible after the desired behavior occurs.

Table 13.1 Guidelines for Positive Reinforcement and Punishment

Positive Reinforcement

- Clearly identify desired work behaviors.
- Maintain a diverse inventory of rewards.
- Inform everyone what must be done to get rewards.
- Recognize individual differences when allocating rewards.
- Follow the laws of immediate and contingent reinforcement.

Punishment

- Tell the person what is being done wrong.
- Tell the person what is being done right.
- Make sure the punishment matches the behavior.
- Administer the punishment in private.
- Follow the laws of immediate and contingent reinforcement.

⦀ Punishment connects undesirable behavior with unpleasant consequences.

As a reinforcement strategy, punishment tries to eliminate undesirable behavior by making an unpleasant consequence contingent with its occurrence. To punish an employee, for example, a manager may deny a valued reward—such as verbal praise or merit pay, or deliver an unpleasant outcome—such as a verbal reprimand or pay reduction.

Manager's Library

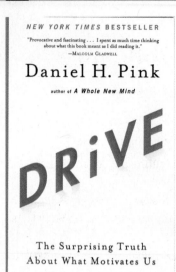

NEW YORK TIMES BESTSELLER

"Provocative and fascinating . . . I spent as much time thinking about what this book meant as I did reading it."
—MALCOLM GLADWELL

Daniel H. Pink

author of *A Whole New Mind*

DRiVE

The Surprising Truth
About What Motivates Us

■ *DRIVE* BY DANIEL H. PINK

WHAT DRIVES YOU?

Two human drives are well described in motivation theory. One is our self-guided biological drive for food, water, and sex—survival and procreation. The second is our drive to respond to rewards and punishment from external sources, or "extrinsic motivation." For example, you may get a job to buy groceries and provide for your family, work overtime if offered bonus pay, and avoid errors if threatened termination.

In the book *Drive* (2009, Riverhead Books), author Daniel Pink argues that more attention should be given to a third drive he calls "intrinsic motivation." It includes our desire to do activities because we enjoy and are gratified by them. They give us purpose and satisfy our need to do what we choose and value without others telling us. We do them not because we need to (buy groceries), or have to (avoid errors), but because we want to (enjoy work).

Pink uses the term "Motivation 3.0" to reflect this third drive and recommends that managers change reward systems in order to improve opportunities for intrinsic motivation. He points out that the economy has shifted from algorithmic work—routine, ruled-based work like product assembly, toward heuristic work—knowledge-driven, creative work that requires intuition and self-direction. Reward systems need to shift too. Extrinsic rewards like pay that drive algorithmic work might appeal to heuristic workers initially. But once a "baseline" level of security is achieved, motivation becomes more linked to things that excite and give them purpose.

Some companies tap intrinsic motivation by giving workers free time, perhaps 20% or so, to engage in projects they choose with colleagues. This allows them to engage in self-guided work while applying favorite skills in a meaningful setting. Many innovations have emerged from these approaches.

REFLECT AND REACT

Do you do most activities because you have to or because you want to? Make a list of activities within each category. What rewards or punishments from others drive you to do things that you have to? Why do you do the things you want to? How would you feel if you went two weeks doing only things that you had to? And, by the way, a lot of people are still doing routine algorithmic work in this economy. Can Pink's ideas with Motivation 3.0 also apply well with algorithmic workers?

Like positive reinforcement, punishment can be done poorly or it can be done well. All too often, it is done both too frequently and poorly. If you look again at Table 13.1, you'll find advice on how to best handle punishment when it is necessary.

Whether talking about using punishment or positive reinforcement, some people complain about the underlying reinforcement principles. They believe that any use of operant conditioning techniques ignores the individuality of people, restricts their freedom of choice, and fails to recognize they can be motivated by things other than extrinsic rewards. Critics view this as inappropriate manipulation and control of human behavior. Others agree that reinforcement involves the control of behavior but argue that control is part of every manager's job. The ethical issue, they say, isn't whether to use reinforcement principles, but whether or not we use them well—in the performance context of the organization and in everyday living.[27] How about you? Do you see reinforcement theory as full of useful insights, or as something to be feared?

STUDY GUIDE

Takeaway 13.3
How Does Reinforcement Influence Motivation to Work?

Terms to Define

Extinction

Law of contingent reinforcement

Law of effect

Law of immediate reinforcement

Negative reinforcement

Operant conditioning

Positive reinforcement

Punishment

Shaping

Rapid Review

- Reinforcement theory views human behavior as determined by its environmental consequences.
- The law of effect states that behavior followed by a pleasant consequence is likely to be repeated; behavior followed by an unpleasant consequence is unlikely to be repeated.
- Managers use strategies of positive reinforcement and negative reinforcement to strengthen desirable behaviors.
- Managers use strategies of punishment and extinction to weaken undesirable work behaviors.
- Positive reinforcement and punishment both work best when applied according to the laws of contingent and immediate reinforcement.

Questions for Discussion

1. Is operant conditioning a manipulative way to influence human behavior?
2. When is punishment justifiable as a reinforcement strategy?
3. Is it possible for a manager, or parent, to only use positive reinforcement?

Be Sure You Can

- explain the law of effect and operant conditioning
- illustrate how positive reinforcement, negative reinforcement, punishment, and extinction can influence work behavior
- explain the reinforcement technique of shaping
- describe how managers can use the laws of immediate and contingent reinforcement when allocating rewards
- list ways to make punishment effective

What Would You Do?

You can predict with great confidence that when Jason comes to a meeting of your student team, he will spend most of his time cracking jokes, telling stories, and otherwise entertaining other team members. He doesn't do any real work. In fact, his behavior makes it hard for the team to accomplish much in its meetings. But Jason's also a talented guy. How can you put reinforcement theory to work here and turn Jason into a solid team contributor?

TestPrep 13

Multiple-Choice Questions

1. Maslow's progression principle stops working at the level of _____ needs.

(a) growth

(b) self-actualization

(c) achievement

(d) self-esteem

2. Lower-order needs in Maslow's hierarchy correspond to _____ needs in ERG theory.

(a) growth

(b) affiliation

(c) existence

(d) achievement

3. A worker high in need for _____ power in McClelland's theory tries to use power for the good of the organization.

(a) position

(b) expert

(c) personal

(d) social

4. In the _____ theory of motivation, an individual who feels underrewarded relative to a co-worker might be expected to reduce his or her work efforts in the future.

(a) ERG

(b) acquired needs

(c) two-factor

(d) equity

5. Which of the following is a correct match?

(a) McClelland–ERG theory

(b) Skinner–reinforcement theory

(c) Vroom–equity theory

(d) Locke–expectancy theory

6. In Herzberg's two-factor theory, base pay is considered a/an _____ factor.

(a) hygiene

(b) satisfier

(c) equity

(d) higher-order

7. The expectancy theory of motivation says that Motivation = Expectancy × Instrumentality × _____.

(a) Rewards

(b) Valence

(c) Equity

(d) Growth

8. When a team member shows strong ego needs in Maslow's hierarchy, the team leader should find ways to link this person's work with _____.

(a) compensation tied to team performance

(b) individual praise and recognition

(c) social interaction with other team members

(d) challenging individual performance goals

9. When someone has a high and positive "expectancy" in expectancy theory of motivation, this means that the person _____.

(a) believes he can achieve performance expectations

(b) highly values the rewards being offered

(c) sees a performance–reward link

(d) believes rewards are equitable

10. The law of _____ states that behavior followed by a positive consequence is likely to be repeated, whereas behavior followed by an undesirable consequence is not likely to be repeated.

(a) reinforcement

(b) contingency

(c) goal setting

(d) effect

11. When a job allows a person to do a complete unit of work, it is high on which core characteristic?

(a) task identity

(b) task significance

(c) task autonomy

(d) feedback

12. _____ is a positive reinforcement strategy that rewards successive approximations to a desirable behavior.

(a) Extinction

(b) Negative reinforcement

(c) Shaping

(d) Merit pay

13. The purpose of negative reinforcement as an operant conditioning technique is to _____.

(a) punish bad behavior

(b) discourage bad behavior

(c) encourage desirable behavior

(d) cancel the effects of shaping

14. The premise of reinforcement theory is:

    (a) behavior is a function of environment

    (b) motivation comes from positive expectancy

    (c) higher-order needs stimulate hard work

    (d) rewards considered unfair are de-motivators

15. Both Barry and Marissa are highly motivated students. Knowing this, I can expect them to be _____.

    (a) hard working   (b) high performing

    (c) highly satisfied   (d) highly dissatisfied

Short-Response Questions

16. What preferences does a person high in the need for achievement bring to the workplace?

17. How can a team leader use goal-setting theory in working with individual team members?

18. What are three ways a worker might react to perceived negative inequity over a pay raise?

19. How can shaping be used to encourage desirable work behaviors?

Integration and Application Question

20. I overheard a conversation between two Executive MBA students. One was telling the other: "My firm just contracted with Musak to have mood music piped into the offices at various times of the workday." The other replied: "That's a waste of money; there should be better things to do if the firm is really interested in increasing motivation and performance." **Question:** Is the second student right or wrong, and why?

StepsforFurtherLearning

Many learning resources are found at the end of the book and online within WileyPLUS.

Don't Miss These Selections from the **Skill-Building Portfolio**

■ **SELF-ASSESSMENT 13:** *Two-Factor Profile*

■ **TEAM PROJECT 13:** *CEO Pay*

■ **CLASS EXERCISE 13:** *Why We Work*

Don't Miss This Selection from **Cases for Critical Thinking**

■ **CHAPTER 13 CASE**

Panera Bread: Staying Ahead of Long-Term Trends

Snapshot Panera's success has come partly from its ability to predict long-term trends and orient the company toward innovation to fulfill consumers' desires. Its self-perception as a purveyor of artisan bread well predated the current national trend for fresh bread and the explosion of artisan bakeries throughout metropolitan America. For Panera Bread, a company able to successfully spot long-term trends in the food industry, artisan-style bread served with deli sandwiches and soups is a combination proven to please the hungry masses.

Panera has demonstrated that sticking to company ideals while successfully forecasting and then leading the response to long-term industry trends will please customers time and time again. The low-carb craze didn't faze Panera, but can this company continue to navigate the changing dietary trends in today's unstable market?

"The way a team plays as a whole determines its success. You may have the greatest bunch of individual stars in the world, but if they don't play together, the club won't be worth a dime."
Former UCLA coach John Wooden

Teams and Teamwork

Two Heads Really Can Be Better Than One

Management Live

Team Contributions and *Lost*

Picture a mysterious island and a group of random strangers brought together by a plane crash. There is little hope of rescue. You've probably been there before, at least vicariously. It's the setting for the hit television series *Lost*.

In episode 5 of season 1 a doctor, Jack Shephard (Matthew Fox), strikes off on his own to deal with personal demons. He ends up discovering a source of clean water and realizes it is the key to keeping everyone alive.

Upon returning to the crash site, Jack finds several of the survivors fighting for control of the remaining bottled water. He interrupts the fight and delivers what becomes the guiding mantra of the series—"live together, die alone." Jack implores each person to figure out what they can contribute to the good of all, and then make the commitment to everyone else that they'll really do it.

If you watch *Lost* episodes, you'll find quite a bit going on about the lessons of teamwork and **team contributions**. Team success always depends on members contributing in a wide variety of ways to help the team reach its goals. Most teams underperform not because they lack talent and energy. They do poorly because members can't overcome the difficulties of working together.

Pick a recent team experience of yours. Make a good realistic assessment of the teamwork that took place—the good parts and the rough spots. What could you have contributed that would have helped the team? This chapter has lots of ideas on teamwork and team success. As you read on, make becoming a strong team contributor a personal development goal.

YOUR CHAPTER 14 TAKEAWAYS

1. Understand the importance of teams and teamwork.

2. Identify the building blocks of successful teamwork.

3. Understand how managers create and lead high-performance teams.

WHAT'S INSIDE

Explore Yourself
More on team contributions

Role Models
Amazon's Jeff Bezos bets big on teams

Ethics Check
Social loafing is closer than you think

Facts to Consider
Unproductive meetings are major time wasters

Manager's Library
Crowdsourcing by Jeff Howe

Takeaway 14.1
Why Is It Important to Understand Teams and Teamwork?

ANSWERS TO COME

- Teams offer synergy and other benefits to organizations and their members.
- Teams often suffer from common performance problems.
- Organizations are networks of formal teams and informal groups.
- Organizations use committees, task forces, and cross-functional teams.
- Virtual teams are increasingly common in organizations.
- Self-managing teams are a form of job enrichment for groups.

WE ARE ALL PART OF TEAMS EVERY DAY, AND IT'S TIME TO RECOGNIZE A BASIC FACT: Teams are hard work, but they are worth it. The beauty of teams is accomplishing something far greater than what's possible for an individual alone. Indeed, two heads can be better than one. But the key word is "can." While we all know that teams can be great, they're often not. Have you ever heard someone say "Too many cooks spoil the broth" or "A camel is an elephant put together by a committee"?

So let's start this discussion realistically. On one level there seems little to debate. Groups and teams have a lot to offer organizations. But at another level you have to sometimes wonder if the extra effort is really worth it. There are times when teams can be more pain than gain. There's a lot to learn about them, their roles in organizations, and how we participate in and help lead them for real performance gains.[1]

Teams offer synergy and other benefits to organizations and their members.

A **team** is a small group of people with complementary skills who work together to accomplish shared goals while holding each other mutually accountable for performance results.[2] Teams are essential to organizations of all types and sizes. Many tasks are well beyond the capabilities of individuals alone.[3] And in this sense, **teamwork**, people actually working together to accomplish a shared goal, is a major performance asset.[4]

The term **synergy** means the creation of a whole that exceeds the sum of its parts. When teams perform well, it's because of synergy that pools many diverse talents and efforts to create extraordinary results.

Check research on success in the NBA. Scholars find that both good and bad basketball teams win more the longer the players have been together. Why? A "teamwork effect" creates wins because players know one another's moves and playing tendencies. Shift to the hospital operating room. Scholars notice the same heart surgeons have lower death rates for similar procedures performed in hospitals where the surgeons did more operations. Why? A teamwork effect—the doctors had more time working together with the surgery teams—

A **team** is a collection of people who regularly interact to pursue common goals.

Teamwork is the process of people actively working together to accomplish common goals.

Synergy is the creation of a whole greater than the sum of its individual parts.

anesthesiologists, nurses, and other surgical technicians. They say it's not only the surgeon's skills that count; the skills of the team and the time spent working together count too.[5]

Don't forget—teams are not only good for performance, they're also good for their members.[6] Just as in life overall, being part of a work team or informal group can strongly influence our attitudes and behaviors. The personal relationships can help with job performance—making contacts, sharing ideas, responding to favors, and bypassing roadblocks. And being part of a team often helps satisfy important needs that are unfulfilled in the regular work setting or life overall. Teams provide members with social relationships, security, a sense of belonging, and emotional support.

> ## Why Teams Are Good for Organizations
>
> - More resources for problem solving
> - Improved creativity and innovation
> - Improved quality of decision making
> - Greater commitment to tasks
> - Increased motivation of members
> - Better control and work discipline
> - More individual need satisfaction

Teams often suffer from common performance problems.

Notwithstanding all the positive talk, we all know that working in teams isn't always easy or productive. Problems not only happen; they are common.[7] One of the most troublesome is **social loafing**—the presence of one or more "free-riders" who slack off and allow other team members to do most of the work.[8] For whatever reason, perhaps the absence of spotlight on personal performance, individuals sometimes work less hard, not harder, when they are part of a group.

What can a team leader do when someone is free-riding? The possibilities include a variety of actions to make individual contributions more visible—rewarding individuals for their contributions, making task assignments more interesting, and keeping group size small so that free-riders are more noticeable. This makes the loafers more susceptible to pressures from peers and to critical leader evaluations. And if you've ever considered free-riding as a team member, think again. You may get away with it in the short term, but your reputation will suffer and sooner or later it will be "pay back" time.

Other common problems of teams include personality conflicts and work style differences that disrupt relationships and accomplishments. Sometimes group members battle over goals or competing visions. Sometimes they withdraw from active participation due to uncertainty over tasks and relationships. Ambiguous agendas or ill-defined problems can cause teamwork fatigue. And, motivation often falls when teams work too long on the wrong things, and end up having little to show for it.

Finally, not everyone is always ready to jump in and do a great job on a team. This might be due to personality or high need for individual achievement. It may also stem from conflicts with other work deadlines and personal priorities. Low enthusiasm for group work may also result from bad past experiences on poorly organized and run teams, as well as from meetings that seem to lack purpose. These and other difficulties can easily turn the great potential of teams into frustration and failure.

Social loafing is the tendency of some people to avoid responsibility by free-riding in groups.

Ethics Check

■ SOCIAL LOAFING IS CLOSER THAN YOU THINK

Psychology study: A German researcher asks people to pull on a rope as hard as they can. First, individuals pull alone. Second, they pull as part of a group. Results show people pull harder when working alone than when working as part of a team. Such social loafing is the tendency to reduce effort when working in groups.

Faculty office: A student wants to speak with the instructor about his team's performance on the last group project. There were four members, but two did almost all of the work. The two loafers largely disappeared, showing up only at the last minute to be part of the formal presentation. His point is that the team was disadvantaged because the two free-riders caused a loss of performance capacity.

Telephone call from the boss: "John, I really need you to serve on this committee. Will you do it? Let me know tomorrow." In thinking about this, I ponder: I'm overloaded, but I don't want to turn down the boss. I'll accept but let the committee members know about my situation. I'll be active in discussions and try to offer viewpoints and perspectives that are helpful. However, I'll let them know up front that I can't be a leader or volunteer for any extra work.

YOU DECIDE

Whether you call it social loafing, free-riding, or just plain old slacking off, the issue is the same. What right do some people have to sit back in team situations and let other people do all or most of the work? Is this ethical? Does everyone in a group have an ethical obligation to do his or her fair share of the work? And when it comes to John, does the fact that he is going to be honest with the other committee members make any difference? Isn't he still going to be a loafer that gets credit with the boss for serving on the committee? Would it be more ethical for him to decline becoming a part of this committee?

⫴ Organizations are networks of formal teams and informal groups.

A **formal team** is officially recognized and supported by the organization.

A **formal team** is officially designated for a specific organizational purpose. You'll find such teams described by different labels on organization charts—examples are *departments* (e.g., market research department), *work units* (e.g., audit unit), *teams* (e.g., customer service team), or *divisions* (e.g., office products division).

Formal teams are headed by supervisors, managers, department heads, team leaders, and the like. It is common, in fact, to describe organizations as interlocking networks of teams in which managers and leaders play "linking pin" roles.[9] This means that they serve both as head of one work team and as a regular member in the next-higher-level one. It's important to recognize, as shown here, that

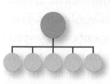 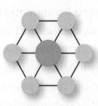  

Supervisor   Network facilitator   Helpful participant   External coach

{ WORKERS AROUND THE WORLD SAY MOST MEETINGS ARE "INEFFECTIVE."

Facts to Consider

■ UNPRODUCTIVE MEETINGS ARE MAJOR TIME WASTERS

A survey of some 38,000 workers around the world links low productivity with bad meetings, poor communication, and unclear goals.

- 69% of meetings attended are considered ineffective.
- 32% of workers complain about team communication.
- 31% complain about unclear objectives and priorities.

YOUR THOUGHTS?

Do these data match your experiences with team meetings? Given the common complaints about meetings, what can a team leader do to improve them? Think about the recent meetings you have attended. In what ways were the best meetings different from the worst ones? Did your behavior play a significant role in both these cases?

---

managers play more than one role in groups and teams. Although often serving as the supervisor or team leader, they also act as network facilitators, helpful participants, and external coaches.

The informal structure of an organization also consists of **informal groups**. They emerge from natural or spontaneous relationships, not required ones. Some are *interest groups* whose members pursue a common cause, such as a women's career network. Some are *friendship groups* that develop for a wide variety of personal reasons, including shared hobbies and other nonwork interests. Others are *support groups* in which members basically help one another out in work and personal affairs.

> An **informal group** is unofficial and emerges from relationships and shared interests among members.

‖ Organizations use committees, task forces, and cross-functional teams.

You will find many types of formal teams and groups in organizations.[10] A **committee** brings together people outside of their daily job assignments to work in a small team for a specific purpose. The task agenda is focused and ongoing. For example, an organization may have standing committees for diversity and compensation.[11] A designated head or chairperson typically leads the committee and is held accountable for its performance.

> A **committee** is designated to work on a special task on a continuing basis.

Project teams or **task forces** put people together to work on common problems, but on a temporary rather than continuing basis. Project teams, for example, might be formed to develop a new product or service, redesign workflows, or provide specialized consulting for a client.[12] A task force might be formed to address employee retention problems or come up with ideas for improving work schedules.[13]

> A **project team** or **task force** is convened for a specific purpose and disbands after completing its task.

The **cross-functional team** brings together members from different functional units.[14] They are supposed to work together on specific problems or tasks,

> A **cross-functional team** operates with members who come from different functional units of an organization.

An **employee involvement team** meets on a regular basis to help achieve continuous improvement.

A **quality circle** is a team of employees who meet periodically to discuss ways of improving work quality.

Members of a **virtual team** work together and solve problems through computer-based interactions.

sharing information and exploring new ideas. They are expected to help knock down the "walls" that otherwise separate departments and people in the organization. Tom's of Maine, for example, uses "Acorn Groups"—symbolizing the fruits of the stately oak tree—to help launch new products. Members work on new ideas from concept to finished product. The goal is to minimize problems and maximize efficiency through cross-departmental cooperation.[15]

Some organizations also use **employee involvement teams**. These groups of workers meet on a regular basis with the goal of using their expertise and experience for continuous improvement. The **quality circle**, for example, is a team that meets regularly to discuss and plan specific ways to improve work quality.[16]

‖ Virtual teams are increasingly common in organizations.

A vice president for human resources at Marriott once called electronic meetings "the quietest, least stressful, most productive meetings you've ever had."[17] She was talking about a type of group that is increasingly common in today's organizations—the **virtual team**.[18] Its members work together and solve problems through computer-mediated rather than face-to-face interactions. The constant emergence of new technologies is making virtual collaboration both easier and more common. At home it may be Skype or Facebook; at the office it's likely to be any number of in-house or other web-based meeting resources.[19]

As you probably realize already from working in college study teams, virtual teamwork has many advantages. The virtual environment allows teamwork by people who may be located at great distances from one another. This offers cost and time efficiencies. It makes it easy to widely share lots of information, keep records of team activities, and maintain databases. And, it can help reduce interpersonal problems that might otherwise occur when team members are dealing face-to-face with controversial issues.[20]

{ VIRTUAL TEAMS NEED THE RIGHT MEMBERS, GOALS, FEEDBACK, AND TECHNOLOGY.

Tips to Remember

■ STEPS TO SUCCESSFUL VIRTUAL TEAMS

- Select team members high in initiative and capable of self-starting.
- Select members who will join and engage the team with positive attitudes.
- Select members known for working hard to meet team goals.
- Begin with social messaging that allows members to exchange information about one another to personalize the process.

- Assign clear goals and roles so that members can focus while working alone and also know what others are doing.
- Gather regular feedback from members about how they think the team is doing and how it might do better.
- Provide regular feedback to team members about team accomplishments.
- Make sure the team has the best technology.

Are there any downsides to virtual teams? Yes, for sure. They often occur for the same reasons as in other groups.[21] Social loafing can still occur, goals may be unclear, meeting requests may be too frequent. Members of virtual teams can also have difficulties establishing good working relationships. The lack of face-to-face interaction limits the role of emotions and nonverbal cues in the communication, and may depersonalize member relations.[22] Yet as more people gain experience, teams working in virtual space rather than face-to-face are proving their performance potential.[23] In fact, they're becoming a way of organizational life.

Self-managing teams are a form of job enrichment for groups.

In a growing number of organizations, traditional work units of supervisors and subordinates are being replaced with **self-managing teams**. Sometimes called *autonomous work groups*, these are teams whose members have been given collective authority to make many decisions about how they work, ones previously made by higher-level managers.[24] The expected advantages include better performance, decreased costs, and higher morale.

As shown in **Figure 14.1**, the "self-management" responsibilities of self-managing teams include planning and scheduling work, training members in various tasks, distributing tasks, meeting performance goals, ensuring high quality, and solving day-to-day operating problems. In some settings the team's authority may even extend to "hiring" and "firing" its members when necessary. A key feature is multitasking, in which team members each have the skills to perform several different jobs.

Members of a **self-managing team** have the authority to make decisions about how they share and complete their work.

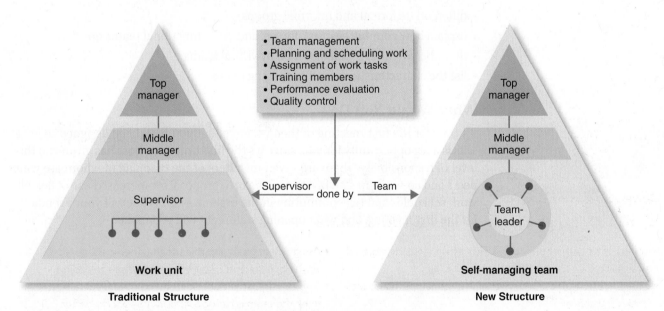

FIGURE 14.1 What Are the Management Implications of Self-Managing Teams?
Members of self-managing teams make decisions together on team membership, task plans and job assignments, training and performance evaluations, and quality control. Because they essentially manage themselves in these ways, they no longer need a traditional supervisor or department head. Instead, the team leader performs this role with the support of team members. The team leader and team as a whole report to the next higher level of management and are held accountable for performance results.

Takeaway 14.1
Why Is It Important to Understand Teams and Teamwork?

Terms to Define

Committee

Cross-functional team

Employee involvement team

Formal team

Informal group

Project team

Quality circle

Self-managing team

Social loafing

Synergy

Task force

Team

Teamwork

Virtual team

Rapid Review

- A team consists of people with complementary skills working together for shared goals and holding one another accountable for performance.
- Teams benefit organizations by providing for synergy that allows the accomplishment of tasks that are beyond individual capabilities alone.
- Social loafing and other problems can limit the performance of teams.
- Organizations use a variety of formal teams in the form of committees, task forces, project teams, cross-functional teams, and virtual teams.
- Self-managing teams allow team members to perform many tasks previously done by supervisors.

Questions for Discussion

1. Do committees and task forces work better when they are given short deadlines?
2. Are there some things that should be done only by face-to-face teams, not virtual ones?
3. Why do people in teams often tolerate social loafers?

Be Sure You Can

- define "team" and "teamwork"
- describe the roles managers play in teams
- explain synergy and the benefits of teams
- discuss social loafing and other potential problems of teams
- differentiate formal and informal groups
- explain how committees, task forces, and cross-functional teams operate
- describe potential problems faced by virtual teams
- list the characteristics of self-managing teams

What Would You Do?

It's time for the first meeting of the task force that you have been assigned to lead. This is a big opportunity for you, since it's the first time your boss has given you this level of responsibility. There are seven members of the team, all of whom are your peers and co-workers. The task is to develop a proposal for increased use of flexible work schedules and telecommuting in the organization. What will your agenda be for the first meeting, and what opening statement will you make?

Takeaway 14.2
What Are the Building Blocks of Successful Teamwork?

ANSWERS TO COME

- Teams need the right members and other inputs to be effective.
- Teams need the right processes to be effective.
- Teams move through different stages of development.
- Team performance is affected by norms and cohesiveness.
- Team performance is affected by task and maintenance roles.
- Team performance is affected by communication networks.

AFTER TALKING ABOUT THE TYPES OF TEAMS IN ORGANIZATIONS, IT'S TIME TO talk about the teamwork that can make them successful.[25] Look at Figure 14.2. It diagrams a team as an open system that, like the organization itself, transforms a variety of inputs into outputs.[26] It also shows that an **effective team** should be accomplishing three output goals—task performance, member satisfaction, and team viability.[27]

The first outcome of an effective team is high *task performance*. When you are on a team, ask: Did we accomplish our tasks and meet expectations? The second

An **effective team** achieves high levels of task performance, membership satisfaction, and future viability.

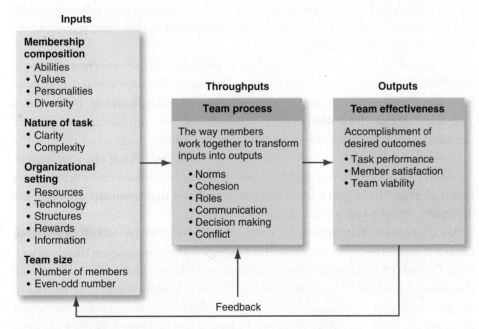

FIGURE 14.2 What Are the Foundations of Team Effectiveness?
An effective team achieves high levels of task performance and member satisfaction, and remains viable for the future. The foundations of effectiveness begin with inputs—things such as membership composition, nature of the task, resources and support in the organizational setting, and team size. The foundations of effectiveness further rest with team process—how well the members utilize their talents and other inputs to create the desired outputs. Key process factors on any team include the stages of development, norms and cohesion, task and maintenance activities, communication, and decision making.

outcome of an effective team is *member satisfaction*. Ask: Are we individually and collectively pleased with our participation in the process? The third outcome of an effective team is *viability for future action*. Ask: Can this team be successful again in the future?[28]

You might hear an effective team described as one that has "the right players in the right seats on the same bus, headed in the same direction."[29] The open-systems model in Figure 14.2 shows this thinking. A team's effectiveness is influenced by inputs—getting the right players and putting them in the right seats, and by process—making sure everyone knows they're on the same bus and headed in the same direction. You can remember the implications with this **team effectiveness equation**.

Team Effectiveness = Quality of Inputs + (Process Gains − Process Losses)

⫿ Teams need the right members and other inputs to be effective.

The foundations for team effectiveness are set when a team is formed. The better the inputs, you might say, the more likely that the team will achieve success. One of the most important inputs of any group is the nature of the membership. You can think of a team's **membership composition** as human capital available in its mix of abilities, skills, backgrounds, and experiences. For anyone creating a team, this raises one of the most important decisions to be made: Just who should be selected to be on the team?

In an ideal world, managers carefully form teams by choosing team members whose talents and interests fit well with the job to be done. If you were in charge of a new team, wouldn't you want to start this way? It makes good sense, but research raises some interesting issues.

It turns out that the most creative teams include a mix of experienced people and those who haven't worked together before.[30] The experienced members have the connections while the newcomers add fresh thinking. Researchers also warn about risks when team members are too similar in background, training, and experience. Such teams tend to underperform even though the members may feel very comfortable with one another.[31] What are your experiences on this issue? Do you get along better in teams whose members are pretty much all alike? Have you encountered problems on teams whose members are diverse?

Another input that influences team effectiveness is the *nature of the task*. Clearly defined tasks make it easier for team members to combine their work efforts. Complex tasks require more information exchange and intense interaction than do simpler tasks. Think task complexity the next time you fly. And check out the ground crews. You should notice some similarities between them and teams handling pit stops for NASCAR racers. In fact, if you fly United Airlines, there's a good chance the members of the ramp crews have been through "Pit Crew U." United is among many organizations sending employees to Pit Instruction & Training in Mooresville, North Carolina. Real racing crews at this facility have trained United's ramp workers to work under pressure while meeting the goals of teamwork, safety, and job preparedness. The goal is better teamwork to reduce aircraft delays and service inadequacies.[32]

Membership composition is the mix of abilities, skills, backgrounds, and experiences among team members.

Predictably, the *organizational setting* influences team outputs. A key issue here is support—how well the organization supports the team in terms of information, material resources, technology, organization structures, available rewards, and even physical space. Having support, as we have all probably experienced, can make a big difference in how well we perform in groups and individually.

Team size also makes a difference. The number of potential interactions increases geometrically as teams increase in size. This affects how members communicate, work together, handle disagreements, and reach agreements. So how big should a team be? In general, teams larger than six or seven members can be difficult to manage for the purpose of creative problem solving. Amazon.com's founder and CEO Jeff Bezos is a great fan of teams. But he has a simple rule when it comes to team size: If creativity is a goal, no team should be larger than two pizzas can feed.[33] Also, when voting is required, teams with odd numbers of members help to prevent ties.

{ AMAZON'S CEO SAYS "IF TWO PIZZAS AREN'T ENOUGH TO FEED A TEAM, IT'S TOO BIG."

Role Models

■ AMAZON'S JEFF BEZOS BETS BIG ON TEAMS

Amazon.com's founder and CEO Jeff Bezos is one of America's top businesspersons and a technology visionary. He's also a great fan of teams. Bezos coined a simple rule when it comes to sizing the firm's product development teams: If two pizzas aren't enough to feed a team, it's too big.

The business plan for Amazon originated while Bezos was driving cross-country. He started the firm in his garage, and even when the worth of his Amazon stock grew to $500 million, he was still driving a Honda and living in a small apartment in downtown Seattle.

Bezos is clearly a unique personality and also one with a great business mind. His goal with Amazon was to "create the world's most customer-centric company, the place where you can find and buy anything you want online." Many would say he has already succeeded.

If you go to Amazon.com and click on the "Gold Box" at the top, you'll be tuning in to his vision. It's a place for special deals, lasting only an hour and offering everything from a power tool to a new pair of shoes. If you join Amazon Prime and "One-Click" your way to free shipping and a hassle-free checkout, you're benefiting from his vision as well. And, of course, there's the Kindle e-reader. Not only did it become Amazon's best selling product ever, it made electronic books an everyday reality—one that competitors have been racing to

also take advantage of. Such innovations don't just come out of the blue. They're part and parcel of the management philosophy Bezos has instilled at the firm.

The Gold Box, One-Click, Kindle, and other Amazon successful innovations are products of many teams that are "small" and "fast-moving" "innovation engines." These teams typically have five to eight members and thrive on turning new ideas into business potential.

Bezos views Amazon's two-pizza teams as a way of fighting bureaucracy and decentralizing, even as the company grows large and very complex. He is also a fan of what he calls fact-based decisions. He says they help to "overrule the hierarchy. The most junior person in the company can win an argument with the most senior person with fact-based decisions."

WHAT'S THE LESSON HERE?

Don't expect to spot a stereotyped corporate CEO in Jeff Bezos. His standard office attire is still blue jeans and a blue-collared shirt. A family friend describes him and his wife as "very playful people." Perhaps "playful" is another word for the two-pizza team, as long as its members also keep their eyes on keeping the business successful. What do you think?

Team process is the way team members work together to accomplish tasks.

||| Teams need the right processes to be effective.

Although having the right inputs available to a team is important, it's not a guarantee of success. Team process counts, too. This is the heart of teamwork—the way the members of any team actually work together as they transform inputs into outputs. Also called *group dynamics*, the process aspects of any group or team include how members get to know one another, develop expectations and loyalty, communicate, handle conflicts, and make decisions.

Again, don't forget the equation: Team Effectiveness = Quality of Inputs × (Process Gains − Process Losses). A positive process takes full advantage of group inputs and creates gains that raise team effectiveness. But any problems with group process can quickly drain energies and create losses that reduce effectiveness. When the internal dynamics fail in any way, team effectiveness quickly suffers. Haven't you been on teams where people seemed to spend more time dealing with personality conflicts than with the task?

||| Teams move through different stages of development.

A synthesis of research suggests that five distinct phases occur in the life cycles of teams.[34] Known as the stages of team development, they are:

1. *Forming*—a stage of initial orientation and interpersonal testing
2. *Storming*—a stage of conflict over tasks and working as a team
3. *Norming*—a stage of consolidation around task and operating agendas
4. *Performing*—a stage of teamwork and focused task performance
5. *Adjourning*—a stage of task completion and disengagement

An effective team meets and masters key process challenges as it moves through each of these stages. One of the challenges is membership diversity. As shown in the nearby figure, diverse teams often experience process complications that can hurt effectiveness. But if they are well handled, real benefits are possible. Diverse teams expand the variety of talents, ideas, perspectives, and experiences available for problem solving.[35] This can help improve long-term performance.

The *forming stage of team development* is one of initial task orientation and interpersonal testing. New members are likely to ask: What can or does the team offer me? What will they ask me to contribute? Can my efforts serve team needs while also meeting my needs? In this stage, people begin to identify with other members and with the team itself. They focus on getting acquainted, establishing interpersonal relationships, discovering what is considered acceptable behavior, and learning how others perceive the team's task. Difficulties in the forming stage tend to be greater in more culturally and demographically diverse teams.

The *storming stage of team development* is a period of high emotionality. Tension often emerges between members over tasks and interpersonal concerns. There may be periods of conflict, outright hostility, and even infighting as some individuals try to impose their preferences on others. But this is also the stage where members start to clarify task agendas and understand one another. Attention begins to shift toward mastering obstacles, and team members start looking for ways to meet team goals while also satisfying individual needs. As the prior figure shows, the storming stage is part of a "critical zone" in team development where process failures cause lasting problems but process successes set the foundations for future effectiveness.

Cooperation is an important issue for teams in the *norming stage of team development*. At this point, members of the team begin to better coordinate their efforts as a working unit and operate with shared rules of conduct. The team feels a sense of leadership, with each member starting to play a useful role. Most interpersonal hostilities give way to a precarious balancing of forces as norming builds initial integration. Norming is also part of the critical zone of team development. When it is well managed, team members are likely to develop initial feelings of closeness and a sense of shared expectations. This helps protect the team from disintegration while members continue their efforts to work well together.

Teams in the *performing stage of team development* are mature, organized, and well functioning. This is a stage of total integration in which team members are able to creatively deal with complex tasks and interpersonal conflicts. The team has a clear and stable structure, members are motivated by team goals, and the process scores high on the criteria of team maturity shown in Figure 14.3.[36]

The *adjourning stage of team development* is the final stage for temporary committees, task forces, and project teams. Here, team members prepare to achieve closure and disband, ideally with a sense that they have accomplished important goals.

		Very poor			Very good	
1.	Trust among members	1	2	3	4	5
2.	Feedback mechanisms	1	2	3	4	5
3.	Open communications	1	2	3	4	5
4.	Approach to decisions	1	2	3	4	5
5.	Leadership sharing	1	2	3	4	5
6.	Acceptance of goals	1	2	3	4	5
7.	Valuing diversity	1	2	3	4	5
8.	Member cohesiveness	1	2	3	4	5
9.	Support for each other	1	2	3	4	5
10.	Performance norms	1	2	3	4	5

FIGURE 14.3 What Are the Criteria for Assessing the Process Maturity of a Team?
Teams vary greatly in the degree of maturity they achieve and demonstrate in day-to-day behavior. These criteria are helpful for assessing the development and maturity of a team as it moves through various phases—from forming to storming to norming to performing. We would expect that teams would start to show strong positives on these criteria as members gain experience with one another in the norming stage of team development. We would expect teams to have consistently strong positive scores in the performing stage.

{ TEAMS OFTEN UNDERPERFORM BECAUSE MEMBERS ARE STRUGGLING WITH PROCESS DIFFICULTIES.

Explore Yourself

■ TEAM CONTRIBUTIONS

If teams and teamwork are a major part of how organizations operate today, **team contributions** have to be considered one of the most essential career skills.

We need to be able to contribute as team members in many different ways so that our teams can reach their performance potential. But experience proves time and time again that teams often underperform or, at least, lose time and effectiveness as members struggle with a variety of process difficulties.

Take a good, hard look at the teams that you participate in. While so doing, make a realistic self-assessment of your team contributions as well as those of other members. Ask: How can the insights of this chapter help me build team skills so that I can help turn teamwork potential into real team achievements?

Get to know yourself better by taking the self-assessment on **Team Leader Skills** and completing the other activities in the *Exploring Management* **Skill-Building Portfolio**.

‖ Team performance is affected by norms and cohesiveness.

A **norm** is a behavior, rule, or standard expected to be followed by team members.

Have you ever felt pressure from other group members when you do something wrong—come late to a meeting, fail to complete an assigned task, or act out of character? What you are experiencing is related to group **norms, or behaviors expected of team members.**[37] A norm is a rule or standard that guides behavior. And when a norm is violated, team members are usually pressured to conform. In the extreme, violating a norm can result in expulsion from the group or social ostracism.

Any number of norms can be operating in a group at any given time. During the forming and storming stages of development, norms often focus on expected attendance and levels of commitment. By the time the team reaches the performing stage, norms have formed around adaptability, change, and desired levels of achievement. And without a doubt, one of the most important norms for any team is the **performance norm**. It defines the level of work effort and performance that team members are expected to contribute.

The **performance norm** defines the effort and performance contributions expected of team members.

It shouldn't surprise you that teams with positive performance norms are more successful than those with negative performance norms. But how do you build teams with the right norms? Actually, there are a number of things leaders can and should do.[38]

- Act as a positive role model.
- Reinforce the desired behaviors with rewards.
- Control results by performance reviews and regular feedback.
- Train and orient new members to adopt desired behaviors.
- Recruit and select new members who exhibit the desired behaviors.
- Hold regular meetings to discuss progress and ways of improving.
- Use team decision-making methods to reach agreement.

Cohesiveness is the degree to which members are attracted to and motivated to remain part of a team.

Whether the team members will accept and conform to norms is largely determined by **cohesiveness, the degree to which members are attracted to and motivated to remain part of a team.**[39] Members of a highly cohesive team value their membership. They try to conform to norms and behave in ways that meet the expectations of other members, and they get satisfaction from doing so. In this way, at least, a highly cohesive team is good for its members. But does the same hold true for team performance?

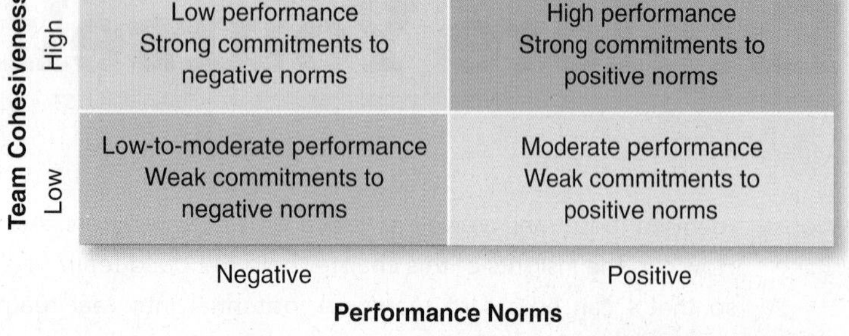

Figure 14.4 shows that teams perform best when the performance norm is positive and cohesiveness is high. In this best-case scenario, cohesion results in conformity to the positive norm, which ultimately benefits team performance. When the performance norm is negative in a cohesive team, however, high conformity to the norm creates a worst-case scenario. In this situation, members join together in restricting their efforts and performance contributions.

	Negative	Positive
High	Low performance Strong commitments to negative norms	High performance Strong commitments to positive norms
Low	Low-to-moderate performance Weak commitments to negative norms	Moderate performance Weak commitments to positive norms

Team Cohesiveness (vertical axis) / Performance Norms (horizontal axis)

FIGURE 14.4 How Do Norms and Cohesiveness Influence Team Performance?
Group norms are expected behaviors for team members; cohesiveness is the strength of attraction members feel toward the team. When cohesiveness is high, conformity to norms is high. Positive performance norms in a highly cohesive group create a desirable situation, with high-performance outcomes likely. However, negative performance norms in a highly cohesive group can be troublesome; conformity by members to the negative norms creates low-performance outcomes.

What are the implications of this relationship between norms and cohesiveness? Basically it boils down to this: Each of us should be aware of what can be done to build both positive norms and high cohesiveness in our teams. In respect to cohesiveness, this means such things as keeping team size as small as possible, working to gain agreements on team goals, increasing interaction among members, rewarding team outcomes rather than individual performance, introducing competition with other teams, and putting together team members who are very similar to one another.

Team performance is affected by task and maintenance roles.

Research on the group process identifies two types of activities that are essential if team members are to work well together over time.[40] **Task activities** contribute directly to the team's performance purpose; **maintenance activities** support the emotional life of the team as an ongoing social system. Although you might expect that these are things that team leaders or managers should be doing, this is only partially correct. In fact, all team members should share the responsibilities for task and maintenance leadership.

The concept of **distributed leadership** in teams makes every member continually responsible for both recognizing when task or maintenance activities are needed, and taking actions to provide them. Leading through task activities involves making an effort to define and solve problems and advance work toward performance results. Without task activities, such as initiating agendas and sharing information, teams have difficulty accomplishing their objectives. Leading through maintenance activities, such as encouraging others and reducing tensions, helps strengthen and perpetuate the team as a social system.

As shown below, both task and maintenance activities stand in distinct contrast to dysfunctional or **disruptive behaviors**. These include obvious self-serving behaviors that you often see and perhaps even engage in yourself—things such as aggressiveness, excessive joking, and nonparticipation. Think about this the next time one of your groups is drifting in the direction of ineffectiveness. Think also what you and others can do to correct things.

A **task activity** is an action taken by a team member that directly contributes to the group's performance purpose.

A **maintenance activity** is an action taken by a team member that supports the emotional life of the group.

Distributed leadership is when any and all members contribute helpful task and maintenance activities to the team.

Disruptive behaviors are self-serving and cause problems for team effectiveness.

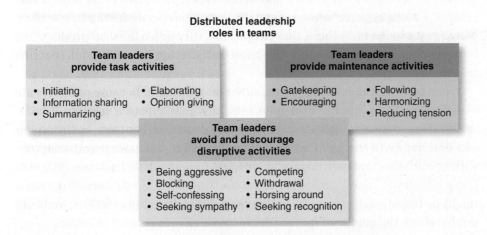

Distributed leadership roles in teams

Team leaders provide task activities
- Initiating
- Information sharing
- Summarizing
- Elaborating
- Opinion giving

Team leaders provide maintenance activities
- Gatekeeping
- Encouraging
- Following
- Harmonizing
- Reducing tension

Team leaders avoid and discourage disruptive activities
- Being aggressive
- Blocking
- Self-confessing
- Seeking sympathy
- Competing
- Withdrawal
- Horsing around
- Seeking recognition

Team performance is affected by communication networks.

Teams use the different communication networks shown in Figure 14.5 as they work and interact together.[41] In a **decentralized communication network**, all members communicate directly with one another. Sometimes called the *all-channel* or *star* structure, this arrangement works well for tasks that require lots of creativity, information processing, and problem solving. Use of a decentralized communication network creates an *interacting team* in which all members actively work together and share information. Member satisfaction on successful interacting teams is usually high.

A **decentralized communication network** allows all members to communicate directly with one another.

FIGURE 14.5
What Communication Networks Are Used in Teams?
Members of teams communicate and interact together in different ways. A decentralized structure is where all members communicate with one another. It works best when tasks are complex and the need for information sharing is high. When tasks are simple and easily broken down into small parts, a centralized structure works well. It coordinates members' communications through one central point. A restricted communication network sometimes forms when subgroups break off to do separate work or due to member alienation. Any lack of communication between the subgroups can create performance problems.

PATTERN	DIAGRAM	CHARACTERISTICS
Decentralized communication network Interacting Team	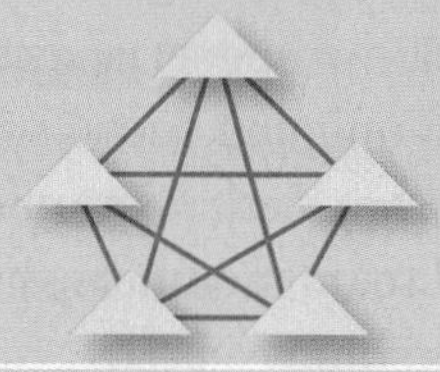	High interdependency around a common task Best at complex tasks
Centralized communication network Coacting Team	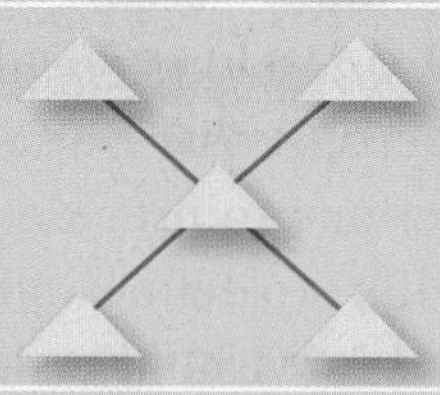	Independent individual efforts on behalf of common task Best at simple tasks
Restricted communication network Counteracting Team	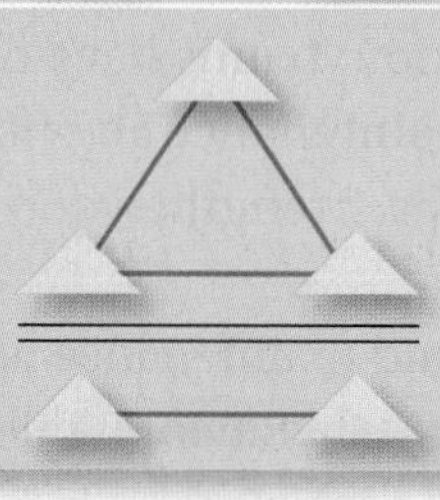	Subgroups in disagreement with one another Slow task accomplishment

When tasks are more routine and less demanding, team members can often divide up the work and then simply coordinate the final results. This is best done with a **centralized communication network**, sometimes called the *wheel* or *chain* structure. It has a central "hub" through which one member, often the team leader, collects information from and distributes information to all others. This creates a *coacting team* whose members work independently and pass completed tasks to the hub. There, they are put together into a finished product. The hub member often experiences the most satisfaction on successful coacting teams.

In a **centralized communication network**, communication flows only between individual members and a hub or center point.

When teams break into subgroups, either on purpose or because members are experiencing issue-specific disagreements, this may create a **restricted communication network**. Left unmanaged, this *counteracting team* environment can deteriorate to the point where subgroups fail to adequately communicate with one another and even engage in outwardly antagonistic relations. Although these situations create problems, there are times when counteracting teams might be intentionally set up to encourage conflict, increase creativity, and help double check the quality of specific decisions or chosen courses of action.

Subgroups in a **restricted communication network** contest one anothers' positions and restrict interactions with one another.

STUDY GUIDE

Takeaway 14.2
What Are the Building Blocks of Successful Teamwork?

Terms to Define

Centralized communication network

Cohesiveness

Decentralized communication network

Disruptive behaviors

Distributed leadership

Effective team

Maintenance activity

Membership composition

Norm

Performance norm

Restricted communication network

Task activity

Team effectiveness equation

Team process

Rapid Review

- An effective team achieves high levels of task performance, member satisfaction, and team viability.
- Important team input factors include the membership characteristics, nature of the task, organizational setting, and group size.
- A team matures through various stages of development, including forming, storming, norming, performing, and adjourning.
- Norms are the standards or rules of conduct that influence the behavior of team members; cohesion is the attractiveness of the team to its members.
- In highly cohesive teams, members tend to conform to norms; the best situation is a team with positive performance norms and high cohesiveness.
- Distributed leadership occurs when team members step in to provide helpful task and maintenance activities and discourage disruptive activities.
- Effective teams make use of alternative communication networks and interaction patterns to best complete tasks.

Questions for Discussion

1. What happens if a team can't get past the storming stage?
2. What can a manager do to build positive performance norms on a work team?
3. Why would a manager ever want to reduce the cohesion of a work group?

Be Sure You Can

- list the outputs of an effective team
- identify inputs that influence team effectiveness
- discuss how diversity influences team effectiveness
- list five stages of group development
- explain how norms and cohesion influence team performance
- list ways to build positive norms and change team cohesiveness
- illustrate task, maintenance, and disruptive activities in teams
- describe how groups use decentralized and centralized communication networks

What Would You Do?

For quite some time now, you've been concerned about a drop in the performance of your work team. Although everyone seems to like one another, the "numbers" in terms of measured daily accomplishments are on the decline. It's time to act. What will you look at, and why, to determine where and how steps might be taken to improve the effectiveness of this work team?

Takeaway 14.3
How Can Managers Create and Lead High-Performance Teams?

ANSWERS TO COME

- Team building helps team members learn to better work together.
- Team performance is affected by use of decision-making methods.
- Team performance suffers when groupthink leads to bad decisions.
- Team performance benefits from good conflict management.

THERE'S QUITE A BIT OF AGREEMENT ABOUT THE CHARACTERISTICS OF HIGH-performance teams. Here's a quick summary of what we know.[42] They have clear and elevating goals. They are results-oriented and their members are hardworking. They have high standards of excellence in a collaborative team culture. They get solid external support and recognition for their accomplishments. And they have strong and principled leaders. It's a great list, isn't it? But how do we get and stay there?

Although we know that high-performance teams generally share the characteristics noted above, not all teams reach this level of excellence. Just as in the world of sports, there are many things that can go wrong and cause problems for work teams.

⦀ Team building helps team members learn to better work together.

One of the ways to grow capacity for long-term team effectiveness is a practice known as **team building**. This is a set of planned activities used to analyze the functioning of a team and then make changes to increase its operating effectiveness.[43] Most systematic approaches to team building begin with awareness that a problem may exist or may develop within the team. Members then work together to gather data and fully understand the problem. Action plans are made and implemented. Results are evaluated by team members. As difficulties or new problems are discovered, the team-building process recycles.

There are many ways to gather data on team functioning, including structured and unstructured interviews, questionnaires, team meetings, and reality experiences. Regardless of the method used, the basic principle of team building remains the same—a careful and collaborative assessment of team inputs, processes, and results. It works best when all members participate in data gathering and analysis, and collectively decide on actions to be taken.

Team building can be done with or without the help of outside consultants. It can also be done in the workplace or in off-site locations. It is increasingly popular, for example, to engage in outdoor activities—obstacle courses or special events—to create enthusiasm for a team building experience. One trainer says: "We throw clients into situations to try and bring out the traits of a good team."[44]

Team building involves activities to gather and analyze data on a team and make changes to increase its effectiveness.

Fast Lanes for NASCAR Teams

The Beauty Is in the Teamwork

When a NASCAR driver pulls in for a pit stop, the pit crew must jump in to perform multiple tasks flawlessly and in perfect order and unison. A second gained or lost can be crucial to a NASCAR driver's performance. "You can't win a race with a 12-second stop, but you can lose it with an 18-second stop," says pit crew coach Trent Cherry.

Pit crew members execute intricate maneuvers while taking care of tire changes, car adjustments, fueling, and related matters on a crowded pit lane. Each crew member is an expert at one task but fully aware of how it fits with every other. Duties are carefully scripted for each peak individual performance and choreographed to fit together seamlessly at the team level. If the jacker is late, for example, the wheel changer can't pull the wheel.

The best crews plan and practice over and over again, getting ready for the big test of race day performance. The crew chief makes sure that everyone is in shape, well trained, and ready to go. "I don't want seven all-stars," Trent Cherry says, "I want seven guys who work as a team."

FIND INSPIRATION

NASCAR pit crews don't just get together and "wing it" on race days. Members are carefully selected for their skills and attitudes. Teams practice, practice, and practice. And, the pit crew leader doesn't hesitate to make changes when things aren't going well. Is this a model for teams everywhere?

Decision making is the process of making choices among alternative courses of action.

▥ Team performance is affected by use of decision-making methods.

The best teams don't limit themselves to just one **decision-making** method. Edgar Schein, a respected scholar and consultant, describes six ways teams make decisions.[45] He and other scholars note that teams ideally choose and use methods that best fit the problems at hand.[46] But mistakes are often made.

In *decision by lack of response*, one idea after another is suggested without any discussion taking place. When the team finally accepts an idea, all alternatives have been bypassed and discarded by simple lack of response rather than by critical evaluation. In *decision by authority rule*, the leader, manager, committee head, or some other authority figure makes a decision for the team. Although time-efficient, the quality of the decision depends on whether the authority figure has the necessary information. Its implementation depends on how well other team members accept the top-down approach. In *decision by minority rule*, two or three people dominate by "railroading" the team into a decision. How often have you heard: "Does anyone object? Okay, let's go ahead with it."

One of the most common ways teams make decisions, especially when early signs of disagreement arise, is *decision by majority rule*. Although consistent with democratic methods, it is often used without awareness of potential downsides. When votes are taken some people will be "winners" and others will be "losers." In all likelihood, you've been on the losing side at times. How did it

Keys to Consensus Decisions

- Don't argue blindly; consider others' reactions to your points.
- Don't change your mind just to reach quick agreement.
- Avoid conflict reduction by voting, coin tossing, bargaining.
- Keep everyone involved in the decision process.
- Allow disagreements to surface so that things can be deliberated.
- Don't focus on winning versus losing; seek acceptable alternatives.
- Discuss assumptions, listen carefully, and encourage inputs by all.

Consensus is reached when all parties believe they have had their say and been listened to, and agree to support the group's final decision.

feel? If you're like me, it may have made you feel left out, unenthusiastic about supporting the majority decision, and even hoping for a future chance to win.

Teams are often encouraged to try for *decision by* **consensus**. This is where full discussion leads to most members favoring one alternative, with the other members agreeing to support it. Even those opposed to the decision know that the others listened to their concerns. Consensus doesn't require unanimity, but it does require that team members be able to argue, debate, and engage in reasonable conflict, while still listening to and getting along with one another.[47]

A *decision by unanimity* means all team members agree on the course of action to take. This is the ideal state of affairs but it is also very difficult to reach. One of the reasons that teams sometimes turn to authority decisions, majority voting, or even minority decisions is the difficulty of managing team processes to achieve consensus or unanimity.

Team performance suffers when groupthink leads to bad decisions.

Groupthink is a tendency for highly cohesive teams to lose their evaluative capabilities.

How often have you held back stating your views in a meeting, agreed to someone else's position when it really seemed wrong, or gone along with a boss's suggestions even though you disagreed?[48] If and when you do these things, you are likely trapped by **groupthink**, the tendency for members of highly cohesive groups to lose their critical evaluative capabilities.[49] It occurs when teams strive too hard to reach agreement and avoid disagreement.[50]

Teams suffering groupthink often fit the description shown in Table 14.1—*Symptoms of Groupthink*. They act this way because members try to hold the group together and maintain harmony at all costs. They don't do anything that might detract from feelings of goodwill. Instead of raising critical questions about a suggested course of action, for example, they hold them back. But when members publicly agree with a suggestion while privately having serious doubts about it, groupthink often delivers a bad decision.

Table 14.1 Symptoms of Groupthink

Illusions of invulnerability—Members assume that the team is too good for criticism or is beyond attack.

Rationalizing unpleasant and disconfirming data—Members refuse to accept contradictory data or to thoroughly consider alternatives.

Belief in inherent group morality—Members act as though the group is inherently right and above reproach.

Stereotyping competitors as weak, evil, and stupid—Members refuse to look realistically at other groups.

Applying direct pressure to deviants to conform to group wishes—Members refuse to tolerate anyone who suggests the team may be wrong.

Self-censorship by members—Members refuse to communicate personal concerns to the whole team.

Illusions of unanimity—Members accept consensus prematurely, without testing its completeness.

Mind guarding—Members protect the team from hearing disturbing ideas or outside viewpoints.

Psychologist Irving Janis first described groupthink using well-known historical blunders—the lack of preparedness of U.S. naval forces for the Japanese attack on Pearl Harbor, and the failed Bay of Pigs invasion under President Kennedy.[51] It has also been linked to flawed U.S. decision making during the Vietnam war, events leading up to the NASA space shuttle disasters, and failures of intelligence agencies regarding the presence of weapons of mass destruction in Iraq.

But, be aware, groupthink isn't limited to big government or big corporate decision making. It appears all too often in any team, at any level, in all sorts of organizations. Hasn't it been part of your experience?

When you are leading or are part of team heading toward groupthink, don't think there's no way out. Janis notes, for example, that after suffering the Bay of Pigs fiasco, President Kennedy approached the Cuban missile crisis quite differently. He purposely did not attend some cabinet discussions and allowed the group to deliberate without him. His absence helped the cabinet members talk

Manager's Library

■ *CROWDSOURCING* BY JEFF HOWE

IS "CROWDSOURCING" THE WAVE OF THE FUTURE?

How would you define a collection of individuals working together to achieve a common purpose? To "digital immigrants"—people who are discovering and adapting to Internet use—the response is typically an "organization." But to "digital natives"—people born during the Internet Age—the reply might be an "online community." In the past, newspaper editors gathered staffs to determine the news. But nowadays, online "bloggers," "discussion boards," and "trending now" topics provide much of the news content that is consumed.

In the book *Crowdsourcing* (2008, Crown Business), author Jeff Howe discusses how the Internet has shifted the paradigm of organizations, teamwork, and innovation. He believes past generations of workers viewed teamwork as physical actions of paid experts, guided by managers telling them what to do. But new generations may view teamwork as primarily a virtual effort of unpaid volunteers, guided by popular opinion that permits them to do what they enjoy. For example, Henry Ford once directed automobile assembly by paying laborers in a Detroit factory. Today, "hobbyists" from across the globe compile encyclopedias on Wikipedia.com for free.

Howe calls this "crowdsourcing"—Internet teamwork that draws on talents of amateurs to create value comparable to companies of paid experts. Marketocracy.com produces "crowd wisdom" by aggregating 70,000 investors into portfolio management, tracking trends to generate stock tips. Digg.com uses "crowd voting" of six million user ratings to promote top news stories, while Kiva.org relies on "crowd funding" to gather financing from individuals for small business loans. Wikipedia uses "crowd creation" to create and update an online encyclopedia.

Howe believes crowdsourcing shifts an organization's approach to intellectual capital. Beliefs were that small numbers of like-minded professionals innovated in closed settings, and ideas advanced slowly under secrecy. Crowdsourcing allows large audiences of diverse hobbyists to generate ideas in digital transparency, and innovations accelerate quickly in open examination. So, many organizations now supplement standard knowledge work by crowdsourcing as well.

REFLECT AND REACT

How might crowdsourcing work for routine subjects like book editing and video surveillance? How about for complex subjects like crime investigation and alternative energy development? How might contributors be paid for crowdsourcing? Should the crowd remain anonymous, or be identified? Should the crowd be led or guided? And by the way, is there a risk of groupthink in crowdsourcing?

more openly and be less inclined to try and say things consistent with his own thinking. When a decision was finally reached, the crisis was successfully resolved.

In addition to having the leader absent for some team discussions, Janis has other advice on how to get a team that is moving toward groupthink back on track.[52] You can assign one member to act as a critical evaluator or "devil's advocate" during each meeting. Subgroups can be assigned to work on issues and then share their findings with the team as a whole. Outsiders can be brought in to observe and participate in team meetings, and offer their advice and viewpoints on both team processes and tentative decisions. And, the team can hold a "second chance" meeting after an initial decision is made to review, change, and even cancel it. With actions like these available, there's no reason to let groupthink lead a team down the wrong pathways.

‖ Team performance benefits from good conflict management.

In interpersonal relationships and on a team, the ability to deal with conflicts is critical. But "conflict" is one of those words like "communication" or "power." We use it a lot, but rarely think it through to the specifics.

At its core **conflict** involves disagreements among people. And in our experiences, it appears in two quite different forms.[53] **Substantive conflict** involves disagreements over such things as goals and tasks, the allocation of resources, the distribution of rewards, policies and procedures, and job assignments. You are in a substantive conflict with a teammate when, for example, each of you wants to solve a problem by following a different strategy. **Emotional conflict** results from feelings of anger, distrust, dislike, fear, and resentment as well as relationship problems. You know this form of conflict as a clash of personalities or emotions—when you don't want to agree with another person just because you don't like or are angry with him or her.

With all this potential for conflict in and around teams, how do you and others deal with it? Most people respond to conflict through different combinations of cooperative and assertive behaviors.[54] Figure 14.6 shows how this results in five conflict management styles—avoidance, accommodation, competition, compromise, and collaboration.[55]

In **avoidance**, everyone withdraws and pretends that conflict doesn't really exist, hoping that it will simply go away. You might think of this as teammates mad about a missed deadline and each unwilling to mention it to the other. In **accommodation**, peaceful coexistence is the goal. Differences are played down and areas of agreement are highlighted, even though the real cause for the conflict doesn't get addressed. Both avoidance and accommodation are forms of *lose-lose conflict*. No one achieves her or his true desires, and the underlying conflict remains unresolved, often to recur in the future.

In **competition**, one party wins through superior skill or outright domination. Although the first example that may come to mind is sports, competition is common in work teams. It occurs as authoritative command by team leaders and as railroading or minority domination by team members. In **compromise**, trade-offs are made, with each party giving up and gaining something of value. Both competition and compromise are forms of *win-lose conflict*. Each party strives to gain at the

Conflict is a disagreement over issues of substance and/or an emotional antagonism.

Substantive conflict involves disagreements over goals, resources, rewards, policies, procedures, and job assignments.

Emotional conflict results from feelings of anger, distrust, dislike, fear, and resentment as well as from personality clashes.

Avoidance pretends that a conflict doesn't really exist.

Accommodation, or smoothing, plays down differences and highlights similarities to reduce conflict.

Competition, or authoritative command, uses force, superior skill, or domination to win a conflict.

Compromise occurs when each party to the conflict gives up something of value to the other.

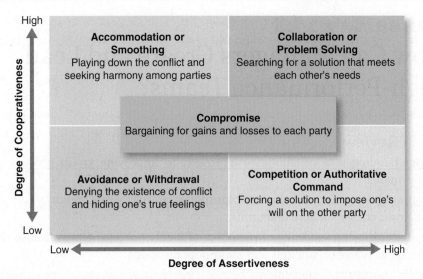

FIGURE 14.6 What Are the Five Common Styles of Conflict Management?
In conflict situations, a combination of cooperative and aggressive behaviors results in five possible conflict management styles. Competition occurs when aggression dominates our behavior, and accommodation occurs when cooperation dominates. Avoidance occurs with both low aggression and cooperation, whereas compromise occurs with moderate amounts of both. When both cooperation and aggression are high, true collaboration and problem solving are more likely to occur.

other's expense. But whenever one party loses something, seeds for future conflict remain in place.

Unlike the prior methods, **collaboration** tries to find and address the problem and reconcile the real differences underlying a conflict. As you would expect, it is often time-consuming and stressful. But it's also the most effective conflict management style in terms of real conflict resolution. Collaboration turns a difficult situation into a *win-win conflict*. Things are resolved to everyone's mutual benefit—no avoiding, no smoothing, no domination, and no compromising. A real agreement is reached. From experience, you should recognize that this approach depends on the willingness of everyone to dig in, confront the issues, and openly and honestly discuss them. When it works, collaboration eliminates the underlying causes of a conflict and creates positive conditions for future teamwork.

The small box is a reminder that each of the five conflict management styles can be useful.[56] Most of us probably use each at least some of the time. But we should make good choices, being sure to fit our style to the requirements of each unique conflict situation. It's also worth remembering that unresolved or suppressed conflicts often sow the seeds for future conflicts. Only true **conflict resolution**, characteristic of the collaborative style, eliminates the underlying causes of a conflict in ways that should prevent similar conflicts in the future.

Collaboration, or problem solving, involves working through conflict differences and solving problems so everyone wins.

Conflict resolution is the removal of the substantive and/or emotional reasons for a conflict.

When to Use Alternative Conflict Management Strategies

- *Collaboration, or problem solving,* is the preferred way to gain true conflict resolution when time and cost permit.
- *Avoidance, or withdrawal,* may be used when an issue is trivial, when more important issues are pressing, or when people need to cool down temporarily and regain perspective.
- *Competition, or authoritative command,* may be used when quick and decisive action is vital or when unpopular actions must be taken.
- *Accommodation, or smoothing,* may be used when issues are more important to others than to yourself or when you want to build "credits" for use in later disagreements.
- *Compromise* may be used to arrive at temporary settlements of complex issues or to arrive at expedient solutions when time is limited.

STUDY GUIDE

Takeaway 14.3
How Can Managers Create and Lead High-Performance Teams?

Terms to Define

Accommodation

Avoidance

Brainstorming

Collaboration

Competition

Compromise

Conflict

Conflict resolution

Consensus

Decision making

Emotional conflict

Groupthink

Substantive conflict

Team building

Rapid Review

- Team building is a collaborative approach to improving group process and performance.
- Teams can make decisions by lack of response, authority rule, minority rule, majority rule, consensus, and unanimity.
- Groupthink is the tendency of members of highly cohesive teams to lose their critical evaluative capabilities and make poor decisions.
- Conflict occurs as disagreements between people over substantive or emotional issues.
- Tendencies toward cooperativeness and assertiveness create the interpersonal conflict management styles of avoidance, accommodation, compromise, competition, and collaboration.

Questions for Discussion

1. How does consensus differ from unanimity in group decision making?
2. Is groupthink found only in highly cohesive teams, or could it exist in pre-cohesive ones?
3. When is it better to avoid conflict rather than directly engage in it?

Be Sure You Can

- describe how team building might help one of your groups
- list and discuss the different ways groups make decisions
- define the term "groupthink" and identify its symptoms
- list at least four ways teams can avoid groupthink
- differentiate substantive and emotional conflict
- explain the conflict management styles of avoidance, accommodation, competition, compromise, and collaboration

What Would You Do?

The members of the executive compensation committee that you are chairing show a high level of cohesiveness. It's obvious that they enjoy being part of the committee and are proud to be on the board of directors. But the committee is about to approve extraordinarily high bonuses for the CEO and five other senior executives. This is occurring at a time when executive pay is getting lots of criticism from the press, unions, and the public at large. What can you do to make sure groupthink isn't causing this committee to potentially make a bad decision?

TestPrep 14

Multiple-Choice Questions

1. _____ occurs when a group of people is able to achieve more than its members could by working individually.

(a) Distributed leadership

(b) Consensus

(c) Team viability

(d) Synergy

2. One of the recommended strategies for dealing with a group member who engages in social loafing is to _____.

(a) redefine tasks to make individual contributions more visible

(b) ask another member to encourage this person to work harder

(c) give the person extra rewards and hope he or she will feel guilty

(d) just forget about it

3. An effective team is defined as one that achieves high levels of task performance, high member satisfaction, and _____.

(a) resource efficiency

(b) team viability

(c) group consensus

(d) creativity

4. In the open-systems model of teams, the _____ is an important input factor.

(a) communication network

(b) decision-making method

(c) performance norm

(d) diversity of membership

5. A basic rule of team dynamics might be stated this way: The greater the _____ in a team, the greater the conformity to norms.

(a) membership diversity

(b) cohesiveness

(c) task clarity

(d) competition among members

6. The team effectiveness equation states the following: Team Effectiveness = Quality of Inputs × (_____ − Process Losses).

(a) Process Gains

(b) Leadership Impact

(c) Membership Ability

(d) Problem Complexity

7. Members of a team become more motivated and better able to deal with conflict during the _____ stage of team development.

(a) forming

(b) norming

(c) performing

(d) adjourning

8. A team member who does a good job at summarizing discussion, offering new ideas, and clarifying points made by others is providing leadership by contributing _____ activities to the group process.

(a) required

(b) task

(c) disruptive

(d) maintenance

9. A team performing very creative and unstructured tasks is most likely to succeed using _____.

(a) a decentralized communication network

(b) decisions by majority rule

(c) decisions by minority rule

(d) more task than maintenance activities

10. One way for a manager to build positive norms within a team is to _____.

(a) act as a positive role model

(b) increase group size

(c) introduce groupthink

(d) isolate the team

11. The best way to try to increase the cohesiveness of a team would be to _____.
    (a) start competition with other groups
    (b) add more members
    (c) reduce isolation from other groups
    (d) increase the diversity of members

12. A _____ decision is one in which all members agree on the course of action to be taken.
    (a) consensus
    (b) unanimous
    (c) majority
    (d) synergy

13. Groupthink is most likely to occur in teams that are _____.
    (a) large in size
    (b) diverse in membership
    (c) high performing
    (d) highly cohesive

14. When people are highly cooperative but not very assertive in a conflict situation, the likelihood is that they will be using which conflict management style?
    (a) avoidance
    (b) authoritative
    (c) accommodation
    (d) collaboration

15. The interpersonal conflict management style with the greatest potential for true conflict resolution is _____.
    (a) compromise
    (b) competition
    (c) avoidance
    (d) collaboration

Short-Response Questions

16. What are the major differences among a task force, an employee involvement group, and a self-managing team?

17. How can a manager influence team performance by modifying group inputs?

18. How do cohesiveness and performance norms together influence team performance?

19. What are two symptoms of groupthink and two possible remedies for them?

Integration and Application Question

20. Mariel Espinoza has just been appointed manager of a production team operating the 11 p.m. to 7 a.m. shift in a large manufacturing firm. An experienced manager, Mariel is pleased that the team members seem to really like and get along well with one another, but she notices that they also appear to be restricting their task outputs to the minimum acceptable levels.

    Question: How might Mariel improve this situation?

Steps*for*FurtherLearning

Many learning resources are found at the end of the book and online within WileyPLUS.

Don't Miss These Selections from the **Skill-Building Portfolio**

■ **SELF-ASSESSMENT 14:** *Team Leader Skills*

■ **CLASS EXERCISE 14:** *Understanding Team Dynamics*

■ **TEAM PROJECT 14:** *Superstars on the Team*

Don't Miss This Selection from **Cases for Critical Thinking**

■ **CHAPTER 14 CASE**
  Pixar: Animated Geniuses

Snapshot Pixar's movies—including the *Toy Story* movies, *The Incredibles, Cars, Ratatouille,* and *Up*—have succeeded largely because Pixar has focused on employing computer graphics (CG) technology to make the characters, scenery, and minute details as realistic as possible.

This is a direct result of the synergy between Pixar's creative teams, who develop the story and characters, and its technical teams who program—and frequently develop—the animation software used to breathe life into each movie. Each forces the other to innovate, and together they successfully balance the latest technology with a back-to-basics focus on interesting characters in compelling stories.

Make notes here on what you've learned about yourself from this chapter.

■ **LEARNING JOURNAL 14**

A survey at the University of New Hampshire showed that 65% of business students sent text messages during classes; 49% felt guilty about it; 36% said it should be prohibited.

Communication

Listening Is the Key to Understanding

Management Live

Communication/Networking and *The Devil Wears Prada*

Who wears Prada? In the hit movie *The Devil Wears Prada* there is no doubt that it is Miranda Priestly (Meryl Streep). She's quite a contrast to her new assistant Andrea Sachs (Anne Hathway). "Andy" is clearly out of her element when it comes to working in the fashion industry. As an assistant to the demanding Miranda, editor-in-chief of *Runway* magazine, she frequently finds herself assigned to impossible tasks.

In one scene Andy is sent to retrieve sketches from designer James Holt (Daniel Sunjata) and gets buried in a party. She meets famed writer Christian Thompson (Simon Baker), and their conversation centers on career talk. But it's easy to see that Thompson has other motives. While Andy recognizes this to a degree, she also realizes this relationship could have real value in terms of helping her meet Miranda's "impossible demands."

There are many work themes in this movie, from good boss/bad boss issues to everyday "how do you get along in a tough job" insights. The next time you watch it, however, check how the various players use **communication and networking** skills—not the kind you do on Facebook or Twitter, but the face-to-face variety.

Management consultant William C. Byham says it is important to forge "deliberate connections" on the job. These connections become networks for learning, collaboration, and work accomplishment. They help us build all-important social capital, the capacity to enlist the help and support of others when it is needed.

YOUR CHAPTER 15 TAKEAWAYS

1. Understand the nature of communication and when it is effective.

2. Identify the major barriers to effective communication.

3. Discuss ways to improve communication with people at work.

WHAT'S INSIDE

Explore Yourself
More on communication and networking

Role Models
The Limited's Linda Heasley gives others reasons to work with her

Ethics Check
In France, it's bloggers beware

Facts to Consider
Employees should worry about electronic monitoring

COL LAB ORA TION

Manager's Library
Collaboration by Morten Hansen

Takeaway 15.1
What Is Communication and When Is It Effective?

ANSWERS TO COME

- Communication is a process of sending and receiving messages with meanings attached.
- Communication is effective when the receiver understands the sender's messages.
- Communication is efficient when it is delivered at low cost to the sender.
- Communication is persuasive when the receiver acts as the sender intends.

COMMUNICATION IS AT THE HEART OF THE MANAGEMENT PROCESS. YOU MIGHT think of it as the glue that binds together the four functions of planning, organizing, leading, and controlling.[1] Planning is accomplished and plans are shared through the communication of information. Organizing identifies and structures communication linkages among people and positions. Leading uses communication to achieve positive influence over organization members and stakeholders. And, controlling relies on communication to process information to assess and measure performance results.

In the above respects and many more, managers act as information nerve centers. They are continually gathering information, processing it, using it for problem solving, and sharing it with others.[2] They are also entwined in complex webs of interpersonal networks through which they implement work priorities and agendas.[3] As Pam Alexander, former CEO of Ogilvy Public Relations Worldwide, says: "Relationships are the most powerful form of media. Ideas will only get you so far these days. Count on personal relationships to carry you further."[4]

In many ways communication is all about building something all managers need—**social capital.** It is the capacity to attract support and help from others to get things done. Whereas intellectual capital is basically what you know, social capital comes from who you know and how well you relate to them.

Given all this, would it surprise you that when the American Management Association asked members to rate the communication skills of their managers, only 22.1% rated them "high"?[5] The respondents also rated their bosses only slightly above average on transforming ideas into words, credibility, listening and asking questions, and written and oral presentations.[6] And even though communication skills regularly top the lists of characteristics looked for by corporate recruiters, why is it that 81% of college professors in one survey rated high school graduates as "fair" or "poor" in writing clearly?

Take the nearby communication quick-check. Can you convince a recruiter that you have the communication skills necessary for success in your career field? Strength in these skills should help differentiate you from others wanting the same job or internship. But how do you stack up? What work do you have left to do in these areas?

Social capital is the capacity to attract support and help from others in order to get things done.

Communication Quick-Check—Rate Your Skills

- Use e-mail and social media well
- Write concise memos, letters, reports
- Network with peers and mentors
- Run meetings, contribute to meetings
- Give persuasive presentations
- Able to give and receive feedback

⫴ Communication is a process of sending and receiving messages with meanings attached.

Communication is an interpersonal process of sending and receiving symbols with messages attached to them. Although the definition sounds simple and commonsense enough, there is a lot of room for error when we actually implement the process. There are many places where things can go wrong and our communications end up misunderstood or poorly received.

Figure 15.1 summarizes the key elements in the communication process. A *sender* encodes an intended message into meaningful symbols, both verbal and nonverbal. He or she sends the *message* through a *communication channel* to a *receiver*, who then decodes or interprets its meaning. This *interpretation* may or may not match the sender's original intentions. When present, *feedback* reverses the process and conveys the receiver's response back to the sender.

Communication is the process of sending and receiving symbols with meanings attached.

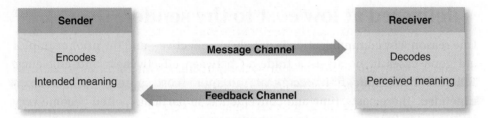

FIGURE 15.1 What Are the Major Elements in the Process of Interpersonal Communication?
The communication process begins when a sender encodes an intended meaning into a message. This message is then transmitted through a channel to a receiver. The receiver next decodes the message into perceived meaning. Finally, the receiver may transmit feedback back to the sender. The communication process is effective when the perceived meaning of the receiver is the same as the intended meaning of the sender.

A useful way to describe the communication process shown in the figure is as a series of questions. "Who?" (sender) "says what?" (message) "in what way?" (channel) "to whom?" (receiver) "with what result?" (interpreted meaning). To check the outcome it's important to ask yet another important question: Do receiver and sender understand things in the same ways?

⫴ Communication is effective when the receiver understands the sender's messages.

The ability to communicate well both orally and in writing is a critical managerial skill and the foundation of effective leadership. Through communication, people exchange and share information, and influence one another's attitudes, behaviors, and understandings. Communication allows managers to establish and maintain interpersonal relationships, listen to others, deal with conflicts, negotiate, and otherwise gain the information needed to make decisions. But all this assumes that the communication goes as intended.

As much as communication is part of our everyday lives, we often fail in using it to our best advantage. One problem is that we take our abilities for granted and end up being disappointed when the process breaks down. Another is that we are too busy, or too lazy, to invest enough time in making sure that the process really works. These problems point to issues of "effectiveness" and "efficiency" in the communication process.

In **effective communication** the receiver fully understands the intended meaning.

In management, we say that **effective communication** occurs when the receiver fully understands the sender's intended message. In other words, the intended meaning matches the received meaning. As you well know, this outcome doesn't always happen.

How often have you wondered what an instructor really wants in an assignment or struggled to understand a point during class lecture? How often have you been angry when a friend or loved one just "didn't seem to get" your message and, unfortunately, didn't respond in the desired way? And, how often have you sent an SMS or e-mail, or left a voice message, only to receive back a confused or even angry reply that wasn't at all appropriate to your intended message? These are all examples of well-intentioned communications that weren't effective. Things don't have to be this way. But it does take effort to achieve effective communication in work and personal affairs.

||| Communication is efficient when it is delivered at low cost to the sender.

Efficient communication occurs at minimum cost to the sender.

One reason why communication is not always effective—and the prior examples are good cases in point—is a trade-off between effectiveness and efficiency. **Efficient communication** occurs at minimum cost in terms of resources expended. These costs, time and convenience, in particular, often become very influential in how we choose to communicate.

{ "I LIKE TO KNOW THE BAD NEWS AS SOON AS YOU KNOW IT . . . I PROMISE NO RECRIMINATIONS."

Role Models

■ THE LIMITED'S LINDA HEASLEY GIVES OTHERS REASONS TO WORK WITH HER

Would you like to work for a boss who encourages you to keep your eyes open for other job opportunities? Well, that's exactly what Linda Heasley's team at The Limited heard. As president and CEO, she says it's her job to "re-recruit them every day and give them a reason to choose to work for us and for me as opposed to anyone else." She describes this approach as part of a leadership philosophy based on the belief that "it's not about me . . . it's very much about the team."

Newcomers to Heasley's team are advised to follow a 90-day rule when it comes to communication. Based on her experience living in Thailand as a high school exchange student, she believes in taking the first 90 days to "watch and listen," trying "not to talk at meetings," and working to build relationships. And when it comes to performance, she also says: "I like to know the bad news as soon as you know it—I promise no recriminations—but I will expect to know what we could've avoided so it doesn't happen again."

Heasley took over The Limited when the company's stores were struggling for profitability. She acted decisively to refocus on core target customers while reducing costs and remodeling sales spaces. And she focused on recruiting staff who would find excitement in the challenges ahead. When asked what she looks for in hiring, Heasley highlights things like passion, curiosity, energy, willingness to take risks, and a sense of humor. During interviews she uses proven questions to try to draw out job candidates and discover their capabilities. She might ask "What books have you read lately?" or "Can you describe a challenging situation you've been in and where you took a controversial position?"

WHAT'S THE LESSON HERE?

Linda Heasley seems very comfortable with herself and her role as president and CEO of this major company. Can you see where communication is one of her strengths? Would you respond well to a leader like this? In what respects might Heasley become a role model for your personal leadership approach someday?

Picture your instructor speaking individually, face-to-face, with each student about this chapter. Although most likely very effective, it would certainly be inefficient in terms of the cost of his or her time. This is why we often send text messages, leave voice-mail messages, chat online, and use e-mail rather than speak directly with other people. These alternatives are more efficient than one-on-one and face-to-face communications. They may also allow us to avoid the discomfort of dealing with a difficult matter face-to-face. But while quick and easy, are these efficient communications always effective?

The next time you have something important to communicate, you might pause and consider the trade-offs between effectiveness and efficiency. A low-cost approach such as a text message may save time, but it may not result in the other party getting the real intended meaning. By the same token, an effective communication may not always be efficient. If a team leader visits each team member individually to explain a new change in procedures, this may guarantee that everyone truly understands the change. It will also take a lot of the leader's time. A team meeting is much more efficient. In these and other ways, potential give and take between effectiveness and efficiency must be recognized in communication.

||| Communication is persuasive when the receiver acts as the sender intends.

In personal life and at work we often want not just to be heard, but to be followed. We want our communication to "persuade" the other party to believe or behave in a specific way that we intend. **Persuasive communication** gets someone else to accept, support, and act consistent with the sender's message.[7]

Persuasive communication presents a message in a manner that causes others to accept and support it.

If you agree that managers get most things done through other people, you should also agree that managers must be very good at persuasive communication. Yet scholar and consultant Jay Conger believes that many

{RECRUITERS GIVE THESE SKILLS HIGH PRIORITY WHEN SCREENING CANDIDATES FOR COLLEGE INTERNSHIPS AND FIRST JOBS.

Explore Yourself

■ COMMUNICATION AND NETWORKING

Effective **communication and networking** skills are essential for turning ideas into actions, being credible, listening and asking questions, and giving written and oral presentations. You might think that the attention given to them as critical management and career skills is overdone. But such attention is warranted.

Recruiters give these skills high priority when screening candidates for college internships and first jobs. Employers consider it essential that workers be able to communicate well both orally and in writing and be able to network with others for collaboration and work accomplishment.

This chapter offers many insights to help you develop communication and networking skills. They are key foundations of one's social capital, or capacity to enlist the help and support of others when needed. Communication and networking are ways of getting work done with the support of other people.

Get to know yourself better by taking the self-assessment on **Feedback and Assertiveness** and completing the other activities in the *Exploring Management* **Skill-Building Portfolio.**

Jay-Z Raps to a Business Empire

Talent Points Way to Corporate Power

Decisions . . . hunches . . . achievements? It's all about being tuned into the environment.

That's a message well learned years ago by a young rapper just breaking into the music scene and calling himself Jay-Z. He could have been doing something else with his time, but he wasn't; he could have stopped with the music, but he didn't. As his lyrics state: "No lie, just know I chose my own fate. I drove by the fork in the road and went straight." Now past the age of 40, he's still rapping, but his rare talent with communication is serving him well in more ways than this one.

Born Shawn Carter, Jay-Z started as a street busker, went on to get his own label Roc-A-Fella Records, made lots more music, won 10 Grammy awards, and became CEO of Def Jam Records. But the Jay-Z story doesn't end with hip-hop. He turned a talent for communication into shrewd entrepreneurship that includes not only Roc Nation, the latest incarnation of Roc-A-Fella Records, but also part ownership of the New Jersey Nets, the marketing firm Translation, and brand partnerships with the likes of Hewlett-Packard and Microsoft. His hard work and success have led to a listing as one of *Forbes* magazine's "Richest People in America," and he tells the story in his first book, *Decoded*.

Was it luck that moved him toward fame and fortune or something else? Raw talent alone isn't enough to succeed in the music business. At some point, as with all occupations, success happens when talent is partnered with insight, intuition, and an ability to make the right decisions. Jay-Z obviously made the connections and uses his communication skills to great business advantage.

FIND INSPIRATION

"This guy from out in the projects who didn't graduate from high school is now living this sort of life," he says. "And this is how he got there." Jay-Z's lyrics don't always tell an easy story or recommend a solution. But they do make the case for how communication can partner with other talents and positive goals to help create career success.

Credible communication earns trust, respect, and integrity in the eyes of others.

managers "confuse persuasion with bold stands and aggressive arguing."[8] This sounds a lot like the so-called "debates" that we watch on television as advocates of different political viewpoints face off against one another. A lot is said, some of it quite aggressively, but little in the way of influence on the other speaker or the listening audience really takes place. An overly confrontational or uncompromising approach can also raise questions about one's credibility.

Conger goes on to define **credible communication** as that which earns trust, respect, and integrity in the eyes of others. He says it is a learned skill, one based on the personal powers of expertise and reference. And without credibility, he claims there is little chance for successful persuasion.

The late Sam Walton, Walmart's founder, was considered a master of persuasive communication. Consider an example—classic Walton in action.[9] Sam stops by to visit a Memphis store and calls everyone to the front, saying: "Northeast Memphis, you're the largest store in Memphis, and you must have the best floor-cleaning crew in America. This floor is so clean, let's sit down on it." Picture this. Walton is kneeling casually while wearing his Walmart baseball cap. He congratulates the employees on their fine work. "I thank you. The company is so proud of you we can hardly stand it," he says. "But, you know that confounded Kmart is getting better, and so is Target. So what's our challenge?" Walton answers his own question: Customer service. Can't you just see everyone present taking his message to heart?

STUDY GUIDE

Takeaway 15.1
What Is Communication and When Is It Effective?

Terms to Define

Communication

Credible communication

Effective communication

Efficient communication

Persuasive communication

Social capital

Rapid Review

- **Communication** is the interpersonal process of sending and receiving symbols with messages attached to them.
- **Effective communication** occurs when the sender and the receiver of a message both interpret it in the same way.
- **Efficient communication** occurs when the sender conveys the message at low cost.
- **Persuasive communication** results in the recipient acting as the sender intends.
- **Credibility** earned by expertise and good relationships is essential to persuasive communication.

Questions for Discussion

1. Why do recruiters place so much emphasis on the communications skills of job candidates?
2. Can you describe a work situation where it's okay to accept less communication effectiveness in order to gain communication efficiency?
3. What can a manager do to gain the credibility needed for truly persuasive communication?

Be Sure You Can

- describe the communication process and identify its key components
- define and give an example of effective communication
- define and give an example of efficient communication
- explain why an effective communication is not always efficient
- explain the role of credibility in persuasive communication

What Would You Do?

Your boss just sent a text message that he wants you at a meeting starting at 3 p.m. Your daughter is performing in a program at her elementary school at 2:45 p.m., and she wants you to attend. You're out of the office making sales calls and have scheduled appointments to put you close to the school in the early afternoon. The office is a long way across town. Do you call him, text him, or send him an e-mail? What exactly will you say in your communication to him?

Takeaway 15.2
What Are the Major Barriers to Effective Communication?

ANSWERS TO COME

- Poor use of channels makes it hard to communicate effectively.
- Poor written or oral expression makes it hard to communicate effectively.
- Failure to spot nonverbal signals makes it hard to communicate effectively.
- Physical distractions make it hard to communicate effectively.
- Status differences make it hard to communicate effectively.

Noise is anything that interferes with the communication process.

WHEN YOSHIHIRO WADA WAS PRESIDENT OF MAZDA CORPORATION, HE USED interpreters when meeting with representatives of the firm's U.S. joint venture partner, Ford. He estimated that he lost 20% of his intended meaning in the exchange between himself and the interpreter, and another 20% between the interpreter and the Americans.[10]

These and other language problems are to be expected in international business. It's not easy to communicate in a second language, and messages do get lost in translation. But do you recognize how problems creep into everyday communications, not just the international or cross-cultural ones?

Look at Figure 15.2. It updates our description of the communication process to include **noise**—anything that interferes with the effectiveness of communication. Common sources of noise that often create communication barriers include poor choice of channels, poor written or oral expression, failure to recognize nonverbal signals, physical distractions, and status differences.

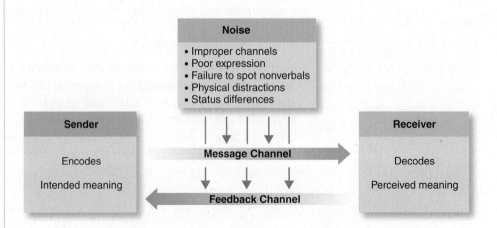

FIGURE 15.2 How Does Noise Interfere with the Communication Process?
Among the types of noise that can interfere with the effectiveness of communication, the following are well worth noting: Semantic problems in the forms of poor written or oral expression, the absence of feedback, improper choice and use of communication channels, physical distractions, status differences between senders and receivers, and cultural differences can all in one way or another complicate the communication process. Unless these factors are given attention, they can reduce communication effectiveness.

Poor use of channels makes it hard to communicate effectively.

People communicate with one another using a variety of **communication channels**, or mediums used to carry the message.[11] A poor choice of channel often causes problems because of differences in **channel richness**, the capacity to carry information in an effective manner.[12] We all need to understand the limits of the possible channels and choose wisely when using them for communication.

The small figure shows that face-to-face communication is very high in richness. These channels are personal and can help create a supportive, even inspirational, relationship between sender and receiver. They work especially well when we need to convey complex or difficult messages, and when we need immediate feedback. Written channels like memos, e-mails, and text messages are much less rich. They are impersonal, one-way interactions with limited opportunity for feedback.

A **communication channel** is the medium used to carry a message.

Channel richness is the capacity of a communication channel to effectively carry information.

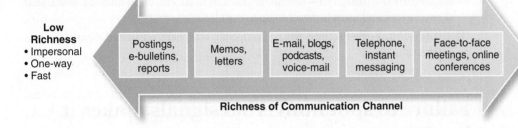

Richness of Communication Channel

Poor written or oral expression makes it hard to communicate effectively.

A survey of 150 companies by the National Commission on Writing found that over one-third of their employees were considered deficient in writing skills and that employers were spending over $3 billion each year on remedial training.[14] Consider the following "bafflegab" found among some executive communications.

> *A business report said:* "Consumer elements are continuing to stress the fundamental necessity of a stabilization of the price structure at a lower level than exists at the present time." *Why couldn't the report say:* "Consumers want prices to come down and stay down."?
>
> *A manager said:* "Substantial economies were affected in this division by increasing the time interval between distributions of data-eliciting forms to business entities." *Why couldn't the manager say:* "The division saved money by sending out fewer surveys."?

It takes a lot of practice to write a concise letter or report, or deliver a great oral presentation. There's no getting around it, good writing and good speaking are products of plain old hard work.[13] But it's well worth the investment. How many drafts do you write for memos, letters, and reports? Are you getting so used to texting that you can't write a proper sentence? How often do you practice for an oral presentation? Are you well informed on the tips that follow in Table 15.1?

Table 15.1 **Essential Ingredients of Successful Presentations**

Be prepared—Know what you want to say; know how you want to say it; rehearse saying it.

Set the right tone—Focus on your audience; make eye contact and act pleasantly and confidently.

Sequence your points—State your purpose, make important points, follow with details, and then summarize.

Support your points—Give specific reasons for your points; state them in understandable terms.

Accent the presentation—Use good visual aids; provide supporting handouts when possible.

Add the right amount of polish—Attend to details; have room, materials, and arrangements ready to go.

Check the technology—Check everything ahead of time; make sure it works and know how to use it.

Don't bet on the Internet—Beware of plans to make real-time Internet visits; save sites on a disk and use a browser to open the file.

Be professional—Be on time; wear appropriate attire; act organized, confident, and enthusiastic.

Failure to spot nonverbal signals makes it hard to communicate effectively.

Nonverbal communication takes place through gestures, expressions, posture, and even use of interpersonal space.

The ways we use **nonverbal communication** can also work for or against our communication effectiveness. It takes place through hand movements, facial expressions, body posture, eye contact, and the use of interpersonal space.[15] And it can be a powerful means of transmitting messages.

Research shows that up to 55% of a message's impact comes through nonverbal communication.[16] A good listener, for example, knows how to read the "body language" of a speaker while listening to the words being spoken. In fact, a potential side effect of the growing use of electronic media is that the added value of reading nonverbal signals, such as gestures, voice intonation, or eye movements, gets lost.

Think of how nonverbal signals play out in your own communications. A simple hand gesture, for example, can show whether someone is positive or negative, excited or bored, or even engaged or disengaged while interacting with you.[17] Sometimes our body may be "talking" even as we otherwise maintain silence. And when we do speak, our body may "say" different things than our words convey. This is called a **mixed message**, when a person's words communicate one thing while his or her nonverbal actions communicate something else.

A **mixed message** results when words communicate one message while actions, body language, or appearance communicates something else.

Status differences make it hard to communicate effectively.

The risk of ineffective communication is high when people are communicating upward in organizations—with their boss in particular. Haven't you heard people say things like this? "Criticize my boss? I'd get fired." "It's her company, not mine." "I can't tell him that; he'll just get mad at me."

We have to be realistic; the hierarchy of authority is always a potential barrier to effective communication between lower and higher levels in organizations. It causes a tendency known as **filtering**—the intentional distortion of information to make it appear favorable to the recipient. You know this as "telling the boss or instructor what he or she wants to hear." And it's more common than many people think. Consultant Tom Peters calls it "Management Enemy Number 1." He also says that "once you become a boss you will never hear the unadulterated truth again."[18]

Whether caused by fear of retribution for bringing bad news, an unwillingness to identify personal mistakes, or just a general desire to please, the end result of filtering is the same. Lower levels "cleanse" the information sent to higher levels. Then the higher levels, although well intentioned, make poor decisions because the information used is inaccurate or incomplete.

⫴ Physical distractions make it hard to communicate effectively.

Don't neglect how *physical distractions* can disrupt communication. Have you ever tried to talk with someone—perhaps your boss—about an important matter, only to have that conversation interrupted by phone calls? Any number of distractions, from drop-in visitors to instant messages to ringing cell phones, can interfere with the effectiveness of a communication attempt. Some of these distractions are evident in the following conversation between an employee, George, and his manager.[19]

> Okay, George, let's hear your problem [phone rings, boss picks it up, promises to deliver a report "just as soon as I can get it done"]. Uh, now, where were we—oh, you're having a problem with your technician. She's [manager's secretary brings in some papers that need his immediate signature; secretary leaves]—you say she's overstressed lately, wants to leave. I tell you what, George, why don't you [phone rings again, lunch partner drops by], uh, take a stab at handling it yourself. I've got to go now.

Besides what may have been poor intentions in the first place, the manager in this example did not do a good job of communicating with George. This problem could easily have been avoided or at least minimized through proper planning. Adequate time should have been set aside for the meeting; instructions could have been given to avoid interruptions such as telephone calls and drop-in visitors. The big lesson here is: Plan ahead. When someone needs to communicate with you, set aside adequate time, choose the right location, and take steps to avoid interruptions—including turning the cell phone off.

Takeaway 15.2
What Are the Major Barriers to Effective Communication?

Terms to Define

Channel richness

Communication channel

Filtering

Mixed message

Noise

Nonverbal communication

Rapid Review

- Noise interferes with the effectiveness of communication.
- Poor choice of channels can reduce communication effectiveness.
- Poor written or oral expression can reduce communication effectiveness.
- Failure to accurately read nonverbal signals can reduce communication effectiveness.
- Filtering caused by status differences can reduce communication effectiveness.

Questions for Discussion

1. When is texting not an appropriate way to convey a message in a work situation?
2. If someone just isn't a good writer or speaker, what can he or she do to improve communication skills?
3. How can a higher-level manager avoid the problem of filtering when lower-level staffers pass information upward to her?

Be Sure You Can

- list common sources of noise that can interfere with effective communication
- discuss how the choice of channels influences communication effectiveness
- give examples of poor language choices in written and oral expression
- clarify the notion of mixed messages and how nonverbals affect communication
- explain how filtering operates in upward communication

What Would You Do?

As the senior member of your work team, the other members have come to you and pointed out that there is no possibility that they can complete the current project on time. In fact, they expect to be at least two weeks late. This is a "pet" project for your boss, and your understanding is that she has a lot riding on its success for her career advancement. She is aloof and very formal in her dealings with you. Now you're in the middle. What actions will you take and why?

Takeaway 15.3
How Can We Improve Communication with People at Work?

ANSWERS TO COME

- Active listening helps people say what they really mean.
- Constructive feedback is specific, timely, and relevant.
- Office spaces can be designed to encourage interaction and communication.
- Transparency and openness ensure that accurate information is shared.
- Appropriate use of technology can facilitate more and better communication.
- Sensitivity and etiquette can improve cross-cultural communication.

COMMUNICATION! MOST OF US PROBABLY GET IT RIGHT SOME OF THE TIME BUT also make our fair share of mistakes. That's what happened to Richard Herlich. Before participating in workshops held at the Center for Creative Leadership, or CCL,[20] he said: "I thought I had the perfect style." But in feedback sessions following role-playing exercises, he learned that wasn't how others saw him. He was actually perceived as aloof and a poor communicator. Back on his new job as a director of marketing, Richard made it a point to meet with his team, discuss his style, and become more involved in their projects.

With so much room for error, don't you wonder how we ever communicate effectively? Fortunately, there are a number of things we can do to give things the best possible chance. They include active listening, constructive use of feedback, opening upward communication channels, understanding the use of space, utilizing technology, and valuing diversity.

⦀ Active listening helps people say what they really mean.

When people talk, they are trying to communicate something. That "something" may or may not be what they are saying. This is why managers must be so good at listening. According to the late John Wooden, legendary UCLA men's basketball coach, "Many leaders don't listen. We'd all be a lot wiser if we listened more—not just hearing the words, but listening and not thinking about what you are going to say."[21]

Active listening is the process of taking action to help others say what they really mean.[22] It requires being sincere while listening to someone, and trying to find the full meaning of a message. It also involves being disciplined, controlling one's emotions, and withholding premature evaluations that turn off rather than turn on the other party's willingness to communicate.

Active listening helps the source of a message say what he or she really means.

The contrast in how a "passive" listener and an "active" listener might act is shown in these alternative workplace conversations.

Question 1: "Don't you think employees should be promoted on the basis of seniority?"

Passive listener's response: "No, I don't!"

Active listener's response: "It seems to you that they should, I take it?"

Question 2: "What does the supervisor expect us to do about these out-of-date computers?"

>*Passive listener's response:* "Do the best you can, I guess."
>
>*Active listener's response:* "You're pretty disgusted with those machines, aren't you?"

The prior examples help show how active listening can facilitate communication in difficult circumstances, rather than discourage it. But it isn't easy to do. As you think further about active listening skills, keep these rules in mind.[23]

1. *Listen for message content:* Try to hear exactly what content is being conveyed in the message.
2. *Listen for feelings:* Try to identify how the source feels about the content in the message.
3. *Respond to feelings:* Let the source know that her or his feelings are being recognized.
4. *Note all cues:* Be sensitive to nonverbal and verbal messages; be alert for mixed messages.
5. *Paraphrase and restate:* State back to the source what you think you are hearing.

⦀ Constructive feedback is specific, timely, and relevant.

When Lydia Whitfield was a marketing vice president at Avaya, she was surprised when she asked one of her managers for feedback. He said: "You're angry a lot." Whitfield learned that "What he and other employees saw as my anger, I saw as my passion."[24]

Feedback is the process of telling other people how you feel about something they did or said, or about the situation in general. And, like active listening, the art of giving feedback is an indispensable skill. When poorly given, critical feedback can easily come off as threatening and create more resentment than positive action. When feedback is well delivered (see Tips), however, the receiver is more likely to listen and carefully consider the message.[25]

> **Feedback** is the process of telling someone else how you feel about something that person did or said.

{ WHEN WE TRY TO GIVE FEEDBACK, NOT EVERYONE WANTS TO LISTEN.

Tips to Remember

■ HOW TO GIVE CONSTRUCTIVE FEEDBACK

- *Choose the right time*—Give feedback at a time when the receiver seems most willing or able to accept it.
- *Be genuine*—Give feedback directly and with real feeling, based on trust between you and the receiver.
- *Be specific*—Make feedback specific rather than general; use clear and recent examples to make points.

- *Stick to the essentials*—Make sure the feedback is valid; limit it to things the receiver can be expected to do something about.
- *Keep it manageable*—Give feedback in small doses; never give more than the receiver can handle at any particular time.

‖ Office spaces can be designed to encourage interaction and communication.

Look at the following figures and think about your office and those of persons you often visit. What messages do the layouts and furnishings send to visitors? It's not only individual offices that count in this respect. Architects and consultants help executives build entire office spaces that are conducive to the intense, multilevel, and cross-functional communications desired today.

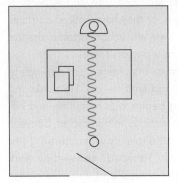

"I am the boss!"

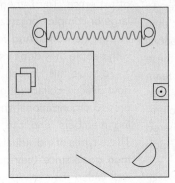

"I am the boss, but let's talk"

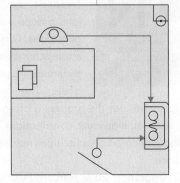

"Forget I'm the boss, let's talk"

The way we use space, **proxemics**, is an important but sometimes neglected influence on communication.[26] We know that physical distance between people conveys varying intentions in terms of intimacy, openness, and status as they communicate with one another. But we might not be as sensitive to how the physical layout of an office can do the same things.

When former Google executive Tim Armstrong became CEO of AOL, for example, one of his first decisions was to remove the glass doors separating the executive offices from other workers. The only way to open them previously had been with a company key card.[27] And at b&a advertising in Dublin, Ohio, "open space" supports the small ad agency's emphasis on creativity; after all, its Web address is www.babrain.com. Face-to-face communication is the rule to the point where internal e-mail among employees is banned at b&a. There are no offices or cubicles, and all office equipment is portable. Desks have wheels so that informal meetings can happen by people repositioning themselves for spontaneous collaboration. Even the formal meetings are held "standing up" in the company kitchen.[28]

> **Proxemics** is the study of the way we use space.

‖ Transparency and openness ensure that accurate and timely information is shared.

HCL Industries is a large technology outsourcing firm. CEO Vineet Nayar believes that one of his most important tasks is to create a "culture of trust." And to do that, he says, you have to create transparency. At HCL this means that the firm's financial information is fully posted on the internal Web site. Nayar says "We put all the dirty linen on the table." Transparency also means that the results of 360° feedback reviews for HCL's 3,800 managers, including Nayar's, are posted on the internal Web site. And when managers present plans to the top management team, Nayar insists that they get posted too so that others can read and comment

Manager's Library

■ *COLLABORATION* BY MORTEN HANSEN

IS THE SUM OF THE PARTS GREATER THAN THE WHOLE?

Human beings are social creatures and prefer to join groups rather than go it alone. Organizations attempt to capture these dynamics using team goals. The results can sometimes be impressive, but the process is often problematic. Ideally, the sum of individual contributions gathered through sharing should exceed any outcomes reached by individuals working alone.

In the book *Collaboration* (2009, Harvard Business Press), author Morten Hansen suggests that group efforts often fail and are more costly than their results justify. He thinks managers assign collaborative projects too frivolously since there is a belief that teamwork is always better than individual assignment. But it isn't, and can be costly to organizations in terms of time, expense, and lost productivity. His research finds that "good collaboration" is possible under the proper conditions and can improve sales, reduce costs, and enhance efficiency in organizations. Managers must recognize the barriers that prevent beneficial team interactions and work to overcome them.

Hansen lists four communication problems for team members. First, individuals are hesitant to reach out to others for help since they believe in self-reliance. Second, people are unwilling to help others since they fear it will diminish their power of expertise. Third, members are unable to find experts in large or complex organizations, or they have limited contacts in their networks. And four, they are uncomfortable sharing with people they don't know on a personal level.

To solve this Hansen believes managers must appreciate how difficult collaboration is and limit its use. He thinks improved organizational sharing begins with recruiting and hiring members who can overcome communication barriers. These types of individuals are able to unify with others in common goals since they possess "T-shaped" skills—they work well within their discipline (the vertical bar), but also across other disciplines (the horizontal bar). Managers can also encourage members to build and use personal networks within the organization to alleviate discomfort. Collaborative results should then sum to greater values than individual outcomes.

REFLECT AND REACT

How have the four communication barriers affected teams that you've been on? Would it have been possible to select members that wouldn't have had these problems? Why is it that team projects in a course can create problems or generate poor results compared with individual projects?

Communication transparency involves being honest and openly sharing accurate and complete information.

In open-book management managers provide employees with essential financial information about their employers.

on them. Why? By the time a plan is approved, it's likely to be a good one, because of the "massive collaborative learning that took place."[29]

Communication transparency involves being honest and openly sharing accurate and complete information about the organization and workplace affairs. It's absence is evident when managers try to hide such information and restrict the access of organizational members to it. Whereas lack of transparency creates conditions for distrust and harmful rumor, full transparency may have a positive impact on trust and employee engagement.

Transparency and openness in communication is a characteristic of **open-book management,** where managers provide employees with essential financial information about their companies. This willingness to open the books was evident in the HCL Industries example. At Bailard, Inc., a private investment firm, openness extends to salaries. If you want to know what others are making at the firm, all you need to do is ask the chief financial officer. The firm's co-founder and CEO Thomas Bailard says this approach is a good way to defeat office politics. "As a manager," he says, "if you know that your compensation decisions are essentially going to be public, you have to have pretty strong convictions about any decision you make."[30]

Underground Boss Opens Communication Channels

CEO Stephen Martin "went underground" at a firm in England for two weeks. He posed with an assumed name as an office worker and kept his ears and eyes open wide while going about his daily work. After the experience, Martin said: "They (workers) said things to me that they never would have told their manager". . . . "Our key messages were just not getting through to people" . . . "We were asking the impossible of some of them." But when he shared these concerns with the firm's managers, the response was: "They never told us that!"

⫴ Appropriate use of technology can facilitate more and better communication.

Knowing how and when to use e-mail, text messaging, and social networking is now a top issue in workplace communications. But the goal always has to be appropriate—not inappropriate—use. "Thnx for the IView! I Wud Luv to Work 4 U!!;)" may be quite understandable "textspeak" for some people, but it isn't the follow-up message that most employers like to receive from job candidates.[31]

When Tory Johnson, President of Women for Hire Inc., received a thank-you note by e-mail from an intern candidate, it included "hiya," "thanx," three exclamation points—"!!!," and two emoticons ☹ ☺. She says: "That e-mail just ruined it for me." The risk of everyday shorthand in e-mails and texting is that we become too casual overall in its use, forgetting that how a message is received is in large part determined by the receiver. Even though textspeak and emoticons are the norm in social networks, for example, staffing executives at KPMG, which hires hundreds of new college grads and interns each year, consider them "not professional."

Communication technology has created another force to be reckoned with—the **electronic grapevine**. Electronic messages fly with speed and intensity around organizations and the Internet at large, assisted by blogs, chat rooms, tweets, and more. The results can be functional when the information is accurate and useful, but dysfunctional when the information is false, distorted, malicious, or rumor based.

Not too long ago a YouTube video appeared showing two Domino's Pizza employees doing all sorts of nasty things to sandwiches they were making for delivery. It went viral, and Domino's faced a crisis of customer confidence. Although the video was pulled by one of its creators—who apologized for "faking" how they worked—both employees were fired. But negative chat had already spread around the Internet, and the Domino's brand was damaged. The firm's management finally created a Twitter account to present its own view of the situation and posted a YouTube video message from the CEO.[32]

Millennial text to Baby Boomer:

Omg sorry abt mtg nbd 4 now b rdy nxt time g2g ttl

Baby Boomer text to Millennial:

Missed you at meeting. It was important. Don't forget next one. Stop by office.

The **electronic grapevine** uses computer technologies to transmit information around informal networks inside and outside of organizations.

{ 65% OF EMPLOYERS BLOCK SOME WEBSITES
FROM INTERNAL VIEWING.

Facts to Consider

■ EMPLOYEES SHOULD WORRY ABOUT ELECTRONIC MONITORING

An American Management Association survey of 304 U.S. companies found the following:

- 66% monitor Internet connections.
- 65% block Web sites: pornography (96%), games (61%), social networking (61%), shopping/auction (27%), and sports (21%).
- 45% track keystrokes and keyboard time.
- 43% store and review computer files.
- 43% monitor e-mail.
- 45% monitor telephone time and numbers dialed.

- >25% have fired employees for misuse of e-mail.
- >30% have fired employees for misuse of the Internet.

YOUR THOUGHTS?

Is this type of employer "snooping" justified? What boundaries should be set on employer invasion of employee privacy? Is there anything special about the fact that in the advertising industry the majority of executives thought personal Web surfing was alright?

When the CEO of Facebook, Mark Zuckerberg, says that privacy is "no longer a social norm," it's time to take the issue very seriously in personal affairs and at work. Employers are concerned that too much work time gets spent with personal texting, Web browsing, and social networking.[33] Employees are concerned that employers are eavesdropping, but they can also be casual and inappropriate in how they act and what they put out on the Web. Consider this tweet that became an Internet sensation: "Cisco just offered me a job! Now I have to weigh the utility of a fatty paycheck against the daily commute to San Jose and hating the work."[34] What would you do if you were the recruiter who had just made this job offer?

The best advice on electronic privacy is still pretty simple and well worth remembering. Don't ever assume you have it, and act accordingly.

⫴ Sensitivity and etiquette can improve cross-cultural communication.

After taking over as the first American to be CEO of the Dutch publisher Wolters Kluwer, Nancy McKinstry initiated major changes—cutting staff, restructuring divisions, and investing in new business areas. She first described the new strategy as "aggressive" in speaking with her management team. But after learning the word wasn't well received by Europeans, she switched to "decisive."[35] "I was coming across as too harsh, too much of a results-driven American to the people I needed to get on board," says McKinstry. It was a nice lesson in cross-cultural communication.

Without a doubt cultural differences are a ready source of potential problems in communication. But keep in mind that you don't have be doing international business or taking a foreign vacation for this point to be relevant. Think about it—going to work, to class, and out to shop is a cross-cultural journey for most of us today.

You should recall that **ethnocentrism** is a major source of intercultural difficulties. It is the tendency to consider one's culture superior to any and all others. Any such tendencies can hurt cross-cultural communication in at least three ways. First, they may cause someone to not listen well to what others have to say. Second, they may cause someone to address or speak with others in ways that alienate them. And third, they may involve use of inappropriate stereotypes.

Just recognizing tendencies toward ethnocentrism is helpful. You can spot it in conversations as arrogance in tone, manners, gestures, and words. But success in cross-cultural communication also takes sensitivity and a willingness to learn about how different people see, do, and interpret things. This involves **cultural etiquette**, the use of appropriate manners, language, and behaviors when communicating with people from other cultures.

Knowing the etiquette helps us avoid basic cross-cultural mistakes. Messages can easily get lost in translation, as advertising miscues often demonstrate. A Pepsi ad in Taiwan that intended to say "the Pepsi generation" came out as "Pepsi will bring your ancestors back from the dead." A KFC ad in China intended to convey "finger lickin' good" came out as "eat your fingers off."[36] Nonverbals are important too. The American "thumbs-up" sign is an insult in Ghana and Australia. Signaling "okay" with thumb and forefinger circled together is not okay in parts of Europe. Whereas we wave "hello" with an open palm, in West Africa it's an insult suggesting the other person has five fathers.[37]

> **Ethnocentrism** is the tendency to consider one's culture superior to any and all others.

> **Cultural etiquette** is use of appropriate manners and behaviors in cross-cultural situations.

Sample Cultural Variations in Nonverbal Communications

- *Eye movements* (*oculesics*)—Chinese and Japanese may show anger only in their eyes, a point often missed by Westerners.
- *Touching* (*haptics*)—Asian cultures typically dislike touching behaviors; Latin cultures tend to use them in communicating.
- *Body motions* (*kinesics*)—Gestures, shrugs, and blushes can mean different things; "thumbs up" means "A-OK" in America but is vulgar in the Middle East.

{ SHE SAYS THAT SHE WAS "DOOCED"—A TERM USED TO DESCRIBE BEING FIRED FOR WHAT ONE WRITES IN A BLOG.

Ethics Check

■ IN FRANCE, IT'S BLOGGERS BEWARE

It is easy and tempting to set up your own blog, write about your experiences and impressions, and then share your thoughts with others online. So, why not do it?

Catherine Sanderson, a British citizen living and working in Paris, might have asked this question before launching her blog, *Le Petite Anglaise*. At one point it was so "successful" that she had 3,000 readers. But, the Internet diary included reports on her experiences at work—and her employer wasn't happy when it became public knowledge.

Even though Sanderson was blogging anonymously, her photo was on the site, and the connection was eventually discovered. Noticed, too, was her running commentary about bosses, colleagues, and life at the office. One boss,

she wrote, "calls secretaries 'typists.'" A Christmas party was described in detail, including an executive's "unforgivable faux pas."

It's all out now and Sanderson is upset. She says that she was "dooced"—a term used to describe being fired for what one writes in a blog. She wants financial damages and confirmation of her rights, on principle, to have a private blog.

YOU DECIDE

Just what are the ethics issues here—from the blogger's and the employer's perspectives? What rights do workers have when it comes to communicating in public about their work experiences and impressions?

STUDY GUIDE

Takeaway 15.3
How Can We Improve Communication with People at Work?

Terms to Define

Active listening

Communication transparency

Cultural etiquette

Electronic grapevine

Ethnocentrism

Feedback

Open-book management

Proxemics

Rapid Review

- Active listening, through reflecting back and paraphrasing, can help overcome barriers and improve communication.
- Organizations can design and use office architecture and physical space to improve communication.
- Information technology, such as e-mail, instant messaging, and intranets, can improve communication in organizations, but it must be well used.
- Ethnocentrism, a feeling of cultural superiority, can interfere with cross-cultural communication; with sensitivity and cultural etiquette it can be improved.

Questions for Discussion

1. Which rules for active listening do you think most people break?
2. Is transparency in communications a sure winner, or could a manager have problems with it?
3. How could you redesign your office space, or that of your instructor or boss, to make it more communication-friendly?

Be Sure You Can

- role play the practice of active listening
- list the rules for giving constructive feedback
- explain how space design influences communication
- identify ways technology utilization influences communication
- explain the concept of cultural etiquette

What Would You Do?

The restaurant you own and manage is being hit hard by a bad economy. The number of customers is down, as is the amount of the average dinner bill. Previously you've maintained a staff of 12, but it's obvious that you're going to have to cut back so that the payroll covers no more than 8. One of the staff has just told you that someone is tweeting that the restaurant is going to close its doors after the weekend. Everyone is "buzzing" about the news. How do you deal with this situation?

TestPrep 15

Multiple-Choice Questions

1. Who is responsible for encoding a message in the communication process?

    (a) sender

    (b) receiver

    (c) observer

    (d) consultant

2. Issues of "respect" and "integrity" are associated with _____ in communication.

    (a) noise

    (b) filtering

    (c) credibility

    (d) ethnocentrism

3. Which is the best example of a supervisor making feedback descriptive rather than evaluative?

    (a) You are a slacker.

    (b) You are not responsible.

    (c) You cause me lots of problems.

    (d) You have been late to work three days this month.

4. When interacting with an angry co-worker who is complaining about a work problem, a manager skilled at active listening would most likely try to _____.

    (a) suggest that the conversation be held at a better time

    (b) point out that the conversation would be better held at another location

    (c) express displeasure in agreement with the co-worker's complaint

    (d) rephrase the co-worker's complaint to encourage him to say more

5. When the intended meaning of the sender and the interpreted meaning of the receiver are the same, communication is _____.

    (a) effective   (b) persuasive

    (c) passive   (d) efficient

6. What happens when a communication is persuasive?

    (a) The receiver understands the message.

    (b) The sender feels good about the message.

    (c) The receiver acts as the sender intended.

    (d) The sender becomes a passive listener.

7. How can a manager build credibility for persuasive communications?

    (a) Make sure rewards for compliance with requests are clear.

    (b) Make sure penalties for noncompliance with requests are clear.

    (c) Make sure everyone knows who the boss is.

    (d) Make sure to establish good relationships with others.

8. One of the rules for giving constructive feedback is to make sure that it is always _____.

    (a) general rather than specific

    (b) indirect rather than direct

    (c) given in small doses

    (d) delivered at a time convenient for the sender

9. When a worker receives an e-mail memo from the boss with information about changes to his job assignment and ends up confused because he doesn't understand it, the boss has erred by making a bad choice of _____ for communicating the message.

    (a) words   (b) channels

    (c) nonverbals   (d) filters

10. The safest conclusion about privacy in electronic communications is _____.

    (a) it's guaranteed by law

    (b) it's not a problem

    (c) it really doesn't exist

    (d) it can be password protected

11. A/An _____ is higher in channel richness than a/an _____.

(a) memo; voice-mail

(b) letter; video conference

(c) instant message; e-mail

(d) voice mail; telephone conversation

12. The negative effects of status differences on communication between lower and higher levels in organizations show up in the form of _____.

(a) filtering

(b) MBWA

(c) ethnocentrism

(d) passive listening

13. A manager who understands the influence of proxemics in communication is likely to _____.

(a) avoid sending mixed messages

(b) arrange work spaces to encourage interaction

(c) be very careful choosing written words

(d) send frequent e-mail messages to team members

14. When a person's words say one thing but his or her body language suggests something quite different, the person is sending _____.

(a) a mixed message

(b) noise

(c) social capital

(d) destructive feedback

15. If a visitor to a foreign culture makes gestures commonly used at home even after learning that they are offensive to locals, the visitor can be described as _____.

(a) a passive listener

(b) ethnocentric

(c) more efficient than effective

(d) an active listener

Short-Response Questions

16. What is the goal of active listening?

17. Why do managers sometimes make bad decisions based on information received from their subordinates?

18. What are four errors managers might make when trying to give constructive feedback to others?

19. How does ethnocentrism influence cross-cultural communication?

Integration and Application Questions

20. Glenn was recently promoted to be the manager of a new store being opened by a large department store chain. He wants to start out right by making sure that communications are always good between him, the six department heads, and the 50 full-time and part-time sales associates. He knows he'll be making a lot of decisions in the new job, and he wants to be sure that he is always well informed about store operations. He always wants to make sure everyone is always "on the same page" about important priorities. Put yourself in Glenn's shoes.

Questions: What should Glenn do right from the start to ensure that he and the department managers communicate well with one another? How can he open up and maintain good channels of communication with the sales associates?

Steps*for*FurtherLearning

Many learning resources are found at the end of the book and online within WileyPLUS.

Don't Miss These Selections from the **Skill-Building Portfolio**

- **SELF-ASSESSMENT 15:** *Feedback and Assertiveness*
- **CLASS EXERCISE 15:** *Communication and Teamwork Dilemmas*
- **TEAM PROJECT 15:** *How Words Count*

Don't Miss This Selection from **Cases for Critical Thinking**

- **CHAPTER 15 CASE**
  Twitter: Redefining Communication

Snapshot Whether or not you tweet, there's no denying that Twitter's having a profound effect on the way we communicate with each other and the outside world.

Is the popular microblogging service reinventing communication or just abbreviating it? Do tweets contribute to the conversation or dumb it down?

Many social media researchers, sociologists, and corporate marketing experts are asking themselves the same question: Does Twitter enable effective communication, or is it a distraction?

"It adds a layer of information and connection to people's lives that wasn't there before," Evan Williams says. "It has the potential to be a really substantial part of how people keep in touch with each other."

Make notes here on what you've learned about yourself from this chapter.

- **LEARNING JOURNAL 15**

A day at work, a trip to the store, a visit with friends—all bring diversity into our lives. Even a walk across the college campus can be a trip around the world, if you're willing to take it.

Diversity and Global Cultures

16

There Are New Faces in the Neighborhood

Management Live

Diversity Maturity and *Finding Forrester*

Finding Forrester is an intriguing story about the relationship between an aging and reclusive Caucasian writer—William Forrester (Sean Connery), and a young African-American from the projects—Jamal Wallace (Rob Brown). Jamal first enters Forrester's apartment through a fire escape window. It is the fulfillment of a dare by friends. Forrester catches Wallace, who escapes by running out the front door. Later, they come face-to-face in the apartment when Wallace writes a 5,000-word essay to appease the reclusive tenant.

The two become fast friends, but only after Forrester tests Wallace's mettle by pretending to be racist. He is anything but that. But Wallace's literature professor, Robert Crawford (F. Murray Abraham), is racist. He finds it hard to believe that Wallace, a star athlete, can perform in the class as well as he does on the basketball court.

The roles of Forrester and Crawford provide excellent examples of differing levels of **diversity maturity,** the ability to respect and work with others who may be ethnically and culturally different. Personal attitudes and actions stem from our diversity maturity. When Forrester invites Wallace into his apartment it is clear he already trusts the young man. When Crawford refers to Wallace's "previous education" and "background," it is evident that he is biased.

Most of us have inherent bias. Give yourself a good honest self-check on diversity maturity. If the results are not what you hoped, begin to think about what you can do to improve.

YOUR CHAPTER 16 TAKEAWAYS

1. Understand what we need to know about diversity in the workplace.

2. Understand what we need to know about diversity among global cultures.

WHAT'S INSIDE

Explore Yourself
More on diversity maturity

Role Models
David Segura Is Hispanic Business Entrepreneur of the Year

Ethics Check
Fair-Trade Fashion

Facts to Consider
Employee morale varies around the world.

Manager's Library
Half the Sky by Nicholas D. Kristof and Sheryl WuDunn

Takeaway 16.1
What Should We Know About Diversity in the Workplace?

ANSWERS TO COME

- There is a business case for diversity.
- Inclusive organizational cultures value and support diversity.
- Organizational subcultures can create diversity challenges.
- Minorities and women suffer diversity bias in many situations.
- Managing diversity should be a top leadership priority.

IN CHAPTER 1 WE FIRST DISCUSSED DIVERSITY IN RESPECT TO AGE, RACE, ETHNICITY, gender, physical ability, and sexual orientation. A broad definition of workplace **diversity** would also include differences in such areas as religious beliefs, education, experience, family status, national cultures, and perhaps more.[1] In his book *Beyond Race and Gender,* diversity consultant R. Roosevelt Thomas Jr. goes so far as to say that "diversity includes everyone ... white males are as diverse as their colleagues."[2] He also says that diversity is good for organizations, a source of competitive advantage. Picture an organization whose diverse employees possess a mix of talents and perspectives, and reflect the firm's customers and clients. Wouldn't this be good for business?

> **Diversity** describes race, gender, age, and other individual differences.

⦀ There is a business case for diversity.

Research reported in the *Gallup Management Journal* shows that establishing a racially and ethnically inclusive workplace is good for morale. In a study of 2,014 American workers, those who felt included were more likely to stay with their employers and recommend them to others. Survey questions asked such things as "Do you always trust your company to be fair to all employees?" "At work, are all employees always treated with respect?" "Does your supervisor always make the best use of employees' skills?"[3] The New York research group Catalyst also reports that companies with a greater percentage of women on their boards outperform those whose boards have the lowest female representation.[4]

Studies and evidence like that just cited point toward what some call a strong "business case for diversity."[5] Thomas Kochan and his colleagues at MIT agree. But, they found in their research that the hoped-for advantages are gained only when managers make diversity a priority through training and supportive human resource practices.[6] They say:

> To be successful in working with and gaining value from diversity requires a sustained, systemic approach and long-term commitment. Success is facilitated by a perspective that considers diversity to be an opportunity for everyone in an organization to learn from each other how better to accomplish their work and an occasion that requires a supportive and cooperative organizational culture as well as group leadership and process skills that can facilitate effective group functioning.

Inclusive organizational cultures value and support diversity.

Just how do managers go about leveraging diversity in the workplace? Many organizations seem to be good or relatively good at attracting new employees of diverse backgrounds to join, but they aren't always successful in keeping them for the long term. This problem of high employee turnover among minorities and women has been called the *revolving door syndrome*.[7] It can reflect a lack of **inclusivity** in the employing organizations—the degree to which they are open to anyone who can perform a job, regardless of race, sexual preference, gender, or other diversity attribute.[8]

Look around. Think about how people are treating those who differ from themselves. What about your experiences at school and at work? Are you and others always treated with respect and inclusion? Or do you sense at times disrespect and exclusion?

The model for inclusivity is the **multicultural organization** that displays commitments to diversity like those in Table 16.1—*Characteristics of Multicultural Organizations*.[9] One such organization is Xerox, the first *Fortune* 500 firm to have an African-American woman, Ursula Burns, as CEO and also the first to have one woman succeed another as CEO. When praising Burns's appointment, Ilene Lang, head of the nonprofit Catalyst, which supports women in business, said: "Most companies have one woman who might be a possibility to become CEO; Xerox has a range of them." The firm has an Executive Diversity Council, runs diversity leadership programs, and evaluates managers on how well they recruit and develop employees from underrepresented groups. Harvard professor David Thomas says Xerox has "a culture where having women and people of color as candidates for powerful jobs has been going on for two decades."[10]

Inclusivity is how open the organization is to anyone who can perform a job.

A **multicultural organization** is based on pluralism and operates with inclusivity and respect for diversity.

Table 16.1 Characteristics of Multicultural Organizations

Pluralism—Members of minority and majority cultures influence key values and policies.

Structural integration—Minority-culture members are well represented at all levels and in all responsibilities.

Informal network integration—Mentoring and support groups assist career development of minority-culture members.

Absence of prejudice and discrimination—Training and task force activities support the goal of eliminating culture-group biases.

Minimum intergroup conflict—Members of minority and majority cultures avoid destructive conflicts.

Organizational subcultures can create diversity challenges.

We have to be realistic in facing up to the challenges in creating truly multicultural organizations. It isn't always easy to get the members of a workforce to really respect and work well with one another. One of the reasons is the existence of **organizational subcultures**, informal groupings of persons that form around such things as gender, age, race and ethnicity, and even job functions. People can get so caught up in their subcultures that they identify and interact mostly with others who are like themselves. They may develop tendencies toward **ethnocentrism**, acting in ways that suggest that their subculture is superior to all others. All of this creates diversity challenges that can make it harder for people to work well together.

Organizational subcultures are groupings of people based on shared demographic and job identities.

Ethnocentrism is the belief that one's membership group or subculture is superior to all others.

Occupational subcultures form among people doing the same kinds of work.

Occupational subcultures develop as people form shared identities around the work that they do. Some employees may consider themselves "systems people" who are very different from "those marketing people" and even more different still from "those finance people." Even at school, in course project groups, have you noticed how students tend to identify with their majors? Don't some look down on others they consider to be pursuing "easy" majors and view their majors as the superior ones?

Ethnic or national subcultures form among people from the same races, language groupings, regions, and nations.

Differences in **ethnic or national subcultures** exist among people from various races, language groups, regions, and countries. And as we all know, it can sometimes be hard to work well with persons whose backgrounds are very different from our own. The best understanding is most likely gained through direct contact and from being open-minded. Although one may speak in everyday conversations about "African-American" or "Latino" or "Anglo" cultures, one has to wonder: Are these subcultures truly understood?[11] If improved cross-cultural understandings can help people work better across national boundaries, how can we create the same understandings to help people from different racial subcultures work better together?

Gender subcultures form among people of the same gender.

Gender subcultures form from shared identities among persons of the same gender. Some research shows, for example, that when men work together the subculture reflects a competitive atmosphere. Sports metaphors are common, and games and stories often deal with winning and losing.[12] When women work together, a rather different subculture may form with more emphasis on personal relationships and collaboration.[13]

Generational subcultures form among people in similar age groups.

Age is the basis for **generational subcultures** in organizations.[14] Harris and Conference Board polls report that younger workers tend to be more dissatisfied

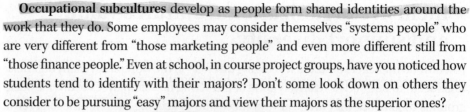

{ "... A COMPANY IS AT ITS BEST WHEN IT FULLY UTILIZES THE TALENTS OF ALL BACKGROUNDS AND ETHNICITIES."

Role Models

■ DAVID SEGURA IS HISPANIC BUSINESS ENTREPRENEUR OF THE YEAR

David Segura grew up in a family of executives. His grandparents were Mexican immigrants, finding work in the automotive industry, and his father worked at Ford Motor Company. And after graduating from the University of Michigan–Dearborn with a degree in computer science he, too, joined Ford. But Segura wanted more—a business of his own.

After doing some IT consulting, Segura founded VisionIT Inc., with $100 and one client. Today his firm is a $225+ million company serving many Fortune 500 clients. It provides IT staffing, managed services, and consulting services based on what Segura calls the FAST approach—**f**ocused on clients, **a**gile, **s**treamlined, and rich with **t**alented people. About being successful in the technology industry, where Hispanics are not well represented, Segura says: "VisionIT is a firm of much diversity and we are showing that a company is at its best when it fully utilizes the talents of all backgrounds and ethnicities."

Hispanic Business magazine named Segura its Hispanic Entrepreneur of the Year, based on the success of his firm and

his commitment to the community. When accepting the award, he said it was a "truly humbling experience" and thanked the VisionIT team "whose shared vision and commitment made this day possible." Segura has also received the Ernst & Young Entrepreneur of the Year award.

When Segura became an entrepreneur he saw it as a way to have a positive impact on society. He continues to pursue that impact not only by running a successful large business, but also by helping young people enter the world of IT through college scholarships and company internships.

WHAT'S THE LESSON HERE?

David Segura is a great example of entrepreneurial success, and he's also a role model for younger members of the Hispanic and minority communities. He has succeeded in an industry that isn't well represented by Hispanics, showing that cultural diversity can be a real business advantage. How good are you at embracing such diversity and engaging people of different cultures?

than older workers.[15] They are also described as more short-term oriented, giving higher priority to work-life balance, and expecting to hold several jobs during their careers.[16] Imagine the conflicts that can occur when members of todays college generation go to work for older managers who grew up with quite different life experiences and even values. Have you had a conflict with a parent, perhaps over a lifestyle or authority issue, that might foreshadow similar ones you might encounter at work someday?

⫾ Minorities and women suffer diversity bias in many situations.

The term "diversity" basically means the presence of differences, and that's potentially challenging in its own right. But diversity issues in organizations are further complicated because such differences and subcultures are often distributed unequally in the power structure. Let's be honest. Most senior executives in large businesses are still older, white, and male. There is more diversity among lower and middle levels of most organizations than at the top. And for some women and minority workers, the **glass ceiling** depicted in Figure 16.1 can be a real barrier to career advancement.[17]

The **glass ceiling** is a hidden barrier to the advancement of women and minorities.

Minorities and women can face diversity challenges that range from misunderstandings, to lack of sensitivity, to glass ceiling limitations, to outright job discrimination and various types of harassment. Data from the U.S. Equal Employment Opportunity Commission (EEOC), for example, report that sex discrimination is a factor in an increasing number of bias suits filed by workers. Sexual harassment in the form of unwanted sexual advances, requests for sexual favors, and sexually laced communications is another problem. One survey found some 45% of minority respondents had experienced abuse as targets of offensive jokes and conversations in the workplace. The EEOC also reports an increase in filings of pregnancy and pay discrimination complaints. A senior executive expressed her surprise upon finding out that the top performer in her work group, an African-American male, was paid 25% less than anyone else. This wasn't because his pay had been cut to that level; it was because his pay increases had always trailed those given to white co-workers. The differences added up significantly over time, but no one noticed or stepped forward to make the adjustment.[18]

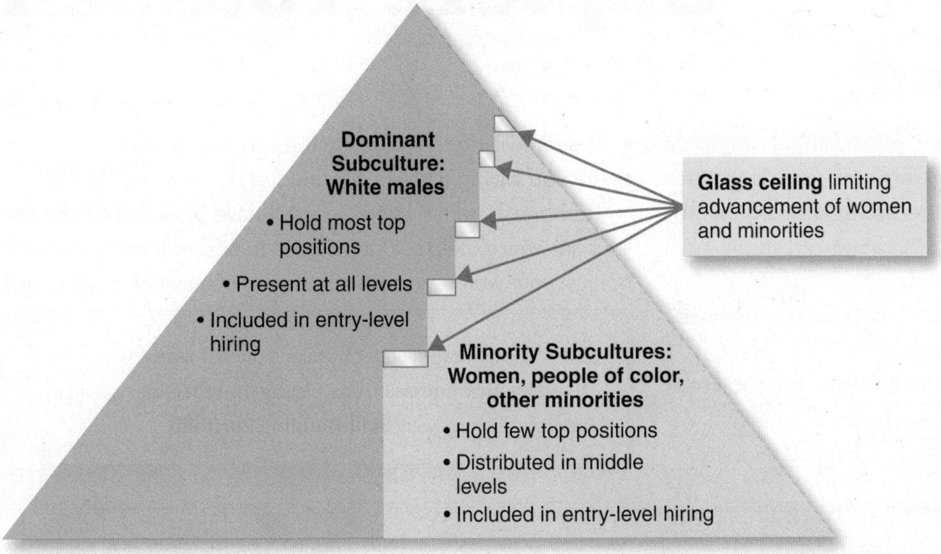

FIGURE 16.1
How Do Glass Ceilings Constrain Career Advancement for Women and Minorities? Organizations consist of a majority culture (often white males) and minority cultures (including women, people of color, and other minorities). It is likely that members of the majority culture will dominate higher management levels. One of the potential consequences is a "glass ceiling" effect that, although not publicized, acts as a barrier that sometimes makes it hard for women and minorities to advance and gain entry into higher management ranks.

Dominant Subculture: White males
• Hold most top positions
• Present at all levels
• Included in entry-level hiring

Glass ceiling limiting advancement of women and minorities

Minority Subcultures: Women, people of color, other minorities
• Hold few top positions
• Distributed in middle levels
• Included in entry-level hiring

Biculturalism is when minority members adopt characteristics of majority cultures in order to succeed.

People respond to bad treatment at work in different ways. Some may challenge the system by filing complaints, pursuing harassment and discrimination charges, or taking legal action. Some may quit to look for better positions elsewhere or to pursue self-employment opportunities. Some may try to "fit in," to adapt through **biculturalism** by displaying majority culture characteristics that seem necessary to succeed in the work environment. For example, gays, lesbians, bisexuals, and transgenders might hide their sexual orientations and gender identities; an African-American or Hispanic manager might avoid using words or phrases that white colleagues would consider subculture slang; a woman might use football or baseball metaphors in conversations with men to gain acceptance into male-dominated career networks.

‖ Managing diversity should be a top leadership priority.

What can leaders and managers do so that people under their care are treated inclusively? The answer begins with a willingness to recognize that, regardless of their backgrounds, most workers want the same things. They want respect for their talents; they want to be fairly treated; they want to be able to work to the best of their abilities; they want to achieve their full potential. Meeting these expectations requires the best in diversity leadership.

The small figure describes what R. Roosevelt Thomas calls a continuum of leadership approaches to diversity.[19] At one end is *affirmative action*. Here, leadership commits the organization to hiring and advancing minorities and women. You might think of this as advancing diversity by increasing the representation of diverse members in the organization's workforce. But this is only a partial solution, and the revolving door syndrome may

Affirmative Action
Create upward mobility for minorities and women

Valuing Differences
Build quality relationships with respect for diversity

Managing Diveristy
Achieve full utilization of diverse human resources

{ ARE YOU WILLING TO COPE WITH TENSIONS
IN ADDRESSING DIVERSITY?

Explore Yourself

■ DIVERSITY MATURITY

Today's organizations and the nature of our global workforce demand **diversity maturity** from anyone who is serious about career success. Being mature about diversity means being able to answer a confident "yes" to questions such as these:

- Do you accept responsibility for improving your performance?
- Do you understand diversity concepts?
- Do you make decisions about others based on their abilities?
- Do you understand that diversity issues are complex?
- Are you able to cope with tensions in addressing diversity?

- Are you willing to challenge the way things are?
- Are you willing to learn continuously?

Be honest; admit where you still have work left to do. Use your answers to help set future goals to ensure that your actions, not just your words, consistently display positive diversity values.

Get to know yourself better by taking the self-assessment on **Diversity Awareness** and completing the other activities in the *Exploring Management* **Skill-Building Portfolio**.

New Continent Attracts Walmart Global Giant

Dear Walmart: "Welcome to South Africa."

When Walmart closed the deal to buy 51% ownership of South Africa's Massmart, it joined forces with an established and successful retailer. And the decision was strategic. "The more we learn about South Africa and the surrounding countries, the more we are convinced that this is an important region with attractive growth characteristics," says Doug McMillon, head of Walmart International. It's a belief confirmed by Massmart's local record. "Yeah, people here love it," says one of the store's sales persons, "by midday there is a stampede through the doors."

Massmart operates 288 stores, mostly in South Africa but also in 14 other southern African countries. The firm has prospered from a growing middle class and an acceptance by locals of the "shopping mall" experience. Walmart hopes to join right in. But the firm also plans to find the right fit with African cultures with the assistance of its local partner. All expectations are that the local management will be retained and valued.

CEO Grant Pattison says Massmart will operate with regional sensitivity. This means that Walmart's corporate culture, which originated in founder Sam Walton's hometown of Bentonville, Arkansas, will have some adapting to do. "Not everyone comes in the morning and does the rah-rah thing," says Pattison. "Not everyone does the Walmart cheer."

FIND INSPIRATION

It's a long way from Arkansas to South Africa, and it's a big step across cultures. But that's the nature of business these days, and we all have to be prepared to work well across diverse cultural boundaries. How experienced are you at cross-cultural relationships, whether in the neighborhood or while traveling? What do you need to know to succeed in a globally connected world of work?

even negate some of its positive impact. Thomas says that the "assumption is that once you get representation, people will assimilate. But we're actually seeing that people are less willing to assimilate than ever before."[20]

A step beyond affirmative action is what Thomas calls *valuing diversity*. Here, a leader commits the organization to education and training programs designed to help people better understand and respect differences. The goal is to teach people of diverse backgrounds more about one another and how to work well together. Thomas says this training should help us deal with "similarities, differences and tensions." And it should help us answer a fundamental question: "Can I work with people who are qualified that are not like me?"[21]

The final step in Thomas's continuum is **managing diversity**. A leader who actively manages diversity is always seeking ways to make an organization truly multicultural and inclusive—and keep it that way. For example, Eastman Kodak has been praised by *Business Ethics* magazine for "leading-edge anti-discrimination policies toward gay, bisexual, and transgender employees." It has also received a perfect score from the Human Rights Campaign for its efforts to end sexual discrimination.[22]

As pointed out earlier regarding the business case for diversity, Thomas argues quite forcibly that leaders have a performance incentive to embrace managing diversity.[23] A diverse workforce offers a rich pool of talents, ideas, and viewpoints that can help solve complex problems. A diverse workforce also aligns well with needs and expectations of diverse customers and stakeholders.[24] Michael R. Losey, former president of the Society for Human Resource Management (SHRM), says, "Companies must realize that the talent pool includes people of all types, including older workers; persons with disabilities; persons of various religious, cultural, and national backgrounds; persons who are not heterosexual; minorities; and women."[25]

Managing diversity is building an inclusive work environment that allows everyone to reach his or her potential.

STUDY GUIDE

Takeaway 16.1
What Should We Know About Diversity in the Workplace?

Terms to Define

Biculturalism

Diversity

Ethnic or national subcultures

Ethnocentrism

Gender subcultures

Generational subcultures

Glass ceiling

Inclusivity

Managing diversity

Multicultural organization

Occupational subcultures

Organizational subcultures

Rapid Review

- Workforce diversity can improve business performance by expanding the talent pool of the organization and establishing better understandings of customers and stakeholders.
- Inclusivity is a characteristic of multicultural organizations that values and respects diversity of their members.
- Organizational subcultures, including those based on occupational, functional, ethnicity, nationality, age, and gender differences, can create diversity challenges.
- Minorities and women can suffer diversity bias in such forms as job and pay discrimination, sexual harassment, and the glass ceiling effect.
- A top leadership priority should be managing diversity to develop an inclusive work environment within which everyone is able to reach their full potential.

Questions for Discussion

1. What subcultures do you see operating at work and/or in school, and how do they affect relationships and daily events?
2. What are some of the things organizations and leaders can do to reduce diversity bias faced by minorities and women in the workplace?
3. What does the existence of an affirmative action policy say about an organization's commitment to diversity?

Be Sure You Can

- identify major diversity trends in American society
- explain the business case for diversity
- explain the concept of inclusivity
- list characteristics of multicultural organizations
- identify subcultures common to organizations
- discuss the types of employment problems faced by minorities and women
- explain Thomas's concept of managing diversity

What Would You Do?

One of your co-workers brought along his friend to lunch. When discussing his new female boss, the friend says: "It really irritates me not only that she gets the job just because she's a woman, but she's also Hispanic. There's no way that someone like me had a chance given her pedigree. And she now has the gall to act as if we're all one big happy team and the rest of us should accept her leadership. As for me, I'll do my best to make it difficult for her to succeed." It was uncomfortable for you just to hear this. Your co-worker looks dismayed but isn't saying anything. What do you do? Just let the comment go, or something more?

Takeaway 16.2
What Should We Know About Diversity Among Global Cultures?

ANSWERS TO COME

- Culture shock comes from discomfort in cross-cultural situations.
- Cultural intelligence is the capacity to adapt to foreign cultures.
- The "silent" languages of cultures include context, time, and space.
- Hofstede identifies five value differences among national cultures.
- Country clusters show cultural differences.

A TRIP TO THE GROCERY STORE, A DAY SPENT AT WORK, A VISIT TO OUR CHILDREN'S schools—all are possible opportunities for us to have cross-cultural experiences. And you have to admit, there are a lot of new faces in the neighborhood. At my university even a walk across campus can be a trip around the world, but we have to be willing to take it. How about you? Do you greet, speak with, and actively engage people of other cultures? Or are you shy, hesitant, and even inclined to avoid them?[26]

‖ Culture shock comes from discomfort in cross-cultural situations.

Maybe it is a bit awkward to introduce yourself to an international student or foreign visitor to your community. Maybe the appearance of a Muslim woman in a headscarf or a Nigerian man in a long overblouse is unusual to the point of being intimidating. Maybe, too, when we do meet or work with someone from another culture, we experience something well known to international travelers as **culture shock**. This is a feeling of confusion and discomfort when in or dealing with an unfamiliar culture.

Global businesses are concerned about culture shock because they need their employees to be successful as they travel and work around the world. Perhaps this understanding might also be applied to our everyday cross-cultural experiences right here at home. Listed below are stages that are often encountered as someone adjusts to the unfamiliar setting of a new culture. The assumption is that knowing about the stages can help us better deal with them.[27]

- *Confusion*—First contacts with the new culture leave you anxious, uncomfortable, and in need of information and advice.
- *Small victories*—Continued interactions bring some "successes," and your confidence grows in handling daily affairs.
- *Honeymoon*—This is a time of wonderment, cultural immersion, and even infatuation, with local ways viewed positively.
- *Irritation and anger*—This is a time when the "negatives" overwhelm the "positives" and the new culture becomes a target of your criticism.
- *Reality*—This is a time of rebalancing; you are able to enjoy the new culture while accommodating its less desirable elements.

Culture shock is the confusion and discomfort that a person experiences when in an unfamiliar culture.

{ THE HIGHEST MORALE IS FOUND AMONG
WORKERS IN THE NETHERLANDS

Facts to Consider

■ EMPLOYEE MORALE VARIES AROUND THE WORLD

A worldwide study shows that the morale of workers varies from one country to the next. FDS International of the United Kingdom surveyed 13,832 workers in 23 countries. Here is how selected countries ranked based on employee reports of job satisfaction, quality of employer-employee relations, and work-life balance.

    Top-Ranked—1. Netherlands, 2. Ireland and Thailand, 3. Switzerland, 4. Denmark, 5. United Kingdom.

    Some Others—10. United States, 11. Canada, 12. Poland, 13. Korea, 14. Australia, 15. Japan.

YOUR THOUGHTS?

Why do you think employee morale in the United States and Canada trails that of other countries such as the Netherlands, Ireland, and Switzerland? Why might one Asian country such as Thailand score very high in employee morale and another such as Korea score much lower? Are there cultural factors that might make a difference in how employees respond to a survey about their workplace morale?

⦀ Cultural intelligence is the capacity to adapt to foreign cultures.

A U.S. businessman once went to meet a Saudi Arabian official. He sat in the office with crossed legs and the sole of his shoe exposed. He didn't know this is a sign of disrespect in the local culture. He passed documents to the host using his left hand, which Muslims consider unclean. And, he declined when coffee was offered. This suggested criticism of the Saudi's hospitality. What was the price for these cultural miscues? A $10 million contract was lost to a Korean executive better versed in Saudi ways.[28]

    Some might say that this American's behavior was ethnocentric, so self-centered that he ignored and showed no concern for the culture of his Arab host. Others might excuse him as suffering from culture shock. Maybe he was so uncomfortable upon arrival in Saudi Arabia that all he could think about was offering his contract and leaving as quickly as possible. Still others might give him the benefit of the doubt. It could have been that he was well intentioned but didn't have time to learn about Saudi culture before making the trip.

    Regardless of the possible reasons for the cultural miscues, they still worked to the businessman's disadvantage. There is also no doubt that he failed to show **cultural intelligence**—the ability to adapt and adjust to new cultures.[29] People with cultural intelligence have high cultural self-awareness and are flexible in dealing with cultural differences. In cross-cultural situations they are willing to learn from what is unfamiliar, and modify their behaviors to act with sensitivity toward other cultures' ways. In other words, someone high in cultural intelligence views cultural differences not as threats but as learning opportunities.

    Cultural intelligence is probably a good indicator of someone's capacity for success in international assignments and in relationships with persons of different cultures. How would you rate yourself? Could cultural intelligence be one of your important personal assets?

Cultural intelligence is the ability to adapt to new cultures.

Workers who make mistakes in Haier's Chinese factories are made to stand on special footprints and publicly criticize themselves by pointing out what they did wrong and what lessons they have learned. When this practice was implemented at a new factory in South Carolina, American workers protested—they thought it was humiliating. But Haier executives didn't force the Americans to accept this practice; they changed their approach. American workers now stand in the footprints as public recognition when they do exceptional work. Because the Chinese managers listened and learned from their experiences, they ended up with a local practice that fits both corporate values and the local culture.

The "silent" languages of cultures include context, time, and space.

It is easy to recognize differences in the spoken and written languages used by people around the world. And foreign-language skills can open many doors to cultural understanding. But anthropologist Edward T. Hall points out that there are other "silent" languages of culture that are also very significant.[30]

If we look and listen carefully, Hall believes we should recognize how cultures differ in the ways their members use language in communication.[31] In **low-context cultures** most communication takes place via the written or spoken word. This is common in the United States, Canada, and Germany, for example. As the saying goes: "We say (or write) what we mean, and we mean what we say."

Low-context cultures emphasize communication via spoken or written words.

In **high-context cultures** things are different. What is actually said or written may convey only part, and sometimes a very small part, of the real message. The rest must be interpreted from nonverbal signals and the situation as a whole—things such as body language, physical setting, and even past relationships among the people involved. Dinner parties and social gatherings in high-context cultures allow potential business partners to get to know one another. Only after the relationships are established is it possible to make business deals.

High-context cultures rely on nonverbal and situational cues as well as spoken or written words in communication.

Hall also notes that the way people approach and deal with time varies across cultures. He describes a **monochronic culture** as one in which people tend to do one thing at a time. This is typical of the United States, where most businesspeople schedule a meeting for one person or group to focus on one issue for an allotted time period.[32] And if someone is late for one of those meetings or brings an uninvited guest, we tend not to like it.

In **monochronic cultures** people tend to do one thing at a time.

Members of a **polychronic culture** are more flexible about time and who uses it. They often try to work on many different things at once, perhaps not in any particular order. An American visitor (monochronic culture) to an Egyptian client (polychronic culture) may be frustrated, for example, by interruptions as the client deals with people continually flowing in and out of his office.

In **polychronic cultures** people accomplish many different things at once.

In addition, Hall points out that cultures vary in how they value and use space. He describes cultural tendencies in terms of **proxemics,** or how people use space to communicate. Americans tend to like and value their own space, perhaps as

Proxemics is the study of how people use interpersonal space.

■ FAIR-TRADE FASHION

Perhaps you're one of a growing number of consumers who like to shop "fair trade." Does it feel good when you buy coffee, for example, that is certified as grown by persons who were paid fairly for their labor? But what about clothing?

At least one retailer wants to be considered as selling fair-trade fashion. Fair Indigo, launched by former executives of major fashion retailers, presents itself as "a new clothing company with a different way of doing business" that wants to "create stylish, high-quality clothes while paying a fair and meaningful wage to the people who produce them." Pointing out that there is no certifying body for fair-trade apparel, Fair Indigo offers this guarantee: "We will therefore guarantee that every employee who makes our clothing is paid a fair wage, not just a legal minimum wage, as is the benchmark in the industry."

Fair Indigo's representatives travel the globe searching for small factories and cooperatives that meet their standards. By doing so, they're bucking industry trends in outsourcing and contract manufacturing. Fair Indigo's CEO, Bill Bass, says: "The whole evolution of the clothing and manufacturing industry has been to drive prices and wages down, shut factories and move work to countries with lower wages. We said, 'we're going to reverse this and push wages up.'"

YOU DECIDE

Are you willing to pay a bit more for a fair-trade product? And what do you think about Fair Indigo's business model? Is it "fashion" that sells apparel, or fashion plus conditions of origin? Is Fair Indigo at the forefront of the next new wave of value creation in retailing—fair-trade fashion?

---

much space as they can get. We like big offices, big homes, big yards; we get uncomfortable in tight spaces and when others stand too close to us in lines. When someone "talks right in our face," we don't like it; the behavior may even be interpreted as an expression of anger.

If you visit Japan you'll notice the difference in proxemics very quickly. Space is precious in Japan; it is respected and its use is carefully planned. Small, tidy homes, offices, and shops are the norm; gardens are tiny but immaculate; public spaces are carefully organized for most efficient use.

⫴ Hofstede identifies five value differences among national cultures.

Understanding the silent languages just discussed is a good place to start in cultural appreciation, but cultures are still more complex. Scholars offer many models and useful perspectives.[33] One of the most discussed is Geert Hofstede, who explores value differences among national cultures.[34] His work began with a study of employees of a U.S.-based corporation operating in 40 countries. Hofstede identified the four cultural dimensions of power distance, uncertainty avoidance, individualism-collectivism, and masculinity-femininity.[35] Later studies resulted in the addition of a fifth dimension, time orientation.[36] Figure 16.2 shows a sample of how national cultures varied in his research. Can you see why Hofstede's cultural dimensions can be significant in business and management?

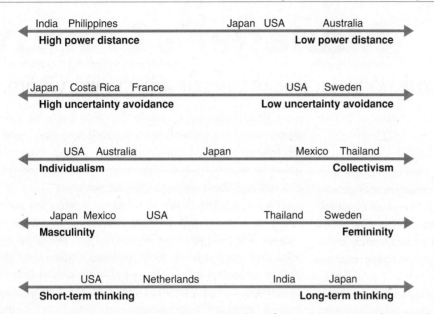

FIGURE 16.2 **How Do Countries Compare on Hofstede's Five Dimensions of National Cultures?**
Countries vary on Hofstede's five dimensions of value differences in national cultures. For example, Japan scores somewhat comparatively higher on power distance and substantially higher on uncertainty avoidance and masculinity; the United States is much more individualistic and short-term oriented. The implications of such cultural differences can be significant. Imagine what they might mean when international business executives try to make deals around the world or when representatives of national governments try to work out problems.

Power distance is the degree to which a society accepts or rejects the unequal distribution of power in organizations and society. In high power distance cultures such as Japan, we expect to find great respect for age, status, and titles. Could this create problems for an American visitor used to the informalities of a more moderate power distance culture, and perhaps accustomed to first names and casual dress in the office?

Uncertainty avoidance is the degree to which a society tolerates or is uncomfortable with risk, change, and situational uncertainty. In high uncertainty avoidance cultures, such as France, one would expect to find a preference for structure, order, and predictability. Could this be one of the reasons why the French seem to favor employment practices that provide job security?

Individualism-collectivism is the degree to which a society emphasizes individual accomplishments and self-interests, versus collective accomplishments and the interests of groups. In Hofstede's data the United States had the highest individualism score of any country. Don't you find the "I" and "me" words used a lot in our conversations and meetings? I'm always surprised how often they occur in student team presentations. What are the implications of our cultural tendency toward individualism when we try to work with people from more collectivist national cultures?

Masculinity-femininity is the degree to which a society values assertiveness and materialism, versus feelings, relationships, and quality of life.[37] You might think of it as a tendency to emphasize stereotypical masculine or feminine traits and attitudes toward gender roles. Visitors to Japan, with the highest masculinity score in Hofstede's research, may be surprised at how restricted career

Power distance is the degree to which a society accepts unequal distribution of power.

Uncertainty avoidance is the degree to which a society tolerates risk and uncertainty.

Individualism-collectivism is the degree to which a society emphasizes individuals and their self-interests.

Masculinity-femininity is the degree to which a society values assertiveness and materialism.

Manager's Library

◼ *HALF THE SKY* BY NICHOLAS KRISTOF AND SHERYL WUDUNN

WOMAN AREN'T THE PROBLEM: THEY'RE THE SOLUTION

An ancient Chinese proverb claims that "women hold up half the sky." But the harsh reality is that women are oppressed throughout the developing world in ways that most Westerners are oblivious to. Sex trafficking, rape, and maternal mortality—death after childbirth—are but a few gender-specific human rights routinely violated in third world countries.

In the book *Half the Sky*, authors Nicolas Kristof and Sheryl WuDunn outline the prevalence of indignities suffered by poor, uneducated women around the globe. They offer well-thought-out ideas for eliminating that injustice, and equate the modern oppression of women worldwide to that of slavery. They argue that since slavery was legal, it was readily identified and defeated. However, inhumane treatments of underprivileged women are illegal and continue despite the rule of law.

Kristof and WuDunn, both Pulitzer Prize-winning journalists, state that "gendercide"—the daily slaughter of girls in the developing world—takes more lives in one decade than any genocide did in the entire 20th century. The authors travel the world writing and working to fight oppressive practices, but are resigned to harsh realities. Victimized women are poor, uneducated, and powerless in their societies. Crimes against them are hidden from the developing world, and often tolerated in their male-dominated cultures. Even subjugated females react in disdain when the authors intervene, proclaiming "these are our problems, not yours!"

This book offers practical solutions in what the authors frame as a moral and political movement to emancipate women. They suggest that Westerners first recognize injustices, then speak against them. Ordinary citizens can initiate change by volunteering with global organizations that fight oppression, or simply joining e-mail lists. The authors believe that educating maltreated women—teaching them their moral rights and the economic means to maintain independence—are key. They advocate for female leadership in countries with masculine power structures.

REFLECT AND REACT

Are our diversity initiatives toward women properly focused on a global scale? For example, is it more important to increase the ranks of female executives in *Fortune* 500 corporations, or to stop global "gendercide"? Do you agree that moral and economic education can empower poor, uneducated women to stand against injustice? And by the way, does the plight of victimized women get lost sometimes when we are too quick to embrace and accept so-called cultural differences?

Time orientation is the degree to which a society emphasizes short-term or long-term goals.

The **ecological fallacy** assumes that a generalized cultural value applies equally well to all members of the culture.

opportunities can be for women.[38] The *Wall Street Journal* comments: "In Japan, professional women face a set of socially complex issues—from overt sexism to deep-seated attitudes about the division of labor." One female Japanese manager says: "Men tend to have very fixed ideas about what women are like.[39]

Time orientation is the degree to which a society emphasizes short-term or long-term goals and gratifications.[40] Americans are notorious for being impatient and wanting quick, even instantaneous, gratification. Even our companies are expected to achieve short-term results; those failing to meet quarterly financial targets often suffer immediate stock price declines. Many Asian cultures are quite the opposite, valuing persistence and thrift, being patient and willing to work for long-term success.

Although Hofstede's ideas are insightful, his five value dimensions offer only a ballpark look at national cultures, a starting point at best. And Hofstede himself warns that we must avoid the **ecological fallacy**.[41] This is acting with the mistaken assumption that a generalized cultural value, such as individualism in American culture or masculinity in Japanese culture, applies always and equally to all members of the culture.

⫼ Country clusters show cultural differences.

In project GLOBE, short for Global Leadership and Organizational Behavior Effectiveness, a team of international researchers led by Robert House convened to study leadership, organizational practices, and diversity among world cultures.[42] They studied 62 countries and discovered they fall into ten culture clusters. Countries within a cluster tend to share societal culture practices with one another, while also differing in many ways from countries in other clusters.

GLOBE researchers use nine dimensions to describe the culture clusters.[43] Two dimensions are direct fits with Hofstede: *power distance*, which is higher in Confucian Asia and lower in Nordic Europe, and *uncertainty avoidance*, which is high in Germanic Europe and low in the Middle East.

Three other GLOBE dimensions are similar to Hofstede's. *Gender egalitarianism* is the degree to which a culture minimizes gender inequalities, similar to Hofstede's masculinity-femininity. It is high in Eastern and Nordic Europe and low in those of the Middle East. *Future orientation* is the degree to which members of a culture are willing to look ahead, delay gratification, and make investments for longer-term payoffs, similar to Hofstede's time orientation. Germanic and Nordic Europe are high on future orientation; Latin America and the Middle East are low. *Institutional collectivism* is the extent to which a society emphasizes and rewards group action and accomplishments versus individual ones, similar to Hofstede's individualism-collectivism. Confucian Asia and Nordic Europe score high in institutional collectivism, while Germanic and Latin Europe score low.

> ## Project GLOBE culture clusters
>
> - *Latin America*—Brazil, Ecuador, Mexico
> - *Anglo*—Australia, England, United States
> - *Latin Europe*—France, Italy, Spain
> - *Nordic Europe*—Denmark, Finland, Sweden
> - *Germanic Europe*—Germany, the Netherlands, Switzerland
> - *Eastern Europe*—Greece, Hungary, Russia
> - *Confucian Asia*—China, Japan, Singapore
> - *Southern Asia*—India, Malaysia, Philippines
> - *Sub-Saharan Africa*—Nigeria, South Africa, Zambia
> - *Middle East*—Egypt, Kuwait, Turkey

The remaining four GLOBE dimensions offer additional insights. *In-group collectivism* is the extent to which people take pride in their families and organizational memberships, acting loyal and cohesive regarding them. This runs high in Latin America and the Middle East; it tends to be low in Anglo and Germanic Europe. *Assertiveness* is the extent to which a culture emphasizes competition and assertiveness in social relationships, valuing behavior that is tough and confrontational as opposed to showing modesty and tenderness. Cultures in Eastern and Germanic Europe score high in assertiveness; those in Nordic Europe and Latin America score low.

Performance orientation is the degree of emphasis on performance excellence and improvements. Anglo and Confucian Asia cultures tend to be high in performance orientation. *Humane orientation* reflects tendencies in a society for people to emphasize fairness, altruism, generosity, and caring as they deal with one another. It tends to be high in Southern Asia and Sub-Saharan Africa, and to be low in Latin and Germanic Europe.

Takeaway 16.2
What Should We Know About Diversity Among Global Cultures?

Terms to Define

Cultural intelligence

Culture shock

Ecological fallacy

High-context culture

Individualism-collectivism

Low-context culture

Masculinity-femininity

Monochronic culture

Polychronic culture

Power distance

Proxemics

Time orientation

Uncertainty avoidance

Rapid Review

- People can experience culture shock due to the discomfort experienced in cross-cultural situations.
- Cultural intelligence is an individual capacity to understand, respect, and adapt to cultural differences.
- Hall's silent languages of culture include the role of context in communication, time orientation, and use of interpersonal space.
- Hofstede's five dimensions of value differences in national cultures are power distance, uncertainty avoidance, individualism-collectivism, masculinity-femininity, and time orientation.
- Countries tend to fall into culture clusters, with cultures more similar within than across the clusters.

Questions for Discussion

1. Should religion be included on Hall's list of the silent languages of culture?
2. Which of Hofstede's cultural dimensions might pose the greatest challenges to U.S. managers working in Asia, the Middle East, or Latin America?
3. Even though cultural differences are readily apparent around the world, is the trend today for cultures to converge and become more like one another?

Be Sure You Can

- explain culture shock and how people may respond to it
- differentiate low-context and high-context cultures, monochronic and poly-chronic cultures
- list Hofstede's five dimensions of value differences among national cultures
- contrast American culture with that of other countries on each of Hofstede's dimensions
- identify similarities and differences between the Hofstede and Project GLOBE cultural dimensions

What Would You Do?

You've just been asked to join a team being sent to China for 10 days to discuss a new software development project with your firm's Chinese engineers. It's your first trip to China or Asia. In fact, you've only been to Europe as part of a study tour when in college. The trip is scheduled four weeks from today. What can you do to prepare for the trip and for your work with Chinese colleagues? What worries you the most about the trip and how well you'll do under the circumstances?

TestPrep 16

Multiple-Choice Questions

1. Which statement is most consistent with arguments that diversity is good for organizations?
   (a) Having a diverse workforce guarantees success.
   (b) Diversity is easy to manage because it is already valued by all people.
   (c) Diverse workforces are good at dealing with diverse customers.
   (d) When workforces are diverse, organizations can spend less on training.

2. When members of minority cultures feel that they have to behave similar to the ways of the majority culture, this tendency is called _____.
   (a) biculturalism
   (b) particularism
   (c) the glass ceiling effect
   (d) multiculturalism

3. The beliefs that older workers are not creative and prefer routine, low-stress jobs are stereotypes that might create bad feelings among members of different _____ subcultures in organizations.
   (a) gender   (b) generational
   (c) functional   (d) ethnic

4. Among the three leadership approaches to diversity identified by Thomas, which one is primarily directed at making sure that minorities and women are hired by the organization?
   (a) equal employment opportunity
   (b) affirmative action
   (c) valuing diversity
   (d) managing diversity

5. Pluralism and the absence of discrimination and prejudice in policies and practices are two important hallmarks of _____.
   (a) the glass ceiling effect
   (b) a multicultural organization
   (c) quality circles
   (d) affirmative action

6. _____ means that an organization fully integrates members of minority cultures and majority cultures.
   (a) Equal employment opportunity
   (b) Affirmative action
   (c) Symbolic leadership
   (d) Pluralism

7. When members of the marketing department stick close to one another, as well as share jokes and even a slang language, the likelihood is that a/an _____ subculture is forming.
   (a) occupational   (b) generational
   (c) gender   (d) ethnic

8. When someone experiences culture shock on a study abroad trip, the first stage is likely to be one of anxiety caused by confusion in the new cultural setting. What is the next stage in culture shock?
   (a) Experiencing a sense of confidence from small victories in dealing with differences.
   (b) Displaying outright irritation and anger at the ways of this new culture.
   (c) Wanting to give up and go home immediately.
   (d) Accepting reality and enjoying the good and bad aspects.

9. When dealing with proxemics as a silent language of culture, what is the issue of most concern?
   (a) How people use the spoken word to communicate.
   (b) How people use nonverbal to communicate.
   (c) How people use time to communicate.
   (d) How people use space to communicate.

10. In _____ cultures, members tend to do one thing at a time; in _____ cultures, members tend to do many things at once.
    (a) monochronic; polychronic
    (b) universal; particular
    (c) collectivist; individualist
    (d) neutral; affective

11. When a foreign visitor to India attends a dinner and criticizes as "primitive" the local custom of eating with one's fingers, he or she can be described as acting in a/an _____ way.

   (a) culturally intelligent   (b) polychronic

   (c) monochronic   (d) ethnocentric

12. In a high-context culture we would expect to find _____.

   (a) low uncertainty avoidance

   (b) high power distance

   (c) use of monochronic time

   (d) emphasis on nonverbal and verbal communication

13. It is common in Malaysian culture for people to value teamwork and to display great respect for authority. Hofstede would describe this culture as high in both _____.

   (a) uncertainty avoidance and feminism

   (b) universalism and particularism

   (c) collectivism and power distance

   (d) long-term orientation and masculinity

14. On which dimension of national culture did the United States score highest and Japan score highest in Hofstede's original survey research?

   (a) masculinity, femininity

   (b) long-term, short-term

   (c) individualism, masculinity

   (d) high uncertainty avoidance, collectivism

15. If someone commits what Hofstede calls the "ecological fallacy," what are they likely to be doing?

   (a) Disregarding monochronic behavior.

   (b) Assuming all members of a culture fit the popular stereotype.

   (c) Emphasizing proxemics over time orientation.

   (d) Forgetting that cultural intelligence can be learned.

Short-Response Questions

16. What is the difference between valuing diversity and managing diversity?

17. How can subculture differences create diversity challenges in organizations?

18. If you were asked to give a short class presentation on the "silent languages" of culture, what cultural issues would you talk about and what examples would you give?

19. In what ways can the power distance dimension of national culture become an important issue in management?

Integration and Application Questions

20. A friend in West Virginia owns a small manufacturing firm employing about 50 workers. His son spent a semester in Japan as an exchange student. Upon return, he said to his dad: "Boy, the Japanese really do things right; everything is organized in teams; decisions are made by consensus, with everyone participating; no one seems to disagree with anything the bosses say. I think we should immediately start more teamwork and consensus decision making in our factory."

Questions: The friend asks you for advice. Using insights from Hofstede's framework, what would you say to him? What differences in the Japanese and American cultures should be considered in this situation, and why?

Steps *for* FurtherLearning

Many learning resources are found at the end of the book and online within WileyPLUS.

Don't Miss These Selections from the **Skill-Building Portfolio**

■ **SELF-ASSESSMENT 16:** *Diversity Awareness*

■ **CLASS EXERCISE 16:** *Alligator River Story*

■ **TEAM PROJECT 16:** *Job Satisfaction Around the World*

Don't Miss This Selection from **Cases for Critical Thinking**

■ **CHAPTER 16 CASE**

Toyota: Looking Far into the Future

Toyota's success in the American auto market is no accident. The company has used strategies honed since the 1950s to earn and retain customer satisfaction by producing superior vehicles within a highly efficient production environment. Two core philosophies guide Toyota's business: (1) creating fair, balanced, mutually beneficial relationships with both suppliers and employees, and (2) strictly adhering to a just-in-time (JIT) manufacturing principle.

By substituting discipline and efficiency for fanfare, Toyota has quietly earned a long-standing reputation for the reliability and quality of all of its models. Although the company's domestic competitors have taken notice and now use many of Toyota's proven methods, their financial difficulties make it hard to keep up the fight.

Make notes here on what you've learned about yourself from this chapter.

■ **LEARNING JOURNAL 16**

...rnational Labour Organization reports there are ...ion child laborers worldwide; 115 million of them ...azardous conditions.

Globalization and International Business

Going Global Isn't Just for Travelers

Management Live

Cultural Awareness and *The Amazing Race*

The popular reality series *The Amazing Race* pits teams of players in an around-the-world competition. Each week, contestants race to complete cultural and physical challenges. They face grueling travel demands within and between countries, and face unfamiliar languages and customs. To top it off, sleep and eating schedules are thrown off by global time differences.

One thing becomes painfully clear as the race episodes unfold. Many of the participants do not know a lot about other countries in the world.

Like most of us, race contestants have grown used to the values and patterns of home. And that's understandable. But, if you watch closely, you'll see that their lack of **cultural awareness** sometimes reflects attitudes of superiority. As the race teams come face-to-face with one new culture after another, however, they learn a lot about themselves in the process.

When Nat Strand and Kat Chang won the $1 million prize, they were the first female team to do so. Their journey took them to 30 cities across four continents for a total of 32,000 miles. They crossed a lot of national and cultural boundaries along the way, much as today's global organizations do.

There's no better time to check your cultural awareness than now. This chapter discusses many ways you can put it to work in today's global economy. And there may well be a million dollar payoff for success in your future—measured in career success!

YOUR CHAPTER 17 TAKEAWAYS

1. Discuss ways that globalization affects international business.

2. Understand what global corporations are and how they work.

WHAT'S INSIDE

Explore Yourself
More on cultural awareness

Role Models
Les Wexner makes sure Limited Brands has its passport

Ethics Check
Nationalism and protectionism

Facts to Consider
Corruption and bribes haunt global business

Manager's Library
Hot, Flat and Crowded 2.0 by Thomas Friedman

Takeaway 17.1
How Does Globalization Affect International Business?

ANSWERS TO COME

- Globalization involves the growing interdependence of the world's economies.
- Globalization creates a variety of international business opportunities.
- International business is done by global sourcing, import/export, licensing, and franchising.
- International business is done by joint ventures and wholly owned subsidiaries.
- International business is complicated by different legal and political systems.

THERE IS NO DOUBT THAT OUR GLOBAL COMMUNITY IS RICH WITH INFORMATION, opportunities, controversies, and complications. We get on the spot news delivered from around the world right to our smart phones. When crises like the Japanese tsunami or people's demonstrations in Egypt and Syria happen, social media like Twitter and Facebook join major news networks in getting the information out instantaneously. It is possible to board a plane in New York and fly nonstop to Beijing, China, or Mumbai, India, or Cape Town, South Africa. Colleges and universities offer a growing variety of study-abroad programs. In the business world an international MBA is an increasingly desirable credential.

Speaking of the business side of things, here are some conversation starters. Ben & Jerry's Ice Cream is owned by the British-Dutch firm Unilever; Anheuser-Busch is now owned by the Belgian firm InBev; Mercedes builds M-class vehicles in Alabama; India's Tata Group owns Jaguar, Land Rover, and Tetley Tea. Japan's Honda, Nissan, and Toyota get 80% to 90% of their profits from sales in America, while 60% of components for Boeing's new 787 Dreamliner are made by foreign firms. Nike earns the majority of its sales outside the U.S., and has manufacturing contracts with over 120 factories in China alone.[1]

The growing power of global businesses affects all of us in roles as citizens, consumers, and career-seekers. If in doubt, take a look at what you are wearing. It's hard to find a garment or a shoe that is really "Made in America." What about your T-shirt? Where did you buy it? Where was it made? Where will it end up?

In a fascinating book called *The Travels of a T-Shirt in the Global Economy*, economist Pietra Rivoli tracks the origins and disposition of a T-shirt that she bought while on a vacation to Florida.[2] As shown in Figure 17.1, the common T-shirt lives a complicated global life. The life of Rivoli's T-shirt begins with cotton grown in Texas. It moves to China, where the cotton is processed and white T-shirts are manufactured. These are imported by a U.S. firm that silk-screens them and sells them to retail shops for resale to American customers. When customers like Rivoli donate used T-shirts to charity, they're sold to a recycler. In this case the recycler sells them to a vendor in Africa who distributes them to local markets, where they are sold yet again to new customers.

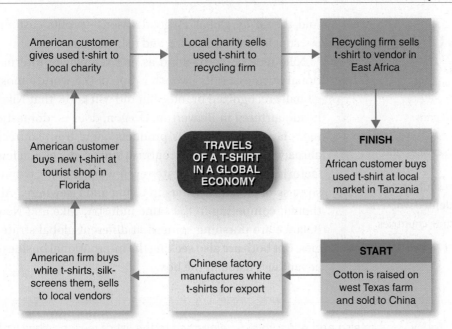

FIGURE 17.1

How Does a T-Shirt Travel Through the World's Global Economy?
This sketch shows the T-shirt beginning as cotton grown in Texas that is shipped to China, where it is processed and white T-shirts are manufactured. The white shirts come back to the United States, where they are silk-screened and sold to retail shops for resale to customers. If customers donate used T-shirts to a charity, they may go to a recycler who sells them to vendors in other countries, where the used T-shirts get sold again to local customers.

Globalization involves the growing interdependence of the world's economies.

These travels of a T-shirt leave little doubt that this is the age of the **global economy** where resource supplies, product markets, and business competition are worldwide in scope.[3] It is also a time when daily living is heavily influenced by the forces of **globalization**, defined in earlier chapters as the process of growing interdependence among the components in the global economy.[4] Harvard scholar and consultant Rosabeth Moss Kanter describes globalization as "one of the most powerful and pervasive influences on nations, businesses, workplaces, communities, and lives."[5]

What about your work and career plans? Do you have a good idea of how much globalization affects your life? If you come to Ohio, where I live, you'll find a growing number of people working for foreign firms.[6] They hold jobs created by **insourcing**, ones provided domestically by foreign employers. At last count there were more than 6 million such jobs in the U.S. economy.

Outsourcing is the other side of the job story. It shifts jobs to foreign locations to save costs by taking advantage of lower-wage skilled labor. John Chambers, CEO of Cisco Systems Inc., pretty much lays it on the line for all of us when he says: "I will put my jobs anywhere in the world where the right infrastructure is, with the right educated workforce, with the right supportive government."[7] As you may well know, not everyone is pleased to hear messages like these.

Globalization creates a variety of international business opportunities.

Firms like Cisco, Sony, Ford, and IKEA are large **international businesses**. They conduct for-profit transactions of goods and services across national boundaries. Such businesses, from small exporters and importers to the huge multinational corporations, form the foundations of world trade. They move raw materials, finished products, and specialized services from one country to another in the global economy.

In the **global economy**, resources, markets, and competition are worldwide in scope.

Globalization is the process of growing interdependence among elements of the global economy.

Insourcing is the creation of domestic jobs by foreign employers.

Outsourcing shifts local jobs to foreign locations to take advantage of lower-wage labor in other countries.

An **international business** conducts commercial transactions across national boundaries.

Why Businesses Go Global

- *Profits*—gain profits through expanded operations.
- *Customers*—enter new markets to gain customers.
- *Suppliers*—get access to products, services, and materials.
- *Capital*—get access to financial resources.
- *Labor*—get access to low-cost, talented workers.
- *Risk*—spread assets among multiple countries.

And, they all "go global" for good reasons—profits, customers, suppliers, capital, labor, and risk management.[8]

Nike may come to mind as an exemplar of international businesses; its swoosh is one of the world's most globally recognized brands. But did you know that Nike, headquartered in Beaverton, Oregon, does no domestic manufacturing? All of its products come from sources abroad. New Balance, by contrast, still produces at a few factories in the United States even while making extensive use of global suppliers in China and elsewhere.[9] Although competing in the same industry, Nike and New Balance are pursuing somewhat different global strategies. But both are also seeking the international business advantages listed in the box.

Today you can also add *economic development* to the list of reasons why businesses go global. An example is found in Rwanda where coffee giants Green Mountain Coffee Roasters, Peet's Coffee & Tea, and Starbucks work with the nonprofit TechnoServe. Its goal is to help raise the incomes for African coffee farmers by improving their production and marketing methods. Partner firms send advisors to teach coffee growers how to meet their global standards. It's a win-win. The global firm gets a quality product at a good price, the growers gain skills and market opportunities, and the local economy improves. Peet's director of coffee purchasing, Shirin Moayyad, says: "If they produce a high-quality product we'll pay more for it."

‖ International business is done by global sourcing, import/export, licensing, and franchising.

Not only is there more than one reason for getting into international business, there are several ways of doing it. And getting started with the forms of international business can be relatively easy.

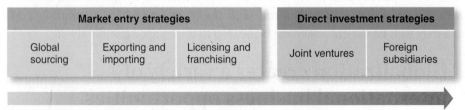

Market entry strategies			Direct investment strategies	
Global sourcing	Exporting and importing	Licensing and franchising	Joint ventures	Foreign subsidiaries

Increasing involvement in ownership and control of foreign operations

In **global sourcing**, firms purchase materials or services around the world for local use.

A common first step in international business is **global sourcing**, where a business purchases materials, manufacturing components, or services from around the world. This is basically taking advantage of international wage gaps by contracting for low-cost goods and services in foreign locations.

In automobile manufacturing, for example, global sourcing may mean getting designs from Italy, instrument panels from Mexico, antilock braking systems from Germany, and electronics from Malaysia. In services, it may mean setting up customer-support call centers in the Philippines, contracting for computer software engineers in Russia, or having medical X-rays read by physicians in India. And for those selling toys, shoes, electronics, clothing, and more—China is the top outsourcing destination. Some call it the factory for the world.[10]

A lot of international business involves **exporting**—selling locally made products in foreign markets, and **importing**—buying foreign-made products and selling them in domestic markets. Because the growth of export industries creates local jobs, you'll often read and hear about governments supporting these types of business initiatives.

Another form of international business is the **licensing** agreement, where foreign firms pay a fee for rights to make or sell another company's products in a specified region. The license typically grants access to a unique manufacturing technology, special patent, or trademark. One of the business risks of licensing is counterfeiting.[11] New Balance, for example, licensed a Chinese supplier to produce one of its brands. Even after New Balance revoked the license, the supplier continued to produce and distribute "New Barlun" shoes around Asia. New Balance ended up facing costly and complex litigation in China's courts.[12]

In **franchising**, a foreign firm buys the rights to use another's name and operating methods in its home country. When companies such as McDonald's or Subway franchise internationally, they sell facility designs, equipment, product ingredients, recipes, and management systems to foreign investors. They also typically retain certain product and operating controls to protect their brand's image.

China Manufactures for the World

- 70% of the world's umbrellas
- 60% of the world's buttons
- 72% of U.S. shoes
- 50% of U.S. appliances
- 80% of U.S. toys

In **exporting**, local products are sold abroad.

Importing is the process of acquiring products abroad and selling them in domestic markets.

In **licensing**, one firm pays a fee for rights to make or sell another company's products.

In **franchising**, a firm pays a fee for rights to use another company's name and operating methods.

{ NATIONAL ECONOMIES ARE NOW GLOBAL; BUSINESS IS NOW GLOBAL; OUR PERSONAL THINKING MUST BE GLOBAL AS WELL.

Explore Yourself

■ CULTURAL AWARENESS

The forces of globalization are often discussed in respect to job migration, outsourcing, currency fluctuations, and the fortunes of global corporations. Yet it is important to remember that globalization is best understood and dealt with in a context of **cultural awareness**.

It's only natural that we become used to the ways of our culture. But many of these same values and patterns of behavior can be called into question when we work and interact with persons from different cultures.

Although very comfortable for us, our ways of doing things may seem strange and even, at the extreme, offensive to others who come from different cultural backgrounds. It's only natural, too, for cultural differences to be frustrating and even threatening when we come face-to-face with them.

National economies are now global; business is now global; our personal thinking must be global as well.

Get to know yourself better by taking the **Global Intelligence** self-assessment and completing other activities in the *Exploring Management* **Skill-Building Portfolio**.

International business is done by joint ventures and wholly owned subsidiaries.

A **joint venture** operates in a foreign country through co-ownership with local partners.

Sooner or later, some firms that are active in international business decide to make costly direct investments in operations in foreign countries. One way to do this is by a **joint venture**. This is a co-ownership arrangement in which the foreign and local partners agree to pool resources, share risks, and jointly operate the new business. Sometimes the joint venture is formed when a foreign partner buys part ownership in an existing local firm. In other cases it is formed when the foreign and local partners start an entirely new operation together.

In a **global strategic alliance**, each partner hopes to achieve through cooperation things they couldn't do alone.

International joint ventures are types of **global strategic alliances** in which foreign and domestic partners cooperate for mutual gains. Each partner hopes to get from the alliance things they couldn't do or would have a hard time doing alone. For the local partner an alliance may bring access to technology and opportunities to learn new skills. For the outside partner an alliance may bring access to new markets and customers, and the expert assistance of locals that understand them.[13]

Joint ventures were the business forms of choice for the world's large automakers when they decided to pursue major operations in China. Recognizing the local complexities, they decided it was better to cooperate with local partners than try to enter the Chinese markets on their own. Of course, such joint venture deals pose potential risks. And loss of technology is a big one. Not long ago, GM executives noticed that a new car from a fast-growing local competitor looked very similar to one of their models. This competitor was partially owned by GM's Chinese joint venture partner and GM claims its design was copied. The competitor denied it and continued its plans to export the cars, called "Cherys," to global markets including the United States.[14]

A **foreign subsidiary** is a local operation completely owned by a foreign firm.

A **greenfield venture** establishes a foreign subsidiary by building an entirely new operation in a foreign country.

In contrast to the international joint venture, which is a cross-border partnership, a **foreign subsidiary** is a local operation completely owned and controlled by a foreign firm. It might be a local firm that was purchased in its entirety or it might be a brand-new operation built from start as a **greenfield venture**. Decisions to set up foreign subsidiaries are most often made only after foreign firms have gained experience in the local environment through earlier joint ventures.

{ MAKE SURE THAT YOUR JOINT VENTURE PARTNER
HAS A REPUTATION FOR GOOD ETHICS.

Tips to Remember

■ CHECKLIST FOR CHOOSING A GOOD JOINT VENTURE PARTNER

- Familiar with your firm's major business
- Employs a strong local workforce
- Values its customers
- Values its employees
- Has strong local market for its own products

- Has record of good management
- Has good profit potential
- Has sound financial standing
- Has reputation for ethical decision making
- Has reputation for socially responsible practices

{ "WE EXPECT OUR SUPPLIERS TO PROMOTE AN ENVIRONMENT OF DIGNITY, RESPECT AND OPPORTUNITY."

Role Models

■ LES WEXNER MAKES SURE LIMITED BRANDS HAS ITS PASSPORT

This is a shopping test. What do Victoria's Secret, C. O. Bigelow, Bath & Body Works, White Barn Candle Co., La Senza, and Henri Bendel have in common? The answer is they all trace their roots back to 1963 and a small women's clothing store in Columbus, Ohio. That single store has grown into Limited Brands, one of the world's most admired fashion retailers; Leslie Wexner, its founder, chairman, and CEO, is a member of the retail CEOs all-star team. He's been praised as a "pioneer of specialty brands" and someone with special retailing "vision and focus."

This is a global business test. Where does Limited Brands get its products? The answer is anywhere in the world where it can get quality at low cost. Under Wexner's leadership, the firm has been a major participant in the world of global sourcing. To ensure quality and protect its brand, Limited's supplier and subcontractor relationships are guided by a "What We Stand For" policy designed to ensure ethical operations. The policy states in part: "We expect our suppliers to promote an environment of dignity, respect and opportunity; provide safe and healthy working conditions; offer fair compensation through wages and other benefits; hire workers of legal age,

who accept employment on a voluntary basis; and maintain reasonable working hours."

Interestingly enough, Wexner has been slow to open stores in other countries. He calls the U.S. market the Limited's "golden goose" and says other retailers have erred by focusing their eyes abroad and neglecting markets at home. But when sales of a Victoria's Secret store in the São Paulo, Brazil, airport hit $10 million, Wexner had to take notice. You can expect to see more international stores opening soon.

Standing behind the displays and the fashion at Limited Brands is a global operation that depends on vast worldwide networks of suppliers and subcontractors.

WHAT'S THE LESSON HERE?

As with other international firms, the Limited's global reach must be well managed, and its ethical standards must be maintained. Any misstep will quickly be met by bad press, public criticism, a damaged reputation, and consumer defections. What can a leader do to ensure ethical practices in the complex world of global business practices?

⦀ International business is complicated by different legal and political systems.

As you might imagine, the more home-country and host-country laws differ, the more difficult and complex it is for international businesses to operate successfully. And the greater the depth of foreign involvement, the more complex it becomes to understand and adapt to local ways. Intel, for example, was fined $1.45 billion by the European Union for breaking its antitrust laws. Neelie Kroes, then vice president of the European Commission, said: "Intel has harmed millions of European consumers by deliberately acting to keep competitors out of the market for computer chips for many years."[15]

Common legal problems faced by international businesses involve incorporation practices and business ownership; negotiation and implemention of contracts with foreign parties; handling of foreign exchange; and intellectual property—patents, trademarks, and copyrights.

The issue of intellectual property is particularly sensitive these days. You might know this best in terms of concerns about movie and music downloads, photocopying of books and journals, and sale of fake designer fashions. Many Western

Ethics Check

■ NATIONALISM AND PROTECTIONISM

The headline read "Bolivia Seizes Control of Oil and Gas Fields." The announcement said: "We are beginning by nationalizing oil and gas; tomorrow we will add mining, forestry, and all natural resources, what our ancestors fought for."

The country's president, Evo Morales, set forth new terms that gave a state-owned firm 82% of all revenues, leaving 18% for the foreign firms. He said: "Only those firms that respect these new terms will be allowed to operate in the country." The implicit threat was that any firms not willing to sign new contracts would be sent home.

While foreign governments described this nationalization as an "unfriendly move," Morales considered it patriotic. His position was that any existing contracts with the state were in violation of the constitution, and that Bolivia's natural resources belonged to its people.

YOU DECIDE

If you were the CEO at one of these global firms, do you resist and raise the ethics of honoring your "old" contracts with the Bolivian government? Or do you comply with the new terms being offered? And as an everyday citizen of the world, can you disagree that a country has a right to protect its natural resources from exploitation by foreigners? Just what are the ethics of Morales's decision?

The **World Trade Organization (WTO)** is a global institution established to promote free trade and open markets around the world.

Most favored nation status gives a trading partner the most favorable treatment for imports and exports.

Tariffs are taxes governments levy on imports from abroad.

Nontariff barriers are nontax policies that governments enact to discourage imports, such as quotas and import restrictions.

Protectionism is a call for tariffs and favorable treatments to protect domestic firms from foreign competition.

businesses know it as lost profits due to their products or designs being copied and sold as imitations by foreign firms. After a lengthy and complex legal battle, for example, Starbucks won a major intellectual property case it had taken to the Chinese courts. A local firm was using Starbucks' Chinese name, "Xingbake" (*Xing* means "star" and *bake* is pronounced "bah kuh"), and was also copying its café designs.[16]

When international businesses believe they are being mistreated in foreign countries, or when local companies believe foreign competitors are disadvantaging them, their respective governments might take the cases to the **World Trade Organization (WTO)**. The 140 members of the WTO give one another **most favored nation status**—the most favorable treatment for imports and exports. Members also agree to work together within its framework to try to resolve some international business problems.

Even though WTO members are supposed to give one another most favored nation status, trade barriers are still common. They include outright **tariffs** or taxes that governments impose on imports. They also include **nontariff barriers** that discourage imports in nontax ways such as quotas and government import restrictions.

Yet another trade barrier emerges as outright **protectionism**—the attempt by governments to protect local firms from foreign competition and save jobs for local workers. You will see such issues reflected in many political campaigns and debates. And the issues aren't easy. Government leaders face internal political dilemmas involving the often-conflicting goals of seeking freer international trade while still protecting domestic industries. Such dilemmas can make it difficult for countries to reach international agreements on trade matters and hard for the WTO to act as a global arbiter of trade issues.

STUDY GUIDE

Takeaway 17.1
How Does Globalization Affect International Business?

Terms to Define

Exporting

Foreign subsidiary

Franchising

Global economy

Global sourcing

Global strategic alliance

Globalization

Greenfield venture

Importing

Insourcing

International business

Joint venture

Licensing

Most favored nation status

Nontariff barriers

Outsourcing

Protectionism

Tariffs

World Trade Organization (WTO)

Rapid Review

- The forces of globalization create international business opportunities to pursue profits, customers, capital, and low-cost suppliers and labor in different countries.
- The least costly ways of doing business internationally are to use global sourcing, exporting and importing, and licensing and franchising.
- Direct investment strategies to establish joint ventures or wholly owned subsidiaries in foreign countries represent substantial commitments to international operations.
- Environmental differences, particularly in legal and political systems, can complicate international business activities.
- The World Trade Organization (WTO) is a global institution established to promote free trade and open markets around the world.

Questions for Discussion

1. Why would a government want to prohibit a foreign firm from owning more than 49% of a local joint venture?
2. Are joint ventures worth the risk of being taken advantage of by foreign partners, as with GM's "Chery" case in China?
3. What aspects of the U.S. legal environment might prove complicated for a Russian firm starting new operations in the United States?

Be Sure You Can

- explain how globalization impacts our lives
- list five reasons that companies pursue international business opportunities
- describe and give examples of how firms do international business by global sourcing, exporting/importing, franchising/licensing, joint ventures, and foreign subsidiaries
- discuss how differences in legal environments can affect businesses operating internationally
- explain the purpose of the World Trade Organization

What Would You Do?

China beckons! Your new design for a revolutionary golf putter has turned out to be a big hit with your friends and players on the local golf courses. So, you decide to have them manufactured in China for sale around the world. The question is: How do you start? What form of international business would be best for you at this point and why? What worries do you have about doing business with a Chinese supplier? How can you learn more about potential complications in the Chinese business environment?

Takeaway 17.2
What Are Global Corporations and How Do They Work?

ANSWERS TO COME

- Global corporations or MNCs do substantial business in many countries.
- The actions of global corporations can be controversial at home and abroad.
- Managers of global corporations face a variety of ethical challenges.
- Planning and controlling are complicated in global corporations.
- Organizing can be difficult in global corporations.
- Leading is challenging in global corporations.

IF YOU TRAVEL ABROAD THESE DAYS, MANY OF YOUR FAVORITE BRANDS AND products will travel with you. You can have a McDonald's sandwich in 119 countries, follow it with Häagen-Dazs ice cream in some 50 countries, and then brush up with Procter & Gamble's Crest in 80 countries. Economists even use the "Big Mac" index to track purchasing power parity among the world's currencies. A recent index listed $3.71 in the U.S., $2.18 in China, and $4.79 in the Euro area.[17]

Global corporations or MNCs do substantial business in many countries.

A **global corporation** or **multinational corporation** or **multinational corporation (MNC)** has extensive international business dealings in many foreign countries.

A **global corporation** or **multinational corporation (MNC)** has extensive international operations in many foreign countries and derives a substantial portion of its sales and profits from international sources.[18] The world's largest MNCs are identified in annual listings such as *Fortune* magazine's Global 500 and the *Financial Times'* FT Global 500. They include names very familiar to consumers, such as Walmart, BP, Toyota, Nestlé, BMW, Hitachi, Caterpillar, Sony, and Samsung. Also on the list are some you might not recognize such as big oil and gas producers like PetroChina (China), Gazprom (Russia), Total (France), and Petrobas (Brazil).[19]

A **transnational corporation** is an MNC that operates worldwide on a borderless basis.

Top managers of some multinationals are trying to move their firms toward becoming **transnational corporations.** That is, they would like to operate worldwide without being identified with one national home.[20] When you buy Nestlé's products, for example, do you have any idea that it is a registered Swiss company? The firm's executives view the entire world as their domain for acquiring resources, locating production facilities, marketing goods and services, and establishing brand image. They seek total integration of global operations, try to make major decisions from a global perspective, and have top managers from many different countries.

Most MNCs still retain strong national identifications even while operating around the world. Is there any doubt in your mind that Walmart and HP are "American" firms whereas Nissan and Sony are "Japanese"? Most likely not, but that may not be the way their executives would like the firms viewed. And by the way, which company is really more American—the Indian giant Tata Group, which gets more than 50% of its revenues from North America, or IBM, which gets 65% of its revenues outside of the United States?[21]

‖ The actions of global corporations can be controversial at home and abroad.

Does a company's nationality matter to the domestic economy? Does it matter to an American whether local jobs come from a domestic giant such as Verizon or a foreign one such as Honda?[22] What about the power global firms wield in the world economy? Quite often now we hear concerns about a **globalization gap** in which large multinationals gain disproportionately from the forces of globalization while smaller firms and many countries do not.[23] The United Nations reports that they hold one-third of the world's productive assets and control 70% of world trade. Revenues of Exxon/Mobil, for example, are equivalent to Egypt's GDP; Finland's budget is 20% less than the annual sales of its premier multinational Nokia.[24]

Ideally, global corporations and the countries that host their foreign operations should all benefit. But as Figure 17.2 shows, things can go both right and wrong in MNC–host country relationships. While the economic power of global firms is undoubtedly good for business leaders and investors, it can be threatening to small and less developed countries and their domestic industries.

MNCs may complain that the host country bars it from taking profits out of country, overprices local resources, and imposes restrictive government rules. Host countries may accuse the MNCs of hiring the best local talent, failing to respect local customs, making too much profit, and failing to transfer really useful technology.[25] Another complaint is that MNCs may use unfair practices, such as below-cost pricing, to drive local competitors out of business. This is one of the arguments in favor of *protectionism*, discussed earlier as the use of laws and practices to protect a country's domestic businesses from foreign competitors.

MNCs can also run into difficulties in their home or headquarters countries. If a multinational cuts local jobs and then moves or outsources the work to another country, local government and community leaders will quickly criticize the firm for its lack of social responsibility. After all, they will say, shouldn't you be creating local jobs and building the local economy? Perhaps you might agree with this view. But can you see why business executives might disagree?

The **globalization gap** involves large global firms gaining disproportionately from the global economic versus smaller firms and many countries.

MNC-HOST COUNTRY RELATIONSHIPS	MNC-HOST COUNTRY RELATIONSHIPS	
What should go right	*What can go wrong*	
Mutual benefits	**Host-country complaints about MNCs**	**MNC complaints about host countries**
Shared opportunities with potential for • Growth • Income • Learning • Development	• Excessive profits • Economic domination • Interference with government • Hires best local talent • Limited technology transfer • Disrespect for local customs	• Profit limitations • Overpriced resources • Exploitative rules • Foreign exchange restrictions • Failure to uphold contracts

FIGURE 17.2 What Can Go Right and Wrong in Relationships Between Global Corporations and Their Host Countries?
When things go right, both the global corporation, or MNC, and its host country gain. The global firm gets profits or resources, and the host country often sees more jobs and employment opportunities, higher tax revenues, and useful technology transfers. But when things go wrong, each finds ways to blame the other.

⫿ Managers of global corporations face a variety of ethical challenges.

Corruption involves illegal practices to further one's business interests.

The **Foreign Corrupt Practices Act** makes it illegal for U.S. firms and their representatives to engage in corrupt practices overseas.

The ethical aspects of international business are often in the news, and it sometimes involves outright **corruption**. This occurs when employees or representatives of MNCs resort to illegal practices such as bribes to further their business interests in foreign countries. The **Foreign Corrupt Practices Act** (FCPA) makes it illegal for U.S. firms and their representatives to engage in corrupt practices overseas. This prohibits them from paying or offering bribes or excessive commissions, including nonmonetary gifts, to foreign officials or employees of state-run companies in return for business favors.[26]

Although the FCPA makes sense, critics claim that it fails to recognize the realities of business as practiced in many foreign nations. They believe it puts U.S. companies at a competitive disadvantage because they can't offer the same "deals" as businesses from other nations—deals that the locals may regard as standard business practices. What do you think? Should U.S. legal standards apply to American companies operating abroad? Or should they be allowed to practice business in whatever way the local setting considers acceptable?

Sweatshops employ workers at very low wages, for long hours, and in poor working conditions.

The fact is that even the most well-intentioned MNCs can end up in troublesome relationships with their global suppliers. Global businesses sometimes end up working with local firms best described as **sweatshops**, places in which employees work at low wages for long hours and in poor, even unsafe, conditions.[27] Microsoft, for example, faced complaints about workers being abused in a factory in China that supplies some of its electronic devices. The National Labor Committee, a U.S.-based human rights advocacy organization, claimed that the Chinese factory owners were overworking employees and housing them in bad conditions. Microsoft's response was to send independent auditors "to conduct a complete and thorough investigation."[28]

Child labor is the full-time employment of children for work otherwise done by adults.

Another possibility is that global firms end up working with contractors who use **child labor**, the full-time employment of children for work otherwise done by adults.[29] As you might guess, the owners of such places might be in a good position to offer low prices to foreign companies buying their products. But just because the factory is legal by local standards, does this justify doing business with its owners? Steve Dowling, an Apple spokesperson, says that Apple regularly audits suppliers "to make sure they comply with Apple's strict standards" and that the firm also conducts "extensive training programs to educate workers about their right to a safe and respectful work environment." One Apple audit discovered that three of its foreign contractors had used underage workers.[30]

⫿ Planning and controlling are complicated in global corporations.

Setting goals, making plans, controlling results—all of these standard management functions can become quite complicated in the international arena. Picture a home office somewhere in the United States, say, Chicago. The MNC's foreign operations are scattered in Asia, Africa, South America, and Europe. Somehow, planning and controlling must span all locations, meeting both home office needs and those of foreign affiliates.

{ TRANSPARENCY INTERNATIONAL SEEKS A WORLD FREE OF CORRUPTION AND BRIBES.

Facts to Consider

■ CORRUPTION AND BRIBES HAUNT GLOBAL BUSINESS

If you want a world free of corruption and bribes, you have a lot in common with the nonprofit activist organization Transparency International. From its headquarters in Berlin, TI publishes regular surveys and reports on corruption and bribery around the world. Here are some recent data.

Corruption: Best and worst out of 180 countries in perceived corruption in doing business.

> *Best*—1. New Zealand, 2. Denmark, 3. (tie) Sweden/ Singapore, 5. Switzerland
>
> *Worst*—180. Somalia, 179. Afghanistan, 178. Myanmar, 177. Sudan, 176. Iraq
>
> *In Betweens*—19. USA, 32. Spain, 55. Greece, 63. Saudi Arabia, 75. Brazil

Bribery: Best and worst of 20 countries in likelihood of home-country firms' willingness to pay bribes abroad. (& = ties)

> *Best*—Belgium & Canada, Netherlands & Switzerland, Germany
>
> *Worst*—Russia, China, Mexico, India, Italy & Brazil
>
> *In Betweens*—Australia, France & United States, Spain, South Korea & Taiwan

YOUR THOUGHTS?

What patterns do you detect in these data, if any? Does it surprise you that the United States didn't make the "best" lists? How would you differentiate between the terms "corruption" and "bribery" as they apply in international business?

One planning issue in international business is **currency risk**, or fluctuations in foreign exchange rates. Companies such as McDonald's and HP, for example, make a lot of sales abroad. These sales are in foreign currencies. But as exchange rates vary, the dollar value of sales revenues goes up and down and profits are affected. Companies have to plan for the potential positive and negative impacts of exchange rate fluctuations.

When the dollar is weak against the euro, it takes more in dollars to buy one euro. This is bad for American consumers who must pay more to buy European products; it's good for European consumers who pay less for American ones. This is also good for American companies who make lots of sales in euros and then get more when exchanging them for dollars. But suppose the dollar strengthens against the euro? Is this good or bad for firms with large sales in euro-zone countries? The boxed example shows that it's bad.

Global businesses must also deal with control issues of **political risk**, potential losses because of instability and political changes in foreign countries. The major threats of political risk today come from terrorism, civil wars, armed conflicts, shifting government systems through elections or forced takeovers, and new laws and economic policies. An example is the surprise nationalization of Bolivia's oil and gas industries as described in the earlier ethics check. Although such things can't be prevented, they can be anticipated to some extent by a planning technique called **political-risk analysis**. It tries to forecast the probability of disruptive events that can threaten the security of a foreign investment. Given the world we now live in, can you see the high stakes of such analysis?

Currency risk is possible loss because of fluctuating exchange rates.

Scenario 1: Weak dollar
> 1 $US = 0.75 euro
> Euro sales = €100,000
> U.S. take-home revenue = $133,000

Scenario 2: Strong dollar
> 1 $US = 1.25 euros
> Euro sales = €100,000
> U.S. take-home revenue = $80,000

Political risk is possible loss because of instability and political changes in foreign countries.

Political-risk analysis forecasts how political events may impact foreign investments.

Organizing can be difficult in global corporations.

Even after plans are in place, it isn't easy to organize for international operations. In the early stages of international activities, businesses often appoint someone or a specific unit to handle them. But as global business expands, a more complex arrangement is usually necessary.

One possible choice for organizing an MNC is the *global area structure* shown in Figure 17.3. It arranges production and sales functions into separate geographical units and puts top managers in charge—such as Area Manager Africa or Area Manager Europe. This allows business in major areas of the world to be run by executives with special local expertise.

FIGURE 17.3

How Can Multinational Corporations Organize for Success in Their Global Operations?
When the international side of a business grows, the structure often gets complicated. One approach is a global area structure, which assigns senior managers to oversee all product operations in major parts of the world. Another is the global product structure, in which area specialists advise other senior managers on business practices in their parts of the world.

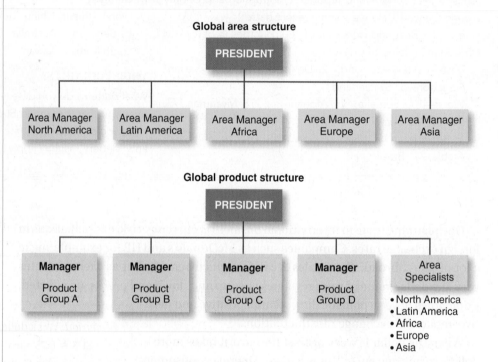

Another organizing option is the *global product structure*, also shown in the figure. It gives worldwide responsibilities to product group managers who are assisted by area specialists who work as part of the corporate staff. These specialists provide expert guidance on the cultures, markets, and unique conditions of various countries or regions.

Leading is challenging in global corporations.

As executives in businesses and other types of organizations press forward with global initiatives, the challenges of leading diverse workforces and dealing with customers across national and cultural borders have to be mastered. There is no doubt the forces of globalization and the growth of international businesses are creating needs for more **global managers**, ones aware of international developments and competent in working across cultures.[31] In fact, the *Wall Street Journal* calls it a business imperative and says that global companies need managers who "understand different countries and cultures" and "intuitively understand the markets they are trying to penetrate."[32]

A **global manager** is culturally aware and informed on international affairs.

A truly global manager is always inquisitive and informed of international events and trends in our ever-changing world, such as those featured throughout this book. A truly global manager is also culturally sensitive and aware. And, a truly global manager is highly skilled in leadership competencies that travel well across cultural boundaries.

Some evidence-based findings on global leadership skills are shown in the small box.[33] It turns out that universal facilitators of leadership success are things like being trustworthy, informed, communicative, and inspiring. Regardless of where they live and work, people tend to like leaders who give them confidence and are good with teamwork. But things like being a loner and acting irritable, uncooperative, and autocratic are viewed negatively across cultures. They are universal inhibitors of leadership success.

So now we come back to you. Are you willing to admit that the world isn't just for traveling anymore, and to embrace it as a career opportunity? Is it possible that you might stand out to a potential employer as someone with the leadership skills to excel as a global manager?

Universal *Facilitators* of Leadership Success

- Acting trustworthy, just, honest
- Showing foresight, planning
- Being positive, dynamic, motivating
- Inspiring confidence
- Being informed and communicative
- Being a coordinator and team builder

Universal *Inhibitors* of Leadership Success

- Being a loner
- Acting uncooperative
- Being irritable
- Acting autocratic

Manager's Library

■ *HOT, FLAT, AND CROWDED 2.0* BY THOMAS FRIEDMAN

WILL GREEN BECOME THE NEW RED, WHITE, AND BLUE?

Is it time for America to rebrand itself and begin 'living the life' differently? Its economic and consumptive lifestyle relies on cheap energy from fossil fuels like coal and oil. These are disappearing natural resources that also produce pollution. Could a new "green" United States emerge in place of the old "red, white, and blue"?

In the book *Hot, Flat, and Crowded 2.0* (2008, Farrar, Straus and Giroux), author Thomas Friedman argues that rising temperatures globally (hot), growing numbers of people with consumptive lifestyles (flat), and swelling populations (crowded) converge to create five threats to national economies built upon fossil fuel use. He predicts unstable energy markets, repressive dictatorships in oil rich countries, climate change, exploitation of natural resources in poor countries, and biodiversity loss of species and forests containing valuable medical and scientific resources for humankind.

Friedman challenges America to lead a global revolution in green energy production utilizing clean power, energy efficient systems, and conservation ethics toward the natural world. He offers strategies such as regulating automobile fuel efficiency at 60 mpg, boosting coal-fired power plant efficiency by 60% and capturing its carbon, building nuclear power plants, and increasing wind power to displace coal plants and produce hydrogen fuel. He thinks America can leverage its innovation, entrepreneurship, and idealism and turn these threats into opportunities.

Friedman envisions an energy Internet of "smart" homes and devices where one national power grid links utility companies to programmable appliances and cars. Machines would communicate with the grid, adjusting energy needs and use times to level demand, and idle cars could give back stored energy. These realities are feasible in the first half of the 21st century. He believes the U.S. can emerge from coal and oil dependence as the world's leading power, and profit by selling its new lifestyle to countries around the world that would be green with envy.

REFLECT AND REACT

How can product manufacturers reuse, recycle, or reduce materials used in consumer goods? Is it possible to grow the world's population and biodiversity at once? How could oil and gas taxes provide incentives for innovations in clean energies like solar, wind, or nuclear? And by the way, does the price of gas or electricity reflect its environmental or human health costs?

STUDY GUIDE

Takeaway 17.2
What Are Global Corporations and How Do They Work?

Terms to Define

Child labor

Corruption

Currency risk

Expatriate workers

Foreign Corrupt
Practices Act

Global corporation
or multinational
corporation (MNC)

Global manager

Globalization gap

Political risk

Political-risk analysis

Sustainable
development

Sweatshop

Transnational
corporation

Rapid Review

- A global business or multinational corporation (MNC) has extensive operations in several foreign countries; a transnational corporation attempts to operate without national identity and with a worldwide strategy.
- Global firms benefit host countries by paying taxes, bringing in new technologies, and creating employment opportunities; they can also harm host countries by interfering with local government and politics, extracting excessive profits, and dominating the local economy.
- The Foreign Corrupt Practices Act prohibits representatives of U.S. international businesses from engaging in corrupt practices abroad.
- Planning and controlling global operations must take into account such things as currency risk and political risk in changing environmental conditions.
- Organizing for global operations often involves use of a global product structure or a global area structure.
- Leading global operations requires universal leadership skills and global managers who are capable of working in different cultures and countries.

Questions for Discussion

1. Should becoming a transnational corporation be the goal of all MNCs?
2. Is there anything that global firms and host governments can do to avoid conflicts and bad feelings with one another?
3. Are laws such as the Foreign Corrupt Practices Act unfair to American companies trying to compete around the world?

Be Sure You Can

- differentiate a multinational corporation from a transnational corporation
- list common host-country complaints and three home-country complaints about MNC operations
- explain the international business challenges of corruption, sweatshops, and child labor
- discuss the implications of political risk for global businesses
- differentiate the global area structure and global product structure
- list possible competencies of global managers

What Would You Do?

You've just read in the newspaper that one of your favorite brands of sports shoes is being investigated for being made in sweatshop conditions at factories in Asia. It really disturbs you, but the shoes are great! One of your friends says it's time to boycott the brand, but you're not sure. Will you engage in a personal boycott or not, and why? Furthermore, why is it that major global firms can often get away with these behaviors?

TestPrep 17

Multiple-Choice Questions

1. In addition to gaining new markets, businesses go international in the search for _____.
   - (a) political risk
   - (b) protectionism
   - (c) lower labor costs
   - (d) most favored nation status

2. When Rocky Brands bought 70% ownership of a manufacturing company in the Dominican Republic, Rocky was engaging in which form of international business?
   - (a) import/export
   - (b) licensing
   - (c) foreign subsidiary
   - (d) joint venture

3. When Limited Brands buys cotton in Egypt and has pants sewn from it in Sri Lanka according to designs made in Italy and then sells the pants in the United States, this is a form of international business known as _____.
   - (a) licensing
   - (b) importing
   - (c) joint venturing
   - (d) global sourcing

4. When foreign investment creates new jobs that are filled by local domestic workers, some call the result _____ as opposed to the more controversial notion of outsourcing.
   - (a) globalization
   - (b) insourcing
   - (c) joint venturing
   - (d) licensing

5. When a Hong Kong firm makes an agreement with the Walt Disney Company to use the Disney logo and legally make jewelry in the shape of Disney cartoon characters, Disney is engaging in a form of international business known as _____.
   - (a) exporting
   - (b) licensing
   - (c) joint venturing
   - (d) franchising

6. One major difference between an international business and a transnational corporation is that the transnational tries to operate _____.
   - (a) without a strong national identity
   - (b) in at least six foreign countries
   - (c) with only domestic managers at the top
   - (d) without corruption

7. The Foreign Corrupt Practices Act makes it illegal for _____.
   - (a) U.S. businesses to work with subcontractors running foreign sweatshop operations
   - (b) foreign businesses to pay bribes to U.S. government officials
   - (c) U.S. businesses to make "payoffs" abroad to gain international business contracts
   - (d) foreign businesses to steal intellectual property from U.S. firms operating in their countries

8. The World Trade Organization, or WTO, would most likely become involved in disputes between countries over _____.
   - (a) exchange rates
   - (b) ethnocentrism
   - (c) nationalization
   - (d) tariffs and protectionism

9. The athletic footwear maker New Balance discovered that exact copies of its running shoe designs were on sale in China under the name "New Barlun." This is an example of a/an _____ problem in international business.
   - (a) most favored nation
   - (b) global strategic alliance
   - (c) joint venture
   - (d) intellectual property rights

10. When the profits of large international businesses are disproportionately high relative to those of smaller firms and even the economies of some countries, this is called _____.
    (a) return on risk for business investment
    (b) the globalization gap
    (c) protectionism
    (d) most favored nations status

11. If a new government comes into power and seizes all foreign assets in the country without any payments to the owners, the loss to foreign firms is considered a _____ risk of international business.
    (a) franchise
    (b) political
    (c) currency
    (d) corruption

12. Who gains most when the dollar weakens versus a foreign currency such as the Brazilian Real?
    (a) American consumers of Brazilian products.
    (b) Brazilian firms selling products in America.
    (c) American firms selling products in Brazil.
    (d) Brazilian consumers of European products.

13. Which of the following is identified by researchers as a universal inhibitor of leadership success across cultures?
    (a) Being positive.
    (b) Acting autocratic.
    (c) Being a good planner.
    (d) Acting trustworthy.

14. If an international business firm has separate vice presidents in charge of its Asian, African, and European divisions, it is most likely using a global _____ structure.
    (a) product
    (b) functional
    (c) area
    (d) matrix

15. Which country is often called "the factory for the world"?
    (a) China
    (b) Germany
    (c) Brazil
    (d) United States

Short-Response Questions

16. What is the difference between a joint venture and a wholly owned subsidiary?

17. List three reasons why host countries sometimes complain about MNCs.

18. What does it mean in an international business sense if a U.S. senator says she favors "protectionism"?

19. What is the difference between currency risk and political risk in international business?

Integration and Application Question

20. Picture yourself sitting in a discussion group at the local bookstore and proudly signing copies of your newly published book, *Business Transitions in the New Global Economy*. A book buyer invites a comment from you by stating: "I am interested in your point regarding the emergence of transnational corporations. But, try as I might, a company like Ford or Procter & Gamble will always be 'as American as Apple pie' for me."

    Questions: How would you respond in a way that both (a) clarifies the difference between a multinational and a transnational corporation, and (b) explains reasons why Ford or P&G may wish not to operate as or be viewed as "American" companies?

Steps*for*FurtherLearning

Many learning resources are found at the end of the book and online within WileyPLUS.

Don't Miss These Selections from the **Skill-Building Portfolio**

■ **SELF-ASSESSMENT 17:** *Global Intelligence*

■ **CLASS EXERCISE 17:** *American Football*

■ **TEAM PROJECT 17:** *Globalization Pros and Cons*

Don't Miss This Selection from **Cases for Critical Thinking**

■ **CHAPTER 17 CASE**
Harley-Davidson—Style and Strategy Have Global Reach

Snapshot Although the company had been exporting motorcycles ever since it was founded, it was not until the late 1980s that Harley-Davidson management began to think seriously about international markets. New ads were developed specifically for different markets, and rallies were adapted to fit local customs. The company also began to actively recruit and develop dealers in Europe and Japan. It purchased a Japanese distribution company and built a large parts warehouse in Germany.

Harley is currently the number one motorcycle brand in five European countries, and number two in four countries. This sustained buying has earned Harley four consecutive quarters of sales and market share growth in Europe. Harley has learned from its international activities and continues to make inroads in overseas markets including China and India.

Make notes here on what you've learned about yourself from this chapter.

■ **LEARNING JOURNAL 17**

"I found my dream job and passion when I was 11—and I still have it. I love what I do and I am good at it, which makes me incredibly lucky and blessed." Buddy Valestro, reality TV's "Cake Boss."

Entrepreneurship and Small Business

18

Taking Risks Can Make Dreams Come True

Management Live

Risk Taking and *The Bourne Ultimatum*

In *The Bourne Ultimatum*, FBI chief Pamela Landy (Joan Allen) is trying to track down someone who leaked highly classified intelligence information to a British newspaper reporter. The reporter is dead and was last seen with rogue CIA operative Jason Bourne (Matt Damon). Bourne is a highly trained killer who is looking for Neil Daniels (Colin Stinton), the individual responsible for the leak.

Landy's team makes contact with Daniels's assistant, Nicky Parsons (Julia Stiles), while Bourne is in the office. In a play to put Bourne at ease, Landy reveals to Parsons that the CIA is looking for him but that she doesn't believe he has anything to do with the leak.

Landy has taken a gamble that Bourne will trust her and make contact. Does the gamble pay off? That's the ultimate question for anyone who's just taken a risk.

Successful entrepreneurs have a tendency toward **risk taking**, but this does not mean they charge blindly into situations. They're not gamblers. They take calculated risks using information and experience to guide them. But taking risks does mean there is always a chance for failure. The true mark of an accomplished entrepreneur and risk taker is the ability to learn from mistakes and continue trying.

Your career will have its share of risks. Think about the many complexities of the present job environment and your plans for career success. Could your ability to deal with risk be a personal strength and competency?

YOUR CHAPTER 18 TAKEAWAYS

1. Understand the nature of entrepreneurship and entrepreneurs.

2. Discuss small business and how to start one.

WHAT'S INSIDE

Explore Yourself
More on risk taking

Role Models
Michelle Greenfield makes power from the sun

Ethics Check
Entrepreneurship and philanthropy

Facts to Consider
Minority entrepreneurs are on the move

Manager's Library
In-N-Out Burger by Stacy Perman

Takeaway 18.1
What Is Entrepreneurship and Who Are Entrepreneurs?

ANSWERS TO COME

- Entrepreneurs are risk takers who spot and pursue opportunities
- Entrepreneurs often share similar backgrounds and experiences
- Entrepreneurs often share similar personality traits
- Women and minority entrepreneurs are growing in numbers
- Social entrepreneurs seek novel solutions to pressing social problems

NEED A JOB? WHY NOT CREATE ONE?[1] THAT'S WHAT JENNIFER WRIGHT DID AFTER the financial crisis shut down her work as a credit analyst. While back at school in an MBA program, she worked with a friend's idea for a better pizza box and entered it in an entrepreneurship competition. The "green box," as she calls it, breaks into plates and a storage container before it goes for recycling. She got "incredibly positive" feedback and seed funding to start her business—GreenBox NY.

Retired, feeling a bit old, and want to do more? Not to worry. People aged 55–64 are the most entrepreneurially active in the United States. Realizing that he needed "someplace to go and something to do" after retirement, Art Koff, now 74, started RetiredBrains.com. It's a job board for retirees and gets thousands of hits a day. It also employs seven people and keeps Koff as busy as he wants to be.

Struggling with work-life balance as a mother? Concerned about child nutrition? You might find flexibility and opportunity in entrepreneurship. Denise Devine was a financial executive with Campbell Soup Co. Now she has her own company, Froose Brands, that provides nutritional drinks and foods for kids. Called *mompreneurs,* women like Devine are finding opportunity in market niches for healthier products they spot as moms. Says Devine: "As entrepreneurs we're working harder than we did, but we're doing it on our own schedules."

Female, thinking about starting a small business, but don't have the money? Get creative and reach out. You might find help with organizations like Count-Me-In, started by co-founders Nell Merlino and Iris Burnett. It provides micro-credit loans from $500 to $10,000 to help women start and expand small businesses. Its unique credit scoring system doesn't hold things such as a divorce, time off to raise a family, or age against applicants—all things that might discourage conventional lenders. Merlino says: "Women own 38% of all businesses in this country, but still have far less access to capital than men because of today's process."[2]

These examples all involve a personal quality that is much valued in today's challenging economic times—**entrepreneurship**, a form of risk taking to achieve business success. People like Jennifer Wright, Art Koff, and Denise Devine acted on their ideas to create something new for society. They are **entrepreneurs**, persons who are willing to take risks to pursue opportunities that others either fail to recognize or view as problems or threats.

Entrepreneurship is risk-taking behavior in pursuit of business success.

An **entrepreneur** is willing to pursue opportunities in situations that others view as problems or threats.

Entrepreneurs are risk takers who spot and pursue opportunities.

H. Wayne Huizenga, former owner of AutoNation, Blockbuster Video, and the Miami Dolphins, and a member of the Entrepreneurs' Hall of Fame, describes being an entrepreneur this way: "An important part of being an entrepreneur is a gut instinct that allows you to believe in your heart that something will work even though everyone else says it will not." You say, "I am going to make sure it works. I am going to go out there and make it happen."[3] In business we talk about this as an entrepreneur's skill at gaining **first-mover advantage**, moving faster than competitors to spot, exploit, and enter a new market or an unrecognized niche in an existing one.

So who are these entrepreneurs and who might become one someday? To begin the discussion take a look at Table 18.1—*Debunking Common Myths About Entrepreneurs.*[4]

A **first-mover advantage** comes from being first to exploit a niche or enter a market.

Table 18.1 Debunking Common Myths About Entrepreneurs

- *Entrepreneurs are born, not made.*
  Not true! Talent gained and enhanced by experience is a foundation for entrepreneurial success.
- *Entrepreneurs are gamblers.*
  Not true! Entrepreneurs are risk takers, but the risks are informed and calculated.
- *Money is the key to entrepreneurial success.*
  Not true! Money is no guarantee of success. There's a lot more to it than that; many entrepreneurs start with very little.
- *You have to be young to be an entrepreneur.*
  Not true! Age is no barrier to entrepreneurship; with age often come experience, contacts, and other useful resources.
- *You have to have a degree in business to be an entrepreneur.*
  Not true! But it helps to study and understand business fundamentals.

With the myths out of the way, let's meet some real entrepreneurs, people who built successful long-term businesses from good ideas and hard work.[5] As you read about these creative and confident individuals, think about how you might apply their experiences to your own life and career. After all, it could be very nice to be your own boss someday.

Anita Roddick

In 1973, Anita Roddick was a 33-year-old housewife looking for a way to support herself and her two children. She spotted a niche for natural-based skin and health care products, and started mixing and selling them from a small shop in Brighton, England. The Body Shop PLC has grown to some 1,500 outlets in 47 countries with 24 languages, selling a product every half-second to one of its 86 million customers. Known for her commitment to human rights, the environment, and economic development, the late Roddick believed in business social responsibility, saying: "If you think you're too small to have an impact, try going to bed with a mosquito."

||| Earl Graves

With a vision and a $175,000 loan, Earl G. Graves Sr. started *Black Enterprise* magazine in 1970. That success grew into the diversified business information company Earl G. Graves Ltd.—a multimedia company covering television, radio, and digital media including BlackEnterprise.com. Among his many accomplishments—named by *Fortune* Magazine as one of the 50 most powerful and influential African Americans in corporate America, recipient of the Lifetime Achievement Award from the National Association of Black Journalists, and selection for the Junior Achievement Worldwide U.S. Business Hall of Fame. He has written a best-selling book, *How to Succeed in Business Without Being White,* and is a member of many business and nonprofit boards. The business school at his college alma mater, Baltimore's Morgan State University, is named after him. Graves says: "I feel that a large part of my role as publisher of *Black Enterprise* is to be a catalyst for black economic development in this country."

||| David Thomas

Have you had your Wendy's today? A lot of people have, and there's quite a story behind it. The late David Thomas opened the first Wendy's restaurant in Columbus, Ohio, in November 1969. It's still there, although there are also about 5,000 others now operating around the world. What began as the founder's dream to own one restaurant grew into a global enterprise. Thomas went on to become one of the best-known entrepreneurs and was often called "the world's most famous hamburger cook." But there's more to Wendy's than profits and business performance. The company strives to help its communities, with a special focus on schools and schoolchildren. An adopted child, Thomas founded the Dave Thomas Foundation for Adoption.

||| Caterina Fake and Stewart Butterfield

From idea to buyout, it only took 16 months. That's quite a benchmark for would-be Internet entrepreneurs. Welcome to the world of Flickr, started by Caterina Fake and her husband Stewart Butterfield. They took the notion of online photo sharing and turned Flickr in real time into an almost viral Internet phenomenon. They also built the firm in the online environment without needing start-up capital. They got the necessary financing from their families, friends, and angel investors. The payoff came when Yahoo! bought them out for $30 million. Fake's latest venture is Hunch.com, a Web site designed to help people make decisions—e.g., should I buy that Porsche? Stewart, meanwhile, started a gaming studio called Tiny Speck. Its first game, Glitch, is free-to-play.

||| Entrepreneurs often share similar backgrounds and experiences.

Although we might think of all entrepreneurs as founding a new business that achieves large-scale success, many operate on a smaller and less public scale. Entrepreneurs also include those who buy a local Subway Sandwich or Papa John's franchise, open a small retail shop selling used video games or bicycles, or start a self-employed service business such as financial planning, editorial services, or management consulting.[6] But what makes these entrepreneurs tick? Check out the Cake Boss featured in the chapter opening photo. Look again at the prior stories. Do you see any patterns?

Researchers tell us that most entrepreneurs are very self-confident, determined, self-directing, resilient, adaptable, and driven by excellence.[7] A report in the *Harvard Business Review* suggests that they have strong interests in both "creative production" and "enterprise control." *Entrepreneurs like to start things*—creative production. They enjoy working with the unknown and finding unique solutions to problems. *Entrepreneurs also like to run things*—enterprise control. They enjoy making progress toward a goal. They thrive on independence and the sense of mastery that comes with success.[8]

Research finds that entrepreneurs tend to have unique backgrounds.[9] *Childhood experiences and family environment* seem to make a difference. Evidence links entrepreneurs with parents who were entrepreneurial and self-employed. Similarly, entrepreneurs are often raised in families that encourage responsibility, initiative, and independence. Another pattern is found in *career or work history*. Entrepreneurs who try one venture often go on to others, and prior work experience in the same business area or industry is helpful.

Entrepreneurs also tend to blossom during certain *windows of career opportunity*. Most start their business between the ages of 22 and 45, an age spread that seems to allow for risk taking. However, age is no barrier to entrepreneurship. When Tony DeSio was 50, he founded the Mail Boxes Etc. chain. He sold it for $300 million when he was 67 and suffering from heart problems. Within a year he launched PixArts, another franchise chain based on photography and art.[10] When asked by a reporter what he liked most about entrepreneurship, DeSio replied: "Being able to make decisions without having to go through layers of corporate hierarchy—just being a master of your own destiny."

Lest we forget, entrepreneurs are also found within larger organizations. Called **intrapreneurs**, they are people who step forward and take a risk to introduce a new product or process or to pursue innovations that can change the organization in significant ways.

Intrapreneurs display entrepreneurial behavior as employees of larger firms.

{ THERE'S PROBABLY A BIT OF ENTREPRENEUR IN EACH OF US.

Explore Yourself

■ RISK TAKING

Entrepreneurship plays an important role in local economies and the nation as a whole. It can also be a pathway to personal success. There's probably a bit of entrepreneur in each of us. Just how much probably depends on our tendency toward **risk taking**. This is a willingness to take action to achieve a goal even in the face of uncertainty. How would others describe you in this regard? How would you describe yourself?

Get to know yourself better by taking the self-assessment on **Entrepreneurship Orientation** and completing the other activities in the *Exploring Management* **Skill-Building Portfolio**.

Entrepreneurs often share similar personality traits.

While we can't say that there is bona-fide entrepreneurial personality, we can say that researchers do agree that entrepreneurs often share similar personality traits and characteristics. How about it, is it possible that your personality has aspects in common with those of successful entrepreneurs? Look at the figure. How many of the boxes could you put a check next to and say with confidence—"yes, that's me for sure"?[11]

Here's some more detail on the personality traits and characteristics often shared by entrepreneurs. Although the list isn't definitive or limiting, we can be confident in assuming that the more of these traits possessed by someone, the more likely it is to find them trying entrepreneurship at some point in their careers.[12]

- *Internal locus of control:* Entrepreneurs believe that they are in control of their own destiny; they are self-directing and like autonomy.
- *High energy level:* Entrepreneurs are persistent, hardworking, and willing to exert extraordinary efforts to succeed.
- *High need for achievement:* Entrepreneurs are motivated to accomplish challenging goals; they thrive on performance feedback.
- *Tolerance for ambiguity:* Entrepreneurs are risk takers; they tolerate situations with high degrees of uncertainty.
- *Self-confidence:* Entrepreneurs feel competent, believe in themselves, and are willing to make decisions.
- *Passion and action orientation:* Entrepreneurs try to act ahead of problems; they want to get things done and not waste valuable time.
- *Self-reliance and desire for independence:* Entrepreneurs want independence; they are self-reliant; they want to be their own bosses, not work for others.
- *Flexibility:* Entrepreneurs are willing to admit problems and errors, and willing to change a course of action when plans aren't working.

Women and minority entrepreneurs are growing in numbers.

Although background and personality help set the stage, it sometimes takes an outside stimulus or a special set of circumstances to awaken one's entrepreneurial tendencies. When economists speak about entrepreneurs, they differentiate between those who are driven by the desire for new opportunities and those who are driven by absolute need. Those in the latter group pursue **necessity-based entrepreneurship**. They start new ventures because they see no other employment options or they find career doors closed, perhaps due to hitting glass ceilings.

For women and minorities, entrepreneurship sometimes becomes a way to strike out on their own and gain economic independence. Anita Roddick, featured

Necessity-based entrepreneurship occurs when people start new ventures because they have few or no other employment options.

Facts to Consider

■ MINORITY ENTREPRENEURS ARE ON THE MOVE

Minority entrepreneurship is one of the fastest-growing sectors of our economy. Consider these facts and trends:

- There are close to 6 million minority-owned firms in America (29% of all business) and they contribute $1 trillion annually to the economy.
- Minority-owned firms employ some 6 million workers, with the largest employers Asian-owned (2.9 million jobs), Hispanic owned (1.9 million jobs), and African-American owned (921,000 jobs).
- In the last census of small businesses, those owned by African Americans had grown by 45%, by Hispanics 31%, and by Asians 24%.

- If minority business ownership was proportionate to their share of the U. S. population, they would number more than 8 million firms and provide more than 17 million jobs.
- Minority businesses export to 41 countries on six continents, and generate twice the export activity of non-minority firms.

YOUR THOUGHTS?

How can we explain the growth of minority-owned businesses? Is minority entrepreneurship a way to fight economic disparities in society? What special obstacles do minorities and women face on their pathways toward entrepreneurship? What can be done about it?

---

earlier, once said that she started the first Body Shop store because she needed "to create a livelihood for myself and my two daughters, while my husband, Gordon, was trekking across the Americas."[13]

Women already own close to 8 million businesses in the United States, and their firms are expected to create one-third of all new jobs by 2018. Many women business owners say they started their firms after realizing they could do for themselves what they were already doing for other employers.[14]

One survey of women leaving private-sector employment to pursue entrepreneurship reports 33% believing they were not being taken seriously by their prior employer and 29% having experienced "glass ceiling" issues. A report entitled *Women Business Owners of Color: Challenges and Accomplishments*, discusses the motivations of women of color to pursue entrepreneurship because of glass ceiling problems. These include not being recognized or valued by their prior employers, not being taken seriously, and seeing others promoted ahead of them.[15]

About 5.8 million business in America are owned by minority entrepreneurs and these firms are significant sources of job creation for the economy. In one five-year period their growth rate was 46% versus 18% for all firms, and the number of employees for minority-owned firms rose by 27% versus less than 1% for all firms. Yet even with this record of accomplishment the obstacles to minority entrepreneurship are real and shouldn't be underestimated, just as is the case for female entrepreneurs. An example is the critical area of start-up financing. Less than 1% of the available venture capital in the U.S. goes to minority entrepreneurs. The Minority Business Development Agency of the Department of Commerce is well aware of this and other problems. As part of its mission to support the development of minority-owned small and medium-sized firms, the MBDA has set up a nationwide network of 40 business development centers with the goal of helping them grow in "size, scale, and capacity."[16]

Manager's Library

■ *IN-N-OUT BURGER* BY STACY PERMAN

THE ALL-AMERICAN BURGER NEVER GOES OUT OF STYLE

In 1948, Harry and Esther Snyder opened a small hamburger stand beside a busy road in Los Angeles, California. They were eager to make ends meet and, after years of sacrifice during the depression and war, people were in the mood to get about and enjoy life. Driving cars to roadside stands was a novel idea. Their restaurant, In-N-Out Burger, is now a successful family-owned chain of 250 drive-through stores.

In the book *In-N-Out Burger* (2009, HarperCollins), author Stacy Perman profiles the Snyder's values and the investment they put into every In-N-Out burger, employee, and customer. She claims their dedication to quality, reinvestment in employees, and joy in delighting customers has generated an "uncopyable" competitive advantage. In-N-Out stores meet McDonald's stores revenues but do so without advertising, franchising, financing debt, paying minimum wage, or sacrificing quality for volume, speed, and price.

Part of the In-N-Out difference is a focus on quality—right from the beef to the service. Another part is genuine interest in employees: Called associates, they are paid well above minimum wage and train at In-N-Out University. New stores open only after managers have been groomed. Perman says In-N-Out has unrivaled loyal customers and a "cult like" following.

REFLECT AND REACT

Do you agree with Perman that In-N-Out Burger is doing things in ways that create an "uncopyable" advantage in its industry? Are these things that could be copied by entrepreneurs setting out to gain success in other industries?

⫴ Social entrepreneurs seek novel solutions to pressing social problems.

> A **social entrepreneur** takes risks to find new ways to solve pressing social problems.

In an earlier discussion in Chapter 3 on ethics and social responsibility we identified **social entrepreneurs** as persons whose entrepreneurial ventures involve novel ways to help solve pressing social problems.[17] You can think of these problems as the likes of poverty, illiteracy, poor health, and even social oppression. Social entrepreneurs share many characteristics with other entrepreneurs, including backgrounds and personalities. But there is one big difference. Instead of the profit motive, they are driven by a social mission.[18] They want to start and run organizations that improve society and help make lives better for people who are disadvantaged.

There's probably quite a bit of social entrepreneurship taking place in your community. Sadly, it often gets little notice. Most attention often goes to business entrepreneurs making lots of money—or trying to do so. Yet there are many examples you can find of people who have made the commitment to social entrepreneurship. Deborah Sardone, for example, owns a housekeeping service in Texas. After noticing that her clients with cancer really struggled with everyday household chores, she started Cleaning for a Reason. It's a nonprofit that networks with cleaning firms around the country that are willing to offer free home cleaning to cancer patients.[19]

Fast Company magazine says social entrepreneurs run enterprises with "innovative thinking that can transform lives and change the world." It celebrates them with its prestigious Honor Roll of Social Enterprises of the Year. Here are some recent winners.[20]

- Chip Ransler and Manoj Sinha tackled the lack of power faced by many of India's poor villagers. As University of Virginia business students, they realized that 350 million of the people without reliable electricity lived in the country's rice-growing regions. And in those regions, tons of rice husks were being discarded with every harvest. Ransler and Sinha sought a way to create biogas from the husks and use the gas to fuel small power plants. They succeeded, and Husk Power Systems is a reality. But with more than 125,000 villages suffering a lack of power, Ransler says "there's a lot of work to be done."

- Rose Donna and Joel Selanikio were concerned about public health problems in sub-Saharan Africa. After noting that developing nations are often bogged down in the paperwork of public health, they created software to make the process quicker and more efficient. The UN, the World Health Organization, and the Vodafone Foundation are now helping their firm, Data-Dyne, move the program into 22 more African nations.

What drives people like those in the prior examples to pursue entrepreneurship for social gains instead of money? Can you think of ideas that could turn social entrepreneurship by yourself and others into positive impact on your local community?

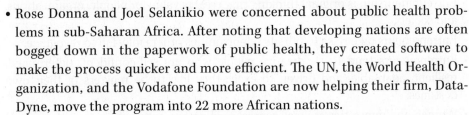

{ CAN SMALL BUSINESSES BUILT ON CARING CAPITALISM SURVIVE BIG BUSINESS BUYOUTS?

Ethics Check

■ ENTREPRENEURSHIP AND PHILANTHROPY

Would you buy shoes just because their maker is pledged to philanthropy? Blake Mycoskie wants you to. Back in 2002, he was participating with his sister in the reality TV show *The Amazing Race*. It whetted his appetite for travel, and he visited Argentina in 2006. There he came face-to-face with lots of young children without shoes, and he had a revelation: He would return home and start a sustainable business that would help address the problem.

Mycoskie launched TOMS (short, he says, for "better tomorrow") to sell shoes made in a classic Argentinean style. But there's a twist—for each pair of shoes it sells, the firm donates a pair to needy children. Blake calls this One for One, a "movement" that involves "people making everyday choices that improve the lives of children." After giving away its one-millionth pair of shoes, Mycoskie renamed the company One for One.

One for One's business model can be described as caring capitalism or profits with principles. Two other names associated with this approach are Ben & Jerry's Ice Cream and Tom's of Maine. But each of these firms was sold to a global enterprise—

Unilever for Ben & Jerry's and Colgate-Palmolive for Tom's of Maine. The expectation was that the corporate buyers wouldn't compromise on the founders' core values and social goals. Who knows what the future holds if One for One grows to the point where corporate buyers loom.

The state of Maryland recently passed a law creating the "benefit corporation" as a new legal entity. It is designed to protect firms like One for One whose charters spell out special values. It also requires them to report their social benefit activities and impact.

YOU DECIDE

What about it? Is Blake's business model one that others should adopt? Is it ethical to link personal philanthropic goals with the products that your business sells? And if an entrepreneurial firm is founded on a caring capitalism model, is it ethical for a future corporate buyer to reduce or limit the emphasis on social benefits? Is Maryland's benefit corporation approach the way we should be heading?

STUDY GUIDE

Takeaway 18.1
What Is Entrepreneurship and Who Are Entrepreneurs?

Terms to Define

Entrepreneur

Entrepreneurship

First-mover advantage

Intrapreneur

Necessity-based entrepreneurship

Social entrepreneur

Rapid Review

- Entrepreneurship is original thinking that creates value for people, organizations, and society.
- Entrepreneurs take risks to pursue opportunities others may fail to recognize.
- Entrepreneurs tend to be creative people who are self-confident, determined, resilient, adaptable, and driven to excel; they like to be masters of their own destinies.
- Women and minorities are well represented among entrepreneurs, with some of their motivation driven by necessity or the lack of alternative career options.
- Social entrepreneurs apply their energies to create innovations that help to solve important problems in society.

Questions for Discussion

1. Does an entrepreneur always need to have first-mover advantage in order to succeed?
2. Are there any items on the list of entrepreneurial characteristics that are "must-haves" for someone to succeed in any career, not just entrepreneurship?
3. Could growth of necessity-driven entrepreneurship be an indicator of some deeper problems in our society?

Be Sure You Can

- explain the concept of entrepreneurship
- explain the concept of first-mover advantage
- explain why people such as Caterina Fake and Earl Graves might become entrepreneurs
- list personal characteristics often associated with entrepreneurs
- explain trends in entrepreneurship by women and minorities
- explain what makes social entrepreneurs unique

What Would You Do?

After reading the examples in this chapter, you're struck by the potential for you to try entrepreneurship. Indeed, you're thinking now that it would be very nice to be your own boss, do your own thing, and make a decent living in the process. But how do you get started? One possibility is to start with ideas passed around among your friends and family. Or perhaps there's something that has been on your mind as a great possible business idea. So, tell us about it. What ideas do you have? What would you like to pursue and why?

Takeaway 18.2

What Should We Know About Small Businesses and How to Start One?

ANSWERS TO COME

- Small businesses are mainstays of the economy.
- Small businesses must master three life-cycle stages.
- Family-owned businesses can face unique challenges.
- Most small businesses fail within five years.
- Assistance is available to help small businesses get started.
- A small business should start with a sound business plan.
- There are different forms of small business ownership.
- There are different ways of financing a small business.

THE U.S. SMALL BUSINESS ADMINISTRATION (SBA) DEFINES A **SMALL BUSINESS** AS one that is independently owned and operated and that does not dominate its industry.[21] It also has 500 or fewer employees, with the number varying a bit by industry. Almost 99% of U.S. businesses meet this definition. Some 87% employ fewer than 20 persons. And interestingly enough, recent data show that business owners rank highest among 10 other occupations in terms of contentment. This includes things like physical and mental health, job satisfaction, and quality of life overall.[22] As to what it's like to be a small business owner, "I'm still excited to get up and go to work every day," says Roger Peugot, who owns a 14-employee plumbing firm. He adds: "Even when things get tough, I'm still in control."[23]

> A **small business** has fewer than 500 employees, is independently owned and operated, and does not dominate its industry.

⦀ Small businesses are mainstays of the economy.

Most nations rely on their small business sector. Why? Among other things, small businesses offer major economic advantages. In the United States, for example, small businesses employ some 52% of private workers, provide 51% of private-sector output, receive 35% of federal government contract dollars, and provide as many as 7 out of every 10 new jobs in the economy.[24] Smaller businesses are especially prevalent in the service and retailing sectors of the economy. Higher costs of entry make them less common in other industries such as manufacturing and transportation.

And then there's the Internet. Have you looked at the action on eBay recently? Can you imagine how many people might now be running small trading businesses from their homes? If you're one of them, you're certainly not alone. The SBA believes that some 85% of small firms are already conducting business over the Internet.[25] Even established "bricks-and-mortar" small retailers are finding the Internet ripe with opportunities. That's what happened to Rod Spencer and

Role Models

■ MICHELLE GREENFIELD MAKES POWER FROM THE SUN

When she was named as a recipient of the Ohio Department of Development's Keys to Success Award, Michelle Greenfield said, "It's exciting. It's kind of nice to be recognized as a good business owner. The goal is not to have the award, the goal is to have a good business and do well." She and her husband Geoff certainly do have a good business; it's called Third Sun Solar Wind and Power, Ltd.

Although the company's products are certainly timely today, they were a bit ahead of the market in the beginning. The Greenfields began by building a rural home that used no electricity in rural Athens County, Ohio. Solar power was the replacement, and they have yet to pay an electric utility bill.

As friends became interested, they helped others get into solar power and the business kept growing from there. It has been ranked by *Inc.* magazine as the 32nd-fastest-growing energy business in the United States. Third Sun is the largest provider of solar energy systems in the Midwest and has experienced a 390% growth in three years. Quite a story for an idea that began with a sustainable home!

Soon after its birth, Third Sun moved into the Ohio University Innovation Center, a business incubator dedicated to helping local firms grow and prosper. Michelle says that they lived very frugally in their rural home and this helped them start the business on a low budget; they have also benefited from tapping the local workforce in a university town and from having MBA students work with their firm in consulting capacities. As the company grew, Geoff focused on technical issues while Michelle spent most of her time on the business and managerial ones. She's now the CEO and, although primarily concerned with strategic issues as the firm grows, still keeps involved by helping the firm's 21 employees with other aspects of the business. "I do a lot of marketing," she says, "I do speaking engagements . . . I serve on the Board of Directors of Green Energy Ohio."

WHAT'S THE LESSON HERE?

Michelle is especially proud of her accomplishments and says: "I think it's nice to be able to point out that there are women in the field that also have enough brains to be successful." She also points out that the name "Third Sun" was chosen to represent a "third son" for the couple, one requiring lots of nurturing in order to help it grow big and strong. Michelle seems to have mastered the test of entrepreneurship and is helping to save our planet as well. Could more people follow her path?

---

his S&S Sports Cards store in Worthington, Ohio. In fact, he closed the store not because business was bad but because it was really good. When his Internet sales greatly exceeded in-store sales, Spencer decided to follow the world of e-commerce. He now works from home, saving the cost of renting retail space and hiring store employees. "I can do less business overall," Rod says, "and make a higher profit."[26]

‖ Small businesses must master three life-cycle stages.

The typical small business moves through recognizable life-cycle stages.[27] The new firm begins with the *birth stage*, where the entrepreneur struggles to get the new venture established and survive long enough to really test the marketplace. The firm then passes into the *breakthrough stage*, where the business model begins to work well, growth takes place, and the complexity of the business expands significantly. Next is the *maturity stage*, where the entrepreneur experiences

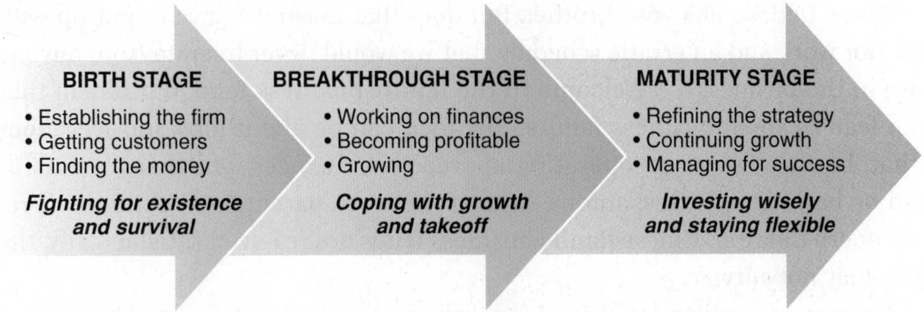

BIRTH STAGE
- Establishing the firm
- Getting customers
- Finding the money

Fighting for existence and survival

BREAKTHROUGH STAGE
- Working on finances
- Becoming profitable
- Growing

Coping with growth and takeoff

MATURITY STAGE
- Refining the strategy
- Continuing growth
- Managing for success

Investing wisely and staying flexible

FIGURE 18.1 What Are the Stages in the Life Cycle of an Entrepreneurial Firm?
It is typical for small businesses to move through three life-cycle stages. During the *birth* stage, the entrepreneur focuses on getting things started—bringing a product to market, finding initial customers, and earning enough money to survive. *Breakthrough* is a time of rapid growth when the business model really starts working well. Growth often slows in the *maturity* stage, where financial success is realized but also where the entrepreneur often needs to make adjustments to stay successful in a dynamic marketplace.

market success and financial stability but also has to face competitive challenges in a dynamic environment.

As shown in Figure 18.1, small business owners often face somewhat different management dilemmas as their firms move through these life-cycle stages. When they experience growth, including possible diversification or global expansion, they can encounter problems making the transition from entrepreneurial leadership to professional strategic leadership. The entrepreneur brings the venture into being and sees it through the early stages of life; the professional manages and leads the venture into maturity as an ever-evolving and perhaps still-growing corporate enterprise. If the entrepreneur is incapable of meeting or unwilling to meet the firm's leadership needs in later life-cycle stages, continued business survival and success may well depend on the business being sold or management control being passed to professionals.

⫼ Family-owned businesses can face unique challenges.

Among the reasons given for getting started in small businesses, you'll find the owners saying they were motivated to be their own bosses, be in control of their own futures, fulfill dreams, and become part of a family-owned business.[28] Indeed, **family businesses**, those owned and financially controlled by family members, represent the largest percentage of businesses operating worldwide. The Family Firm Institute reports that family businesses account for 78% of new jobs created in the United States and provide 60% of the nation's employment.[29]

Family businesses must master the same challenges as other small or large businesses, such as devising strategy, achieving competitive advantage, and ensuring operational excellence. When everything goes right, the family firm can be an ideal situation. Everyone works together, sharing values and a common goal: doing well to support the family. But things don't always turn out this way or stay this way. Changes and complications often test the family bonds, especially as a business changes hands over successive generations.

Family businesses are owned and financially controlled by family members.

A **family business feud** can lead to small business failure.

The **succession problem** is the issue of who will run the business when the current head leaves.

A **succession plan** describes how the leadership transition and related financial matters will be handled.

"Okay, Dad, so he's your brother. But does that mean we have to put up with inferior work and an erratic schedule that we would never tolerate from anyone else in the business?"[30] Welcome to the **family business feud**, a problem that can lead to small business failure. The feud can be about jobs and who does what, business strategy, operating approaches, finances, or other matters. It can be between spouses, among siblings, between parents and children. It really doesn't matter. Unless family business feuds are resolved satisfactorily, the firm may not survive.

A survey of small and midsized family businesses indicated that 66% planned on keeping the business within the family.[31] The management question is: Upon leaving, how will the current head of the company distribute assets and determine who will run the business? This introduces the **succession problem**, how to handle the transfer of leadership from one generation to the next. The data on succession are eye-opening. About 30% of family firms survive to the second generation; 12% survive to the third generation; only 3% are expected to survive beyond that.[32]

If you were the owner of a successful family business, what would you do? Wouldn't you want to have a **succession plan** that clearly spells out how leadership transition and related matters, including financial ones, are to be handled when the time for changeover occurs?

‖ Most small businesses fail within five years.

Does the prospect of starting your own small business sound good? It should, but a word of caution is called for as well. What the last figure on life-cycle stages didn't show is a very common event—small business failure.

Small businesses have a scary high failure rate. The SBA reports that as many as 60% to 80% of new businesses fail in their first five years of operation.[33] Part of this might be explained as a "counting" issue. The government counts as a "failure" any business that closes, whether it is due to the death or retirement of an owner, the sale to someone else, or the inability to earn a profit. Nevertheless, the fact remains: A lot of small business start-ups just don't make it.

The recent economic downturn was especially hard on small firms.[34] Reports are that over 4 million closed in one three-month period, with most facing major sales revenue and credit problems. Beth Wood, a family business expert with MassMutual, says: "They've seen reductions in top line revenue that they just can't react fast enough to." And reflecting on problems with her family restaurant, former owner Georgia Roussos said: "You had to discount so heavily to get someone in the door that it just wasn't profitable anymore." When the restaurant finally closed, her family suffered emotionally not just for themselves but for their former employees as well; 55 people, some serving as long as 35 years, lost their jobs.

Look at the next figure and consider the many possible causes of small business failures.[35] Most of the failures result from poor judgment and management mistakes made by entrepreneurs and owners. So if you decide to launch your own venture someday, you'll need to learn from these mistakes. This is just as important as studying success stories.

‖ Assistance is available to help small businesses get started.

Individuals who start small businesses face a variety of challenges. And even though the prospect of being part of a new venture is exciting, the realities of working through complex problems during setup and the early life of the business can be especially daunting. Fortunately, there is often some assistance available to help entrepreneurs and owners of small businesses get started.

One way that start-up difficulties can be managed is through participation in a **business incubator**. These are special facilities that offer space, shared administrative services, and management advice at reduced costs with the goal of helping new businesses get successfully established. Some incubators are focused on specific business areas such as technology, light manufacturing, or professional services; some are located in rural areas, while others are urban based; some focus only on socially responsible businesses.

Regardless of their focus or location, business incubators share the common goal of increasing the survival rates for new business start-ups. They want to help build new businesses that will create new jobs and expand economic opportunities in their local communities. In the incubators, small businesses are nurtured and assisted so that they can grow quickly and become healthy enough to survive on their own.

A **business incubator** is a facility that offers services to help new businesses get established.

Y Combinator is a business incubator located in Mountain View, California. It was founded by Paul Graham with a focus on Web start-ups. Graham says his premise is "to apply mass-production techniques to founding of a start-up." In the Y Combinator, which supports about 10 start-ups at any given time, entrepreneurs get offices, regular meetings with Graham and other business experts, and access to potential investors. They also receive $15,000 grants in exchange for the incubator taking a 6% ownership stake; Y Combinator hopes to capture a significant return on such investments as the new businesses succeed.[36]

Small Business Development Centers offer guidance to entrepreneurs and small business owners on how to set up and manage business operations.

A **business plan** describes the direction for a new business and the financing needed to operate it.

Another source of assistance for small business development is the U. S. Small Business Administration. Because small businesses play such significant roles in the economy, the SBA works with state and local agencies as well as the private sector to support a network of over 1,100 **Small Business Development Centers** nationwide.[37] These SBDCs offer guidance to entrepreneurs and small business owners, actual and prospective, on how to set up and manage business operations. They are often associated with colleges and universities, and they give students a chance to work as consultants with small businesses at the same time that they pursue their academic programs. If you are inclined toward small business, why not check out your local SBDC?

A small business should start with a sound business plan.

When people start new businesses or even start new units within existing ones, they can greatly benefit from another type of plan—a sound **business plan**. This plan describes the goals of the business and the way it intends to operate, ideally in ways that can help obtain any needed start-up financing.[38] Although there is no single template for a successful business plan, most would agree on the general framework presented in Tips to Remember.[39]

Banks and other financiers want to see a business plan before they loan money or invest in a new venture. Senior managers want to see a business plan before they allocate scarce organizational resources to support a new entrepreneurial project. You should also want a small business plan. The detailed and disciplined thinking helps sort out your ideas, map strategies, and pin down your business model. Says Ed Federkeil, who founded a small business called California Custom Sport Trucks: "It gives you direction instead of haphazardly sticking your key in the door every day and saying—'What are we going to do?'"[40]

{ THE DISCIPLINE OF WRITING A BUSINESS PLAN CAN INCREASE THE LIKELIHOOD OF SUCCESS.

Tips to Remember

■ WHAT TO INCLUDE IN A BUSINESS PLAN

- *Executive summary*—business purpose, highlights of plan
- *Industry analysis*—nature of industry, economic trends, legal or regulatory issues, risks
- *Company description*—mission, owners, legal form
- *Products and services*—major goods or services, uniqueness vis-à-vis competition
- *Market description*—size, competitor strengths and weaknesses, five-year sales goals
- *Marketing strategy*—product characteristics, distribution, promotion, pricing

- *Operations description*—manufacturing or service methods, suppliers, controls
- *Staffing*—management and worker skills needed and available, compensation, human resource systems
- *Financial projection*—cash flow projections 1–5 years, break-even points
- *Capital needs*—amount needed, amount available, amount being requested
- *Milestones*—timetable for completing key stages of new venture

There are different forms of small business ownership.

One of the important choices when starting a new venture is the legal form of ownership. There are a number of alternatives and each has its own advantages and disadvantages.

A **sole proprietorship** is simply an individual or a married couple that pursues business for a profit. The business often operates under a personal name, such as "Tiaña Lopez Designs." Because a sole proprietorship is simple to start, run, and terminate, it is the most common form of U.S. small business ownership. If you choose this form, however, you have to remember—any owner of a sole proprietorship is personally liable for all business debts and claims.

A **partnership** is formed when two or more people contribute resources to start and operate a business together. Most are set up with legal and written agreements that document what each party contributes as well as how profits and losses are to be shared. You would be ill advised to enter into a serious partnership without such an agreement. But once the choice is made to go the partnership route, there are two alternatives.

In a **general partnership**, the simplest and most common form, the owners share day-to-day management and responsibilities for debts and losses. This differs from a **limited partnership**, consisting of a general partner and one or more "limited" partners. The general partner runs the business; the limited partners do not participate in day-to-day management. All partners share in profits, but their losses are limited to the amounts of their investments. This limit to one's liabilities is a major advantage. You'll notice that many professionals, such as accountants and attorneys, work in *limited liability partnerships*—designated as LLP—because they limit the liability of one partner in case of negligence by any others.

A **corporation**, commonly identified by the "Inc." designation in a name, is a legal entity that exists separately from its owners. Corporations are legally chartered by the states in which they are registered, and they can be for-profit, such as Microsoft Inc., or not-for-profit, such as Catalyst Inc. There are two major advantages in choosing to incorporate: (1) it grants the organization certain legal rights—for example, to engage in contracts, and (2) the corporation is responsible for its own liabilities. This gives the firm a life of its own and separates the owners from personal liability. The major disadvantages are the legal costs of setting up the corporation and the complex documentation required to operate as one.

Recently, the **limited liability corporation (LLC)** has gained popularity. It combines the advantages of sole proprietorship, partnership, and corporation. It functions as a corporation for liability purposes and protects the assets of owners against claims made against the company. For tax purposes, it functions as a partnership in the case of multiple owners and as a sole proprietorship in the case of a single owner.

A **sole proprietorship** is an individual pursuing business for a profit.

A **partnership** is when two or more people agree to contribute resources to start and operate a business together.

In a **general partnership**, owners share management and responsibility for debts and losses.

In a **limited partnership** owners shares profits but responsibility for losses is limited to original investments.

A **corporation** is a legal entity that exists separately from its owners.

A **limited liability corporation (LLC)** combines the advantages of the sole proprietorship, partnership, and corporation.

There are different ways of financing a small business.

Starting a new venture takes money. Unless you possess personal wealth that you are willing to risk, that money has to be raised. The two most common ways to raise it are debt financing and equity financing.

Debt financing involves borrowing money from another person, a bank, or a financial institution. This is a loan that must be paid back over time with interest. A loan also requires collateral that pledges business assets or personal assets, such as a home, as security in case of default. You borrow money with a promise to repay both the loan amount and interest. If you can't pay, the security is lost up to the amount of the outstanding loan.

Equity financing gives ownership shares to outsiders in return for their financial investments. In contrast to debt financing, this money does not need to be paid back. Instead, the investor assumes the risk of potential gains and losses based on the performance of the business. But in return for taking that risk, the equity investor gains something—part of your original ownership. The amount of ownership and control given up is represented in the number and proportion of ownership shares transferred to the equity investors.

When businesses need equity financing in fairly large amounts, from the tens of thousands to the millions of dollars, they often turn to **venture capitalists**. These are individuals and companies that pool capital to invest in new ventures. The hope is that their equity stakes rise in value and can be sold for a profit when the business becomes successful. Venture capitalists can sometimes be quite aggressive in wanting active management roles to make sure the business grows in value as soon as possible. This value is often tapped by an **initial public offering (IPO)**. This is when shares in the business are sold to the public at large, most likely beginning to trade on a major stock exchange.

When an IPO is successful, the market bids up the share price, thus increasing the value of the original shares held by the venture capitalist and the entrepreneur. Google's IPO went public at $85 per share. Check out the current price for a GOOG share on the NASDAQ today and you'll find it worth considerably more. Wouldn't it have been nice to be in on that original IPO? And how about Facebook or Zynga? They're the hotly anticipated IPOs of the moment. Check out their valuations and follow them from IPO to the daily stock reports.

When venture capital isn't available or isn't yet interested, entrepreneurs may try to find an **angel investor**. This is a wealthy individual who invests in return for equity in a new venture. Angel investors are especially helpful in the late birth and early breakthrough stages of a new venture. Once they jump in, it can raise the confidence and interests of the venture capitalists, thus making it easier to attract even more funding. When Liz Cobb wanted to start her sales compensation firm, Incentive Systems, for example, she contacted 15 to 20 venture capital firms. Only 10 interviewed her, and all of those turned her down. However, after she located $250,000 from two angel investors, the venture capital firms renewed their interest, allowing her to obtain her first $2 million in financing. Her firm grew to employ over 70 workers.[41] This isn't quite a Google story, but it's still a good one.

Debt financing involves borrowing money from another person, a bank, or a financial institution.

Equity financing gives ownership shares to outsiders in return for their financial investments.

Venture capitalists make large investments in new ventures in return for an equity stake in the business.

An **initial public offering (IPO)** is an initial selling of shares of stock to the public at large.

An **angel investor** is a wealthy individual willing to invest in return for equity in a new venture.

STUDY GUIDE

Takeaway 18.2
What Should We Know About Small Businesses and How to Start One?

Terms to Define

Angel investor

Business incubator

Business plan

Corporation

Debt financing

Equity financing

Family business

Family business feud

General partnership

Initial public offering (IPO)

Limited liability corporation (LLC)

Limited partnership

Partnership

Small business

Small business development centers

Sole proprietorship

Succession plan

Succession problem

Venture capitalists

Rapid Review

- Small businesses constitute the vast majority of businesses in the United States and create 7 out of every 10 new jobs in the economy.
- Small businesses have a high failure rate; as many as 60% to 80% of new businesses fail in their first five years of operation.
- Small businesses owned by family members can suffer from the succession problem of transferring leadership from one generation to the next.
- A business plan describes the intended nature of a proposed new business, how it will operate, and how it will obtain financing.
- Proprietorships, partnerships, and corporations are different forms of business ownership, with each offering advantages and disadvantages.
- New ventures can be financed through debt financing in the form of loans and through equity financing, which involves the exchange of ownership shares in return for outside investment.
- Venture capitalists and angel investors invest in new ventures in return for an equity stake in the business.

Questions for Discussion

1. Given the economic importance of small businesses, what could local, state, and federal governments do to make it easier for them to prosper?
2. If you were asked to join a small company, what would you look for as potential success indicators in its business plan?
3. Why might the owner of a small but growing business want to be careful when accepting big investments from venture capitalists?

Be Sure You Can

- state the SBA definition of small business
- list the life-cycle stages of a small business
- list several reasons why many small businesses fail
- discuss the succession problem in family-owned businesses
- list the major elements in a business plan
- differentiate the common forms of small business ownership
- differentiate debt financing and equity financing
- explain the roles of venture capitalists and angel investors in new venture financing

What Would You Do?

At this point, your start-up textbook-rating Web site is attracting potential investors. One angel investor is willing to put up $150,000 to help move things to the next level. But presently you and your two co-founders haven't done anything to legally structure the business. You've operated on personal resources and a "handshake" agreement among friends. What's the best course of action to legally set up the company? What's your best option for getting the financing needed for future growth while still protecting your ownership?

Multiple-Choice Questions

1. An entrepreneur who thrives on uncertainty displays _____.
   (a) high tolerance for ambiguity
   (b) internal locus of control
   (c) need for achievement
   (d) action orientation

2. _____ is a personality characteristic common among entrepreneurs.
   (a) External locus of control
   (b) Inflexibility
   (c) Self-confidence
   (d) Low self-reliance

3. When a new business is quick to capture a market niche before competitors, this is _____.
   (a) intrapreneurship
   (b) an initial public offering
   (c) succession planning
   (d) first-mover advantage

4. Almost _____% of U.S. businesses meet the definition of "small business."
   (a) 40   (b) 99
   (c) 75   (d) 81

5. A small business owner who wants to pass the business to other family members after retirement or death should prepare a _____ plan.
   (a) retirement   (b) succession
   (c) partnership   (d) liquidation

6. A common reason new small businesses often fail is _____.
   (a) the owner lacks experience and business skills
   (b) there is too much government regulation
   (c) the owner tightly controls money and finances
   (d) the business grows too slowly

7. A pressing problem faced by a small business in the birth or start-up stage is _____.
   (a) gaining acceptance in the marketplace
   (b) finding partners for expansion

(c) preparing the initial public offering
(d) getting management professional skills

8. A venture capitalist that receives an ownership share in return for investing in a new business is providing _____ financing.
   (a) debt   (b) equity
   (c) limited   (d) corporate

9. In _____ financing, the business owner borrows money as a loan that must be repaid.
   (a) debt   (b) equity
   (c) partnership   (d) limited

10. If you start a small business and want to avoid losing any more than the original investment, what form of ownership is best?
    (a) sole proprietorship
    (b) general partnership
    (c) limited partnership
    (d) corporation

11. The first element in a good business plan is _____.
    (a) an industry analysis
    (b) a marketing strategy
    (c) an executive summary
    (d) a set of performance milestones

12. Trends in U.S. small businesses show _____.
    (a) a growing number owned by minorities
    (b) fewer small businesses using the Internet
    (c) large businesses creating more jobs
    (d) fewer small businesses family owned

13. A _____ protects small business owners from personal liabilities for losses.
    (a) sole proprietorship
    (b) franchise
    (c) limited partnership
    (d) corporation

14. _____ take ownership shares in a new venture in return for start-up funds.

(a) Business incubators

(b) Angel investors

(c) SBDCs

(d) Intrapreneurs

15. _____ makes social entrepreneurship unique.

(a) Lack of other career options

(b) Focus on international markets

(c) Refusal to finance by loans

(d) Commitment to solving social problems

Short-Response Questions

16. What is the relationship between diversity and entrepreneurship?

17. What major challenges are faced at each life cycle stage of an entrepreneurial firm?

18. What are the advantages of a limited partnership form of ownership?

19. What is the difference, if any, between a venture capitalist and an angel investor?

Integration and Application Question

20. You have a great idea for an Internet-based start-up business. A friend advises you to clearly link your business idea to potential customers and then describe it well in a business plan. "You won't succeed without customers, she says, and you'll never get a chance if you can't attract financial backers with a good business plan." **Questions:** What questions will you ask and answer to ensure that you are customer-focused in this business? What are the major areas that you would address in your initial business plan?

StepsforFurtherLearning

Many learning resources are found at the end of the book and online within WileyPLUS.

Don't Miss These Selections from the **Skill-Building Portfolio**

■ **SELF-ASSESSMENT 18:** *Entrepreneurship Orientation*

■ **TEAM PROJECT 18:** *Community Entrepreneurs*

■ **CLASS EXERCISE 18:** *Entrepreneurs Among Us*

Don't Miss This Selection from **Cases for Critical Thinking**

■ **CHAPTER 18 CASE**

In-N-Out Burger: Building a Better Burger

Snapshot At face value, In-N-Out Burger seems like a modest enterprise—only four food items on the menu, little to no advertising. For more than sixty years, In-N-Out has focused on providing customers the basics—fresh, well-cooked food served quickly in a sparkling clean environment—and has made consistency and quality their hallmarks.

In addition to making the best burgers around, In-N-Out's other primary successful trait is its insistence on playing by its own rules. A fierce entrepreneurial streak ran through the Snyders, In-N-Out's founding family, and from the sock-hop décor to the secret menu to its treatment of employees as long-term partners instead of disposable resources, the chain prefers to focus on its formula for success instead of conventional definitions like shareholder return or IPOs.

Self-Assessment 1: **Personal Career Readiness**[1]

Instructions

Use this scale to rate yourself on the following list of personal characteristics.

S = Strong, I am very confident with this one.
G = Good, but I still have room to grow.
W = Weak, I really need work on this one.
U = Unsure, I just don't know.

_____ 1. *Resistance to stress:* The ability to get work done even under stressful conditions
_____ 2. *Tolerance for uncertainty:* The ability to get work done even under ambiguous and uncertain conditions
_____ 3. *Social objectivity:* The ability to act free of racial, ethnic, gender, and other prejudices or biases
_____ 4. *Inner work standards:* The ability to personally set and work to high performance standards
_____ 5. *Stamina:* The ability to sustain long work hours
_____ 6. *Adaptability:* The ability to be flexible and adapt to changes
_____ 7. *Self-confidence:* The ability to be consistently decisive and display one's personal presence
_____ 8. *Self-objectivity:* The ability to evaluate personal strengths and weaknesses and to understand one's motives and skills relative to a job
_____ 9. *Introspection:* The ability to learn from experience, awareness, and self-study
_____ 10. *Entrepreneurism:* The ability to address problems and take advantage of opportunities for constructive change

Scoring

Give yourself 1 point for each S, and 1/2 point for each G. Do not give yourself points for W and U responses. Total your points and enter the result here: _____.

Interpretation

This assessment offers a self-described *profile of your management foundations*. Are you a perfect 10 or something less? There shouldn't be too many 10s around. Also ask someone else to assess you on this instrument. You may be surprised at the results, but the insights are well worth thinking about. The items on the list are skills and personal characteristics that should be nurtured now and throughout your career.

Self-Assessment 2: **Managerial Assumptions**

Instructions

Use the space in the left margin to write "Yes" if you agree with the statement or "No" if you disagree with it. Force yourself to take a "yes" or "no" position for every statement.

1. Are good pay and a secure job enough to satisfy most workers?
2. Should a manager help and coach subordinates in their work?
3. Do most people like real responsibility in their jobs?
4. Are most people afraid to learn new things in their jobs?
5. Should managers let subordinates control the quality of their work?
6. Do most people dislike work?
7. Are most people creative?
8. Should a manager closely supervise and direct the work of subordinates?
9. Do most people tend to resist change?
10. Do most people work only as hard as they have to?
11. Should workers be allowed to set their own job goals?
12. Are most people happiest off the job?
13. Do most workers really care about the organization they work for?
14. Should a manager help subordinates advance and grow in their jobs?

Scoring

Count the number of "yes" responses to items 1, 4, 6, 8, 9, 10, 12; write that number here as [**X** = _____].
Count the number of "yes" responses to items 2, 3, 5, 7, 11, 13, 14; write that score here as [**Y** = _____].

Interpretation

This assessment examines your orientation toward Douglas McGregor's Theory X (your "X" score) and Theory Y (your "Y" score) assumptions. Consider how your X/Y assumptions might influence how you behave toward other people at work. What self-fulfilling prophecies are you likely to create?

Self-Assessment 3: Terminal Values Survey[2]

Instructions

1. Read the following list of things people value. Think about each value in terms of its importance as a guiding principle in your life.

A comfortable life	An exciting life	A sense of accomplishment
A world at peace	A world of beauty	Equality
Family security	Freedom	Happiness
Inner harmony	Mature love	National security
Pleasure	Salvation	Self-respect
Social recognition	True friendship	Wisdom

2. "*Circle*" six of these 18 values to indicate that they are *most important* to you. If you can, rank order these most important values by writing a number above them—with "1" = the most important value in my life, and so on through "6."

3. "*Underline*" the six of these 18 values that are *least important* to you.

Interpretation

Terminal values reflect a person's preferences concerning the ends to be achieved. They are the goals individuals would like to achieve in their lifetimes. As you look at the items you have selected as most and least important, what major differences exist among the items in the two sets? Think about this and then answer the following questions.

A) What does your selection of most and least important values say about you as a person?

B) What does your selection of most and least important values suggest about the type of work and career that might be best for you?

C) Which values among your most and least important selections might cause problems for you in the future—at work and/or in your personal life? What problems might they cause and why? How might you prepare now to best deal with these problems in the future?

D) How might your choices of most and least important values turn out to be major strengths or assets for you—at work and/or in your personal life, and why?

Self-Assessment 4: Intuitive Ability[3]

Instructions

Answer each of the following questions.

1. Do you prefer to: **(a)** be given a problem and left free to do it? **(b)** get clear instructions on how to solve a problem before starting?
2. Do you prefer to work with colleagues who are: **(a)** realistic? **(b)** imaginative?
3. Do you most admire: **(a)** creative people? **(b)** careful people?
4. Do your friends tend to be: **(a)** serious and hardworking? **(b)** exciting and emotional?
5. When you ask for advice on a problem, do you: **(a)** seldom or never get upset if your basic assumptions are questioned? **(b)** often get upset with such questions?
6. When you start your day, do you: **(a)** seldom make or follow a specific plan? **(b)** usually make and follow a plan?
7. When working with numbers, do you make factual errors: **(a)** seldom or never? **(b)** often?
8. Do you: **(a)** seldom daydream and really not enjoy it? **(b)** often daydream and enjoy it?
9. When working on a problem, do you: **(a)** prefer to follow instructions or rules? **(b)** often enjoy bypassing instructions or rules?
10. When trying to put something together, do you prefer: **(a)** step-by-step assembly instructions? **(b)** a picture of the assembled item?
11. Do you find that people who irritate you most appear to be: **(a)** disorganized? **(b)** organized?
12. When an unexpected crisis comes up, do you: **(a)** feel anxious? **(b)** feel excited by the challenge?

Scoring

Total the a responses for 1, 3, 5, 6, 11; [A = _____].

Total the b responses for 2, 4, 7, 8, 9, 10, 12; [B = _____].

Your *intuitive score* is A + B. The highest score is 12.

Self-Assessment 5: Time Management Profile[4]

Instructions

Indicate Y (yes) or N (no) for each item. Be frank; let your responses describe an accurate picture of how you tend to respond to these kinds of situations.

1. When confronted with several items of similar urgency and importance, I tend to do the easiest one first.
2. I do the most important things during that part of the day when I know I perform best.
3. Most of the time I don't do things someone else can do; I delegate this type of work to others.
4. Even though meetings without a clear and useful purpose upset me, I put up with them.
5. I skim documents before reading them and don't complete any that offer a low return on my time investment.
6. I don't worry much if I don't accomplish at least one significant task each day.
7. I save the most trivial tasks for that time of day when my creative energy is lowest.
8. My workspace is neat and organized.
9. My office door is always "open"; I never work in complete privacy.
10. I schedule my time completely from start to finish every workday.
11. I don't like "to-do" lists, preferring to respond to daily events as they occur.
12. I "block" a certain amount of time each day or week to be dedicated to high-priority activities.

Scoring and Interpretation

Count the number of Y responses to items 2, 3, 5, 7, 8, 12. [Enter that score here _____.] Count the number of N responses to items 1, 4, 6, 9, 10, 11. [Enter that score here _____.] Add together the two scores.

The higher the total score, the closer your behavior matches recommended time management guidelines. Reread those items where your response did not match the desired one. Why don't they match? Are there reasons for your action tendencies? Think about what you can do to be more consistent with time management guidelines.

Self-Assessment 6: Internal/External Control[5]

Instructions

Circle either a or b to indicate the item you most agree with in each pair of the following statements.

1. **(a)** Promotions are earned through hard work and persistence.
   (b) Making a lot of money is largely a matter of breaks.
2. **(a)** Many times the reactions of teachers seem haphazard to me.
   (b) In my experience I have noticed that there is usually a direct connection between how hard I study and the grades I get.
3. **(a)** The number of divorces indicates that more and more people are not trying to make their marriages work.
   (b) Marriage is largely a gamble.
4. **(a)** It is silly to think that one can really change another person's basic attitudes.
   (b) When I am right, I can convince others.
5. **(a)** Getting promoted is really a matter of being a little luckier than the next guy.
   (b) In our society, an individual's future earning power is dependent on his or her ability.
6. **(a)** If one knows how to deal with people, they are really quite easily led.
   (b) I have little influence over the way other people behave.
7. **(a)** In my case, the grades I make are the results of my own efforts; luck has little or nothing to do with it.
   (b) Sometimes I feel that I have little to do with the grades I get.
8. **(a)** People such as I can change the course of world affairs if we make ourselves heard.
   (b) It is only wishful thinking to believe that one can really influence what happens in society at large.
9. **(a)** Much of what happens to me is probably a matter of chance.
   (b) I am the master of my fate.
10. **(a)** Getting along with people is a skill that must be practiced.
    (b) It is almost impossible to figure out how to please some people.

Scoring

Give yourself 1 point for 1b, 2a, 3a, 4b, 5b, 6a, 7a, 8a, 9b, 10a. Total scores of: 8–10 = high *internal* locus of control, 6–7 = moderate *internal* locus of control, 5 = *mixed* locus of control, 3–4 = moderate *external* locus of control, 0–2 = high *external* locus of control.

Interpretation

This instrument offers an impression of your tendency toward an *internal locus of control or external locus of control*. Persons with a high internal locus of control tend to believe they have control over their own destinies. They may be most responsive to opportunities for greater self-control in the workplace. Persons with a high external locus of control tend to believe that what happens to them is largely in the hands of external people or forces. They may be less comfortable with self-control and more responsive to external controls in the workplace.

Self-Assessment 7: Handling Facts and Inferences[6]

Instructions

1. Read the following report.

   A well-liked college instructor had just completed making up the final examination and had turned off the lights in the office. Just then a tall, broad figure with dark glasses appeared and demanded the examination. The professor opened the drawer. Everything in the drawer was picked up, and the individual ran down the corridor. The president was notified immediately.

2. Indicate whether you think the following observations are true (T), false (F), or doubtful in that it may be either true or false (?). Judge each observation in order. Do not reread the observations after you have indicated your judgment, and do not change any of your answers.

   1. The thief was tall, broad, and wore dark glasses.
   2. The professor turned off the lights.
   3. A tall figure demanded the examination.
   4. The examination was picked up by someone.
   5. The examination was picked up by the professor.
   6. A tall, broad figure appeared after the professor turned off the lights in the office.
   7. The man who opened the drawer was the professor.
   8. The professor ran down the corridor.
   9. The drawer was never actually opened.
   10. Three persons are referred to in this report.

Scoring

The correct answers in reverse order (starting with 10) are: ?, F, ?, ?, T, ?, ?, T, T, ?.

Interpretation

To begin, ask yourself if there was a difference between your answers and the correct ones. If so, why? Why do you think people, individually or in groups, may answer these questions incorrectly? Good planning depends on good decision making by the people doing the planning. Being able to distinguish "facts" and understand one's "inferences" are important steps toward improving the planning process. Involving others to help do the same can frequently assist in this process.

Self-Assessment 8: Empowering Others[7]

Instructions

Think of times when you have been in charge of a group—this could be a full-time or part-time work situation, a student work group, or whatever. Complete the following questionnaire by recording how you feel about each statement according to this scale.

   1 = Strongly disagree   2 = Disagree   3 = Neutral   4 = Agree   5 = Strongly agree

When in charge of a team, I find that

1. Most of the time other people are too inexperienced to do things, so I prefer to do them myself.
2. It often takes more time to explain things to others than to just do them myself.
3. Mistakes made by others are costly, so I don't assign much work to them.
4. Some things simply should not be delegated to others.
5. I often get quicker action by doing a job myself.
6. Many people are good only at very specific tasks, so they can't be assigned additional responsibilities.
7. Many people are too busy to take on additional work.
8. Most people just aren't ready to handle additional responsibilities.
9. In my position, I should be entitled to make my own decisions.

Scoring

Total your responses and enter the score here [_____].

Interpretation

This instrument gives an impression of your willingness to delegate. Possible scores range from 9 to 45. The lower your score, the more willing you appear to be to delegate to others. Willingness to delegate is an important managerial characteristic: It is how you—as a manager—can empower others and give them opportunities to assume responsibility and exercise self-control in their work. With the growing importance of horizontal organizations and empowerment in the new workplace, your willingness to delegate is worth thinking about seriously.

Self-Assessment 9: Tolerance for Ambiguity[8]

Instructions

Rate each of the following items on this seven-point scale.

strongly agree   1   2   3   4   5   6   7   strongly disagree

_____ **1.** An expert who doesn't come up with a definite answer probably doesn't know too much.

_____ **2.** There is really no such thing as a problem that can't be solved.

_____ **3.** I would like to live in a foreign country for a while.

_____ **4.** People who fit their lives to a schedule probably miss the joy of living.

_____ **5.** A good job is one where what is to be done and how it is to be done are always clear.

_____ **6.** In the long run it is possible to get more done by tackling small, simple problems rather than large, complicated ones.

_____ **7.** It is more fun to tackle a complicated problem than it is to solve a simple one.

_____ **8.** Often the most interesting and stimulating people are those who don't mind being different and original.

_____ **9.** What we are used to is always preferable to what is unfamiliar.

_____ **10.** A person who leads an even, regular life in which few surprises or unexpected happenings arise really has a lot to be grateful for.

_____ **11.** People who insist upon a yes or no answer just don't know how complicated things really are.

_____ **12.** Many of our most important decisions are based on insufficient information.

_____ **13.** I like parties where I know most of the people more than ones where most of the people are complete strangers.

_____ **14.** The sooner we all acquire ideals, the better.

_____ **15.** Teachers or supervisors who hand out vague assignments give a chance for one to show initiative and originality.

_____ **16.** A good teacher is one who makes you wonder about your way of looking at things.

Scoring

To obtain a score, first *reverse* your scores for items 3, 4, 7, 8, 11, 12, 15, and 16 (i.e., a rating of 1 = 7, 2 = 6, 3 = 5, etc.).

Next add up your scores for all 16 items. The higher your total, the higher your indicated tolerance for ambiguity.

Self-Assessment 10: Performance Appraisal Assumptions[9]

Instructions

In each of the following pairs of statements, check the one that best reflects your assumptions about performance evaluation.

1. **(a)** a formal process that is done annually
   (b) an informal process done continuously

2. **(a)** a process that is planned for subordinates
   (b) a process that is planned with subordinates

3. **(a)** a required organizational procedure
   (b) a process done regardless of requirements

4. **(a)** a time to evaluate subordinates' performance
   (b) a time for subordinates to evaluate their manager

5. **(a)** a time to clarify standards
   (b) a time to clarify the subordinate's career needs

6. **(a)** a time to confront poor performance

   (b) a time to express appreciation

7. **(a)** an opportunity to clarify issues and provide direction and control

   (b) an opportunity to increase enthusiasm and commitment

8. **(a)** only as good as the organization's forms

   (b) only as good as the manager's coaching skills

Interpretation

In general, the a responses show more emphasis on the *evaluation* function of performance appraisal. This largely puts the supervisor in the role of documenting a subordinate's performance for control and administrative purposes. The b responses show a stronger emphasis on the *counseling* or *development* function. Here, the supervisor is concerned with helping the subordinate do better and with learning from the subordinate what he or she needs to be able to do better.

Self-Assessment 11: Least Preferred Co-Worker Scale[10]

Instructions

Think of all the different people with whom you have ever worked—in jobs, in social clubs, in student projects, or whatever. Next, think of the one person with whom you could work least well—that is, the person with whom you had the most difficulty getting a job done. This is the one person—a peer, boss, or subordinate—with whom you would least want to work. Describe this person by circling numbers at the appropriate points on each of the following pairs of bipolar adjectives. Work rapidly. There is no right or wrong answer.

Pleasant	8	7	6	5	4	3	2	1		Unpleasant
Friendly	8	7	6	5	4	3	2	1		Unfriendly
Rejecting	1	2	3	4	5	6	7	8		Accepting
Tense	1	2	3	4	5	6	7	8		Relaxed
Distant	1	2	3	4	5	6	7	8		Close
Cold	1	2	3	4	5	6	7	8		Warm
Supportive	8	7	6	5	4	3	2	1		Hostile
Boring	1	2	3	4	5	6	7	8		Interesting
Quarrelsome	1	2	3	4	5	6	7	8		Harmonious
Gloomy	1	2	3	4	5	6	7	8		Cheerful
Open	8	7	6	5	4	3	2	1		Guarded
Backbiting	1	2	3	4	5	6	7	8		Loyal
Untrustworthy	1	2	3	4	5	6	7	8		Trustworthy
Considerate	8	7	6	5	4	3	2	1		Inconsiderate
Nasty	1	2	3	4	5	6	7	8		Nice
Agreeable	8	7	6	5	4	3	2	1		Disagreeable
Insincere	1	2	3	4	5	6	7	8		Sincere
Kind	8	7	6	5	4	3	2	1		Unkind

Scoring

This is called the "least-preferred co-worker scale" (LPC). Compute your LPC score by totaling all the numbers you circled; enter that score here [LPC = _____].

Interpretation

The LPC scale is used by Fred Fiedler to identify a person's dominant leadership style. Fiedler believes that this style is a relatively fixed part of one's personality and is therefore difficult to change. This leads Fiedler to his contingency views, which suggest that the key to leadership success is finding (or creating) good "matches" between style and situation.

    If your score is 73 or above on the LPC scale, Fiedler considers you a "relationship-motivated" leader; if it is 64 or below on the scale, he considers you a "task-motivated" leader. If your score is between 65 and 72, Fiedler leaves it up to you to determine which leadership style is most accurate.

Self-Assessment 12: Stress Test[11]

Instructions

Complete the following questionnaire. Circle the number that best represents your tendency to behave on each bipolar dimension.

Am casual about appointments	1 2 3 4 5 6 7 8	Am never late for appointments
Am not competitive	1 2 3 4 5 6 7 8	Am very competitive
Never feel rushed	1 2 3 4 5 6 7 8	Always feel rushed
Take things one at a time	1 2 3 4 5 6 7 8	Try to do many things at once
Do things slowly	1 2 3 4 5 6 7 8	Do things fast
Express feelings	1 2 3 4 5 6 7 8	"Sit on" feelings
Have many interests	1 2 3 4 5 6 7 8	Have few interests but work

Scoring

Total the numbers circled for all items, and multiply this by 3; enter the result here [_____].

Points	Personality Type
120+	A+
106−119	A
100−105	A−
90−99	B+
below 90	B

Self-Assessment 13: Two-Factor Profile

Instructions

On each of the following dimensions, distribute a total of 10 points between the two options. For example:

Summer weather	(7)	(3)	Winter weather
1. Very responsible job	(_)	(_)	Job security
2. Recognition for work accomplishments	(_)	(_)	Good relations with co-workers
3. Advancement opportunities at work	(_)	(_)	A boss who knows his/her job well
4. Opportunities to grow and learn on the job	(_)	(_)	Good working conditions
5. A job that I can do well	(_)	(_)	Supportive rules, policies of employer
6. A prestigious or high-status job	(_)	(_)	A high base wage or salary

Scoring

Summarize your total score for all items in the *left-hand column* and write it here. MF = _____
Summarize your total score for all items in the *right-hand column* and write it here. HF = _____

Interpretation

The MF score indicates the relative importance that you place on the motivating, or satisfier, factors in Herzberg's two-factor theory. This shows how important job content is to you. The HF score indicates the relative importance that you place on hygiene, or dissatisfier, factors in Herzberg's two-factor theory. This shows how important job context is to you.

Self-Assessment 14: Team Leader Skills[12]

Instructions

Consider your experiences in groups and work teams. Ask: "What skills do I bring to team leadership situations?" Then complete the following inventory by rating yourself on each item using this scale.

> 1 = Almost never   2 = Seldom   3 = Sometimes   4 = Usually   5 = Almost always

_____ **1.** I facilitate communications with and among team members between team meetings.

_____ **2.** I provide feedback/coaching to individual team members on their performance.

_____ **3.** I encourage creative and out-of-the-box thinking.

_____ **4.** I continue to clarify stakeholder needs/expectations.

_____ **5.** I keep team members' responsibilities and activities focused within the team's objectives and goals.

_____ **6.** I organize and run effective and productive team meetings.

_____ **7.** I demonstrate integrity and personal commitment.

_____ **8.** I have excellent persuasive and influence skills.

_____ **9.** I respect and leverage the team's cross-functional diversity.

_____**10.** I recognize and reward individual contributions to team performance.

_____**11.** I use the appropriate decision-making style for specific issues.

_____**12.** I facilitate and encourage border management with the team's key stakeholders.

_____**13.** I ensure that the team meets its team commitments.

_____**14.** I bring team issues and problems to the team's attention and focus on constructive problem solving.

_____**15.** I provide a clear vision and direction for the team.

Scoring and Interpretation

Add your scores for the items listed next to each dimension below to get an indication of your potential strengths and weaknesses on seven dimensions of team leadership. The higher the score, the more confident you are on the particular skill and leadership capability. When considering the score, ask yourself if others would rate you the same way.

1, 9	Building the team
2, 10	Developing people
3, 11	Team problem solving/decision making
4, 12	Stakeholder relations
5, 13	Team performance
6, 14	Team process
7, 8, 15	Providing personal leadership

Self-Assessment 15: Feedback and Assertiveness[13]

Instructions

For each statement below, decide which of the following answers best fits you.

1 = Never true   2 = Sometimes true   3 = Often true   4 = Always true

_____ **1.** I respond with more modesty than I really feel when my work is complimented.

_____ **2.** If people are rude, I will be rude right back.

_____ **3.** Other people find me interesting.

_____ **4.** I find it difficult to speak up in a group of strangers.

_____ **5.** I don't mind using sarcasm if it helps me make a point.

_____ **6.** I ask for a raise when I feel I really deserve it.

_____ **7.** If others interrupt me when I am talking, I suffer in silence.

_____ **8.** If people criticize my work, I find a way to make them back down.

_____ **9.** I can express pride in my accomplishments without being boastful.

_____**10.** People take advantage of me.

_____**11.** I tell people what they want to hear if it helps me get what I want.

_____**12.** I find it easy to ask for help.

_____**13.** I lend things to others even when I don't really want to.

_____**14.** I win arguments by dominating the discussion.

_____**15.** I can express my true feelings to someone I really care for.

_____**16.** When I feel angry with other people, I bottle it up rather than express it.

_____**17.** When I criticize someone else's work, they get mad.

_____**18.** I feel confident in my ability to stand up for my rights.

Scoring and Interpretation

Aggressiveness tendency score—Add items 2, 5, 8, 11, 14, and 17.

Passiveness tendency score—Add items 1, 4, 7, 10, 13, and 16.

Assertiveness tendency score—Add items 3, 6, 9, 12, 15, and 18.

The maximum score in any single area is 24. The minimum score is 6. Try to find someone who knows you well. Have this person complete the instrument also as it relates to you. Compare his or her impression of you with your own score. What is this telling you about your behavior tendencies in social situations?

Self-Assessment 16: Diversity Awareness

Instructions

Indicate O for often, S for sometimes, and N for never in response to each of the following questions as they pertain to where you work or go to school.

1. How often have you heard jokes or remarks about other people that you consider offensive?
2. How often do you hear men "talk down" to women in an attempt to keep them in an inferior status?
3. How often have you felt personal discomfort as the object of sexual harassment?
4. How often do you work or study with persons of different ethnic or national cultures?
5. How often have you felt disadvantaged because members of ethnic groups other than yours were given special treatment?
6. How often have you seen a woman put in an uncomfortable situation because of unwelcome advances by a man?
7. How often does it seem that African Americans, Hispanics, Caucasians, women, men, and members of other minority demographic groups seem to "stick together" during work breaks or other leisure situations?
8. How often do you feel uncomfortable about something you did and/or said to someone of the opposite sex or a member of an ethnic or racial group other than yours?
9. How often do you feel efforts are made in this setting to raise the level of cross-cultural understanding among people who work and/or study together?
10. How often do you step in to communicate concerns to others when you feel actions and/or words are used to the disadvantage of minorities?

Interpretation

There are no correct answers for the Diversity Awareness Checklist. The key issue is the extent to which you are sensitive to diversity issues in the workplace or university. Are you comfortable with your responses? How do you think others in your class responded? Why not share your responses with others and examine different viewpoints on this important issue?

Self-Assessment 17: Global Intelligence[14]

Instructions

Use the following scale to rate yourself on these 10 items.

   1 = Very poor   2 = Poor   3 = Acceptable   4 = Good   5 = Very good

1. I understand my own culture in terms of its expectations, values, and influence on communication and relationships.
2. When someone presents me with a different point of view, I try to understand it rather than attack it.
3. I am comfortable dealing with situations where the available information is incomplete and the outcomes unpredictable.
4. I am open to new situations and am always looking for new information and learning opportunities.
5. I have a good understanding of the attitudes and perceptions toward my culture as they are held by people from other cultures.
6. I am always gathering information about other countries and cultures and trying to learn from them.
7. I am well informed regarding the major differences in the government, political, and economic systems around the world.
8. I work hard to increase my understanding of people from other cultures.
9. I am able to adjust my communication style to work effectively with people from different cultures.
10. I can recognize when cultural differences are influencing working relationships, and I adjust my attitudes and behavior accordingly.

Interpretation

To be successful in the global economy, you must be comfortable with the cultural diversity that it holds. This requires a global mindset that is receptive to and respectful of cultural differences, global knowledge that includes the continuing quest to know and learn more about other nations and cultures, and global work skills that allow you to work effectively across cultures.

Scoring

The goal is to score as close to a perfect 5 as possible on each of the three dimensions of global intelligence. Develop your scores as follows:

- Items (1 + 2 + 3 + 4)/4 = _____ **Global Mindset Score**—The extent to which you are receptive to and respectful of cultural differences.
- Items (5 + 6 + 7)/3 = **Global Knowledge Score**—Your openness to know and learn more about other nations and cultures.
- Items (8 + 9 + 10)/3 = **Global Work Skills Score**—Your capacity to work effectively across cultures.

Self-Assessment 18: Entrepreneurship Orientation[15]

Instructions

Answer each of the following questions.

1. What portion of your college expenses did you earn (or are you earning)?

   (a) 50% or more **(b)** less than 50% **(c)** none

2. In college, your academic performance was/is

   (a) above average. **(b)** average. **(c)** below average.

3. What is your basic reason for considering opening a business?

   (a) I want to make money. **(b)** I want to control my own destiny. **(c)** I hate the frustration of working for someone else.

4. Which phrase best describes your attitude toward work?

   (a) I can keep going as long as I need to; I don't mind working for something I want. **(b)** I can work hard for a while, but when I've had enough, I quit. **(c)** Hard work really doesn't get you anywhere.

5. How would you rate your organizing skills?

   (a) superorganized **(b)** above average **(c)** average **(d)** I do well to find half the things I look for.

6. You are primarily a(n)

   (a) optimist. **(b)** pessimist. **(c)** neither.

7. You are faced with a challenging problem. As you work, you realize you are stuck. You will most likely

   (a) give up. **(b)** ask for help. **(c)** keep plugging; you'll figure it out.

8. You are playing a game with a group of friends. You are most interested in

   (a) winning. **(b)** playing well. **(c)** making sure that everyone has a good time. **(d)** cheating as much as possible.

9. How would you describe your feelings toward failure?

   (a) Fear of failure paralyzes me. **(b)** Failure can be a good learning experience. **(c)** Knowing that I might fail motivates me to work even harder. **(d)** "Damn the torpedoes! Full speed ahead."

10. Which phrase best describes you?

    (a) I need constant encouragement to get anything done. **(b)** If someone gets me started, I can keep going. **(c)** I am energetic and hardworking—a self-starter.

11. Which bet would you most likely accept?

    (a) a wager on a dog race **(b)** a wager on a racquetball game in which you play an opponent **(c)** Neither. I never make wagers.

12. At the Kentucky Derby, you would bet on

    (a) the 100-to-1 long shot. **(b)** the odds-on favorite. **(c)** the 3-to-1 shot. **(d)** none of the above.

Scoring

Give yourself 10 points each for answers 1a, 2a, 3c, 4a, 5a, 6a, 7c, 8a, 9c, 10c, 11b, 12c; total the scores and enter the result here [I = _____].

Give yourself 8 points each for answers 3b, 8b, 9b; enter total here [II = _____].

Give yourself 6 points each for answers 2b, 5b; enter total here [III = _____].

Give yourself 5 points for answer 1b; enter result here [IV = _____].

Give yourself 4 points for answer 5c; enter result here [V = _____].

Give yourself 2 points each for answers 2c, 3a, 4b, 6c, 9d, 10b, 11a, 12b; enter total here [VI = _____].

The other answers are worth 0 points.

Total your summary scores for I + II + III + IV + V + VI and enter the result here: My Entrepreneurship Potential Score is _____.

Interpretation

This assessment offers an impression of your *entrepreneurial profile (EP)*. It compares your characteristics with those of typical entrepreneurs, according to this profile: 100+ = Entrepreneur extraordinaire; 80–99 = Entrepreneur; 60–79 = Potential entrepreneur; 0–59 = Entrepreneur in the rough.

Class Exercise 1: My Best Manager[1]

Preparation

Working alone, make a list of the *behavioral attributes* that describe the "best" manager you have ever had. This could be someone you worked for in a full-time or part-time job, summer job, volunteer job, student organization, or elsewhere. If you have trouble identifying an actual manager, make a list of behavioral attributes of the manager you would most like to work for in your next job.

Instructions

Form into teams as assigned by your instructor, or work with a nearby classmate. Share your list of attributes and listen to the lists of others. Be sure to ask questions and make comments on items of special interest. Work together in your team to create a master list that combines the unique attributes of the "best" managers experienced by members of your group. Have a spokesperson share that list with the rest of the class for further discussion.

Class Exercise 2: Evidence-Based Management Quiz[2]

Instructions

1. For each of the following questions, answer T (true) if you believe the statement is backed by solid research evidence or F (false) if you do not believe it is an evidence-based statement.

    _____ **1.** Intelligence is a better predictor of job performance than having a conscientious personality.

    _____ **2.** Screening job candidates for values results in higher job performance than screening for intelligence.

    _____ **3.** A highly intelligent person will have a hard time performing well in a low-skill job.

    _____ **4.** "Integrity tests" are good predictors of whether employees will steal, be absent, or take advantage of their employers in other ways.

    _____ **5.** Goal setting is more likely to result in improved performance than is participation in decision making.

    _____ **6.** Errors in performance appraisals can be reduced through proper training.

    _____ **7.** People behave in ways that show pay is more important to them than what they indicate on surveys.

2. Share your answers with others in your assigned group. Discuss the reasons members chose the answers they did; arrive at a final answer to each question for the group as a whole.

3. Compare your results with these answers "from the evidence."

4. Engage in a class discussion of how "commonsense" answers can sometimes differ from answers provided by "evidence." Ask: What are the implications of this discussion for management practice?

Class Exercise 3: Confronting Ethical Dilemmas

Preparation

Read and indicate your response to each of the situations below.

1. Ron Jones, vice president of a large construction firm, receives in the mail a large envelope marked "personal." It contains a competitor's cost data for a project that both firms will be bidding on shortly. The data are accompanied by a note from one of Ron's subordinates saying: "This is the real thing!" Ron knows that the data could be a major advantage to his firm in preparing a bid that can win the contract. What should he do?

2. Kay Smith is one of your top-performing subordinates. She has shared with you her desire to apply for promotion to a new position just announced in a different division of the company. This will be tough on you since recent budget cuts mean you will be unable to replace anyone who leaves, at least for quite some time. Kay knows this and, in all fairness, has asked your permission before she submits an application. It is rumored that the son of a good friend of your boss is going to apply for the job. Although his credentials are less impressive than Kay's, the likelihood is that he will get the job if she doesn't apply. What will you do?

3. Marty Jose got caught in a bind. She was pleased to represent her firm as head of the local community development committee. In fact, her supervisor's boss once held this position and told her in a hallway conversation, "Do your best and give them every support possible." Going along with this, Marty agreed to pick up the bill (several hundred dollars) for a dinner meeting with local civic and business leaders. Shortly thereafter, her supervisor informed everyone that the entertainment budget was being eliminated in a cost-saving effort. Marty, not wanting to renege on supporting the community development committee, was able to charge the dinner bill to an advertising budget. Eventually, an internal auditor discovered the charge and reported it to you, the personnel director. Marty is scheduled to meet with you in a few minutes. What will you do?

Instructions

Working alone, make the requested decisions in each of these incidents. Think carefully about your justification for the decision. Meet in a group assigned by your instructor. Share your decisions and justifications in each case with other group members. Listen to theirs. Try to reach a group consensus on what to do in each situation and why. Be prepared to share the group decisions, and any dissenting views, in general class discussion.

Class Exercise 4: Lost at Sea[3]

Consider This Situation

You are adrift on a private yacht in the South Pacific when a fire of unknown origin destroys the yacht and most of its contents. You and a small group of survivors are now in a large raft with oars. Your location is unclear, but you estimate that you are about 1,000 miles south-southwest of the nearest land. One person has just found in her pockets five $1 bills and a packet of matches. Everyone else's pockets are empty. The items below are available to you on the raft.

	Individual ranking	Team ranking	Expert ranking
Sextant	_____	_____	_____
Shaving mirror	_____	_____	_____
5 gallons water	_____	_____	_____
Mosquito netting	_____	_____	_____
1 survival meal	_____	_____	_____
Maps of Pacific Ocean	_____	_____	_____
Floatable seat cushion	_____	_____	_____
2 gallons oil-gas mix	_____	_____	_____
Small transistor radio	_____	_____	_____
Shark repellent	_____	_____	_____
20 square feet black plastic	_____	_____	_____
1 quart 20-proof rum	_____	_____	_____
15 feet nylon rope	_____	_____	_____
24 chocolate bars	_____	_____	_____
Fishing kit	_____	_____	_____

Instructions

1. *Working alone,* rank the 15 items in order of their importance to your survival (1 is most important and 15 is least important).

2. *Working in an assigned group,* arrive at a "team" ranking of the 15 items. Appoint one person as team spokesperson to report your team ranking to the class.

3. *Do not write in column 3* until your instructor provides the "expert" ranking.

Class Exercise 5: The Future Workplace

Instructions

Form groups as assigned by the instructor. Brainstorm to develop a master list of the major characteristics you expect to find in the workplace in the year 2020. Use this list as background for completing the following tasks:

1. Write a one-paragraph description of what the typical "Workplace 2020" manager's workday will be like.

2. Draw a "picture" representing what the "Workplace 2020" organization will look like.

3. Summarize in list form what you consider to be the major planning implications of your future workplace scenario for management students today. That is, explain what this means in terms of using academic and extracurricular activities to best prepare for success in this future scenario.

4. Choose a spokesperson to share your results with the class as a whole and explain their implications for the class members.

Class Exercise 6: Stakeholder Maps

Preparation

Review the discussion of organizational stakeholders in the textbook. (1) Make a list of the stakeholders that would apply to all organizations—for example, local communities, employees, and customers. What others would you add to this starter listing? (2) Choose one organization that you are familiar with from each list below. (3) Draw a map of key stakeholders for each organization. (4) For each stakeholder indicate its major interest in the organization. (5) For each organization make a list of possible conflicts among stakeholders that the top manager should recognize.

Nonprofit	Government	Business
Elementary school	Local mayor's office	Convenience store
Community hospital	State police	Movie theater
Church	U.S. Senator	National retailer
University	Internal Revenue Service	Local pizza shop
United Way	Homeland Security agency	Urgent care medical clinic

Instructions

In groups assigned by your instructor, choose one organization from each list. Create "master" stakeholder maps for each organization, along with statements of stakeholder interests and lists of potential stakeholder conflicts. Assume the position of top manager for each organization. Prepare a "stakeholder management plan" that represents the high-priority issues the manager should be addressing with respect to the stakeholders. Make a presentation to the class for each of your organizations and engage in discussion about the importance and complexity of stakeholder analysis.

Class Exercise 7: Strategic Scenarios[4]

Preparation

In today's turbulent economic climate, it is no longer safe to assume that an organization that was highly successful yesterday will continue to be so tomorrow—or that it will even be in existence. Changing times exact the best from strategic planners. Think about the situations currently facing the following well-known organizations. Think, too, about the futures they may face.

McDonald's	Ford	Sony
Apple Computer	Nordstrom	Electronic Arts
Yahoo.com	National Public Radio	AT&T
Ann Taylor	*The New York Times*	Federal Express

Instructions

Form into groups as assigned by your instructor. Choose one or more organizations from the prior list (or as assigned) and answer the following questions for the organization:

1. What in the future might seriously threaten the success, perhaps the very existence, of this organization? As a group, develop at least three such *future scenarios*.
2. Estimate the probability (0 to 100%) of each future scenario occurring.
3. Develop a strategy for each scenario that will enable the organization to successfully deal with it.
4. Thoroughly discuss these questions within the group and arrive at your best possible consensus answers. Be prepared to share and defend your answers in general class discussion.

Class Exercise 8: Organizational Metaphors

Instructions

1. Start by answering the following questions using this scale:

   5 = strongly agree   4 = agree somewhat   3 = undecided   2 = disagree somewhat   1 = strongly disagree

   I prefer to work in an organization where:

   _____ 1. Goals are defined by those in higher levels.

   _____ 2. Work methods and procedures are specified.

   _____ 3. Top management makes important decisions.

_____ **4.** My loyalty counts as much as my ability to do the job.

_____ **5.** Clear lines of authority and responsibility are established.

_____ **6.** Top management is decisive and firm.

_____ **7.** My career is pretty well planned out for me.

_____ **8.** I can specialize.

_____ **9.** My length of service is almost as important as my level of performance.

_____ **10.** Management is able to provide the information I need to do my job well.

_____ **11.** A chain of command is well established.

_____ **12.** Rules and procedures are adhered to equally by everyone.

_____ **13.** People accept the authority of a leader's position.

_____ **14.** People are loyal to their boss.

_____ **15.** People do as they have been instructed.

_____ **16.** People clear things with their boss before going over his or her head.

2. Total your scores for all questions. Enter the score here [_____].

3. Interpretation. This assessment measures your preference for working in an organization designed along "organic" or "mechanistic" lines. The higher your score (above 64), the more comfortable you are with a mechanistic design; the lower your score (below 48), the more comfortable you are with an organic design. Scores between 48 and 64 can go either way.

4. Form into groups and compare scores and organizational design preferences. Discuss areas of similarity and difference. Prepare a report to the class that summarizes the organizational design preferences within your group and also highlights arguments for and against organic and mechanistic organizations as places to work.

Class Exercise 9: Force-Field Analysis

Instructions

1. Form into your class discussion groups and review this model of force-field analysis—the consideration of forces driving in support of a planned change and forces resisting the change.

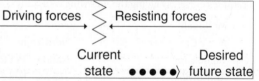

2. Use force-field analysis and make lists of driving and resisting forces for one of the following situations:

(a) Because of rapid advances in Web-based computer technologies, the possibility exists that the course you are presently taking could be, in part, offered online. This would mean a reduction in the number of required class sessions but an increase in students' responsibility for completing learning activities and assignments through computer mediation. The dean wants all faculty to put at least part of their courses online.

(b) A new owner has just taken over a small walk-in-and-buy-by-the-slice pizza shop in a college town. There are presently eight employees, three of whom are full-time and five of whom are part-time. The shop is open seven days a week from 10:30 a.m. to midnight. The new owner believes there is a market niche available for late-night pizza and would like to stay open each night until 4 a.m. She wants to make the change as soon as possible.

(c) A situation assigned by the instructor.

3. Choose the three driving forces that are most significant for the proposed change. For each force, develop ideas on how it could be further increased or mobilized in support of the change.

4. Choose the three resisting forces that are most significant for the proposed change. For each force, develop ideas on how it could be reduced or turned into a driving force.

5. Be prepared to participate in a class discussion led by your instructor.

Class Exercise 10: Upward Appraisal[5]

Instructions

Form into work groups as assigned by the instructor. The instructor will then leave the room. As a group, complete the following tasks:

1. Within each group create a master list of comments, problems, issues, and concerns about the course experience to date that members would like to communicate to the instructor.

2. Select one person from the group to act as a spokesperson who will give your feedback to the instructor when he or she returns to the classroom.

3. Before the instructor returns, the spokespersons from each group should meet to decide how the room should be physically arranged (placement of tables, chairs, etc.) for the feedback session. This arrangement should allow the spokespersons and instructor to communicate while they are being observed by other class members.

4. While the spokespersons are meeting, members remaining in the groups should discuss what they expect to observe during the feedback session.

5. The classroom should be rearranged. The instructor should be invited in.

6. Spokespersons should deliver feedback to the instructor while observers make notes.

7. After the feedback session is complete, the instructor will call on observers for comments, ask the spokespersons for their reactions, and engage the class in general discussion about the exercise and its implications.

Class Exercise 11: Leading by Participation[6]

Preparation

Read each of the following vignettes. Write in the margin whether you think the leader should handle the situation with:

I = an individual or authority decision   C = a consultative decision   G = a group decision

Vignette I

You are the leader of a large team laying an oil pipeline. It is now necessary to estimate your expected rate of progress in order to schedule material deliveries to the next field site. You know the nature of the terrain you will be traveling and have the historical data needed to compute the mean and variance in the rate of speed over the type of terrain. Given these two variables, it is a simple matter to calculate the earliest and latest times at which materials and support facilities will be needed at the next site. It is important that your estimate be reasonably accurate; underestimates result in idle teams, and overestimates result in materials being tied up for a period of time before they are to be used. Progress has been good, and your team stands to receive substantial bonuses if the project is completed ahead of schedule.

Vignette II

You are supervising the work of 12 engineers. Their formal training and work experience are very similar, permitting you to use them interchangeably on projects. Yesterday, your manager informed you that a request had been received from an overseas affiliate for four engineers to go abroad on extended loan for a period of six to eight months. He argued and you agreed that for a number of reasons this request should be filled from your group. All your engineers are capable of handling this assignment, and from the standpoint of present and future projects, there is no particular reason that any one should be retained over any other. The problem is complicated by the fact that the overseas assignment is in what is generally regarded in the company as an undesirable location.

Vignette III

You are the head of a staff unit reporting to the vice president of finance. She has asked you to provide a report on the firm's current portfolio, including recommendations for changes in the selection criteria. Doubts have been raised about the efficiency of the existing system in the current market conditions, and there is dissatisfaction with rates of return. Your own specialty is the bond market, and it is clear to you that a detailed knowledge of the equity market, which you lack, would greatly enhance the value of the report. Four members of your staff are specialists in different segments of the equity market and possess a vast amount of knowledge about the intricacies of investment. However, they seldom agree on the best way to achieve anything when it comes to the stock market. Although conscientious as well as knowledgeable, they have major differences when it comes to investment philosophy and strategy. The report is due in six weeks. You have already begun to familiarize yourself with the firm's current portfolio and have been provided by management with a specific set of constraints that any portfolio must satisfy. Your immediate problem is to come up with some alternatives to the firm's present practices and select the most promising ones for detailed analysis in your report.

Instructions

Form groups as assigned by the instructor. Share your choices with other group members and try to achieve a consensus on how the leader should best handle each situation. Refer back to the Vroom–Jago "leader-participation" theory presented in this chapter. Analyze each vignette according to their ideas. Do you come to any different conclusions? If so, why? Nominate a spokesperson to share your results in general class discussion.

Class Exercise 12: Job Satisfaction Preferences[7]

Preparation

Rank the following items from 1 = least important to 9 = most important to your future job satisfaction.

My job will be satisfying when:

_____ 1. It is respected by other people.

_____ 2. It encourages continued development of knowledge and skills.

_____ 3. It provides job security.

_____ 4. It provides a feeling of accomplishment.

_____ 5. It provides the opportunity to earn a high income.

_____ 6. It is intellectually stimulating.

_____ 7. It rewards good performance with recognition.

_____ 8. It provides comfortable working conditions.

_____ 9. It permits advancement to high administrative responsibility.

Instructions

Form into groups as designated by your instructor. Within each group, the men should develop a consensus ranking of the items as they think women ranked them. The reasons for the rankings should be shared and discussed so they are clear to everyone. The women in the group should not participate in this ranking task. They should listen to the discussion and be prepared to comment later in class discussions. A spokesperson for the men in the group should share the group's rankings with the class.

Optional Instructions

Form into groups consisting entirely of men or women. Each group should meet and decide which of the work values members of the opposite sex will rank first. Do this again for the work value ranked last. The reasons should be discussed, along with the reasons why each of the other values probably was not ranked first—or last. A spokesperson for each group should share group results with the rest of the class.

Class Exercise 13: Why We Work[8]

Preparation

Read this "ancient story."

In days of old, a wandering youth happened upon a group of men working in a quarry. Stopping by the first man, he said: "What are you doing?" The worker grimaced and groaned as he replied: "I am trying to shape this stone, and it is backbreaking work." Moving to the next man, the youth repeated the question. This man showed little emotion as he answered: "I am shaping a stone for a building." Moving to the third man, our traveler heard him singing as he worked. "What are you doing?" asked the youth. "I am helping to build a cathedral," the man proudly replied.

Instructions

In groups assigned by your instructor, discuss this short story. (1) Ask and answer the question: "What are the motivation and job design lessons of this ancient story?" (2) Have members of the group role-play each of the stonecutters as they are answering this additional question: "Why are you working?" Have someone in the group be prepared to report and share the group's responses with the class as a whole.

Class Exercise 14: Understanding Team Dynamics[9]

Preparation

Think about your course work team, a team you are involved with in another campus activity, or any other team situation suggested by your instructor. Use this scale to indicate how often each of the following statements accurately reflects your experience in the group.

1 = always   2 = frequently   3 = sometimes   4 = never

_____ 1. My ideas get a fair hearing.

_____ 2. I am encouraged to offer innovative ideas and take risks.

_____ 3. Diverse opinions within the group are encouraged.

_____ 4. I have all the responsibility I want.

_____ 5. There is a lot of favoritism shown in the group.

_____ 6. Members trust one another to do their assigned work.

_____ 7. The group sets high standards of performance excellence.

_____ 8. People share and change jobs a lot in the group.

_____ 9. You can make mistakes and learn from them in this group.

_____ 10. This group has good operating rules.

Instructions

Form groups as assigned by your instructor. Ideally, this will be the group you have just rated. Have all group members share their ratings, and then make one master rating for the group as a whole. Circle the items for which there are the biggest differences of opinion. Discuss those items and try to find out why they exist. In general, the better a group scores on this instrument, the higher its creative potential. If everyone has rated the same group, make a list of the five most important things members can do to improve its operations in the future. Nominate a spokesperson to summarize the group discussion for the class as a whole.

Class Exercise 15: Communication and Teamwork Dilemmas[10]

Instructions

1. Identify from the list below the three activities that you find most uncomfortable when part of a team.

   (a) Telling a friend that she or he must stop coming late to team meetings

   (b) Pointing out to a team member that his or her poor performance is hurting the team

   (c) Asking teammates to comment on your criticism of the consensus that seems to be emerging on a particular issue

   (d) Telling a teammate who has problems working with others on the team that he or she has to do something about it

   (e) Responding to a team member who has just criticized your performance

   (f) Responding to a team member who has just criticized your attitude toward the team

   (g) Responding to a team member who becomes emotional and defensive when you criticize his or her performance

   (h) Having a teammate challenge you to justify your contributions to a discussion

2. Form three-person teams as assigned by your instructor. Identify the three behaviors with which each person indicates the most discomfort.

3. Have each team member practice performing these behaviors with another member, while the third member acts as an observer. Be direct, but try to perform the behavior in an appropriate way. Listen to feedback from the observer and try the behaviors again, perhaps with different members of the group practicing each behavior.

4. When finished, discuss the overall exercise and be prepared to share highlights of the exercise with the rest of the class.

Class Exercise 16: Alligator River Story[11]

Preparation

Read this story.

There lived a woman named Abigail who was in love with a man named Gregory. Gregory lived on the shore of a river. Abigail lived on the opposite shore of the same river. The river that separated the two lovers was teeming with dangerous alligators. Abigail wanted to cross the river to be with Gregory. Unfortunately, the bridge had been washed out by a heavy flood the previous week. So she went to ask Sinbad, a riverboat captain, to take her across. He said he would be glad to if she would consent to go to bed with him prior to the voyage. She promptly refused and went to a friend named Ivan to explain her plight. Ivan did not want to get involved at all in the situation. Abigail felt her only alternative was to accept Sinbad's terms. Sinbad fulfilled his promise to Abigail and delivered her into the arms of Gregory. When Abigail told Gregory about her amorous escapade in order to cross the river, Gregory cast her aside with disdain. Heart-sick and rejected, Abigail turned to Slug with her tale of woe. Slug, feeling compassion for Abigail, sought out Gregory and beat him brutally. Abigail was overjoyed at the sight of Gregory getting his due. As the sun set on the horizon, people heard Abigail laughing at Gregory.

Instructions

1. After reading the story, rank the five characters in the story beginning with the one you consider the most offensive and ending with the one you consider the least objectionable. That is, the character who seems to be the most reprehensible to you should be entered first in the list, then the second most reprehensible, and so on, with the least reprehensible or objectionable being entered fifth. Of course, you will have your own reasons as to why you rank them in the order that you do. Very briefly note these, too.

2. Form groups as assigned by your instructor (at least four persons per group with gender mixed). Each group should:

   (a) Elect a spokesperson for the group

   (b) Compare how the group members have ranked the characters

   (c) Examine the reasons used by each of the members for their rankings

   (d) Seek consensus on a final group ranking

3. After completing the prior steps, discuss in the group the outcomes and reasons for agreement or disagreement on the rankings. Pay particular attention to any patterns that emerge.

4. Have a spokesperson be prepared to discuss the results of the exercise and the discussion within your group with the rest of the class.

Class Exercise 17: American Football

Instructions

Form into groups as assigned by the instructor. In the group, do the following:

1. Discuss American football—the rules, the way the game is played, the way players and coaches behave, and the roles of owners and fans.

2. Use American football as a metaphor to explain the way U.S. corporations run and how they tend to behave in terms of strategies and goals.

3. Prepare a class presentation for a group of visiting Japanese business executives. In this presentation, use the metaphor of American football to (1) explain American business strategies and practices to the Japanese and (2) critique the potential strengths and weaknesses of the American business approach in terms of success in the global marketplace.

Class Exercise 18: Entrepreneurs Among Us[12]

Michael Gerber, author and entrepreneur, says: "The entrepreneur in us sees opportunities everywhere we look, but many people see only problems everywhere they look."

Instructions

1. Think about the people you know and deal with. Who among them is the best example of a successful entrepreneur? Write down their name and also a brief justification for your choice.

2. Think about your personal experiences, interests, and ideas that might be sources of personal entrepreneurship. Jot down a few notes that set forth some tentative plans for turning at least one into an actual accomplishment.

3. Form teams as assigned by the instructor. Within the team share both (a) your example of a successful entrepreneur and (b) your personal entrepreneurship plan.

4. Choose one as your team's "exemplar" entrepreneurs to share with the class at large. Focus on the entrepreneur as a person, the entrepreneur's business or nonprofit venture, what factors account for success and/or failure in this case, and what the entrepreneur contributes to the local community.

5. Choose one of the entrepreneurship plans from among your teammates and be prepared to share and explain it as well with the class at large.

Team Project 1: Managing Millennials

Question

What should Baby Boomers know about members of the Millennial generation to best manage them in the workplace?

Instructions

- Gather insights regarding the work and career preferences, values, and expectations of members of these different generational subcultures—specifically, Baby Boomers, Generation Xers, and Millennials.
- Analyze the points of potential difference between Baby Boomers and Millennials. What advice can you give to a Baby Boomer manager on how to best deal with a Millennial worker? What advice can you give the Millennial on how to best deal with a Baby Boomer boss?
- Analyze the points of potential difference between Baby Boomers and Generation Xers. What advice can you give to a Baby Boomer manager on how to best deal with a Generation X worker? What advice can you give the Generation Xer on how to best deal with a Baby Boomer boss?
- Analyze the points of potential difference between Millennials and Generation Xers. What advice can you give to a Generation X manager on how to best deal with a Millennial worker? What advice can you give the Millennial on how to best deal with a Generation X boss?

Team Project 2: Management in Popular Culture

You'll notice that the chapter openers in this book bring in movies and television shows from our popular culture. Lots of them have situations and themes that deal with things like leadership, team dynamics, attitudes, personalities—all the major topics of this textbook. The point is: Management learning is everywhere; we just have to look for it.

Question

What management insights are available in various elements of our popular culture and reflected in our everyday living?

Instructions

- Listen to music. Pick out themes that reflect important management concepts and theories. Put them together in a multimedia report that presents your music choices and describes their messages about management and working today.
- Watch television. Look again for the management themes. In a report, describe what popular television programs have to say about management and working. Also consider TV advertisements. How do they use and present workplace themes to help communicate their messages?
- Read the comics looking for management themes. Compare and contrast management and working in two or three popular comic strips.
- Read a best-selling novel. Find examples of management and work themes in the novel. Report on what the author's characters and their experiences say about people at work.

Team Project 3: Organizational Commitment to Sustainability

Instructions

In your assigned work teams do the following.

1. Agree on a definition of "sustainability" that should fit the operations of any organization.
2. Brainstorm audit criteria that can be used to create a Commitment to Sustainability Scorecard (CSS) that can be used to assess the sustainability practices of an organization.
3. Formalize your list of criteria and then create a formal CSS worksheet that can be used to conduct an actual audit. Be sure that an organization being audited would not only receive scores on individual dimensions or categories of sustainability performance but also receive a total overall "Sustainability Score" that can be compared with results for other organizations.
4. Present and defend your CSS to the class at large.
5. Use feedback received from the class presentation to revise your CSS to be used in an actual organizational sustainability audit.
6. Use your CSS to conduct a sustainability audit for a local organization.

Team Project 4: Crisis Management Realities

Question

What types of crises do business leaders face and how do they deal with them?

Instructions

- Identify three crisis events from the recent local, national, and international business news.
- Read at least three different news reports on each crisis, trying to learn as much as possible about its specifics, how it was dealt with, what the results were, and the aftermath of the crisis.
- For each crisis, use a balance sheet approach to list sources or causes of the conflict and management responses to it. Analyze the lists to see if there are any differences based on the nature of the crisis faced in each situation. Also look for any patterns in the responses to them by the business executives.
- Score each crisis (from 1 = low to 5 = high) in terms of how successfully it was handled. Be sure to identify the criteria that you use to describe "success" in handling a crisis situation. Make a master list of "Done Rights" and "Done Wrongs" in crisis management.
- Summarize the results of your study into a report on "Realities of Crisis Management."

Team Project 5: Personal Career Planning[1]

Instructions

1. Complete the following activities and bring the results to class. Your work should be in a written form suitable for grading.

    Activity 1: Strengths and Weaknesses Inventory   Different occupations require special talents, abilities, and skills. Each of us, you included, has a repertoire of existing strengths and weaknesses that are "raw materials" we presently offer a potential employer. Actions can (and should!) be taken over time to further develop current strengths and to turn weaknesses into strengths. Make a list identifying your most important strengths and weaknesses in relation to the career direction you are likely to pursue upon graduation. Place a * next to each item you consider most important to focus on for continued personal development.

    Activity 2: Five-Year Career Objectives   Make a list of three career objectives that you hope to accomplish within five years of graduation. Be sure they are appropriate given your list of personal strengths and weaknesses.

    Activity 3: Five-Year Career Action Plans   Write a specific action plan for accomplishing each of the five objectives. State exactly what you will do, and by when, in order to meet each objective. If you will need special support or assistance, identify what it is and state how you will obtain it. An outside observer should be able to read your action plan for each objective and end up feeling confident that he or she knows exactly what you are going to do and why.

2. In class, form into groups as assigned by the instructor. Share your career-planning analysis with the group and listen to those of others. Participate in a discussion that examines any common patterns and major differences among group members. Take advantage of any opportunities to gather feedback and advice from others. Have one group member be prepared to summarize the group discussion for the class as a whole.

Team Project 6: After Meeting/Project Review[2]

Instructions

1. Complete the following assessment after participating in a meeting or a group project.

    1. How satisfied are *you* with the outcome of the meeting project?

    Not at all satisfied   1   2   3   4   5   6   7   Totally satisfied

    2. How do you think *other members of the meeting/project group would rate you* in terms of your *influence* on what took place?

    No influence   1   2   3   4   5   6   7   Very high influence

    3. In your opinion, how *ethical* was any decision that was reached?

    Highly *un*ethical   1   2   3   4   5   6   7   Highly ethical

    4. To what extent did you feel "*pushed into*" going along with the decision?

    Not pushed into it at all   1   2   3   4   5   6   7   Very pushed into it

    5. How *committed* are *you* to the agreements reached?

    Not at all committed   1   2   3   4   5   6   7   Highly committed

    6. Did you understand what was expected of you as a member of the meeting or project group?

    Not at all clear   1   2   3   4   5   6   7   Perfectly clear

    7. Were participants in the meeting/project group discussion listening to each other?

    Never   1   2   3   4   5   6   7   Always

    8. Were participants in the meeting/project group discussion honest and open in communicating with one another?

    Never   1   2   3   4   5   6   7   Always

9. Was the meeting/project completed efficiently?

Not at all 1 2 3 4 5 6 7 Very much

10. Was the outcome of the meeting/project something that you felt proud to be a part of?

Not at all 1 2 3 4 5 6 7 Very much

2. Make sure that everyone in your group completed this assessment for the same team project.

3. Each person in the group should then take the "mirror test." They should ask: (a) What are my thoughts about my team and my contributions to the team, now that the project is finished? (b) What could I do in future situations to end up with a "perfect" score after a meeting or after a project review?

4. Share results of both the assessment and mirror test with one another. Discuss their implications: (a) for the future success of the group on another project and (b) for the members as they go forward to work with other groups on other projects in the future.

5. Be prepared to share your team project results with the class as a whole.

Team Project 7: Contrasting Strategies

Starbucks is the dominant name among coffee kiosks—how does Dunkin Donuts compete? Google has become the world's search engine of choice—can Bing ever catch up? Does it make a difference to you whether you shop for books at Amazon or Barnes & Noble, or buy gasoline from BP, Shell, or the local convenience store?

Question

How do organizations in the same industry fare when they pursue somewhat or very different strategies?

Instructions

1. Look up recent news reports and analyst summaries for each of the following organizations:

    Coach and Kate Spade . . . Southwest Airlines and Delta Airlines . . . *New York Times* and *USA Today* . . . Electronic Arts and Take 2 Interactive . . . National Public Radio and Sirius . . . Coca-Cola and PepsiCo

2. Use this information to write a short description of the strategies that each seems to be following in the quest for performance success.

3. Compare the strategies for each organizational pair, with the goal of identifying whether or not one organization has a strategic advantage in the industry.

4. Try to identify other pairs of organizations and do similar strategic comparisons for them.

5. Prepare a summary report highlighting (a) the strategy comparisons and (b) those organizations whose strategies seem best positioned for competitive advantage.

Team Project 8: Network "U"

Instructions

Form into groups as assigned by the instructor. In the group do the following:

1. Discuss the concept of the network organization structure as described in the textbook.

2. Create a network organization structure for your college or university. Identify the "core staffing" and what will be outsourced. Identify how outsourcing will be managed.

3. Draw a diagram depicting the various elements in your Network "U."

4. Identify why Network "U" will be able to meet two major goals: (a) create high levels of student learning and (b) operate with cost efficiency.

5. Present and justify your design for Network "U" to the class.

Team Project 9: Organizational Culture Walk

Question

What organizational cultures do we encounter and deal with every day, and what are their implications for employees, customers, and organizational performance?

Instructions

1. In your team make two lists. List A should identify the things that represent the core cultures of organizations. List B should identify the things that represent the observable cultures of organizations. For each item on the two lists, identify one or more indicators that you might use to describe this aspect of the culture for an actual organization.

2. Take an *organizational culture walk* through a major shopping area of your local community. Choose at least three business establishments. Visit each as customers. As you approach, put your "organizational culture senses" to work. Start gathering data on your Lists A and B. Keep gathering it while you are at the business and right through your departure. Take good notes and gather your thoughts together after leaving. Do this for each of the three organizations you choose.

3. Analyze and compare your data to identify the major cultural attributes of the three organizations and how they influence customers and organizational performance.

4. Use your results to make some general observations and report on the relationship between organizational cultures and performance as well as among organizational cultures, employee motivation, and customer satisfaction.

Team Project 10: The Future of Labor Unions

Question

What is the future for labor unions in America?

Instructions

1. Perform library research to identify trends in labor union membership in the United States.

2. Analyze the trends to identify where unions are gaining and losing strength; develop possible explanations.

3. Consider talking with members of labor unions in your community to gather their viewpoints.

4. Consider examining data on labor union trends in other countries.

5. Prepare a report that uses the results of your research to answer the project question.

Team Project 11: Leadership Believe-It-Or-Not

You would think leaders would spend lots of time talking with the people who make products and deliver services, trying to understand problems and asking for advice. But *Business Week* reports a survey that shows quite the opposite. Persons with a high school education or less are asked for advice by only 24% of their bosses; for those with a college degree, the number jumps to 54%.

Question

What stories do your friends, acquaintances, family members, and you tell about their bosses that are truly hard to believe?

Instructions

1. Listen to others and ask others to talk about the leaders they have had or presently do have. What strange-but-true stories are they telling?

2. Create a journal that can be shared with class members that summarizes, role-plays, or otherwise communicates the real-life experiences of people whose bosses sometimes behave in ways that are hard to believe.

3. For each of the situations in your report, try to explain the boss's behaviors.

4. Also for each of the situations, assume that you observed or heard about it as the boss's supervisor. Describe how you would "coach" or "counsel" the boss in order to turn the situation into a "learning moment" for positive leadership development.

Team Project 12: Difficult Personalities

Question

What personalities cause the most problems when people work together in teams, and what can be done to best deal with them?

Instructions

1. Do a survey of friends, family, co-workers, and even the public-at-large to get answers to these questions:

   1. When you work in a team, what personalities do you have the most difficulty dealing with?

   2. How do these personalities affect you, and how do they affect the team as a whole?

   3. In your experience and for each of the "difficult personalities" that you have described, what have you found to be the best way of dealing with them?

   4. How would you describe your personality, and are there any circumstances or situations in which you believe others could consider your personality "difficult" to deal with?

   5. Do you engage in any self-management when it comes to your personality and how it fits when you are part of a team?

2. Gather the results of your survey, organize them for analysis, and then analyze them to see what patterns and insights your study has uncovered.

3. Prepare a report to share your study with the rest of your class.

Team Project 13: CEO Pay

Question
What is happening in the area of executive compensation and what do you think about it?

Instructions
1. Check the latest reports on CEO pay. Get the facts and prepare a brief report as if you were writing a short, informative article for *Fortune* magazine. The title of your article should be "Status Report: Where We Stand Today on CEO Pay."

2. Address the equity issue: Are CEOs paid too much, especially relative to the pay of average workers?

3. Address the pay-for-performance issue: Do corporate CEOs get paid for performance or for something else? What do the researchers say? What do the business periodicals say? Find some examples to explain and defend your answers to these questions.

4. Address the social responsibility issue: Should CEOs accept pay that is many times the amounts that workers receive?

5. Take a position: Should a limit be set on CEO pay? If not, why not? If yes, what type of limit should be set? Who, if anyone, should set these limits—the government, company boards of directors, or someone else?

Team Project 14: Superstars on the Team

During a period of reflection following a down cycle for his teams, Sasho Cirovski, head coach of the University of Maryland's men's soccer, came to a realization. "I was recruiting talent," he said, "I wasn't doing a very good job of recruiting leaders." With a change of strategy, his teams moved back to top-ranked national competition.

Question
What do you do with a "superstar" on your team?

Instructions
1. Everywhere you look—in entertainment, in sports, and in business—a lot of attention these days goes to the superstars. What is the record of teams and groups with superstars? Do they really outperform the rest?

2. What is the real impact of a superstar's presence on a team or in the workplace? What do they add? What do they cost? Consider the potential cost of having a superstar on a team in the equation Benefits − Cost = Value. What is the bottom line of having a superstar on the team?

3. Interview the athletic coaches on your campus. Ask them the previous questions about superstars. Compare and contrast their answers. Interview players from various teams. Ask them the same questions.

4. Develop a set of guidelines for creating team effectiveness in a situation where a superstar is present. Be thorough and practical.

Team Project 15: How Words Count

Question
What words do people use in organizations that carry meanings that create unintended consequences for the speaker?

Research Directions
1. Brainstorm with others to make a list of words that you have used or heard used by people and that cause other persons to react or respond negatively and even with anger toward the person speaking them?

2. For each word on the list write its "positive" meaning and "negative" meaning.

3. Choose two or three of the words that seem especially significant. Write role-plays that display speakers using each word in the positive sense in conversations and in which the words are interpreted positively by the receivers.

4. For these same words, write role-plays that display speakers using each word conversationally with positive intentions but in which they are interpreted negatively by the receiver.

5. Explain the things that make a difference in how the same words are interpreted by receivers.

6. Draft a report that explains how people in organizations can avoid getting trapped unintentionally in problems caused by poor choice and/or use of words in their conversations.

Team Project 16: Job Satisfaction Around the World

Question

Does job satisfaction vary around the world, and does it reflect differences in national cultures?

Instructions

1. Gather together recent reports on job satisfaction among workers in the United States.
2. Gather similar data on workers in other countries—for example, Canada, the United Kingdom, Germany, Brazil, Mexico, Japan, India.
3. Compare the job satisfaction data across countries to answer the project question.
4. Consider pursuing your results further by researching how the various countries compare on working conditions, labor laws, and related matters. Use this information to add context to your findings.
5. Prepare a report to share your study with the rest of your class.

Team Project 17: Globalization Pros and Cons

In his book *The World Is Flat*, Thomas L. Friedman says: "...the more your culture easily absorbs foreign ideas and best practices and melds those with its local traditions—the greater advantages you will have in a flat world."[3] Friedman is talking about a world in which the forces of globalization have ushered in a completely new world that nations, companies, and people must both understand and learn how to best deal with.

Question

"Globalization" is frequently in the news. You can easily read or listen to both advocates and opponents. What is the bottom line? Is globalization good or bad, and for whom?

Instructions

1. What does the term "globalization" mean? Review various definitions and find the common ground.
2. Read and study the scholarly arguments about globalization. Summarize what the scholars say about the forces and consequences of globalization in the past, present, and future.
3. Examine current events relating to globalization. Summarize the issues and arguments. What is the positive side of globalization? What are the negatives that some might call its "dark" side?
4. Consider globalization from the perspective of your local community or one of its major employers. From their perspectives, is globalization a threat or an opportunity, and why?
5. Take a position on globalization. State what you believe to be the best course for government and business leaders to take. Justify your position.

Team Project 18: Community Entrepreneurs

Entrepreneurs are everywhere. Some might live next door, many own and operate the small businesses of your community, and you might even be one.

Question

Who are the entrepreneurs in your community and what are they accomplishing?

Instructions

1. Read the local news, talk to your friends and other locals, and think about where you shop. Make a list of the businesses and other organizations that have an entrepreneurial character. Be as complete as possible—look at both businesses and nonprofits.
2. For each of the organizations, do further research to identify the persons who are the entrepreneurs responsible for them.
3. Contact as many of the entrepreneurs as possible and interview them. Try to learn how they got started, why, what they encountered as obstacles or problems, and what they learned about entrepreneurship that could be passed along to others. Add to these questions a list of your own: What do you want to know about entrepreneurship?
4. Analyze your results for class presentation and discussion. Look for patterns and differences in terms of entrepreneurs as persons, the entrepreneurial experience, and potential insights into business versus social entrepreneurship.
5. Consider writing short cases that summarize the "founding stories" of the entrepreneurs you find especially interesting.

Case 1: Trader Joe's: Keeping a Cool Edge

The average Trader Joe's stocks only a small percentage of the products of local super- markets in a space little larger than a corner store. How did this neighborhood market grow to earnings of $8.5 billion, garner supe- rior ratings, and become a model of manage- ment? Take a walk down the aisles of Trader Joe's and learn how sharp attention to the fundamentals of retail management made this chain more than the average Joe.

From Corner Store to Foodie Mecca

In more than 344 stores across the United States, hundreds of thousands of custom- ers are treasure hunting. Driven by gourmet tastes but hungering for deals, they are led by cheerful guides in Hawaiian shirts who point them to culinary discoveries such as ahi jerky, ginger granola, and baked jala- peño cheese crunchies.

It's just an average day at Trader Joe's, the gourmet, specialty, and natural-foods store that offers staples such as milk and eggs along with curious, one-of-a-kind foods at below-average prices in almost thirty states. Foodies, hipsters, and reces- sionistas alike are attracted to the chain's charming blend of low prices, tasty treats, and laid-back but enthusiastic customer service. Shopping at Trader Joe's is less a chore than it is immersion into another culture. In keeping with its whimsi- cal faux-nautical theme, crew members

and managers wear loud tropical-print shirts. Chalkboards around every corner unabashedly announce slogans such as, "You don't have to join a club, carry a card, or clip coupons to get a good deal."

"When you look at food retailers," says Richard George, professor of food market- ing at St. Joseph's University, "there is the low end, the big middle, and then there is the cool edge—that's Trader Joe's." But how does Trader Joe's compare with other stores with an edge, such as Whole Foods? Both obtain products locally and from all over the world. Each values employees and strives to offer the highest quality. However, there's no mistaking that Trader Joe's is cozy and intimate, whereas Whole Foods' spacious stores offer an abundance of choices. By limiting its stock and sell- ing quality products at low prices, Trader Joe's sells twice as much per square foot than other supermarkets. Most retail mega-markets, such as Whole Foods, carry between 25,000 and 45,000 products; Trader Joe's stores carry only around 4,000. But this scarcity benefits both Trader Joe's and its customers. According to Swarth- more professor Barry Schwartz, author of *The Paradox of Choice: Why Less Is More,* "Giving people too much choice can result in paralysis. . . . [R]esearch shows that the more options you offer, the less likely peo- ple are to choose any."

Trader Joe's didn't always stand for brie and baguettes at peanut butter and jelly prices. In 1958, the company began life in Los Angeles as a chain of 7-Eleven–style cor- ner stores. Striving to differentiate his stores from those of his competitors in order to survive in a crowded marketplace, founder "Trader" Joe Coulombe, vacationing in the Caribbean, reasoned that consumers are more likely to try new things while on vaca- tion. He transformed his stores into oases of value by replacing humdrum sundries with exotic, one-of-a-kind foods priced persuasively below those of any reasonable competitor. In 1979, he sold his chain to the Albrecht family, German billionaires and owners of an estimated 8,400 Aldi markets in the United States and Europe.

The Albrechts shared Coulombe's relent- less pursuit of value, a trait inseparable from Trader Joe's success. Recent annual sales are estimated at $8.5 billion, landing Trader Joe's in the top third of Supermarket News's Top 75 Retailers. Because it's not easy competing with such giants as Whole Foods and Dean & DeLuca, the company applies its pursuit of value to every facet of management. By keeping stores comparatively small—they average about 10,000 square feet—and shy- ing away from prime locations, Trader Joe's keeps real estate costs down. The chain prides itself on its thriftiness and cost-saving measures, proclaiming, "Every penny we save is a penny you save" and "Our CEO doesn't even have a secretary."

Trader Giotto, Trader José, Trader Ming, and Trader Darwin

Trader Joe's strongest weapon in the fight to keep costs low may also be its greatest appeal to customers: its stock. The com- pany follows a deliciously simple approach to stocking stores: (1) search out tasty, unusual foods from all around the world; (2) contract directly with manufacturers; (3) label each product under one of several catchy house brands; and (4) maintain a small stock, making each product fight for its place on the shelf. This common-sense, low-overhead approach to retail serves Trader Joe's well, embodying its commit- ment to aggressive cost-cutting.

Most Trader Joe's products are sold under a variant of their house brand—dried pasta under the "Trader Giotto's" moniker, frozen enchiladas under the "Trader Jose's" label, vitamins under "Trader Darwin's," and so on. But these store brands don't sacrifice quality—readers of Consumer Reports awarded Trader Joe's house brands top marks. The house brand success is no accident. According to Trader Joe's President Doug Rauch, the company pursued the strategy to "put our destiny in our own hands."

But playing a role in this destiny is no easy feat. Ten to fifteen new products debut each week at Trader Joe's—and the company maintains a strict "one in, one out" policy. Items that sell poorly or whose costs rise get the heave-ho in favor of new blood, something the company calls the "gangway factor." If the company hears that customers don't like something about a product, out it goes. In just such a move, Trader Joe's phased out single-ingredient products (such as spinach and garlic) from China. "Our customers have voiced their concerns about products from this region and we have listened," the company said in a statement, noting that items would be replaced with "products from other regions until our customers feel as confident as we do about the quality and safety of Chinese products."

Conversely, discontinued items may be brought back if customers are vocal enough, making Trader Joe's the model of an open system. "We feel really close to our customers," says Audrey Dumper, vice president of marketing for Trader Joe's East. "When we want to know what's on their minds, we don't need to put them in a sterile room with a swinging bulb. We like to think of Trader Joe's as an economic food democracy." In return, customers keep talking, and they recruit new converts. Word-of-mouth advertising has lowered the corporation's advertising budget to approximately 0.2% of sales, a fraction of the 4% spent by supermarkets.

Trader Joe's connects with its customers because of the culture of product knowledge and customer involvement that its management cultivates among store employees. Most shoppers recall instances when helpful crew members took the time to locate or recommend particular items. Despite the lighthearted tone suggested by marketing materials and in-store ads, Trader Joe's aggressively courts friendly, customer-oriented employees by writing job descriptions highlighting desired soft skills ("ambitious and adventurous, enjoy smiling and have a strong sense of values") as much as actual retail experience.

Those who work for Trader Joe's earn more than their counterparts at other chain grocers. In California, Trader Joe's employees can earn almost 20% more than counterparts at supermarket giants Albertsons or Safeway. Starting benefits include medical, dental, and vision insurance; company-paid retirement; paid vacation; and a 10% employee discount. Assistant store managers earn a compensation package averaging $94,000 a year, and store managers' packages average $122–132,000. One analyst estimates that a Wal-Mart store manager earning that much would need to run an outlet grossing six or seven times that of an average Trader Joe's.

Outlet managers are highly compensated, partly because they know the Trader Joe's system inside and out (managers are hired only from within the company). Future leaders enroll in training programs such as Trader Joe's University that foster in them the loyalty necessary to run stores according to both company and customer expectations, teaching managers to imbue their part-timers with the customer-focused attitude shoppers have come to expect.

If Trader Joe's has any puzzling trait, it's that the company is more than a bit media-shy. Executives have granted no interviews

since the Aldi Group took over. Company statements and spokespersons have been known to be terse—the company's leases even stipulate that no store opening may be formally announced until a month before the outlet opens!

The future looks bright for Trader Joe's. More outlets are planned up and down the East Coast and in the Midwest, and the company continues to break into markets hungry for reasonably priced gourmet goodies. But will Trader Joe's struggle to sustain its international flavor in the face of shrinking discretionary income, or will the allure of cosmopolitan food at provincial prices continue to tempt consumers?

Discussion Questions

1. Of the six "must have" managerial skills listed in Chapter 1, which do you think is the most important for a store manager of Trader Joe's? Why?

2. This is a German company operating in America and sourcing products from around the world. What are the biggest risks that international ownership and global events pose for Trader Joe's performance effectiveness and performance efficiency?

3. In a casual and nontraditional work environment such as the one at Trader Joe's, what are the keys to a team leader or supervisor becoming an effective manager?

4. FURTHER RESEARCH Study news reports to find more information on Trader Joe's management and organization practices. Look for comparisons with its competitors and try to identify whether or not Trader Joe's has the right management approach and business model for continued success. Are there any internal weaknesses or external competitors or industry forces that might cause future problems?

Case 2: Zara International: Fashion at the Speed of Light

Spotted! Kate Middleton wears a cream Reiss dress for her engagement photo with Prince William. Within a few days, hundreds of European women were searching out the same look. Welcome to fast fashion, a trend that sees clothing retailers frequently purchasing small quantities of merchandise to stay on top of emerging trends. In this world of "hot today, gauche tomorrow," no company does fast fashion better than Zara International. Shoppers in 77 countries are fans of Zara's knack for bringing the latest styles from sketchbook to clothing rack at lightning speed—and reasonable prices.

In Fast Fashion, Moments Matter

Because style-savvy customers expect shorter and shorter delays from runway to store, Zara International employs a creative team of 200 professionals to help it keep up with the latest fashions. It takes just two weeks for the company to update existing garments and get them into its stores; new pieces hit the market twice a week.

Defying the recession with its cheap-and-chic Zara clothing chain, Zara's parent company Inditex posted strong sales gains. Low prices and a rapid response to fashion trends are enabling it to challenge Gap Inc. for top ranking among global clothing vendors. The improved results highlight how Zara's formula continues to work even in the economic downturn. The chain specializes in lightning-quick turnarounds of the latest designer trends at prices tailored to the young—about $27 an item. Louis Vuitton fashion director Daniel Piette described Zara as "possibly the most innovative and devastating retailer in the world."

Inditex Group shortens the time from order to arrival by a complex system of just-in-time production and inventory reporting that keeps Zara ahead. Their distribution centers can have items in European stores within 24 hours of receiving an order, and in American and Asian stores in under 48 hours. "They're a fantastic case study in terms of how they manage to get product to their stores so quick," said Stacey Cartwright, CFO of Burberry Group PLC. "We are mindful of their techniques."

Inditex's history in fabrics manufacturing made it good business sense to internalize as many points in the supply chain as possible. Design, production, distribution, and retail sales are all controlled by Inditex to optimize the flow of goods, without having to share profits with wholesalers or intermediary partners. Customers win by having access to new fashions while they're still fresh off the runway. During a Madonna concert tour in Spain, Zara's quick turnaround let young fans at the last show wear Madonna's outfit from the first one.

Twice a week Zara's finished garments are shipped to logistical centers that all simultaneously distribute product to stores worldwide. These small production batches help the company avoid the risk of oversupply. Because batches always contain new products, Zara's stores perpetually energize their inventories. Most clothing lines are not replenished. Instead they are replaced with new designs to create scarcity value—shoppers cannot be sure that designs in stores one day will be available the next.

Store managers track sales data with handheld computers. They can reorder hot items in less than an hour. This lets Zara know what's selling and what's not; when a look doesn't pan out, designers promptly put together new products. According to Dilip Patel, U.K. commercial director for Inditex, new arrivals are rushed to store sales floors still on the black plastic hangers used in shipping. Shoppers who are in the know recognize these designs as the newest of the new; soon after, any items left over are rotated to Zara's standard wood hangers.

Inside and out, Zara's stores are specially dressed to strengthen the brand. Inditex considers this to be of the greatest importance—because that is where shoppers ultimately decide which fashions make the cut. In a faux shopping street in the basement of the company's headquarters, stylists craft and photograph eye-catching layouts that are e-mailed every two weeks to store managers for replication.

Zara stores sit on some of the world's glitziest shopping streets—including New York's Fifth Avenue, near the flagship stores of leading international fashion brands—which make its reasonable prices stand out. "Inditex gives people the most up-to-date fashion at accessible prices, so it is a real alternative to high-end fashion lines," said Luca Solca, senior research analyst with Sanford C. Bernstein in London. That is good news for Zara as many shoppers trade down from higher-priced chains.

Catfights on the Catwalk

Zara is not the only player in fast fashion. Competition is fierce, but Zara's overwhelming success (recent quarterly net profits were up 63%) has the competition in its rear-view mirror: Inditex recently surpassed Gap as the world's leading clothing retailer by sales. Only time will tell if super-chic Topshop's entry into the American market causes a wrinkle in Zara's success.

Some fashion analysts are referring to all of this as the democratization of fashion: bringing high(er) fashion to low(er) income shoppers. According to James Hurley, a senior research analyst with New York-based Telsey Advisory Group LLC, big-box discount stores such as Target and Walmart are emulating Zara's ability to study emerging fashions and knock out look-a-likes in a matter of weeks. "In general," Hurley said, "the fashion cycle is becoming sharper and more immediately accessible."

A Single Fashion Culture

With a network of over 1,500 stores around the world, Zara International is Inditex's largest and most profitable brand, bringing home 72% of international sales and nearly 67% of revenues. The first Zara outlet opened shop in 1975 in La Coruña. It remained solely a Spanish chain until opening a store in Oporto, Portugal, in 1988. The brand reached the United States and France in 1989 and 1990 with outlets in New York and Paris, respectively. Zara went into mainland China in 2001, expanded into India in 2009, and began online sales one year later.

Essential to Zara's growth and success are Inditex's 100-plus textile design, manufacturing, and distribution companies that employ more than 92,000 workers. The Inditex group began in 1963 when Amancio Ortega Gaona, chairman and founder of Inditex, got his start in textile manufacturing. After a period of growth, he assimilated Zara into a new holding company, Industria de Diseño Textil. Inditex has a tried-and-true strategy for entering new markets: start with a handful of stores and gain a critical mass of customers. Generally, Zara is the first Inditex chain to break ground in new countries, paving the way for the group's other brands, including Pull and Bear, Massimo Dutti, and Bershka.

Inditex farms out much of its garment production to specialist companies, located on the Iberian Peninsula, which it often supplies with its own fabrics. Although some pieces and fabrics are purchased in Asia—many undyed or only partly finished—the company manufactures about half of its clothing in its hometown of La Coruña, Spain.

H&M, one of Zara's top competitors, uses a slightly different strategy. Around one quarter of its stock is made up of fast-fashion items that are designed in-house and farmed out to independent factories. As at Zara, these items move quickly through the stores and are replaced often by fresh designs. But H&M also keeps a large inventory of basic, everyday items sourced from inexpensive Asian factories.

Inditex CEO Pablo Isla believes in cutting expenses wherever and whenever possible. Zara spends just 0.3% of sales on ads, making the 3–4% typically spent by rivals seem excessive in comparison. Isla disdains markdowns and sales, as well.

Few can criticize the results of Isla's frugality. Inditex recently opened 343 stores in a single year and was named Retailer of the Year during the World Retailer Congress meeting, after raking in net profits of almost $2 billion. Perhaps most important in an industry based on image, Inditex secured bragging rights as Europe's largest fashion retailer by overtaking H&M. According to José Castellano, Inditex's deputy chairman, the group plans to double in size in the coming years while making sales of more than $15 billion. He envisions most of this growth taking place in Europe—especially in trend-savvy Italy.

Fashion of the Moment

Although Inditex's dominance of fast fashion seems virtually complete, it isn't without its challenges. For instance, keeping production so close to home becomes difficult when an increasing number of Zara stores are far-flung across the globe. "The efficiency of the supply chain is coming under more pressure the farther abroad they go," notes Nirmalya Kumar, a professor at London Business School.

Analysts worry that Inditex's rapid expansion may pressure its business. The rising number of overseas stores, they warn, adds cost and complexity and is straining its operations. Inditex may no longer be able to manage everything from Spain. But Inditex isn't worried. By closely managing costs, Inditex says its current logistics system can handle its growth until 2012.

José Luis Nueno of IESE, a business school in Barcelona, agrees that Zara is here to stay. Consumers have become more demanding and more arbitrary, he says—and fast fashion is better suited to these changes. But does Zara International have what it takes to succeed in the hypercompetitive world of fast fashion? Or is the company trying to expand too quickly?

Discussion Question

1. In what ways are elements of the classical management approaches evident at Zara International?

2. How do you see operations management in practice at Zara?

3. How can systems concepts and the notion of contingency thinking explain the success of some of Zara's distinctive practices?

4. FURTHER RESEARCH Gather the latest information on competitive trends in the apparel industry, and the latest actions and innovations of Zara. Is the firm continuing to do well? Is it adapting in ways needed to stay abreast of both its major competition and the pressures of a changing global economy? Is Inditex still providing worthy management benchmarks for other firms to follow?

Case 3: Patagonia: Leading a Green Revolution

How has Patagonia managed to stay both green and profitable at a time when the economy is down, consumers are tight for cash, and "doing the profitable thing" is not necessarily doing the right thing? How has Patagonia achieved its success without compromising their ideals?

Twelve hundred Walmart buyers, a group legendary for their tough-as-nails negotiating tactics, sit in rapt attention in the company's Bentonville, AR, headquarters. They're listening to a small man in mustard yellow corduroy sportcoat lecture them on the environmental impact of Walmart's purchasing choices.

He's not criticizing the company, per se—*he's criticizing them.* Yet when he finishes speaking, the buyers leap to their feat and applaud enthusiastically.

Such is the authenticity of Yvon Chouinard. Since founding Patagonia in 1972, he's built it into one of the most successful outdoor clothing companies, and one that is steadfastly committed to environmental sustainability.

It's hard to discuss Patagonia without constantly referencing Chouinard, because for all practical purposes, the two are one. Where Chouinard ends, Patagonia begins. Chouinard breathes life into the company, espousing the outdoorsy athleticism of Patagonia's customers. In turn, Patagonia's business practices reflect Chouinard's insistence on minimizing environmental

impact, even at the expense of the bottom line.

Taking Risks to Succeed

For decades, Patagonia has been at the forefront of a cozy niche: high-quality, performance-oriented outdoor clothes and gear sold at top price points. Derided as *Pradagonia* or *Patagucci* by critics, the brand is aligned with top-shelf labels like North Face and Royal Robbins. Patagonia clothes are designed for fly fishermen, rock climbers, and surfers. They are durable, comfortable, and sustainably produced. And they are not cheap.

It seems counterintuitive, almost dangerous, to market a $400 raincoat in a down economy. But the first thing you learn about Yvon Chouinard is that he's a risk taker. The second thing you learn is that he's usually right. "Corporations are real weenies," he says. "They are scared to death of everything. My company exists, basically, to take those risks and prove that it's a good business."

And it is a good business. With recent annual revenues of $314.5 million, Patagonia succeeds by staying true to Chouinard's vision. "They've become the Rolls-Royce of their product category," says Marshal Cohen, chief industry analyst with market research firm NPD Group. "When people were stepping back, and the industry became copycat, Chouinard didn't sell out,

lower prices, and dilute the brand. Sometimes, the less you do, the more provocative and true of a leader you are."

Chouinard concurs. "I think the key to surviving a conservative economy is quality," he says. "The number one reason is that in a recession, consumers stop being silly. Instead of buying fashion, they'll pay more for a multifunctional product that will last a long time."

Ideal Corporate Behavior

Chouinard is not shy about espousing the environmentalist ideals intertwined with Patagonia's business model. "It's good business to make a great product, and do it with the least amount of damage to the planet," he says. "If Patagonia wasn't profitable or successful, we'd be an environmental organization."

In many ways, Patagonia is an environmental organization. The company has a library of working documents, published online for the world to see, that guides employees in making sustainable decisions in even the most mundane office scenarios. Its mission statement: "Build the best product, cause no unnecessary harm, use business to inspire and implement solutions to the environmental crisis."

Patagonia's solutions extend well beyond the lip service typically given by profitable corporations. The company itself holds an annual environmental campaign; last year's was *Our Common Waters.*

Chouinard has cofounded a number of external environmental organizations, including *1% For the Planet*, which secures pledges from companies to donate 1% of annual sales to a worldwide network of nearly 2,400 environmental causes. To date, more than 1,350 companies participate, raising more than $20 million in 2010.

The name comes from Patagonia's thirty-year practice of contributing 10% of pre-tax profits or 1% of sales—whichever is *greater*—to environmental groups each year. Whatever you do, don't call it a handout. "It's not a charity," Chouinard flatly states. "It's a cost of doing business. We use it to support civil democracy."

Another core value at Patagonia is providing opportunities for motivated volunteers to devote themselves to sustainable causes. Employees can leave their jobs for up to two months to volunteer full-time for the environmental cause of their choice, while continuing to receive full pay and benefits from Patagonia. And every eighteen months, the company hosts the Tools for Grassroots Activists Conference, where it invites a handful of participants to engage in leadership training, much of it derived from the advocacy experiences of Patagonia management.

Growing Green

Patagonia has demonstrated a remarkable ability to thrive even despite the unplanned obsolescence of several of its key products. What makes this even more notable is that Chouinard is often the force driving his own best sellers out of the marketplace.

Chouinard Equipment, Ltd., Patagonia's precursor, was a successful vendor in America's nascent rock climbing community. Chouinard himself was well known on the circuit, having made the first successful climbs of several previously unconquered Californian peaks. For more than a decade, Chouinard had been hand forging his own steel pitons (pegs driven into rock or ice to support climbers) that were far more durable than the soft iron pitons coming from Europe. Because his pitons could be used again and again, climbing was suddenly more affordable and less of a fringe activity.

But during a 1970 ascent of El Capitan, Chouinard saw that the very invention that brought his company success was also irreparably damaging the wilderness he so loved. Though Chouinard Equipment's pitons brought more climbers into the sport, the climbers tended to follow the same routes. And the constant hammering and removal of steel pitons was scarring the delicate rock face of these peaks.

Ignoring the fact that pitons were a mainstay of their success, Chouinard and partner Tom Frost decided to phase themselves out of the piton business. Two years later, the company coupled a new product—aluminum chocks that could be inserted or removed by hand—with a fourteen-page essay in their catalog on the virtues of *clean climbing*. A few months later, demand for pitons had withered and orders for chocks outstripped supplies.

Fast forward nearly twenty years. Chouinard Equipment spinoff Patagonia is a booming manufacturer of outdoor clothing. And though they'd seen success with products woven with synthetic threads, the majority of their items were still spun with natural fibers like cotton and wool. Patagonia commissioned an external audit of the environmental impact of their four major fibers, anticipating bad news about petroleum-derived nylon and polyester.

Instead, they were shocked to learn that the production of cotton, a mainstay of the American textile market for hundreds of years, had a more negative impact on the environment than any of their other fibers. The evidence was clear: destructive soil and water pollution, unproven but apparent health consequences for fieldworkers, and the astounding statistic that 25% of all toxic pesticides used in agriculture are spent in the cultivation of cotton.

To Chouinard and Patagonia, the appropriate response was equally clear: Source organic fibers for all sixty-six of their cotton clothing products. They gave themselves until 1996 to complete the transition, which was a manageable lead time of eighteen months.

But due to the advance nature of fashion production, they had only four months to lock in fabric suppliers. Worse, at the time, there wasn't enough organic cotton being commercially produced to fill their anticipated fabric needs.

Taking a page from their own teaching on grassroots advocacy, Patagonia representatives went directly to organic cotton farmers, ginners, and spinners, seeking pledges from them to increase production, dust off dormant processing equipment, and do whatever it would take to line up enough raw materials to fulfill the company's promise to its customers and the environment.

Not surprisingly, Patagonia met its goal, and every cotton garment made since 1996 has been spun from organic cotton.

Sustaining Momentum

At 72, Chouinard can't helm Patagonia forever. But that's not to say he isn't continuing to find better ways for Patagonia to do business. "I think entrepreneurs are like juvenile delinquents who say, 'This sucks. I'll do it my own way,'" he says. "I'm an innovator because I see things and think I can make it better. So I try it. That's what entrepreneurs do."

Patagonia's next major project is their Common Threads initiative. To demonstrate that it's possible to minimize the number of Patagonia clothes that wind up in landfills, the company is committing to making clothes built to last, fixing wear-and-tear items for consumers that can be repaired, and collecting and recycling worn-out fashions as efficiently and responsibly as possible.

"It'll be in the front of the catalog—our promise that none of our stuff ever ends up in a landfill," Chouinard says. "We'll make sure of it with a liberal repair policy and by accepting old clothing for recycling. People will talk about it, and we'll gain business like crazy."

It's doubtful that Chouinard will ever stop thinking about how Patagonia can responsibly innovate and improve. "Right now, we're trying to convince zipper companies to make teeth out of polyester or nylon synths, which can be recycled infinitely," he says. "Then we can take a jacket and melt the whole thing down back to its original polymer to make more jackets."

Despite his boundless enthusiasm for all things green, he admits that no process is truly sustainable. "I avoid using that word as much as I can," he says.

He pauses for a moment. "I keep at it, because it's the right thing to do."

Discussion Questions

1. While Patagonia has a history of putting sustainability ahead of profits, it cannot do so at the expense of operating capital. Based on what you learned about Patagonia's ideals, how do you think the company determines what possible ventures will be both practical and environmentally friendly?

2. What could Patagonia do today to confirm that Yvon Chouinard's ideals become a permanent part of the company's culture after he leaves the company?

3. Imagine you were asked by Yvon Chouinard to propose a new sustainability initiative for Patagonia. What would you choose, and why?

4. FURTHER RESEARCH Business decisions can often be a compromise between ethics and profitability, even for a company with the idealism of Patagonia. Research Patagonia's and see if you can find a business decision that appeared to put profits ahead of the company's publicly stated environmental goals. Explain why you think that company made this decision and the competing factors you believe were involved.

Case 4: Amazon: One E-Store to Rule Them All

Even its logo was updated to symbolize that Amazon.com sells almost anything you can think of, from A to Z.

And that only takes into account Amazon's U.S. presence. At latest count, customers in seven other countries, including China, Japan, and France, can access Amazon sister sites built especially for them. Amazon's 31 "fulfillment centers" around the world enclose more than 9 million square feet of operating space.

So what's next? Growth. Bezos continues to diversify Amazon's product offerings and broaden its brand by partnering with existing retailers to add new product lines. It's a win-win proposition for a multitude of companies—including Target, Toys 'R' Us, and Wine.com. The companies profit from the additional exposure and sales (without undercutting their existing business), and Amazon's brand thrives from the opportunity to keep customers who might otherwise shop elsewhere.

Traditional Content, Layers of Value

Beyond simply finding more and more products to sell, Bezos realized that to prevent his brand from becoming stagnant, he would have to innovate, creating new levels of service to complement existing products. "We have to say, 'What kind of innovation can we layer on top of that that will be meaningful for our customers?'" Bezos said.

So far, much of this innovation has come from the depth of the free content available to Amazon customers. Far from being a loss leader, Amazon's free content spurs sales and reinforces customers' perception of Amazon's commitment to customer service.

As David Meerman Scott put it in eContent, "Here is the flip side of free in action—a smart content company figuring out how to get people to contribute compelling content for free and then building a for-profit business model around it. Amazon.com has built a huge content site by having all of the content provided to it for no cost. Of course, Amazon.com makes money by selling products based on the contributed content on the site—another example of the flip side of free."

Tete a Tete with Cupertino

In recent years, Amazon has found itself squaring off against Apple in all realms of

Amazon.com has soared ahead of other online merchants. What the firm can't carry in its 29 worldwide warehouses, affiliated retailers distribute for it. Not content to rest on past laurels, CEO Jeff Bezos has introduced a number of Amazon products, including a set-top box and several versions of the Kindle. But will the investments pay off?

The Rocket Takes Off

Like a rocket propelled by jet fuel, Internet commerce has shot off the launch pad. No matter what the product is that may set a shopper's heart aflutter, some up-and-coming marketer has likely already set up a specialty e-store selling it. But one online vendor has grander aspirations: why stop at selling one line of products—or two, or twenty—when customers can instead be offered the equivalent of an online Mall of America?

From its modest beginning in Jeff Bezos's garage in 1995, Amazon.com has quickly sprouted into the most megalithic online retailer. Once Bezos saw that Amazon could outgrow its role as an immense book retailer, he began to sell CDs and DVDs.

Barnes & Noble: Adapting to an Uncertain Future

Seeing the electronic writing on the wall, Barnes and Noble recently named William Lynch, the executive behind many of its recent e-publishing successes, as CEO. In less than two years with B&N, Lynch acquired top e-book retailer Fictionwise, launched B&N's e-bookstore, and debuted the Nook, the company's answer to Amazon's Kindle.

"We're morphing into the future," says B&N chairman Leonard Riggio. "We need someone who has a vision of the new space, somebody who can recruit great people in technology. We have to be more than a retail bookseller."

Like many brick-and-mortar businesses, B&N is increasingly relying on online traffic to make up for declining year-on-year retail sales. Lynch currently helms America's biggest physical bookseller, but he faces tooth-and-nail competition from Amazon for print and e-book market share. And with the meteoric success of the iPad, B&N must also contend with Apple's comfy 30% cut on every e-book sale.

Given Apple's "take it or leave it" negotiating tactics, it's no surprise that Lynch has admirers in the publishing world.

"It's important that our largest retailer has someone at the helm who has a lot of digital experience," says Brian Murray, CEO of HarperCollins Publishers, "because this business is transforming quickly."

digital entertainment. First, by launching its Amazon MP3 music downloading service and, in a move of digital one-upmanship, offering all of its tracks from the Big 4 record labels without proprietary digital rights management (DRM) software, allowing the files to be played on any MP3 player. Amazon also bought top-shelf audio book vendor Audible.com for $300 million, adding more than 85,000 audio titles to its arsenal; it later added shoe and clothing merchant Zappos.com for $928 million.

The company introduced the Amazon Unbox, which allows customers to purchase or rent thousands of movies and television shows from most major networks. In another snub to Apple, Unbox files initially could only be played on Windows-compatible devices, putting Apple computers and the Apple TV out of the action. Amazon touts the content as roughly that of DVD quality, though occupying only half as much space. Using a cable broadband connection, Unbox subscribers can expect to begin to watch it after five minutes or so of downloading.

Although Amazon still sells a considerable number of Apple's iPods, in 2007 it unveiled a new device that existed completely outside Apple's catalog—the Amazon Kindle. Part e-book reader, part tablet, the Kindle can download and store e-books, RSS feeds, Microsoft Word documents, and digital pictures in most major formats. Bezos sees this as a natural evolution of technology. "Books are the last bastion of analog," he said to *Newsweek*. "Music and video have been digital for a long time, and short-form reading has been digitized, beginning with the early Web. But long-form reading really hasn't." He must be right, because Amazon now sells more Kindle books than paperback books.

Not wanting to exclude Apple fans entirely, Amazon's free Kindle app lets users read Kindle titles on their iOS devices. Three years after the first Kindle hit the market, Apple debuted the iPad and sucked most of the oxygen out of the e-reader market. To stay in the fight, Amazon was forced to slash the Kindle's price. And while Kindle fans abound, some critics say that price is the only point on which Kindle truly competes with the iPad.

But Amazon customers are nothing if not loyal. And over the years, Amazon has made a tidy profit selling its customers magazine subscriptions. Given the magazine industry's sudden interest in digital publishing, Apple recently revised its publishing rules to make it easier for magazines to offer readers in-app subscription renewals . . . so long as Apple keeps 30% of the profits. Coupled with new rules that prohibit iOS publishers from taking customers to external sites (and thus out of Apple's iBook store) to purchase e-books, Merrill Lynch analysts suggest that unless Amazon finds a workaround, the changes could cost $80–160 million in lost revenue.

Looking Ahead

It seems hard to catch Bezos not being upbeat. Even as Amazon's stock values fluctuate, he still believes that customer service, not the stock ticker, defines the Amazon experience. "I think one of the things people don't understand is we can build more shareholder value by lowering product prices than we can by trying to raise margins," he says. "It's a more patient approach, but we think it leads to a stronger, healthier company. It also serves customers much, much better."

In just over a decade, Amazon.com has grown from a one-man operation into a global giant of commerce. By forging alliances to ensure that he has what customers want and making astute purchases, Jeff Bezos has made Amazon the go-to brand for online shopping. But with its significant investments in new media and services, does the company risk spreading itself too thin? Will customers continue to flock to Amazon, the go-to company for their every need?

Discussion Questions

1. In what ways does Bezos's decision to develop and deliver the Kindle show systematic and intuitive thinking?

2. Would you describe Amazon's position in the digital entertainment market as certain, risky, or uncertain? Why?

3. Which decision errors and traps are the greatest threats to the success of Bezos's decision making as Amazon's CEO, and why?

4. FURTHER RESEARCH What are the latest initiatives coming out of Amazon? How do they stack up in relation to actual or potential competition? How has the Zappos acquisition turned out? Is Bezos making the right decisions as he guides the firm through today's many business and management challenges?

Case 5: Nordstrom: Planning a Better Inventory

When profit margins are low, how has Nordstrom managed to stay profitable heads and tails above the competition? It brought time-honored retail practices—keep customers happy and manage your inventory tightly—into a new era.

There aren't many bridesmaid dresses for 6′2″ women. Julie learned that when she was asked to be the sole bridesmaid in her best friend's wedding. Her friend found the perfect dress. Julie ordered it, and when it arrived it didn't fit. That is, it *really* didn't fit. The bride took it well. "I don't care what you choose," she said. "Just find the exact same dress."

Weeks before the wedding, Julie desperately scoured shopping web sites only to find few tall sizes and no similar styles. Out of choices and nearly out of hope, she checked Nordstrom's web site. Using their online tools to filter dresses by size, color, and even occasion, she found a near match for The Dress. "So now," Julie says with a smile, "whenever I need a party dress, that's the first place I look."

That's just the kind of customer loyalty Nordstrom hoped to inspire with its recent $150+ million investment in an ultramodern inventory management system. The upgrade, spearheaded by the fourth generation of Nordstrom family members in corporate leadership, accomplished two key goals: correlate purchasing with demand to keep inventory as lean as possible, and present both customers and sales associates with a comprehensive view of Nordstrom's entire inventory, including every store and warehouse.

Keep It Profitable, Keep It Lean

Items don't stay in stock very long at Nordstrom stores these days, and that's the point. In stock items should fluctuate with demand, but the chain is currently turning inventory about twice as fast as its competitors, thanks to strong help from web sales. Nordstrom keeps items in its inventory for an average of 62 days, compared to competitors Macy's for 119 days and Saks for 140 days.

Not only does the company turn existing stock over quickly, but they plan purchasing for future seasons to align tightly with anticipated demand. To counteract the "hopeful" nature of buyers and merchandisers, says Pete Nordstrom, president of merchandising, a departmental buyer would be limited from ordering 10% more of a product if sales slumped 5% in the previous two months, for instance.

Instead of relying on one-day sales, coupon blitzes, or marking down entire lines of product like Macy's, Nordstrom prefers to discount only certain items. A few years ago, the company installed "markdown optimization" software to assist planning more profitable and productive sale prices. According to retail analyst Patricia Edwards, this helps Nordstrom calculate what will sell better at a 25% discount instead of a profit-gouging 35% discount, and forecast which single items should be marked down.

And if a style gets stale, the company can ship it off to its Nordstrom Rack outlet stores. This kind of demand planning is part of Nordstrom's long-term investment in efficiency. "If we can identify what is not performing and move it out to bring in fresh merchandise," says Pete Nordstrom, "that's a decision we want to make."

Total inventory should slide according to overall demand, and by recent accounts, Nordstrom has this mastered. It shrank its recent year-end inventory per square foot 12%, nearly lockstep with a 12.5% decline in fourth-quarter sales.

Perpetual Inventory

It's an axiom of sales: When a customer wants to spend money with you, make it as easy as possible. Nordstrom associates had this down to a science for in-stock items. But until recently, if the customer wanted another color, size, or model, employees didn't have the tools to see what choices were available at neighboring stores.

A customer who fell in love with a pair of candy red Prada pumps one day might return twenty-four hours later to find her Nordstrom store out of her size. While inventory naturally fluctuates, Nordstrom associates couldn't easily locate a pair in another store or verify when they'd return to stock. And in an era of booming online sales, Nordstrom realized they were likely to lose such a customer faster than you could say, "I'll just Google that."

That changed in 2009, when Nordstrom integrated the inventory of each of its stores into its website. After an immense overhaul of the chain's inventory management processes, customers at their laptops and associates behind sales counters see the same thing—the entire inventory of Nordstrom's 115 stores presented as one selection, which the company refers to as *perpetual inventory*.

The upgrade was an immediate hit. As of launch day, Nordstrom found that the percentage of customers who purchased products after searching the website for an

Zappos: How Zappos Did It

The brain child of Tony Hsieh, Zappos.com launched in 1999, selling only shoes. By 2001, gross sales had reached $8.6 million. That number nearly quadrupled to $32 million in 2002 and continues to earn more than $1 billion annually since 2008. By that time, Zappos carried more than 1,300 brands and 2 million total products, including shoes, handbags, clothes, housewares, electronics, and jewelry.

And it had also caught the eye of Amazon's Jeff Bezos. He liked what he was seeing and spent $928 million to buy the firm for Amazon's business stable in 2009. Today, the company is one of *Fortune's* 15 Best Companies to Work For.

The blog search engine *Land* calls Zappos "the poster child for how to connect with customers online." Online resources such as Facebook and Twitter help the company connect with their customers, distributors, employees, and other businesses.

The company's relentless pursuit of the ultimate customer experience is the stuff of legend. Zappos offers extremely fast shipping at no cost and will cover the return shipping if you are dissatisfied for any reason at any time.

Hsieh feels employees have to be free to be themselves. That means no-call times or scripts for customer service representatives, regular costume parties, and parades and decorations in each department. Customer service reps are given a lot of leeway to make sure every customer is an enthusiastic customer.

Zappos' past success comes down to the company's culture and the unusual amount of openness Hsieh encourages among employees, vendors, and other businesses. "If we get the culture right," he says, "most of the other stuff, like the brand and the customer service will just happen. With most companies, as they grow, the culture goes downhill. We want the culture to grow stronger and stronger as we grow."

Now that Zappos is part of Amazon, will it still prosper and grow? Will the company continue to put customers first?

---

item doubled. It also learned that multichannel customers—those who shop from Nordstrom in more than one way—spend on average of four times more than one-source customers. This profit more than offsets the cost of hiring additional shipping employees to wrap and mail items from each store.

So now Nordstrom doesn't have to turn away the customer who spied that pair of candy red Pradas; she can order them online or in her local store, and they'll be shipped to her door directly from a store that has them in stock, even if it's located across the country.

"Customer service is not just a friendly, helpful, knowledgeable salesperson helping you buy something," says Robert Spector, retail expert and author of *The Nordstrom Way*. "Part of customer service is having the right item at the right size at the right price at the right time. And that's something perpetual inventory will help with."

Better yet, Nordstrom's finding that after integrating store inventory into its website, inventory is selling faster, and more profitably, than before. "If we're out of something on the website, it's probably late in the season and the stores are trying to clear it out," says Jaime Nordstrom, president of Nordstrom Direct. "By pulling merchandise from the store, you've now dramatically lessened the likelihood that you'll take a markdown."

One Step Ahead of the Competition

Fast-turning inventories are a sign a retailer is well managed, making it more attractive to investors, especially in an uncertain economy. "If Nordstrom were a car," says retail analyst Patricia Edwards, "it would be a hybrid Cadillac Escalade that gets twenty miles per gallon instead of the normal twelve."

But success has been hard fought. Since its inception in 1901, the Nordstrom name has been synonymous with customer service *par excellence*. And for decades, having top-notch salespeople, carrying the right brands, and developing lasting relationships with customers did the trick.

"The old, classic Nordstrom way is that if you sell more stuff, that compensates for any deficiency you may have in terms of technology," says Robert Spector. "They didn't want to replace the high touch with the high-tech," and they faced striking "that balance between having up-to-date systems and giving that personal service."

"Traditional retailers have traditional ways of doing things," echoes Adrianne Shapira, Goldman Sachs retail analyst, "and sometimes those barriers are hard to break down."

But Nordstrom's investments in inventory planning and tracking have paid handsome dividends. Its operating margin—operating income as a percentage of sales—measured nearly 9% last year, Bloomberg reports, as compared with Macy's 5.6% and Saks' negative return.

"If I am going to put my money behind a retailer in this rocky economic environment, I want it to be one of the best-run companies out there," Patricia Edwards says. "Nordstrom is one of those."

Discussion Questions

1. How does Nordstrom use demand forecasting to minimize leftover inventory?

2. What benchmarks could Nordstrom use to assess the success of its web-based inventory integration?

3. How might Nordstrom apply the concept of participatory planning to product purchasing? What groups should be involved?

4. FURTHER RESEARCH Imagine you have been asked to develop a long-range plan to extend Nordstrom's inventory management overhaul into the future. What changes, revisions, or updates would you plan for the company? What stretch goals come to mind?

Case 6: Electronic Arts: Inside Fantasy Sports

Electronic Arts is one of the largest and most profitable third-party video game makers. Exclusive contracts with professional sports teams have enabled it to dominate the sports gaming market. But as gaming has shifted from consoles to laptops, phones, and tablets, it is struggling to stay relevant. Can EA regain the pole position in a crowded and contentious market?

Founded in 1982 by William "Trip" Hawkins, an early director of strategy and marketing for Apple Computer, EA gained quick distinction for its detail-oriented sports titles compatible with the Nintendo and Sega platforms. Although EA has also received good reviews for its strategy and fighting games, it left its heart on the gridiron, diamond, court, or any other playing field long ago. Says EA Sports marketing chief Jeffrey Karp, "We want to be a sports company that makes games."

Ad Revenue In, Ad Revenue Out

Word of mouth may still be the most trusted form of advertising, and EA has always depended on fans to spread its gaming gospel. But in a highly competitive—and lucrative—gaming market, EA knows better than to skimp on brand building: it spends two to three times as much marketing and advertising a title as it does developing it. EA knows its audience, and it promotes as heavily to *Game Informer* readers as it does to subscribers of ESPN's *The Magazine*.

The realism of EA's graphics set it apart from competitors long ago, but the energy and talent used to depict that realism might be wasted if EA games didn't include the one element fans most want to see: their favorite players. However, top athletes aren't cheap, and neither are their virtual depictions. Players such as Tiger Woods, Donovan McNabb, and Carmelo Anthony expect a tidy sum to promote any product, including video games that use their likenesses. EA spends $100 million annually—three times its ad budget—to license athletes, players' associations, and teams. It's a complex dance: the *FIFA Soccer* game requires 350 different licenses from a total of 18 club leagues, 40 national teams, and 11,000 players. Cheap? Anything but. EA knows that, simply put, players got game.

Paying to Be Seen

Even the most dedicated *Madden* fans may wonder whether the sports video gaming market has enough muscle to shoulder EA's gargantuan costs. Enter the promotional alliance. Just as EA pays to license the use of NFL logos in its games, big-name sports companies such as Nike and Reebok pay to the tune of $3.5 million a year to get their logos on digital players. One game, *NBA Live*, offers players the opportunity to switch up the color and style of players' logo-friendly footwear. The shoe styles may be virtual, but the value of brand recognition is very real for companies that pony up for sponsorship.

Such brand reinforcement isn't limited to sports games either. EA's *Need for Speed Underground* 2, a fast-paced racing game, takes endorsement beyond the omnipresent billboard ads and vehicle logos found in typical driving simulators. Here players receive "text messages" on the screen suggesting game hints, each bearing the AT&T logo. The significance may be lost on adults, but for a younger generation raised on instant messaging, the placement makes perfect sense.

It makes financial sense, too. A recent poll by Nielsen Entertainment and Activision indicates that this kind of placement may result in notable improvements in both brand recall and favorable brand perception. "I think truly that no other media type can deliver the persuasion that in-game ads can if executed properly," said Michael Dowling, general manager at Nielsen Entertainment, Los Angeles.

Losing Ground in a Crowded Market

Until recently, EA's devotion to sports games was a winning asset—it dominated the market as the world's largest video-game publisher. But a funny thing happened on the way to the bank—over the course of a few short years, the gaming market radically changed. Now EA finds itself in third place behind two strong competitors whose successes represent areas in which EA needs to double down to stay in the game.

Blame the Wii. Or blame *Guitar Hero*. Both led popular interest in gaming away from complex sports games played with standard controllers to new types of games, and new ways of interacting with consoles. Nintendo's Wii has been tremendously popular, and although EA has several successful titles for the platform, many of the top games—like *Wii Sports Resort and Super Mario Galaxy 2*—are published by Nintendo itself. The nontraditional controller lends itself to movement-based games, not EA's button-mashing bread and butter.

Emerging nearly parallel with the Wii was the popularity of *Guitar Hero* and *Rock Band*. It didn't take long for casual gamers to take up cheap plastic guitars and drum sets, leaving their traditional controllers to gather dust in the corner. Small gaming shop Harmonix pulled double duty in this market,

Zynga: Building an Army of Social Gamers

Approximately two million farmers in the U.S. engage in backbreaking labor from before sunrise until well after sunset—plowing land, harvesting crops, raising livestock. Another 30 million farmers do the same without ever getting dirty or climbing onto a tractor.

Welcome to FarmVille, the massively popular Facebook and iOS app by Zynga. While FarmVille earns Zynga most of its press, the company still packs an impressive roster of online games: Mafia Wars, Café World, and Zynga Poker, to name a few.

In just over three years, Zynga's earned some impressive stats—including more than 50 million daily users and nearly $500 million in investment funding—and is undoubtedly the most successful developer for the Facebook platform.

"Games are no longer just for geeks," says Brian Reynolds, Zynga's chief game designer, noting that the social focus of their games keep users in touch with everyone from "people [they] care about" to "those they wouldn't normally have conversations with."

And it's working. While other online gaming shops have struggled to commoditize their products, Zynga recently earned a cool $850 million, mostly from vending virtual goods like cows, bushes, and power-ups. In the meantime, they're developing secondary revenue streams from sponsorships and licensed accessories.

Will Zynga's bubble burst, or will they continue to rule Facebook while expanding into iOS and other mobile platforms? Log on and see!

---

first publishing *Guitar Hero*, then selling it to EA adversary Activision, only to follow up with the arguably better *Rock Band* series. EA came to the party late; sensing the market for rock-along music games was sufficiently saturated, it resorted to striking a deal with Harmonix to help distribute *Rock Band*.

While the Wii's popularity seems to have peaked for the time being and plastic instruments are on their way out (parent company Viacom recently sold Harmonix for the bargain-basement price of $50), these emerging trends ultimately diluted EA's chokehold on the popular gaming market. Meanwhile, Activision found a comfortable home with the Wii, scoring big hits with several *Guitar Hero* titles and hitting the bullseye by porting their massively successful *Call of Duty* franchise.

And then there's Apple. When Steve Jobs launched the iPhone/iPod Touch App Store in the summer of 2008, he decreed that one-third of the first 500 apps would be games. Before long, specs improved in iOS devices to make them serious portable gaming machines. The iPad improved iOS gaming with a large, high-resolution screen, and the App Store suddenly became a self-sufficient gaming platform faster than you can say *Angry Birds*.

At the same time, Facebook was coming into its own as a singular destination for simple but time-swallowing games. Together, these platforms heralded a new way of acquiring and playing games in which EA had little to no experience: digital distribution. Quick on the draw, however, was Zynga, an upstart publisher who quickly dominated Facebook games with *FarmVille* and *FrontierVille*, among others. Games on iOS and Facebook are portable, easy, and you can step away from them as long as you like and pick up just where you left off. That kind of gaming is worlds away from EA's traditions, and it's forced the company to do some serious reckoning on its future.

As of today, EA is the third-place publisher behind Activision and Zynga, and while things are starting to look up, it's a long, hard road back to the top. CEO John Riccitiello even admitted recently, "What we've described as a two-year comeback is clearly taking longer."

EA knows that the road to riches is paved with recurring sales. And though it's annualized releases of many of popular sports titles for some time, they haven't done so for the growing market of massive multiplayer online games (MMOG), which Activision has been lucratively exploiting for years with *Call of Duty* and *World of Warcraft*. EA hopes to catch up with the release of *Star Wars: The Old Republic*.

And the company is showing signs that it's shifting gears to compete successfully in the new gaming landscape. It spent $300 million last year to snatch up social gaming developer Playfish, and news is out that it's planning to bring *Madden* to Facebook. EA's digital distribution business, which it's been quietly building, recently soared 30 percent in one quarter. And though this lead might not hold, EA is the leading publisher for iPhone, iPad, and Windows Phone.

Playing for Keeps

Despite its wild success in the video game market, Electronic Arts faces substantial challenges to its power by competing game companies, the cost of doing business, and even dissatisfied gamers. Can EA overcome these threats and continue producing the sports franchises that brought the company considerable success?

Discussion Questions

1. How can feedforward, concurrent, and feedback controls help Electronic Arts meet its quality goals for video games?

2. What output standards and input standards would be appropriate for the control process as applied to video game production?

3. Can you see the principle of management by exception at play in any of EA's recent business decisions? Why or why not?

4. FURTHER RESEARCH What is the latest in Electronic Arts' quest to regain its former glory as the top gaming publisher? How well is EA positioned for future competitive advantage? Overall, is EA's executive team still on "top of its game?"

Case 7: Dunkin' Donuts: Betting Dollars on Donuts

Once a niche company operating in the northeast, Dunkin' Donuts is opening hundreds of stores and entering new markets. At the same time, the java giant is broadly expanding both its food and its coffee menus to ride the wave of fresh trends, appealing to a new generation of customers. But is the rest of America ready for Dunkin' Donuts? Can the company keep up with its own rapid growth? With Starbucks rethinking its positioning strategy and McDonald's offering a great tasting coffee at a reasonable price, Dunkin' Donuts is hoping they "Kin Do It."

Serving the Caffeinated Masses

There's a lot more to a coffee shop than just change in the tip jar. Some 500 billion cups of coffee are consumed every year, making it the most popular beverage globally. Estimates indicate that more than 107 million Americans drink a total of 400 million cups of coffee a day. And with Starbucks driving tastes for upscale coffee, some customers may wonder whether any coffee vendors remember the days when drip coffee came in only two varieties—regular and decaf. But Dunkin' Donuts does, and it's betting dollars to donuts that consumers nationwide will embrace its reputation for value, simplicity, and a superior Boston Kreme donut.

Winning New Customers

Most of America has had an occasional relationship with the Dunkin' Donuts brand through its almost 6,600 domestic outlets, which have their densest cluster in the northeast and a growing presence in the rest of the country. But the brand has also managed to carve out an international niche, not only in expected markets such as Canada and Brazil, but also in some unexpected ones, including Qatar, South Korea, Pakistan, and the Philippines.

If the company has its way, in the future you won't have to go very far to pick up a box of donuts. "We're only represented large-scale in the northeastern market," said Jayne Fitzpatrick, strategy officer for Dunkin' Brands, mentioning plans to expand "as aggressively" as possible. "We're able to do that because we're a franchise system, so access to operators and capital is easier." How aggressively? According to John Fassak, vice president of business development, the company expanded into 29 new markets last year alone. Sample cities in the Midwest reveal heavy investment: 36 new stores recently opened in Milwaukee, with more than 100 planned in St. Louis and 30 in central Ohio.

What Would Consumers Think?

None of Dunkin' Donuts' moves makes much difference unless consumers buy into the notion that the company has the culinary imperative to sell more than its name suggests. If plans prove successful, more customers than ever may flock to indulge in the company's breakfast-to-go menu. If they don't, the only thing potentially worse for Dunkin' Donuts than diluted coffee could be a diluted brand image. After 60 years, the company has a reputation for doing two things simply and successfully—coffee and donuts. Even when consumers see the line of products expand into what was once solely the realm of the company's competitors, they may be unconvinced that Dunkin' Donuts is the shop to go to for breakfast.

For most of its existence, Dunkin' Donuts' main product focus has been implicit in its name: donuts, and coffee in which to dip them. First-time customers acquainted with this simple reputation were often overwhelmed by the wide varieties of donuts stacked end-to-end in neat, mouthwatering rows. Playing catch-up to the rest of the morning market, Dunkin' Donuts has only recently joined the breakfast sandwich game.

According to spokesperson Andrew Mastroangelo, Dunkin' Donuts sells approximately one billion cups of coffee a year, for 63% of the company's annual store revenue. Considering that coffee is the most profitable product on the menu, it's a good bet that those margins give the company room to experiment with its food offerings.

Changing Course to Follow Demand

Faced with the challenge of maintaining a relevant brand image in the face of fierce and innovative competition, Dunkin' Donuts pursued a time-honored business tradition—following the leader. The company now offers a competitive variety of espresso-based drinks complemented with a broad number of sugar-free flavorings, including caramel, vanilla, and Mocha Swirl. Ever-increasing competition in the morning meal market made an update to Dunkin' Donuts' food selection inevitable. The company currently focuses on bagel and croissant-based breakfast sandwiches, as well as its Oven-Toasted line, including flatbread sandwiches and personal pizzas.

On Every Corner

Starbucks is known for its aggressive dominance of the coffee marketplace. When competitors opened a new store in town, Starbucks didn't worry. It just opened a new store across the street, in a vigorous one-upmanship that conquered new ground and deterred competitors. But many who have struggled to compete with Starbucks have had to do so with limited resources or only a few franchises. Not so with Dunkin' Donuts, whose parent brand, Dunkin' Brands, also owns Baskin-Robbins. Starbucks, which faced slow sales and weak earnings growth as customers cut back on spending, shut down more than 600 U.S. locations as part of a broader plan to revive the company.

Simple Food for Simple People

Dunkin Donuts' history of offering simple and straightforward morning snacks has given it the competitive advantage of distinction as the anti-Starbucks—earnest and without pretense. Like Craftsman tools and Levi's jeans, the company appeals to simple, modest, and cost-conscious customers.

The Sweet Spot Has a Jelly Center

Dunkin' Donuts is trying to grow in all directions, reaching more customers in more places with more products. According to Fassak, achieving proper retail placement can be a delicate balance. Although Dunkin' Donuts often partners with a select group of grocery retailers—such as Stop & Shop and Walmart—to create a store-within-a-store concept, the company won't set up shop in just any grocery store. "We want to be situated in supermarkets that provide a superior overall customer experience," he said. "Of course, we also want to ensure that the supermarket is large enough to allow us to provide the full expression of our brand . . . which includes hot and iced coffee, our line of high-quality espresso beverages, donuts, bagels, muffins, and even our breakfast sandwiches." Furthermore, the outlet's location within the supermarket is critical for a successful relationship. "We

want to be accessible and visible to customers, because we feel that gives us the best chance to increase incremental traffic and help the supermarket to enhance their overall performance," Fassak said.

But why stop at grocery stores? Taking this philosophy a step further, Dunkin' Donuts has also entered the lodging market with their first hotel restaurant at the Great Wolf Lodge in Concord, North Carolina—one of North America's largest indoor water parks. Dunkin' Donuts offers a variety of store models to suit any lodging property, including full retail shops, kiosks, and self-serve hot coffee stations perfect for gift shops and general stores, snack bars, and convention registration areas. Who knows where they'll pop up next?

The launch into the lodging market coincides with Dunkin' Donuts' worldwide expansion program. Steadily and strategically expanding, Dunkin' Donuts unveiled the brand's first-ever theme park restaurant at Hershey Park, new coffee kiosks at sporting venues such as Fenway Park and the TD Banknorth (Boston) Garden, and new stores at airports including Boston, Dallas-Fort Worth, and New York City.

The company is banking on these mutually beneficial partnerships to help it achieve widespread marketplace prominence. Dunkin' Donuts is a nationally known brand with a long reputation for quality, giving the company the benefit of not having to work hard to earn many customers' trust. And if Dunkin' Donuts can find the sweet spot by being within most consumers' reach while falling just short of a Big Brother-like omnipresence, the company's strategy of expansion may well reward it very handsomely.

But this strategy is not without its risks. In the quest to appeal to new customers, offering too many original products and placements could dilute the essential brand appeal and alienate long-time customers who respect simplicity and authenticity. On the other hand, new customers previously

unexposed to Dunkin' Donuts might see it as "yesterday's brand."

If Dunkin' Donuts' executives focus too narrowly on franchising new stores, they might not be aware of issues developing in long-standing or even recently established stores. Some older franchises seem long overdue for a makeover, especially when compared to the Starbucks down the block.

In order to keep up with the latest health concerns, it has reformulated its food and beverages according to its DDSMART criteria so that they meet at least one of these criteria: 25% fewer calories, or 25% less sugar, fat, saturated fat, or sodium than comparable fare. The company has even begun shifting its donut production from individual stores into centralized production facilities designed to serve up to 100 stores apiece.

For the time being, Dunkin' Donuts seems determined in its quest for domination of the coffee and breakfast market. Will Dunkin' Donuts strike the right balance of products and placement needed to mount a formidable challenge against competitors?

Discussion Questions

1. What does a Porter's Five Forces analysis reveal about the industry in which Dunkin' Donuts and Starbuck's compete, and what are its strategic implications for Dunkin' Donuts?

2. In what ways is Dunkin' Donuts presently using strategic alliances, and how could cooperative strategies further assist with its master plan for growth?

3. Do you see evidence of strategic leadership in Dunkin's U.S. expansion plans? If so, how?

4. FURTHER RESEARCH Gather information on industry trends, as well as current developments with Dunkin' Donuts and its competitors. Use this information to build an up-to-date SWOT analysis for Dunkin' Donuts. If you were the CEO of the firm, what would you consider to be the strategic management implications of this analysis, and why?

Case 8: Nike: Spreading Out to Stay Together

Nike is indisputably a giant in the athletics industry. But the Portland, Oregon, company has grown large precisely because it knows how to stay small. By focusing on its core competencies—and outsourcing all others—Nike has managed to become a sharply focused industry leader. But can it stay in front?

What Do You Call a Company of Thinkers?

It's not a joke or a Buddhist riddle. Rather, it's a conundrum about one of the most successful companies in the United States—a company known worldwide for its products, none of which it actually makes. This begs two questions: If you don't make anything, what do you actually do? If you outsource everything, what's left?

A whole lot of brand recognition, for starters. Nike, famous for its trademark Swoosh, is still among the most recognized brands in the world and is an industry leader

in the $122 billion U.S. sports footwear and apparel market. And its 35% market share dominates the global athletic shoe market.

Since captivating the shoe-buying public in the early 1980s with legendary spokesperson Michael Jordan, Nike continues to outpace the athletic shoe competition while spreading its brand through an ever-widening universe of sports equipment, apparel, and paraphernalia. The ever-present Swoosh graces everything from bumper stickers to sunglasses to high school sports uniforms.

Not long after Nike's introduction of Air Jordans, the first strains of the "Just Do It" ad campaign sealed the company's reputation as a megabrand. When Nike made the strategic image shift from simply selling products to embodying a love of sport, discipline, ambition, practice, and all other desirable traits of athleticism, it became among the first in a long line of brands to represent itself as aiding customers in their self-expression as part of its marketing strategy.

Advertising has played a large part in Nike's continued success. Nike recently spent $2.3 billion annually on advertising, and since 2004 has annually invested 11–13% of revenue in marketing. Portland ad agency Wieden + Kennedy has been instrumental in creating and perpetuating Nike's image—so much so that the agency has a large division in-house at Nike headquarters. This intimate relationship between the two companies allows the agency's creative designers to focus solely on Nike work and gives them unparalleled access to executives, researchers, and anyone else who

might provide advertisers with their next inspiration for marketing greatness.

What's Left, Then?

Although Nike has cleverly kept its ad agency nestled close to home, it has relied on outsourcing many nonexecutive responsibilities in order to reduce overhead. It can be argued that Nike, recognizing that its core competency lies in the design—not the manufacturing—of shoes, was wise to transfer production overseas.

But Nike has taken outsourcing to a new level, barely producing any of its products in its own factories. All of its shoes, for instance, are made by subcontractors. Nike claims that this allocation of production hasn't hurt the quality of the shoes but it has challenged Nike's reputation among fair-trade critics.

After initial allegations of sweatshop labor surfaced at Nike-sponsored factories, the company reached out and tried to reason with its more moderate critics. But this approach failed, and Nike found itself in the unenviable position of trying to defend its outsourcing practices while withholding the location of its favored production shops from the competition.

Boldly, in a move designed to turn critics into converts, Nike posted information on its website detailing every one of the more than 700 factories it uses to make shoes, apparel, and other sporting goods. It released the data in conjunction with a comprehensive new corporate responsibility report summarizing the environmental and labor situations of its contract factories.

"This is a significant step that will blow away the myth that companies can't release their factory names because it's proprietary information," said Charles Kernaghan, executive director of the National Labor Committee, a New York-based anti-sweatshop group that has been no friend to Nike over the years. "If Nike can do it, so can WalMart and all the rest."

Jordan Isn't Forever

Knowing that shoe sales alone wouldn't be enough to sustain continued growth, Nike decided, in a lateral move, to learn more about its customers' interests and involvement in sports, identifying what needs it might be able to fill. Nike's success in the running category, for example, was largely driven by the Apple iPod-linked Nike Plus, which now ranks as the world's largest running club. The technology not only motivates runners with music and tracking their pace, but it also uploads their times and distances into a global community of runners online, creating a social-networking innovation that lets runners race in different countries.

Banking on the star power of its Swoosh, Nike has successfully branded apparel, sporting goods, sunglasses, and even an MP3 player made by Philips. Like many large companies who have found themselves at odds with the possible limitations of their brands, Nike realized that it would have to master the one-two punch: identifying new needs and supplying creative and desirable products to fill those needs.

In fitting with the times, Nike's head designer, John R. Hoke III, is encouraging his designers to develop environmentally sustainable designs. This may come as a surprise to anyone who has ever thought about how much foam and plastic goes into the average Nike sneaker, but a corporate-wide mission called "Considered" has designers rethinking the materials used to put the spring in millions of steps. Nike built a software program—the Environmental Apparel Design Tool—to help its designers make environmentally friendly design and material choices, and it recently released the program for the use of other design companies.

Nike even launched a line of environmentally sustainable products under the same name, all of them built under the principle established in the Considered program. "I'm very passionate about this idea," Hoke said. "We are going to challenge ourselves to think a little bit differently about the way we create products." The jerseys it recently provided for World Cup teams, for instance, were partly made from recycled plastic bottles.

Nipping at Nike's Heels

Despite Nike's success and retention of its market share, things haven't been a bed of roses in the past few years. When CEO Phil Knight decided to step down, he handed the reins to Bill Perez, former CEO of S.C. Johnson and Sons, who became the first outsider recruited for the executive tier since Nike's founding in 1968. But after barely a year with Perez on the job, Knight, who remained in the inner circle in his position as chairman of the board, decided Perez couldn't "get his arms around the company." Knight accepted Perez's resignation and promoted Mark Parker, a 27-year veteran who was then co-president of the Nike brand, as a replacement.

And pressures are mounting from outside its Beaverton, Oregon, headquarters. German rival adidas drew a few strides closer to Nike when it purchased Reebok for approximately $3.8 billion. Joining forces will help the brands negotiate shelf space and other sales issues in American stores and will aid the adidas group in its price discussions with Asian manufacturers. With recent combined global sales of nearly $15 billion, the new supergroup of shoes isn't far off from Nike's $19 billion.

According to Jon Hickey, senior vice president of sports and entertainment marketing for the ad agency Mullen, Nike has its "first real, legitimate threat since the '80s. There's no way either one would even approach Nike, much less overtake them, on their own." But now, adds Hickey, "Nike has to respond. This new, combined entity has a chance to make a run. Now, it's game on."

But when faced with a challenge, Nike simply knocks its bat against its cleats and steps up to the plate. "Our focus is on growing our own business," said Nike spokesman Alan Marks. "Of course we're in a competitive business, but we win by staying focused on our strategies and our consumers. And from that perspective nothing has changed."

Putting It All Together

Nike has balanced its immense size and tremendous pressures to remain successful by leveraging a decentralized corporate structure. Individual business centers—such as research, production, and marketing—are free to focus on their core competencies without worrying about the effects of corporate bloat.

A recent organizational change is part of a wider Nike restructuring that may result in an overall reduction of up to 5% of the company's workforce. "This new model sharpens our consumer focus and will allow us to make faster decisions, with fewer management layers," said Charlie Denson, President of the Nike Brand.

Nike has found continued marketplace success by positioning itself not simply as a sneaker company but as a brand that fulfills the evolving needs of today's athletes. Will Nike continue to profit from its increasingly decentralized business model, or will it spread itself so thin that its competition will overtake it?

Discussion Questions

1. When Nike CEO Phil Knight stepped down and handed the top job to Bill Perez, he stayed on as chairman of the board. In what ways could Knight's continued presence on the board have created an informal structure that prevented Perez from achieving full and complete leadership of Nike?

2. How can Nike utilize both traditional and newer organization structures to support the firm's heavy strategic commitment to outsourcing?

3. Does Nike's in-house collaboration with ad agency Wieden + Kennedy qualify as a strategic alliance or an outsourcing alliance? Explain your reasoning.

4. FURTHER RESEARCH Gather information on Nike's recent moves and accomplishments, and those of its rival, adidas. Are both firms following the same strategies and using the same structures to support them? Or is one doing something quite different from the other? Based on what you learn, what do you predict for the future? Can Nike stay on top, or is adidas destined to be the next industry leader?

Case 9: Apple: People and Design Create the Future

Over a span of more than 30 years, Apple Computer—now simply known as Apple, Inc.—paradoxically existed both as one of America's greatest business successes and as a company that sometimes failed to realize its potential. Apple, Inc. ignited the personal computer industry in the 1970s, bringing such behemoths as IBM and Digital Equipment almost to their knees; stagnated when a series of CEOs lost opportunities; and rebounded tremendously since the return of its co-founder and former CEO, Steve Jobs. The firm represents a fascinating microcosm of American business as it continues to leverage its strengths while reinventing itself.

Corporate History

The history of Apple Inc. is a history of passion, whether on the part of its founders, its employees, or its loyal users. It was begun by a pair of Stevens who, from an early age, had an interest in electronics. Steven Wozniak and Steven Jobs initially put their skills to work at Hewlett Packard and Atari, respectively. But then Wozniak constructed his first personal computer—the Apple I—and, along with Jobs, created Apple Computer on April 1, 1976.

Right from the start, Apple exhibited an extreme emphasis on new and innovative styling in its computer offerings. Jobs took a personal interest in the development of new products, including the Lisa and the first, now legendary, Macintosh, or "Mac."

The passion that Apple is so famous for was clearly evident in the design of the Mac. Project teams worked around the clock to develop the machine and its operating system, Mac OS. The use of graphical icons to create simplified user commands was an immensely popular alternative to the command-line structure of DOS found on IBM's first PCs.

When Apple and IBM began to clash head-on in the personal computer market, Jobs recognized the threat and realized that it was time for Apple to "grow up" and be run in a more businesslike fashion. In early 1983, he persuaded John Sculley, at that time president of Pepsi-Cola, to join Apple as president. The two men clashed almost from the start, with Sculley eventually ousting Jobs from the company.

The launch of the Mac reinvigorated Apple's sales. However, by the 1990s, IBM PCs and clones were saturating the personal computer market. Furthermore, Microsoft launched Windows 3.0, a greatly improved version of the Wintel operating system, for use on IBM PCs and clones.

In 1991 Apple had contemplated licensing its Mac operating system to other computer manufacturers, making it run on Intel-based machines, but the idea was nixed by then chief operating officer Michael Spindler in a move that would ultimately give Windows the nod to dominate the market.

Innovative Design to the Rescue

Apple continued to rely on innovative design to remain competitive in the 1990s. It introduced the popular PowerBook notebook computer line, as well as the unsuccessful Newton personal digital assistant. Sculley was forced out and replaced by Michael Spindler. He oversaw a number of innovations, including the PowerMac family—the first Macs based on the PowerPC chip, an extremely fast processor co-developed with IBM and Motorola. In addition, Apple finally licensed its operating system to a number of Mac-cloners, although never in significant numbers.

After a difficult time in the mid-1990s, Spindler was replaced with Gil Amelio, the former president of National Semiconductor. This set the stage for one of the most famous returns in corporate history.

Jobs's Return

After leaving Apple, Steven Jobs started NeXT computer, which produced an advanced personal computer with a sleek, innovative design. The computer entered the market late in the game, required proprietary software and never gained a large following. Jobs then cofounded the Pixar computer-animation studio which coproduced a number of movies with Walt Disney Studios, including the popular Toy Story.

In late 1996, Apple purchased NeXT, and Jobs returned to Apple in an unofficial capacity as advisor to the president. When Amelio resigned, Jobs accepted the role of "interim CEO" of Apple Computer and wasted no time in making his return felt. One of the first things he did was to announce an alliance with Apple's former rival, Microsoft. In exchange for $150 million in Apple stock, Microsoft and Apple would share a five-year patent cross-license for their graphical interface operating systems. He revoked licenses allowing the production of Mac clones and started selling Macs over the Web through the Apple Store.

Beginning with the iMac and the iBook, its laptop cousin, Jobs has continually introduced a series of increasingly popular products that have captured the buying public's imagination. Upon their release, the iPod, MacBook, Apple TV, and iPhone instantly spawned imitators that mimicked the look of these products, but they couldn't duplicate Apple's acute ability to integrate design with usability. Once again, Apple became an industry innovator by introducing certifiably attractive—and powerful—consumer electronics products. And though Macs only account for 4.6% of the global computer market, Apple took home nearly 30% of all dollars spent on computers in the U.S. last year. It also tends to earn more revenue per computer sold than its value-priced competitors.

What Does the Future Hold?

When Verizon debuted a CDMA (Code Division Multiple Access)-compatible iPhone in early 2011, U.S. customers hot for the #1 smartphone suddenly gained a choice among two competing carriers. But iPhone's CDMA compatibility has bigger implications for the world market—now that iPhone is available on the two major mobile phone technologies, there's nary a network in the world on which iPhone won't run. Though it's already available in ninety-three countries, CDMA spells good news for iPhone's global domination.

Drawing on the intuitive touch interface of iPhone, iPad captured the pent-up demand of consumers seeking the ideal tablet. Apple is selling an estimated 4.5 million iPads each quarter, and it's quickly become the fastest-selling electronic device ever. Not only that, but Apple's left few crumbs on the table for new tablet competitors Motorola, Blackberry, and Samsung: According to *PC World*, iPad accounts for 93% of all tablets sold. Analysts and bloggers closely watch for blurry mobile phone photos surreptitiously taken by Apple parts suppliers for a glimpse of features the next model might sport; on the eve of the iPad 2 announcement, journalists were already speculating what the third iPad model might look like.

Given the rapid success of Apple's iOS devices, it's natural to wonder if there's a future for Mac desktops and laptops. For the time being, the answer seems to be, "Of course!" Mac sales outpaced PC sales three to one last year, jumping 28.5% in one quarter, with business sales improving 66.3%.

But reviews of the newest version of the Mac operating system, OS X Lion, indicate what's in store for Apple's computers. During rare public comments, Apple reps have been clear that iOS is the future of Apple, and OS X Lion has a number of features taken directly from the iOS playbook, including a redesigned Mail program that mimics iPad's screen apps, and new multi-touch gestures for trackpads.

Apple has also introduced its iCloud wireless data Sync service. iCloud stores music, photos, apps, calendars, documents, and more. And it wirelessly and automatically pushes them to all of the user's devices.

Inevitable Changes in Leadership

Casting an ominous shadow on the company are Steve Jobs's multiple medical leaves of absence. Jobs is inextricably linked to Apple's initial success, revitalization, and chief creative innovations. Analysts and investors alike wildly speculate on Apple's ability to stay on its creative course without Jobs at the helm.

Chief Operating Officer Tim Cook has handled Apple's day-to-day operations on and off for the last four years. Some analysts think that, health willing, Jobs may transition into an advisory role, focusing on products and strategy and Cook would formally become CEO.

Although able to quietly work miracles, Cook has not been credited with the long-term vision or showmanship of Steve Jobs. Instead he is known as a capable and hard-working executive who has been at the top ranks of Apple for years and understands the company and its products inside and out.

Steve Jobs's leaves of absences remind us that no leader, no matter how innovative or charismatic, will be with a company forever. Do you think Steve Jobs is really the key to Apple's success, or can the firm continue to succeed without him? And, what should Jobs himself be doing now to help prepare the firm for this eventuality?

Discussion Questions

1. What examples can you find that illustrate Apple's core culture and observable culture elements: stories, heroes, symbols, rites and rituals?

2. Should Apple's board of directors be expecting Jobs to push transformational change or incremental change, or both, at this point in time? Why?

3. How could organization development be used to help the iPhone development teams make sure that they are always working together in the best ways as they pursue the next generations of iPhones and innovative product extensions?

4. FURTHER RESEARCH Review what the analysts are presently saying about Apple. Make a list of all of the praises and criticisms, organize them by themes, and then put them in the priority order you would tackle if taking over from Steve Jobs as Apple's new CEO. In what ways can the praises and criticisms be used to create a leadership agenda for positive change and continuous improvement?

Case 10: Netflix: Making Movie Magic

How can the most successful video-delivery company beat its already unbelievable one-day turnaround time? By making a growing portion of its immense catalog available for instant download. Netflix leverages emerging technologies, superior customer service, and an ever-growing subscriber base to transform the traditional video-rental model into a 21st-century on-demand concept.

The Open Secret of Success

What's the most exciting piece of mail you've received lately? Ask more than twenty million customers in the United States and Canada, and they'll probably reply that it's a little red-and-white envelope from Netflix. More than 1.5 million DVDs are in transit on any given day, requiring the company to stock more than 55 million DVDs to keep up with customer demand.

What accounts for Netflix's success? CEO Reed Hastings believes the key to the sustained growth of the Los Gatos, California, company is no secret at all—it thrives because of its renowned customer service. Though Netflix took second place this year, it's annually beat out such heavies as Amazon, Apple, and Target in eight straight e-commerce customer satisfaction surveys conducted by ForeSee Results.

According to Netflix spokesman Steve Swasey, the company keeps its top place by continuously improving operations—both title selection and customer convenience. These qualities make Netflix absolutely magnetic to new subscribers—the company added more customers its most recent quarter than the entire prior year.

Netflix customers have posted more than three billion movie reviews on its Web site to date; an average customer has posted about two hundred. In return, Netflix recommends movies to customers based on their renting habits. About 60% of its members choose new rentals based on these recommendations. To improve the tool used to generate these recommendations, Netflix organized a contest to gather its members' ideas. The prize: one million dollars.

Netflix claims that its members rent twice as many movies as they did before joining the service. Given their recent sales figures, it comes as little surprise. At the end of the most recent fiscal year, Netflix earned $2.1 billion in revenue *despite* spending 1/3 less on marketing than the prior year.

Netflix's Instant Viewing, which streams any of 17,000 movies and television shows to customers' computers, is widely thought to represent the company's future. Within thirty seconds of beginning a download, customers can roll the opening credits. Unlike in Apple's iTunes Store, Netflix customers can wait as long as they want before finishing a streamed movie. Since opening up the service, Netflix has quadrupled its inventory of streaming content.

And it's not just Netflix's inventory that's constantly growing. To date, U.S. customers can choose from more than 200 Netflix-compatible devices, including TVs, gaming consoles, Blu-Ray players, and set-top boxes. It's a logical move, according to David Cohen, executive vice president and U.S. director of digital communications at Interpublic Group's Universal McCann. "The ability to have thousands, if not millions, of content options delivered to your box is certainly the way of the future," he said.

Some customers even help Netflix expand into markets it has overlooked. A few small libraries are quietly using Netflix to expand their interlibrary loan capabilities. Video stores have caught on, too. One

Redbox: Will Customers Wait for New Releases?

What was built on burgers, purchased with coins, and expanded to be in more than 26,000 places at once? One hint: it's bright red and eats dollar bills.

Redbox, the company behind the DVD- and Blu-Ray-renting kiosks found in grocery stores, restaurants, and even the Empire State Building, came to light as a project funded by McDonald Ventures (a collection of brands outside the Golden Arches' core interests). Coinstar bought nearly half the company in 2005, finishing the purchase almost four years later.

Its business model—renting customers the most popular new releases without absorbing the overhead of retail stores—was custom tailored for the "watch it in the theater today, rent it tomorrow" release schedule movie studios prefer. But studios want their share of DVD sales,

too. So Universal, 20th Century Fox, and Warner Bros. cut Redbox and other outlets off from renting hot releases until they've been out 28 days, long enough for film buffs to make the bulk of their DVD purchases.

It was a crushing blow to Redbox, as part of their revenue comes from selling new releases to customers who'd rather keep their rented copy of, say, *The Social Network*. Redbox responded by cultivating new deals with Sony, Paramount, and Lionsgate.

"We are an engine for growth," insists Redbox president Mitch Lowe. "As an important customer of the studios, we provide a significant revenue stream for their businesses. Simply put, our growth can lead to theirs."

---

discreet Massachusetts store owner claims to rent ten to fifteen Netflix discs a month, which saves him more than $2,000 in yearly inventory expenses. "It's nice to be able to offer the latest foreign title that no one has heard of," he said.

Slaying the Dragons

Giving customers what they want, Netflix has beaten back competition from some of the biggest names in media. By allowing customers to keep DVDs as long as they like, Netflix undermined the concept of late fees, which had represented a major source of profits for traditional rental companies. And as instant viewing continues to grow in popularity among Netflix customers, the concept is not catching on everywhere— Walmart closed the curtains on its own movie download service.

Netflix recently hiked the price of subscription plans that include DVDs and streaming, highlighting the company's shift from discs to online video but leaving many customers angry. "It is expected and unfortunate that our DVD subscribers who also use streaming don't like our price change, which can be as much as a 60% increase," Netflix said in its earning release. The company acknowledged that "some subscribers will cancel Netflix or downgrade their Netflix plan, [but] we expect most to stay with us."

Putting People Up Front

So, what does the future hold for Netflix? CEO Reed Hastings makes no bones

about the business model: "If one thinks about Netflix as a DVD rental business," he says, "one is right to be scared; if one thinks of Netflix as an online movie service with multiple different delivery models, then one's a lot less scared. We're only now beginning to deliver the proof points behind that second vision." To "deliver" on this promise, Hastings is now betting as much on people as on his business vision and high technology.

Perks, compensation, and freedom are mainstays of Netflix's commitment to hiring and retaining the best people in the industry. When dealing with competitors such as Apple, Blockbuster, and Amazon, a lot is on the line in the wars for talent. As to salaries, Hastings says: "We're unafraid to pay high." And interestingly, pay isn't linked with performance in the sense of "merit."

Salaries are pegged to job markets to ensure that Netflix pay is always the best around. If you're top talent, you get top salary and are given the freedom to put your talents to work making Netflix's strategy succeed. But if you're something less than a top performer, say, just "average," there isn't room at the company. "At most companies," says Hastings, "average performers get an average raise. At Netflix they get a generous severance package."

Netflix not only hires carefully and well, it offers a unique and highly productive work environment rich in features that appeal to today's high-tech and high-talent workers. Its human resource plan

is as creative as its business model: pay higher-than-average salaries; let employees choose how much of their compensation is paid in cash and how much in stock options; encourage each employee to recruit three others they would "love" to work with; let employees take as much time off and vacation as they think they need; limit work rules, maximize work freedom, and make everyone responsible for the choices he or she makes.

Hastings has a lot riding on his human resource strategy. Does Netflix have the right vision for the future?

Discussion Questions

1. What performance appraisal method would you recommend to make sure that only the "best" are kept on the Netflix team?

2. What are the limitations and risks of Hastings' human resource management practices?

3. How does Netflix's compensation policies encourage high performance?

4. FURTHER RESEARCH Check up on Hastings and Netflix. How is the firm doing right now? How has it changed since the case information was prepared? Are the human resource management practices described here still active at the firm? What else is Netflix doing to create human capital for sustained competitive advantage?

Case 11: SAS: Business Decisions at the Speed of Information

Leadership isn't just about style and charisma. Key players need to make sense of massive amounts of information and successfully predict how and where their organization should go next. Learn how SAS, the most popular business analytics software, helps leaders do just that.

Dr. Bruce Bedford is a learned man. He spent years pursuing collegiate and postgraduate education. After leaving school, he joined Oberweis Dairy and is currently its vice president of marketing analytics and consumer insight. He uses complex diagnostic tools to study the intricacies of Oberweis's business and suggest micro-adjustments that could have million-dollar outcomes. Recently, he was tasked with a career-defining challenge: Stop milk bottle fraud.

It echoes an episode of *Seinfeld* where Kramer and Newman hatched a scheme to take thousands of recyclable bottles to Michigan to redeem them for a nickel more than in New York. But bottle fraud cuts into dairy companies' profits, and Dr. Bedford is investigating it using high-tech software that combines predictive modeling, data mining, and state-of-the-art visualization tools. Sounds like *CSI*? It's more like SAS.

Powerful Tools, Rapid Responses

Short for *Statistical Analysis System*, SAS (pronounced *sass*) is a set of integrated software tools that help decision makers cope with unwieldy amounts of unrelated data. "It is a very powerful tool," says Mu Hu, director of customer relationship management for Golfsmith. "I can pretty much do anything with SAS."

At its core is Base SAS—a set of analyzing, reporting, and data output tools that compile and present information stored in tables or databases. Base SAS can interpret data from almost any source—like spreadsheets, sales records, or annual reports—so that non-programmers can make business decisions based on that information.

Companies can couple Base SAS with more than two hundred specialized software tools intended for specific applications or industries. Examples include tools for supply chain analysis, K–12 teacher evaluation, and anti-money laundering.

SAS is the primary product of the SAS Institute, the self-described "leader in business analytics software." While SAS is its primary product, the company has developed a peripheral business around supporting and training SAS users. Anthony J. Barr wrote the first version of SAS in 1966, incorporating the SAS Institute in 1976 with co-contributors James Goodnight, John Sall, and Jane T. Helwig. Since then, with Goodnight at the helm, it's gained an impressive roster of clients: 92 of the top 100 Fortune Global 500 companies, more than 45,000 businesses, universities, and government agencies, with customers in 121 different countries.

A New Way of Making Old Decisions

To understand the success of SAS, you must first grasp the concept of business analytics. According to Michael J. Beller and Alan Barnett, business analytics is the "continuous iterative exploration and investigation of past business performance to gain insight and drive business planning." It chiefly focuses on "developing new insights and understanding of business performance based on data and statistical methods."

Business analytics help an organization's leaders and researchers understand why something is happening, what might happen next, what will happen if trends continue, and what the optimum result or decision might be.

This focused measurement of business data has been employed since the late 19th century. But since the widespread implementation of business computing systems that began in the late 1960s, organizations have been collecting exponentially more data and have sought to analyze it to more effectively model business possibilities. This lead to the advent of computer-based decision support systems like SAS, as well as other tools like enterprise resource planning (ERP) systems and data warehouses.

For Every Problem, a Solution

SAS brings an organization's decision makers the data they need to solve a problem in the absence of sufficient expertise or information. For example, Mu Hu and Golfsmith used SAS to shrink data merging costs by 50% and reduce time spent preparing marketing campaign results by 70%. Using other data gleaned from SAS, they increased their direct mail response rates from 10% to 60%.

Business leaders often need to interpret separate sets of information to effectively forecast market conditions or gain greater organizational insight. "We had a lot of islands of data without any sort of enterprise information view of the college," says Dr. Jim Riha, director of enterprise business intelligence for Oklahoma City Community College (OCCC), noting his desire for "a more consistent and improved view of the organization." Using SAS, Riha can "bring additional insight to the right people at the right time, while changing the focus from arguing about data

Sungard: Risky Business

Risk. The word summarizes a variety of uncomfortable situations a manager must grapple with. *How likely is this to happen, and what would be the cost if it did?*

SaaS (software as a service) provider Sungard wants to help leaders and decision-makers accurately analyze and manage the risks inherent in any organization's day-to-day and long-term operation.

Like competitor SAS, Sungard produces a family of specialized software products that help organizations collect, organize, and make sense of large amounts of data in order to better understand the factors that affect their business. Though Sungard offers software solutions for a variety of business needs—such as process management, wealth management, and data administration—its risk management programs are especially valued by organizations that operate in complex regulatory environments.

And as the sources of risk grow, so do Sungard's solutions: The company recently partnered with SiteQuest Technologies to release Protogent Social Media Surveillance, a program that scans social media sites like Twitter, Facebook, and LinkedIn for employee-posted content, verifying that it meets regulatory requirements and internal social media policies.

"We don't want to have to review every post about a weekend, local sporting events or weather," says James Cella, SiteQuest's president. "Social network updates are personal in nature, but at the same time, compliance departments have a responsibility to review business content."

to having a better understanding of the issues and making more informed decisions."

And too often, leaders don't get to choose when they must make a key business decision, and they need the right data in order to act quickly. "We need to maintain rapid access to our global data to make informed decisions, and it has to be done cost-effectively," says John Wise, senior director of Informatics at drug developer Daiichi Sankyo. "We want to spend money on drug development, not IT."

Stu Harvey, executive director of planning and research at OCCC, concurs. "The real value comes when you are empowering people with data to make efficient, effective decisions earlier."

Making the Complex Simple(r)

While leadership may come naturally to some managers, predictive analytics and data mining often do not. And though the SAS Institute takes great pains to make its tools user-friendly for non-programmers, it recognizes that SAS administrators and end-users alike need help from time to time.

Beyond the knowledge base and documentation you expect to find behind any major program, SAS Institute goes to great lengths to provide a constant stream of support for its users. Employees write more than 30 SAS blogs, many focused on tips, tricks, and shortcuts. The SAS web site is chock full of useful sample queries, webinars, and articles with titles like, "Jedi SAS tricks" and "The Bayes theorem, explained to an above-average squirrel".

Inspiring Loyalty

Though competitors like Cognos, Oracle, and SAP are trying to catch up to SAS by rapidly gobbling up smaller business intelligence companies, SAS still leads the pack. And most of its success derives from its extremely dedicated staff. The company attracts and keeps brainpower through such perks as private offices for every employee and a 35-hour work week. The company snatches up thousands of undeveloped acres near its North Carolina headquarters, which it sells to employees at a steep discount so they'll establish roots nearby. And the corporate campus is a small town unto itself—it boasts a state-of-the art nursery school, health center, and even private junior and senior high schools.

Mark Moorman, SAS program manager for business intelligence, summarizes the strategy as, "We're willing to take care of you if you're willing to take care of us." It must be working: Employee turnover is less than 4% per year, compared with 15% turnover at typical U.S. software houses.

Customers are equally enamored with the company. In fact, 95% of companies renew their annual lease of SAS software. That's likely because CEO Jim Goodnight lets customers tell him where the company should go next. Users rave about SAS's technical support representatives, who are required to record every product improvement users suggest. These suggestions are sorted, ranked, and sent to customers via the annual SASware Ballot. The results are analyzed (doubtlessly using SAS), and the top ten results are nearly always put into action. "It's an amazingly effective business practice, listening to your customers," says Goodnight.

At the end of the day, customers like OCCC's Stu Harvey stick with SAS because it enables them to make key conclusions independently. "We want people using this and making decisions on their own," he says. "People will be using data and feedback from these wonderful automated systems to change the way they do things."

Discussion Questions

1. Explain why House's path-goal theory might affect an organization's decision to adopt a business analytics tool like SAS.

2. How could access to SAS data affect an employee's high- or low-LMX relationship with their leader?

3. A leader with which leadership style would be most likely to seek out analytical results from SAS? Why?

4. FURTHER RESEARCH The success of a leader can be influenced as much by her access to correct, pertinent information as her leadership style. Describe a situation in which a leader would serve her organization best by utilizing analytical information provided by SAS, even if the choice to do so goes against her personal leadership style. Then describe a situation in which an organization would benefit more from a leader's personal style than her interpretation of analytical data.

Case 12: Facebook: Social Networking Is Big Business

Social networking web sites are a dime a dozen these days, so how does Facebook stay at the top? By expanding its user base and working with developers and advertisers to create fresh content that keeps users at the site for hours on end. But can Facebook keep up the growth while deflecting concerns about its leadership?

The Perception Counts

Mark Zuckerberg wants you to think differently about Facebook. Unlike most other young Silicon Valley CEOs, he's got experience in managing the kind of changes in perception he hopes to bring about. In 2006 he opened Facebook with plans to convince advertisers—and developers—that social networking was more than kids' stuff. Zuckerberg hopes to persuade these same two groups that Facebook is firmly seated at the top and successfully expanding into global markets.

Though Zuckerberg and Facebook have generated their share of controversy in recent years, there's no denying that Facebook has been a runaway success. It is the third most trafficked site on the Web, falling behind only Google and Microsoft. It is by far the most popular social networking site. Currently, more than two-thirds of Facebook users are outside college.

Applications for Every User

Regardless of age or profession, what keeps users coming back to Facebook? The site relies on a host of internally and externally developed applications that integrate directly into the site to keep visitors' eyes glued to Facebook for hours on end. Video is an extremely popular recent addition: the site ranks sixth for online video watching, and it directs more users to videos than the second biggest search provider.

Facebook sees the bleak economy as reason to press ahead with its plans for aggressive growth. The company is gearing up for more acquisitions, hiring rapidly, and rolling out new advertising programs. Moving beyond traditional online ads—the text and pictorial banners that show up on most Web sites—they believe that they can stand out among the crowd. Facebook began rolling out "engagement ads" encouraging users to respond to the pitches by commenting, sharing virtual gifts, or becoming fans of the ads

themselves. By serving approximately one billion display ads, Facebook's online advertising earned it $1.86 billion last year; $740 million of that came from major household brands like Coca-Cola and Procter & Gamble.

As much as advertisers need Facebook users' page views, Facebook wants to keep those advertisers as loyal customers. Facebook ads accounted for approximately 5% of all online ad buys last year and is expected to climb to 8% this year. Facebook ads can sell as inexpensively as two cents per 1,000 impressions—less than a similar buy at Yahoo! The pressure is on Facebook to continue to differentiate itself from other social networking sites, according to Jeff Ratner, a managing partner at WPP's MindShare Interaction. If not, "Facebook doesn't look that different," he said. "It just becomes another buy, and there are cheaper, more efficient ways to reach eyes."

But the best potential for amassing page views and click-throughs lies in Facebook's integrated applications. The site's photo viewing app, for example—the number one photo sharing application on the Web—receives more than two billion photos uploaded to the site each month, with 750 million uploaded last New Year's Eve weekend. Some 6,600,000 developers and entrepreneurs are involved in developing what the company is calling the Facebook Platform. More than 95% of its members have used at least one application built on the Facebook Platform, and advertisers are betting that they can improve that statistic.

Facebook notes that users install more than 25 million apps each day, and the vast number of them are games. While Zynga is the clear leader in Facebook gaming, users can choose among thousands of adventure, racing, word, and—yes—zombie games.

Changing Perceptions

On several occasions during his reign at Facebook, the youthful Zuckerberg has fought the common Silicon Valley stereotype of young CEOs who are brash and unripe to lead. His flat rejection of Yahoo!'s $1 billion bid to buy Facebook was criticized by some as a lost opportunity, so he's working to create a professional impression for his company by hiring some experienced Web personalities. Zuckerberg persuaded Sheryl Sandberg to leave Google, where she had developed cash

LinkedIn: Social Networking's All Grown Up

According to LinkedIn CEO Jeff Weiner, the case for his company as a preferred social networking tool to Facebook comes down to two words: Keg stands.

"While many of us in college probably were at parties having a good time, doing things like keg stands," Weiner says, "I don't know that many of us would look forward to having a prospective employer have access to pictures of those events."

LinkedIn was specifically created to help users foster professional relationships, and in many ways it seems like the older, more mature sibling to Facebook. Whereas Facebook emphasizes the sheer number of friends you acquire, LinkedIn emphasizes *relationships*, classifying your connections by whether you know someone directly or if they know someone you know (a *second-degree connection*). Presenting users with a hierarchical network of possible contacts offers them the chance to get in touch with someone desirable—a hiring manager or possible mentor—through a trusted mutual source.

Even its monetizing strategy seems more grown up than Facebook's: Instead of generating income via ad impressions (measured by the total time a user spends in Facebook), LinkedIn earns income from providing networking and hiring services to its individual and corporate members.

Forbes writer Bruno Aziza lauds how LinkedIn mines its own data for users' benefit instead of just for its own: "Using clever algorithms, members can be presented with insights [to] connect with others more efficiently. They allow you to visualize a possible future and prompt you to act on it."

cows Adwords and Adsense, to join Facebook as chief operating officer. Fourteen years older than her boss, Sandberg is charged with bringing a mature personality to the laidback, collegiate work environment. To do this, she is integrating performance reviews, refining the recruiting model, and developing a mature, sustainable advertising program that will support Facebook as it evolves. "I'm hopeful that we play a significant role in pushing the envelope [with] awareness building," Sandberg said. "How we get there, I don't think we know yet."

Noting that visitors to the site tripled after Facebook unveiled its international presence, the company is continuing its international growth. Facebook translated its content into seventy different languages, with more to come soon. This is critical, because about 70% of Facebook's 500 million active users live outside the United States. Whereas MySpace specializes in locally themed subsites, Facebook has opted to simply translate its entire site for non-English speakers. "Through the translations we are seeing mass adoption in those markets," said Javier Olivan, an international manager at Facebook, adding that because the site is by its nature a tool for communication, Facebook doesn't need to spend much energy localizing it. "The translation approach allows us to support literally every language in the world," Olivan said.

And to head off the efforts of other social networking sites, Facebook makes data available to users from outside of the site with its Facebook Connect program. Facebook Connect allows users to import their Facebook profiles into other Web sites and synchronize their friend lists. Changes appear in real time as users modify their Facebook profiles, and users have "total control" of website permissions to access Facebook data, according to the company.

But some users fear that Facebook considers "total control" to be a relative term. Facebook's settings default to a state where all users' comments and content are open to the entire Web—even Web searches. Many users complained about having to dig through a myriad of confusing menus in order to change their privacy settings to what they actually considered "private."

Late last year, the *Wall Street Journal* reported that many of the most popular Facebook apps were transmitting personal information—users' names and sometimes even their friends' names—to dozens of advertising and Internet tracking companies. Tens of millions of users' accounts were compromised, including those who had set their privacy options at the strictest possible settings. In this case, it was the app developers who were sending users' data, but earlier last year, Facebook was also caught transmitting similar identifying information itself. Though Facebook halted these practices when major media outlets brought the leaks to worldwide attention, privacy advocates are concerned that Facebook would knowingly or unknowingly permit such breaches in the first place.

What Do You Think?

Despite all of its successes, the management team of Facebook knows that they have serious work ahead in order to change the perception of advertisers, developers, and even some users regarding their ability to lead Facebook successfully and profitably into the future of social networking. Will adding experienced management alter advertisers' stereotypes about youthful Silicon Valley CEOs? Can Facebook overcome the bad impression being communicated about its privacy gaffes?

Discussion Questions

1. Can effective communication be achieved among users of social networking sites such as Facebook?

2. Do you believe that Facebook has had problems managing users' privacy, or is this an instance of the selective perception of a few upset users? What influenced your answer?

3. Sheryl Sandberg is under pressure to bring a mature edge to Facebook. What are the most significant challenges that she most likely faces when communicating with her younger peers at the firm, and how would you advise her to best deal with them?

4. FURTHER RESEARCH Find as much information as you can about Mark Zuckerberg. Does he have what it takes to lead Facebook at this stage in its life? Is he making the right choices in terms of "communicating" himself and his firm to the world? What constructive feedback would you give him as an executive coach?

Case 13: Panera Bread Company: Staying Ahead of Long-Term Trends

Panera Bread is in the business of satisfying customers. With fresh-baked breads, gourmet soups, and efficient service, the franchise has surpassed all expectations for success. But how did a startup food company get so big, so fast? By watching and carefully timing market trends.

French Roots, American Tastes

What's so exciting about bread and soup? For some people, it conjures up images of bland food that soothes an upset stomach. Others think of the kind of simple gruel offered to jailed prisoners in movies. But for Panera Bread, a company able to successfully spot long-term trends in the food industry, artisan-style bread served with deli sandwiches and soups is a combination proven to please the hungry masses.

Despite its abundance of restaurants, Panera Bread is a relatively new company, known by that name only since 1997. Its roots go back to 1981, when Louis Kane and Ron Shaich founded Au Bon Pain Company Inc., which merged Kane's three existing Au Bon Pain stores with Shaich's Cookie Jar store. The chain of French-style bakeries offered baguettes, coffee, and sandwiches served on either French bread or croissants. It soon became the dominant operator in the bakery-café category on the East Coast. To expand its domestic presence, Au Bon Pain purchased the Saint Louis Bread Company, a Missouri-based chain of about 20 bakery-cafés, in 1993. It renovated the Saint Louis Bread Company stores, renamed them Panera Bread, and their sales skyrocketed.

Executives at Au Bon Pain invested heavily toward building the new brand. In 1999, Panera Bread was spun off as a separate company. Since then, the firm has sought to distinguish itself in the soup-and-sandwich restaurant category. Its offerings have grown to include not only a variety of soups and sandwiches, but also soufflés, salads, panini, breakfast sandwiches, and a variety of pastries and sweets. Most of the menu offerings somehow pay homage to the company name and heritage—bread. Panera takes great pride in noting that its loaves are handmade and baked fresh daily. To conserve valuable real estate in the retail outlets, as well as to reduce the necessary training for new employees, many bread doughs are manufactured off-site at one of the company's 17 manufacturing plants. The dough is then delivered daily by trucks—driving as many as 9.7 million miles per year—to the stores for shaping and baking. At this point, there are more than 1,450 Panera Bread bakery-cafés in 40 states and Canada. Franchise stores outnumber company-owned outlets by approximately one-third.

Modern Tastes, Modern Trends

Panera's success has come partly from its ability to predict long-term trends and orient the company toward innovation to fulfill consumers' desires. Its self-perception as a purveyor of artisan bread well predated the current national trend (now rebounded from the brief low-carb craze) for fresh bread and the explosion of artisan bakeries throughout metropolitan America.

Consumers' desire for organic and all-natural foods, once thought to be a marginal market force, has become the norm. Keenly positioning itself at the forefront of retail outlets supporting this trend, Panera recently introduced a children's menu called Panera Kids. Kids can choose from items such as peanut butter and jelly, grilled cheese, and yogurt, and the all-natural and organic foods will please choosy parents.

In addition, Panera proactively responded to unease in the marketplace about the negative impact of trans fats on a healthy diet by voluntarily removing trans fats from its menu. "Panera recognized that trans fat was a growing concern to our customers and the medical community; therefore we made it a priority to eliminate it from our menu," said Tom Gumpel, director of bakery development for Panera Bread. Though reformulating the menu incurred unexpected costs, all Panera menu items are now free from trans fats, except for some small amounts that occur naturally in dairy and meat products, as well as in some condiments.

TOMS: Get One, Give One

While traveling through Argentina in 2006, Blake Mycoskie saw firsthand that shoeless children were suffering from cuts, sores, and infections from soil-transmitted diseases. Worse, if their school required shoes as part of the official uniform, these children were denied from attending classes.

"I was so overwhelmed by the spirit of the South American people, especially those who had so little," Mycoskie says. "And I was instantly struck with the desire—the responsibility—to do more."

Influenced by the simple but effective design of Argentina's traditional *alpargata*, Blake returned to the U.S. and founded TOMS Shoes. Its commitment: Provide shoes to needy children around the world. Through its One for One program, the company donates a pair of TOMS shoes for each pair purchased. TOMS sold 10,000 pairs its first year, and has donated more than one million pairs to date through NGOs, charities, and non-profits.

"When someone asks customers about [the shoes], they'll tell the whole story of the company," Mycoskie says. "They feel good that a child somewhere is wearing shoes because they bought some."

In 2011, Blake announced the next chapter of his One for One Company—saving people's sight worldwide. According to Mycoskie, most cases of blindness and visual impairment can be prevented or treated. He notes that of the nearly 284 million visually impaired people, about 90% live in developing countries. Through the sale of sunglasses, Blake hopes TOMS will improve as many lives as possible. For each pair of glasses sold, TOMS will provide one person with the eye care he or she needs.

According to Ron Shaich, former CEO and now executive chairman of the board of Panera, "Real success never comes by simply responding to the day-to-day pressures; in fact, most of that is simply noise. The key to leading an organization is understanding the long-term trends at play and getting the organization ready to respond to it."

And let's not forget, we are a coffee nation. For customers who just want to come in, grab a quick cup, and get out, Panera has just the thing. In many stores, coffee customers can avoid the normal line and head straight for the cash register, where they can pick up a cup, drop a small fee into a nearby can, and go directly to the java station. Caffeine-crazed customers can avoid the maddening line during a morning rush and cut the wait for that first steaming sip.

What Makes a Customer Stay?

Panera learned from mega-competitor Starbucks that offering wireless Internet access can make customers linger after their initial purchase, thus increasing the likelihood of a secondary purchase.

Now most of its stores offer customers free Wi-Fi access. According to spokesperson Julie Somers, the decision to offer Wi-Fi began as a way to separate Panera from the competition and to exemplify the company's welcoming atmosphere. "We are the kind of environment where all customers are welcome to hang out," Somers said. "They can get a quick bite or a cup of coffee, read the

paper or use a computer, and stay as long as they like. And in the course of staying, people may have a cappuccino and a pastry or a soup." She went on to note that the chief corporate benefit to offering Wi-Fi is that wireless customers tend to help fill out the slow time between main meal segments. Executive Vice President Neal Yanofsky concurred. "We just think it's one more reason to come visit our cafés," he said. And wireless users' tendency to linger is just fine with him. "It leads to food purchases," he concluded. And he's right—the average Panera store has an annualized unit volume of $2 million.

Profits Rise Along with the Dough

All of Panera's attention to the monitoring of trends has paid off handsomely. Since Panera went public, the company's stock has grown thirteenfold, creating more than $1 billion in shareholder value. *BusinessWeek* recognized Panera as one of its "100 Hot Growth Companies." And even more recently, the *Wall Street Journal* recognized the company as the top performer in the Restaurants and Bars category for one-year returns (63% return), five-year returns (42% return), and ten-year returns (32% return) to shareholders. In addition, a Sandleman & Associates survey of customer satisfaction ranked Panera at the top of the list for eight years in a row, beating out 120 other competitors.

Sticking It Out

Through wise financial management, Panera Bread found itself in the enviable position of

having no debt and $150 million in the bank. Taking advantage of a weak U.S. real estate market, the company opened nearly 80 new stores last year. With a debt-free balance sheet, the company plans to better position itself for the end of the financial crisis.

Panera Bread has demonstrated that sticking to company ideals while successfully forecasting, and then leading the response to long-term industry trends will please customers time and time again. The low-carb craze didn't faze Panera, but can this company continue to navigate the changing dietary trends in today's unstable market?

Discussion Questions

1. How might consumers' perception of Panera's menu and atmosphere affect their dining experience and tendencies to return as customers?

2. Describe how stereotypes about the fast food industry might positively and negatively impact Panera.

3. What are Panera's competitive advantages? Can any of them be deemed "sustainable"?

4. FURTHER RESEARCH Find data reporting on how Panera's sales were affected by the recent economic downturn in the U.S. economy. See if the effects were different in various regions of the country. Does Panera have special strengths that help it deal better than others with challenges such as those posed by a declining economy?

Case 14: Pixar: Animated Geniuses

Pixar has delivered a series of wildly successful animated movies featuring plucky characters and intensely lifelike animation. Yet some of the most memorable ones—*Toy Story, Finding Nemo,* and *The Incredibles*—were almost never made. Find out how Apple guru Steve Jobs, whose company struggled to stay alive during its early years, took these upstarts of animation to success.

"The Illusion of Life"

Though the story is far from over, it might seem like a fairytale ending of sorts for John Lasseter, Pixar's creative head, who went from being fired from his position as a Disney animator in the early 80s to running Disney's animation wing with Pixar cohead Edwin Catmull. Lasseter provided the creative direction for Pixar as it grew from an offshoot of Lucasfilm production company into the world's most successful computer animation company.

Pixar's movies—including the *Toy Story* movies, *The Incredibles, Cars, Ratatouille,* and *Up*—have succeeded largely because of Lasseter's focus on employing computer graphics (CG) technology to make the characters, scenery, and minute details as realistic as possible. "Character animation isn't the fact that an object looks like a character or has

a face and hands," Lasseter said. "Character animation is when an object moves like it is alive, when it moves like it is thinking and all of its movements are generated by its own thought processes. . . . It is the thinking that gives the illusion of life."

This "illusion of life" is a direct result of the synergy between Pixar's creative teams, who develop the story and characters, and its technical teams who program—and frequently develop—the animation software used to breathe life into each movie. Each forces the other to innovate, and together they successfully balance the latest technology with a back-to-basics focus on interesting characters in compelling stories. "Pixar has such a thoughtful approach, both from a storyline and business perspective," said Ralph Schackart, analyst with William Blair & Co LLC, "I don't think anyone has quite figured out how to do it like them."

In an industry abounding with delight in others' misfortune, some might be surprised that Pixar's old-fashioned approach to moviemaking has succeeded. But Disney CEO Bob Iger believes the opposite. "There is not an ounce of cynicism in Pixar's films," Iger told *Fortune.* "And in a world that is more cynical than it should be, that's pretty refreshing. I think it's a critical ingredient to the success of Pixar's films."

Another unique quality of Pixar is that—unlike competitor DreamWorks Animation SKG—it does not limit its creative products to the animated movies it releases. The studio shares its technical advances with the greater CG community through white papers and technology partnerships, such as its RenderMan software and hardware.

Perhaps Pixar's closest competitor is DreamWorks, headed by former Disney impresario Jeffrey Katzenberg and backed by media luminaries Steven Spielberg and David Geffen. Other smaller American animation companies such as Orphanage, Wild Brain Inc., and CritterPix Inc. face challenging budgets, limited technology, and tighter deadlines. And in the event these upstarts do manage a theatrical release, they've got a hard act to follow—Pixar grosses a domestic average of $258 million per movie.

An Uphill Battle

Pixar came to life in the early 1980s within a computer graphics division of Lucasfilm, George Lucas's production company. The *Star Wars* director hired the brightest computer programmers he could find to fill the small but growing need in Hollywood for CG graphics. Two of Lucas's programmers, Ed Catmull and Alvy Ray Smith, had developed a number of impressive CG technologies. Enter John Lasseter, just let go by Disney because his intense interest in computer animation wasn't shared by management. At an animation conference, Catmull and Smith tapped Lasseter to work with them on a number of digital animation shorts. One, *The Adventures of André & Wally B.,* was the very first character-animation cartoon done with a computer.

Then came Steve Jobs, who had just left Apple Computer and was looking for a new technology venture. He purchased the division, which he named Pixar, for $5 million, investing another $5 million to make it financially soluble. During Jobs's tenure, Pixar created about one short film a year and slowly broke into producing television commercials. Jobs sought to capitalize on Pixar's inventive sprit by licensing its RenderMan software and selling its Pixar Image Computer. But at $130,000 each, the rendering computers were a difficult sell, even in Hollywood. RenderMan sold only slightly better, earning it a reputation as niche software—especially because the program's primary customer was Disney.

DreamWorks: DreamWorks Delights

DreamWorks Animation SKG began as an ambitious attempt by media moguls Steven Spielberg, Jeffrey Katzenberg, and David Geffen (forming the SKG present on the bottom of the DreamWorks logo) to create a new Hollywood studio. The company was founded after Katzenberg was fired from—you guessed it—the Walt Disney Company. The DreamWorks studio was officially founded on October 12, 1994, with financial backing of $33 million from each of the three main partners and $500 million from Microsoft co-founder Paul Allen.

DreamWorks Animated SKG is devoted to producing high-quality family entertainment through the use of computer-generated, or CG, animation. With world-class creative talent and technological capabilities, DreamWorks was the first to release two CG animated feature films a year. With each film they strive to tell great stories with a level of sophistication that appeal to both children and adults.

In keeping with the importance of cooperation and teamwork, the open spaces and unique amenities at DreamWorks enhance the collaborative nature of the studio. In fact, the lagoon is a favorite gathering spot for informal meetings. When the fountains are turned off, it doubles as an amphitheater which can hold all employees. To showcase their talents, employees can contribute to on-campus art shows and craft fairs, allowing all to appreciate their fellow employees' abilities.

Its team efforts have paid off. Starting with its first full-length animated feature, *Antz*, DreamWorks has produced more than ten films with box-office grosses totaling more than $100 million each. Its endearing films have included *Bee Movie*, *Monsters vs. Aliens*, and *How to Train Your Dragon*. To date, its most successful release is *Shrek 2*, the third highest grossing film of all time.

Never one to rely on past success, DreamWorks created a new division, MoonBoy Animation, with plans to produce television content. Can DreamWorks make a successful transition to the small screen?

Although Jobs aggressively sought to build Pixar's reputation in the animation industry, it was still an uphill battle. He invested more than $50 million in keeping the company afloat, refusing to concede defeat and even releasing Alvy Smith after repeated personality conflicts. Slowly, Hollywood began to take notice of Pixar. Disney expressed interest in having Pixar develop a feature-length animated movie, and Pixar agreed to animate and produce *Toy Story*.

Tired of pouring money into keeping it afloat, Steve Jobs toyed with selling the company. He entertained offers from Oracle, Microsoft, and, curiously enough, the greeting-card company Hallmark. But Jobs held out. "We should have failed," says Smith, "Steve just would not suffer a defeat." The release of *Toy Story* proved his instincts right—the groundbreaking movie earned $362 million worldwide, shattering records for box-office earnings by animated movies. *A Bug's Life* followed, and although the movie did well, especially for an animated feature, it's worth noting that every Pixar release since has done even better.

Acutely aware of a string of failures for its own animated movies, Disney entered into talks to buy Pixar. Lasseter and Catmull were pleasantly surprised when Disney not only purchased Pixar, but also placed the Pixar honchos at the top of Disney's stagnant animation department. The duo moved to dump the top-down development process they say was in place at the studio, favoring instead the collaborative approach at Pixar that famously empowers the creative talent as much as the studio executives. Transplanting some of Pixar's successful processes meant opening up spaces in the mazes of the Disney animation building to allow more chance encounters between employees, and to give animators and other creative types more input in the overall story ideas and the direction of projects.

The sale went through for $7.4 billion, and suddenly Steve Jobs became Disney's single largest shareholder.

Things are bright for Pixar. The company brought home two Oscars for *Toy Story 3*, one for—you guessed it—Best Animated Feature. (Pixar films have won this Oscar four years in a row, and six of the last ten years.) Never one to rest on its laurels, the company continues to actively invest in software and technology, the tools that have made possible the lifelike rendering that is the hallmark of Pixar movies. But Pixar will have to stay sharp to stave off competition from the junior animation firms that are quickly forging alliances with major production companies to put out feature-length films of their own. Wild Brain, for instance, inked a five-picture deal with Dimension Films, a unit of Miramax (owned by, of all companies, Disney).

But a good part of Pixar's success stems from its ability to generate intriguing stories that warm the hearts of audiences. And according to Ralph Schackart, analyst with William Blair & Co LLC, that's where Pixar has it made: "It all starts with the story. You or I can go buy off-the-shelf software and make an animated film. The barrier to entry for this industry is the story."

Discussion Questions

1. How do you think the changes that John Lasseter and Edwin Catmull made to Disney's animation department affected that team's effectiveness?

2. Pixar relies heavily on creative people who are motivated to do their best under production schedules that can sometimes be stressful. How does this create challenges in maintaining effective team performance?

3. Pixar struggled in its early days. Steve Jobs was tempted to sell it when it was necessary to invest more money to keep it afloat. How did his action and the events that contributed to Pixar's success increase team cohesiveness?

4. FURTHER RESEARCH Some predict that Pixar's best days are over and that it will be hard for it to stay creative as a Disney business. What are the facts? In what ways is its current performance consistent with or different from the predictions, and why?

Case 15: Twitter: Redefining Communication

Whether or not you tweet, there's no denying that Twitter's having a profound effect on the way we communicate with each other and the outside world. Is the popular microblogging service reinventing communication or just abbreviating it? Do tweets contribute to the conversation or dumb it down? Let's take a look in more than 140 characters.

Tweets, RTs, and DMs were conceived on a playground slide during a burrito-fueled brainstorming session by employees of podcasting company Odeo. Jack Dorsey (*@jack*), now Twitter's chairman, suggested the idea of using short, SMS-like messages to connect with a small group.

"[W]e came across the word *twitter*, and it was just perfect," Dorsey says. "The definition was 'a short burst of inconsequential information' and 'chirps from birds'. And that's exactly what the product was."

Dorsey developed a working prototype, initially used internally by Odeo employees, and refined the concept before releasing the first public version on July 15, 2006. Three months later, sensing the magnitude of Dorsey's invention, Dorsey and other members of Odeo, including current product strategist Evan Williams (*@ev*) and creative director Biz Stone (*@biz*), formed Obvious Corporation and neatly acquired Odeo and all of its assets, including Twitter.com, from Odeo's shareholders and investors.

Who Uses It?

Demographically speaking, there's a better chance that your mom's on Twitter than you. Unlike other social media tools, Twitter use skews unusually toward older users who might not have previously dipped their toes into social networking. According to industry analyst Jeremiah Owyang, "Adults are just catching up to what teens have been doing for years." Web analysis site *comScore* points out that only 11% of Twitter's users are between 12–17.

Like any popular social media tool, Twitter's also become a vehicle for communicating (sometimes) carefully crafted messages of self-promotion, attracting the usual suspects like corporations (*@starbucks*), politicians (*@BarackObama*), social organizations (*@amnesty*), and musicians (*@ladygaga*). And don't forget astronauts: *@Astro_TJ* sent the first off-Earth tweet on January 22, 2010, from the International Space Station. By late November, ISS passengers sent an average of a dozen tweets each day from their communal account, *@NASA_Astronauts*.

A Growing Chorus of Tweets

In Twitter's first full year on the web, its relatively small user base sent around 400,000 tweets per quarter. After a buoyant reception by attendees of the 2007 SXSW Festival, during which the daily tweet average jumped from 20,000 to 60,000, the service leapfrogged to post 100 million tweets per quarter the next year.

At a recent count, Twitter boasted 175 million registered users sending 95 million tweets per day. This compares closely to the estimated one billion messages sent daily through Facebook Chat. The topics that rule water cooler chatter—sports, gossip, and politics—also drive tweet counts through the roof.

At times during Twitter's dramatic initial spurts of growth, the company struggled to maintain uptime. Users have been quick to curse the Fail Whale, an image of a blissful cetacean being carried out of the ocean by birds that Twitter displays when service interruptions arise. "Too many tweets!" the image reads, and though the site has a recent uptime average of 99.7%, downtimes are particularly noticeable (but not tweetable) during tech industry gatherings like San Francisco's Macworld.

To Tweet, or Not to Tweet?

Twitter's 140-character limit keeps tweets terse and to the point. But there's no guarantee they'll be pertinent. "Using Twitter for literate communication is about as likely as firing up a CB radio and hearing some guy recite the *Iliad*," gripes tech writer Bruce Sterling.

Market research firm Pear Analytics captured 2,000 U.S. and British tweets sent during daytime hours (11 AM–5 PM CST) over two weeks and assigned each message one of six labels according to its content. The two largest categories, pointless babble (small talk) and conversation, comprised 78% of all tweets.

"For many people, the idea of describing your blow-by-blow activities in such detail is absurd," concurs writer Clive Thompson. "Why would you subject your friends to your daily minutiae?"

But avid Twitter users argue that while not all tweets are gems, the service has its place in digital culture. Social network researcher Danah Boyd (*@zephoria*) criticized Pear Analytics's results, pointing out that pointless babble could be better characterized as *social grooming*, where tweeters "want to know what the people around them are thinking and doing and feeling."

Yammer: Microblogging Goes Corporate

Yammer

Like Twitter, microblogging tool Yammer was originally developed for internal use in a Silicon Valley startup—in this case, genealogy company Geni. And like the developers at Odeo, Geni founder David Sacks liked Yammer so much he spun it off into its own company.

But the comparisons end there. Whereas Twitter lets users blast bite-sized comments about their daily foibles openly across the Internet, Yammer users can only see posts by coworkers within their own company. Added features include uploading directory information, creating groups to help teams communicate privately, and uploading files and links to share one-on-one.

In many ways, Yammer sounds like it was dreamt up by a corporate compliance offi-cer—it's secure, private, and data is stored off site. So it's no surprise that Yammer clients include more than 100,000 businesses, including 80% of the Fortune 500. And it's not just for corporations: Departments within the U.S., U.K., and Australian governments are also reaping the benefits.

"Companies that use Yammer have employees that feel more engaged," says David Sacks. "They feel more connected to their coworkers, they feel more connected to the company's mission."

Twitter's low overhead translates into instantaneous communication, and for some users, that's part of the appeal to "Twitter lets me hear from a lot of people in a very short period of time," says tech evangelist Robert Scoble (@Scobleizer).

During recent conflicts in Iran, Tunisia, Egypt, and Syria residents tweeted instantaneous reports of fast-moving situations. And because international users can tweet over SMS, residents could sent short messages and photos at times when Internet bandwidth was slow to nonexistent. After Egypt forced local Internet providers to temporarily cease service, Google and Twitter teamed up to create a voice-to-tweet service; by calling one of three Egyptian phone numbers, callers could leave a voice-mail message, which Arabic-speaking volunteers would translate and post to Twitter with the hashtag #egypt.

"It adds a layer of information and connection to people's lives that wasn't there before," Evan Williams says. "It has the potential to be a really substantial part of how people keep in touch with each other."

Changing Interpersonal Communication

Many social media researchers, sociologists, and corporate marketing experts are asking themselves the same question: Does Twitter enable effective communication, or is it a distraction?

Soren Gordhamer notes five ways in which Twitter is changing interpersonal communication. These include making communication transparent (messages are broadcast on the Web for all to see), codifying stages of communication (quick thoughts warrant a tweet; if you need to communicate more, send a DM or, if it's a really long message, an email), and the relationship between a growing network of communication partners and the subsequent brevity of messages (the more people you keep in touch with, each message will be shorter on the average).

While the immediacy of tweets makes group and one-on-one Twitter conversations less personal in some ways, Twitter's use of hashtags helps users gain an intimate understanding of a particular topic by grouping similar tweets. Whether they're discussing Memorial Day plans or civil unrest, hashtags provide an aggregation of live, up-to-the-minute microreports. Critics of the "Twitter as layman's journalism" movement note that tweets prioritize speed over accuracy—just because something was tweeted doesn't make it true.

Corporate Tweeters, Start Your Engines

In a recent survey, 81% of businesses queried responded that social media marketing generated exposure for their business. While only 35% surveyed indicated that social media helped them close business deals, it's clear that social tools like Twitter are good for business . . . when used properly. Dell's Twitter promotions helped sell $6.5 million in tech gear. And New Orleans-based Naked Pizza brought in 15% of its April business from an exclusive-to-Twitter promotion.

The immediacy of tweeting can lend itself to impulsive communication, and organizations must be watchful that corporate tweets don't cross any lines. Companies are advised to register their name, affiliated brands, and even executives' names down to C-level team members with Twitter simply to protect themselves from name spoofing.

Many social media strategists confirm that effective Twitter communication comes down to one very human element: trust. "Trust is the currency of social media," says consultant Joel Postman. "Without it, social media is worthless as a tool with which to engage customers."

Discussion Questions

1. Do you think Twitter's 140-character limit for tweets is a barrier to effective communication? Why or why not?

2. For what kinds of messages would Twitter be an appropriate communication channel?

3. How could Twitter improve communication within an organization?

4. FURTHER RESEARCH Imagine you have been tasked with analyzing the "official" tweets of a competing company in order to discern their social media strategy. Choose a company with a Twitter presence and select fifty consecutive tweets to analyze. What is the company attempting to communicate with its tweets? Do they tend to be public or intended for individuals? What proportion of their tweets are retweets? Do they tweet Twitter-only deals or specials? Based on this analysis, how would you define this company's social media strategy?

Case 16: Toyota: Looking Far into the Future

By borrowing the best ideas from American brands and innovating the rest itself, Toyota has become a paragon of auto manufacturing efficiency. Its vehicles are widely known for their quality and longevity—and Toyota's sales numbers are the envy of the American Big Three. Here is how Toyota became so efficient at producing high-quality automobiles.

Buy "American"?

"Buy American" used to be a well-known slogan encouraging U.S. car buyers to purchase domestic models assembled in America. Those who still tout the motto have likely done a good bit of head-scratching over how to classify Toyota—a Japanese company sited in rural America that employs American workers to use American-made parts to produce vehicles sold in the United States. What to think when this Japanese brand achieves a product quality far superior to long-known American brands? And Toyota has surged ahead of General Motors to rank number one in global auto sales for three years in a row.

Quality by Design

Toyota's success and growth in the American auto market is no accident. The company has used strategies honed since the 1950s to earn and retain customer satisfaction by producing superior vehicles within a highly efficient production environment. From the home office to factories to showrooms, two core philosophies guide Toyota's business: (1) creating fair, balanced, mutually beneficial relationships with both suppliers and employees, and (2) strictly adhering to a just-in-time (JIT) manufacturing principle.

Collaboration over Competition

Over the decades, American auto manufacturers developed relationships with their suppliers that emphasized tense competition, price-cutting, and the modification of suppliers' production capacities with the changing needs of the domestic market. Year after year, parts suppliers had to bid to renew contracts in a process that valued year-to-year price savings over long-term relationships.

Domestic manufacturers, notorious for changing production demands mid-season to comply with late-breaking market dynamics or customer feedback, forced suppliers to turn to double or triple shifts to keep up with capacity and thus can't avoid the problems—quality slips, recalls, line shutdowns, layoffs—that ultimately slow the final assembly of vehicles. When a carmaker doesn't know what it wants, suppliers have little chance of keeping up. This system of industry dynamics proved susceptible to new approaches from Japanese competitors.

Toyota's model of supply-chain management displays an exclusive commitment to parts suppliers, well-forecast parts orders that are not subject to sways in the market, and genuine concern for the success of suppliers. In the *Financial Times*, M. Reza Vaghefi noted that supply-chain relationships among Asian manufacturers are based on a complex system of cooperation and equity interests. "Asian values, more so than in [W]estern cultures, traditionally emphasize the collective good over the goals of the individual," he said. "This attitude clearly supports the synergistic approach of supply chain management and has encouraged concern for quality and productivity."

Visiting American auto plants and seeing months' worth of excess parts waiting to be installed taught Toyota the benefit of having only enough supplies on hand to fulfill a given production batch. Toyota plans its production schedules months in advance, dictating regularly scheduled parts shipments from its suppliers. Suppliers benefit by being able to predict long-range demand for products, scheduling production accordingly. This builds mutual loyalty between suppliers and the carmaker—almost as if suppliers are a part of Toyota. The fit and finish in Toyota vehicles is precise because its suppliers can afford to focus on the quality of their parts. And consumers notice: Toyota vehicles consistently earn high marks for customer satisfaction and retain their resale value better than almost any others.

Keep It Lean

Early Toyota presidents Toyoda Kiichiro and Ohno Taiichi are considered the fathers of the Toyota Production System (TPS), known widely by the JIT moniker as "lean production." Emphasizing quality and efficiency at all levels, it drives nearly all aspects of decision making at Toyota.

Simply put, TPS is "all about producing only what's needed and transferring only what's needed," said Teruyuki Minoura, senior managing director at Toyota. He likened it to a "pull" system—in which workers fetch only that which is immediately needed—as opposed to a traditional "push" system. "Producing what's needed means producing the right quantity of what's needed," he continued. "The answer is a flexible system that allows the line to produce what's necessary when it's necessary. If it takes six people to make a certain quantity of an item and there is a drop in the quantity required, then your system should let one or two of them drop out and get on with something else."

To achieve maximum efficiency, workers at Toyota plants must be exceptionally

Ford: The Assembly Line Goes Global

It's a big world. But as far as Ford is concerned, it just got a little smaller.

Since taking over as CEO of Ford Motor Company, one of Alan Mulally's chief pursuits has been to produce a truly global car—one that is built using nearly identical parts in a nearly identical style, and marketed to global audiences using nearly identical marketing campaigns.

To many auto executives, including some top brass at Ford, the idea seemed sheer folly. But Mulally holds that automakers have gone to expensive and unnecessary lengths in the past to reconfigure cars for individual world regions.

"Why are we doing it this way?" asks Mulally. "Because we believe the customer requirements are going to be more the same around the world than they are different."

Mulally chose the Focus as the first global platform, largely because of the worldwide desire for compact cars. Designers settled a middle ground of design and features that should please everyone from style-driven Americans to conservative Chinese buyers. Mulally and Ford heir William C. Ford, Jr. even recently unveiled a battery-powered hatchback model that will directly compete with the Chevy Volt and Nissan Leaf.

"If we [are] going to be world-class, we need to pull together and leverage and use our global assets around the world to create a powerhouse 'One Ford,'" says Mulally. "It's exactly why we are here."

knowledgeable about all facets of a vehicle's production, able to change responsibilities as needed. "An environment where people have to think brings with it wisdom, and this wisdom brings with it kaizen [the notion of continuous improvement]," noted Minoura. "If asked to produce only one unit at a time, to produce according to the flow, a typical line worker is likely to be flummoxed. It's a basic characteristic of human beings that they develop wisdom from being put under pressure."

Keeping Up with the Times

No vehicle represents Toyota's innovation better than the Prius. Now in its tenth year in North America, the Prius has been wildly successful in the U.S. and has come to represent a new generation of fuel-sipping cars and the environmentally-conscious consumers who clamor for them. Worldwide, Prius sales recently topped two million, and the car sells in over 70 countries and regions.

The devastating earthquake and tsunami in Japan have affected the production of the Prius, however. Factories were damaged, and the Prius's plants located in the region of the country hit hardest by ongoing power outages may continue to cause production delays.

On the other hand, no other Toyota vehicle has come to represent the challenges of adapting to a changing sales landscape as its Tundra pickup truck has. Hoping to make gains over the sales of domestic pickups, Toyota built a Tundra plant in Texas to prove that its trucks were as All-American as those made by the Big Three. But bad became worse when—already 60% over budget—truck sales began to decline as the price of oil rose. Contractors and builders, prime candidates for pickups, began to think twice about new pickup purchases; the San Antonio plant began to run well under capacity.

Despite its best efforts, Toyota suffered some of the same ills as General Motors, Ford, and Chrysler. Instead of sending its workers home, as Detroit's Big Three car makers often do, Toyota kept them at the plants. Employees spent their days in training sessions designed to sharpen their job skills and find better ways to assemble vehicles.

For several years, Toyota faced "a significant lack of production work for a significant number of workers," said Sean McAlinden, an economist for Automotive Research. He estimated the wage cost of idling the assembly lines at Toyota's two plants at $35 million a month. Toyota pledged to never lay off any of its full-time, nonunion employees. Jim Lentz, president of Toyota U.S. sales unit, said that the company believes keeping employees on the payroll and using the time to improve their capabilities is the best move in the long run. Norm Bafunno, president of Toyota Motor Manufacturing Indiana, reports that plant leadership used the downtime to sharpen fundamental skills and implement hundreds of improvements, resulting in an ultimate cost savings of $7 million.

Gaining the Lead, One Vehicle at a Time

By substituting discipline and efficiency for fanfare, Toyota has quietly earned a long-standing reputation for the reliability and quality of all of its models. Although the company's domestic competitors have taken notice and now use many of Toyota's proven methods, their financial difficulties make it hard to keep up the fight. In such a fierce market, can Toyota maintain the self-control to stay on top?

Discussion Questions

1. How might a cell phone manufacturer, an elementary school, and the local post office each benefit from using Toyota's concept of kaizen?

2. Do you believe that a U.S. automaker would keep auto assembly employees on the payroll when the line is stopped? Use Hofstede's five dimensions of value differences to explain your answer.

3. Does Toyota value its human resources more than do its U.S. rivals? Is this management approach to people a result of Toyota's business philosophy or its cultural values?

4. FURTHER RESEARCH Toyota isn't alone as a major Asian competitor to the U.S. automakers. Do some investigation; who else is in the picture and what countries are they from? Are the other Asian automakers using operations techniques and values similar to those found at Toyota, or are they bringing new ones into play?

Case 17: Harley-Davidson: Style and Strategy Have Global Reach

Harley-Davidson celebrated a century in business with a year-long International Road Tour. The party culminated in the company's hometown, Milwaukee. Harley is a true American success story. Once near death in the face of global competition, Harley reestablished itself as the dominant maker of big bikes in the United States. However, success breeds imitation and Harley once again faces a mixture of domestic and foreign competitors encroaching on its market. Can it meet the challenge?

Harley's Roots

When Harley-Davidson was founded in 1903, it was one of more than 100 firms producing motorcycles in the United States. The U.S. government became an important customer for the company's high-powered, reliable bikes, using them in both world wars.

By the 1950s, Harley-Davidson was the only remaining American manufacturer. But by then British competitors were entering the market with faster, lighter-weight bikes. And Honda Motor Company of Japan began marketing lightweight bikes in the United States, moving into middleweight vehicles in the 1960s. Harley initially tried to compete by manufacturing smaller bikes, but had difficulty making them profitably. The company even purchased an Italian motorcycle firm, Aermacchi, but many of its dealers were reluctant to sell the small Aermacchi Harleys.

Consolidation and Renewal

American Machine and Foundry Co. (AMF) took over Harley in 1969, expanding its portfolio of recreational products. AMF increased production from 14,000 to 50,000 bikes per year. This rapid expansion led to significant problems with quality, and better-built Japanese motorcycles began to take over the market. Harley's share of its major U.S. market—heavyweight motorcycles—was only 23%.

A group of 13 managers bought Harley-Davidson back from AMF in 1981 and began to turn the company around with the rallying cry "The Eagle Soars Alone." As Richard Teerlink, former CEO of Harley, explained, "The solution was to get back to detail. The key was to know the business, know the customer, and pay attention to detail." The key elements in this process were increasing quality and improving service to customers and dealers. Management kept the classic Harley style and focused on the company's traditional strength—heavyweight and super heavyweight bikes.

In 1983, the Harley Owners Group (H.O.G.) was formed; H.O.G. membership now exceeds one million members and 1,400 chapters worldwide. Also in 1983, Harley-Davidson asked the International Trade Commission (ITC) for tariff relief on the basis that Japanese manufacturers were stockpiling inventory in the United States and providing unfair competition. The request was granted and a tariff relief for five years was placed on all imported Japanese motorcycles that were 700 cc or larger. By 1987 Harley was confident enough to petition the ITC to have the tariff lifted because the company had improved its ability to compete with foreign imports.

Once Harley's image had been restored, the company began to increase production. The firm opened new facilities in Franklin, Milwaukee, and Menomonee Falls, Wisconsin; Kansas City, Missouri; and York, Pennsylvania; and opened a new assembly plant in Manaus, Brazil.

In the 1980s, the average Harley purchaser was in his late thirties, with an average household income of over $40,000. Teerlink didn't like the description of his customers as "aging" baby boomers: "Our customers want the sense of adventure that they get on our bikes. . . . Harley-Davidson doesn't sell transportation, we sell transformation. We sell excitement, a way of life."

However, the average age and income of Harley riders has continued to increase. Recently, the median age of a Harley rider was 47, and the median income exceeded $80,000. The company also created a line of Harley accessories available through dealers or by catalog, all adorned with the Harley-Davidson logo. These jackets, caps, T-shirts, and other items became popular with nonbikers as well. In fact, the clothing and accessories had a higher profit margin than the motorcycles; nonbike products made up as much as half of sales at some dealerships.

International Efforts

Although the company had been exporting motorcycles ever since it was founded, it was not until the late 1980s that Harley-Davidson management began to think seriously about international markets. Traditionally, the company's ads had been translated word for word into foreign languages. New ads were developed specifically for different markets, and rallies were adapted to fit local customs.

The company also began to actively recruit and develop dealers in Europe and Japan. It purchased a Japanese distribution company and built a large parts warehouse in Germany. And Harley learned from its international activities. Recognizing, for example, that German motorcyclists rode at high speeds—often more than 100 mph—the company began studying ways to give Harleys a smoother ride and emphasizing accessories that would give riders more protection.

Harley continues to make inroads in overseas markets. Although the worldwide economic slowdown has attenuated Harley sales somewhat, and export sales are down about 10%, the company has made unexpected inroads in European markets. European buyers haven't had it as rough as their American counterparts, and they're turning their tastes away from Japanese motorcycles and toward premium American labels. Harley is currently the number one motorcycle brand in five European countries, and number two in four countries. This sustained buying has earned Harley four consecutive quarters of sales and market share growth in Europe.

Given that interest in sport bikes is waning, Harley motorcycles are among America's fastest-growing exports to Japan. Harley's Japanese subsidiary adapted the company's marketing approach to Japanese tastes, even producing shinier and more complete tool kits than those available in the United States. Harley bikes have long been considered symbols of prestige in Japan; many Japanese enthusiasts see themselves as rebels on wheels.

The company has also made inroads into the previously elusive Chinese market, with the first official Chinese Harley-Davidson dealership opening its doors just outside downtown Beijing. To break into this emerging market, Harley partnered with China's Zongshen Motorcycle Group,

which makes more than one million small-engine motorcycles each year. Like other Harley stores, the Chinese outlet stocks bikes, parts and accessories, and branded merchandise, and offers post-sales service. Despite China's growing disposable income, the new store has several hurdles ahead of it, including riding restrictions imposed by the government in urban areas.

Harley's even announced a major production expansion into India, where it's chosen to build its second-ever assembly plant outside the U.S. While most parts will still be fabricated in the U.S. by domestic workers, they'll be shipped to the north Indian state of Haryana for assembly for the rapidly growing Indian market.

Harley seeks to grow its brand internationally from 30% to 40% by 2014, and it sees the Indian and Pakistani markets as key to achieving this goal. Despite the obvious cost of shipping parts halfway around the globe, it's still a win for Harley: Indian consumers pay nearly twice the normal international cost for fully assembled vehicles because India's import duties are so high. Anoop Prakesh, managing director for Harley-Davidson India, estimates that building the bikes nearby could cut import duty tariffs by around 80%.

The Future

Although its international sales have grown, the domestic market still represents more than 60% of Harley's sales. Given the climbing price of gas, Harley is uniquely positioned to take advantage of this economic factor. Many riders report in-town fuel consumption rates in excess of 40 miles per gallon. Analyst Todd Sullivan notes, "I know plenty of F-150, Suburban, and Silverado drivers who ride Harleys. They are doubling or even tripling their gas mileage and savings by making the switch."

Executives attribute Harley's success to loyal customers and the Harley-Davidson name. "It is a unique brand that is built on personal relationship and deep connections with customers, unmatched riding experiences, and proud history," says Jim Ziemer, Harley's outgoing president and chief executive.

However, Harley-Davidson has been in a fight not just with the recession and a sharp consumer spending slowdown, but also the aging of its customer base, and a credit crisis that has made it difficult for both the motorcycle maker and its loyal riders to get financing. With 17 consecutive years of increased production, marked with record revenues and earnings, will the future for Harley be bright?

Discussion Questions

1. If you were CEO of Harley-Davidson, how would you compare the advantages and disadvantages of using exports, joint ventures, and wholly owned subsidiaries as ways of expanding international sales?

2. Given Harley's legacy of quality and craftsmanship, what complications might the Chinese business environment pose for the firm to manufacture there?

3. Now that more Harley bikes are being built outside the U.S. than ever before, what qualities of global managers should the company seek for its assembly plant management?

4. FURTHER RESEARCH Is it accurate to say that Harley is "still on top" of its game? How is the company doing today in both domestic and global markets? Who are its top competitors in other parts of the world, and how is Harley faring against them?

Case 18: In-N-Out Burger: Building a Better Burger

At face value, In-N-Out Burger seems like a modest enterprise—only four food items on the menu, little to no advertising. So how has this West Coast chain achieved near-cult status among regular joes and foodies alike? For more than sixty years, In-N-Out has focused on providing customers the basics—fresh, well-cooked food served quickly in a sparkling clean environment—and has made consistency and quality their hallmarks.

Or So In-N-Out Would Have You Think

Walk into any of the 258 In-N-Out Burger locations, and you'll only find four food items on the menu: Hamburger, Cheeseburger, Double-Double and French Fries. You can wash those down with a Coke or a milkshake.

But stand next to the ordering counter long enough, and you'll hear customers recite a litany of curious requests. None are on the menu, but sure enough, the cashier rings each one up with a smile: *Animal Style* (a mustard-cooked patty with extra pickles, cheese, spread, and grilled onions), *Flying Dutchman* (two patties, two slices of cheese, no bun or garnish), *Protein Style* (heavy on the fixings, wrapped in lettuce instead of a bun), or any permutation of patties and cheese slices up to a 4 × 4 (four patties and four slices of cheese barely contained in one

bun). The open secret of the secret menu is only part of what keeps customers coming back for more.

A Simple Formula for Success

In-N-Out's motto is straightforward: "Give customers the freshest, highest quality foods you can buy and provide them with friendly service in a sparkling clean environment." And so is the chain's formula for success—it only makes a few food items, it consistently makes them well, and it earns the trust of its customers by not deviating from this premise.

Robert LePlae, head of creative giant McCann Erickson, commends In-N-Out's ability to consistently execute their simple-but-effective concept of *fast food done right.* "They don't abuse the privilege that they have built up with their customers," he says. "They haven't commercialized the 'secret menu'. There is a powerful trust between the company and the customers that is deeply ingrained."

In-N-Out's former CFO, Steve Tanner, agrees that honesty is the best policy: "If you have to tell somebody you're something, you're probably not."

In addition to making the best burgers around, In-N-Out's other primary successful trait is its insistence on playing by its own rules. A fierce entrepreneurial streak ran through the Snyders, In-N-Out's

founding family, and from the sock-hop décor to the secret menu to its treatment of employees as long-term partners instead of disposable resources, the chain prefers to focus on its formula for success instead of conventional definitions like shareholder return or IPOs.

The funny thing is, it works. Unwilling to grow at a speed that would sacrifice quality or consistency of the customer experience, In-N-Out has resisted going public or franchising. Yet—or maybe, because of this—they best rivals Burger King and McDonald's in per-store sales.

All in the Family

Harry Snyder and his wife Esther opened the first In-N-Out Burger in Baldwin Park, CA, in 1948. Unlike other carhop-oriented fast food restaurants of the era, Harry installed a two-way speaker through which drivers could order without leaving their car, thus creating California's first drive-thru hamburger stand. Harry brought sons Rich and Guy to work at an early age, where the boys learned their father's insistence on complementing fresh, promptly-cooked food with great customer service.

The Snyder's second restaurant opened three years later, and franchising continued slowly until 1976, when Rich took over after his father's death. At that time, In-N-Out managed eighteen locations throughout California.

Though he was only twenty-four when he became CEO, Rich Snyder had big plans for In-N-Out. The next seventeen years would see Rich expand In-N-Out into new cities but still maintain exacting control over the quality of both ingredients and employees.

Harry and Rich understood that you can't truthfully attest to the quality of your ingredients unless you've inspected them yourself. So with the help of younger brother Guy, one of Rich's first projects was to build a commissary in Baldwin Park, CA, where all In-N-Out's ingredients are inspected for quality and prepared for distribution to their stores. The commissary location in part explains why In-N-Out restaurants are clustered in the American Southwest: establishing locations longer than one day's drive from the commissary is "not even negotiable," executive Carl Van Fleet told the *Orange County Register*

Sprinkles: Leading a Sweet Trend

Candace Nelson's big break came courtesy of two of the world's most famous women, 300 cupcakes, and a sleepless red-eye flight. It started when Barbra Streisand bought a dozen cupcakes from Nelson's new bakery, Sprinkles, for her friend Oprah Winfrey. Soon after, Nelson

received a 2 PM call from one of Winfrey's producers with a last-minute order: bring 300 cupcakes to Chicago for an appearance the next morning on Breakfast with Oprah.

"You can't say no to Oprah," Nelson jokes. The investment-banker-turned-baker arrived at Oprah's studios with shopping bags full of her gourmet cupcakes—coconut, red velvet, and Madagascar vanilla, topped with Sprinkles' requisite half-inch-thick sheet of buttercream frosting. Like many before her, Nelson soon benefited from Oprah's magic touch—cupcake sales at the Beverly Hills bakery jumped 50% to 1,500 per day. And at $3.50 per cupcake, it was sweet news for Nelson and her husband, Charles, who co-owns the Sprinkles chain.

At Sprinkles, the line stretches out the door and around the block. Tourists and locals alike often wait well over a half-hour—longer than a cupcake takes to bake and cool—for a taste of one of Sprinkles' 23 custom flavors, only 13 of which are offered each day. Favorites such as dark chocolate and red velvet are available every day, but specialty flavors such as chai latte, carrot cake, and peanut butter chocolate appear sporadically throughout the week.

With seventeen Sprinkles outlets scheduled to open in five countries, Nelson has a lot to smile about. "That's why I went into the cupcake business," she says. "I'm in this little cupcake bubble where everyone is smiling ear to ear."

---

in 2006, as doing so would require longer delivery runs or additional processing hubs, both of which could reduce quality control. (Yet a few years later, In-N-Out caved to consumer demand and built a second patty plant in Dallas, TX, to support their inevitable expansion into the Lone Star state.)

Unlike Harry, who hoped employees would transfer skills learned at In-N-Out to a "better" job, Rich thought differently: "Why let good people move on when you can use them to help your company grow?" Knowing that his expansion plans would require a pool of talented and loyal store managers, Rich opened In-N-Out University in 1984. Store associates had to please hungry diners, show initiative, and exhibit strong decision-making skills for at least one year before being invited to attend the management training program. Reasoning that the same high-tech tools for performance analysis employed by pro sports teams could also improve his team, Rich videotaped trainees to analyze their performance and produced training films.

The Best Advertising Is Free

Whether by preference or accident, In-N-Out's infrequent forays into paid advertising are oblique at best—with radio ads that simply tout, "In-N-Out, In-N-Out. That's what a hamburger's all about," and holiday

ads that explain the meaning of the holidays instead of the weekly specials.

You're more likely to see a simple visual ad for In-N-Out. Like other stores in the early days of roadside diners, the company placed locations along interstate off ramps, relying on their yellow boomerang logo and plain billboards reading, "In-N-Out Burger 2.5 Miles Ahead" to draw customers.

For years they gave customers free bumper stickers with the company's name, thousands of which were modified by rabid fans to say, "In-N-Out urge." Stores have also sold clothing bearing the company logo.

"Their marketing is really brilliant," concedes Robert LePlae. "The best marketing is word of mouth, and they have that. You can't get that through traditional media."

Because the company has long been press and advertising shy, and because their burgers aren't available in most of the U.S., In-N-Out has cultivated a considerable mystique around ultimately simple products.

William Martin, who composed In-N-Out University's training regimen, says that during his time with the company, the Snyders and other top brass were definitely conscious of the magic surrounding their brand. "They were all aware of it, and they loved it," he says. "But they had no explanation for it."

Discussion Questions

1. Rich Snyder was twenty-four years old when he assumed leadership of In-N-Out

after his father passed away. Do you think his young age was an asset or a liability for his leadership? Or did it matter in the first place?

2. In an era of jalapeno poppers and extreme fajitas, do you view In-N-Out's long-term strategy of offering only four, simple food items as risky? Why or why not?

3. Do you think an entrepreneur could walk into a bank today and expect to receive financing for a business plan based on In-N-Out's extremely simple menu? Why or why not?

4. FURTHER RESEARCH Imagine you were asked by In-N-Out Burger to modernize its advertising mix while maintaining the modesty and simplicity that's characterized its brand for over sixty years. With a partner, craft an advertising concept that speaks to In-N-Out's core values: quality, consistency, friendliness, and cleanliness. How would you illustrate this concept to consumers? Explain why you would choose to include or exclude TV, print, radio, or online advertising based on your premise. How would you pitch this concept to In-N-Out's marketing department in a way that would emphasize In-N-Out's core values?

Test Prep 1

Multiple Choice

1. d.   **2.** c.   **3.** b.   **4.** b.   **5.** b.   **6.** d.   **7.** a.   **8.** d.   **9.** c.   **10.** a.   **11.** c.   **12.** a.   **13.** c.
14. c.   **15.** a.

Short Response

16. Prejudice involves holding a negative stereotype or irrational attitude toward a person who is different from one's self. Discrimination occurs when such prejudice leads to decisions that adversely affect the other person in his or her job or in advancement opportunities at work or in his or her personal life.

17. The "free agent economy" is one where there is a lot of job-hopping and people work for several different employers over a career, rather than just one. This relates not only to the preferences of the individuals but also the nature of organizational employment practices. As more organizations reduce the hiring of full-time workers in favor of more part-timers and independent contractors, this creates fewer long-term job opportunities for potential employees. Thus they become "free agents" who sell their services to different employers on a part-time and contract basis.

18. You will typically find that top managers are more oriented toward the external environment than the first-level or lower-level managers. This means that top managers must be alert to trends, problems, and opportunities that can affect the performance of the organization as a whole. The first-line or lower manager is most concerned with the performance of his or her immediate work unit, and managing the people and resources of the unit on an operational day-to-day basis. Top management is likely to be more strategic and long term in orientation.

19. Planning sets the objectives or targets that one hopes to accomplish. Controlling measures actual results against the planning objectives or targets, and makes any corrections necessary to better accomplish them. Thus, planning and controlling work together in the management process, with planning setting the stage for controlling.

Integration & Application

20. I consider myself "effective" as a manager if I can help my work unit achieve high performance and the persons in it to achieve job satisfaction. In terms of skills and personal development, the framework of essential management skills offered by Katz is a useful starting point. At the first level of management, technical skills are important and I would feel capable in this respect. However, I would expect to learn and refine these skills even more through my work experiences. Human skills, the ability to work well with other people, will also be very important. Given the diversity anticipated for this team, I will need good human skills and I will have to keep improving my capabilities in this area. One area of consideration here is emotional intelligence, or my ability to understand how the emotions of myself and others influence work relationships. I will also have a leadership responsibility to help others on the team develop and utilize these skills so that the team itself can function effectively. Finally, I would expect opportunities to develop my conceptual or analytical skills in anticipation of higher-level appointments. In terms of personal development I should recognize that the conceptual skills will increase in importance relative to the technical skills as I move upward in management responsibility, while the human skills are consistently important.

Test Prep 2

Multiple Choice

1. a.   **2.** b.   **3.** c.   **4.** a.   **5.** c.   **6.** b.   **7.** d.   **8.** b.   **9.** a.   **10.** a.   **11.** c.   **12.** a.   **13.** c.
14. b.   **15.** b.

Short Response

16. You can see scientific management principles operating everywhere, from UPS delivery, to fast-food restaurants, to order-fulfillment centers. In each case the workers are trained to perform highly specified job tasks that are carefully engineered to be the most efficient. Their supervisors try to keep the process and workers well supported. In some cases the workers may be paid on the basis of how much work they accomplish in a time period, such as a day or week. The basic principles are to study the job, identify the most efficient job tasks and train the workers, and then support and reward the workers for doing them well.

17. According to the deficit principle, a satisfied need is not a motivator of behavior. The social need, for example, will motivate only if it is deprived or in deficit. According to the progression principle, people move step by step up Maslow's hierarchy as they strive to satisfy their needs. For example, esteem need becomes activated only after the social need is satisfied. Maslow also suggests, however, that the progression principle stops operating at the level of self-actualization; the more this need is satisfied, the stronger it gets.

18. The Hawthorne effect occurs when people singled out for special attention tend to perform as expected. An example would be giving a student a lot of personal attention in class with the result that he or she ends up studying harder and performing better. This is really the same thing as McGregor's notion of the self-fulfilling prophesy with the exception that he identified how it works to both the positive and the negative. When managers, for example, have positive assumptions about people, they tend to treat them well and the people respond in ways that reinforce the original positive thinking. This is a form of the Hawthorne effect. McGregor also pointed out that negative self-fulfilling prophesies result when managers hold negative assumptions about people and behave accordingly.

19. Contingency thinking takes an "if–then" approach to situations. It seeks to modify or adapt management approaches to fit the needs of each situation. An example would be to give more customer contact responsibility to workers who want to satisfy social needs at work, while giving more supervisory responsibilities to those who want to satisfy their esteem or ego needs.

Integration & Application

20. A bureaucracy operates with a strict hierarchy of authority, promotion based on competency and performance, formal rules and procedures, and written documentation. Enrique can do all of these things in his store. However, he must be careful to meet the needs of the workers and not to make the mistake identified by Argyris—failing to treat them as mature adults. While remaining well organized, the store manager has room to help workers meet higher order esteem and self-fulfillment needs, as well as to exercise autonomy under Theory Y assumptions. Enrique must also be alert to the dysfunctions of bureaucracy that appear when changes are needed or when unique problems are posed or when customers want to be treated personally. The demands of these situations are difficult for traditional bureaucracies to handle, due to the fact that they are set up to handle routine work efficiently and impersonally, with an emphasis on rules, procedures, and authority.

Test Prep 3

Multiple Choice

1. a. 2. c. 3. d. 4. a. 5. c. 6. b. 7. c. 8. b. 9. a. 10. a. 11. b. 12. b. 13. d.
14. c. 15. d.

Short Response

16. Distributive justice means that everyone is treated the same, that there is no discrimination based on things like age, gender, and sexual orientation. An example would be a man and a woman who both apply for the same job. A manager violates distributive justice if he interviews only the man and not the woman as well, or vice versa. Procedural justice means that rules and procedures are fairly followed. For example, a manager violates distributive justice if he or she punishes one person for coming to work late while ignoring late behavior by another person with whom he or she regularly plays golf.

17. The "spotlight questions" for double-checking the ethics of a decision are: "How would I feel if my family finds out?" "How would I feel if this were published in the local newspaper or on the Internet?" "What would the person you know or know of who has the strongest character and best ethical judgment do in this situation?"

18. The rationalizations include believing that (1) the behavior is not really illegal, (2) the behavior is really in everyone's best interests, (3) no one will find out, and (4) the organization will protect you.

19. The "virtuous circle" concept of social responsibility holds that social responsibility practices do not hurt the bottom line and often help it; when socially responsible actions result in improved financial performance, this encourages more of the same actions in the future—a virtuous circle being created.

Integration & Application

20. If the manager adopts a position of cultural relativism, there will be no perceived problem in working with the Tanzanian firm. The justification would be that as long as it is operating legally in Tanzania, that makes everything okay. The absolutist position would hold that the contract should not be taken because the factory conditions are unacceptable at home and therefore are unacceptable anywhere. The cultural relativism position can be criticized because it makes it easy to do business in places where people are not treated well; the absolutist position can be criticized as trying to impose one's values on people in a different cultural context.

Test Prep 4

Multiple Choice

1. b. 2. c. 3. a. 4. c. 5. d. 6. a. 7. b. 8. c. 9. c. 10. c. 11. a. 12. a. 13. b.
14. d. 15. b.

Short Response

16. An optimizing decision represents the absolute "best" choice of alternatives. It is selected from a set of all known alternatives. A satisficing decision selects the first alternative that offers a "satisfactory" choice, not necessarily the absolute best choice. It is selected from a limited or incomplete set of alternatives.

17. A risk environment is one in which things are not known for sure—all of the possible decision alternatives, all of the possible consequences for each alternative—but they can be estimated as probabilities. For example, if I take a new job with a new employer, I can't know for certain that it will turn out as I expect, but I could be 80% sure that I'd like the new responsibilities, or only 60% sure that I might get promoted within a year. In an uncertain environment, things are so speculative that it is hard to even assign such probabilities.

18. A manager using systematic thinking is going to approach problem solving in a logical and rational fashion. The tendency will be to proceed in a linear step-by-step manner, handling one issue at a time. A manager using intuitive thinking will be more spontaneous and open in problem solving. He or she may jump from one stage in the process to the other and deal with many different things at once.

19. Escalating commitment is the tendency of people to keep investing in a previously chosen course of action, continuing to pursue it, even though it is not working. This is a human tendency to try and make things work by trying harder, investing more time, effort, resources, etc. In other words, I have decided in the past to pursue this major in college; I can't be wrong, can I? The feedback from my grades and course satisfaction suggests it isn't working, but I'm doing it now so I just need to make it work, right? I'll just stick with it and see if things eventually turn out okay. In this example, I am making a decision to continue with the major that is most likely an example of escalating commitment.

Integration & Application

20. This is what I would say. On the question of whether a group decision is best or an individual decision is best, the appropriate answer is probably: It all depends on the situation. Sometimes one is preferable to the other; each has its potential advantages and disadvantages. If you are in a situation where the problem being addressed is unclear, the information needed to solve it is uncertain, and you don't have a lot of personal expertise, the group approach to decision making is probably best. Group decisions offer advantages like bringing more information and ideas to bear on a problem; they often allow for more creativity; and they tend to build commitments among participants to work hard to implement any decisions reached. On the other hand, groups can be dominated by one or more members, and they can take a lot of time making decisions. Thus, when time is short, the individual decision is sometimes a better choice. However, it is important that you, as this individual, are confident that you have the information needed to solve the problem or can get it before making your decision.

Test Prep 5

Multiple Choice

1. d. 2. a. 3. b. 4. b. 5. d. 6. c. 7. a. 8. d. 9. b. 10. a. 11. c. 12. b. 13. d. 14. b. 15. c.

Short Response

16. The five steps in the formal planning process are (1) define your objectives, (2) determine where you stand relative to objectives, (3) develop premises about future conditions, (4) identify and choose among action alternatives to accomplish objectives, and (5) implement action plans and evaluate results.

17. Planning facilitates controlling because the planning process sets the objectives and standards that become the basis for the control process. If you don't have objectives and standards, you have nothing to compare actual performance with; consequently, control lacks purpose and specificity.

18. Contingency planning essentially makes available optional plans that can be quickly implemented if things go wrong with the original plan. Scenario planning is a longer-term form of contingency planning that tries to project several future scenarios that might develop over time and to associate each scenario with plans for best dealing with it.

19. Participation is good for the planning process, in part because it brings to the process a lot more information, diverse viewpoints, and potential alternatives than would otherwise be available if just one person or a select group of top managers are doing the planning. Furthermore and very importantly, through participation in the planning process, people develop an understanding of the final plans and the logic used to arrive at them, and they develop personal commitments to trying to follow through and work hard to make implementation of the plans successful.

Integration & Application

20. Benchmarking is the use of external standards to help evaluate one's own situation and develop ideas and directions for improvement. Curt and Rich are both right to a certain extent about its potential value for them. Rich is right in suggesting that there is much to learn by looking at what other bookstores are doing really well. The bookstore owner/manager might visit other bookstores in other towns that are known for their success. By observing and studying the operations of those stores and then comparing his store to them, the owner/manager can develop plans for future action. Curt is also right in suggesting that there is much to be learned potentially from looking outside the bookstore business. They should look at things like inventory management, customer service, and facilities in other settings—not just bookstores; they should also look outside their town as well as within it.

Test Prep 6

Multiple Choice

1. a.   **2.** a.   **3.** d.   **4.** b.   **5.** b.   **6.** c.   **7.** c.   **8.** d.   **9.** a.   **10.** b.   **11.** c.   **12.** a.   **13.** b.
14. a.   **15.** c.

Short Response

16. The Army's "after-action review" takes place after an action or activity has been completed. This makes it a form of "feedback" control. The primary purpose is to critique the action/activity and try to learn from it so that similar things in the future can be done better and so that the people involved can be best trained.

17. One way to use clan control in a TQM context would be to set up small teams or task forces called "Quality Circles" that bring together persons from various parts of the work place with a common commitment to quality improvements. You can ask these teams or QCs to meet regularly to discuss quality results and options, and to try and maintain a continuous improvement momentum in their work areas. The members should ideally get special quality training. They should also be expected to actively serve as quality champions in their own work areas to implement continuous quality improvements and come up with ideas for new ones.

18. The just-in-time inventory approach reduces the carrying costs of inventories. It does this by trying to have materials arrive at a work station just in time to be used. When this concept works perfectly, there are no inventory carrying costs. However, even if it is imperfect and some inventory ends up being stockpiled, it should still be less than that which would otherwise be the case. But as the recent tsunami and nuclear disaster in Japan showed, firms that are too reliant on JIT in their supply chains must prepare for the risk of disruptions when crises and natural disasters occur.

19. The four questions to ask when developing a balanced scorecard are: (1) *Financial Performance*—To improve financially, how should we appear to our shareholders? (2) *Customer Satisfaction*—To achieve our vision, how should we appear to our customers? (3) *Internal Process Improvement*—To satisfy our customers and shareholders, at what internal business processes should we excel? (4) *Innovation and Learning*—To achieve our vision, how will we sustain our ability to change and improve?

Integration & Application

20. I would begin the speech by describing MBO as an integrated planning and control approach. I would also clarify that the key elements in MBO are objectives and participation. Any objectives should be clear, measurable, and time defined. In addition, these objectives should be set with the full involvement and participation of the employees; they should not be set by the manager and then told to the employees. Given this, I would describe how each business manager should jointly set objectives with each of his or her employees and jointly review progress toward their accomplishment. I would suggest that the employees should work on the required activities while staying in communication with their managers. The managers, in turn, should provide any needed support or assistance to their employees. This whole process could be formally recycled at least twice per year.

Test Prep 7

Multiple Choice

1. a.   **2.** b.   **3.** b.   **4.** c.   **5.** a.   **6.** b.   **7.** c.   **8.** a.   **9.** c.   **10.** d.   **11.** d.   **12.** c.   **13.** a.
14. b.   **15.** b.

Short Response

16. A corporate strategy sets long-term direction for an enterprise as a whole. Functional strategies set directions so that business functions such as marketing and manufacturing support the overall corporate strategy. A corporate strategy sets long-term direction for an enterprise as a whole. Functional strategies set directions so that business functions such as marketing and manufacturing support the overall corporate strategy.

17. If you want to sell at lower prices than competitors and still make a profit, you have to have lower operating costs (profit $\times$ revenues = costs). Also, you have to be able to operate at lower costs in ways that are hard for your competitors to copy. This is the point of a cost leadership strategy—always seeking ways to lower costs and operate with greater efficiency than anyone else.

18. A question mark in the BCG matrix has a low market share in a high growth industry. This means that there is a lot of upside potential, but for now it is uncertain whether or not you will be able to capitalize on it. Thus, hard thinking is required. If you are confident, the recommended strategy is growth; if you aren't, it would be retrenchment, to allow resources to be deployed into more promising opportunities.

19. Strategic leadership is the ability to enthuse people to participate in continuous change, performance enhancement, and the implementation of organizational strategies. The special qualities of the successful strategic leader include the ability to make tradeoffs, create a sense of urgency, communicate the strategy, and engage others in continuous learning about the strategy and its performance responsibilities.

Integration & Application

20. A SWOT analysis is useful during strategic planning. It involves the analysis of organizational strengths and weaknesses, and of environmental opportunities and threats. Such a SWOT analysis in this case would help frame Kim's thinking about the current and future positioning of her store, particularly in respect to possible core competencies and competitive opportunities and threats. Then she can use Porter's competitive strategy model for further strategic refinements. This involves the possible use of three alternative strategies: differentiation, cost leadership, and focus. In this situation, the larger department store seems better positioned to follow the cost leadership strategy. This means that Kim may want to consider the other two alternatives. A differentiation strategy would involve trying to distinguish Kim's products from those of the larger store. This might involve a "made in America" theme or an emphasis on leather or canvas or some other type of clothing material. A focus strategy might specifically target college students and try to respond to their tastes and needs rather than those of the larger community population. This might involve special orders and other types of individualized service for the college student market.

Test Prep 8

Multiple Choice

1. b. **2.** c. **3.** b. **4.** a. **5.** b. **6.** c. **7.** b. **8.** a. **9.** c. **10.** b. **11.** c. **12.** b. **13.** c.
14. b. **15.** c.

Short Response

16. An organization chart depicts the formal structure of the organization. This is the official picture of the way things are supposed to be. However, the likelihood is that an organization chart quickly becomes out of date in today's dynamic environments. So one issue is whether or not the chart one is viewing actually depicts the current official structure. Second, there is a lot more to the way things work in organizations than what is shown in the organization chart. People are involved in a variety of informal networks that create an informal structure. It operates as a shadow lying above or behind the formal structure and also influences operations. Both the formal structure and informal structure must be understood; at best, an organization chart helps with understanding the formal one.

17. There are two major ways that informal structures can be good for organizations. First, they can help get work done efficiently and well. When people know one another in informal relationships, they can and often do use these relationships as part of their jobs. Sometimes an informal contact makes it a lot easier to get something done or learn how to do something than the formal linkages displayed on an organization chart. Second, being part of informal groups is an important source of potential need satisfaction. Being in an informal network or group can satisfy needs in ways that one's job can't sometimes and can add considerably to the potential satisfactions of the work experience.

18. The matrix structure is organized in a traditional functional fashion in the vertical dimension. For example, a business might have marketing, human resources, finance, and manufacturing functions. On the horizontal dimension, however, it is organized divisionally in a product or project fashion, with a manager heading up each special product or project. Members from the functional departments are assigned to permanent cross-functional teams for each product or project. They report vertically to their functional bosses and horizontally to their product/project bosses. This two-boss system is the heart of the matrix organization.

19. An organic design tends to be quicker and more flexible because it is very strong in lateral communication and empowerment. People at all levels are talking to one another and interacting as they gather and process information and solve problems. They don't wait for the vertical structure and "bosses" to do these things for them. This means that as the environment changes they are more likely to be on top of things quickly. It also means that when problems are complex and difficult to solve, they will work with multiple people in various parts of the organization to best deal with them.

Integration & Application

20. A network structure often involves one organization "contracting out" aspects of its operations to other organizations that specialize in them. The example used in the text was of a company that contracted out its mailroom services. Through the formation of networks of contracts, the organization is reduced to a core of essential employees whose expertise is concentrated in the primary business areas. The contracts are monitored and maintained in the network to allow the overall operations of the organization to continue even though they are not directly accomplished by full-time employees. There are many possibilities for doing something similar in a university. In one model, the core staff would be the faculty. They would be supported by a few administrators who managed contracts with outsourcing firms for things such as facilities maintenance, mail, technology support, lawns maintenance, food services, housing services, and even things like development, registrar, and student affairs. Another model would have the administrators forming a small core staff who contract out for the above and, in addition, for faculty who would be hired "as needed" and on contracts for specific assignments.

Test Prep 9

Multiple Choice

1. a.   **2.** c.   **3.** d.   **4.** b.   **5.** b.   **6.** c.   **7.** a.   **8.** c.   **9.** c.   **10.** b.   **11.** d.   **12.** c.   **13.** c.   **14.** b.   **15.** b.

Short Response

16. The core values that might be found in high-performance organizational cultures include such things as emphasize performance excellence, innovation, social responsibility, integrity, worker involvement, customer service, and teamwork.

17. First, process innovations result in better ways of doing things. Second, product innovations result in the creation of new or improved goods and services. Third, business model innovations result in new ways of making money for the firm.

18. Lewin's three phases of planned change are unfreezing, changing, and refreezing. In terms of the change leadership challenges, the major differences in attention would be as follows: unfreezing—preparing a system for change; changing—moving or creating change in a system; and refreezing—stabilizing and reinforcing change once it has occurred.

19. In general, managers can expect that others will be more committed and loyal to changes that are brought about through shared power strategies. Rational persuasion strategies can also create enduring effects if they are accepted. Force-coercion strategies tend to have temporary effects only.

Integration & Application

20. In any change situation, it is important to remember that successful planned change occurs only when all three phases of change—unfreezing, changing, and refreezing—have been taken care of. Thus, I would not rush into the changing phase. Rather, I would work with the people involved to develop a felt need for change based on their ideas and inputs as well as mine. Then I would proceed by supporting the changes and helping to stabilize them into everyday routines. I would also be sensitive to any resistance and respect that resistance as a signal that something important is being threatened. By listening to resistance, I would be in a position to better modify the change to achieve a better fit with the people and the situation. Finally, I would want to take maximum advantage of the shared power strategy, supported by rational persuasion, and with limited use of force-coercion (if it is used at all). By doing all of this, I would like my staff to feel empowered and committed to constructive improvement through planned change. Throughout all of this I would strive to perform to the best of my ability and gain trust and credibility with everyone else; in this way I would be a positive role model for change.

Test Prep 10

Multiple Choice

1. a.   **2.** b.   **3.** c.   **4.** b.   **5.** b.   **6.** b.   **7.** a.   **8.** d.   **9.** b.   **10.** a.   **11.** d.   **12.** d.   **13.** a.   **14.** a.   **15.** b.

Short Response

16. Orientation activities introduce a new employee to the organization and the work environment. This is a time when the individual may develop key attitudes and when performance expectations will also be established. Good orientation communicates positive attitudes and expectations and reinforces the desired organizational culture. It formally introduces the individual to important policies and procedures that everyone is expected to follow.

17. Mentoring is when a senior and experienced individual adopts a newcomer or more junior person with the goal of helping him or her develop into a successful worker. The mentor may or may not be the individual's immediate supervisor. The mentor meets with the individual and discusses problems, shares advice, and generally supports the individual's attempts to grow and perform. Mentors are considered very useful for persons newly appointed to management positions.

18. Any performance assessment approach should be both valid and reliable. To be valid it must measure accurately what it claims to measure—whether that is some aspect of job performance or personal behavior. To be reliable it must deliver the same results consistently—whether applied by different raters to the same person or when measuring the same person over time. Valid and reliable assessments are free from bias and as objective as possible.

19. The graphic rating scale simply asks a supervisor to rate an employee on an established set of criteria, such as quantity of work or attitude toward work. This leaves much room for subjectivity and debate. The behaviorally anchored rating scale asks the supervisor to rate the employee on specific behaviors that had been identified as positively or negatively affecting performance in a given job. This is a more specific appraisal approach and leaves less room for debate and disagreement.

Integration & Application

20. As Sy's supervisor, you face a difficult but perhaps expected human resource management problem. Not only is Sy influential as an informal leader, he also has considerable experience on the job and in the company. Even though he is experiencing performance problems using the new computer system, there is no indication that he doesn't want to work hard and continue to perform for the company. Although retirement is an option, Sy may also be transferred, promoted, or simply terminated. The latter response seems unjustified and may cause legal problems. Transferring Sy, with his agreement, to another position could be a positive move; promoting Sy to a supervisory position in which his experience and networks would be useful is another possibility. The key in this situation seems to be moving Sy out so that a computer-literate person can take over the job, while continuing to utilize Sy in a job that better fits his talents. Transfer and/or promotion should be actively considered both in his and in the company's best interests.

Test Prep 11

Multiple Choice

1. b.   **2.** b.   **3.** a.   **4.** d.   **5.** a.   **6.** c.   **7.** c.   **8.** a.   **9.** a.   **10.** b.   **11.** d.   **12.** d.   **13.** a.   **14.** d.   **15.** a.

Short Response

16. Position power is based on reward, coercion or punishment, and legitimacy or formal authority. Managers, however, need to have more power than that made available to them by the position alone. Thus, they have to develop personal power through expertise and reference. This personal power is essential in helping managers get things done beyond the scope of their position power alone.

17. Leadership situations are described by Fiedler according to: Position power—how much power the leader has in terms of rewards, punishments, and legitimacy; leader-member relations—the quality of relationships between the leader and followers; task structure—the degree to which the task is clear and well defined, or open ended and more ambiguous. Highly favorable situations are high in position power, have good leader-member relations, and have structured tasks; highly unfavorable situations are low in position power, have poor leader-member relations, and have unstructured tasks.

18. According to House's path-goal theory, the following combinations are consistent with successful leadership. Participative leadership works well, for example, when performance incentives are low and people need to find other sources of need satisfaction. Through participation the leader gains knowledge that can help identify important needs and possible ways of satisfying them other than through the available performance incentives. Directive leadership works well, for example, when people aren't clear about their jobs or goals. In these cases the leader can step in and provide direction that channels their efforts toward desired activities and outcomes.

19. Servant leadership is basically other-centered and not self-centered. A servant leader is concerned with helping others to perform well so that the organization or group can ultimately do good things for society. The person who accepts the responsibilities of servant leadership is good at empowering others so that they can use their talents while acting independently to do their jobs in the best possible ways.

Integration & Application

20. In his new position, Marcel must understand that the transactional aspects of leadership are not sufficient enough to guarantee him long-term leadership effectiveness. He must move beyond the effective use of task-oriented and people-oriented behaviors—the "transactional" side of leadership, and demonstrate through his behavior and personal qualities the capacity to inspire others and lead with moral integrity—the "transformational" side. A transformational leader develops a unique relationship with followers in which they become enthusiastic, highly loyal, and high achievers. Marcel needs to work very hard to develop positive relationships with the team members. But he must add to this a moral and ethical dimension. He must emphasize in those relationships high aspirations for performance accomplishments, enthusiasm, ethical behavior, integrity and honesty in all dealings, and a clear vision of the future. By working hard with this agenda and by allowing his personality to positively express itself in the team setting, Marcel should make continuous progress as an effective and moral leader.

Test Prep 12

Multiple Choice

1. c.   **2.** d.   **3.** b.   **4.** a.   **5.** d.   **6.** a.   **7.** b.   **8.** a.   **9.** b.   **10.** a.   **11.** b.   **12.** d.   **13.** d.   **14.** d.   **15.** c.

Short Response

16. All of the Big Five personality traits are relevant to the workplace. To give some basic examples, consider the following. Extroversion suggests whether or not a person will reach out to relate and work well with others. Agreeableness suggests whether or not a person is open to the ideas of others and willing to go along with group decisions. Conscientiousness suggests whether someone can be depended on to meet commitments and perform agreed-upon tasks. Emotional stability suggests whether or not someone will be relaxed and secure, or uptight and tense, in work situations. Openness suggests whether someone will be open to new ideas or resistant to change.

17. The Type A personality is characteristic of people who bring stress on themselves by virtue of personal characteristics. These tend to be compulsive individuals who are uncomfortable waiting for things to happen, who try to do many things at once, and who generally move fast and have difficulty slowing down. Type A personalities can be stressful for both the individuals and the people around them. Managers must be aware of Type A personality tendencies in their own behavior and among others with whom they work. Ideally, this awareness will help the manager take precautionary steps to best manage the stress caused by this personality type.

18. The halo effect occurs when a single attribute of a person, such as the way he or she dresses, is used to evaluate or form an overall impression of the person. Selective perception occurs when someone focuses in a situation on those aspects that reinforce or are most consistent with his or her existing values, beliefs, or experiences.

19. Job satisfaction is an attitude that reflects how people feel about their jobs, work settings, and the people with whom they work. A typical job satisfaction survey might ask people to respond to questions about their pay, co-worker relationships, quality of supervisor, nature of the work setting, and the type of work they are asked to do. These questions might be framed with a scale ranging from "very satisfied" to "not satisfied at all" for each question or job satisfaction dimension.

Integration & Application

20. Scott needs to be careful. Although there is modest research support for the relationship between job satisfaction and performance, there is no guarantee that simply doing things to make people happier at work will cause them to be higher performers. Scott needs to take a broader perspective on this issue and his responsibilities as a manager. He should be interested in job satisfaction for his therapists and do everything he can to help them to experience it. But he should also be performance oriented and understand that performance is achieved through a combination of skills, support, and motivation. He should be helping the therapists to achieve and maintain high levels of job competency. He should also work with them to find out what obstacles they are facing and what support they need—things that perhaps he can deal with in their behalf. All of this relates as well to research indications that performance can be a source of job satisfaction. And finally, Scott should make sure that the therapists believe they are being properly rewarded for their work since rewards are shown by research to have an influence on both job satisfaction and job performance.

Test Prep 13

Multiple Choice

1. b. **2.** c. **3.** d. **4.** d. **5.** b. **6.** a. **7.** b. **8.** b. **9.** a. **10.** d. **11.** a. **12.** c. **13.** c.
14. a. **15.** a.

Short Response

16. People high in need for achievement will prefer work settings and jobs in which they have (1) challenging but achievable goals, (2) individual responsibility, and (3) performance feedback.

17. One way for a team leader to use goal-setting principles in working with team members is to engage them in a process of joint goal-setting and performance review. In an earlier chapter on planning and controlling, this type of approach was described as "management by objectives." It is really a good application of goal-setting theory. Participation of both team leader and team member in goal setting offers an opportunity to choose goals to which the member will respond and which also will serve the team and organization as a whole. Furthermore, through goal setting, the team leader and team member can identify performance standards or targets. Progress toward these targets can be positively reinforced by the team leader. This type of approach harnesses the power of goal-setting theory by putting the team leader and team member together in a process where specific, challenging, and measureable goals can be set, and the team member can feel that he or she has helped set them.

18. When perceived inequity exists an individual might (1) quit the job, (2) speak with the boss to try and increase rewards to the point where the inequity no longer exists, or (3) decide to reduce effort to the level that seems consistent with the rewards being received.

19. Shaping encourages the formation of desirable work behaviors by rewarding successive approximations to those behaviors. In this sense, the behavior doesn't have to be perfect to be rewarded—it just has to be moving in the right direction. Over time and with a change of reinforcement scheduling from continuous to intermittent, such rewards can end up drawing forth the desired behavior.

Integration & Application

20. The use of Muzak would be considered improvement in a hygiene factor under Herzberg's two-factor theory. Thus it would not be a source of greater work motivation and performance. Herzberg suggests that job content factors are the satisfiers or motivators. Based in the job itself, they represent such things as responsibility, sense of achievement, and feelings of growth. Job context factors are considered sources of dissatisfaction. They are found in the job environment and include such things as base pay, technical quality of supervision, and working conditions. Whereas improvements in job context such as introduction of Muzak make people less dissatisfied, improvements in job content are considered necessary to motivate them to high-performance levels.

Test Prep 14

Multiple Choice

1. d.　　**2.** a.　　**3.** b.　　**4.** d.　　**5.** b.　　**6.** a.　　**7.** c.　　**8.** b.　　**9.** a.　　**10.** a.　　**11.** a.　　**12.** b.　　**13.** d.
14. c.　　**15.** d.

Short Response

16. In a task force, members are brought together to work on a specific assignment. The task force usually disbands when the assignment is finished. In an employee involvement group, perhaps a quality circle, members are brought together to work on an issue or task over time. They meet regularly and always deal with the same issue/task. In a self-managing team, the members of a formal work group provide self-direction. They plan, organize, and evaluate their work, share tasks, and help one another develop skills; they may even make hiring decisions. A true self-managing team does not need the traditional "boss" or supervisor, since the team as a whole takes on the supervisory responsibilities.

17. Input factors can have a major impact on group effectiveness. In order to best prepare a group to perform effectively, a manager should make sure that the right people are put in the group (maximize available talents and abilities), that these people are capable of working well together (membership characteristics should promote good relationships), that the tasks are clear, and that the group has the resources and environment needed to perform up to expectations.

18. A group's performance can be analyzed according to the interaction between cohesiveness and performance norms. In a highly cohesive group, members tend to conform to group norms. Thus, when the performance norm is positive and cohesion is high, we can expect everyone to work hard to support the norm—high performance is likely. By the same token, high cohesion and a low performance norm will act similarly—low performance is likely. With other combinations of norms and cohesion, the performance results will be more mixed.

19. The book lists several symptoms of groupthink along with various strategies for avoiding groupthink. For example, a group whose members censure themselves to refrain from contributing "contrary" or "different" opinions and/or whose members keep talking about outsiders as "weak" or the "enemy" may be suffering from groupthink. This may be avoided or corrected, for example, by asking someone to be the "devil's advocate" for a meeting and by inviting in an outside observer to help gather different viewpoints.

Integration & Application

20. Mariel is faced with a highly cohesive group whose members conform to a negative or low-performance norm. This is a difficult situation that is ideally resolved by changing the performance norm. In order to gain the group's commitment to a high-performance norm, Mariel should act as a positive role model for the norm. She must communicate the norm clearly and positively to the group. She should not assume that everyone knows what she expects of them. She may also talk to the informal leader and gain his or her commitment to the norm. She might carefully reward high-performance behaviors within the group. She may introduce new members with high-performance records and commitments. And she might hold group meetings in which performance standards and expectations are discussed, with an emphasis on committing to new high-performance directions. If attempts to introduce a high-performance norm fail, Mariel may have to take steps to reduce group cohesiveness so that individual members can pursue higher-performance results without feeling bound by group pressures to restrict their performance.

Test Prep 15

Multiple Choice

1. a.　　**2.** c.　　**3.** d.　　**4.** d.　　**5.** a.　　**6.** c.　　**7.** d.　　**8.** c.　　**9.** b.　　**10.** c.　　**11.** c.　　**12.** a.　　**13.** b.
14. a.　　**15.** b.

Short Response

16. The manager's goal in active listening is to help the subordinate say what he or she really means. To do this, the manager should carefully listen for the content of what someone is saying, paraphrase or reflect back what the person appears to be saying, remain sensitive to nonverbal cues and feelings, and not be evaluative.

17. Well-intentioned managers can make bad decisions when they base decisions on bad information. Because of the manager's position of authority in the organization, those below him or her may be reluctant to communicate upward information that they believe the manager doesn't want to hear. Thus, they may filter the information to make it as agreeable to the manager as possible. As a result of this filtering of upward communication, the manager may end up with poor or incomplete information and subsequently make bad decisions.

18. The four major errors in giving constructive feedback would be (1) being general rather than specific, (2) choosing a poor time, (3) including in the message irrelevant things, and (4) overwhelming the receiver with too much information at once.

19. Ethnocentrism is when a person views his or her own culture as superior to others. It can interfere with cross-cultural communication when the ethnocentrism leads the person to ignore cultural signals that indicate his or her behavior is inappropriate or offensive by local cultural standards. With the ethnocentric attitude of cultural superiority, the individual is inclined not to change personal ways or display the sensitivity to local cultural ways that are necessary to effective communication.

Integration & Application

20. Glenn can do a number of things to establish and maintain a system of communication with his employees and for his department store branch. To begin, he should, as much as possible, try to establish a highly interactive style of management based upon credibility and trust. Credibility is earned through building personal power through expertise and reference. With credibility, he might set the tone for the department managers by using MBWA—"managing by wandering around." Once this pattern is established, trust will build between him and other store employees, and he should find that he learns a lot from interacting directly with them. Harold should also set up a formal communication structure, such as bimonthly store meetings, where he communicates store goals, results, and other issues to the staff, and in which he listens to them in return. An e-mail system whereby Glenn and his staff could send messages to one another from their workstation computers would also be beneficial.

Test Prep 16

Multiple Choice

1. c. 2. a. 3. b. 4. b. 5. b. 6. d. 7. a. 8. a. 9. d. 10. a. 11. d. 12. d. 13. c.
14. c. 15. b.

Short Response

16. An approach of valuing diversity shows through leadership a commitment to helping people understand their differences, often through education and training programs. An approach of managing diversity, according to Roosevelt Thomas, is a step beyond in that it is where the leadership commits to changing the culture of the organization to empower everyone and create a fully inclusive environment where human resources are respected and fully utilized.

17. There are numbers of subcultures that form in organizations and can become the source of perceived differences as people work with one another across subculture boundaries. Examples of common organizational subcultures include those based on age, gender, profession, and work function. If younger workers stereotype older workers as uncreative and less ambitious, a team consisting of an age mix of members might experience some difficulties. This illustrates an example of problems among generational subcultures.

18. The anthropologist Edward Hall identified communication context, time, and space as silent languages of culture. High-context cultures rely on nonverbal and situational cues as well as the spoken word to convey messages, whereas low-context cultures are more focused on what is being said. An American business person might press an Indonesian client to sign a contract immediately, whereas the body language of the client might say she doesn't want to, even though she is offering a reluctant "okay" in their conversation. Monochromic cultures deal with time in a linear fashion while polychromic cultures view it as more non-linear and dynamic. Whereas the American schedules time, saves time, and tries to meet time deadlines (monochromic behavior), a Mexican might be less concerned about time budgeting like this and more likely to act flexibly in terms of time schedules and engagements. Proxemics involves the use of space in communication. If you observe Americans in conversation there is likely to be a modest amount of distance maintained between speakers. But in Italy the conversation is likely to take place in much closer face-to-face conditions, and this would likely make the American a bit uncomfortable.

19. Organizations are power structures, and the way people view and respond to power differences in organizations can be very significant in how they operate. In a national culture where power distance is high, there would be a tendency in organizations to respect persons of authority—perhaps defer to them, use job titles and formal greetings, and refrain from challenging their views in public meetings. In a low or moderate power distance culture, by contrast, there might be more informality in using first names without job titles and being more casual in relationships and even in public disagreements with views expressed by senior people.

Integration & Application

20. The friend must recognize that the cultural differences between the United States and Japan may affect the success of group-oriented work practices such as quality circles and work teams. The United States was the most individualistic culture in Hofstede's study of national cultures; Japan is much more collectivist. Group practices such as the quality circle and teams are natural and consistent with the Japanese culture. When introduced into a more individualistic culture, these same practices might cause difficulties or require some time for workers to get used to. At the very least, the friend should proceed with caution, discuss ideas for the new practices with the workers before making any changes, and then monitor the changes closely so that adjustments can be made to improve them as the workers gain familiarity with them and have suggestions of their own.

Test Prep 17

Multiple Choice

1. c. **2.** d. **3.** d. **4.** b. **5.** b. **6.** a. **7.** c. **8.** d. **9.** d. **10.** b. **11.** b. **12.** c. **13.** b.
14. c. **15.** a.

Short Response

16. In a joint venture the foreign corporation and the local corporation each own a portion of the firm—e.g., 75% and 25%. In a wholly owned subsidiary the foreign firm owns the local subsidiary in its entirety.

17. The relationship between an MNC and a host country should be mutually beneficial. Sometimes, however, host countries complain that MNCs take unfair advantage of them and do not include them in the benefits of their international operations. The complaints against MNCs include taking excessive profits out of the host country, hiring the best local labor, not respecting local laws and customs, and dominating the local economy. Engaging in corrupt practices is another important concern.

18. If a Senator says she favors "protectionism" in international trade, it basically means that she wants to make sure that domestic American firms are protected against foreign competitors. In other words, she doesn't want foreign companies coming into America and destroying through competition the local firms. Thus, she wants to protect them in some ways such as imposing import tariffs on the foreign firms' products or imposing legal restrictions on them setting up businesses in America.

19. Currency risk in international business involves the rise and fall of currencies in relationship with one another. For an American company operating in Japan, currency risk involves the value of the dollar vis-à-vis the yen. When the dollar falls relative to the yen (requiring more of them to buy 1 yen), it means that buying products and making investments in Japan will be more costly; the "risk" of this eventuality needs to be planned for when business relationships are entered in foreign countries. Political risk is the potential loss in one's investments in foreign countries due to wars or political changes that might threaten the assets. An example would be a Socialist government coming into power and deciding to "nationalize" or take over ownership of all foreign companies.

Integration & Application

20. This issue of MNC vs. transnational is growing in importance. When a large global company such as Ford or IBM is strongly associated with a national identity, the firm might face risk in international business when foreign consumers or governments are angry at the firm's home country; they might stop buying its products or make it hard for them to operate. When the MNC has a strong national identity, its home constituents might express anger and create problems when the firm makes investments in creating jobs in other countries. Also, when the leadership of the MNC views itself as having one national home, it might have a more limited and even ethnocentric approach to international operations. When a firm operates as a transnational, by contrast, it becomes a global citizen and, theoretically at least, is freed from some potential problems identified here. Because a transnational views the world as its home, furthermore, its workforce and leadership are more likely to be globally diverse and have broad international perspectives on the company and its opportunities.

Test Prep 18

Multiple Choice

1. a. **2.** c. **3.** d. **4.** b. **5.** b. **6.** a. **7.** a. **8.** b. **9.** a. **10.** c. **11.** c. **12.** a. **13.** d.
14. b. **15.** d.

Short Response

16. Entrepreneurship is rich with diversity. It is an avenue for business entry and career success that is pursued by many women and members of minority groups. Data show almost 40% of U.S. businesses are owned by women. Many report leaving other employment because they had limited opportunities. For them, entrepreneurship made available the opportunities for career success that they lacked. Minority-owned businesses are one of the fastest-growing sectors, with the growth rates highest for Hispanic-owned, Asian-owned, and African American-owned businesses in that order.

17. The three stages in the life cycle of an entrepreneurial firm are birth, breakthrough, and maturity. In the birth stage, the leader is challenged to get customers, establish a market, and find the money needed to keep the business going. In the breakthrough stage, the challenges shift to becoming and staying profitable and managing growth. In the maturity stage, a leader is more focused on revising/maintaining a good business strategy and more generally managing the firm for continued success and possibly more future growth.

18. The limited partnership form of small business ownership consists of a general partner and one or more "limited partners." The general partner(s) play an active role in managing and operating the business; the limited partners do not. All contribute resources of some value to the partnership for the conduct of the business. The advantage of any partnership form is that the partners may share in profits, but their potential for losses is limited by the size of their original investments.

19. A venture capitalist is an individual or group of individuals that invests money in new start-up companies and gets a portion of ownership in return. The goal is to sell their ownership stakes in the future for a profit. An angel investor is a type of venture capitalist, but on a smaller and individual scale. This is a person who invests in a new venture, taking a share of ownership, and also hoping to gain profit through a future sale of the ownership.

Integration & Application

20. The friend is right—it takes much forethought and planning to prepare the launch of a new business venture. In response to the question of how to ensure that you are really being customer-focused in the new start-up, I would ask and answer the following questions to frame my business model with a strong customer orientation. "Who are my potential customers? What market niche am I shooting for? What do the customers in this market really want? How do these customers make purchase decisions? How much will it cost to produce and distribute my product/service to these customers? How much will it cost to attract and retain customers?" Following an overall executive summary, which includes a commitment to this customer orientation, I would address the following areas in writing up my initial business plan. The plan would address such areas as company description—mission, owners, and legal form—as well as an industry analysis, product and services description, marketing description and strategy, staffing model, financial projections with cash flows, and capital needs.

Glossary

3 Ps of organizational performance The 3 Ps of organizational performance are profit, people, and planet.

360° feedback 360° feedback includes superiors, subordinates, peers, and even customers in the appraisal process.

A

accommodation Accommodation, or smoothing, plays down differences and highlights similarities to reduce conflict.

accountability Accountability is the requirement to show performance results to a supervisor.

active listening Active listening helps the source of a message say what he or she really means.

affirmative action Affirmative action is an effort to give preference in employment to women and minority group members.

after-action review After-action review is a structured review of lessons learned and results accomplished through a completed project, task force assignment, or special operation.

age discrimination Age discrimination penalizes an employee in a job or as a job applicant for being over the age of 40.

agenda setting Agenda setting identifies important action priorities.

amoral manager An amoral manager fails to consider the ethics of her or his behavior.

analytics Analytics is the systematic use and analysis of data to solve problems and make informed decisions.

anchoring and adjustment heuristic The anchoring and adjustment heuristic adjusts a previously existing value or starting point to make a decision.

angel investor An angel investor is a wealthy individual willing to invest in return for equity in a new venture.

assessment center An assessment center examines how job candidates handle simulated work situations.

attitude An attitude is a predisposition to act in a certain way.

attribution Attribution is the process of creating explanations for events.

authoritarianism Authoritarianism is the degree to which a person defers to authority and accepts status differences.

authority decision An authority decision is made by the leader and then communicated to the group.

autocratic leader An autocratic leader acts in unilateral command-and-control fashion.

availability heuristic The availability heuristic uses readily available information to assess a current situation.

avoidance Avoidance pretends that a conflict doesn't really exist.

B

B2B business strategy A B2B business strategy uses IT and Web portals to link organizations vertically in supply chains.

B2C business strategy A B2C business strategy uses IT and Web portals to link businesses with customers.

balanced scorecard A balanced scorecard measures performance on financial, customer service, internal process, and innovation and learning goals.

BCG Matrix The BCG Matrix analyzes business opportunities according to market growth rate and market share.

behavioral decision model The behavioral decision model describes decision making with limited information and bounded rationality.

behaviorally anchored rating scale (BARS) A behaviorally anchored rating scale (BARS) uses specific descriptions of actual behaviors to rate various levels of performance.

benchmarking Benchmarking uses external comparisons to gain insights for planning.

best practices Best practices are methods that lead to superior performance.

biculturalism Biculturalism is when minority members adopt characteristics of majority cultures in order to succeed.

board of directors Members of a board of directors are elected by stockholders to represent their ownership interests.

bona fide occupational qualifications Bona fide occupational qualifications are employment criteria justified by capacity to perform a job.

bonus pay Bonus pay plans provide one-time payments based on performance accomplishments.

breakeven analysis Breakeven analysis performs what-if calculations under different revenue and cost conditions.

breakeven point The breakeven point occurs where revenues just equal costs.

budget A budget is a plan that commits resources to projects or activities.

bureaucracy A bureaucracy is a rational and efficient form of organization founded on logic, order, and legitimate authority.

bureaucratic control Bureaucratic control influences behavior through authority, policies, procedures, job descriptions, budgets, and day-to-day supervision.

business incubator A business incubator is a facility that offers services to help new businesses get established.

business model innovations Business model innovations result in ways for firms to make money.

business plan A business plan describes the direction for a new business and the financing needed to operate it.

business strategy A business strategy identifies how a division or strategic business unit will compete in its product or service domain.

C

career development Career development is the process of managing how a person grows and progresses in a career.

career planning Career planning is the process of matching career goals and individual capabilities with opportunities for their fulfillment.

centralization With centralization, top management keeps the power to make most decisions.

centralized communication network In a centralized communication network, communication flows only between individual members and a hub or center point.

certain environment A certain environment offers complete information on possible action alternatives and their consequences.

change leader A change leader tries to change the behavior of another person or social system.

changing Changing is the phase where a planned change actually takes place.

channel richness Channel richness is the capacity of a communication channel to effectively carry information.

Chapter 11 bankruptcy Chapter 11 bankruptcy protects an insolvent firm from creditors during a period of reorganization to restore profitability.

charismatic leader A charismatic leader develops special leader-follower relationships and inspires followers in extraordinary ways.

child labor Child labor is the full-time employment of children for work otherwise done by adults.

clan control Clan control influences behavior through social norms and peer expectations.

classical decision model The classical decision model describes decision making with complete information.

classical view of CSR The classical view of CSR is that business should focus on the pursuit of profits.

coaching Coaching occurs as an experienced person offers performance advice to a less experienced person.

code of ethics A code of ethics is a formal statement of values and ethical standards.

coercive power Coercive power achieves influence by punishment.

cognitive dissonance Cognitive dissonance is discomfort felt when attitude and behavior are inconsistent.

cognitive style Cognitive style is the way an individual deals with information while making decisions.

cohesiveness Cohesiveness is the degree to which members are attracted to and motivated to remain part of a team.

collaboration Collaboration, or problem solving, involves working through conflict differences and solving problems so everyone wins.

collective bargaining Collective bargaining is the process of negotiating, administering, and interpreting a labor contract.

commercializing innovation Commercializing innovation is the process of turning new ideas into salable products.

committee A committee is designated to work on a special task on a continuing basis.

communication Communication is the process of sending and receiving symbols with meanings attached.

communication channel A communication channel is the medium used to carry a message.

communication transparency Communication transparency involves being honest and openly sharing accurate and complete information.

commutative justice Commutative justice focuses on the fairness of exchanges or transactions.

competition Competition, or authoritative command, uses force, superior skill, or domination to win a conflict.

competitive advantage A competitive advantage is an ability to outperform rivals.

complacency trap The complacency trap is being lulled into inaction by current successes or failures.

compressed workweek A compressed workweek allows a worker to complete a full-time job in less than five days.

compromise Compromise occurs when each party to the conflict gives up something of value to the other.

concentration Growth through concentration means expansion within an existing business area.

conceptual skill A conceptual skill is the ability to think analytically and solve complex problems.

concurrent control Concurrent control focuses on what happens during the work process.

confirmation error Confirmation error is when we attend only to information that confirms a decision already made.

conflict Conflict is a disagreement over issues of substance and/or an emotional antagonism.

conflict resolution Conflict resolution is the removal of the substantive and/or emotional reasons for a conflict.

consensus Consensus is reached when all parties believe they have had their say and been listened to, and agree to support the group's final decision.

constructive stress Constructive stress is a positive influence on effort, creativity, and diligence in work.

consultative decision A consultative decision is made by a leader after receiving information, advice, or opinions from group members.

contingency leadership perspective The contingency leadership perspective suggests that what is successful as a leadership style varies according to the situation and the people involved.

contingency planning Contingency planning identifies alternative courses of action to take when things go wrong.

contingency thinking Contingency thinking tries to match management practices with situational demands.

contingency workers Contingency workers or permatemps work part-time hours on a longer-term basis.

continuous improvement Continuous improvement involves always searching for new ways to improve work quality and performance.

control charts Control charts are graphical ways of displaying trends so that exceptions to quality standards can be identified.

controlling Controlling is the process of measuring performance and taking action to ensure desired results.

co-opetition Co-opetition is the strategy of working with rivals on projects of mutual benefit.

core competency A core competency is a special strength that gives an organization a competitive advantage.

core culture The core culture is found in the underlying values of the organization.

core values Core values are beliefs and values shared by organization members.

corporate governance Corporate governance is oversight of a company's management by a board of directors.

corporate social responsibility Corporate social responsibility is the obligation of an organization to serve its own interests and those of its stakeholders.

corporate strategy A corporate strategy sets long-term direction for the total enterprise.

corporation A corporation is a legal entity that exists separately from its owners.

corruption Corruption involves illegal practices to further one's business interests.

cost-benefit analysis Cost-benefit analysis involves comparing the costs and benefits of each potential course of action.

cost leadership strategy A cost leadership strategy seeks to operate with lower costs than competitors.

CPM/PERT CPM/PERT is a combination of the critical path method and the program evaluation and review technique.

creativity Creativity is the generation of a novel idea or unique approach that solves a problem or crafts an opportunity.

credible communication Credible communication earns trust, respect, and integrity in the eyes of others.

crisis A crisis is an unexpected problem that can lead to disaster if not resolved quickly and appropriately.

critical-incident technique The critical-incident technique keeps a log of someone's effective and ineffective job behaviors.

critical path The critical path is the pathway from project start to conclusion that involves activities with the longest completion times.

cross-functional team A cross-functional team operates with members who come from different functional units of an organization.

crowdsourcing Crowdsourcing is strategic use of the Internet to engage customers and potential customers in providing opinions and suggestions on products and their designs.

cultural etiquette Cultural etiquette is use of appropriate manners and behaviors in cross-cultural situations.

cultural intelligence Cultural intelligence is the ability to adapt to new cultures.

cultural relativism Cultural relativism suggests there is no one right way to behave; cultural context determines ethical behavior.

culture shock Culture shock is the confusion and discomfort that a person experiences when in an unfamiliar culture.

currency risk Currency risk is possible loss because of fluctuating exchange rates.

customer structure A customer structure groups together people and jobs that serve the same customers or clients.

D

debt financing Debt financing involves borrowing money from another person, a bank, or a financial institution.

decentralization With decentralization, top management allows lower levels to help make many decisions.

decentralized communication network A decentralized communication network allows all members to communicate directly with one another.

decision A decision is a choice among possible alternative courses of action.

decision making Decision making is the process of making choices among alternative courses of action.

decision-making process The decision-making process begins with identification of a problem and ends with evaluation of implemented solutions.

deficit principle Maslow's deficit principle is that people act to satisfy needs for which a satisfaction deficit exists; a satisfied need doesn't motivate behavior.

delegation Delegation is the process of entrusting work to others.

democratic leader A democratic leader encourages participation with an emphasis on task and people.

departmentalization Departmentalization is the process of grouping together people and jobs into work units.

destructive stress Destructive stress is a negative influence on one's performance.

differentiation strategy A differentiation strategy offers products that are unique and different from those of the competition.

discrimination Discrimination actively denies women and minorities the full benefits of organizational membership.

disruptive behaviors Disruptive behaviors are self-serving and cause problems for team effectiveness.

distributed leadership Distributed leadership is when any and all members contribute helpful task and maintenance activities to the team.

distributive justice Distributive justice focuses on treating people the same regardless of personal characteristics.

diversification Growth through diversification means expansion by entering related or new business areas.

diversity Diversity describes race, gender, age, and other individual differences.

divestiture Divestiture involves selling off parts of the organization to refocus attention on core business areas.

division of labor The division of labor means that people and groups perform different jobs.

divisional structure A divisional structure groups together people working on the same product, in the same area, or with similar customers.

downsizing Downsizing decreases the size of operations.

E

e-business strategy An e-business strategy strategically uses the Internet to gain competitive advantage.

ecological fallacy The ecological fallacy assumes that a generalized cultural value applies equally well to all members of the culture.

economic order quantity The economic order quantity method places new orders when inventory levels fall to predetermined points.

effective communication In effective communication the receiver fully understands the intended meaning.

effective manager An effective manager successfully helps others achieve high performance and satisfaction in their work.

effective team An effective team achieves high levels of task performance, membership satisfaction, and future viability.

efficient communication Efficient communication occurs at minimum cost to the sender.

electronic grapevine The electronic grapevine uses computer technologies to transmit information around informal networks inside and outside of organizations.

emotional conflict Emotional conflict results from feelings of anger, distrust, dislike, fear, and resentment as well as from personality clashes.

emotional intelligence (EI) Emotional intelligence (EI) is the ability to manage our emotions in leadership and social relationships.

emotions Emotions are strong feelings directed toward someone or something.

employee assistance programs Employee assistance programs help employees cope with personal stresses and problems.

employee engagement Employee engagement is a strong sense of belonging and connection with one's work and employer.

employee involvement team An employee involvement team meets on a regular basis to help achieve continuous improvement.

empowerment Empowerment gives people job freedom and power to influence affairs in the organization.

entrepreneur An entrepreneur is willing to pursue opportunities in situations that others view as problems or threats.

entrepreneurship Entrepreneurship is risk-taking behavior in pursuit of business success.

environmental capital or **natural capital** Environmental capital or natural capital is the storehouse of natural resources—atmosphere, land, water, and minerals—that we use to sustain life and produce goods and services for society.

equal employment opportunity (EEO) Equal employment opportunity (EEO) is the right to employment and advancement without regard to race, sex, religion, color, or national origin.

equity financing Equity financing gives ownership shares to outsiders in return for their financial investments.

escalating commitment Escalating commitment is the continuation of a course of action even though it is not working.

ethical behavior Ethical behavior is "right" or "good" in the context of a governing moral code.

ethical dilemma An ethical dilemma is a situation that, although offering potential benefit or gain, is also unethical.

ethical frameworks Ethical frameworks are well-thought-out personal rules and strategies for ethical decision making.

ethical imperialism Ethical imperialism is an attempt to impose one's ethical standards on other cultures.

ethics Ethics set moral standards of what is "good" and "right" behavior in organizations and in our personal lives.

ethics training Ethics training seeks to help people understand the ethical aspects of decision making and to incorporate high ethical standards into their daily behavior.

ethnic or national subcultures Ethnic or national subcultures form among people from the same races, language groupings, regions, and nations.

ethnocentrism Ethnocentrism is the belief that one's membership group or subculture is superior to all others.

evidence-based management Evidence-based management involves making decisions based on hard facts about what really works.

existence needs Existence needs are desires for physiological and material well-being.

expectancy Expectancy is a person's belief that working hard will result in high task performance.

expert power Expert power achieves influence by special knowledge.

exporting In exporting, local products are sold abroad.

external control External control occurs through direct supervision or administrative systems.

extinction Extinction discourages a behavior by making the removal of a desirable consequence contingent on its occurrence.

F

family business feud A family business feud can lead to small business failure.

family businesses Family businesses are owned and financially controlled by family members.

family-friendly benefits Family-friendly benefits help employees achieve better work-life balance.

feedback Feedback is the process of telling someone else how you feel about something that person did or said.

feedback control Feedback control takes place after completing an action.

feedforward control Feedforward control ensures clear directions and needed resources before the work begins.

filtering Filtering is the intentional distortion of information to make it more favorable to the recipient.

first-line managers First-line managers supervise people who perform nonmanagerial duties.

first-mover advantage A first-mover advantage comes from being first to exploit a niche or enter a market.

flexible benefits Flexible benefits programs allow choice to personalize benefits within a set dollar allowance.

flexible working hours Flexible working hours give employees some choice in daily work hours.

focused cost leadership strategy A focused cost leadership strategy seeks the lowest costs of operations within a special market segment.

focused differentiation strategy A focused differentiation strategy offers a unique product to a special market segment.

force-coercion strategy A force-coercion strategy pursues change through formal authority and/or the use of rewards or punishments.

forecasting Forecasting attempts to predict the future.

Foreign Corrupt Practices Act The Foreign Corrupt Practices Act makes it illegal for U.S. firms and their representatives to engage in corrupt practices overseas.

foreign subsidiary A foreign subsidiary is a local operation completely owned by a foreign firm.

formal structure Formal structure is the official structure of the organization.

formal team A formal team is officially recognized and supported by the organization.

framing error Framing error is solving a problem in the context perceived.

franchising In franchising, a firm pays a fee for rights to use another company's name and operating methods.

free-agent economy In a free-agent economy people change jobs more often, and many work on independent contracts with a shifting mix of employers.

fringe benefits Fringe benefits are nonmonetary forms of compensation such as health insurance and retirement plans.

functional chimneys, or functional silos, problem The functional chimneys, or functional silos, problem is a lack of communication and coordination across functions.

functional plan A functional plan identifies how different parts of an enterprise will contribute to accomplishing strategic plans.

functional strategy A functional strategy guides activities within one specific area of operations.

functional structure A functional structure groups together people with similar skills who perform similar tasks.

fundamental attribution error The fundamental attribution error overestimates internal factors and underestimates external factors as influences on someone's behavior.

G

gain sharing Gain sharing allows employees to share in cost savings or productivity gains realized by their efforts.

Gantt chart A Gantt chart graphically displays the scheduling of tasks required to complete a project.

gender similarities hypothesis The gender similarities hypothesis holds that males and females have similar psychological makeups.

gender subcultures Gender subcultures form among people of the same gender.

general partnership In a general partnership, owners share management responsibilities.

generational subcultures Generational subcultures form among people in similar age groups.

geographical structure A geographical structure brings together people and jobs performed in the same location.

glass ceiling effect The glass ceiling effect is an invisible barrier limiting career advancement of women and minorities.

glass ceiling The glass ceiling is a hidden barrier to the advancement of women and minorities.

global corporation or multinational corporation (MNC) A global corporation or multinational corporation (MNC) has extensive international business dealings in many foreign countries.

global economy In the global economy, resources, markets, and competition are worldwide in scope.

global manager A global manager is culturally aware and informed on international affairs.

global sourcing In global sourcing, firms purchase materials or services around the world for local use.

global strategic alliance In a global strategic alliance, each partner hopes to achieve through cooperation things they couldn't do alone.

globalization gap The globalization gap involves large global firms gaining disproportionately from the global economy versus smaller firms and many countries.

globalization Globalization is the worldwide interdependence of resource flows, product markets, and business competition.

globalization strategy A globalization strategy adopts standardized products and advertising for use worldwide.

governance Governance is oversight of top management by a board of directors or board of trustees.

graphic rating scale A graphic rating scale uses a checklist of traits or characteristics to evaluate performance.

green innovation or sustainable innovation Green innovation or sustainable innovation reduces the carbon footprint of an organization or its products.

greenfield venture A greenfield venture establishes a foreign subsidiary by building an entirely new operation in a foreign country.

group decision A group decision is made by group members themselves.

groupthink Groupthink is a tendency for highly cohesive teams to lose their evaluative capabilities.

growth needs Growth needs are desires for continued psychological growth and development.

growth strategy A growth strategy involves expansion of the organization's current operations.

H

halo effect A halo effect uses one attribute to develop an overall impression of a person or situation.

Hawthorne effect The Hawthorne effect is the tendency of persons singled out for special attention to perform as expected.

hierarchy of objectives In a hierarchy of objectives, lower-level objectives help to accomplish higher-level ones.

high-context cultures High-context cultures rely on nonverbal and situational cues as well as spoken or written words in communication.

higher-order needs Higher-order needs are esteem and self-actualization needs in Maslow's hierarchy.

high-performance organization A high-performance organization consistently achieves excellence while creating a high-quality work environment.

human capital Human capital is the economic value of people with job-relevant abilities, knowledge, ideas, energies, and commitments.

human relations A human relations leader emphasizes people over tasks.

human resource management (HRM) Human resource management (HRM) is the process of attracting, developing, and maintaining a high-quality workforce.

human skill A human skill is the ability to work well in cooperation with other people.

hygiene factor A hygiene factor is found in the job context, such as working conditions, interpersonal relations, organizational policies, and salary.

I

immoral manager An immoral manager chooses to behave unethically.

importing Importing is the process of acquiring products abroad and selling them in domestic markets.

impression management Impression management tries to create desired perceptions in the eyes of others.

improvement objectives Improvement objectives document intentions to improve performance in a specific way.

inclusivity Inclusivity is how open the organization is to anyone who can perform a job.

incremental change Incremental change bends and adjusts existing ways to improve performance.

independent contractors Independent contractors are hired on temporary contracts and are not part of the organization's permanent workforce.

individualism view In the individualism view, ethical behavior advances long-term self-interests.

individualism-collectivism Individualism-collectivism is the degree to which a society emphasizes individuals and their self-interests.

informal group An informal group is unofficial and emerges from relationships and shared interests among members.

informal structure The informal structure is the set of unofficial relationships among an organization's members.

information competency Information competency is the ability to gather and use information to solve problems.

initial public offering (IPO) An initial public offering (IPO) is an initial selling of shares of stock to the public at large.

innovation Innovation is the process of taking a new idea and putting it into practice.

input standard An input standard measures work efforts that go into a performance task.

insourcing Insourcing is the creation of domestic jobs by foreign employers.

instrumental values Instrumental values are preferences regarding the means to desired ends.

instrumentality Instrumentality is a person's belief that various outcomes will occur as a result of task performance.

integrity Integrity in leadership is honesty, credibility, and consistency in putting values into action.

intellectual capital Intellectual capital is the collective brainpower or shared knowledge of a workforce.

interactional justice Interactional justice is the degree to which others are treated with dignity and respect.

interactive leadership Interactive leadership is strong on communication, participation, and dealing with problems by teamwork.

internal control, or self-control Internal control, or self-control, occurs as people exercise self-discipline in fulfilling job expectations.

international business An international business conducts commercial transactions across national boundaries.

intrapreneurs Intrapreneurs display entrepreneurial behavior as employees of larger firms.

intuitive thinking Intuitive thinking approaches problems in a flexible and spontaneous fashion.

inventory control Inventory control ensures that inventory is only big enough to meet immediate needs.

ISO 14001 ISO 14001 is a global quality standard that certifies organizations that set environmental objectives and targets, account for the environmental impact of their activities, and continuously improve environmental performance.

J

job burnout Job burnout is physical and mental exhaustion from work stress.

job design Job design is the allocation of specific work tasks to individuals and groups.

job discrimination Job discrimination occurs when someone is denied a job or job assignment for non-job-relevant reasons.

job enrichment Job enrichment increases job content by adding work planning and evaluating duties normally performed by the supervisor.

job migration Job migration occurs when global outsourcing shifts from one country to another.

job satisfaction Job satisfaction is the degree to which an individual feels positive about a job and work experience.

job sharing Job sharing splits one job between two people.

joint venture A joint venture operates in a foreign country through co-ownership with local partners.

justice view In the justice view, ethical behavior treats people impartially and fairly.

Just-in-time scheduling (JIT) Just-in-time scheduling (JIT) routes materials to workstations just in time for use.

K

knowledge workers Knowledge workers add value to organizations through their intellectual capabilities.

L

labor contract A labor contract is a formal agreement between a union and an employer about the terms of work for union members.

labor union A labor union is an organization that deals with employers on the workers' collective behalf.

lack-of-participation error Lack-of-participation error is failure to include the right people in the decision-making process.

laissez-faire leader A laissez-faire leader is disengaged, showing low task and people concerns.

law of contingent reinforcement Law of contingent reinforcement—deliver the reward only when desired behavior occurs.

law of effect The law of effect states that behavior followed by pleasant consequences is likely to be repeated; behavior followed by unpleasant consequences is not.

law of immediate reinforcement Law of immediate reinforcement—deliver the reward as soon as possible after the desired behavior occurs.

leadership Leadership is the process of inspiring others to work hard to accomplish important tasks.

leadership style Leadership style is the recurring pattern of behaviors exhibited by a leader.

leading Leading is the process of arousing enthusiasm and inspiring efforts to achieve goals.

legitimate power Legitimate power achieves influence by formal authority.

licensing In licensing, one firm pays a fee for rights to make or sell another company's products.

lifelong learning Lifelong learning is continuous learning from daily experiences.

limited liability corporation (LLC) A limited liability corporation (LLC) combines the advantages of the sole proprietorship, partnership, and corporation.

limited partnership A limited partnership consists of a general partner who manages the business and one or more limited partners.

liquidation Liquidation occurs when a business closes and sells its assets to pay creditors.

locus of control Locus of control is the extent to which one believes what happens is within one's control.

long-range plans Long-range plans usually cover three years or more.

low-context cultures Low-context cultures emphasize communication via spoken or written words.

lower-order needs Lower-order needs are physiological, safety, and social needs in Maslow's hierarchy.

M

machiavellianism Machiavellianism is the degree to which someone uses power manipulatively.

maintenance activity A maintenance activity is an action taken by a team member that supports the emotional life of the group.

management by exception Management by exception focuses attention on differences between actual and desired performance.

management process The management process is planning, organizing, leading, and controlling the use of resources to accomplish performance goals.

management science and **operational research** Management science and operational research apply mathematical techniques to solve management problems.

manager A manager is a person who supports and is responsible for the work of others.

managing by objectives Managing by objectives is a process of joint objective setting between a superior and a subordinate.

managing diversity Managing diversity is building an inclusive work environment that allows everyone to reach his or her potential.

market control Market control is essentially the influence of market competition on the behavior of organizations and their members.

masculinity-femininity Masculinity-femininity is the degree to which a society values assertiveness and materialism.

matrix structure A matrix structure combines functional and divisional approaches to emphasize project or program teams.

MBWA Managers using MBWA spend time out of their offices, meeting and talking with workers at all levels.

mechanistic designs Mechanistic designs are bureaucratic, using a centralized and vertical structure.

membership composition Membership composition is the mix of abilities, skills, backgrounds, and experiences among team members.

mentoring Mentoring assigns early-career employees as protégés to more senior ones.

merit pay Merit pay awards pay increases in proportion to performance contributions.

middle managers Middle managers oversee the work of large departments or divisions.

mission The mission is the organization's reason for existence in society.

mixed message A mixed message results when words communicate one message while actions, body language, or appearance communicate something else.

monochronic In monochronic cultures people tend to do one thing at a time.

mood contagion Mood contagion is the spillover of one's positive or negative moods onto others.

moods Moods are generalized positive and negative feelings or states of mind.

moral absolutism Moral absolutism suggests ethical standards apply universally across all cultures.

moral leadership Moral leadership has integrity and appears to others as "good" or "right" by ethical standards.

moral manager A moral manager makes ethical behavior a personal goal.

moral rights view In the moral rights view, ethical behavior respects and protects fundamental rights.

most favored nation status Most favored nation status gives a trading partner the most favorable treatment for imports and exports.

motion study Motion study is the science of reducing a job or task to its basic physical motions.

motivation Motivation accounts for the level, direction, and persistence of effort expended at work.

multicultural organization A multicultural organization is based on pluralism and operates with inclusivity and respect for diversity.

multiperson comparison A multiperson comparison compares one person's performance with that of others.

N

necessity-based entrepreneurship Necessity-based entrepreneurship occurs when people start new ventures because they have few or no other employment options.

need A need is a physiological or psychological deficiency that a person wants to satisfy.

need for achievement Need for achievement is the desire to do something better, to solve problems, or to master complex tasks.

need for affiliation Need for affiliation is the desire to establish and maintain good relations with people.

need for power Need for power is the desire to control, influence, or be responsible for other people.

negative reinforcement Negative reinforcement strengthens a behavior by making the avoidance of an undesirable consequence contingent on its occurrence.

network structure A network structure uses IT to link with networks of outside suppliers and service contractors.

networking Networking involves building and maintaining positive relationships with other people.

noise Noise is anything that interferes with the communication process.

nonprogrammed decision A nonprogrammed decision applies a specific solution that has been crafted to address a unique problem.

nontariff barriers Nontariff barriers are nontax policies that governments enact to discourage imports, such as quotas and import restrictions.

nonverbal communication Nonverbal communication takes place through gestures, expressions, posture, and even use of interpersonal space.

norm A norm is a behavior, rule, or standard expected to be followed by team members.

O

objectives Objectives are specific results that one wishes to achieve.

observable culture The observable culture is what you see and hear when walking around an organization.

occupational subcultures Occupational subcultures form among people doing the same kinds of work.

open-book management In open-book management managers provide employees with essential financial information about their employers.

open system An open system transforms resource inputs from the environment into product outputs.

operant conditioning Operant conditioning is the control of behavior by manipulating its consequences.

operating objectives Operating objectives are specific results that organizations try to accomplish.

operational plan or **tactical plan** An operational plan or tactical plan sets out ways to implement a strategic plan.

operations management Operations management is the study of how organizations produce goods and services.

optimizing decision An optimizing decision chooses the alternative providing the absolute best solution to a problem.

organic designs Organic designs are adaptive, using a decentralized and horizontal structure.

organization chart An organization chart describes the arrangement of work positions within an organization.

organization structure Organization structure is a system of tasks, reporting relationships, and communication linkages.

organizational citizenship behaviors Organizational citizenship behaviors are things people do to go the extra mile in their work.

organizational culture Organizational culture is a system of shared beliefs and values guiding behavior.

organizational design Organizational design is the process of configuring organizations to meet environmental challenges.

organizational subcultures Organizational subcultures are groupings of people based on shared demographic and job identities.

organizing Organizing is the process of assigning tasks, allocating resources, and coordinating work activities.

orientation Orientation familiarizes new employees with jobs, co-workers, and organizational policies and services.

output standard An output standard measures performance results in terms of quantity, quality, cost, or time.

outsourcing Outsourcing shifts local jobs to foreign locations to take advantage of lower-wage labor in other countries.

P

participatory planning Participatory planning includes the persons who will be affected by plans and/or who will be asked to implement them.

partnership A partnership is when two or more people agree to contribute resources to start and operate a business together.

pay discrimination Pay discrimination occurs when men and women are paid differently for doing equal work.

perceived negative inequity Perceived negative inequity is discomfort felt over being harmed by unfair treatment.

perceived positive inequity Perceived positive inequity is discomfort felt over benefitting from unfair treatment.

perception Perception is the process through which people receive and interpret information from the environment.

performance appraisal Performance appraisal is the process of formally evaluating performance and providing feedback to a job holder.

performance norm The performance norm defines the effort and performance contributions expected of team members.

performance opportunity A performance opportunity is a situation that offers the possibility of a better future if the right steps are taken.

performance threat A performance threat is a situation where something is wrong or likely to be wrong.

personal development objectives Personal development objectives document intentions to accomplish personal growth, such as expanded job knowledge or skills.

personal wellness Personal wellness is the pursuit of a personal health-promotion program.

personality Personality is the profile of characteristics making a person unique from others.

person-organization fit Person-organization fit is the match of individual values, interests, and behavior with the organizational culture.

persuasive communication Persuasive communication presents a message in a manner that causes others to accept and support it.

plan A plan is a statement of intended means for accomplishing objectives.

planning Planning is the process of setting performance objectives and determining how to accomplish them.

policy A policy is a standing plan that communicates broad guidelines for decisions and action.

political risk Political risk is possible loss because of instability and political changes in foreign countries.

political-risk analysis Political-risk analysis forecasts how political events may impact foreign investments.

polychronic cultures In polychronic cultures people accomplish many different things at once.

positive reinforcement Positive reinforcement strengthens a behavior by making a desirable consequence contingent on its occurrence.

power distance Power distance is the degree to which a society accepts unequal distribution of power.

power Power is the ability to get someone else to do something you want done.

pregnancy discrimination Pregnancy discrimination penalizes a woman in a job or as a job applicant for being pregnant.

prejudice Prejudice is the display of negative, irrational attitudes toward women or minorities.

problem solving Problem solving involves identifying and taking action to resolve problems.

procedural justice Procedural justice focuses on the fair application of policies and rules.

procedure A procedure or rule precisely describes actions to take in specific situations.

process innovations Process innovations result in better ways of doing things.

product innovations Product innovations result in new or improved goods or services.

product structure A product structure groups together people and jobs working on a single product or service.

profit sharing Profit sharing distributes to employees a proportion of net profits earned by the organization.

programmed decision A programmed decision applies a solution from past experience to a routine problem.

progression principle Maslow's progression principle is that a need at any level becomes activated only after the next-lower-level need is satisfied.

project management Project management makes sure that activities required to complete a project are planned well and accomplished on time.

project team or **task force** A project team or task force is convened for a specific purpose and disbands after completing its task.

projection Projection assigns personal attributes to other individuals.

projects Projects are one-time activities with many component tasks that must be completed in proper order and according to budget.

protectionism Protectionism is a call for tariffs and favorable treatments to protect domestic firms from foreign competition.

proxemics Proxemics is the study of the way we use space.

punishment Punishment discourages a behavior by making an unpleasant consequence contingent on its occurrence.

Q

quality circle A quality circle is a team of employees who meet periodically to discuss ways of improving work quality.

quality of work life Quality of work life is the overall quality of human experiences in the workplace.

R

rational persuasion strategy A rational persuasion strategy pursues change through empirical data and rational argument.

realistic job previews Realistic job previews provide job candidates with all pertinent information about a job and organization.

recruitment Recruitment is a set of activities designed to attract a qualified pool of job applicants.

referent power Referent power achieves influence by personal identification.

refreezing Refreezing is the phase at which change is stabilized.

relatedness needs Relatedness needs are desires for satisfying interpersonal relationships.

reliability Reliability means that a selection device gives consistent results over repeated measures.

representativeness heuristic The representativeness heuristic assesses the likelihood of an occurrence using a stereotyped set of similar events.

restricted communication network Subgroups in a restricted communication network contest one anothers' positions and restrict interactions with one another.

restructuring Restructuring reduces the scale or mix of operations.

retrenchment strategy A retrenchment strategy changes operations to correct weaknesses.

reverse innovation Reverse innovation recognizes the potential for valuable innovations to be launched from lower organizational levels and diverse locations, including emerging markets.

reverse mentoring In reverse mentoring, younger and newly hired employees mentor senior executives, often on the latest developments with digital technologies.

reward power Reward power achieves influence by offering something of value.

risk environment A risk environment lacks complete information but offers probabilities of the likely outcomes for possible action alternatives.

S

satisficing decision A satisficing decision chooses the first satisfactory alternative that presents itself.

satisfier factor A satisfier factor is found in job content, such as a sense of achievement, recognition, responsibility, advancement, or personal growth.

scalar chain principle The scalar chain principle states that organizations should operate with clear and unbroken lines of communication top to bottom.

scenario planning Scenario planning identifies alternative future scenarios and makes plans to deal with each.

scientific management Scientific management emphasizes careful selection and training of workers and supervisory support.

selection Selection is choosing whom to hire from a pool of qualified job applicants.

selective perception Selective perception focuses attention on things consistent with existing beliefs, needs, actions.

self-efficacy Self-efficacy is a person's belief that they are capable of performing a task.

self-fulfilling prophecy A self-fulfilling prophecy occurs when a person acts in ways that confirm another's expectations.

self-management Self-management is the ability to understand oneself, exercise initiative, accept responsibility, and learn from experience.

self-managing team Members of a self-managing team have the authority to make decisions about how they share and complete their work.

self-monitoring Self-monitoring is the degree to which someone is able to adjust behavior in response to external factors.

self-serving bias Self-serving bias underestimates internal factors and overestimates external factors as influences on someone's behavior.

servant leadership Servant leadership means serving others and helping them use their talents to help organizations best serve society.

shamrock organization A shamrock organization operates with a core group of full-time long-term workers supported by others who work on contracts and part time.

shaping Shaping is positive reinforcement of successive approximations to the desired behavior.

shared power strategy A shared power strategy pursues change by participation in assessing change needs, values, and goals.

short-range plans Short-range plans usually cover a year or less.

Six Sigma Six Sigma is a quality standard of 3.4 defects or less per million products or service deliveries.

skunkworks Skunkworks are special creative units set free from the normal structure for the purpose of innovation.

small business A small business has fewer than 500 employees, is independently owned and operated, and does not dominate its industry.

Small Business Development Centers Small Business Development Centers offer guidance to entrepreneurs and small business owners on how to set up and manage business operations.

social business A social business is one in which the underlying business model directly addresses a social problem.

social capital Social capital is the capacity to attract support and help from others in order to get things done.

social entrepreneurs Social entrepreneurs take business risks to find novel ways to solve pressing social problems.

social innovation Social innovation is business innovation driven by a social conscience.

social loafing Social loafing is the tendency of some people to avoid responsibility by free-riding in groups.

social media strategy A social media strategy uses social media to better engage with an organization's customers, clients, and external audiences in general.

social network analysis Social network analysis identifies the informal structures and their embedded social relationships that are active in an organization.

social responsibility audit A social responsibility audit measures and reports on an organization's performance in various areas of corporate social responsibility.

socialization Socialization is the process through which new members learn the culture of an organization.

socioeconomic view of CSR The socioeconomic view of CSR is that business should focus on contributions to society, not just on making profits.

sole proprietorship A sole proprietorship is an individual pursuing business for a profit.

span of control Span of control is the number of persons directly reporting to a manager.

spotlight questions Spotlight questions highlight the risks of public disclosure of one's actions.

stakeholders Stakeholders are people and institutions most directly affected by an organization's performance.

stereotype A stereotype assigns attributes commonly associated with a group to an individual.

stock options Stock options give the right to purchase shares at a fixed price in the future.

strategic alliance In a strategic alliance, organizations join together in partnership to pursue an area of mutual interest.

strategic control Strategic control makes sure strategies are well implemented and that poor strategies are scrapped or changed.

strategic formulation Strategic formulation is the process of creating strategies.

strategic human resource management Strategic human resource management mobilizes human capital to implement organizational strategies.

strategic intent Strategic intent focuses organizational energies on achieving a compelling goal.

strategic leadership Strategic leadership inspires people to implement organizational strategies.

strategic management Strategic management is the process of formulating and implementing strategies.

strategic plan A strategic plan identifies long-term directions for the organization.

strategy A strategy is a comprehensive plan guiding resource allocation to achieve long-term organization goals.

strategy implementation Strategy implementation is the process of putting strategies into action.

stress Stress is a state of tension experienced by individuals facing extraordinary demands, constraints, or opportunities.

stretch goals Stretch goals are performance targets that we have to work extra hard and stretch to reach.

strong cultures Strong cultures are clear, well defined, and widely shared among members.

substantive conflict Substantive conflict involves disagreements over goals, resources, rewards, policies, procedures, and job assignments.

substitutes for leadership Substitutes for leadership are factors in the work setting that direct work efforts without the involvement of a leader.

subsystem A subsystem is a smaller component of a larger system.

succession plan A succession plan describes how the leadership transition and related financial matters will be handled.

succession problem The succession problem is the issue of who will run the business when the current head leaves.

sustainability Sustainability is a goal that addresses the rights of present and future generations as co-stakeholders of present day natural resources.

sustainable business Sustainable business is where firms operate in ways that both meet the needs of customers and protect or advance the well-being of our natural environment.

sustainable competitive advantage A sustainable competitive advantage is achieved in ways that are difficult to imitate.

sustainable development Sustainable development is making use of natural resources to meet today's needs while also preserving and protecting the environment for use by future generations.

sweatshops Sweatshops employ workers at very low wages, for long hours, and in poor working conditions.

SWOT analysis A SWOT analysis examines organizational strengths and weaknesses, as well as environmental opportunities and threats.

symbolic leader A symbolic leader uses language and symbols and actions to establish and maintain a desired organizational culture.

synergy Synergy is the creation of a whole greater than the sum of its individual parts.

systematic thinking Systematic thinking approaches problems in a rational and analytical fashion.

T

tariffs Tariffs are taxes governments levy on imports from abroad.

task activity A task activity is an action taken by a team member that directly contributes to the group's performance purpose.

team A team is a collection of people who regularly interact to pursue common goals.

team building Team building involves activities to gather and analyze data on a team and make changes to increase its effectiveness.

team process Team process is the way team members work together to accomplish tasks.

team structure A team structure uses permanent and temporary cross-functional teams to improve lateral relations.

teamwork Teamwork is the process of people actively working together to accomplish common goals.

technical skill A technical skill is the ability to use expertise to perform a task with proficiency.

telecommuting Telecommuting involves using IT to work at home or outside the office.

terminal values Terminal values are preferences about desired end states.

theory X Theory X assumes people dislike work, lack ambition, are irresponsible, and prefer to be led.

theory Y Theory Y assumes people are willing to work, accept responsibility, are self-directed, and are creative.

time orientation Time orientation is the degree to which a society emphasizes short-term or long-term goals.

top managers Top managers guide the performance of the organization as a whole or of one of its major parts.

total quality management (TQM) Total quality management (TQM) commits to quality objectives, continuous improvement, and doing things right the first time.

transactional leadership Transactional leadership directs the efforts of others through tasks, rewards, and structures.

transformational change Transformational change results in a major and comprehensive redirection of the organization.

transformational leadership Transformational leadership is inspirational and arouses extraordinary effort and performance.

transnational corporation A transnational corporation is an MNC that operates worldwide on a borderless basis.

transnational firm A transnational firm tries to operate globally without having a strong national identity.

triple bottom line The triple bottom line of organizational performance includes financial, social, and environmental criteria.

two-tier wage systems Two-tier wage systems pay new hires less than workers already doing the same jobs with more seniority.

Type A personality A Type A personality is oriented toward extreme achievement, impatience, and perfectionism.

U

uncertain environment An uncertain environment lacks so much information that it is difficult to assign probabilities to the likely outcomes of alternatives.

uncertainty avoidance Uncertainty avoidance is the degree to which a society tolerates risk and uncertainty.

unfreezing Unfreezing is the phase during which a situation is prepared for change.

unity of command principle The unity of command principle states that a worker should receive orders from only one boss.

upside-down pyramid The upside-down pyramid view puts customers at the top of the organization being served by workers who are supported by managers below them.

utilitarian view In the utilitarian view, ethical behavior delivers the greatest good to the most people.

V

valence Valence is the value a person assigns to work-related outcomes.

validity Validity means that scores on a selection device have demonstrated links with future job performance.

value-based management Value-based management actively develops, communicates, and enacts shared values.

values Values are broad beliefs about what is appropriate behavior.

venture capitalists Venture capitalists make large investments in new ventures in return for an equity stake in the business.

vertical integration Growth through vertical integration occurs by acquiring suppliers or distributors.

virtual organization A virtual organization uses information technologies to operate as a shifting network of alliances.

virtual team Members of a virtual team work together and solve problems through computer-based interactions.

virtuous circle A virtuous circle exists when corporate social responsibility leads to improved financial performance that leads to more social responsibility.

vision A vision clarifies the purpose of the organization and expresses what it hopes to be in the future.

visionary leadership Visionary leadership brings to the situation a clear sense of the future and an understanding of how to get there.

W

whistleblowers Whistleblowers expose misconduct of organizations and their members.

withdrawal behaviors Withdrawal behaviors include absenteeism (not showing up for work) and turnover (quitting one's job).

work sampling Work sampling evaluates applicants as they perform actual work tasks.

workforce diversity Workforce diversity describes differences among workers in gender, race, age, ethnicity, religion, sexual orientation, and able-bodiedness.

work-life balance Work-life balance involves balancing career demands with personal and family needs.

workplace privacy Workplace privacy is the right to privacy while at work.

workplace rage Workplace rage is aggressive behavior toward co-workers or the work setting.

workplace spirituality Workplace spirituality involves practices that create meaning and shared community among organizational members.

World Trade Organization (WTO) The World Trade Organization (WTO) is a global institution established to promote free trade and open markets around the world.

Z

zero-based budget A zero-based budget allocates resources as if each budget was brand new.

Endnotes

Feature Notes 1

Slumdog Millionaire—Information and quotes from Manohla Dargis, "Orphan's Lifeline Out of Hell Could Be a Game Show in Mumbai," *New York Times* (November 12, 2008): movies.nytimes.com; and James Christopher, "Slumdog Millionaire," *The Times* (January 8, 2009): entertainment.timesonline.co.uk.

Role Models—Information and quotes from William M. Bulkeley, "Xerox Names Burns Chief as Mulcahy Retires Early," *Wall Street Journal* (May 22, 2009), pp. B1, B2; and Nanette Byrnes and Roger O. Crockett, "An Historic Succession at Xerox," *Business Week* (June 9, 2008), pp. 18–21.

Ethics Check—Based on incident reported in "FBI Nabs 3 over Coca-Cola Secrets," cnn.com (retrieved July 6, 2006); Betsy McKay, "Coke Employee Faces Charges in Plot to Sell Secrets," *Wall Street Journal* (July 6, 2006), p. B1; and "Man Gets Two Years in Coke Secrets Case," *Wall Street Journal* (June 7, 2007), p. A12. *For your information, here is the rest of the story:* After receiving a similar call, Pepsi executives contacted the FBI. A sting netted three former Coke employees. Coke's CEO thanked his Pepsi rivals for helping fight off "this attack" on its secret. Pepsi replied: "We did what any responsible company would do. Competition can be fierce, but it must also be fair and legal."

Facts to Consider—Information from "The View from the Kitchen Table," *Newsweek* (January 26, 2009), p. 29; and Del Jones, "Women Slowly Gain on Men," *USA Today* (January 2, 2009), p. 6B; Catalyst research reports at www.Catalyst.org; "Nicking the Glass Ceiling," *Business Week* (June 9, 2009), p. 18; Francesco Guerrera and Alan Rappeport, "Women Still to Break Through 'Glass Ceiling' in U.S. Boardroom," *Financial Times*, Kindle Edition (October 19, 2010); "Women on Wall Street Fall Further Behind," *Bloomberg Business Week* (October 11–17, 2010), pp. 46–47.

Endnotes 1

[1] See examples in Carol Hymowitz, "As Managers Climb, They Have to Learn How to Act the Parts," *Wall Street Journal* (November 14, 2005), p. B1.

[2] Information from *Wall Street Journal* (September 21, 2005), p. R4.

[3] For a perspective on the first-line manager's job, see Leonard A. Schlesinger and Janice A. Klein, "The First-Line Supervisor: Past, Present and Future," pp. 370–82, in Jay W. Lorsch (ed.), *Handbook of Organizational Behavior* (Englewood Cliffs, NJ: Prentice-Hall, 1987). Research reported in "Remember Us?" *Economist* (February 1, 1992), p. 71.

[4] For a discussion, see Marcus Buckingham, "What Great Managers Do," *Harvard Business Review* (March 2005). Reprint R0503D.

[5] Ellen Byron, "P&G's Lafley Sees CEOs as Link to World," *Wall Street Journal* (March 23, 2009), p. B6; and Stefan Stern, "What Exactly Are Chief Executives For?" *Financial Times* (May 15, 2009).

[6] Ibid.

[7] John A. Byrne, "Letter from the Editor," *Fast Company* (April 2005), p. 14. Note: When Bloomberg bought *Business Week* in 2009, Byrnes left shortly after to start his own digital media company.

[8] Stewart D. Friedman, Perry Christensen, and Jessica De Groot, "Work and Life: The End of the Zero-Sum Game," *Harvard Business Review* (November/December 1998), pp. 119–29.

[9] Alan M. Webber, "Danger: Toxic Company," *Fast Company* (November 1998), pp. 15–21.

[10] See George Anders, "Overseeing More Employees—With Fewer Managers," *Wall Street Journal* (March 24, 2008), p. B6; and "Women Come on Board," *Business Week* (June 15, 2009), p. 24.

[11] Henry Mintzberg, *The Nature of Managerial Work* (New York: Harper & Row, 1973, and HarperCollins, 1997), p. 60.

[12] Ibid., p. 30.

[13] See, for example, John R. Veiga and Kathleen Dechant, "Wired World Woes: www.Help," *Academy of Management Executive*, vol. 11 (August 1997), pp. 73–79.

[14] For a classic study, see Thomas A. Mahoney, Thomas H. Jerdee, and Stephen J. Carroll, "The Job(s) of Management," *Industrial Relations*, vol. 4 (February 1965), pp. 97–110.

[15] This running example is developed from information from "Accountants Have Lives, Too, You Know," *Business Week* (February 23, 1998), pp. 88–90; Silvia Ann Hewlett and Carolyn Buck Luce, "Off-Ramps and On-Ramps: Keeping Talented Women on the Road to Success," *Harvard Business Review* (March 2005), reprint R0503B; and the Ernst & Young Web site: www.Ey.com.

[16] Information on women and men leaving jobs from Hewlett and Luce, op. cit.

[17] See Mintzberg, op. cit. (1973/1997); Henry Mintzberg, "Covert Leadership: The Art of Managing Professionals," *Harvard Business Review* (November/December 1998), pp. 140–47; and Jonathan Gosling and Henry Mintzberg, "The Five Minds of a Manager," *Harvard Business Review* (November 2003), pp. 1–9.

[18] See Mintzberg, op. cit. (1973/1997); Mintzberg, op. cit. (1998); and Gosling and Mintzberg, op. cit. (2003).

[19] This incident is taken from John P. Kotter, "What Effective General Managers Really Do," *Harvard Business Review* (November/December 1982), pp. 156–57.

[20] Ibid.

[21] Robert L. Katz, "Skills of an Effective Administrator," *Harvard Business Review* (September/October 1974), p. 94.

[22] See Daniel Goleman's books *Emotional Intelligence* (New York: Bantam, 1995) and *Working with Emotional Intelligence* (New York: Bantam, 1998); and his articles "What Makes a Leader," *Harvard Business Review* (November/December 1998), pp. 93–102, and "Leadership That Makes a Difference," *Harvard Business Review* (March/April 2000), pp. 79–90, quote from p. 80.

[23] Quote from "Insuring Success for the Road," *BizEd* (March/April 2005), p. 19.

[24] Henry Mintzberg, "The Manager's Job: Folklore and Fact," *Harvard Business Review*, vol. 53 (July/August 1975), p. 61. See also Mintzberg, op. cit. (1973/1997).

[25] Kenichi Ohmae's books include *The Borderless World: Power and Strategy in the Interlinked Economy* (New York: Harper, 1989); *The End of the Nation State* (New York: Free Press, 1996); *The Invisible Continent: Four Strategic Imperatives of the New Economy* (New York: Harper, 1999), and *The Next Global Stage: Challenges and Opportunities in Our Borderless World* (Upper Saddle River, N.J.: Wharton School Publishing, 2005).

[26] This example is from Thomas Friedman, *The World Is Flat: A Brief History of the 21st Century* (New York: Farrar, Straus & Giroux, 2005), pp. 208–09.

[27] For a discussion of globalization, see Thomas L. Friedman, *The Lexus and the Olive Tree: Understanding Globalization* (New York: Bantam Doubleday Dell, 2000); John Micklethwait and Adrian Woolridge, *A Future Perfect: The Challenges and Hidden Promise of Globalization* (New York: Crown, 2000); and Alfred E. Eckes Jr. and Thomas W. Zeiler, *Globalization and the American Century* (Cambridge, UK: Cambridge University Press, 2003).

[28] Christy Lilly, "Rocky Boots CEO Explains Outsourcing," *Connections* (Ohio University College of Business, 2005), p. 6.

[29] An Internet search will turn up many news articles reporting the details of the Bernie Madoff scandal.

[30] Portions adapted from John W. Dienhart and Terry Thomas, "Ethical Leadership: A Primer on Ethical Responsibility in Management," in John R. Schermerhorn, Jr. (ed.), *Management,* 7th ed. (New York: Wiley, 2002).

[31] See Judith Burns, "Everything You Wanted to Know About Corporate Governance . . . But Didn't Know How to Ask," *Wall Street Journal* (October 27, 2003), pp. R1, R7.

[32] Daniel Akst, "Room at the Top for Improvement," *Wall Street Journal* (October 26, 2004), p. D8; and Herb Baum and Tammy King, *The Transparent Leader* (New York: HarperCollins, 2005).

[33]*Workforce 2000: Work and Workers for the 21st Century* (Indianapolis: Towers Perrin/Hudson Institute, 1987); Richard W. Judy and Carol D' Amico (eds.), *Work and Workers for the 21st Century* (Indianapolis: Hudson Institute, 1997). See Richard D. Bucher, *Diversity Consciousness: Opening Our Minds to People, Cultures, and Opportunities* (Upper Saddle River, NJ: Prentice-Hall, 2000); R. Roosevelt Thomas, "From Affirmative Action to Affirming Diversity," *Harvard Business Review* (March/April 1990), pp. 107–17; and *Beyond Race and Gender: Unleashing the Power of Your Total Workforce by Managing Diversity* (New York: AMACOM, 1992).

[34]June Kronholz, "Hispanics Gain in Census," *Wall Street Journal* (May 10, 2006), p. A6; Phillip Toledano, "Demographics: The Population Hourglass," *Fast Company* (March, 2006), p. 56; June Kronholz, "Racial Identity's Gray Area," *Wall Street Journal* (June 12, 2008), p. A10; "We're Getting Old," *Wall Street Journal* (March 26, 2009), p. D2; Les Christie, "Hispanic Population Boom Fuels Rising U.S. Diversity," *CnnMoney:* www.cnn.com; and Betsy Towner, "The New Face of 501 America," *AARP Bulletin* (June 2009), p. 31; "Los U.S.A.: Latin Population Grows Faster, Spreads Wider," *Wall Street Journal* (March 25, 2011), p. A1.

[35]Information from "Racism in Hiring Remains, Study Says," *Columbus Dispatch* (January 17, 2003), p. B2.

[36]For discussions of the glass ceiling effect, see Ann M. Morrison, Randall P. White, and Ellen Van Velso, *Breaking the Glass Ceiling* (Reading, MA: Addison-Wesley, 1987); Anne E. Weiss. *The Glass Ceiling: A Look at Women in the Workforce* (New York: Twenty First Century, 1999); and Debra E. Meyerson and Joyce K. Fletcher, "A Modest Manifesto for Shattering the Glass Ceiling," *Harvard Business Review* (January/February 2000).

[37]For background, see Taylor Cox, Jr., "The Multicultural Organization," *Academy of Management Executive,* vol. 5 (1991), pp. 34–47; and *Cultural Diversity in Organizations: Theory, Research and Practice* (San Francisco: Berrett-Koehler, 1993).

[38]See "Women Come on Board," *Business Week* (June 15, 2009), p. 24.

[39]Survey data reported in Sue Shellenbarger, "New Workplace Equalizer: Ambition," *Wall Street Journal* (March 26, 2009), p. D5.

[40]Judith B. Rosener, "Women Make Good Managers, So What?" *Business Week* (December 11, 2000), p. 24.

[41]Thomas, op. cit.

[42]*Business Week* (August 8, 1990), p. 50.

[43]See Tom Peters, "The Brand Called You," *Fast Company* (August/September 1997), p. 83.

[44]Charles Handy, *The Age of Unreason* (Cambridge, MA: Harvard Business School Press, 1990). See also Michael S. Malone, *The Future Arrived Yesterday: The Rise of the Protean Organization and What It Means for You* (New York: Crown Books, 2009).

[45]See Gareille Monaghan, "Don't Get a Job, Get a Portfolio Career," *The Sunday Times* (April 26, 2009), p. 15.

[46]Dave Ulrich, "Intellectual Capital 5 Competency 3 Commitment," *Harvard Business Review* (Winter, 1998), pp. 15–26.

[47]Max DePree's books include *Leadership Is an Art* (New York: Dell, 1990) and *Leadership Jazz* (New York: Dell, 1993). See also Herman Miller's home page at www.Hermanmiller.com.

[48]See Peter F. Drucker, *The Changing World of the Executive* (New York: T.T. Times Books, 1982), and *The Profession of Management* (Cambridge, MA: Harvard Business School Press, 1997); and Francis Horibe, *Managing Knowledge Workers: New Skills and Attitudes to Unlock the Intellectual Capital in Your Organization* (New York: Wiley, 1999).

[49]Daniel Pink, *A Whole New Mind: Moving from the Information Age to the Conceptual Age* (New York: Riverhead Books, 2005).

[50]Peters, op. cit.

Feature Notes 2

Life Is Good—Information from Leigh Buchanan, "Life Lessons, Inc." (June 6, 2006): www.inc.com/magazine; "A Fortune Coined from Cheerfulness Entrepreneurship," *Financial Times* (May 20, 2009); and www.lifeisgood.com/about.

Role Models—Information from Miguel Helft, "Yahoo's New Chief Makes Decisive Appearance," *New York Times* (January 16, 2009): www.nytimes.com; and Jessica E. Vascellaro, "Yahoo CEO Set to Install Top-Down Management," *Wall Street Journal* (February 23, 2009), p. B1; "A Question of

Management," *Wall Street Journal* (June 2, 2009), p. R4; and Kermit Pattison, "Yahoo CEO Carol Bartz: 'I'm Just a Manager'," *Fast Company* (August 11, 2010): fastcompany.com.

Ethics Check—This situation was reported in the *Columbus Dispatch* (March 8, 2006), p. D2.

Facts to Consider—Information and quotes from "Generation Gap: On Their Bosses, Millennials Happier than Boomers," *Wall Street Journal* (November 15, 2010), p. B6.

Endnotes 2

[1]A thorough review and critique of the history of management thought, including management in ancient civilizations, is provided by Daniel A. Wren, *The Evolution of Management Thought*, 4th ed. (New York: Wiley, 1993).

[2]For a timeline of 20th-century management ideas, see "75 Years of Management Ideas and Practices: 1922–1997," *Harvard Business Review*, supplement (September/October 1997).

[3]For a sample of this work, see Henry L. Gantt, *Industrial Leadership* (Easton, MD: Hive, 1921; Hive edition published in 1974); Henry C. Metcalfe and Lyndall Urwick (eds.), *Dynamic Administration: The Collected Papers of Mary Parker Follett* (New York: Harper & Brothers, 1940); James D. Mooney, *The Principles of Administration*, rev. ed. (New York: Harper & Brothers, 1947); and Lyndall Urwick, *The Elements of Administration* (New York: Harper & Brothers, 1943) and *The Golden Book of Management* (London: N. Neame, 1956).

[4]References on Taylor's work are from Frederick W. Taylor, *The Principles of Scientific Management* (New York: W. W. Norton, 1967), originally published by Harper & Brothers in 1911. See Charles W. Wrege and Amedeo G. Perroni, "Taylor's Pig-Tale: A Historical Analysis of Frederick W. Taylor's Pig Iron Experiments," *Academy of Management Journal*, vol. 17 (March 1974), pp. 6–27, for a criticism; see Edwin A. Locke, "The Ideas of Frederick W. Taylor: An Evaluation," *Academy of Management Review*, vol. 7 (1982), p. 14, for an examination of the contemporary significance of Taylor's work. See also the biography by Robert Kanigel, *The One Best Way* (New York: Viking, 1997).

[5]Frank Gilbreth, *Motion Study* (New York: Van Nostrand, 1911).

[6]For current examples see Ben Worthen, "Do You Need to Work Faster? Get a Bigger Computer Monitor," *Wall Street Journal* (March 25, 2008), p. B8; and "Plant Seeks Savings with Shot-Clock Approach," *The Messenger*, Athens, Ohio (November 15, 2009), p. A3.

[7]Kanigel, op. cit.

[8]Opening quote from A. M. Henderson and Talcott Parsons (eds. and trans.), *Max Weber: The Theory of Social Economic Organization* (New York: Free Press, 1947), p. 337.

[9] Ibid.

[10]Available in the English language as Henri Fayol, *General and Industrial Administration* [London: Pitman, 1949); subsequent discussion relies on M. B. Brodie, *Fayol on Administration* (London: Pitman, 1949).

[11]M. P. Follett, *Freedom and Coordination* (London: Management Publications Trust, 1949).

[12]Pauline Graham, *Mary Parker Follett—Prophet of Management: A Celebration of Writings from the 1920s* (Boston: Harvard Business School Press, 1995).

[13]Information from "Honesty Top Trait for Chair," *Columbus Dispatch* (January 15, 2003), p. G1.

[14]See Peter F. Drucker, "Looking Ahead: Implications of the Present," *Harvard Business Review* (September/October, 1997), pp. 18–32.

[15]The Hawthorne studies are described in detail in F. J. Roethlisberger and William J. Dickson, *Management and the Worker* (Cambridge, MA: Harvard University Press, 1966); and G. Homans, *Fatigue of Workers* (New York: Reinhold, 1941). For an interview with three of the participants in the relay-assembly test-room studies, see R. G. Greenwood, A. A. Bolton, and R. A. Greenwood, "Hawthorne a Half Century Later: 'Relay Assembly Participants Remember,'" *Journal of Management*, vol. 9 (1983), pp. 217–31.

[16]The criticisms of the Hawthorne studies are detailed in Alex Carey, "The Hawthorne Studies: A Radical Criticism," *American Sociological Review*, vol. 32 (1967), pp. 403–16; H. M. Parsons, "What Happened at Hawthorne?" *Science*, vol. 183 (1974), pp. 922–32; and B. Rice, "The Hawthorne Defect: Persistence of a Flawed Theory," *Psychology Today*, vol. 16 (1982), pp. 70–74. See also Wren, op. cit.

[17]This discussion of Maslow's theory is based on Abraham H. Maslow, *Eupsychian Management* (Homewood, IL: Richard D. Irwin, 1965); and Abraham H. Maslow, *Motivation and Personality*, 2nd ed. (New York: Harper & Row, 1970).

[18]Douglas McGregor, *The Human Side of Enterprise* (New York: McGraw-Hill, 1960).

[19]See Gary Heil, Deborah F. Stevens, and Warren G. Bennis, *Douglas McGregor on Management: Revisiting the Human Side of Enterprise* (New York: Wiley, 2000).

[20]Chris Argyris, *Personality and Organization* (New York: Harper & Row, 1957).

[21]Information on attitude survey in the federal bureaucracy from David E. Rosenbaum, "Study Ranks Homeland Security Dept. Lowest in Morale," *New York Times* (October 16, 2005), p. 17.

[22]Scott Morrison, "Google Searches for Staffing Answers," *Wall Street Journal* (May 19, 2009), p. B1.

[23]Thomas H. Davenport, Jeanne G. Harris, and Robert Morison, *Analytics at Work: Smarter Decisions, Better Results* (Cambridge, MA: Harvard Business Press, 2010).

[24]The ideas of Ludwig von Bertalanffy contributed to the emergence of this systems perspective on organizations. See his article, "The History and Status of General Systems Theory," *Academy of Management Journal*, vol. 15 (1972), pp. 407–26. This viewpoint is further developed by Daniel Katz and Robert L. Kahn in their classic book, *The Social Psychology of Organizations* (New York: Wiley, 1978). For an integrated systems view, see Lane Tracy, *The Living Organization* (New York: Quorum Books, 1994). For an overview, see W. Richard Scott, *Organizations: Rational, Natural, and Open Systems*, 4th ed. (Upper Saddle River, NJ: Prentice Hall, 1998).

[25]See discussion by Scott, op. cit., pp. 66–68.

[26]For an overview, see ibid., pp. 95–97.

[27]W. Edwards Deming, *Quality, Productivity, and Competitive Position* (Cambridge, MA: MIT Press, 1982), and Rafael Aguay, *Dr. Deming: The American Who Taught the Japanese about Quality* (New York: Free Press, 1997).

[28]See Howard S. Gitlow and Shelly J. Gitlow, *The Deming Guide to Quality and Competitive Position* (Englewood Cliffs, NJ: Prentice-Hall, 1987).

[29]See Edward E. Lawler III, Susan Albers Mohrman, and Gerald E. Ledford, Jr., *Employee Involvement and Total Quality Management: Practices and Results in Fortune 1000 Companies* (San Francisco: Jossey-Bass, 1992).

[30]See William C. Bogner, "Tom Peters on the Real World of Business" and "Robert Waterman on Being Smart and Lucky," *Academy of Management Executive*, vol. 16 (2002), pp. 40–50.

[31]See Jim Collins and Jerry I. Porras, *Built to Last* (New York: HarperCollins, 1994); and Jim Collins, *Good to Great* (New York: HarperCollins, 2001). For recent research critical of Collins's work, see Bruce G. Resnick and Timothy L. Smunt, "From Good to Great to . . .," *Academy of Management Perspectives* (November, 2008), pp. 6–12; and Bruce Niendorf and Kristine Beck, "Good to Great, or Just Good?" *Academy of Management Perspectives* (November, 2008), pp. 13–20.

[32]See Bruce G. Resnick and Timothy L. Smunt, "From Good to Great to . . ." *Academy of Management Perspectives* (November, 2008), pp. 6–12; and, "Bruce Niendorf and Kristine Beck, "Good to Great, or Just Good?" *Academy of Management Perspectives* (November, 2008), pp. 13–20.

[33]Jim Collins, *How the Mighty Fall: And Why Some Companies Never Give In* (New York: HarperCollins, 2009).

[34]Jeffrey Pfeffer and Robert I. Sutton, *Hard Facts, Dangerous Half-Truths, and Total Nonsense: Profiting from Evidence-Based Management* (Boston: Harvard Business School Press, 2006); Jeffrey Pfeffer and Robert I. Sutton, "Management Half-Truths and Nonsense," *California Management Review*, vol. 48 (2006), pp. 77–100; and Jeffrey Pfeffer and Robert I. Sutton, "Evidence-Based Management, *Harvard Business Review* (January, 2006), R0601E.

[35]Jeffrey Pfeffer, *The Human Equation: Building Profits by Putting People First* (Boston: Harvard Business School Press, 1998); and Z. Charles O'Reilly III and Jeffrey Pfeffer, *Hidden Value: How Great Companies Achieve Extraordinary Results with Ordinary People* (Boston: Harvard Business School Press, 2000).

[36]Denise M. Rousseau, "On Organizational Behavior," *BizEd* (May/June, 2008), pp. 30–31.

Feature Notes 3

Role Models—Information and quotes from stonyfieldfarms.com, notablebiographies.com, and "25 Rich Ass Greenies Who Made Their Fortune Saving the Environment," earthfirst.com (August 25, 2008).

Facts to Consider—Information from Deloitte LLP, "Leadership Counts: 2007 Deloitte & Touche USA Ethics & Workplace Survey Results," *Kiplinger Business Resource Center* (June, 2007): www.kiplinger.com

Ethics Check—Example and quote from Morice Mendoza, "How to Create a Green Supply Chain," *Financial Times*, Kindle Edition (November 11, 2010).

Whole Foods—Information and quotes from Sarah Skidmore, "Path to Health," *Columbus Dispatch* (January 7, 2010), pp. A10, A11; Stephen Moore, "The Conscience of a Capitalist," *Wall Street Journal* (October 3–4, 2009), p. A11; and "Employees First," *Time* (July 7, 2008), p. 4.

UN Global Leaders Compact—Information from Helen Jones, "CEOs Now Find That Principles and Profits Can Mix Well," *Wall Street Journal* (November 22, 2010), p. R5. *New Profit, Inc.*—Information and quotes from www.newprofit.com.

Endnotes 3

[1]See the discussion by Terry Thomas, John W. Dienhart, and John R. Schermerhorn, Jr., "Leading Toward Ethical Behavior in Business," *Academy of Management Executive*, vol. 18 (May 2004), pp. 56–66.

[2]See the discussion by Lynn Sharpe Paine, "Managing for Organizational Integrity," *Harvard Business Review* (March/April 1994), pp. 106–17.

[3]Desmond Tutu, "Do More Than Win," *Fortune* (December 30, 1991), p. 59.

[4]Ibid.

[5]For an overview, see Linda K. Trevino and Katherine A. Nelson, *Managing Business Ethics*, 3rd ed. (New York: Wiley, 2003).

[6]Information from Sue Shellenbarger, "How and Why We Lie at the Office: From Pilfered Pens to Padded Accounts," *Wall Street Journal* (March 24, 2005), p. D1.

[7]Milton Rokeach, *The Nature of Human Values* (New York: Free Press, 1973). See also W. C. Frederick and J. Weber, "The Values of Corporate Executives and Their Critics: An Empirical Description and Normative Implications," in W. C. Frederick and L. E. Preston (eds.), *Business Ethics: Research Issues and Empirical Studies* (Greenwich, CT: JAI Press, 1990).

[8]Case reported in Michelle Conlin, "Cheating—Or Postmodern Learning?" *Business Week* (May 14, 2007), p. 42.

[9]See Gerald F. Cavanagh, Dennis J. Moberg, and Manuel Velasquez, "The Ethics of Organizational Politics," *Academy of Management Review*, vol. 6 (1981), pp. 363–74; Justin G. Locknecker, Joseph A. McKinney, and Carlos W. Moore, "Egoism and Independence: Entrepreneurial Ethics," *Organizational Dynamics* (Winter 1988), pp. 64–72; and Justin G. Locknecker, Joseph A. McKinney, and Carlos W. Moore, "The Generation Gap in Business Ethics," *Business Horizons* (September/October 1989), pp. 9–14.

[10]Raymond L. Hilgert, "What Ever Happened to Ethics in Business and in Business Schools?" *The Diary of Alpha Kappa Psi* (April 1989), pp. 4–8.

[11]Jerald Greenburg, "Organizational Justice: Yesterday, Today, and Tomorrow," *Journal of Management*, vol. 16 (1990), pp. 399–432; and Mary A. Konovsky, "Understanding Procedural Justice and Its Impact on Business Organizations," *Journal of Management*, vol. 26 (2000), pp. 489–511.

[12]Interactional justice is described by Robert J. Bies, "The Predicament of Injustice: The Management of Moral Outrage," in L. L. Cummings & B. M. Staw (eds.), *Research in Organizational Behavior*, vol. 9 (Greenwich, CT: JAI Press, 1987), pp. 289–319. The example is from Carol T. Kulik & Robert L. Holbrook, "Demographics in Service Encounters: Effects of Racial and Gender Congruence on Perceived Fairness," *Social Justice Research*, vol. 13 (2000), pp. 375–402.

[13]See, for example, M. Fortin and M. R. Fellenz, 2008. Hypocrisies of Fairness: Towards a More Reflexive Ethical Base in Organizational Justice Research and Practice. *Journal of Business Ethics*, vol. 78 (2008), pp. 415–433.

[14]The United Nations Universal Declaration of Human Rights is available online at: http://www.un.org/Overview/rights.html.

[15]Robert D. Haas, "Ethics—A Global Business Challenge," *Vital Speeches of the Day* (June 1, 1996), pp. 506–9.

[16]This discussion is based on Thomas Donaldson, "Values in Tension: Ethics Away from Home," *Harvard Business Review*, vol. 74 (September/October 1996), pp. 48–62.

[17]Ibid; Thomas Donaldson and Thomas W. Dunfee, "Towards a Unified Conception of Business Ethics: Integrative Social Contracts Theory," *Academy of Management Review*, vol. 19 (1994), pp. 252–85.

[18]Developed from Donaldson, op. cit.

[19]Reported in Barbara Ley Toffler, "Tough Choices: Managers Talk Ethics," *New Management*, vol. 4 (1987), pp. 34–39. See also Barbara Ley Toffler, *Tough Choices: Managers Talk Ethics* (New York: Wiley, 1986).

[20]See discussion by Trevino and Nelson, op. cit., pp. 47–62.

[21]Information from Steven N. Brenner and Earl A. Mollander, "Is the Ethics of Business Changing?" *Harvard Business Review*, vol. 55 (January/February 1977).

[22]Deloitte LLP, "Leadership Counts: 2007 Deloitte & Touche USA Ethics & Workplace Survey Results," *Kiplinger Business Resource Center* (June, 2007): www.kiplinger.com.

[23]"Who's to Blame: Washington or Wall Street?" *Newsweek* (March 30, 2009): www.newsweek.com.

[24]This research is summarized by Archie Carroll, "Pressure May Force Ethical Hand," *BGS International Exchange* (Fall 2004), p. 5.

[25]Ibid.

[26]Ibid.

[27]Saul W. Gellerman, "Why 'Good' Managers Make Bad Ethical Choices," *Harvard Business Review*, vol. 64 (July/August, 1986), pp. 85–90.

[28]Stephen Moore, "The Conscience of a Capitalist," *Wall Street Journal* (October 3–4, 2009), p. A11.

[29]Survey results from Del Jones, "48% of Workers Admit to Unethical or Illegal Acts," *USA Today* (April 4, 1997), p. A1.

[30]Lawrence Kohlberg, *The Psychology of Moral Development: The Nature and Validity of Moral Stages (Essays in Moral Development*, Volume 2) (New York: HarperCollins, 1984). See also the discussion by Linda K. Trevino, "Moral Reasoning and Business Ethics: Implications for Research, Education, and Management, *Journal of Business Ethics*, vol. 11 (1992), pp. 445–59.

[31]See, for example, David Bielo, "MBA Programs for Social and Environmental Stewardship," *Business Ethics* (Fall 2005), pp. 22–28.

[32]Alan L. Otten, "Ethics on the Job: Companies Alert Employees to Potential Dilemmas," *Wall Street Journal* (July 14, 1986), p. 17; and "The Business Ethics Debate," *Newsweek* (May 25, 1987), p. 36.

[33]See the Josephson model for ethical decision making: www.josephsoninstitute.org.

[34]Examples from "Whistle-Blowers on Trial," *Business Week* (March 24, 1997), pp. 172–78; and "NLRB Judge Rules for Massachusetts Nurses in Whistle-Blowing Case," *American Nurse* (January/February 1998), p. 7. For a review of whistleblowing, see Marcia P. Micelli and Janet P. Near, *Blowing the Whistle* (Lexington, MA: Lexington Books, 1992); Micelli and Near, "Whistle-blowing: Reaping the Benefits," *Academy of Management Executive*, vol. 8 (August 1994), pp. 65–72; and Cynthia Cooper, *Extraordinary Circumstances* (Hoboken, NJ: Wiley, 2009).

[35]Information from Ethics Resource Center, "Major Survey of America's Workers Finds Substantial Improvements in Ethics": www.ethics.org/releases/nr_2003052l_nbes.html.

[36]Information from James A. Waters, "Catch 20.5: Mortality as an Organizational Phenomenon," *Organizational Dynamics*, vol. 6 (Spring 1978), pp. 3–15.

[37]Information from "Gifts of Gab: A Start-Up's Social Conscience Pays Off," *Business Week* (February 5, 2001), p. F38.

[38]Developed from recommendations of the Government Accountability Project reported in "Blowing the Whistle without Paying the Piper," *Business Week* (June 3, 1991): businessweek.com/archives.

[39]Archie B. Carroll, "In Search of the Moral Manager," *Business Horizons* (March/April, 2001), pp. 7–15.

[40]Kohlberg, op. cit.

[41]Information from corporate Web site: www.gapinc.com/community sourcing/vendor_conduct.htm.

[42]See Marc Gunther, "Can Factory Monitoring Ever Really Work?" *Business Ethics* (Fall 2005), p. 12.

[43]Information from corporate Web site: www.gapinc.com/community sourcing/vendor_conduct.htm.

[44]See David Vogel, *The Market for Virtue: The Potential and Limits of Corporate Social Responsibility* (Washington, D.C.: Brookings Institution Press, 2006); and Thomas et al., op. cit.

[45]For more on this notion, see Alfred A. Marcus and Adam R. Fremeth, "Green Management Matters Regardless," *Academy of Management Perspectives*, vol. 23 (August, 2009), pp. 17–26; and, Jeffrey Pfeffer, "Building Sustainable Organizations: The Human Factor," *Academy of Management Perspectives*, vol. 24 (February, 2010), pp. 34–45.

[46]Joe Biesecker, "What Today's College Graduates Want: It's Not All About Paychecks," *Central Penn Business Journal* (August 10, 2007).

[47]Sarah E. Needleman, "The Latest Office Perk: Getting Paid to Volunteer," *Wall Street Journal* (April 29, 2008), p. D1.

[48]The historical framework of this discussion is developed from Keith Davis, "The Case For and Against Business Assumption of Social Responsibility," *Academy of Management Journal* (June 1973), pp. 312–22; Keith Davis and William Frederick, *Business and Society: Management: Public Policy, Ethics*, 5th ed. (New York: McGraw-Hill, 1984). This debate is discussed by Joel Makower in *Putting Social Responsibility to Work for Your Business and the World* (New York: Simon & Schuster, 1994), pp. 28–33. See also Aneel Karnani, "The Case Against Social Responsibility," *Wall Street Journal* (August 23, 2010); www.usj.com.

[49]The Friedman quotation is from Milton Friedman, *Capitalism and Freedom* (Chicago: University of Chicago Press, 1962); the Samuelson quotation is from Paul A. Samuelson, "Love That Corporation," *Mountain Bell Magazine* (Spring 1971). Both are cited in Davis, op. cit.

[50]See James K. Glassman, "When Ethics Meet Earnings," *International Herald Tribune* (May 24–25, 2003), p. 15; Simon Zaydek, "The Path to Corporate Social Responsibility," *Harvard Business Review* (December 2004), pp. 125–32.

[51]See Makower, op. cit. (1994), pp. 71–75; Sandra A. Waddock and Samuel B. Graves, "The Corporate Social Performance–Financial Performance Link," *Strategic Management Journal* (1997), pp. 303–19: and Vogel, op. cit. (2006).

[52]Michael E. Porter and Mark R. Kramer, "Shared Value: How to Reinvent Capitalism and Unleash a Wave of Innovation and Growth," *Harvard Business Review* (January–February, 2011), pp. 62–77.

[53]Archie B. Carroll, "A Three-Dimensional Model of Corporate Performance," *Academy of Management Review*, vol. 4 (1979), pp. 497–505. Carroll's continuing work in this area is reported in Mark S. Schwartz and Archie B. Carroll, "Corporate Social Responsibility: A Three Domain Approach," *Business Ethics Quarterly*, vol. 13 (2003), pp. 503–30.

[54]See the discussion by Porter and Kramer, op. cit.

[55]Examples from Jim Phillips, "Business Leaders Say 'Green' Approach Doable," *Athens News* (March 27, 2008): www.athensnews.com; "The Bottom Line on Business and the Environment," *Wall Street Journal* (February 12, 2009), p. A7; and Alan G. Robinson and Dean M. Schroeder, "Greener and Cheaper," *Wall Street Journal* (March 23, 2009), p. R4.

[56]Information from Helen Jones, "CEOs Now Find that Principles and Profits Can Mix Well," *Wall Street Journal* (November 22, 2010), p. R5.

[57]Ibid.

[58]Ibid.

[59]Definition from www.sustainablebusiness.com.

[60]www.wbcsd.org.

[61]"Indra Nooyi of Pepsico, View from the Top," *Financial Times*: www.ft.com (February 1, 2010), retrieved March 11, 2010.

[62]"Eco-nomics—Creating Environmental Capital," *Wall Street Journal* (March 8, 2010), p. R1.

[63]From www.iso.org.

[64]Pfeffer, op cit.

[65]Abuses of micro-credit lending have been publicized in the press, and both the microfinance industry as a whole and the Grameen Bank in particular have been criticized by the Bangladesh government. Muhammad Yunus published his own criticism of the industry and defense of the Grameen Bank model in "Sacrificing Microcredit for Megaprofits," *The New York Times* (January 14, 2011): nytimes.com. A Norwegian documentary that aired criticisms of how Yunus and Grameen Bank handled funds has largely been refuted, but Yunus continues to be criticized by the Bangladesh government.

[66]David Bornstein, *How to Change the World—Social Entrepreneurs and the Power of New Ideas* (Oxford, UK: Oxford University Press, 2004).

[67]See Laura D' Andrea Tyson, "Good Works—With a Business Plan," *Business Week* (May 3, 2004), retrieved from Business Week Online (November 14, 2005) at www.Businessweek.com.

[68]Chip Fleiss, "Social Enterprise—the Fiegling Fourth Sector Soapbox," *Financial Times* (June 15, 2009).

[69]Drucker quote referenced and discussed at www.druckersociety.at/repository/newsletter/09/newsletter.html.

Feature Notes 4

Role Models—Information from Kate Klonick, "Pepsi's CEO a Refreshing Change" (August 15, 2006): www.abcnews.com; Diane Brady, "Indra Nooyi: Keeping Cool in Hot Water," *Business Week* (June 11, 2007), special report; Indra Nooyi, "The Best Advice I Ever Got," CNNMoney (April 30, 2008): www.Cnnnmoney.com; "Indra Nooyi," *Wall Street Journal* (November 10, 2008), p. R3; and "Indra Nooyi of PepsiCo," View from the Top, *Financial Times*: www.ft.com (February 1, 2010), retrieved March 11, 2010.

Ethics Check—Story reported in and quotes from *Economist* (June 17, 2006), vol. 379, issue 8482, pp. 65–66, 2p, 1c.

Facts to Consider—Information from "Six Products, Six Carbon Footprints," *Wall Street Journal* (October 6, 2008), p. R3; and, "Walmart Behind on Carbon Goal," *Environmental Reader* (April 18, 2010): www.environmentalleader.com/2011/04/18/.

Zynga—Information from Douglas MacMillan, Peter Burrows, and Spencer E. Ante, "The App Economy," *Business Week* (November 2, 2009), pp. 44–49; Kevin Casey, "Putting Your Money Where Your Mouse Is?" *The Irish Times* (August 6, 2010), p. 6; and zynga.com/about.

Endnotes 4

[1]Information and quotes from "Last Miner Out Hailed as a Shift Boss Who Kept Group Alive," news.blog.cnn.com (October 14, 2010); and Eva Bergara, "Chilean Miners Honored in Ceremony, Football Game," news.yahoo.com (October 25, 2010).

[2]Peter F. Drucker, "Looking Ahead: Implications of the Present," *Harvard Business Review* (September/October 1997), pp. 18–32. See also Shaker A. Zahra, "An Interview with Peter Drucker," *Academy of Management Executive*, vol. 17 (August 2003), pp. 9–12.

[3]For a good discussion, see Watson H. Agor, *Intuition in Organizations: Leading and Managing Productively* (Newbury Park, CA: Sage, 1989); Herbert A. Simon, "Making Management Decisions: The Role of Intuition and Emotion," *Academy of Management Executive*, vol. 1 (1987), pp. 57–64; Orlando Behling and Norman L. Eckel, "Making Sense Out of Intuition," *Academy of Management Executive*, vol. 1 (1987), pp. 57–64; Orlando Behling and Norman L. Eckel, "Making Sense Out of Intuition," *Academy of Management Executive*, vol. 5 (1991), pp. 46–54.

[4]Alan Deutschman, "Inside the Mind of Jeff Bezos," *Fast Company*, Issue 85 (August, 2004); www.fastcompany.com.

[5]Quote from Susan Carey, "Pilot 'in Shock' as He Landed Jet in River," *Wall Street Journal* (February 9, 2009), p. A6.

[6]Based on Carl Jung's typology, as described in Donald Bowen, "Learning and Problem-Solving: You're Never Too Jung," in Donald D. Bowen, Roy J. Lewicki, Donald T. Hall, and Francine S. Hall, eds., *Experiences in Management and Organizational Behavior*, 4th ed. (New York: Wiley, 1997), pp. 7–13; and John W. Slocum Jr., "Cognitive Style in Learning and Problem Solving," in ibid., pp. 349–53.

[7]See Hugh Courtney, Jane Kirkland, and Patrick Viguerie, "Strategy Under Uncertainty," *Harvard Business Review* (November/December 1997), pp. 67–79.

[8]See George P. Huber, *Managerial Decision Making* (Glenview, IL: Scott, Foresman, 1975). For a comparison, see the steps in Xerox's problem-solving process, as described in David A. Garvin, "Building a Learning Organization," *Harvard Business Review* (July/August 1993), pp. 78–91; and the Josephson model for ethical decision making described at www.josephsoninstitute.org/MED/MED-4sevensteppath.htm.

[9]Joseph B. White and Lee Hawkins Jr., "GM Cuts Deeper in North America," *Wall Street Journal* (November 22, 2005), p. A3. See also Rick Wagoner, "A Portrait of My Industry," *Wall Street Journal* (December 6, 2005), p. A20.

[10]See Herbert A. Simon, *Administrative Behavior* (New York: Free Press, 1947); James G. March and Herbert A. Simon, *Organizations* (New York: Wiley, 1958); and Herbert A. Simon, *The New Science of Management Decision* (New York: Harper, 1960).

[11]This figure and the related discussion is developed from conversations with Dr. Alma Acevedo of the University of Puerto Rico at Rio Piedras and her articles "Of Fallacies and Curricula: A Case of Business Ethics," *Teaching Business Ethics*, vol. 5 (2001), pp. 157–170; and "Business Ethics: An Introduction," working paper (2009).

[12]Based on Gerald F. Cavanagh, *American Business Values*, 4th ed. (Upper Saddle River, NJ: Prentice-Hall, 1998).

[13]The third spotlight question is based on the Josephson model for ethical decision making: www.josephsoninstitute.org/MED/MED-4sevensteppath.htm.

[14]Information from "Lonnie Johnson," *USAA Magazine* (Fall, 2007), p. 38; and www.johnsonrd.com.

[15]See, for example, Roger von Oech, *A Whack on the Side of the Head* (New York: Warner Books, 1983) and *A Kick in the Seat of the Pants* (New York: Harper & Row, 1986).

[16]Teresa M. Amabile, "Motivating Creativity in Organizations," *California Management Review*, vol. 40 (Fall, 1997), pp. 39–58.

[17]Developed from discussions by Edward DeBono, *Lateral Thinking: Creativity Step-by-Step* (New York: HarperCollins, 1970); John S. Dacey and Kathleen H. Lennon, *Understanding Creativity* (San Francisco: Jossey-Bass, 1998); and Bettina von Stamm, *Managing Innovation, Design & Creativity* (Chichester, England: Wiley, 2003).

[18]The classic work is Norman R. Maier, "Assets and Liabilities in Group Problem Solving," *Psychological Review*, vol. 74 (1967), pp. 239–49.

[19]This presentation is based on the work of R. H. Hogarth, D. Kahneman, A. Tversky, and others, as discussed in Max H. Bazerman, *Judgment in Managerial Decision Making*, 3rd ed. (New York: Wiley, 1994).

[20]Barry M. Staw, "The Escalation of Commitment to a Course of Action," *Academy of Management Review*, vol. 6 (1981), pp. 577–87; and Barry M. Staw and Jerry Ross, "Knowing When to Pull the Plug," *Harvard Business Review*, vol. 65 (March/April 1987), pp. 68–74.

[21]Quotes from Jeff Kingston, "A Crisis Made in Japan," *Wall Street Journal* (February 6–7, 2010), pp. W1, W2; and Kate Linebaugh, Dionne Searcey, and Norihiko Shirouzu, "Secretive Culture Led Toyota Astray," *Wall Street Journal* (February 10, 2010), pp. A1, A16.

[22]Ibid; and Richard Tedlow, "Toyota Was in Denial. How About You?" *Bloomberg Businessweek* (April 19, 2010), p. 76.

[23]For scholarly reviews, see Dean Tjosvold, "Effects of Crisis Orientation on Managers' Approach to Controversy in Decision Making," *Academy of Management Journal*, vol. 27 (1984), pp. 130–38; and Ian I. Mitroff, Paul Shrivastava, and Firdaus E. Udwadia, "Effective Crisis Management," *Academy of Management Executive*, vol. 1 (1987), pp. 283–92.

[24]Anna Muoio, "Where There's Smoke It Helps to Have a Smoke Jumper," *Fast Company*, vol. 33, p. 290.

Feature Notes 5

Opening photo—Quote from "Japan Widens Evacuation Zone Around Fukushima Nuclear Plant," www.dailytelegraph.com (May 15, 2011).

Role Models—Information from Julie Bennett, "Don Thompson Engineers Winning Role as McDonald's President," *Franchise Times* (February 2008): www.franchisetimes.com.

Facts to Consider—Information from Phred Dvorak, Baob Davis, and Louise Radnofsky, "Firms Confront Boss-Subordinate Love Affairs," *Wall Street Journal* (October 27, 2008), p. B5. Survey data from Society for Human Resource Management.

Zynga—Information from Douglas MacMillan, Peter Burrows, and Spencer E. Ante, "The App Economy," *BusinessWeek* (November 2, 2009), pp. 44–49; Kevin Casey, "Putting Your Money Where Your Mouse Is?" *The Irish Times* (August 6, 2010), p. 6; and, zynga.com/about.

Endnotes 5

[1]*Eaton Corporation Annual Report*, 1985.

[2]Henry Mintzberg, "The Manager's Job: Folklore and Fact," *Harvard Business Review*, vol. 53 (July/August 1975), pp. 54–67; and Henry Mintzberg, "Planning on the Left Side and Managing on the Right," *Harvard Business Review*, vol. 54 (July/August 1976), pp. 46–55.

[3]For a classic study, see Stanley Thune and Robert House, "Where Long-Range Planning Pays Off," *Business Horizons*, vol. 13 (1970), pp. 81–87. For

a critical review of the literature, see Milton Leontiades and Ahmet Teel, "Planning Perceptions and Planning Results," *Strategic Management Journal* vol. 1 (1980), pp. 65–75; and J. Scott Armstrong, "The Value of Formal Planning for Strategic Decisions," *Strategic Management Journal*, vol. 3 (1982), pp. 197–211.

For special attention to the small business setting, see Richard B. Robinson Jr., John A. Pearce II, George S. Vozikis, and Timothy S. Mescon, "The Relationship Between Stage of Development and Small Firm Planning and Performance," *Journal of Small Business Management*, vol. 22 (1984), pp. 45–52; and Christopher Orphen, "The Effects of Long–Range Planning on Small Business Performance: A Further Examination," *Journal of Small Business Management*, vol. 23 (1985), pp. 16–23. For an empirical study of large corporations, see Vasudevan Ramanujam and N. Venkatraman, "Planning and Performance: A New Look at an Old Question," *Business Horizons*, vol. 30 (1987), pp. 19–25.

[4]Quote from Stephen Covey and Roger Merrill, "New Ways to Get Organized at Work," *USA Weekend* (February 6/8, 1998), p. 18. Books by Stephen R. Covey include: *The 7 Habits of Highly Effective People: Powerful Lessons in Personal Change* (New York: Fireside, 1990), and Stephen R. Covey and Sandra Merril Covey, *The 7 Habits of Highly Effective Families: Building a Beautiful Family Culture in a Turbulent World* (New York: Golden Books, 1996).

[5]McDonald's Tech Turnaround," *Harvard Business Review* (November 2004), p. 128.

[6]Information from Carol Hymowitz, "Packed Calendars Rule over Executives," *Wall Street Journal* (June 16, 2008), p. B1.

[7]Quotes from *Business Week* (August 8, 1994), pp. 78–86.

[8]See William Oncken Jr. and Donald L. Wass, "Management Time: Who's Got the Monkey?" *Harvard Business Review*, vol. 52 (September/October 1974), pp. 75–80, and featured as an HBR classic, *Harvard Business Review* (November/December 1999).

[9]For more on the long term, see Danny Miller and Isabelle Le Breton-Miller, *Managing for the Long Run* (Cambridge, MA: Harvard Business School Press, 2005).

[10]See Elliot Jaques, *The Form of Time* (New York: Russak & Co., 1982). For an executive commentary on his research, see Walter Kiechel III, "How Executives Think," *Fortune* (December 21, 1987), pp. 139–44.

[11]See Henry Mintzberg, "Rounding Out the Manager's Job," *Sloan Management Review* (Fall 1994), pp. 1–25.

[12]Excerpts in sample sexual harassment policy from American Express's advice to small businesses at www.americanexpress.com (retrieved November 21, 2005).

[13]Information from "Avoiding a Time Bomb: Sexual Harassment," *Business Week*, Enterprise issue (October 13, 1997), pp. ENT20–21.

[14]Paul Glader, "GE's Immelt to Cite Lessons Learned," *Wall Street Journal* (December 15, 2009), p. B2.

[15]For a thorough review of forecasting, see J. Scott Armstrong, *Long-Range Forecasting*, 2nd ed. (New York: Wiley, 1985).

[16]Forecasts in Stay Informed from "Long-Term Forecasts on EIU Country Data and Market Indicators & Forecasts," *The Economist* Intelligence Unit, www.eiu.com (retrieved November 21, 2005).

[17]Information and quotes from Guy Chazan and Neil King, "BP's Preparedness for Major Crisis Is Questioned," *Wall Street Journal* (May 10, 2010), p. A6; and Ben Casselman and Guy Chazan, "Disaster Plans Lacing at Deep Rigs," *Wall Street Journal*, (May 18, 2010), p. A1.

[18]The scenario-planning approach is described in Peter Schwartz, *The Art of the Long View* (New York: Doubleday/Currency, 1991); and Arie de Geus, *The Living Company: Habits for Survival in a Turbulent Business Environment* (Boston, MA: Harvard Business School Press, 1997).

[19]Ibid.

[20]See, for example, Robert C. Camp, *Business Process Benchmarking* (Milwaukee: ASQ Quality Press 1994); Michael J. Spendolini, *The Benchmarking Book* (New York: AMACOM, 1992); and Christopher E. Bogan and Michael J. English, *Benchmarking for Best Practices: Winning Through Innovative Adaptation* (New York: McGraw-Hill, 1994).

[21]David Kiley, "One Ford for the Whole World," *Business Week* (June 15, 2009), pp. 58–59.

[22]See, for example, Cecile Rohwedder and Keith Johnson, "Pace-setting Zara Seeks More Speed to Fight Its Rising Cheap-Chic Rivals," *Wall Street Journal* (February 20, 2008), pp. B1, B6.

[23]"How Classy Can 7-Eleven Get?" *Business Week* (September 1, 1997), pp. 74–75; and Kellie B. Gormly, "7-Eleven Moving Up a Grade," *Columbus Dispatch* (August 3, 2000), pp. C1–C2.

[24]T. J. Rodgers, with William Taylor and Rick Foreman, "No Excuses Management," *World Executive's Digest* (May 1994), pp. 26–30.

[25]See Paul Ingrassia, "The Right Stuff," *Wall Street Journal* (April 8, 2005), p. D5.

Feature Notes 6

Opening Quote—"Toyota CEO Tells Lawmakers: I'm Deeply Sorry," Associated Press: Moneynews.com (February 24, 2010).

Chick-fil-A—Information and quotes from Daniel Yee, "Chick-fil-A Recipe Winning Customers," *Columbus Dispatch* (September 9, 2006), p. D1; Tom Murphy, "Chick-fil-A plans aggressive product rollout initiatives," *Rocky Mount Telegram* (May 28, 2008): www.rockymounttelegram.com; and "Chick-fil-A Reaches 20,000th Scholarship Milestone" (July 28, 2005), Chick-fil-A press release: www.csrwire.com.

Role Models—Information and quotes from Stacy Perman, "Scones and Social Responsibility," *Business Week* (August 21/28, 2006), p. 38; and www. dancingdeer.com.

Ethics Check—Paul Davidson, "'Climate Has Changed' for Data Privacy," *USA Today* (May 12, 2006), p. B1; Ben Elgin, "The Great Firewall of China," *Business Week* (January 23, 2006), pp. 32–34; Alison Maitland, "Skype Says Text-Messages Censored by Partner in China," *Financial Times* (April 19, 2006), p. 15; and, "Web Firms Criticized Over China," CNN.com (July 20, 2006).

Facts to Consider—Information from Sarah E. Needleman, "Businesses Say Theft by Their Workers Is Up," *Wall Street Journal* (December 11, 2008), p. B8; Michelle Conlin, "To Catch a Corporate Thief," *Business Week* (February 16, 2009), p. 52; Simona Covel, "Small Businesses Face More Fraud in Downturn," *Wall Street Journal* (February 19, 2009), p. B5; "Increase in Data Theft Outstrips Physical Loss," *Financial Times* (October 18, 2010) Kindle Edition.

Endnotes 6

[1]Toyota's problems with quality and product recalls were widely described in the news media during January/February 2010. See, for example, Sharon Terlep and Josh Mitchell, "U.S. Widens Toyota Probe to Electronics," *Wall Street Journal* (February 4, 2010), pp. B1, B12.

[2]Quote from "An Open Letter to Toyota Customers," *Columbus Dispatch* (February 4, 2010), p. A12.

[3]"The Renewal Factor: Friendly Fact, Congenial Controls," *Business Week* (September 14, 1987), p. 105.

[4]Rob Cross and Lloyd Baird, "Technology Is Not Enough: Improving Performance by Building Institutional Memory," *Sloan Management Review* (Spring 2000), p. 73.

[5]Information from Pep Sappal, "Integrated Inclusion Initiative," *Wall Street Journal* (October 3, 2006), p. A2.

[6]Example from George Anders, "Management Guru Turns Focus to Orchestras, Hospitals," *Wall Street Journal* (November 21, 2005), pp. B1, B5.

[7]Information from Leon E. Wynter, "Allstate Rates Managers on Handling Diversity," *Wall Street Journal* (October 1, 1997), p. B1.

[8]Information from Kathryn Kranhold, "U.S. Firms Raise Ethics Focus," *Wall Street Journal* (November 28, 2005), p. B4.

[9]Information from Raju Narisetti, "For IBM, a Groundbreaking Sales Chief," *Wall Street Journal* (January 19, 1998), pp. B1, B5.

[10]Based on discussion by Harold Koontz and Cyril O'Donnell, *Essentials of Management* (New York: McGraw-Hill, 1974), pp. 362–65; see also Cross and Baird, op. cit.

[11]Information from Louis Lee, "I'm Proud of What I've Made Myself Into—What I've Created," *Wall Street Journal* (August 27, 1997), pp. B1, B5; and Jim Collins, "Bigger, Better, Faster," *Fast Company*, vol. 71 (June 2003), p. 74.

[12]See Sue Shellenbarger, "If You Need to Work Better, Maybe Try Working Less," *Wall Street Journal* (September 23, 2009), p. D1.

[13]Douglas McGregor, *The Human Side of Enterprise* (New York: McGraw-Hill, 1960).

[14]This distinction is made in William G. Ouchi, "Markets, Bureaucracies and Clans," *Administrative Science Quarterly*, vol. 25 (1980), pp. 129–41.

[15]Martin LaMonica, "Wal-Mart Readies Long-Term Move into Solar Power," *CNET News.com* (January 3, 2007).

[16]See Dale D. McConkey, *How to Manage by Results*, 3rd ed. (New York: AMACOM, 1976); Stephen J. Carroll Jr. and Henry J. Tosi Jr., *Management by Objectives: Applications and Research* (New York: Macmillan, 1973); and Anthony P. Raia, *Managing by Objectives* (Glenview, IL: Scott, Foresman, 1974).

[17]For a discussion of research on MBO, see Carroll and Tosi, op. cit.; Raia, op. cit; and Steven Kerr, "Overcoming the Dysfunctions of MBO," *Management by Objectives*, vol. 5, no. 1 (1976). Information in part from Dylan Loeb McClain, "Job Forecast: Internet's Still Hot," *New York Times* (January 30, 2001), p. 9.

[18]The work on goal setting and motivation is summarized in Edwin A. Locke and Gary P. Latham, *Goal Setting: A Motivational Technique That Works!* (Englewood Cliffs, NJ: Prentice-Hall, 1984).

[19]McGregor, op. cit.

[20]The "hot stove rules" are developed from R. Bruce McAfee and William Poffenberger, *Productivity Strategies: Enhancing Employee Job Performance* (Englewood Cliffs, NJ: Prentice-Hall, 1982), pp. 54–55. They are originally attributed to Douglas McGregor, "Hot Stove Rules of Discipline," in G. Strauss and L. Sayles (eds), *Personnel: The Human Problems of Management* (Englewood Cliffs, NJ: Prentice-Hall, 1967).

[21]For basic readings on quality control, see Joseph M. Juran, *Quality Control Handbook*, 3rd ed.(New York: McGraw-Hill, 1979) and "The Quality Trilogy: A Universal Approach to Managing for Quality," in H. Costin (ed.), *Total Quality Management* (New York: Dryden, 1994); W. Edwards Deming, *Out of Crisis* (Cambridge, MA: MIT Press, 1986) and "Deming's Quality Manifesto," *Best of Business Quarterly*, vol. 12 (Winter 1990–1991), pp. 6–101; Howard S. Gitlow and Shelly J. Gitlow, *The Deming Guide to Quality and Competitive Position* (Englewood Cliffs, NJ: Prentice-Hall, 1987); and Rafael Aguay, *Dr. Deming: The American Who Taught the Japanese About Quality* (New York: Free Press, 1997).

[22]Aguay, op. cit.; W. Edwards Deming, op. cit. (1986).

[23]Ibid.

[24]"See "Downsides of Just-In-Time Inventory," *Bloomberg BusinessWeek* (March 28–April 3, 2011), pp. 17–18.

[25]Information from Karen Carney, "Successful Performance Measurement: A Checklist," *Harvard Management Update* (No. U9911B), 1999.

[26]Robert S. Kaplan and David P. Norton, "The Balanced Scorecard: Measures That Drive Performance," *Harvard Business Review* (July/August, 2005); see also Robert S. Kaplan and David P. Norton, *The Balanced Scorecard* (Cambridge, MA: Harvard Business School Press, 1996).

Feature Notes 7

Patagonia—Information and quotes from Yvon Chouinard, *Let My People Go Surfing: The Education of a Reluctant Businessman* (New York: Penguin Press HC, 2005); Steve Hamm, "A Passion for the Plan," *Business Week* (August 21/28, 2006), pp. 92–94; and www.patagonia.com/web/us/patagonia.go?assetid=2047&ln=24.

Role Models—Information and quotes from "Who's Who on Obama's New Economic Advisory Board," LA Times Blog (February 6, 2009): www.latimesblogs.latimes.com; "'Diversify' Isn't Just Smart Financial Advice," *Black MBA* (Winter, 2008/2009), p. 54; "*Black Enterprise* Announces 100 Most Powerful African Americans in Corporate America," press release (February 5, 2009): www.biz.yahoo.com/bw; and www.blackentrepreneurprofile.com/fortune-500-ceos (February 23, 2009).

Ethics Check—Life and Death at an Outsourcing Factory: Information and quotes from "Life and Death at the iPad Factory," *Bloomberg Business-Week* (June 7–13, 2010), pp. 35–36.

Facts to Consider—Information from Daniel Costello, "The Drought is Over (At Least for CEOs)," *The New York Times* (April 9, 2011); nytimes.com (accessed May 3, 2011); Joann S. Lublin, "CEO Pay in 2010 Jumped 11%," *Wall Street Journal* (May 9, 2011), p. 81; and, AFL-CIO, "2011 CEO Paywatch," http://www.aflcio.org/.

Endnotes 7

[1]Information and quotes from Marcia Stepanek, "How Fast Is Net Fast?" *Business Week E-Biz* (November 1, 1999), pp. EB52–54.

[2]Keith H. Hammond, "Michael Porter's Big Ideas," *Fast Company* (March 2001), pp. 150–56.

[3]Gary Hamel and C. K. Prahalad, "Strategic Intent," *Harvard Business Review* (May/June 1989), pp. 63–76.

[4]See "Gauging the Walmart Effect," *Wall Street Journal* (December 3–4, 2005), p. A9; and Matthew Boyle, "Walmart's Magic Moment," *Business Week* (June 15, 2009), pp. 58–59.

[5]Geoffrey A. Fowler and Nick Wingfield, "Apple's Showman Takes the Stage," *Wall Street Journal* (March 3, 2011), p. B1.

[6]Michael A. Hitt, R. Duane Ireland, and Robert E. Hoskisson, *Strategic Management: Competitiveness and Globalization* (Minneapolis: West, 1997), p. 197.

[7]See William McKinley, Carol M. Sanchez, and A. G. Schick, "Organizational Downsizing: Constraining, Cloning, Learning," *Academy of Management Executive*, vol. 9 (August 1995), pp. 32–44.

[8]Kim S. Cameron, Sara J. Freeman, and A.K. Mishra, "Best Practices in White-Collar Downsizing: Managing Contradictions," *Academy of Management Executive*, vol. 4 (August 1991), pp. 57–73.

[9]"Overheard," *Wall Street Journal* (April 16, 2009), p. C10; and Geoffrey A. Fowler and Evan Ramstad, "eBay Looks Abroad for Growth," *Wall Street Journal* (April 16, 2009), p. B2.

[10]This strategy classification is found in Hitt et al., op. cit.; the attitudes are from a discussion by Howard V. Perlmutter, "The Tortuous Evolution of the Multinational Corporation," *Columbia Journal of World Business*, vol. 4 (January/February 1969).

[11]Fowler and Ramstad, op. cit., 2009.

[12]Adam M. Brandenburger and Barry J. Nalebuff, *Co-Opetition: A Revolution Mindset that Combines Competition and Cooperation* (New York: Bantam, 1996).

[13]Jonathan Spiva, "BMW ActiveHybrid 7 Review," the dieseldriver.com (July 1, 2010).

[14]See Michael E. Porter, "Strategy and the Internet," *Harvard Business Review* (March 2001), pp. 63–78; and Michael Rappa, *Business Models on the Web* (www.ecommerce.ncsu.edu/business_models.html. February 6, 2001).

[15]See threadless.com

[16]Peter F. Drucker, *Management: Tasks, Responsibilities, Practices* (New York: Harper & Row, 1973), p. 122.

[17]See Laura Nash, "Mission Statements—Mirrors and Windows," *Harvard Business Review* (March/April 1988), pp. 155–56; James C. Collins and Jerry I. Porras, "Building Your Company's Vision," *Harvard Business Review* (September/October 1996), pp. 65–77; and James C. Collins and Jerry I. Porras, *Built to Last: Successful Habits of Visionary Companies* (New York: Harper Business, 1997).

[18]Gary Hamel, *Leading the Revolution* (Boston, MA: Harvard Business School Press, 2000), pp. 72–73.

[19]Collins and Porras, op. cit., 1996 and 1997.

[20]See Peter F. Drucker's views on organizational objectives in his classic books *The Practice of Management* (New York: Harper & Row, 1954) and *Management: Tasks, Responsibilities, Practices* (New York: Harper & Row, 1973). For a more recent commentary, see his article "Management: The Problems of Success," *Academy of Management Executive*, vol. 1 (1987), pp. 13–19.

[21]C. K. Prahalad and Gary Hamel, "The Core Competencies of the Corporation," *Harvard Business Review* (May/June 1990), pp. 79–91; see also Hitt et al., op. cit., pp. 99–103.

[22]For a discussion of Michael Porter's approach to strategic planning, see his books, *Competitive Strategy: Techniques for Analyzing Industries and Competitors* (New York: Free Press, 1980) and *Competitive Advantage: Creating and Sustaining Superior Performance* (New York: Free Press, 1986) and his article, "What Is Strategy?" *Harvard Business Review* (November/December, 1996, pp. 61–78; and Richard M. Hodgetts's interview "A Conversation with Michael E. Porter: A Significant Extension Toward Operational Improvement and Positioning," *Organizational Dynamics* (Summer 1999), pp. 24–33.

[23]See Porter, op. cit. (1980 and 1986).

[24]Information from www.polo.com.

[25]www.vanguard.com.

[26]For more on GE and Jeffrey Immelt, see "The Immelt Revolution," *Business Week* (March 28, 2005), pp. 64–73.

[27]Richard G. Hammermesh, "Making Planning Strategic," *Harvard Business Review*, vol. 64 (July/August 1986), pp. 115–20; and Richard G. Hammermesh, *Making Strategy Work* (New York: Wiley, 1986).

[28]See Gerald B. Allan, "A Note on the Boston Consulting Group Concept of Competitive Analysis and Corporate Strategy," Harvard Business School, Intercollegiate Case Clearing House, ICCH9-175-175 (Boston: Harvard Business School, June 1976).

[29]R. Duane Ireland and Michael A. Hitt, "Achieving and Maintaining Strategic Competitiveness in the 21st Century," *Academy of Management Executive,* vol. 13 (1999), pp. 43–57.

[30]www.patagonia.com/web/us/patagonia.go?assetid=3351.

[31]Hammond, op. cit.

Feature Notes 8

Build-A-Bear—Information and quotes from "Build-A-Bear Workshop, Inc., Funding Universe": www.fundinguniverse.com/company-histories/BuildABear-Workshop-Inc (accessed March 9, 2009); and www.buildabear.com. See also Maxine Clark and Amy Joyner, *The Bear Necessities of Business: Building a Company with Heart* (Hoboken, NJ: Wiley, 2007).

Role Models—Information and quotes from David Kiley, "Ford's Savior?" *Business Week* (March 16, 2009), pp. 31–34; and Alex Taylor III, "Fixing Up Ford," *Fortune* (May 14, 2009).

Facts to Consider—Information and quote from "Bosses Overestimate Their Managing Skills," *Wall Street Journal* (November 1, 2010), p. B10.

Endnotes 8

[1]Henry Mintzberg and Ludo Van der Heyden, "Organigraphs: Drawing How Companies Really Work," *Harvard Business Review* (September/October 1999), pp. 87–94.

[2]Ibid.

[3]The classic work is Alfred D. Chandler, *Strategy and Structure* (Cambridge, MA: MIT Press, 1962).

[4]See Alfred D. Chandler Jr., "Origins of the Organization Chart," *Harvard Business Review* (March/April 1988), pp. 156–57.

[5]"A Question of Management," *Wall Street Journal* (June 2, 2009), p. R4.

[6]Joann S. Lublin, "Chairman-CEO Split Gains Allies," *Wall Street Journal* (March 30, 2009), p. B4.

[7]See David Krackhardt and Jeffrey R. Hanson, "Informal Networks: The Company Behind the Chart," *Harvard Business Review* (July/August 1993), pp. 104–11.

[8]Information from Jena McGregor, "The Office Chart That Really Counts," *Business Week* (February 27, 2006), pp. 48–49.

[9]See Phred Dvorak, "Engineering Firm Charts Ties," *Wall Street Journal* (January 26, 2009): www.wsj.com.

[10]See Kenneth Noble, "A Clash of Styles: Japanese Companies in the U.S.," *New York Times* (January 25, 1988), p. 7.

[11]Information from Ellen Byron, "A New Odd Couple: Google, P&G Swap Workers to Spur Innovation," *Wall Street Journal* (November 19, 2008), pp. A1, A18.

[12]For a discussion of departmentalization, see H. I. Ansoff and R. G. Bradenburg, "A Language for Organization Design," *Management Science,* vol. 17 (August 1971), pp. B705–B731; Mariann Jelinek, "Organization Structure: The Basic Conformations," in Mariann Jelinek, Joseph A. Litterer, and Raymond E. Miles (eds.), *Organizations by Design: Theory and Practice* (Plano, TX: Business Publications, 1981), pp. 293–302; Henry Mintzberg, "The Structuring of Organizations," in James Brian Quinn, Henry Mintzberg, and Robert M. James (eds.), *The Strategy Process: Concepts, Contexts, and Cases* (Englewood Cliffs, NJ: Prentice-Hall, 1988), pp. 276–304.

[13]"A Question of Management," op. cit.

[14]Example reported in "Top Business Teams: A Lesson Straight from Mars," *Time* (February 9, 2009), p. 40; and Howard M. Guttman, *Great Business Teams* (Hoboken, NJ: Wiley, 2009).

[15]These alternatives are well described by Mintzberg, op. cit.

[16]Norihiko Shirouzu, "Toyota Plans a Major Overhaul in U. S.," *Wall Street Journal* (April 10, 2009), p. B3.

[17]Information and quotes from "Management Shake-Up to Create 'Leaner Structure'," *Financial Times* (June 11, 2009).

[18]Information and quote from "Revamped GM Updates Image of Core Brands," *Financial Times* (June 18, 2009).

[19]Excellent reviews of matrix concepts are found in Stanley M. Davis and Paul R. Lawrence, *Matrix* (Reading, MA: Addison-Wesley, 1977); Paul R. Lawrence, Harvey F. Kolodny, and Stanley M. Davis, "The Human Side of the Matrix," *Organizational Dynamics,* vol. 6 (1977), pp. 43–61; and Harvey F. Kolodny, "Evolution to a Matrix Organization," *Academy of Management Review,* vol. 4 (1979), pp. 543–53.

[20]Davis and Lawrence, op. cit.

[21]Susan Albers Mohrman, Susan G. Cohen, and Allan M. Mohrman Jr., *Designing Team-Based Organizations* (San Francisco: Jossey-Bass, 1996).

[22]See Glenn M. Parker, *Cross-Functional Teams* (San Francisco: Jossey-Bass, 1995).

[23]Information from William Bridges, "The End of the Job," *Fortune* (September 19, 1994), pp. 62–74; and Alan Deutschman, "The Managing Wisdom of High-Tech Superstars," *Fortune* (October 17, 1994), pp. 197–206.

[24]See the discussion by Jay R. Galbraith, "Designing the Networked Organization: Leveraging Size and Competencies," in Susan Albers Mohrman, Jay R. Galbraith, Edward E. Lawler III, and Associates, *Tomorrow's Organizations: Crafting Winning Strategies in a Dynamic World* (San Francisco: Jossey-Bass, 1998), pp. 76–102. See also Rupert F. Chisholm, *Developing Network Organizations: Learning from Practice and Theory* (Reading, MA: Addison-Wesley, 1998); and Michael S. Malone, *The Future Arrived Yesterday: The Rise of the Protean Corporation and What It Means for You* (New York: Crown Books, 2009).

[25]See Jerome Barthelemy, "The Seven Deadly Sins of Outsourcing," *Academy of Management Executive,* vol. 17 (2003), pp. 87–98; and Paulo Prada and Jiraj Sheth, "Delta Air Ends Use of India Call Centers," *Wall Street Journal* (April 18–19, 2009), pp. B1, B5.

[26]See the collection of articles by Cary L. Cooper and Denise M. Rousseau (eds.), *The Virtual Organization: Vol. 6, Trends in Organizational Behavior* (New York: Wiley, 2000).

[27]For a discussion of organization theory, see W. Richard Scott, *Organizations: Rational, Natural, and Open Systems,* 4th ed. (Upper Saddle River, NJ: Prentice-Hall, 1998).

[28]For a classic work, see Jay R. Galbraith, *Organizational Design* (Reading, MA: Addison-Wesley, 1977).

[29]David Van Fleet, "Span of Management Research and Issues," *Academy of Management Journal,* vol. 26 (1983), pp. 546–52.

[30]Information and quotes from Ellen Byron and Joann S. Lublin, "Appointment of New P&G Chief Sends Ripples Through Ranks," *Wall Street Journal* (June 11, 2009), P. B3.

[31]Information from Tim Stevens, "Winning the World Over," *Industry Week* (November 15, 1999).

[32]See George P. Huber, "A Theory of Effects of Advanced Information Technologies on Organizational Design, Intelligence, and Decision Making," *Academy of Management Review,* vol. 15 (1990), pp. 67–71.

[33]Developed from Roger Fritz, *Rate Your Executive Potential* (New York: Wiley, 1988), pp. 185–86; Roy J. Lewicki, Donald D. Bowen, Douglas T. Hall, and Francine S. Hall, *Experiences in Management and Organizational Behavior,* 3rd ed. (New York: Wiley, 1988), p. 144.

[34]Max Weber, *The Theory of Social and Economic Organization,* A. M. Henderson (trans.) and H. T. Parsons (ed.) (New York: Free Press, 1974). For classic treatments of bureaucracy, see also Alvin Gouldner, *Patterns of Industrial Bureaucracy* (New York: Free Press, 1954); and Robert K. Merton, *Social Theory and Social Structure* (New York: Free Press, 1957).

[35]Tom Burns and George M. Stalker, *The Management of Innovation* (London: Tavistock, 1961), republished (London: Oxford University Press, 1994). See also Wesley D. Sine, Hitoshi Mitsuhashi, and David A. Kirsch, "Revisiting Burns and Stalker: Formal Structure and New Venture Performance in Emerging Economic Sectors," *Academy of Management Journal,* vol. 49 (2006), pp. 121–32. The Burns and Stalker study was later extended by Paul R. Lawrence and Jay W. Lorsch, *Organizations and Environment* (Boston: Division of Research, Graduate School of Business Administration, Harvard University, 1967).

[36]See Henry Mintzberg, *Structure in Fives: Designing Effective Organizations* (Englewood Cliffs, NJ: Prentice-Hall, 1983).

[37]"What Ails Microsoft?" *Business Week* (September 26, 2005), p. 101.

[38]"Should Microsoft Break Up, on Its Own?" *Wall Street Journal* (November 26–27, 2005), p. B16.

[39]See, for example, Jay R. Galbraith, Edward E. Lawler III, and Associates, *Organizing for the Future* (San Francisco: Jossey-Bass, 1993); and Mohrman et al., op. cit.

[40]Peter Senge, *The Fifth Discipline: The Art and Practice of the Learning Organization* (New York: Doubleday, 1994).

[41]See Rosabeth Moss Kanter, *The Changing Masters* (New York: Simon & Schuster, 1983).

⁴²Barney Olmsted and Suzanne Smith, *Creating a Flexible Workplace: How to Select and Manage Alternative Work Options* (New York: American Management Association, 1989).

⁴³See Allen R. Cohen and Herman Gadon, *Alternative Work Schedules: Integrating Individual and Organizational Needs* (Reading, MA: Addison-Wesley, 1978), p. 125; Simcha Ronen and Sophia B. Primps, "The Compressed Work Week as Organizational Change: Behavioral and Attitudinal Outcomes," *Academy of Management Review,* vol. 6 (1981), pp. 61–74.

⁴⁴Information from Lesli Hicks, "Workers, Employers Praise Their Four-Day Workweek," *Columbus Dispatch* (August 22, 1994), p. 6.

⁴⁵Business for Social Responsibility Resource Center: www.bsr.org/resourcecenter (January 24, 2001); Anusha Shrivastava, "Flextime Is Now Key Benefit for Mom-Friendly Employers," *Columbus Dispatch* (September 23, 2003), p. C2; Sue Shellenbarger, "Number of Women Managers Rises," *Wall Street Journal* (September 30, 2003), p. D2.

⁴⁶"Networked Workers," *Business Week* (October 6, 1997), p. 8; and Diane E. Lewis, "Flexible Work Arrangements as Important as Salary to Some," *Columbus Dispatch* (May 25, 1998), p. 8.

⁴⁷Christopher Rhoads and Sara Silver, "Working at Home Gets Easier," *Wall Street Journal* (December 29, 2005), p. B4.

⁴⁸For a review, see Wayne F. Cascio, "Managing a Virtual Workplace," *Academy of Management Executive,* vol. 14 (2000), pp. 81–90.

⁴⁹Quote from Phil Porter, "Telecommuting Mom Is Part of a National Trend," *Columbus Dispatch* (November 29, 2000), pp. H1, H2.

Feature Notes 9

Netflix—Information and quotes from Brian Steinberg, "Transforming the Movie-Rental Model," *Advertising Age,* vol. 79, no. 1 (January 7, 2008); Nick Wingfield, "Netflix vs. Naysayers," *Wall Street Journal* (March 27, 2008), pp. B1, B2; and Daniel Roth, "Netflix Everywhere: Sorry Cable, You're History," *Wired Magazine* (September 21, 2009): www.wired.com.

Role Models—Information from David A. Price, "From Dorm Room to Wal-Mart," *Wall Street Journal* (March 11, 2009), p. A13; "Huddler.com Interview with CEO and Founder Tom Szaky," www.greenhome.huddler.com/wiki/terracycle; and Tom Szaky, *Revolution in a Bottle* (Knoxville, TN: Portfolio Trade, 2009).

Ethics Check 9—Information and examples from Joe O'Shea, "How a Facebook Update Can Cost You Your Job," *Irish Independent* (September 1, 2010), p. 34.

Facts to Consider—Data reported in "A Saner Workplace," *Business Week* (June 1, 2009), pp. 66–69, and based on excerpt from Claire Shipman and Katty Kay, *Womenomics: Write Your Own Rules for Success* (New York: Harper Business, 2009); and "A to Z of Generation Y Attitudes," *Financial Times* (June 18, 2009).

Endnotes 9

¹See the discussion of Anthropologie in William C. Taylor and Polly LaBarre, *Mavericks at Work: Why the Most Original Minds in Business Win* (New York: William Morrow, 2006).

²Edgar H. Schein, "Organizational Culture," *American Psychologist,* vol. 45 (1990), pp. 109–19. See also Schein's *Organizational Culture and Leadership,* 2nd ed. (San Francisco: Jossey-Bass, 1997); and *The Corporate Culture Survival Guide* (San Francisco: Jossey-Bass, 1999).

³Information and quotes from Christopher Palmeri, "Now for Sale, the Zappos Culture," *Business Week* (January 11, 2010), p. 57.

⁴Jena McGregor, "Zappos' Secret: It's an Open Book," *Business Week* (March 23 & 30, 2009), p. 62.

⁵James Collins and Jerry Porras, *Built to Last* (New York: Harper Business, 1994).

⁶Rajiv Dutta, "eBay's Meg Whitman on Building a Company's Culture," *Business Week* (March 27, 2009): www.businessweek.com.

⁷Wallin Wong, "Noncorporate Culture: Groupon's Rapid Growth Built on Relaxed Workplace, Openness, Creativity," *The Columbus Dispatch* (January 3, 2011), p. A6.

⁸Ibid.

⁹Schein, op. cit. (1997); Terrence E. Deal and Alan A. Kennedy, *Corporate Cultures: The Rites and Rituals of Corporate Life* (Reading, MA: Addison-Wesley, 1982); and Ralph Kilmann, *Beyond the Quick Fix* (San Francisco: Jossey-Bass, 1984).

¹⁰Schein, op. cit. (1997).

¹¹John P. Wanous, *Organizational Entry,* 2nd ed. (New York: Addison-Wesley, 1992).

¹²Scott Madison Patton, "Service Quality, Disney Style" (Lake Buena Vista, FL: Disney Institute, 1997).

¹³This is a simplified model developed from Schein, op. cit. (1997).

¹⁴James C. Collins and Jerry I. Porras, "Building Your Company's Vision," *Harvard Business Review* (September/October 1996), pp. 65–77.

¹⁵See corporate websites.

¹⁶Tom's of Maine example is from Jenny C. McCune, "Making Lemonade," *Management Review* (June 1997), pp. 49–53.

¹⁷See, for example, Lee G. Bolman and Terrence E. Deal, *Reframing Organizations: Artistry, Fourth Edition Choice, and Leadership* (San Francisco: Jossey-Bass, 2008).

¹⁸See Robert A. Giacalone and Carol L. Jurkiewicz (Eds.), *Handbook of Workplace Spirituality and Organizational Performance* (Armonk, NY: M. E. Sharpe, 2003).

¹⁹See Peter F. Drucker, "The Discipline of Innovation," *Harvard Business Review* (November/December 1998), pp. 3–8.

²⁰Peter F. Drucker, *Management: Tasks, Responsibilities, and Practices* (New York: Harper & Row, 1973), p. 797.

²¹See Cortis R. Carlson and William W. Wilmont, *Getting to "Aha"* (New York: Crown Business, 2006).

²²See for example *Bloomberg Business Week* reports on "The World's Most Innovative Companies."

²³See "Green Business Innovations" and "New Life for Old Threads," both in *Business Week* (April 28, 2008), special advertising section.

²⁴*Border Green Energy Team*—Information on Salinee Tavaranan and the Border Green Energy Team is from bget.org.

²⁵Quote from "How to Measure Up," *Kellogg* (Summer, 2009), p. 17.

²⁶David Bornstein, *How to Change the World: Social Entrepreneurs and the Power of New Ideas* (Oxford, U.K.: Oxford University Press, 2004).

²⁷Example from Aubrey Henvetty, "Seeds of Change," *Kellogg* (Summer, 2006), p. 13; and "Amid Turmoil, One Acre Fund Sows Hope in Africa," *Kellogg* (Spring, 2008), p. 7.

²⁸See Gary Hamel, *Leading the Revolution* (Boston, MA: Harvard Business School Press, 2000).

²⁹Based on Edward B. Roberts, "Managing Invention and Innovation," *Research Technology Management* (January/February 1988), pp. 1–19.

³⁰"The Joys and Perils of 'Reverse Innovation'," *Business Week* (October 5, 2009), p. 12.

³¹Ibid. Also, example and quotes from "How to Compete in a World Turned Upside Down," *Financial Times,* Kindle edition (October 6, 2009).

³²Information and quotes from Nancy Gohring, "Microsoft: Stodgy or Innovative? It's All About Perception," *PC World* (July 25, 2008).

³³This discussion is stimulated by James Brian Quinn, "Managing Innovation Controlled Chaos," *Harvard Business Review,* vol. 63 (May/June 1985).

³⁴Quote from www.ideo.com/culture/ (retrieved: March 11, 2009).

³⁵"'Mosh Pits' of Creativity," *Business Week* (November 7, 2005), p. 99.

³⁶Reena Jana, "Brickhouse: Yahoo's Hot Little Incubator," *Business Week* (November, 2007), p. IN 14.

³⁷"How Google Fuels Its Idea Factory," *Business Week* (May 12, 2008), pp. 54–55.

³⁸Kenneth Labich, "The Innovators," *Fortune* (June 6, 1988), pp. 49–64.

³⁹Quote from Brad Stone, "Amid the Gloom, an E-Commerce War," *New York Times* (October 12, 2008): www.nytimes.com.

⁴⁰Quote from Pilita Clark, "Delayed, Not Cancelled," *Financial Times* (December 19, 2009).

⁴¹Reported in Carol Hymowitz, "Task of Managing Changes in Workplace Takes a Careful Hand," *Wall Street Journal* (July 1, 1997), p. B1.

⁴²For an overview, see W. Warner Burke, *Organization Change: Theory and Practice* (Thousand Oaks, CA: Sage, 2002).

⁴³For a discussion of alternative types of change, see David A. Nadler and Michael L. Tushman, *Strategic Organizational Design* (Glenview, Il: Scott, Foresman, 1988); John P. Kotter, "Leading Change: Why Transformation Efforts Fail," *Harvard Business Review* (March/April 1995), pp. 59–67; and Burke, op. cit.

[44]Michael Beer and Nitin Nohria, "Cracking the Code of Change"; *Harvard Business Review* (May–June 2000), pp. 138–141; and "Change Management, An Inside Job," *Economist* (July 15, 2000), p. 61.

[45]Ibid. Beer and Nohria, op. cit.; and "Change Management, An Inside Job," *Economist* (July 15, 2000), p. 61.

[46]Based on Kotter, op. cit.

[47]Beer & Nohria, op. cit.

[48]Kurt Lewin, "Group Decision and Social Change," in G. E. Swanson, T. M. Newcomb, and E. L. Hartley (eds.), *Readings in Social Psychology* (New York: Holt, Rinehart, 1952), pp. 459–473.

[49]This discussion is based on Robert Chin and Kenneth D. Benne, "General Strategies for Effecting Changes in Human Systems," in Warren G. Bennis, Kenneth D. Benne, Robert Chin, and Kenneth E. Corey (eds.), *The Planning of Change*, 3rd ed. (New York: Holt, Rinehart, 1969), pp. 22–45.

[50]The change agent descriptions here and following are developed from an exercise reported in J. William Pfeiffer and John E. Jones, *A Handbook of Structured Experiences for Human Relations Training*, vol. 2 (LaJolla, CA: University Associates, 1973).

[51]Ram N. Aditya, Robert J. House, and Steven Kerr, "Theory and Practice of Leadership: Into the New Millennium," Chapter 6 in Cary L. Cooper and Edwin A. Locke, *Industrial and Organizational Psychology: Linking Theory with Practice* (Malden, MA: Blackwell, 2000).

[52]Information from Mike Schneider, "Disney Teaching Execs Magic of Customer Service," *Columbus Dispatch* (December 17, 2000), p. G9.

[53]Teresa M. Amabile, "How to Kill Creativity," *Harvard Business Review* (September/October 1998), pp. 77–87.

[54]See Jeffrey D. Ford and Laurie W. Ford, "Decoding Resistance to Change," *Harvard Business Review* (April, 2009), pp. 99–103.

[55]John P. Kotter and Leonard A. Schlesinger, "Choosing Strategies for Change," *Harvard Business Review*, vol. 57 (March/April 1979), pp. 109–112.

Feature Notes 10

Working Mother—Information and quote from workingmother.com (retrieved September 29, 2006, and August 1, 2008); see also workingmother.com.

Role Models—Information and quotes from David A. Kaplan, "#1 SAS: The Best Company to Work For," *Fortune* (January 26, 2010), Kindle edition.

Ethics Check—Information from Jennifer Saranow, "Car Dealers Recruit Saleswomen at the Mall," *Wall Street Journal* (April 12, 2006), pp. B1, B3.

Facts to Consider—Information from Joe Light, "Human-Resource Executives Say Reviews Are Off the Mark," *Wall Street Journal* (November 8, 2010), p. B8.

Endnotes 10

[1]See Jeffrey Pfeffer, *The Human Equation: Building Profits by Putting People First* (Boston: Harvard University Press, 1998).

[2]Jeffrey Pfeffer and John F. Veiga, "Putting People First for Organizational Success," *Academy of Management Executive,* vol. 13 (May 1999), pp. 37–48.

[3]Ibid.; and Pfeffer, op. cit. See also James N. Baron and David M. Kreps, *Strategic Human Resources: Frameworks for General Managers* (New York: Wiley, 1999).

[4]Quote from William Bridges, "The End of the Job," *Fortune* (September 19, 1994), p. 68.

[5]Information from "New Face at Facebook Hopes to Map Out a Road to Growth," *Wall Street Journal* (April 15, 2008), pp. B1, B5.

[6]Baron and Kreps, op. cit.

[7]Quotes from Kris Maher, "Human-Resources Directors Are Assuming Strategic Roles," *Wall Street Journal* (June 17, 2003), p. B8.

[8]Ibid.

[9]See also R. Roosevelt Thomas Jr.'s books, *Beyond Race and Gender* (New York: AMACOM, 1999) and (with Marjorie I. Woodruff) *Building a House for Diversity* (New York: AMACOM, 1999); and Richard D. Bucher, *Diversity Consciousness* (Englewood Cliffs, NJ: Prentice-Hall, 2000).

[10]Information from Courtney E. Martin, "Wal-Mart v. Dukes Ruling is Out of Synch with 21st Century Sex Discrimination," *The Christian Science Monitor* (June 22, 2011): csmonitor.com; Dahlia Lithwick, "Class Dismissed: The Supreme Court Decides That the Women of Wal-Mart Can't Have Their Day in Court," slate.com (June 20, 2011); and, "Walmart Statement Regarding Supreme Court Ruling in Dukes Case," corporate press release (June 20, 2011): walmartstores.com/pressromm.

[11]For a discussion of affirmative action, see R. Roosevelt Thomas Jr., "From 'Affirmative Action' to 'Affirming Diversity,'" *Harvard Business Review* (November/December 1990), pp. 107–117.

[12]See the discussion by David A. DeCenzo and Stephen P. Robbins, *Human Resource Management*, 6th ed. (New York: Wiley, 1999), pp. 66–68 and 81–83.

[13]Ibid., pp. 77–79.

[14]See, for example, Melanie Trottman, "Charges of Bias at Work Increase," *Wall Street Journal* (January 12, 2011), p. A2.

[15]Case reported in Sue Shellenbarger, "Work & Family Mailbox," *Wall Street Journal* (March 11, 2009), p. D6.

[16]See Frederick S. Lane, *The Naked Employee: How Technology Is Compromising Workplace Privacy* (New York: Amacom, 2003).

[17]This and other cases are described in Debra Cassens Weiss, "Companies Face 'Legal Potholes' as They Crack Down on Workers' Social Media Posts," ABAJournal.com (posted January 24, 2011).

[18]Information from Sheryl Gay Stolberg, "Obama Signs Equal-Pay Legislation," *New York Times* (January 30, 2009): www.nytimes.com.

[19]"What to Expect When You're Expecting," *Business Week* (May 26, 2008), p. 17.

[20]Ibid; and Madeline Heilman and Tyhler G. Okimoto, "Motherhood: A Potential Source of Bias in Employment Decisions," *Journal of Applied Psychology,* vol. 93, no. 1 (2008), pp. 189–98.

[21]Information and quotes from Jennifer Levitz and Philip Shiskin, "More Workers Cite Age Bias After Layoffs," *Wall Street Journal* (March 11, 2009), pp. D1, D2.

[22]Information from Adam Lashinsky, "Zappos: Life After Acquisition," tech.fortune.cnn.com (November 24, 2010).

[23]"The Smart Way to Hire Workers," *The Economist,* Kindle edition (February 4, 2010).

[24]Ibid.

[25]See Sarah E. Needleman, "Initial Phone Interviews Do Count," *Wall Street Journal* (February 7, 2006), p. 29.

[26]Information and quote from Sarah E. Needleman, "The New Trouble on the Line," *Wall Street Journal* (June 2, 2009): www.wsj.com.

[27]See John P. Wanous, *Organizational Entry: Recruitment, Selection, and Socialization of Newcomers* (Reading, MA: Addison-Wesley, 1980), pp. 34–44.

[28]Josey Puliyenthuruthel, "How Google Searches for Talent," *Business Week* (April 11, 2005), p. 52.

[29]Quote from Ronald Henkoff, "Finding, Training, and Keeping the Best Service Workers," *Fortune* (October 3, 1994), pp. 110–122.

[30]Kimes, op. cit.

[31]See Harry J. Martin, "Lessons Learned," *Wall Street Journal* (December 15, 2008), p. R11.

[32]"A to Z of Generation Y Attitudes," *Financial Times* (June 18, 2009); and "When Three Generations Can Work Better Than One," *Financial Times* (September 16, 2009).

[33]Dick Grote, "Performance Appraisal Reappraised," *Harvard Business Review Best Practice* (1999), Reprint F00105.

[34]See Larry L. Cummings and Donald P. Schwab, *Performance in Organizations: Determinants and Appraisal* (Glenview, IL: Scott, Foresman, 1973).

[35]For a good review, see Gary P. Latham, Joan Almost, Sara Mann, and Celia Moore, "New Developments in Performance Management," *Organizational Dynamics,* vol. 34, no. 1 (2005), pp. 77–87.

[36]See Mark R. Edwards and Ann J. Ewen, *360-Degree Feedback: The Powerful New Tool for Employee Feedback and Performance Improvement* (New York: Amacom, 1996).

[37]Examples are from Jena McGregor, "Job Review in 140 Keystrokes," *Business Week* (March 23 & 30, 2009), p. 58.

[38]Kimes, op. cit.

[39]Timothy Butler and James Waldroop, "Job Sculpting: The Art of Retaining Your Best People," *Harvard Business Review* (September/October 1999), pp. 144–52.

[40]Information from "What Are the Most Effective Retention Tools?" *Fortune* (October 9, 2000), p. S7.

[41]Data reported in "A Saner Workplace," *Business Week* (June 1, 2009), pp. 66–69, and based on excerpt from Claire Shipman and Katty Kay,

Womenomics: Write Your Own Rules for Success (New York: Harper Business, 2009); see also "A to Z of Generation Y Attitudes," op. cit.

⁴²See Betty Friedan, *Beyond Gender: The New Politics of Work and the Family* (Washington, DC: Woodrow Wilson Center Press, 1997); and James A. Levine, *Working Fathers: New Strategies for Balancing Work and Family* (Reading, MA: Addison-Wesley, 1997).

⁴³Data from "A Saner Workplace," op. cit., and based on excerpt from Shipman and Kay, op. cit.

⁴⁴Study reported in Ann Belser, "Employers Using Less-Costly Ways to Retain Workers," *Columbus Dispatch* (June 1, 2008), p. D3.

⁴⁵Information from Sue Shellenbarger, "What Makes a Company a Great Place to Work Today," *Wall Street Journal* (October 4, 2007), p. D1.

⁴⁶Information from ibid.

⁴⁷Examples from Amy Saunders, "A Creative Approach to Work," *Columbus Dispatch* (May 2, 2008), pp. C1, C9; Shellenbarger, op. cit. (2007); and Michelle Conlin and Jay Greene, "How to Make a Microserf Smile," *Business Week* (September 10, 2007), pp. 57–59.

⁴⁸"A Saner Workplace," op. cit.

⁴⁹Quote from Sudeep Reddy, "Wary Companies Rely on Temporary Workers," *Wall Street Journal* (March 6–7, 2010), p. A. 4.

⁵⁰Information and quotes from Peter Coy, Michelle Conlin, and Moira Herbst, "The Disposable Worker," *Business Week* (January 18, 2010), pp. 33–39.

⁵¹Ibid.; and "Don't Call Me Victim," *Business Week* (January 25, 2010), p. 69.

⁵²Michael Orey, "They're Employees, No, They're Not," *Business Week* (November 16, 2009), pp. 73–74.

⁵³See Kaja Whitehouse, "More Companies Offer Packages Linking Pay Plans to Performance," *Wall Street Journal* (December 13, 2005), p. B6.

⁵⁴Ibid.

⁵⁵Erin White, "How to Reduce Turnover," *Wall Street Journal* (November 21, 2005), p. B5.

⁵⁶Ibid.

⁵⁷Information from Susan Pulliam, "New Dot-Com Mantra: 'Just Pay Me in Cash, Please,'" *Wall Street Journal* (November 28, 2000), p. C1.

⁵⁸Nanette Byrnes, "Pain, but No Layoffs at Nucor," *Business Week* (March 26, 2009): www.businessweek.com.

⁵⁹Information from www.intel.com; and "Stock Ownership for Everyone," *Hewitt Associates* (November 27, 2000): www.hewitt.com/hewitt/business/talent/subtalent/con_bckg_global.htm.

⁶⁰"Benefits: For Companies, the Runaway Train Is Slowing Down," *Business Week* (February 16, 2009), p. 15.

⁶¹For reviews, see Richard B. Freeman and James L. Medoff, *What Do Unions Do?* (New York: Basic Books, 1984); Charles C. Heckscher, *The New Unionism* (New York: Basic Books, 1988); and Barry T. Hirsch, *Labor Unions and the Economic Performance of Firms* (Kalamazoo, MI: W.E. Upjohn Institute for Employment Research, 1991).

⁶²U.S. Bureau of Labor Statistics, "Union Members Survey," *News Release* (January 21, 2011): www.ubls.gov.

⁶³Example from Timothy Aeppel, "Pay Scales Divide Factory Floors," *Wall Street Journal* (April 9, 2008), p. B4.

⁶⁴Matthew Dolan, "Ford to Begin Hiring at Much Lower Wages," *Wall Street Journal* (January 26, 2010), p. B1.

Feature Notes 11

Kraft Foods—Information and quotes from Irene Rosenfeld, "Irene Rosenfeld Drives Change with 'Rules of the Road'," *Wall Street Journal*, Special Advertising Section (October 6, 2009), p. A17; David Kesmodel and Ceceilie Rohwedder, "Sugar and Spice: A Clash of Two Change Agents," *Wall Street Journal* (September 8, 2009), p. A17; Ilan Brat, "A Jar of New Vegmite, a Window into Kraft," *Wall Street Journal* (September 30, 2009), pp. B1, B2; and Susan Verfield and Michael Arndt, "Kraft's Sugar Rush," *Business Week* (January 25, 2010), pp. 37–39.

Role Models—Information and quotes from Lorraine Monroe, "Leadership Is About Making Vision Happen—What I Call 'Vision Acts,'" *Fast Company* (March 2001), p. 98; Lorraine Monroe Leadership Institute Web site: www.lorrainemonroe.com. See also Lorraine Monroe, *Nothing's Impossible: Leadership Lessons from Inside and Outside the Classroom* (New York: Public Affairs Books, 1999), and *The Monroe Doctrine: An ABC Guide to What Great Bosses Do* (New York: PublicAffairs Books, 2003).

Ethics Check—The zone of indifference is described by Chester Barnard in *Functions of the Executive* (Cambridge, MA: Harvard University Press, 1971), 30th Anniversary Edition.

Facts to Consider—Information from "Many U.S. Employees Have Negative Attitudes to Their Jobs, Employers and Top Managers," Harris Poll #38 (May 6, 2005), retrieved from www.harrisinteractive.com.

Endnotes 11

¹Abraham Zaleznick, "Leaders and Managers: Are They Different?" *Harvard Business Review* (May/June 1977), pp. 67–78.

²Tom Peters, "Rule #3: Leadership Is Confusing as Hell," *Fast Company* (March 2001), pp. 124–40.

³Quotations from Marshall Loeb, "Where Leaders Come From," *Fortune* (September 19, 1994), pp. 241–42; Genevieve Capowski, "Anatomy of a Leader: Where Are the Leaders of Tomorrow?" *Management Review* (March 1994), pp. 10–17. For additional thoughts, see Warren Bennis, *Why Leaders Can't Lead* (San Francisco: Jossey-Bass, 1996).

⁴See Jean Lipman-Blumen, *Connective Leadership: Managing in a Changing World* (New York: Oxford University Press, 1996), pp. 3–11.

⁵Rosabeth Moss Kanter, "Power Failure in Management Circuits," *Harvard Business Review* (July/August 1979), pp. 65–75.

⁶The classic treatment of these power bases is John R. P. French Jr. and Bertram Raven, "The Bases of Social Power," in Darwin Cartwright (ed.), *Group Dynamics: Research and Theory* (Evanson, IL: Row, Peterson, 1962), pp. 607–13.

⁷For managerial applications of this basic framework, see Gary Yukl and Tom Taber, "The Effective Use of Managerial Power," *Personnel*, vol. 60 (1983), pp. 37–49; and Robert C. Benfari, Harry E. Wilkinson, and Charles D. Orth, "The Effective Use of Power," *Business Horizons*, vol. 29 (1986), pp. 12–16. Gary A. Yukl, *Leadership in Organizations*, 4th ed. (Englewood Cliffs, NJ: Prentice-Hall, 1998), includes "information" as a separate, but related, power source.

⁸James M. Kouzes and Barry Z. Posner, "The Leadership Challenge," *Success* (April 1988), p. 68. See also their books *Credibility: How Leaders Gain and Lose It: Why People Demand It* (San Francisco: Jossey-Bass, 1996); *Encouraging the Heart: A Leader's Guide to Rewarding and Recognizing Others* (San Francisco: Jossey-Bass, 1999); and *The Leadership Challenge: How to Get Extraordinary Things Done in Organizations*, 3rd ed. (San Francisco: Jossey-Bass, 2002).

⁹Quote from Andy Serwer, "Game Changers: Legendary Basketball Coach John Wooden and Starbucks' Howard Schultz Talk About a Common Interest—Leadership," *Fortune* (August 11, 2008): www.cnnmoney.com.

¹⁰Burt Nanus, *Visionary Leadership: Creating a Compelling Sense of Vision for Your Organization* (San Francisco: Jossey-Bass, 1992).

¹¹The early work on leader traits is well represented in Ralph M. Stogdill, "Personal Factors Associated with Leadership: A Survey of the Literature," *Journal of Psychology*, vol. 25 (1948), pp. 35–71. See also Edwin E. Ghiselli, *Explorations in Management Talent* (Santa Monica, CA: Goodyear, 1971); and Shirley A. Kirkpatrick and Edwin A. Locke, "Leadership: Do Traits Really Matter?" *Academy of Management Executive* (1991), pp. 48–60.

¹²See also John W. Gardner's article, "The Context and Attributes of Leadership," *New Management*, vol. 5 (1988), pp. 18–22; John P. Kotter, *The Leadership Factor* (New York: Free Press, 1988); and Bernard M. Bass, *Stogdill's Handbook of Leadership* (New York: Free Press, 1990).

¹³Kirkpatrick and Locke, op. cit. (1991).

¹⁴This terminology comes from Robert R. Blake and Jane Strygley Mouton, *The New Managerial Grid III* (Houston: Gulf Publishing, 1985) and the classic studies by Kurt Lewin and his associates at the University of Iowa. See, for example, K. Lewin and R. Lippitt, "An Experimental Approach to the Study of Autocracy and Democracy: A Preliminary Note," *Sociometry*, vol. 1 (1938), pp. 292–300; K. Lewin, "Field Theory and Experiment in Social Psychology: Concepts and Methods," *American Journal of Sociology*, vol. 44 (1939); and K. Lewin, R. Lippitt, and R. K. White, "Patterns of Aggressive Behavior in Experimentally Created Social Climates," *Journal of Social Psychology*, vol. 10 (1939), pp. 271–301.

¹⁵See Blake and Mouton, op. cit.

¹⁶For a good discussion of this theory, see Fred E. Fiedler, Martin M. Chemers, and Linda Mahar, *The Leadership Match Concept* (New York: Wiley, 1978); Fiedler's current contingency research with the cognitive resource theory

is summarized in Fred E. Fiedler and Joseph E. Garcia, *New Approaches to Effective Leadership* (New York: Wiley, 1987).

[17]Paul Hersey and Kenneth H. Blanchard, *Management and Organizational Behavior* (Englewood Cliffs, NJ: Prentice-Hall, 1988). For an interview with Paul Hersey on the origins of the model, see John R. Schermerhorn Jr., "Situational Leadership: Conversations with Paul Hersey," *Mid-American Journal of Business* (Fall 1997), pp. 5–12.

[18]See Claude L. Graeff, "The Situational Leadership Theory: A Critical View," *Academy of Management Review*, vol. 8 (1983), pp. 285–91; and Carmen F. Fernandez and Robert P. Vecchio, "Situational Leadership Theory Revisited: A Test of an Across-Jobs Perspective," *Leadership Quarterly*, vol. 8 (summer 1997), pp. 67–84.

[19]See, for example, Robert J. House, "A Path-Goal Theory of Leader Effectiveness," *Administrative Sciences Quarterly*, vol. 16 (1971), pp. 321–38; and Robert J. House and Terrence R. Mitchell, "Path-Goal Theory of Leadership," *Journal of Contemporary Business* (Autumn 1974), pp. 81–97. The path-goal theory is reviewed by Bass, op. cit., and Yukl, op. cit. A supportive review of research is offered in Julie Indvik, "Path-Goal Theory of Leadership. A Meta-Analysis," in John A. Pearce II and Richard B. Robinson Jr. (eds.), *Academy of Management Best Paper Proceedings* (1986), pp. 189–92.

[20]See the discussions of path-goal theory in Yukl, op. cit.; and Bernard M. Bass, "Leadership: Good, Better, Best," *Organizational Dynamics* (Winter 1985), pp. 26–40.

[21]See Steven Kerr and John Jermier, "Substitutes for Leadership: Their Meaning and Measurement," *Organizational Behavior and Human Performance*, vol. 22 (1978), pp. 375–403; Jon P. Howell and Peter W. Dorfman, "Leadership and Substitutes for Leadership Among Professional and Non-professional Workers," *Journal of Applied Behavioral Science*, vol. 22 (1986), pp. 29–46.

[22]An early presentation of the theory is F. Dansereau Jr., G. Graen, and W. J. Haga, "A Vertical Dyad Linkage Approach to Leadership Within Formal Organizations: A Longitudinal Investigation of the Role Making Process," *Organizational Behavior and Human Performance*, vol. 13, pp. 46–78.

[23]This discussion is based on Yukl, op. cit., pp. 117–22.

[24]Ibid.

[25]Victor H. Vroom and Arthur G. Jago, *The New Leadership: Managing Participation in Organizations* (Englewood Cliffs, NJ: Prentice-Hall, 1988). This is based on earlier work by Victor H. Vroom, "A New Look in Managerial Decision-Making," *Organizational Dynamics* (Spring 1973), pp. 66–80; and Victor H. Vroom and Phillip Yetton, *Leadership and Decision-Making* (Pittsburgh: University of Pittsburgh Press, 1973).

[26]Vroom and Jago, op. cit.

[27]For a related discussion, see Edgar H. Schein, *Process Consultation Revisited: Building the Helping Relationship* (Reading, MA: Addison-Wesley, 1999).

[28]For a review, see Yukl, op. cit.

[29]See the discussion by Victor H. Vroom, "Leadership and the Decision Making Process," *Organizational Dynamics*, vol. 28 (2000), pp. 82–94.

[30]Survey data from Gallup Leadership Institute, *Briefings Report 2005-01* (Lincoln, NE: University of Nebraska-Lincoln); "The Stat," *Business Week* (September 12, 2005), p. 16; and "U.S. Job Satisfaction Keeps Falling, the Conference Board Reports Today," The Conference Board (February 28, 2005), retrieved from www.conference-board.org.

[31]Among the popular books addressing this point of view are Warren Bennis and Burt Nanus, *Leaders: The Strategies for Taking Charge* (New York: Harper Business 1997); Max DePree, *Leadership Is an Art* (New York: Doubleday, 1989); Kouzes and Posner, op. cit. (2002).

[32]The distinction was originally made by James McGregor Burns, *Leadership* (New York: Harper & Row, 1978) and was further developed by Bernard Bass, *Leadership and Performance Beyond Expectations* (New York: Free Press, 1985), and Bernard M. Bass. "Leadership: Good, Better, Best," *Organizational Dynamics* (Winter 1985), pp. 26–40. See also Bernard M. Bass, "Does the Transactional-Transformational Leadership Paradigm Transcend Organizational and National Boundaries?" *American Psychologist*, vol. 52 (February 1997), pp. 130–39.

[33]See the discussion in Bass, op. cit., 1997.

[34]This list is based on Kouzes and Posner, op. cit.; Gardner, op. cit.

[35]Daniel Goleman, "Leadership That Gets Results," *Harvard Business Review* (March/April 2000), pp. 78–90. See also his books *Emotional Intelligence* (New York: Bantam Books, 1995) and *Working with Emotional Intelligence* (New York: Bantam Books, 1998).

[36]Daniel Goleman, Annie McKee, and Richard E. Boyatzis, *Primal Leadership: Realizing the Power of Emotional Intelligence* (Boston, MA: Harvard Business School Press, 2002), p. 3.

[37]Daniel Goleman, "What Makes a Leader?" *Harvard Business Review* (November/December 1998), pp. 93–102.

[38]Goleman, *Working with Emotional Intelligence*, op. cit. (1998).

[39]Information from "Women and Men, Work and Power," *Fast Company*, issue 13 (1998), p. 71.

[40]Jane Shibley Hyde, "The Gender Similarities Hypothesis," *American Psychologist*, vol. 60, no. 6 (2005), pp. 581–92.

[41]A. H. Eagley, S. J. Daran, and M. G. Makhijani, "Gender and the Effectiveness of Leaders: A Meta-Analysis," *Psychological Bulletin*, vol. 117 (1995), pp. 125–45.

[42]Research on gender issues in leadership is reported in Sally Helgesen, *The Female Advantage: Women's Ways of Leadership* (New York: Doubleday, 1990); Judith B. Rosener, "Ways Women Lead," *Harvard Business Review* (November/December 1990), pp. 119–25; Alice H. Eagley, Steven J. Karau, and Blair T. Johnson, "Gender and Leadership Style Among School Principals: A Meta Analysis," *Administrative Science Quarterly*, vol. 27 (1992), pp. 76–102; Lipman-Blumen, op. cit.; Alice H. Eagley, Mary C. Johannesen-Smith, and Marloes L. van Engen, "Transformational, Transactional and Laissez-Faire Leadership: A Meta-Analysis of Women and Men," *Psychological Bulletin*, vol. 124, no. 4 (2003), pp. 569–591; and Carol Hymowitz, "Too Many Women Fall for Stereotypes of Selves, Study Says," *Wall Street Journal* (October 24, 2005), p. B. 1.

[43]Herminia Ibarra and Otilia Obodaru, "Women and the Vision Thing," *Harvard Business Review* (January, 2009): Reprint R0901E.

[44]Data reported by Rochelle Sharpe, "As Women Rule," *Business Week* (November 20, 2000), p. 75.

[45]Eagley et al., op. cit. (2003); Hymowitz, op. cit.; Rosener, op. cit.; Vroom, op. cit.; and, Ibarra and Obodaru, op. cit.

[46]Rosener, op. cit, (1990).

[47]See research summarized by Stephanie Armour, "Do Women Compete in Unhealthy Ways at Work?" *USA Today* (December 30, 2005), pp. B1–B2.

[48]Quote from "As Leaders, Women Rule," *Business Week* (November 20, 2000), pp. 75–84. Rosabeth Moss Kanter is the author of *Men and Women of the Corporation*, 2nd ed. (New York: Basic Books, 1993).

[49]Del Jones, "Women CEOs Slowly Gain on Corporate America," *USA Today* (January 1, 2009): www.usatoday.com; and Morice Mendoza, "Davos 2009: Where Are the Women?" *Business Week* (January 26, 2009): www.businessweek.com.

[50]Hyde, op. cit.; Hymowitz, op. cit.

[51]For debate on whether some transformational leadership qualities tend to be associated more with female than male leaders, see "Debate: Ways Women and Men Lead," *Harvard Business Review* (January/February 1991), pp. 150–60.

[52]See Thomas et al, op. cit.

[53]"Many U.S. Employees Have Negative Attitudes to Their Jobs, Employers and Top Managers," Harris Poll #38 (May 6, 2005), retrieved from www.harrisinteractive.com.

[54]Information from "The Stat," *Business Week* (September 12, 2005), p. 16.

[55]See Terry Thomas, John R. Schermerhorn Jr., and John W. Dienhart, "Strategic Leadership of Ethical Behavior in Business," *Academy of Management Executive*, vol. 18 (May 2004), pp. 56–66.

[56]Doug May, Adrian Chan, Timothy Hodges, and Bruce Avolio, "Developing the Moral Component of Authentic Leadership," *Organizational Dynamics*, vol. 32 (2003), pp. 247–60.

[57]Peter F. Drucker, "Leadership: More Doing than Dash," *Wall Street Journal* (January 6, 1988), p. 16.

[58]"Information from Southwest CEO Puts Emphasis on Character," *USA Today* (September 26, 2004), retrieved from www.usatoday/money/companies/management on December 12, 2005.

[59]See Drucker, op cit., 1988.

[60]Robert K. Greenleaf and Larry C. Spears, *The Power of Servant Leadership: Essays* (San Francisco: Berrett-Koehler, 1996).

[61]Jay A. Conger, "Leadership: The Art of Empowering Others," *Academy of Management Executive*, vol. 3 (1989), pp. 17–24.

[62]Max DePree, "An Old Pro's Wisdom: It Begins with a Belief in People," *New York Times* (September 10, 1989), p. F2; DePree, op. cit.; David Woodruff, "Herman Miller: How Green Is My Factory," *Business Week* (September 16, 1991), pp. 54–56; and Max DePree, *Leadership Jazz* (New York: Doubleday, 1992).

[63]Lorraine Monroe, "Leadership Is About Making Vision Happen—What I Call 'Vision Acts,'" *Fast Company* (March 2001), p. 98; School Leadership Academy Web site: www.lorrainemonroe.com.

[64]Greenleaf and Spears, op. cit., p. 78.

Feature Notes 12

The Social Network—Eric Ditzian, "The Social Network: The Reviews are In!" mtv.com (October 1, 2010); and Ethan Smith, "'Social Network' Opens at No. 1," *Wall Street Journal* (October 4, 2010), p. B5.

Spanx—Information from Andrew Ward, "Spanx Queen Firms Up the Bottom Line," *Financial Times* (November 30, 2006), p. 7; and Simona Covel, "A Dated Industry Gets a Modern Makeover," *Wall Street Journal* (August 7, 2008), p. B9.

Role Models—Information and quotes from corporate Web sites; The Entrepreneur's Hall of Fame: www.1tbn.com/halloffame.html; Knowledge@Wharton, "The Importance of Being Richard Branson," *Wharton School Publishing* (June 3, 2005): www.whartonsp.com; and Diane Brady, "Richard Branson," *Bloomberg BusinessWeek* (November 22–28, 2010), p. 122.

Facts to Consider—See Linda Grant, "Happy Workers, High Returns," *Fortune* (January 12, 1998), p. 81; Timothy A. Judge, "Promote Job Satisfaction Through Mental Challenge," Chapter 6 in Edwin A. Locke, ed., *The Blackwell Handbook of Organizational Behavior* (Malden, MA: Blackwell, 2004); "U.S. Employees More Dissatisfied with Their Jobs," Associated Press (February 28, 2005), retrieved from www.msnbc.com; "U.S. Job Satisfaction Keeps Falling, the Conference Board Reports Today," *The Conference Board* (February 28, 2005): www.conference-board.org; and, "Grateful to Be Employed, Bored Half to Death," *Bloomberg Businessweek* (June 20–26, 2011), pp. 35–36.

Endnotes 12

[1]This example is reported in *Esquire* (December 1986), p. 243. Emphasis is added to the quotation. Note: Nussbaum became director of the Labor Department's Women's Bureau during the Clinton administration and subsequently moved to the AFL–CIO as head of the Women's Bureau.

[2]See H. R. Schiffman, *Sensation and Perception: An Integrated Approach,* 3rd ed. (New York: Wiley, 1990).

[3]Information from "Misconceptions About Women in the Global Arena Keep Their Numbers Low," Catalyst study: www.catalystwomen.org/home.html.

[4]The classic work is Dewitt C. Dearborn and Herbert A. Simon, "Selective Perception: A Note on the Departmental Identification of Executives," *Sociometry,* vol. 21 (1958), pp. 140–44. See also J. P. Walsh, "Selectivity and Selective Perception: Belief Structures and Information Processing," *Academy of Management Journal,* vol. 24 (1988), pp. 453–70.

[5]Quote from Sheila O'Flanagan, "Underestimate Casual Dressers at Your Peril," *The Irish Times* (July 22, 2005).

[6]See William L. Gardner and Mark J. Martinko, "Impression Management in Organizations," *Journal of Management* (June 1988), pp. 332–43.

[7]Sandy Wayne and Robert Liden, "Effects of Impression Management on Performance Ratings," *Academy of Management Journal* (February 2005), pp. 232–52.

[8]See M. R. Barrick and M. K. Mount, "The Big Five Personality Dimensions and Job Performance: A Meta-Analysis," *Personnel Psychology,* vol. 44 (1991), pp. 1–26.

[9]For a sample of research, see G. M. Hurtz and J. J. Donovan, "Personality and Job Performance: The Big Five Revisited," *Journal of Applied Psychology,* vol. 85 (2000), pp. 869–79; and T. A. Judge and R. Ilies, "Relationship of Personality to Performance Motivation: A Meta-Analytic Review," *Journal of Applied Psychology,* vol. 87 (2002), pp. 797–807.

[10]Carl G. Jung, *Psychological Types,* H. G. Baynes trans. (Princeton, NJ: Princeton University Press, 1971).

[11]I. Briggs-Myers, *Introduction to Type* (Palo Alto, CA: Consulting Psychologists Press, 1980).

[12]See, for example, William L. Gardner and Mark J. Martinko, "Using the Myers-Briggs Type Indicator to Study Managers: A Literature Review and Research Agenda," *Journal of Management,* vol. 22 (1996), pp. 45–83; Naomi L. Quenk, *Essentials of Myers-Briggs Type Indicator Assessment* (New York: Wiley, 2000).

[13]This discussion based in part on John R. Schermerhorn Jr., James G. Hunt, and Richard N. Osborn, *Organizational Behavior,* 9th ed. (New York: Wiley, 2005), pp. 54–60.

[14]J. B. Rotter, "Generalized Expectancies for Internal Versus External Control of Reinforcement," *Psychological Monographs,* vol. 80 (1966), pp. 1–28.

[15]T. W. Adorno, E. Frenkel-Brunswick, D. J. Levinson, and R. N. Sanford, *The Authoritarian Personality* (New York: Harper & Row, 1950).

[16]Niccolo Machiavelli, *The Prince,* trans. George Bull (Middlesex, UK: Penguin, 1961).

[17]See M. Snyder, *Public Appearances/Private Realities: The Psychology of Self-Monitoring* (New York: Freeman, 1987).

[18]See Arthur P. Brief, Randall S. Schuler, and Mary Van Sell, *Managing Job Stress* (Boston: Little, Brown, 1981), pp. 7, 8.

[19]The classic work is Meyer Friedman and Ray Roseman, *Type A Behavior and Your Heart* (New York: Knopf, 1974).

[20]Sue Shellenbarger, "Do We Work More or Not? Either Way, We Feel Frazzled," *Wall Street Journal* (July 30, 1997), p. B1.

[21]See, for example, "Desk Rage," *Business Week* (November 27, 2000), p. 12.

[22]See Hans Selye, *Stress in Health and Disease* (Boston: Butterworth, 1976).

[23]Carol Hymowitz, "Can Workplace Stress Get *Worse?*" *Wall Street Journal* (January 16, 2001), pp. B1, B3.

[24]See Steve M. Jex, *Stress and Job Performance* (San Francisco: Jossey-Bass, 1998).

[25]The extreme case of "workplace violence" is discussed by Richard V. Denenberg and Mark Braverman, *The Violence-Prone Workplace* (Ithaca, NY: Cornell University Press, 1999).

[26]David Gauthier-Villars and Leila Abboud, "In France, CEOs Can Become Hostages," *Wall Street Journal* (April 3, 2009), pp. B1, B4.

[27]See Daniel C. Ganster and Larry Murphy, "Workplace Interventions to Prevent Stress-Related Illness: Lessons from Research and Practice," Chapter 2 in Cary L. Cooper and Edwin A Locke (eds.), *Industrial and Organizational Psychology: Linking Theory with Practice* (Malden, MA: Blackwell Business, 2000); Jonathan D. Quick, Amy B. Henley, and James Campbell Quick, "The Balancing Act—At Work and at Home," *Organizational Dynamics,* vol. 33 (2004), pp. 426–37.

[28]Data from "Michael Mandel, "The Real Reasons You're Working So Hard," *Business Week* (October 3, 2005), pp. 60–70; "Many U.S. Employees Have Negative Attitudes to Their Jobs, Employers and Top Managers," *The Harris Poll #38* (May 6, 2005), retrieved from www.harrisinteractive.com; Sue Shellenbarger, "If You Need to Work Better, Maybe Try Working Less," *Wall Street Journal* (September 23, 2009), pp. D1, D2.

[29]See Melinda Beck, "Stress So Bad It Hurts—Really," *Wall Street Journal* (March 17, 2009), pp. D1, D6.

[30]Information and quote from Joann S. Lublin, "How One Black Woman Lands Her Top Jobs: Risks and Networking," *Wall Street Journal* (March 4, 2003), p. B1.

[31]Martin Fishbein and Icek Ajzen, *Belief, Attitude, Intention and Behavior: An Introduction to Theory and Research* (Reading, MA: Addison-Wesley, 1973).

[32]See Leon Festinger, *A Theory of Cognitive Dissonance* (Palo Alto, CA: Stanford University Press, 1957).

[33]For an overview, see Paul E. Spector, *Job Satisfaction* (Thousand Oaks, CA: Sage, 1997); Timothy A. Judge and Allan H. Church, "Job Satisfaction: Research and Practice," Chapter 7 in Cooper and Locke (eds.), op. cit. (2000); Timothy A. Judge, "Promote Job Satisfaction Through Mental Challenge," Chapter 6 in Edwin A. Locke (ed.), *The Blackwell Handbook of Principles of Organizational Behavior* (Malden, MA: Blackwell, 2004).

[34]Information in Stay Informed from Linda Grant, "Happy Workers, High Returns," *Fortune* (January 12, 1998), p. 81; Judge and Church op. cit. (2004); "U.S. Employees More Dissatisfied with Their Jobs," Associated Press (February 28, 2005), retrieved from www.msnbc.com; "U.S. Job Satisfaction Keeps Falling, the Conference Board Reports Today," *The Conference Board* (February 28, 2005), retrieved from www.conference-board.org; and Salary.com, "Survey Shows Impact of Downturn on Job Satisfaction," *OH&S: Occupational Health and Safety* (February 7, 2009): www.ohsonline.com.

[35]*What Workers Want: A Worldwide Study of Attitudes to Work and Work-Life Balance* (London: FDS International, 2007).

[36]Data reported in "When Loyalty Erodes, So Do Profits," *Business Week* (August 13, 2001), p. 8.

[37]Dennis W. Organ, *Organizational Citizenship Behavior: The Good Soldier Syndrome* (Lexington, MA: Lexington Books, 1988).

[38]See Mark C. Bolino and William H. Turnley, "Going the Extra Mile: Cultivating and Managing Employee Citizenship Behavior," *Academy of Management Executive*, vol. 17 (August 2003), pp. 60–67.

[39]Tony DiRomualdo, "The High Cost of Employee Disengagement" (July 7, 2004): www.wistechnology.com.

[40]These relationships are discussed in Charles N. Greene, "The Satisfaction-Performance Controversy," *Business Horizons*, vol. 15 (1982), pp. 31; Michelle T. Iaffaldano and Paul M. Muchinsky, "Job Satisfaction and Job Performance: A Meta Analysis," *Psychological Bulletin*, vol. 97 (1985), pp. 251–73.

[41]This discussion follows conclusions in Judge, op. cit. (2004). For a summary of the early research, see Iaffaldano and Muchinsky, op. cit.

[42]Daniel Goleman, "Leadership That Gets Results," *Harvard Business Review* (March–April 2000), pp. 78–90. See also his books *Emotional Intelligence* (New York: Bantam Books, 1995) and *Working with Emotional Intelligence* (New York: Bantam Books, 1998).

[43]"Charm Offensive: Why America's CEOs Are So Eager to Be Loved," *BusinessWeek* (June 26, 2006): businessweek.com (retrieved September 20, 2008).

[44]See Robert G. Lord, Richard J. Klimoski, and Ruth Knafer (eds.), *Emotions in the Workplace; Understanding the Structure and Role of Emotions in Organizational Behavior* (San Francisco: Jossey-Bass, 2002); Roy L. Payne and Cary L. Cooper (eds.), *Emotions at Work: Theory Research and Applications for Management* (Chichester, UK: Wiley, 2004); and Daniel Goleman and Richard Boyatzis, "Social Intelligence and the Biology of Leadership," *Harvard Business Review* (September 2008), Reprint R0809E.

[45]J. E. Bono and R. Ilies, "Charisma, Positive Emotions and Mood Contagion," *Leadership Quarterly*, vol. 17 (2006), pp. 317–34; and Goleman and Boyatzis, op. cit.

Feature Notes 13

Role Models—Information and quotes from Julie Flaherty, "A Parting Gift from the Boss Who Cared," *New York Times* (September 28, 2000), pp. C1, C25; Business Wire press release, "Employees of the Butcher Company Share over $18 Million as Owner Shares Benefits of Success" (September 21, 2000); and "Butcher, Charles," *New York Times* (June 20, 2004): www.nytimes.com.

Facts to Consider—Information from "UK Headhunters Pledge New Focus on Gender," *Financial Times*, Kindle Edition (May 11, 2011).

Ethics Check—Information on this situation from Jared Sandberg, "Why You May Regret Looking at Papers Left on the Office Copier," *Wall Street Journal* (June 20, 2006), p. B1.

HopeLab—Information from "HopeLab Video Games for Health," *Fast Company* (December, 2008/ January, 2009), p. 116; and www.hopelab.org.

Endnotes 13

[1]Photo quote on J. K. Rowling from "J. K. Rowling; Learning to Live with Fame, Fortune, and Life without Harry," *The Independent* (July 8, 2007); www.independent.co.uk. Additional information from Melinda Beck, "If at First You Don't Succeed, You're in Excellent Company," *Wall Street Journal* (April 29, 2008), p. D1.

[2]See Abraham H. Maslow, *Eupsychian Management* (Homewood, IL: Richard D. Irwin, 1965); and Abraham H. Maslow, *Motivation and Personality*, 2nd ed. (New York: Harper & Row, 1970). For a research perspective, see Mahmoud A. Wahba and Lawrence G. Bridwell, "Maslow Reconsidered: A Review of Research on the Need Hierarchy," *Organizational Behavior and Human Performance*, vol. 16 (1976), pp. 212–40.

[3]Clayton P. Alderfer, *Existence, Relatedness, and Growth* (New York: Free Press, 1972).

[4]Examples and quotes from Jane Hodges, "A Virtual Matchmaker for Volunteers," *Wall Street Journal* (February 12, 2009), p. D3; Dana Mattioli, "The Laid-Off Can Do Well Doing Good," *Wall Street Journal* (March 17, 2009), p. D1; Elizabeth Garone, "Paying It Forward Is a Full-Time Job," *Wall Street Journal* (March 17, 2009), p. D4.

[5]Developed originally from a discussion in Edward E. Lawler III, *Motivation in Work Organizations* (Monterey, CA: Brooks/Cole Publishing, 1973), pp. 30–36.

[6]For a collection of McClelland's work, see David C. McClelland, *The Achieving Society* (New York: Van Nostrand, 1961); "Business Drive and National Achievement," *Harvard Business Review*, vol. 40 (July/August 1962), pp. 99–112; David C. McClelland, *Human Motivation* (Glenview, IL: Scott, Foresman, 1985); David C. McClelland and Richard E. Boyatsis, "The Leadership Motive Pattern and Long-Term Success in Management," *Journal of Applied Psychology*, vol. 67 (1982), pp. 737–43.

[7]David C. McClelland and David H. Burnham, "Power Is the Great Motivator," *Harvard Business Review* (March/April 1976), pp. 100–10.

[8]The complete two-factor theory is in Frederick Herzberg, Bernard Mausner, and Barbara Block Synderman, *The Motivation to Work*, 2nd ed. (New York: Wiley, 1967); Frederick Herzberg, "One More Time: How Do You Motivate Employees?" *Harvard Business Review* (January/February 1968), pp. 53–62, and reprinted as an *HBR classic* (September/October 1987), pp. 109–20.

[9]Critical reviews are provided by Robert J. House and Lawrence A. Wigdor, "Herzberg's Dual-Factor Theory of Job Satisfaction and Motivation: A Review of the Evidence and a Criticism," *Personnel Psychology*, vol. 20 (Winter 1967), pp. 369–89; and Steven Kerr, Anne Harlan, and Ralph Stogdill, "Preference for Motivator and Hygiene Factors in a Hypothetical Interview Situation," *Personnel Psychology*, vol. 27 (Winter 1974), pp. 109–24. See also Frederick Herzberg, "Workers' Needs: The Same Around the World," *Industry Week* (September 21, 1987), pp. 29–32.

[10]See, for example, Greg R. Oldham and J. Richard Hackman, "Not What It Was and Not What It Will Be: The Future of Job Design Research," *Journal of Organizational Behavior*, vol. 31 (2010), pp. 463–479.

[11]See Herzberg et al., op. cit. (1967). The quotation is from Herzberg, op. cit. (1968).

[12]For a complete description of the core characteristics model, see J. Richard Hackman and Greg R. Oldham, *Work Redesign* (Reading, MA: Addison-Wesley, 1980).

[13]See, for example, J. Stacy Adams, "Toward an Understanding of Inequity," *Journal of Abnormal and Social Psychology*, vol. 67 (1963), pp. 422–36; and J. Stacy Adams, "Inequity in Social Exchange," in vol. 2, L. Berkowitz (ed.), *Advances in Experimental Social Psychology* (New York: Academic Press, 1965), pp. 267–300.

[14]See, for example, J. W. Harder, "Play for Pay: Effects of Inequity in a Pay-for-Performance Context," *Administrative Science Quarterly*, vol. 37 (1992), pp. 321–35.

[15]Information and quotes from Alistair Barr, "A Look at Some of the Most Luxurious Executive Perks," *Columbus Dispatch* (May 24, 2009), p. D1.

[16]Victor H. Vroom, *Work and Motivation* (New York: Wiley, 1964; republished by Jossey-Bass, 1994).

[17]"The Boss: Goal by Goal," *New York Times* (August 31, 2008), p. 10.

[18]The work on goal-setting theory is well summarized in Edwin A. Locke and Gary P. Latham, *Goal Setting: A Motivational Technique That Works!* (Englewood Cliffs, NJ: Prentice Hall, 1984). See also Edwin A. Locke, Kenneth N. Shaw, Lisa A. Saari, and Gary P. Latham, "Goal Setting and Task Performance 1969–1980," *Psychological Bulletin*, vol. 90 (1981), pp. 125–52; Mark E. Tubbs, "Goal Setting: A Meta-Analytic Examination of the Empirical Evidence," *Journal of Applied Psychology*, vol. 71 (1986), pp. 474–83; and Terence R. Mitchell, Kenneth R. Thompson, and Jane George-Falvy, "Goal Setting: Theory and Practice," Chapter 9 in Cary L. Cooper and Edwin A. Locke (eds.), *Industrial and Organizational Psychology: Linking Theory with Practice* (Malden, MA: Blackwell Business, 2000), pp. 211–49.

[19]For a recent critical discussion of goal-setting theory, see Lisa D. Ordonez, Maurice E. Schweitzer, Adam D. Galinsky, and Max H. Bazerman, "Goals Gone Wild: The Systematic Side Effects of Overprescribing Goal Setting," *Academy of Management Perspectives*, vol. 23 (February 2009), pp. 6–16; and Edwin A. Locke and Gary P. Latham, "Has Goal Setting Gone Wild, or Have Its Attackers Abandoned Good Scholarship?" *Academy of Management Perspectives*, vol. 23 (February, 2009), pp. 17–23.

[20]Gary P. Latham and Edwin A. Locke, "Self-Regulation Through Goal Setting," *Organizational Behavior and Human Decision Processes*, vol. 50 (1991), pp. 212–47.

[21]Edwin A. Locke, "Guest Editor's Introduction: Goal-Setting Theory and Its Applications to the World of Business," *Academy of Management Executive*, vol. 18, no. 4 (2004), pp. 124–25.

[22]E. L. Thorndike, *Animal Intelligence* (New York: Macmillan, 1911), p. 244.

[23]B. F. Skinner, *Walden Two* (New York: Macmillan, 1948); *Science and Human Behavior* (New York: Macmillan, 1953); *Contingencies of Reinforcement* (New York: Appleton-Century-Crofts, 1969).

[24]For a good review, see Lee W. Frederickson (ed.), *Handbook of Organizational Behavior Management* (New York: Wiley-Interscience, 1982); Fred Luthans and Robert Kreitner, *Organizational Behavior Modification* (Glenview, IL: Scott-Foresman, 1985); and Andrew D. Stajkovic and Fred Luthans, "A Meta-Analysis of the Effects of Organizational Behavior Modification on Task Performance 1975–95," *Academy of Management Journal*, vol. 40 (1997), pp. 1122–49.

[25]Knowledge@Wharton, "The Importance of Being Richard Branson," *Wharton School Publishing* (June 3, 2005): www.whartonsp.com.

[26]Richard Gibson, "Pitchman in the Corner Office," *Wall Street Journal* (October 24, 2007), p. D10. See also David Novak, *The Education of an Accidental CEO: Lessons Learned from the Trailer Park to the Corner Office* (New York: Crown Business, 2007).

[27]Edwin A. Locke, "The Myths of Behavior Mod in Organizations," *Academy of Management Review*, vol. 2 (October 1977), pp. 543–53.

Feature Notes 14

Role Models—Information and quotes from Robert D. Hof, "Amazon's Risky Bet," *Business Week* (November 13, 2006), p. 52; Jon Neale, "Jeff Bezos," *Business Wings* (February 16, 2007): www.businesswings.com.uk; Alan Deutschman, "Inside the Mind of Jeff Bezos," *Fast Company* (December 19, 2007): www.fastcompany.com/magazine/85; and http://en.wikipedia.org/wiki/Jeff_Bezos.

Ethics Check—Some information from Williams, and Stephen Harkins, "Many Hands Make Light the Work: The Causes and Consequences of Social Loafing," *Journal of Personality and Social Psychology*, vol. 37 (1978), pp. 822–32; and W. Jack Duncan, "Why Some People Loaf in Groups and Others Loaf Alone," *Academy of Management Executive*, vol. 8 (1994), pp. 79–80.

Facts to Consider—Information from "Two Wasted Days at Work," *CNNMoney.com* (March 16, 2005): www.cnnmoney.com.

Endnotes 14

[1]See, for example, Edward E. Lawler III, Susan Albers Mohrman, and Gerald E. Ledford Jr., *Employee Involvement and Total Quality Management: Practices and Results in Fortune 1000 Companies* (San Francisco: Jossey-Bass, 1992); Susan A. Mohrman, Susan A. Cohen, and Monty A. Mohrman, *Designing Team-Based Organizations: New Forms for Knowledge Work* (San Francisco: Jossey-Bass, 1995).

[2]Jon R. Katzenbach and Douglas K. Smith, *The Wisdom of Teams: Creating the High Performance Organization* (Boston: Harvard Business School Press, 1993).

[3]See Edward E. Lawler III, *From the Ground Up: Six Principles for Building the New Logic Corporation* (San Francisco: Jossey-Bass, 1996), p. 131.

[4]Data from Lynda C. McDermott, Nolan Brawley, and William A. Waite, *World-Class Teams: Working Across Borders* (New York: Wiley, 1998), p. 5; survey reported in "Meetings Among Top Ten Time Wasters," *San Francisco Business Times* (April 7, 2003); www.bizjournals.com/sanfrancisco/stories/2003/04/07/daily21.html.

[5]Information from Scott Thurm, "Teamwork Raises Everyone's Game," *Wall Street Journal* (November 7, 2005), p. B7.

[6]Harold J. Leavitt, "Suppose We Took Groups More Seriously," in Eugene L. Cass and Frederick G. Zimmer (eds.), *Man and Work in Society* (New York: Van Nostrand Reinhold, 1975), pp. 67–77.

[7]See Marvin E. Shaw, *Group Dynamics: The Psychology of Small Group Behavior*, 2nd ed. (New York: McGraw-Hill, 1976); Leavitt, op. cit.

[8]A classic work is Bib Latané, Kipling Williams, and Stephen Harkins, "Many Hands Make Light the Work: The Causes and Consequences of Social Loafing," *Journal of Personality and Social Psychology*, vol. 37 (1978), pp. 822–32. See also John M. George, "Extrinsic and Intrinsic Origins of Perceived Social Loafing in Organizations," *Academy of Management Journal* (March 1992), pp. 191–202; and W. Jack Duncan, "Why Some People Loaf in Groups While Others Loaf Alone," *Academy of Management Executive*, vol. 8 (1994), pp. 79–80.

[9]The "linking pin" concept is introduced in Rensis Likert, *New Patterns of Management* (New York: McGraw-Hill, 1962).

[10]See discussion by Susan G. Cohen and Don Mankin, "The Changing Nature of Work," in Susan Albers Mohrman, Jay R. Galbraith, Edward E. Lawler III, and associates, *Tomorrow's Organization: Crafting Winning Capabilities in a Dynamic World* (San Francisco: Jossey-Bass, 1998), pp. 154–78.

[11]Information from "Diversity: America's Strength," special advertising section, *Fortune* (June 23, 1997); and American Express corporate communication (1998).

[12]See Susan D. Van Raalte, "Preparing the Task Force to Get Good Results," *S.A.M. Advanced Management Journal*, vol. 47 (Winter 1982), pp. 11–16; Walter Kiechel III, "The Art of the Corporate Task Force," *Fortune* (January 28, 1991), pp. 104–06.

[13]Developed from Eric Matson, "The Seven Sins of Deadly Meetings," *Fast Company* (April/May 1996), p. 122.

[14]Mohrman et al., op. cit. (1998).

[15]Information from Jenny C. McCune, "Making Lemonade," *Management Review* (June 1997), pp. 49–53.

[16]For a good discussion of quality circles, see Edward E. Lawler III and Susan A. Mohrman, "Quality Circles After the Fad," *Harvard Business Review*, vol. 63 (January/February 1985), pp. 65–71; Edward E. Lawler III and Susan Albers Mohrman, "Employee Involvement, Reengineering, and TQM: Focusing on Capability Development," in Mohrman et al. (1998), pp. 179–208.

[17]William M. Bulkeley, "Computerizing Dull Meetings Is Touted as an Antidote to the Mouth That Bored," *Wall Street Journal* (January 28, 1992), pp. B1, B2.

[18]See Wayne F. Cascio, "Managing a Virtual Workplace," *Academy of Management Executive*, vol. 14 (2000), pp. 81–90.

[19]Robert D. Hof, "Teamwork, Supercharged," *Business Week* (November 21, 2005), pp. 90–92.

[20]See Sheila Simsarian Webber, "Virtual Teams: A Meta-Analysis," http://www.shrm.org/foundation/findings.asp.

[21]See Stacie A. Furst, Martha Reeves, Benson Rosen, and Richard S. Blackburn, "Managing the Life Cycle of Virtual Teams," *Academy of Management Executive*, vol. 18, no. 2 (2004), pp. 6–11.

[22]R. Brent Gallupe and William H. Cooper, "Brainstorming Electronically," *Sloan Management Review* (Winter 1997), pp. 11–21; Cascio, op. cit.

[23]Cascio, op. cit.; Furst et al., op. cit.

[24]See, for example, Paul S. Goodman, Rukmini Devadas, and Terri L. Griffith Hughson, "Groups and Productivity: Analyzing the Effectiveness of Self-Managing Teams," in John R. Campbell and Richard J. Campbell, *Productivity in Organizations* (San Francisco: Jossey-Bass, 1988); Jack Orsbrun, Linda Moran, Ed Musslewhite, and John H. Zenger, with Craig Perrin, *Self-Directed Work Teams: The New American Challenge* (Homewood, IL: Business One Irwin, 1990); Dale E. Yeatts and Cloyd Hyten, *High Performing Self-Managed Work Teams* (Thousand Oaks, CA: Sage, 1997).

[25]See, for example, J. Richard Hackman and Nancy Katz, "Group Behavior and Performance," in Susan T. Fiske, Daniel T. Gilbert, and Gardner Lindzey (eds.), *Handbook of Social Psychology*, 5th ed. (Hoboken, NJ: Wiley, 2010), pp. 1208–51.

[26]Goodman et al., op. cit.; Orsbrun et al., op. cit.; Yeatts and Hyten, op. cit.; and Lawler et al., op. cit., 1992.

[27]For a review of research on group effectiveness, see J. Richard Hackman, "The Design of Work Teams," in Jay W. Lorsch (ed.), *Handbook of Organizational Behavior* (Englewood Cliffs, NJ: Prentice-Hall, 1987), pp. 315–42; and J. Richard Hackman, Ruth Wageman, Thomas M. Ruddy, and Charles L. Ray, "Team Effectiveness in Theory and Practice," in Cary L. Cooper and Edwin A. Locke, *Industrial and Organizational Psychology: Linking Theory with Practice* (Malden, MA: Blackwell, 2000).

[28]For a discussion of effectiveness in the context of top management teams, see Edward E. Lawler III, David Finegold, and Jay A. Conger, "Corporate Boards: Developing Effectiveness at the Top," in Mohrman, op. cit. (1998), pp. 23–50.

[29]Quote from Alex Markels, "Money & Business," *U.S. News online* (October 22, 2006).

[30]"Dream Teams," *Northwestern* (Winter 2005), p. 10; Matt Golosinski, "Teamwork Takes Center Stage," *Northwestern* (Winter 2005), p. 39.

[31]Golosinski, op. cit., p. 39.

[32]Information from Susan Carey, "Racing to Improve," *Wall Street Journal* (March 24, 2006), pp. B1, B6.

[33]Robert D. Hof, "Amazon's Risky Bet," *BusinessWeek* (November 13, 2006), p. 52.

[34]J. Steven Heinen and Eugene Jacobson, "A Model of Task Group Development in Complex Organizations and a Strategy of Implementation," *Academy of Management Review*, vol. 1 (1976), pp. 98–111; Bruce W. Tuckman, "Developmental Sequence in Small Groups," *Psychological Bulletin*, vol. 63 (1965), pp. 384–99; Bruce W. Tuckman and Mary Ann C. Jensen, "Stages of Small-Group Development Revisited," *Group & Organization Studies*, vol. 2 (1977), pp. 419–27.

[35]See Warren Watson, "Cultural Diversity's Impact on Interaction Process and Performance," *Academy of Management Journal*, vol. 16 (1993); Christopher Earley and Elaine Mosakowski, "Creating Hybrid Team Structures: An Empirical Test of Transnational Team Functioning," *Academy of Management Journal*, vol. 5 (February 2000), pp. 26–49; Eric Kearney, Diether Gebert, and Sven C. Voilpel, "When and How Diversity Benefits Teams: The Importance of Team Members' Need for Cognition," *Academy of Management Journal*, vol. 52 (2009), pp. 582–598; and Aparna Joshi and Hyuntak Roh, "The Role of Context in Work Team Diversity Research: A Meta-Analytic Approach," *Academy of Management Journal*, vol. 52 (2009), pp. 599–628.

[36]See, for example, Edgar Schein, *Process Consultation* (Reading, MA: Addison-Wesley, 1988); and Linda C. McDermott, Nolan Brawley, and William A. Waite, *World-Class Teams: Working Across Borders* (New York: Wiley, 1998).

[37]For a good discussion, see Robert F. Allen and Saul Pilnick, "Confronting the Shadow Organization: How to Detect and Defeat Negative Norms," *Organizational Dynamics* (Spring 1973), pp. 13–16.

[38]See Schein, op. cit., pp. 76–79.

[39]Marvin E. Shaw, *Group Dynamics: The Psychology of Small Group Behavior* (New York: McGraw-Hill, 1976).

[40]A classic work in this area is K. Benne and P. Sheets, "Functional Roles of Group Members," *Journal of Social Issues*, vol. 2 (1948), pp. 42–47; see also Likert, op. cit., pp. 166–69; Schein, op. cit., pp. 49–56.

[41]Based on John R. Schermerhorn Jr., James G. Hunt, and Richard N. Osborn, *Organizational Behavior*, 7th ed. (New York: Wiley, 2000), pp. 345–46.

[42]Schein, op. cit., pp. 69–75.

[43]A good overview is William D. Dyer, *Team-Building* (Reading, MA: Addison-Wesley, 1977).

[44]Dennis Berman, "Zap! Pow! Splat!" *Business Week*, Enterprise issue (February 9, 1998), p. ENT22.

[45]Schein, op. cit., pp. 69–75.

[46]Victor H. Vroom and Arthur G. Jago, *The New Leadership: Managing Participation in Organizations* (Englewood Cliffs, NJ: Prentice Hall, 1988); Victor H. Vroom, "A New Look in Managerial Decision-Making," *Organizational Dynamics* (Spring 1973), pp. 66–80; Victor H. Vroom and Phillip Yetton, *Leadership and Decision-Making* (Pittsburgh: University of Pittsburgh Press, 1973).

[47]See Kathleen M. Eisenhardt, Jean L. Kahwajy, and L. J. Bourgeois III, "How Management Teams Can Have a Good Fight," *Harvard Business Review* (July/August 1997), pp. 77–85.

[48]Michael A. Roberto, "Why Making the Decisions the Right Way Is More Important Than Making the Right Decisions," *Ivey Business Journal* (September/October 2005), pp. 1–7.

[49]See Irving L. Janis, "Groupthink," *Psychology Today* (November 1971), pp. 43–46; and *Victims of Groupthink*, 2nd ed. (Boston: Houghton Mifflin, 1982).

[50]See also Michael Harvey, M. Ronald Buckley, Milorad M. Novicevic, and Jonathon R. B. Halbesleben, "The Abilene Paradox After Thirty Years: A Global Perspective," *Organizational Dynamics*, vol. 33 (2004), pp. 215–26.

[51]Janis, op. cit.

[52]Ibid.

[53]Richard E. Walton, *Interpersonal Peacemaking: Confrontations and Third-Party Consultation* (Reading, MA: Addison-Wesley, 1969), p. 2.

[54]See Kenneth W. Thomas, "Conflict and Conflict Management," in M. D. Dunnett (ed.), *Handbook of Industrial and Organizational Behavior* (Chicago: Rand McNally, 1976), pp. 889–935.

[55]See Robert R. Blake and Jane Strygley Mouton, "The Fifth Achievement," *Journal of Applied Behavioral Science*, vol. 6 (1970), pp. 413–27; and Alan C. Filley, *Interpersonal Conflict Resolution* (Glenview, IL: Scott, Foresman, 1975);

and L. David Brown, *Managing Conflict at Organizational Interfaces* (Reading, MA: Addison-Wesley, 1983).

[56]Filley, op. cit.

Feature Notes 15

The Devil Wears Prada—W. C. Byham, "Start Networking Right Away (Even if You Hate It)." *Harvard Business Review*, vol. 22 (January 2009).

Jay-Z—Information and quotes from John Jurgensen, "The State of Jay-Z's Empire," *Wall Street Journal* (October 22, 2010), pp. D1, D2.

Role Models—Information and quotes from Adam Bryant, "Give Your Staff a Reason to Work for You," *International Herald Tribune* (July 5, 2010), p. 17.

Ethics Check—Information from Bridget Jones, "Blogger Fire Fury," CNN.com (July 19, 2006).

Facts to Consider—Information from American Management Association, "Electronic Monitoring & Surveillance Survey" (February 8, 2008): www.press.amanet.org/press-releases; and Liz Wolgemuth, "Why Web Surfing Is a No Problem," *U.S. News & World Report* (August 22, 2008): www.usnews.com/blogs.

Undercover Boss—Information and quotes from "Undercover Boss Gets the Communication Message," *Financial Times* (June 9, 2009).

Endnotes 15

[1]See Henry Mintzberg, *The Nature of Managerial Work* (New York: Harper & Row, 1973 and Harper-Collins, 1997; John P. Kotter, "What Effective General Managers Really Do," *Harvard Business Review*, vol. 60 (November/December 1982), pp. 156–157; and *The General Managers* (New York: Macmillan, 1986).

[2]Mintzberg, op cit.

[3]Kotter, op cit.

[4]"Relationships Are the Most Powerful Form of Media," *Fast Company* (March 2001), p. 100.

[5]Information from American Management Association (AMA), "The Passionate Organization Fast-Response Survey" (September 25–29, 2000), and organization Web site: http://www.amanet.org/aboutama/index.htm.

[6]Survey information from "What Do Recruiters Want?" *BizEd* (November/December 2002), p. 9; "Much to Learn, Professors Say," *USA Today* (July 5, 2001), p. 8D; and AMA, op. cit.

[7]Jay A. Conger, *Winning 'Em Over: A New Model for Managing in the Age of Persuasion* (New York: Simon & Schuster, 1998), pp. 24–79.

[8]This discussion developed from ibid.

[9]Quotations from John Huey, "America's Most Successful Merchant," *Fortune* (September 23, 1991), pp. 46–59; see also Sam Walton and John Huey, *Sam Walton: Made in America: My Story* (New York: Bantam Books, 1993).

[10]*Business Week* (February 10, 1992), pp. 102–08.

[11]See Robert H. Lengel and Richard L. Daft, "The Selection of Communication Media as an Executive Skill," *Academy of Management Executive*, vol. 2 (August 1988), pp. 225–32.

[12]See Ibid.

[13]See Eric Matson, "Now That We Have Your Complete Attention," *Fast Company* (February/March 1997), pp. 124–32.

[14]Information from Sam Dillon, "What Corporate America Can't Build: A Sentence," *New York Times* (December 7, 2004).

[15]David McNeill, *Hand and Mind: What Gestures Reveal About Thought* (Chicago: University of Chicago Press, 1992).

[16]Martin J. Gannon, *Paradoxes of Culture and Globalization* (Los Angeles: Sage, 2008), p. 76.

[17]McNeill, op. cit.

[18]Tom Peters and Nancy Austin, *A Passion for Excellence* (New York: Random House, 1985). "Epigrams and Insights from the Original Modern Guru," *Financial Times*, Kindle edition (March 4, 2010). See also Tom Peters, *The Little Big Things: 163 Ways to Pursue EXCELLENCE* (New York: HarperStudio, 2010).

[19]Adapted from Richard V. Farace, Peter R. Monge, and Hamish M. Russell, *Communicating and Organizing* (Reading, MA: Addison-Wesley, 1977), pp. 97–98.

[20]Examples and quotes from *Business Week* (July 8, 1991), pp. 60–61; www.ccl.org/leadership/programs/profiles/lisaDitullio.aspx (retrieved August 12, 2008); and, Joe Walker, "Executives Learn New Skills to Improve Their Communication," *Wall Street Journal* (May 6, 2010), p. B3.

[21]Quote from Andy Serwer, "Game Changers: Legendary Basketball Coach John Wooden and Starbucks' Howard Schultz Talk about a Common Interest—Leadership," *Fortune* (August 11, 2008): www.cnnmoney.com.

[22]This discussion is based on Carl R. Rogers and Richard E. Farson, "Active Listening" (Chicago: Industrial Relations Center of the University of Chicago, n.d.); see also Carl R. Rogers and Fritz J. Roethlisberger, "Barriers and Gateways to Communication," *Harvard Business Review* (November/December, 2001), Reprint 91610.

[23]Ibid.

[24]Information from Carol Hymowitz, "Managers See Feedback from Their Staffers as Most Valuable," *Wall Street Journal* (August 22, 2000), p. B1.

[25]A useful source of guidelines is John J. Gabarro and Linda A. Hill, "Managing Performance," Note 9-96-022 (Boston, MA: Harvard Business School Publishing, n.d.).

[26]A classic work on proxemics is Edward T. Hall's book *The Hidden Dimension* (Garden City, NY: Doubleday, 1986).

[27]Information from Rachel Metz, "Office Décor First Change by New AOL Executive," *Columbus Dispatch* (May 25, 2009), p. A7.

[28]Amy Saunders, "A Creative Approach to Work," *Columbus Dispatch* (May 2, 2008), pp. C1, C9.

[29]Information and quotes from Adam Bryant, "Creating Trust by Destroying Hierarchy," *Global Edition of the New York Times* (February 15, 2010), p. 19.

[30]Information and quote from Kelly K. Spors, "Top Small Workplaces 2009," *Wall Street Journal* (September 28, 2009), pp. R1–R4.

[31]Information and quotes from Sarah E. Needleman, "Thnx for the IView! I Wud Luv to Work 4 U!!;)," *Wall Street Journal Online* (July 31, 2008).

[32]Stephanie Clifford, "Video Prank at Domino's Taints Brand," *New York Times* (April 16, 2009): www.nytimes.com; and Deborah Stead, "An Unwelcome Delivery," *Business Week* (May 4, 2009), p. 15.

[33]For a review of legal aspects of e-mail privacy, see William P. Smith and Filiz Tabak, "Monitoring Employee E-Mails: Is There Any Room for Privacy?" *Academy of Management Perspectives,* vol. 23 (November, 2009), pp. 33–48.

[34]Information and quotes from Michelle Conlin and Douglas MacMillan, "Managing the Tweets," *Business Week* (June 1, 2009), pp. 20–21.

[35]Information from Carol Hymowitz, "More American Chiefs Are Taking Top Posts at Overseas Concerns," *Wall Street Journal* (October 17, 2005), p. B1.

[36]Examples reported in Martin J. Gannon, *Paradoxes of Culture and Globalization* (Los Angeles: Sage Publications, 2008), p. 80.

[37]Information from Ben Brown, "Atlanta Out to Mind Its Manners," *USA Today* (March 14, 1996), p. 7.

Feature Notes 16

Finding Forrester—Project Implicit (https://implicit.harvard.edu/implicit/).

Role Models—Information and quotes from Joshua Molina, "A Vision for Change: Tech Innovator and Entrepreneur David Segura," HispanicBusiness.com (December 3, 2008): www.hispanicbusiness.com; "2008 Ernst & Young Entrepreneur of the Year: David Segura," *Smart Business Detroit* (July, 2008); and "David Segura Hispanic Business Entrepreneur of the Year," press release, Michigan Minority Business Council (November 13, 2008): www.mmbdc.com.

Ethics Check—Information and quotes from Susan Chandler, "'Fair Trade' Label Enters Retail Market," *Columbus Dispatch* (October 16, 2006), p. G6; and www.fairindigo.com/about.

Facts to Consider—Information from *What Workers Want: A Worldwide Study of Attitudes to Work and Work-Life Balance* (London: FDS International Limited, 2007).

Massmart and Walmart—Information and quotes from Robb M. Stewart, "Wal-Mart Checks Out a New Continent," *Wall Street Journal* (October 27, 2010), pp. B1, B2; and Robb M. Stewart, "Wal-Mart Sets Africa Deal," *Wall Street Journal* (November 30, 2010), p. B2.

Haier Group—Example from Mei Fong, "Chinese Refrigerator Maker Finds U.S. Chilly," *Wall Street Journal* (March 16, 2010), p. C10.

Endnotes 16

[1]Lee Gardenswartz and Anita Rowe, *Managing Diversity: A Complete Desk Reference and Planning Guide* (Chicago: Irwin, 1993).

[2]R. Roosevelt Thomas Jr., *Beyond Race and Gender* (New York: AMACOM, 1992), p. 10; see also R. Roosevelt Thomas Jr., "'From Affirmative Action' to 'Affirming Diversity,'" *Harvard Business Review* (November/December 1990), pp. 107–17; R. Roosevelt Thomas Jr., with Marjorie I. Woodruff, *Building a House for Diversity* (New York: AMACOM, 1999).

[3]Survey reported in "The Most Inclusive Workplaces Generate the Most Loyal Employees," *Gallup Management Journal* (December 2001), retrieved from http://gmj.gallup.com/press_room/release.asp?i=117.

[4]Carol Stephenson, "Leveraging Diversity to Maximum Advantage: The Business Case for Appointing More Women to Boards," *Ivey Business Journal* (September/October 2004), Reprint #9B04TE03, pp. 1–8.

[5]Donald H. Oliver, "Achieving Results Through Diversity: A Strategy for Success," *Ivey Business Journal* (March/April, 2005), Reprint #9B05TB09, pp. 1–6.

[6]Thomas Kochan, Katerina Bezrukova, Robin Ely, Susan Jackson, Aparna Joshi, Karen Jehn, Jonathan Leonard, David Levine, and David Thomas, "The Effects of Diversity on Business Performance: Report of the Diversity Research Network," reported in *SHRM Foundation Research Findings* (retrieved from www.shrm.org/foundation/findings.asp). Full article published in *Human Resource Management*, vol. 42 (2003), pp. 3–21.

[7]Oliver, op. cit.

[8]Gardenswartz and Rowe, op. cit., p. 220.

[9]Taylor Cox Jr., *Cultural Diversity in Organizations* (San Francisco: Berrett Koehler, 1994).

[10]Nanette Byrnes and Roger O. Crockett, "An Historic Succession at Xerox," *Business Week* (June 9, 2008), pp. 18–21.

[11]See Anthony Robbins and Joseph McClendon III, *Unlimited Power: A Black Choice* (New York: Free Press, 1997); and Augusto Failde and William Doyle, *Latino Success: Insights from America's Most Powerful Latino Executives* (New York: Free Press, 1996).

[12]Barbara Benedict Bunker, "Appreciating Diversity and Modifying Organizational Cultures: Men and Women at Work," in Suresh Srivastiva and David L. Cooperrider, *Appreciative Management and Leadership* (San Francisco: Jossey-Bass, 1990), Chapter 5.

[13]See Gary N. Powell, *Women-Men in Management* (Thousand Oaks, CA: Sage, 1993); and Cliff Cheng (ed.), *Masculinities in Organizations* (Thousand Oaks, CA: Sage, 1996). For added background, see also Sally Helgesen, *Everyday Revolutionaries: Working Women and the Transformation of American Life* (New York: Doubleday, 1998).

[14]Information from "Demographics: The Young and the Restful," *Harvard Business Review* (November 2004), p. 25.

[15]"Many U.S. Employees Have Negative Attitudes to Their Jobs, Employers and Top Managers," *The Harris Poll #38* (May 6, 2005), available from www.harrisinteractive.com; and "U. S. Job Satisfaction Keeps Falling," *The Conference Board Reports Today* (February 25, 2005; retrieved from www.conferenceboard.org).

[16]Mayo Clinic, "Workplace Generation Gap: Understand Differences Among Colleagues" (July 6, 2005), retrieved from http://www.cnn.com/HEALTH/library/WL/00045.html).

[17]Information based on "The Conundrum of the Glass Ceiling," op. cit.

[18]Stephanie N. Mehta, "What Minority Employees Really Want," *Fortune* (July 10, 2000), pp. 181–86.

[19]"Bias Cases by Workers Increase 9%," *Wall Street Journal* (March 6, 2008), p. D6; and ibid. See also "The 50 Women to Watch: 2005," *Wall Street Journal* (October 31, 2005), pp. R1–R11.

[20]Thomas, op. cit. (1990, 1992).

[21]Amy Chozick, "Beyond the Numbers," *Wall Street Journal* (November 14, 2005), p. R4.

[22]Thomas, op. cit. (1992), p. 17.

[23]Information from "100 Best Corporate Citizens," *Business Ethics* online (retrieved from www.business-ethics.com, November 1, 2005).

[24]Thomas, op. cit. (1992), p. 17.

[25]Thomas and Woodruff, op. cit. (1999), pp. 211–26.

[26]"Diversity Today: Corporate Recruiting Practices in Inclusive Workplaces," *Fortune* (June 12, 2000), p. S4.

[27]For a good overview, see Richard D. Lewis, *The Cultural Imperative: Global Trends in the 21st Century* (Yarmouth, ME: Intercultural Press, 2002); and Martin J. Gannon, *Understanding Global Cultures* (Thousand Oaks, CA: Sage, 1994).

[28]Based on Bunker, op. cit., pp. 127–49.

[29]Examples reported in Neil Chesanow, *The World-Class Executive* (New York: Rawson Associates, 1985).

[30]P. Christopher Earley and Elaine Mosakowski, "Toward Cultural Intelligence: Turning Cultural Differences into Workplace Advantage," *Academy of Management Executive,* vol. 18 (2004), pp. 151–57.

[31]See Gary P. Ferraro, "The Need for Linguistic Proficiency in Global Business," *Business Horizons* (May/June 1996), pp. 39–46; quote from Carol Hymowitz, "Companies Go Global, but Many Managers Just Don't Travel Well," *Wall Street Journal* (August 15, 2000), p. B1. See also Edward T. Hall, *The Silent Language* (New York: Anchor Books, 1959).

[32]Edward T. Hall, *Beyond Culture* (New York: Doubleday, 1976).

[33]Edward T. Hall, *Hidden Differences* (New York: Doubleday, 1990).

[34]See, for example, Fons Trompenaars, *Riding the Waves of Culture: Understanding Cultural Diversity in Business* (London: Nicholas Brealey Publishing, 1993); Harry C. Triandis, *Culture and Social Behavior* (New York: McGraw-Hill, 1994); Steven H. Schwartz, "A Theory of Cultural Values and Some Implications for Work," *Applied Psychology: An International Review,* vol. 48 (1999), pp. 23–49; Martin J. Gannon, *Understanding Global Cultures,* 3rd ed. (Thousand Oaks, CA: Sage, 2004); and Robert J. House, Paul J. Hanges, Mansour Javidan, Peter W. Dorfman, and Vipin Gupta (eds.), *Culture, Leadership and Organizations: The GLOBE Study of 62 Societies* (Thousand Oaks, CA: Sage Publications, Inc., 2004).

[35]Geert Hofstede, *Culture's Consequences* (Beverly Hills, CA: Sage, 1984), and *Culture's Consequences: Comparing Values, Behaviors, Institutions and Organizations Across Nations,* 2nd ed. (Thousand Oaks, CA: Sage, 2001). See also Michael H. Hoppe, "An Interview with Geert Hofstede," *Academy of Management Executive,* vol. 18 (2004), pp. 75–79.

[36]Geert Hofstede and Michael H. Bond, "The Confucius Connection: From Cultural Roots to Economic Growth," *Organizational Dynamics,* vol. 16 (1988), pp. 4–21.

[37]This dimension is explained more thoroughly by Geert Hofstede et al., *Masculinity and Femininity: The Taboo Dimension of National Cultures* (Thousand Oaks, CA.: Sage, 1998).

[38]Information from "The Conundrum of the Glass Ceiling," op cit.; and "Japan's Diversity Problem," *Wall Street Journal* (October 24, 2005), pp. B1, B5.

[39]"Japan's Diversity Problem," op. cit.

[40]See Hofstede and Bond, op. cit.

[41]See Geert Hofstede, *Culture and Organizations: Software of the Mind* (London: McGraw-Hill, 1991).

[42]This summary is based on Mansour Javidan, P. Dorfman, Mary Sully de Luque, and Robert J. House, "In the Eye of the Beholder: Cross Cultural Lessons in Leadership from Project GLOBE," *Academy of Management Perspectives* (February, 2006), pp. 67–90.

Feature Notes 17

Opening Quote—International Labour Organization, *Facts on Child Labor 2010* (Geneva, Switzerland: April 1, 2010).

The Amazing Race—E. R. Goldstein, "What If 'English Only' Isn't Wrong?", *Wall Street Journal* (August 2010). Retrieved December 8, 2010 from http://online.wsj.com/article/SB10001424052748704002104575290602423212366.html

Role Models—Information and quotes from www.limited.com/feature.jsp; and Time Ferna, "Success of 'Secret' in Brazil Startling," *Columbus Dispatch* (October 24, 2010), pp. D1, D2.

Ethics Check 17—Information from Raul Burgoa, "Bolivia Seizes Control of Oil and Gas Fields," *Bangkok Post* (May 3, 2006), p. B5.

Facts to Consider—Information from Transparency International, "Corruption Perceptions Index 2008" and "Bribe Payers Index" (December 9, 2008), both available from: www.transparency.org.

Rwanda—Information and quote from Steve Hamm, "Into Africa: Capitalism from the Ground Up," *Business Week* (May, 4 2009), pp. 60–61.

Endnotes 17

[1]Sample articles include "Globalization Bites Boeing," *Business Week* (March 24, 2008), p. 32; "One World, One Car, One Name," *Business Week* (March 24, 2008), p. 32; Eric Bellman and Jackie Range. "Indian-Style Mergers: Buy a Brand, Leave it Alone," *Wall Street Journal* (March 22–23, 2008), pp. A9, A14; and David Kiley, "One Ford for the Whole Wide World," *Business Week* (June 15, 2009), pp. 58–59.

[2]Pietra Rivoli, *The Travels of a T-Shirt in the Global Economy,* 2nd ed. (Hoboken, NJ: Wiley, 2009).

[3]See for example Kenichi Ohmae's books *The Borderless World: Power and Strategy in the Interlinked Economy* (New York: Harper, 1989); *The End of the Nation State* (New York: Free Press, 1996); *The Invisible Continent: Four Strategic Imperatives of the New Economy* (New York: Harper, 1999); and *The Next Global Stage: Challenges and Opportunities in Our Borderless World* (Philadelphia: Wharton School Publishing, 2006).

[4]For a discussion of globalization, see Thomas L. Friedman, *The Lexus and the Olive Tree: Understanding Globalization* (New York: Bantam Doubleday Dell, 2000); John Micklethwait and Adrian Woodridge, *A Future Perfect: The Challenges and Hidden Promise of Globalization* (New York: Crown, 2000); and Thomas L. Friedman, *The World Is Flat: A Brief History of the Twenty-First Century* (New York: Farrar, Straus and Giroux, 2005).

[5]Rosabeth Moss Kanter, *World Class: Thinking Locally in the Global Economy* (New York: Simon & Schuster, 1995), preface.

[6]Paul Wilson, "Foreign Companies Big Employers in Ohio," *Columbus Dispatch* (December 26, 2005), p. F6.

[7]Quote from John A. Byrne, "Visionary vs. Visionary," *Business Week* (August 28, 2000), p. 210.

[8]See Mauro F. Guillén and Esteban García-Canal, "The American Model of the Multinational Firm and the 'New' Multinationals from Emerging Economies," *Academy of Management Perspectives,* vol. 23 (2009), pp. 23–35.

[9]Information from newbalance.com/corporate.

[10]Information in box from "Factory to the World," *National Geographic* (May, 2008), p. 170. For how Chinese firms are being affected by the global economic slowdown, see Dexter Roberts, "China's Factory Blues," *Business Week* (April 7, 2008), pp. 78–82.

[11]"Survey: Intellectual Property Theft Now Accounts for 31% of Global Counterfeiting." *Gieschen Consultancy,* February 25, 2005.

[12]Information from "Not Exactly Counterfeit," *Fortune* (April 26, 2006): oney.cnn.com/magazines/fortune.

[13]Criteria for choosing joint venture partners developed from Anthony J. F. O'Reilly, "Establishing Successful Joint Ventures in Developing Nations: A CEO's Perspective," *Columbia Journal of World Business* (Spring 1988), pp. 65–71; and "Best Practices for Global Competitiveness," *Fortune* (March 30, 1998), pp. S1–S3, special advertising section.

[14]Karby Leggett, "U.S. Auto Makers Find Promise—and Peril—in China," *Wall Street Journal* (June 19, 2003), p. B1; "Did Spark Spark a Copycat?" *Business Week* (February 7, 2005), p. 64.

[15]Quote from Charles Forelle and Don Clark, "Intel Fine Jolts Tech Sector," *Wall Street Journal* (May 14, 2009), pp. A1, A14.

[16]"Starbucks Wins Trademark Case," *The Economic Times,* Bangalore (January 3, 2006), p. 8.

[17]This index is reported in *The Economist.* Data in table are from "Bunfight," economist.com (October 14, 2010).

[18]Many newspapers and magazines publish annual lists of the world's largest multinational corporations. *Fortune's* annual listing is available from www.fortune.com.

[19]See Fortune.com and Ftimes.com.

[20]See Peter F. Drucker, "The Global Economy and the Nation-State," *Foreign Affairs,* vol. 76 (September/October 1997), pp. 159–71.

[21]Information from Steve Hamm, "IBM vs. TATA: Which Is More American?" *Business Week* (May 5, 2008), p. 28.

[22]Michael Mandel, "Multinationals: Are They Good for America?," *Business Week* (February 28, 2008): businessweek.com.

[23]Ibid.

[24]"Count: Really Big Business," *Fast Company* (December, 2008/ January, 2009), p. 46.

[25]Adapted from R. Hall Mason, "Conflicts Between Host Countries and Multinational Enterprise," *California Management Review,* vol. 17 (1974), pp. 6, 7.

[26]See Dionne Searcey, "U.S. Cracks Down on Corporate Bribes," *Wall Street Journal* (May 26, 2009), pp. A1–A4.

[27]Marc Gunther, "Can Factory Monitoring Ever Really Work?" *Business Ethics* (Fall 2005), p. 12.

[28]Information and quote from Andrew Morse and Nick Wingfield, "Microsoft Will Investigate Conditions at Chinese Plant," *Wall Street Journal* (April 16, 2010), p. B7.

[29]"An Industry Monitors Child Labor," *New York Times* (October 16, 1997), pp. B1, B9; and Rugmark International Web site: www.rugmark.de.

[30]Information and quote from Andrew Morse and Nick Wingfield, "Apple Audits Labor Practices," *Wall Street Journal* (March 1, 2010), p. B3.

[31]See Robert B. Reich, "Who Is Them?" *Harvard Business Review* (March/April 1991), pp. 77–88.

[32]Carol Hymowitz, "The New Diversity," *Wall Street Journal* (November 14, 2005), p. R1.

[33]This summary is based on Mansour Javidan, P. Dorfman, Mary Sully de Luque, and Robert J. House, "In the Eye of the Beholder: Cross Cultural Lessons in Leadership from Project GLOBE," *Academy of Management Perspectives* (February 2006), pp. 67–90; and Martin J. Gannon, *Paradoxes of Culture and Globalization* (Thousand Oaks, CA: Sage, 2008), p. 52.

Feature Notes 18

Role Models—Information and quotes from Joe Higgins, "Athens Business Owner Presented State Award," *Athens Messenger* (November 18, 2009), p. 3; and Samantha Pirc, "A Local Success Story: Q&A with Michelle Greenfield of Third Sun," *OHIO Today* (Fall/Winter, 2009), pp. 14, 15.

Ethics Check—Information from Jessica Shambora, "The Story Behind the World's Hottest Shoemaker," *Financial Times*, Kindle edition (March 21, 2010); www.toms.com/movement-one-for-one; and John Tozzi, "The Ben & Jerrys' Law: Principles Before Profit," *Bloomberg Businessweek* (April 26–May 2, 2010), pp. 69, 70.

Facts to Consider—Data reported by Karen E. Klein, "Minority Start Ups: A Measure of Progress," *Business Week* (August 25, 2005), retrieved from www.businessweekonline; and press release, Minority Business Development Agency (March 5, 2009): www.mbda.gov; "Minority-Owned Business Growth & Global Reach," U. S. Department of Commerce MBDA: www.mdba.org (revised March, 2011); and, Leah Yomtovian, "The Funding Landscape for Minority Entrepreneurs," *ideacrossing.org* (February 16, 2011).

Endnotes 18

[1]Information and quotes for these examples from Alison Damasi, "No Job? Create One," *Bloomberg Businessweek* (March 22 & 29, 2010), p. 89; Laura Lorber, "Older Entrepreneurs Target Peers," *Wall Street Journal* (February 16, 2010), p. B6; and Dale Buss, "The Mothers of Invention," *Wall Street Journal* (February 8, 2010), p. R7.

[2]Information from "Women Business Owners Receive First-Ever Micro Loans Via the Internet," *Business Wire* (August 9, 2000); Jim Hopkins, "Non-Profit Loan Group Takes Risks on Women in Business," *USA Today* (August 9, 2000), p. 2B; and "Women's Group Grants First Loans to Entrepreneurs," *Columbus Dispatch* (August 10, 2000), p. B2.

[3]Speech at the Lloyd Greif Center for Entrepreneurial Studies, Marshall School of Business, University of Southern California, 1996.

[4]This list is developed from Jeffry A. Timmons, *New Venture Creation: Entrepreneurship for the 21st Century* (New York: Irwin/McGraw-Hill, 1999), pp. 47–48; and Robert D. Hisrich and Michael P. Peters, *Entrepreneurship*, 4th ed. (New York: Irwin/McGraw-Hill, 1998), pp. 67–70.

[5]Information for these profiles from the corporate Web sites; the Entrepreneur's Hall of Fame: www.ltbn.com/halloffame.html; people.forbes.com; Josh Quittner, "The Flickr Founders," *Time* (April 30, 2006): www.time.com (accessed May 17, 2010); and www.hunch.com.

[6]For the top-selling franchises, see "Top 10 Franchises for 2009," *Entrepreneur Magazine* (January, 2009): www.entrepreneur.com.

[7]For a review and discussion of the entrepreneurial mind, see Timmons, op. cit., pp. 219–225.

[8]Timothy Butler and James Waldroop, "Job Sculpting: The Art of Retaining Your Best People," *Harvard Business Review* (September/October 1999), pp. 144–52.

[9]Based on research summarized by Hisrich and Peters, op. cit., pp. 70–74.

[10]Information and quote from Jim Hopkins, "Serial Entrepreneur Strikes Again at Age 70," *USA Today* (August 15, 2000).

[11]See the review by Hisrich and Peters, op. cit.; and Paulette Thomas, "Entrepreneurs' Biggest Problems and How They Solve Them," *Wall Street Journal Reports* (March 17, 2003), pp. R1, R2.

[12]Ibid.

[13]Quote from www.anitaroddick.com/aboutanita.php (accessed April 24, 2010).

[14]"New Census Data Reinforces the Economic Power of Women-Owned Businesses in the U.S. says NAWBO," National Association of Women Business Owners press release (July 15, 2010); nawbo.org; Mark D. Wolf, "Women-Owned Business: America's New Job Creation Engine," *Forbes.com* (January 12, 2010); and *Paths to Entrepreneurship: New Directions for Women in Business* (New York: Catalyst, 1998) as summarized on the National Foundation for Women Business Owners Web site: www.nfwbo.org/key.html.

[15]*Paths to Entrepreneurship*, op. cit.; and *Women Business Owners of Color: Challenges and Accomplishments* (Washington, DC: National Foundation for Women Business Owners, 1998).

[16]Information from www.mbda.gov; and, Leah Yomtovian, "The Funding Landscape for Minority Entrepreneurs," *ideacrossing.org* (February 16, 2011).

[17]David Bornstein, *How to Change the World: Social Entrepreneurs and the Power of New Ideas* (Oxford, U.K.: Oxford University Press, 2004).

[18]See Laura D' Andrea Tyson, "Good Works—With a Business Plan," *Business Week* (May 3, 2004), retrieved from *Business Week Online* (November 14, 2005) at www.businessweek.com.

[19]Examples are from "Growing Green Business," *Northwestern* (Winter, 2007), p. 19; and Regina McEnery, "Cancer Patients Getting the White-Glove Treatment," *Columbus Dispatch* (March 1, 2008).

[20]See "The 10 Best Social Enterprises of 2009," *Fast Company* (December 1, 2009): fastcompany.com.

[21]*The Facts About Small Business 1999* (Washington, DC: U.S. Small Business Administration, Office of Advocacy).

[22]Reported by Sue Shellenbarger, "Plumbing for Joy? Be Your Own Boss," *Wall Street Journal* (September 16, 2009), pp. D1, D2.

[23]Ibid.

[24]See U.S. Small Business Administration Web site: www.sba.gov; and *Statistical Abstract of the United States* (Washington, DC: U.S. Census Bureau, 1999).

[25]"Small Business Expansions in Electronic Commerce," U.S. Small Business Administration, Office of Advocacy (June 2000).

[26]Information from Will Christensen, "Rod Spencer's Sports-Card Business Has Migrated Cyberspace Marketplace," *Columbus Dispatch* (July 24, 2000), p. F1.

[27]Discussion based on "The Life Cycle of Entrepreneurial Firms," in Ricky Griffin (ed.), *Management*, 6th ed. (New York: Houghton Mifflin, 1999), pp. 309–10; and Neil C. Churchill and Virginia L. Lewis, "The Five Stages of Small Business Growth," *Harvard Business Review* (May/June 1993), pp. 30–50.

[28]Information reported in "The Rewards," *Inc. State of Small Business* (May 20–21, 2001), pp. 50–51.

[29]Data reported by The Family Firm Institute: www.ffi.org/looking/factsfb.html.

[30]Conversation from the case "Am I My Uncle's Keeper?" by Paul I. Karofsky (Northeastern University Center for Family Business) and published at www.fambiz.com/contprov.cfm? ContProvCode=NECFB&ID=140.

[31]*Survey of Small and Mid-Sized Businesses: Trends for 2000*, conducted by Arthur Andersen and National Small Business United.

[32]Ibid.

[33]See U.S. Small Business Administration Web site: www.sba.gov.

[34]George Gendron, "The Failure Myth," *Inc.* (January 2001), p. 13. Information and quotes from Dana Mattioli, "Recession Spells End for Many Family Enterprises," *Wall Street Journal* (October 6, 2009), p. B6.

[35]Based on Norman M. Scarborough and Thomas W. Zimmerer, *Effective Small Business Management* (Englewood Cliffs, NJ: Prentice-Hall, 2000), pp. 25–30; and Scott Clark, "Most Small-Business Failures Tied to Poor Management," *Business Journal* (April 10, 2000).

[36]Anne Field, "Business Incubators Are Growing Up," *Business Week* (November 16, 2009), p. 76.

[37]See www.sba.gov/aboutsba.

[38]Developed from William S. Sahlman, "How to Write a Great Business Plan," *Harvard Business Review* (July/August 1997), pp. 98–108.

[39]Marcia H. Pounds, "Business Plan Sets Course for Growth," *Columbus Dispatch* (March 16, 1998), p. 9; see also firm Web site: www.calcustoms.com.

[40]Standard components of business plans are described in many books, such as Linda Pinson, *Anatomy of a Business Plan: The Step-by-Step Guide to Building the Business and Securing Your Company's Future* (Tustin, CA: Out of Your Mind . . . and Into the Marketplace, 2008). Scarborough and Zimmerer, op. cit.; and on Web sites such as American Express Small Business Services, Business Town.com., and BizplanIt.com.

[41]"You've Come a Long Way Baby," *Business Week Frontier* (July 10, 2000).

SKILL-BUILDING PORTFOLIO

Self-Assessment Notes

[1]Some Items included in *Outcome Measurement Project, Phase I and Phase II Reports* (St. Louis: American Assembly of Collegiate Schools of Business, 1986).

[2]Item list from James Weber, "Management Value Orientations: A Typology and Assessment," *International Journal of Value Based Management*, vol. 3, no. 2 (1990), pp. 37–54.

[3]AIM Survey (El Paso, TX: ENFP Enterprises, 1989). Copyright © 1989 by Weston H. Agor. Used by permission.

[4]Suggested by a discussion in Robert Quinn, Sue R. Faerman, Michael P. Thompson, and Michael R. McGrath, *Becoming a Master Manager: A Contemporary Framework* (New York: Wiley, 1990), pp. 75–76.

[5]Julian P. Rotter, "External Control and Internal Control," *Psychology Today* (June, 1971), p. 42. Used by permission.

[6]Joseph A. Devito, *Messages: Building Interpersonal Communication Skills*, 3rd ed. (New York: HarperCollins, 1996), referencing William Haney, *Communicational Behavior: Text and Cases*, 3rd ed. (Homewood, IL: Irwin, 1973). Reprinted by permission.

[7]Questionnaire adapted from L. Steinmetz and R. Todd, *First Line Management*, 4th ed. (Homewood, IL: BPI/Irwin, 1986), pp. 64–67. Used by permission.

[8]Based on S. Budner, "Intolerance of Ambiguity as a Personality Variable," *Journal of Personality*, vol. 30, no. 1 (1962), pp. 29–50.

[9]Developed in part from Robert E. Quinn, Sue R. Faerman, Michael P. Thompson, and Michael R. McGrath, *Becoming a Master Manager! A Contemporary Framework* (New York: Wiley, 1990), p. 187. Used by permission.

[10]Fred E. Fiedler and Martin M. Chemers, *Improving Leadership Effectiveness: The Leader Match Concept*, 2nd ed. (New York: Wiley, 1984). Used by permission.

[11]Adapted from R.W. Bortner, "A Short Rating Scale as a Potential Measure of Type A Behavior, "*Journal of Chronic Diseases*, vol. 22 (1966), pp. 87–91. Used by permission.

[12]Developed from Lynda McDermott, Nolan Brawley, and William Waite, *World-Class Teams: Working Across Borders* (New York: Wiley, 1998).

[13]Douglas T. Hall, Donald D. Bowen, Roy J. Lewicki, and Francine S. Hall, *Experiences in Management and Organizational Behavior*, 2nd ed. (New York: Wiley, 1985). Used by permission.

[14]Developed from "Is Your Company Really Global?" *Business Week* (December 1, 1997).

[15]Instrument adapted from Norman M. Scarborough and Thomas W. Zimmerer, *Effective Small Business Management*, 3rd ed. (Columbus: Merrill, 1991), pp. 26–27.

Class Exercise Notes

[1]Adapted from John R. Schermerhorn Jr., James G. Hunt, and Richard N. Osborn, *Managing Organizational Behavior*, 3rd ed. (New York: Wiley, 1988), pp. 32–33. Used by permission.

[2]Developed from Sara L. Rynes, Tamara L. Giluk, and Kenneth G. Brown, "The Very Separate Worlds of Academic and Practitioner Periodicals in Human Resource Management: Implications for Evidence-Based Management," *Academy of Management Journal*, vol. 50 (October 2008), p. 986.

[3]Adapted from "Lost at Sea: A Consensus-Seeking Task," in the *1975 Handbook for Group Facilitators*. Used with permission of University Associates, Inc.

[4]Suggested by an exercise in John F. Veiga and John N. Yanouzas, *The Dynamics of Organization Theory: Gaining a Macro Perspective* (St. Paul, MN: West, 1979), pp. 69–71.

[5]Developed from Eugene Owens, "Upward Appraisal: An Exercise in Subordinate's Critique of Superior's Performance," *Exchange: The Organizational Behavior Teaching Journal*, vol. 3 (1978), pp. 41–42.

[6]Vignettes from Victor H. Vroom and Arthur G. Jago, *The New Leadership* (Englewood Cliffs, NJ: Prentice-Hall, 1988). Used by permission.

[7]Adapted from Roy J. Lewicki, Donald D. Bowen, Douglas T. Hall, and Francine S. Hall, "What Do You Value in Work?" *Experiences in Management and Organizational Behavior*, 3rd ed. (New York: Wiley, 1988), pp. 23–26. Used by permission.

[8]Developed from Brian Dumaine, "Why Do We Work?" *Fortune* (December 26, 1994), pp. 196–204.

[9]Adapted from William Dyer, *Team Building*, 2nd ed. (Reading, MA: Addison-Wesley, 1987), pp. 123–25.

[10]Suggested by feedback questionnaire in Judith R. Gordon, *A Diagnostic Approach to Organizational Behavior*, 3rd ed. (Boston: Allyn & Bacon, 1991), p. 298.

[11]From Sidney B. Simon, Howard Kirschenbaum, and Leland Howe, *Values Clarification, The Handbook*, rev. ed. © 1991, Values Press, P.O. Box 450, Sunderland, MA. 01375.

[12]Quote from woopidoo.com/businessquotes (retrieved September 16, 2006). See also Michael Gerber, *The E-Myth Revisited: Why Most Small Businesses Don't Work and What to Do About It* (New York: HarperCollins, 2001).

Team Project Notes

[1]Developed in part from Roy J. Lewicki, Donald D. Bowen, Douglas T. Hall, and Francine S. Hall, *Experiences in Management and Organizational Behavior*, 3rd ed. (New York: Wiley, 1988), pp. 261–67. Used by permission.

[2]Developed from Roy J. Lewicki, Donald D. Bowen, Douglas T. Hall, and Francine S. Hall, *Experiences in Management and Organizational Behavior*, 4th ed. (New York: Wiley, 1997), pp. 195–97.

[3]Thomas L. Friedman, *The World Is Flat: A Brief History of the Twenty-First Century* (New York: Farrar, Straus and Giroux, 2005).

Case 1 Bibliography

"Trader Joe's Market." *Supermarket News*. http://supermarketnews.com/profiles/top75/trader_joes_market11/. Accessed 2/6/11.

Beth Kowitt. "Inside the secret world of Trader Joe's." *Fortune*. Posted 8/23/10. http://money.cnn.com/2010/08/20/news/companies/inside_trader_joes_full_version.fortune/index.htm. Accessed 2/6/11.

"Aldi Sud." *Fast Company*. http://www.fastcompany.com/mic/2010/profile/aldi-sumld. Accessed 2/6/11.

"Trader Joe's Store Manager Salary." *GlassDoor.com*. http://www.glassdoor.com/Salary/Trader-Joe-s-Store-Manager-Salaries-E5631_D_KO13,26.htm. Accessed 2/6/11.

www.traderjoes.com/history.html.

Deborah Orr, "The Cheap Gourmet," *Forbes* (April 10, 2006).

Business Week Online (February 21, 2008),

Kerry Hannon, "Let Them Eat Ahi Jerky," *U.S. News & World Report* (July 7, 1997).

Marianne Wilson, "When Less is More," *Chain Store Age* (November 2006).

Supermarket News's Top 75 Retailers (January 12, 2009).

www.traderjoes.com/value.html.

www.traderjoes.com/how_we_do_biz.html.

"Win at the Grocery Game," *Consumer Reports* (October 2006), p. 10.

www.traderjoes.com/tjs_faqs.asp#DiscontinueProducts.

www.latimes.com/business/la-fi-tj12feb12,1,1079460.story.

Jena McGregor, "2004 Customer 1st," *Fast Company* (October 2004).

Irwin Speizer, "The Grocery Chain That Shouldn't Be," *Fast Company* (February 2004).

Heidi Brown, "Buy German," *Forbes* (January 12, 2004).

www.traderjoes.com/benefits.html.

Irwin Speizer, "Shopper's Special," *Workforce Management* (September 2004).

"Retailer Spotlight," *Gourmet Retailer* (June 2006).

http://www.wholefoodsmarket.com/company/index.php.

"Downturn Could Burn Whole Foods," *The Walls Street Journal* (November 3, 2008), pp. B1.

"Employees First!" *Time* (July 7, 2008), p. 4.

http://www.wholefoodsmarket.com/company/index.php.

"Employees First!" *Time* (July 7, 2008), p. 4.

"Downturn Could Burn Whole Foods," *The Wall Street Journal* (November 3, 2008), pp. B1, B9.

Matt Andrejczak, "Have Investors Whet Their Appetite on Whole Foods?" *MarketWatch* (May 19, 2009).

"Downturn Could Burn Whole Foods."

Case 2 Bibliography

Sonya Dowsett. "Zara Owner Inditex Q1 Net Profit Up 63 Percent." *International Business Times.* 6/9/10. http://www.ibtimes.com/articles/27536/20100609/zara-owner-inditex-q1-net-profit-up-63-percent.htm. Accessed 2/6/11.

Julia Caesar. "Zara launches online retail store." *BBC News.* Posted 9/2/10. http://www.bbc.co.uk/news/business-11155437. Accessed DATE.

"Our Group." Inditex. http://www.inditex.com/en/who_we_are/our_group. Accessed 2/6/11.

Inditex Press Dossier: www.inditex.com/en/press/information/press_kit (accessed May 17, 2009).

"Zara Grows as Retail Rivals Struggle," *Wall Street Journal* (March 26, 2009).

"Zara, A Spanish Success Story," CNN (June 15, 2001).

Cecile Rohwedder and Keith Johnson, "Pace-setting Zara Seeks More Speed to Fight Its Rising Cheap-Chic Rivals," *Wall Street Journal* (February, 20, 2008), p. B1.

"Zara: Taking the Lead in Fast-Fashion," *Business Week* (April 4, 2006).

"Zara Grows as Retail Rivals Struggle," *Wall Street Journal* (March 26, 2009).

Diana Middleton, "Fashion for the Frugal," *The Florida Times-Union* (October 1, 2006).

"Who We Are," www.inditex.com/en/who_we_are/timeline (accessed May 18, 2008).

"Shining Examples," *Economist* (June 17, 2006).

"Westfield Looks to Zara for Fuller Figure of $1 bn Australian," *The Australian* (September 3, 2007), p. 3.

"Ortega's Empire Showed Rivals New Style of Retailing," *The Times* (United Kingdom) (June 14, 2007).

Case 3 Bibliography

Monte Burke. "Wal-Mart, Patagonia Team to Green Business." *Forbes.* Posted 5/6/10, 12:20 PM. http://www.forbes.com/forbes/2010/0524/rebuilding-sustainability-eco-friendly-mr-green-jeans.html. Accessed 2/2/11.

Kent Garber. "Yvon Chouinard: Patagonia Founder Fights for the Environment." *U.S. News.* Posted 10/22/09. http://www.usnews.com/news/best-leaders/articles/2009/10/22/yvon-chouinard-patagonia-founder-fights-for-the-environment. Accessed 2/2/11.

"Patagonia." *Inc.* http://www.inc.com/top-workplaces/2010/profile/patagonia-richard-sheahan.html. Accessed 2/3/11.

Jennifer Wang. "Patagonia, From the Ground Up." *Entrepreneur.* Posted 6/10. http://www.entrepreneur.com/magazine/entrepreneur/2010/june/206536.html. Accessed 2/2/11.

"Environmentalism: Our Common Waters." *Patagonia.* http://www.patagonia.com/us/patagonia.go?assetid=1865. Accessed 2/3/11.

"Keep Earth in Business." *1% For the Planet.* http://www.onepercentfortheplanet.org/en/. Accessed 2/3/11.

Kristall Lutz. "What Makes Patagonia 'The Coolest Company on the Planet': Insights from Founder Yvon Chouinard." *Opportunity Green.* Posted 1/27/11. http://opportunitygreen.com/green-business-blog/2011/01/27/what-makes-patagonia-the-coolest-company-on-the-planet-insights-from-founder-yvon-chouinard/. Accessed 2/2/11.

"Environmental Internships." *Patagonia.* http://www.patagonia.com/eu/enSE/patagonia.go?assetid=9153. Accessed 2/3/11.

"Tools for Grassroots Activists Conference." *Patagonia.* http://www.patagonia.com/us/patagonia.go?assetid=15372. Accessed 2/3/11.

"Our History." *Patagonia.* http://www.patagonia.com/us/patagonia.go?assetid=3351. Accessed 2/3/11.

"Introducing the Common Threads Initiative." *Patagonia.* http://www.patagonia.com/us/patagonia.go?assetid=1956. Accessed 2/3/11.

Case 4 Bibliography

"Amazon.com Announces Fourth Quarter Sales Up 36% to $12.95 Billion." *Amazon.* Posted 1/27/11. http://phx.corporate-ir.net/phoenix.zhtml?c=176060&p=irol-newsArticle&ID=1521090&highlight=. Accessed 2/24/11.

Stuart Dredge. "Kindle app for iPhone and iPad may get webby to avoid Apple's new rules." *CNET UK.* Posted 2/24/11, 12:14 PM. http://crave.cnet.co.uk/mobiles/kindle-app-for-iphone-and-ipad-may-get-webby-to-avoid-apples-new-rules-50002913/. Accessed 2/24/11.

Jeffrey A. Trachtenberg. "Barnes & Noble Names Its Web Chief as CEO ." *Wall Street Journal.* Posted 3/19/10. http://online.wsj.com/article/SB10001424052748704207504575129313539265910.html. Accessed 2/20/11.

www.amazon.com.

http://www.amazon.com/Locations-Careers/b?ie=UTF8&node=239366011.

www.jumpstart-it.com/jumpstart-it-on-amazon.html.

Sean O'Neill, "Indulge Your Literary Urge," *Kiplinger's Personal Finance*, vol. 59, no. 8 (August 2005).

"Amazon CEO Takes Long View," *USA Today* (July 6, 2005).

David Meerman Scott, "The Flip Side of Free," *eContent*, vol. 28, no. 10 October 2005.

"New Amazon MP3 Clips Widget Ads to Suite of Digital Product Widgets?" (accessed at http://top10-charts.com/news.php?nid=40273 May 29, 2008).

Thomas Ricker, "Amazon Adds Audible to its Digital Empire" (accessed at http://www.engadget.com/2008/01/31/amazon-adds-audible-to-its-digital-empire/ May 28, 2008).

"Amazon Unbox on TiVo" (accessed at http://www.amazon.com/gp/video/tivo May 29, 2008).

Steven Levy, "The Future of Reading," *Newsweek* (November 26, 2007).

Tim O Reilly, "Why Kindle Should Be an Open Book," *Forbes* (accessed at http://www.forbes.com/2009/02/22/kindle-oreilly-ebooks-technology-breakthroughs_oreilly.html).

http://www.applelinks.com/index.php/more/amazon_launches_optimized_kindle_store_seamlessly_integrated_with_kindle_fo/. Accessed March 4, 2009.

Brad Stone, "The Zappos Way of Managing," *The New York Times* (March 28, 2009).

http://about.zappos.com/zappos-story/looking-ahead-let-there-be-anything-and-everything.

http://about.zappos.com/press-center/zappos-finds-perfect-fit Zappos finds a perfect fit.

Gene Marks, "Many Happy Returns" (accessed at http://www.forbes.com/2009/01/05/zappos-retail-return-ent-manage-cx_gm_0105genemarks returns.html).

http://www.businessweek.com/smallbiz/content/sep2008/sb20080916_288698.htm).

http://about.zappos.com/press-center/workplace-fun-shoe-fits-zappos.

"Zappos Secret: It's an Open Book," *Business Week* (March 23 & 30, 2009).

Case 5 Bibliography

"Nordstrom Beats Macy's and Saks by Moving Inventories." *Bloomberg.* Posted 4/8/09, 4:19 PM. http://www.bloomberg.com/apps/news?pid=news archive&sid=a54WN3jQ6TEs. Accessed 1/18/11.

"Nordstrom Uses Web to Locate Items and Increase Sales." *The New York Times.* Posted 8/23/2010. http://www.nytimes.com/2010/08/24/business/24shop.html. Accessed 1/18/21.

Jake Batsell. "Nordstrom gets in step with tracking its inventory." *The Seattle Times.* Posted 2/10/02. http://community.seattletimes.nwsource.com/archive/?date=20020210&slug=nordstrom10. Accessed 2/7/11.

Case 6 Bibliography

Dean Takahashi. "EA's chief creative officer describes game industry's re-engineering." *GamesBeat.* Posted 8/26/09. http://venturebeat.com/2009/08/26/eas-chief-creative-officer-describes-game-industrys-re-engineering/. Accessed 2/20/11.

Ben Fritz. "Viacom sold Harmonix for $50, saved $50 million on taxes." *Los Angeles Times.* Posted 1/4/11. http://latimesblogs.latimes.com/entertainment newsbuzz/2011/01/viacom-sold-harmonix-for-50-saved-50-million-on-taxes.html. Accessed 2/20/11.

Christopher Grant. "Jobs: 1/3 of iPhone App Store launch apps are games." Website *Joystiq.* Posted 7/10/08. http://www.joystiq.com/2008/07/10/jobs-1-3-of-iphone-app-store-launch-apps-are-games/. Accessed 2/20/11.

Chris Morris. "Video Game Faceoff: EA vs Activision." *CNBC.* Posted 2/11/2010. http://www.cnbc.com/id/35352043/Video_Game_Faceoff_EA_vs_Activision. Accessed 2/20/11.

Mark Serrels. "Digital Distribution: Is EA the Best Prepared Publisher?" *Kotaku.* Posted 2/2/11. http://www.kotaku.com.au/2011/02/digital-distribution-is-ea-the-best-prepared-publisher/. Accessed 2/20/11.

"Numbers." *Zynga*. http://www.zynga.com/about/numbers.php. Accessed 2/20/11.

"Facts." *Zynga*. http://www.zynga.com/about/facts.php. Accessed 2/20/11.

Joab Jackson. "Zynga's Secret to Success: Connecting Casual Friends." *CIO*. Posted 2/15/11. http://www.cio.com/article/664955/Zynga_s_Secret_to_Success_Connecting_Casual_Friends. Accessed 2/20/11.

"EA Reports Fourth Quarter and Fiscal Year 2009 Results," http://news.ea.com/news/ea/20090505006595/en (accessed May 23, 2009).

David Whelan, "Name Recognition," *Forbes* (June 20, 2005).

Martin McEachern, "The Only Game in Town," *Computer Graphics World* (October 2005).

Owen Good, "Lawsuit: Retired NFLers Cheated by EA, Union" (accessed May 23, 2009, at http://kotaku.com/5059011/lawsuit-retired-nflers-cheated-by-ea-union).

"Anti-trust lawsuit over exclusive license contract" (accessed July 9, 2008, at http://www.aolcdn.com/tmz_socumetns/0611_nfl_ea_wm.pdf).

Kenneth Hein, "Gaming Product Placement Gets Good Scores in Study," *Brandweek* (December 5, 2005).

Nick Wingfield, "Electronic Arts Offers $2 Billion for Take-Two," *Wall Street Journal* (February 25, 2008).

Nick Wingfield, "Take-Two's Earnings Report May Be a Coda to EA Offer," *Wall Street Journal* (December 15, 2008).

Software Top 100: "The World's Largest Software Companies" (accessed May 23, 2009, at http://www.softwaretop100.org/).

"Take 2 Interactive Corporate Overview" (accessed at http://ir.take2games.com/).

Case 7 Bibliography

"Guatemala/Mexico." *Frontline World*. http://www.pbs.org/frontlineworld/stories/guatemala.mexico/facts.html. Accessed 2/8/11.

"Company Snapshot." *Dunkin' Donuts*. http://www.dunkindonuts.com/content/dunkindonuts/en/company.html. Accessed 2/8/11.

"Dunkin' Donuts Announces Robust Development Growth in 2010." *Dunkin' Donuts*. Posted 2/3/11. http://news.dunkindonuts.com/dunkin+donuts/dunkin+donuts+news/dunkin+donuts+announces+robust+2010+growth.htm. Accessed 2/8/11.

dunkindonuts.com/aboutus/company/products/CoffeeConsFacts.aspx?Section=company.

Susan Spielberg, "For Snack Chains, Coffee Drinks the Best Way to Sweeten Profits," *Nation's Restaurant News* (June 27, 2005).

www.bizjournals.ocm/boston/gen/company.html?gcode=3AF1302DF8B5463AA3EA890B32D5B9C2.

Kara Kridler, "Dunkin Donuts to Add 150 Stores in Baltimore-Washington Area," *Daily Record* (Baltimore) (May 6, 2005).

Janet Adamy, "As Starbucks Pares Stores, Tension Rises Over Leases," *The Wall Street Journal* (October 13, 2008), p. B1.

http://www.reuters.com/article/pressRelease/idUS133273+14-Apr-2009+PRN20090414.

https://www.dunkindonuts.com/downloads/pdf/DD_Press_Kit.pdf.

http://leadership.wharton.upenn.edu/digest/attachments/BW-EBIZ_How-Fast.pdf.

Janet Adamy, "Starbucks Plays Common Joe," *The Wall Street Journal* (February 9, 2009), p. B3.

http://investor.starbucks.com/phoenix.zhtml?c=99518&p=irol-newsArticle&ID=1267447&highlight.

http://news.starbucks.com/article_display.cfm?article_id=180.

Janet Adamy, "Starbucks Takes Plunge into Instant Coffee," *The Wall Street Journal* (February 13, 2009), p. B8.

Case 8 Bibliography

"Nike Could Grab 6% of Global Sports Apparel Market." *NASDAQ*. Posted 9/21/10. http://community.nasdaq.com/News/2010-09/nike-could-grab-6-of-global-sports-apparel-market.aspx?storyid=37156. Accessed 2/17/11

"Nike." *WikiInvest*. http://www.wikinvest.com/stock/Nike_%28NKE%29. Accessed 2/17/11.

"Nike Furthers Its Commitment to Open Innovation and Sustainability." *Nike*. http://www.nikebiz.com/responsibility/. Accessed 2/17/11.

"Phil Knight." *Forbes*. http://www.forbes.com/profile/Phil-Knight. Accessed 2/17/11.

www.apparelandfootwear.org/Statistics.asp.

articles moneycentral.msn.com/Investigating/CNBC/TVReports/Nike-StarEndorsements.aspx.

nikeresponsibility.com/#workers-facotries/active_factories.

Aaron Bernstein, "Nike Names Names," *BusinessWeek Online* (April 13, 2005). http://adage.com/moy2008/article?article_id=131755.

Stanley Holmes, "Green Foot Forward," *BusinessWeek* (November 28, 2005).

"Nike Replaces CEO After 13 months," *USA Today* (January 24, 2006).

"Just Doing It," *Economist*, vol. 376, no. 8438 (August 6, 2005).

Nike 2008 Annual Report. http://media.corporate-ir.net/media_files/irol/10/100529/ar_08/nike_ar_2008/docs/Nike_AR_2008.pdf downloaded May 28, 2009.

http://www.nikebiz.com/media/pr/2009/05/14_NikeRestructuring Statement.html.

http://www.newbalance.com/corporate/aboutus/corporate_about_ourcompany.php.

Case 9 Bibliography

Sam Abuelsamid. "Mac sales growth continues to surge ahead of PCs 3 to 1." *TUAW*. Posted 11/23/10. http://www.tuaw.com/2010/11/23/mac-sales-growth-continues-to-surge-ahead-of-pcs-3-to-1/. Accessed 2/26/11.

"Locating iPhone Wireless Carriers." *Apple*. Posted 2/25/11. http://support.apple.com/kb/ht1937. Accessed 2/26/11.

Sarah Jacobsson Purewal. "iPad, Fastest-Selling Electronic Device . . . Ever." *PC World*. Posted 10/5/10. http://www.pcworld.com/article/206953/ipad_fastestselling_electronic_deviceever.html. Accessed 2/26/11.

Lexton Snol. "93% of Tablets Sold Are iPads." *PC World*. Posted 2/24/11. http://www.pcworld.com/article/220600/93_of_tablets_sold_are_ipads.html#tk.mod_rel. Accessed 2/26/11.

Apple Inc. home page: http://www.apple.com.

Pixar home page: http://www.pixar.com.

apple20.blogs.fortune.cnn.com/2008/04/01/analyst-apples-us-consumer-market-share-now-21-percent/.

apple20.blogs.fortune.cnn.com/2008/05/19/report-apples-market-share-of-pcs-over-1000-hits-66/.

Brad Stone, "Apple's Chief Takes a Medical Leave."

Peter Burrows, "The Improbable Heroes of Toontown," *BusinessWeek* (May 26, 2008), pp. 81–82.

Case 10 Bibliography

Tracy V. Wilson. "How Netflix Works." *How Stuff Works*. http://electronics.howstuffworks.com/netflix.htm/printable. Accessed 2/16/11.

"Customer Satisfaction with E-Commerce Stalls According to American Customer Satisfaction Index." *MarketWatch*. Posted 2/15/11. http://www.marketwatch.com/story/customer-satisfaction-with-e-commerce-stalls-according-to-american-customer-satisfaction-index-2011-02-15. Accessed 2/16/11.

"Netflix Adds 7.7 Million Subscribers in 2010 to Pass 20 Million." *ReadWriteWeb*. Posted 1/26/11. http://www.readwriteweb.com/archives/netflix_adds_77_million_subscribers_in_2010_to_pas.php. Accessed 2/16/11.

Juan Martinez. "Netflix Q4 2010 revenue jumps 34% despite marketing cut." *Direct Marketing News*. Posted 1/26/11. http://www.dmnews.com/netflix-q4-2010-revenue-jumps-34-despite-marketing-cut/article/195063/. Accessed 2/16/11.

"Media Center." *Netflix*. http://www.netflix.com/MediaCenter. Accessed 2/16/11.

Mark Hefflinger. "Coinstar Buys Rest of DVD Kiosk Firm Redbox for Up to $176M." *DigitalMediaWire*. Posted 2/13/09, 8:28 AM. http://www.dmwmedia.com/news/2009/02/13/coinstar-buys-rest-dvd-kiosk-firm-redbox-$176m. Accessed 2/20/11.

Mitch Lowe. "Redbox Chief: We Are an Engine for Industry Growth." *The Wrap*. Posted 10/2/09, 2:44 PM. http://www.thewrap.com/blog-post/redbox-chief-we-are-engine-industry-growth-8165. Accessed 2/20/11.

Netflix Consumer Press Kit, at http://cdn-0.nflximg.com/us/pdf/Consumer_Press_Kit.pdf (accessed May 27, 2009).

Jennifer Netherby, "Netflix Builds Profit, Subs," *Video Business* (January 21, 2008).

Susanne Ault, "Netflix No. 1 in Online Customer Service," *Video Business* (May 19, 2008).

Mary Brandel, "The 'In' Crowd," *Computerworld* (March 3, 2008).

Danny King, "Netflix Now," *Video Business* (May 1, 2008).

Josh Quittner, "The Idiot Box Gets Smart," *Time*, vol. 171, no. 22 (June 2, 2008).

Brian Steinberg, "Transforming the Movie-Rental Model," *Advertising Age*, vol. 79, no. 1 (January 7, 2008).

Lynn Blumenstein, "Small Libraries Start Using Netflix," *Library Journal*, vol. 133, no. 7 (April 15, 2008).

Daniel McGinn, "Sure, We've Got That!" *Newsweek*, vol. 151, no. 10 (March 10, 2008).

Nick Wingfield, "Netflix vs. Naysayers," *Wall Street Journal* (March 27, 2008), pp. B1, B2.

Michelle Conlin, "Netflix: Flex to the Max," *BusinessWeek* (September 4, 2007), p. 72.

Case 11 Bibliography

"Golfsmith Shoots Well Below Par with Help from SAS." *SAS.* http://www.sas.com/success/golfsmithint.html. Accessed 2/10/11.

"Customer Success." *SAS.* http://www.sas.com/success/. Accessed 2/10/11.

Michael J. Beller and Alan Barnett. "Next Generation Business Analytics". Lightship Partners LLC. http://www.slideshare.net/LightshipPartners/next-generation-business-analytics-presentation. Accessed 2/10/11

Thomas H. Davenport and Jeanne G Harris. *Competing on Analytics: The New Science of Winning.* Harvard Business School Press, 2007.

"Oklahoma City Community College uses SAS Business Analytics to make proactive decisions for student success." *SAS.* http://www.sas.com/success/occc.html. Accessed 2/10/11.

"Daiichi Sankyo demonstrates a significant ROI with SAS Drug Development." *SAS.* http://www.sas.com/success/daiichisankyo.html. Accessed 2/10/11.

Randall Lane. "Pampering the Customers, Pampering the Employees." *Forbes.* Posted 10/14/96, 11:37 AM. http://www.forbes.com/2007/11/08/sas-corestates-goognight-biz-cz_rl_1108sas.html. Accessed 2/10/11.

Michael Shashoua. "SunGard launches social media surveillance." *Risk.net.* Posted 2/7/11. http://www.risk.net/operational-risk-and-regulation/news/2024519/sungard-launches-social-media-surveillance. Accessed 2/21/11.

Case 12 Bibliography

Jackie Cohen. "Facebook Gets More Views Than Yahoo, ComScore Says." *All Facebook.* Posted 12/26/10. http://www.allfacebook.com/facebook-gets-more-views-than-yahoo-comscore-says-2010-12. Accessed 2/17/11.

Jolie O'Dell. "Facebook's Ad Revenue Hit $1.86B for 2010." *Mashable.* Posted 1/17/11. http://mashable.com/2011/01/17/facebooks-ad-revenue-hit-1-86b-for-2010/. Accessed 2/17/11.

Lauren Indvik. "Facebook Users Upload Record-Breaking 750M Photos Over New Year's Weekend." *Mashable.* Posted 1/4/11. http://mashable.com/2011/01/04/facebook-photos-750-million/. Accessed 2/17/11.

"Statistics." *Facebook.* http://www.facebook.com/press/info.php?statistics. Accessed 2/17/11.

Emily Steel and Geoffrey A. Fowler. "Facebook in Privacy Breach." *Wall Street Journal.* Posted 10/18/10. http://online.wsj.com/article/SB10001424052702304772804575558484075236968.html. Accessed 2/17/11.

Alexei Oreskovic. "LinkedIn's secret anti-Facebook weapon: Keg Stands." *Mediafile.* Posted 4/17/10, 4.55 PM. http://blogs.reuters.com/mediafile/2010/11/17/linkedins-secret-anti-facebook-weapon-keg-stands/. Accessed 2/21/11.

Bruno Aziza. "Why LinkedIn Is More Valuable Than Facebook." *Forbes.* Posted 2/16/11. http://blogs.forbes.com/ciocentral/2011/02/16/why-linkedin-is-more-valuable-than-facebook/. Accessed 2/21/11.

Spencer E. Ante, "Facebook's Land Grab in the Face of a Downturn," *BusinessWeek* (December 1, 2008).

Jessi Hempel, "Finding Cracks in Facebook," *Fortune*, vol. 157, no. 11 (May 26, 2008).

Catherine Holahan, "Facebook's New Friends Abroad," *BusinessWeek Online* (May 14, 2008).

Bill Greenwood, "MySpace, Facebook, Google Integrate Data Portability," *Information Today,* vol. 25, no. 6 (June 2008).

"Facebook Exodus," nytimes.com/2009/08/30 (accessed September 3, 2008).

Dan Tynan, "The 25 Worst Web Sites," *PC World* (accessed at http://www.fastcompany.com/magazine/128/myspace-the-sequel.html?page=0%2C1).

Case 13 Bibliography

Barbara Farfan. "Panera Expands in Recession, Leverages Its Strengths in a Weak Economy." *About.com.* http://retailindustry.about.com/od/retailtrendsetters/ig/2010-US-Retail-Store-Openings/Panera-2010-Store-Openings.htm. Accessed 2/17/11.

"TOMS Company Overview." *TOMS.* http://www.toms.com/corporate-info/. Accessed 2/21/11.

JJ Ramberg. "Sole Saver." *Entrepreneur.* Posted 6/08. http://www.entrepreneur.com/magazine/entrepreneur/2008/june/193766.html. Accessed 2/21/11.

http://www.panerabread.com/about/company/.

www.bakingbusiness.com/bs/channel.asp?ArticleID=73003 (accessed August 2, 2006).

"Panera Bread Removes Trans Fat from Menu," Panera Bread press release (February 23, 2006).

Ron Shaich, speech at Annual Meeting 2006, Temple Israel (June 28, 2006).

Ron Miller, "Wi Fi Continues Its Extended Coffee Break," *Information Week* (January 4, 2006). Accessed August 2, 2006.

Jefferson Graham, "As Wi-Fi Spreads, More Free Locations Popping Up," *USA Today* (December 8, 2005) (accessed August 2, 2006, at usatoday.com/tech/wireless/2005-12-08-wi-fi-free_x.htm).

"Panera Bread Recognized as Top Performer in Restaurant Category for One-, Five-, Ten-Year Returns to Shareholders," Panera Bread press release (May 4, 2006).

http://www.bloomberg.com/apps/news?pid=20601087&sid=aFA7bcdaRgL4&refer=home.

Case 14 Bibliography

"Pixar." *Box Office Mojo.* http://www.boxofficemojo.com/franchises/chart/?id=pixar.htm. Accessed 2/28/11.

See David A. Price, *The Pixar Touch* (New York: Knopf, 2008); and Ed Catmull, "How Pixar Fosters Collective Creativity," *Harvard Business Review* (September 2008), Reprint R0809D.

Doug Childers, "Pixar's success is more than just pixel-deep," in *Rich.com* (June 1, 2008).

Greg Sandoval, "New Competitors Challenge Pixar's Animation Domination," *The Sacramento Union* (December 2, 2005).

"How Disney Knew it Needed Pixar," *Fortune*, vol. 153, no. 10 (May 29, 2006).

Pixar corporate Overview at http://www.pixar.com/companyinfo/about_us/overview.htm. Accessed June 8, 2008.

www.worstpreviews.com/review.php?id=758&section=preview.

See Price, op. cit.; Peter Burrow, "The Improbable Heroes of Toontown," *BusinessWeek* (May 26, 2008), p. 82; and Paul Boutin, "An Industry Gets Animated," *Wall Street Journal* (May 14, 2008), p. A19.

Brent Schlender and Christopher Tkaczyk, "Pixar's Magic Man," *Fortune*, vol. 153, no. 10 (May 29, 2006).

David Price, "How Pixar Cheated Death," *Inc.*, vol. 28, no. 6 (June 2006).

Jia Lynn Yang, "How Disney Picked Up Pixar," *Fortune*, vol. 157, no. 9 (May 5, 2008).

Peter Sanders, "Disney Learns Lessons from Pixar," *Wall Street Journal* (October 27, 2008).

Peter Cohen, "Disney Buys Pixar," *Macworld* vol. 23, no. 4 (April 2006).

Case 15 Bibliography

Claire Cain Miller. "Why Twitter's C.E.O. Demoted Himself." *The New York Times.* Posted 10/3010. http://www.nytimes.com/2010/10/31/technology/31ev.html. Accessed 2/14/11.

David Sarno. "Twitter Creator Jack Dorsey Illuminates the Site's Founding Document." *Los Angeles Times.* Posted 2/18/09, 5:04 PM. http://latimesblogs.latimes.com/technology/2009/02/twitter-creator.html. Accessed 2/14/11.

Om Malik. "Odeo RIP. Hello Obvious Corp." *GigaOM.* Posted 10/22/06. http://gigaom.com/2006/10/25/odeo-rip-hello-obvious-corp/. Accessed 2/14/11.

Claire Cain Miller. "Who's Driving Twitter's Popularity? Not Teens." *The New York Times.* Posted 8/5/09. http://www.nytimes.com/2009/08/26/technology/internet/26twitter.html. Accessed 2/14/11.

John Yembrick and Kelly Humphries. "NASA Extends the World Wide Web Out Into Space." *NASA.* Posted 1/22/10. http://www.nasa.gov/home/hqnews/2010/jan/HQ_M10-011_Hawaii221169.html. Accessed 2/14/11.

Claudine Beaumont. "Twitter users send 50 million tweets per day." *The Telegraph*. Posted 2/23/10, 9:15 AM. http://www.telegraph.co.uk/technology/twitter/7297541/Twitter-users-send-50-million-tweets-per-day.html. Accessed 2/14/11.

"Twitter is the best way to discover what's new in your world." *Twitter*. http://twitter.com/about. Accessed 2/15/11.

Claire Cain Miller. "Sports Fans Break Records on Twitter." *The New York Times*. Posted 6/18/10, 6:36. http://bits.blogs.nytimes.com/2010/06/18/sports-fans-break-records-on-twitter/. Accessed 2/14/11.

Jennifer Van Grove. "Twitter Sets New Record: 3,283 Tweets Per Second." *Mashable*. Posted 6/25/10. http://mashable.com/2010/06/25/tps-record/. Accessed 2/4/11.

Maggie Shiels. "Web slows after Jackson's death." *BBC News*. Posted 6/29/09. http://news.bbc.co.uk/2/hi/technology/8120324.stm. Accessed 2/14/11.

David Hamilton. "Twitter's Uptime Has Not Improved." *The WHIR*. Posted 11/19/09. http://www.thewhir.com/web-hosting-news/111909_Twitters_Uptime_Has_Not_Improved_CheckMySitecom. Accessed 2/15/11.

Jason Pontin. "From Many Tweets, One Loud Voice on the Internet." *The New York Times*. Posted 4/22/07. http://www.nytimes.com/2007/04/22/business/yourmoney/22stream.html?_r=1. Accessed 2/14/11.

Ryan Kelly, ed. "Twitter Study Reveals Interesting Results About Usage." *Pear Analytics*. Posted 8/12/09. http://www.pearanalytics.com/blog/wp-content/uploads/2010/05/Twitter-Study-August-2009.pdf. Accessed 2/14/11.

Clive Thompson. "Brave New World of Digital Intimacy." *The New York Times*. Posted 11/5/08. http://www.nytimes.com/2008/09/07/magazine/07awareness-t.html. Accessed 2/14/11.

Danah Boyd. "Twitter: "pointless babble" or peripheral awareness + social grooming?" *Apophoria*. Posted 8/16/09. http://www.zephoria.org/thoughts/archives/2009/08/16/twitter_pointle.html. Accessed 2/14/11.

Soren Gordhamer. "Changing Communication As We Know It: Twitter." *The Huffington Post*. Posted 2/5/10, 1:28 AM. http://www.huffingtonpost.com/soren-gordhamer/changing-communication-as_b_450486.html. Accessed 2/14/11.

Munindra Khaund. "Is Twitter, by changing our communication, changing how we conduct business?" *SlideShare*. http://www.slideshare.net/mkhaund/is-twitterby-changing-our-communication-changing-how-we-conduct-business. Accessed 2/14/11.

Ericka Chickowski. "25 Fast Facts About Twitter in the Workplace." *Baseline*. Posted 9/24/10. http://www.baselinemag.com/c/a/Business-Intelligence/25-Fast-Facts-About-Twitter-in-the-Workplace-212013/. Accessed 2/14/11.

Joel Postman. "Seven rules for establishing a corporate presence on Twitter." *Socialized*. Posted 8/20/08. http://www.socializedpr.com/twitter-seven-rules/. Accessed 2/14/11s

Robert Scoble. "Yammer: Changing the way we communicate at work." *Building43*. Posted 2/9/11. http://www.building43.com/videos/2011/02/15/yammer-changing-the-way-we-communicate-at-work/. Accessed 2/22/11.

Case 16 Bibliography

Norm Bafunno. "Amid sales declines and recalls, TMMI stays the course." *Evansville Courier & Press*. Posted 1/3/11. http://www.courierpress.com/news/2011/jan/03/norm-bafunno/. Accessed 2/17/11.

Bill Vlasic. "Ford's Bet: It's a Small World After All." *The New York Times*. Posted 1/9/10. http://www.nytimes.com/2010/01/10/business/10ford.html. Accessed 2/22/11.

"Toyota Outsells GM, Ford Posts Eye-Popping Loss," *US News & World Reports* (posted online July 24, 2008), wsj.com/mdc/public/page/2_3022-autosales.html.

M. Reza Vaghefi, "Creating Sustainable Competitive Advantage: The Toyota Philosophy and Its Effects," *Mastering Management Online* (October 2001) (accessed January 13, 2006, at www.ftmastering.com/mmo/index.htm).

"Top 10 SUVs, Pickups and Minivans with the Best Residual Value for 2005," *Edmunds.com* (accessed January 14, 2006, at www.edmunds.com/reviews/list/top10/103633/article.html).

"Making Things: The Essence and Evolution of the Toyota Production System," Toyota Motor Corporation (www.toyota.com).

"The 'Thinking' Production System: TPS as a Winning Strategy for Developing People in the Global Manufacturing Environment," Toyota Motor Corporation (www.toyota.com).

money.cnn.com/magazines/fortune/fortune_archive/2006/03/06/8370702/index.htm.

www.toyota.com/about/our_news/product.html.

Rick Newman, "Toyota's Next Turn," *US News & World Report* (posted online June 16, 2008).

Kate Linebaugh, "Idle Workers Busy at Toyota," *Wall Street Journal* (October 13, 2008).

Case 17 Bibliography

"Harley announces fourth straight quarter of sales growth in Europe." *Creative Cycles*. Posted 10/11/10. http://blog.creativecycles.com/harley-announce-fourth-straight-quarter-of-sales-growth-in-europe/. Accessed 2/17/11.

Sara Sidner. "Harley-Davidson to build bikes in India." *CNN*. Posted 11/4/10. http://articles.cnn.com/2010-11-04/world/india.bikes_1_india-market-harley-davidsons-haryana?_s=PM:WORLD. Accessed 2/17/11.

http://www.harley-davidson.com/wcm/Content/Pages/Events/100th_anniversary.jsp?locale=en_US (accessed May 25, 2009).

Malia Boyd, "Harley-Davidson Motor Company," *Incentive* (September 1993), pp. 26–27.

Shrader et al., "Harley-Davidson, Inc.—1991," In Fred David, ed., *Strategic Management*, 4th ed. (New York: Macmillan, 1993), p. 655.

Marktha H. Peak, "Harley-Davidson: Going Whole Hog to Provide Stakeholder Satisfaction," *Management Review*, vol. 82 (June 1993), p. 53.

http://www.motorcyclistonline.com/calendar/122_0709_hog_members_adirondacks/index.html (accessed May 18, 2009).

Kevin Kelly and Karen Miller, "The Rumble Heard Round the World: Harley's," *BusinessWeek* (May 24, 1993), p. 60.

Sandra Dallas and Emily Thornton, "Japan's Bikers: The Tame Ones," *BusinessWeek* (October 20, 1997), p. 159.

http://www.motorcyclistonline.com/newsandupdates/harley_davidson_chinese_motorcycle_market/index.html.

"H-D Cautiously Upbeat over Beijing Dealer," *Dealer News* (May 2006), p. 67.

Harley-Davidson Motorcycles and Customer Data: Registrations (accessed May 20, 2008, at http://investor.harley-davidson.com/registrations.cfm?locale=en_US&bmLocale=en_US).

http://seekingalpha.com/article/75695-high-gas-prices-may-help-harley-davidson-more-evidence (accessed May 21, 2008).

http://www.businessweek.com/investor/content/apr2009/pi20090416_239475_page_2.htm.

Case 18 Bibliography

Stacy Perman. "In-N-Out Burger's Marketing Magic." *Bloomberg Businessweek*. Posted 4/24/09, 12:15 PM. http://www.businessweek.com/smallbiz/content/apr2009/sb20090424_877655.htm. Accessed 2/17/11.

Stacy Perman. "In-N-Out Burger: Professionalizing Fast Food." *Bloomberg Businessweek*. Posted 4/9/09, 5:00 PM. http://www.businessweek.com/magazine/content/09_16/b4127068288029.htm. Accessed 2/17/11.

"In-N-Out Burger to open restaurants in Texas." *OC Register*. Posted 5/26/10. http://articles.ocregister.com/2010-05-26/food/24553290_1_burger-chain-open-restaurants-beef-processing-plant. Accessed 2/17/11.

Frank Pellegrini. "Restaurant Review: The In-N-Out Burger." *TIME*. Posted 8/21/2000. http://www.time.com/time/nation/article/0,8599,53002,00.html. Accessed 2/17/11.

Nancy Luna, "Sprinkles Bakery to Open in Corona del Mar," *The Orange County Register* (May 18, 2006).

Morco R. della Cava, "Cupcake Bakeries Cater to the Kid in Us," *USA Today* (September 18, 2007).

"Cupcake Crazy!" *People in Touch* (July 31, 2006).

http://www.sprinkles.com/flavors.html.

TomKat's Tasty Holiday Treats," *OK Magazine* (December 21, 2007).

Audrey Davidow, "So, Sweetie, I Quit to Bake Cupcakes," *The New York Times* (June 3, 2007).

"Cupcake Bakeries," *USA Today*, op. cit.

"Sprinkles Cupcake Bakery" (accessed May 25, 2008, at www.dmagazine.com).

Joel Stein, "Cupcake Nation," *Time* (August 28, 2006).

Photo Credits

A

Abraham, F. Murray, 383
Adams, Barry, 68
Adams, Hunter "Patch," 179
Alderfer, Clayton, 309–310
Alexander, Pam, 360
Allen, Joan, 423
Allen, Paul, C-29
Alsop, Ron, 242
Amabile, Teresa M., 224
Amelio, Gil, C-19
Aniston, Jennifer, 257
Anthony, Carmelo, C-12
Argyris, Chris, 38, 43
Armstrong, Tim, 373
Aziza, Bruno, C-25

B

Bafunno, Norm, C-33
Bailard, Thomas, 374
Baker, Simon, 359
Ban-Ki-moon, 76
Barnett, Alan, C-22
Barr, Anthony J., C-22
Bartz, Carol, 48, 178, 186
Bass, Bill, 394
Baum, Herb, 21
Bedford, Bruce, C-22
Beller, Michael J., C-22
Benioff, Marc, 164
Bennis, Warren, 258
Beyer, Jon, 223
Bezos, Jeff, 89, 109, 206, 217, 341, C-8–C-9, C-11
Blakely, Sara, 293
Boyd, Danah, C-30
Brandenburger, Adam M., 163
Branson, Richard, 287, 288, 325
Bridges, Jeff, 157
Briggs, Katherine, 291
Briggs-Myers, Isabel, 291
Brooks, Mike, 36
Brown, Rob, 383
Brown, Tim, 217
Bullock, Sandra, 55
Burke, James, 217
Burnett, Iris, 424
Burns, Edward, 111
Burns, Tom, 198
Burns, Ursula, 12, 385
Butcher, Charlie, 324
Butler, Susan Bulkeley, 286
Butterfield, Stewart, 426
Byham, William C., 359
Byrne, John A., 5, 6

C

Carr, Nicholas, 96
Carroll, Archie, 62, 69
Carter, Shawn, 364
Cartwright, Stacey, C-4
Castellano, José, C-5

Cathy, Dan T., 141
Cathy, Truett, 141
Catmull, Ed, C-28, C-29
Cavanaugh, Gerald, 98
Cella, James, C-23
Chambers, John, 405
Chang, Kat, 403
Chappell, Tom, 210
Cherry, Trent, 349
Chouinard, Yvon, 83, 172, C-6–C-7
Christen, Pat, 311
Clark, Maxine, 182
Cohen, David, C-20
Cohen, Herman, 68
Cohen, Marshal, 83, C-6
Collins, Jim, 50
Conger, Jay, 363–364
Connery, Sean, 383
Connolly, Agnes, 68
Cook, Tim, C-19
Coulombe, Joe, C-2–C-3

D

Damon, Matt, 423
Davenport, Thomas, 114
Davis, Steven A., 320
Deming, W. Edwards, 49
Denson, Charlie, C-17
DePew, Tammy, 249
DePree, Max, 25, 277
DeSio, Tony, 427
Devine, Denise, 424
Donaldson, Thomas, 61
Donna, Rose, 431
Donovan, Denis, 233
Dorsey, Jack, C-30
Dowling, Michael, C-12
Dowling, Steve, 414
Downey, Robert, Jr., 230
Dreyfus, Richard, 31
Drucker, Peter, 166
Dumper, Audrey, C-3

E

Eckhardt, Aaron, 257
Eddington, Sir Rod, 219
Edwards, Patricia, C-10, C-11
Enrico, Roger, 97
Erker, Scott, 199

F

Fake, Caterina, 426
Farley, James D., 126
Fassak, John C-14, C-15
Faulk, Woody, 141
Fayol, Henri, 32, 36
Ferguson, Roger W., Jr., 159
Fiedler, Fred, 265–266
Fitzpatrick, Jayne, C-14
Follett, Mary Parker, 38–39
Ford, Henry, 32, 158

Ford, William Clay, Jr., 196, C-33
Fox, Matthew, 331
Friedman, Thomas, 417
Fritz, Justin, 4, 5
Frost, Tom, C-7
Fry, Art, 215

G

Geffen, David, C-28, C-29
Geithner, Timothy, 88–89
George, Richard, C-2
Gladwell, Malcolm, 49
Goleman, Daniel, 16, 273, 300, 301
Goodnight, James, 248, C-22, C-23
Gordhamer, Soren, C-31
Grabowski, Gerry, 248
Graves, Earl, 426
Greenfield, Michelle and Geoff, 434
Greenleaf, Robert, 277
Gumpel, Tom, C-26

H

Haas, Robert, 60
Haeckel, Stephen, 158
Hall, Edward T., 393–394
Handy, Charles, 23–24
Hanks, Tom, 133, 205
Hansen, Morton, 374
Harris, Jeanne, 114
Harvey, Stu, C-23
Hastings, Reed, 207, C-20, C-21
Hawkins, William "Trip," C-12
Hayward, Tony, 124
Heasley, Linda, 362
Hedlund, Garrett, 157
Heigl, Katherine, 111
Helwig, Jane T., C-22
Herlick, Richard, 371
Herzberg, Frederick, 312–313
Hickey, John, C-17
Hillary, Edmund, 98
Hirshberg, Gary, 73
Hofstede, Geert, 394–396
Hoke, John R, III, C-17
Holmes, Deborah K., 11–12, 13
Hopper, Grace, 258
House, Robert, 267–268, 397
Howard, Terrence, 31
Howe, Jeff, 351
Hsieh, Tony, 2, 24, 206, 207, 238, C-11
Hu, Mu, C-22
Huizenga, H. Wayne, 425
Hurley, James, C-5

I

Iger, Bob, C-28
Immelt, Jeffrey, 171
Isla, Pablo, C-3–C-5

J

Jacobs, Bert and John, 39
Jacques, Elliot, 118

Jain, Dipak C., 214
Janis, Irving, 351
Jobs, Steve, 229, C-13, C-18–C-19, C-28, C-29
Johnson, Lonnie, 100
Johnson, Tory, 375
Jordan, Michael, C-16
Jung, Carl, 291

K

Kane, Louis, C-26
Kanno, Noro, 110
Kanter, Rosabeth Moss, 259, 275, 405
Kaplan, Robert S., 150–151
Karp, Jeffrey, C-12
Katz, Robert L., 15–16
Katzenberg, Jeffrey, C-28, C-29
Kelly, Gary, 276
Kennedy, John F., 351
Kernaghan, Charles, C-16
King, Martin Luther, Jr., 256, 272
Kirkpatrik, David, 142
Kirsch, Vanessa, 79
Knight, Phil, C-17
Kochan, Thomas, 384
Koff, Art, 424
Kohlberg, Lawrence, 66
Kotter, John, 14
Kranernkdijk, Stef, 75
Kristof, Nicolas, 396
Kroes, Neelie, 409
Kumar, Nirmalya, C-5

L

Lafley, A.G., 5, 6
Laskawy, Philip A., 11, 13
Lasseter, John, C-28, C-29
Lauren, Ralph, 169
Ledbetter, Lilly, 236
Lentz, Jim, 134, C-33
LePlae, Robert, C-36, C-37
Levinson, Sara, 274
Lewin, Kurt, 221
Locke, Edwin A., 321
Losey, Michael R., 389
Lowe, Challis M., 297
Lowe, Mitch, C-21
Lucas, George, C-28
Lynch, William, C-9

M

Mackey, John, 70
Madoff, Bernie, 20, 54
Madonna, C-4
Marciante, Joe P., 36
Mark, Reuben, 21
Marks, Alan, C-17
Marsh, Kristina, 7
Martin, Stephen, 375
Martin, Wiliam, C-37
Martinez, Angel, 219
Maslow, Abraham, 38, 41–42, 308–309
Mastroangelo, Andrew, C-14
Mayo, Elton, 38, 40
Mays, Jayma, 85
McAdams, Rachel, 85
McAlinden, Sean, C-33

McClaughlin, Paul P., 324
McClelland, David, 310–311
McDonald, Robert A., 12
McGregor, Douglas, 38, 42, 142
McKinstry, Nancy, 376
McMillon, Doug, 389
McNabb, Donovan, C-12
Meisinger, Susan, 233
Melchionda, Gabrielle, 68–69
Merlino, Nell, 424
Michaels, Paul, 186
Middleton, Kate, C-4
Minoura, Teruyuki, C-32
Mintzberg, Henry, 10–11, 13, 17
Moayyad, Shirin, 406
Monroe, Lorraine, 261, 277
Moorman, Mark, C-23
Morales, Evo, 410
Morison, Robert, 114
Mulally, Alan, 196, C-33
Murray, Brian, C-9
Mycoskie, Blake, 431, C-27

N

Nalebuff, Barry J., 163
Nasseri, Mehran, 205
Nayar, Vineet, 373–374
Neath, Gavin, 77
Nelson, Candace, C-37
Nelson, Craig T., 307
Newsham, Margaret, 68
Nitsch, Judith, 120
Nooyi, Indra, 97
Nordstrom, Jaime, C-11
Nordstrom, Pete, C-10
Norton, David P., 150–151
Novak, David, 325
Nueno, José Luis, C-5

O

Obama, Barack, 159
Oher, Michael, 55
Ohmae, Kenichi, 19
Ohno, Taiichi, C-32
Olivan, Javier, C-25
Omidyar, Pam, 311
Ortega Gaona, Amancio, C-5
Osterman, Paul, 192
Ouellette, Lynne, 324
Overton, Rick, 310
Owyang, Jeremiah, C-30

P

Parker, Mark, C-17
Patel, Dev, 3
Patel, Dilip, C-5
Pattison, Grant, 389
Perez, Bill, C-17
Perman, Stacy, 430
Peters, Tom, 369
Pfeffer, Jeffrey, 50, 78–79, 260
Piette, Daniel, C-4
Pincus, Marc, 119
Pink, Daniel H., 326
Porter, Michael, 168–171, 173
Postman, Joel, C-31
Prahalad, C. K., 216

Prakesh, Anoop, C-35
Presley, Elvis, 123

R

Ransler, Chip, 431
Ratner, Jeff, C-24
Rauch, Doug, C-3
Reynolds, Brian, C-13
Riccitiello, John, C-13
Riggio, Leonard, C-9
Riha, Jim, C-22
Rivoli, Pietra, 404
Roddick, Anita, 425, 428–429
Rodgers, T. J., 127
Rokeach, Milton, 57
Rosener, Judith, 23
Rosenfeld, Irene, 374
Rowling, J.K., 306, 308
Rust, Edward B., Jr., 16–17

S

Sacks, David, C-31
Sall, James, C-22
Sandberg, Sheryl, 233, C-24–C-25
Sanderson, Catherine, 377
Sardone, Deborah, 430
Saverin, Eduardo, 283
Schacht, Henry, 134
Schackart, Ralph, C-28, C-29
Schiavo, Beth, 7
Schmidt, Eric, 217
Schwartz, Barry, C-2
Scoble, Robert, C-31
Scott, David Meerman, C-8
Seator, Laine, 309, 310
Segura, David, 386
Selanikio, Joel, 431
Shaich, Ron, C-26, C-27
Shapira, Adrianne, C-11
Shawn, Wallace, 307
Simon, Herbert, 96
Sinha, Manoj, 431
Smith, Adam, 32
Smith, Alvy Ray, C-28, C-29
Snyder, Guy, C-36
Snyder, Harry and Esther, 430, C-36
Snyder, Rich, C-36, C-37
Solca, Luca, C-5
Somers, Julie, C-27
Spector, Robert, C-11
Spencer, Rod, 433–434
Spielberg, Steven, C-28, C-29
Spindler, Michael, C-18–C-19
Stalker, George, 198
Stone, Biz, C-30
Strand, Nat, 403
Streep, Meryl, 359
Sullenberger, Chesley, 89–90
Sullivan, Todd, C-35
Sunjata, Daniel, 359
Sutton, Robert, 50
Swasey, Steve, C-20
Szaky, Tom, 223

T

Tator, Robin, 223
Tavaranan, Saline, 204, 214

Taylor, Frederick, 32–33
Teerlink, Richard, C-34, C-35
Thomas, David (Harvard professor), 385
Thomas, David (Wendy's founder), 426
Thomas, R. Roosevelt, 23, 384,
    388–389
Thompson, Clive, C-30
Thompson, Don, 120
Toyoda, Akio, 105, 132
Toyoda, Kiichiro, C-32
Tuohy, Leigh Anne, 55
Tutu, Desmond, 56

U

Urzua, Luis, 84, 86, 104

V

Vaghefi, M. Reza, C-32
Valestro, Buddy, 422

Van der Veer, Jeroen, 125
Van Fleet, Carl, C-36–C-37
Vroom, Victor, 318, 319

W

Wada, Yoshida, 366
Walton, Sam, 364, 389
Weber, Max, 32, 34–35, 198
Weiner, Jeff, C-25
Welch, Jack, 127, 220, 222–223
Wexner, Lex, 409
Wilde, Olivia, 157
Wiliams, Evan, C-30
Winfrey, Oprah, 293
Winklevoss, Cameron, 283
Winklevoss, Tyler, 283
Wise, John, C-22
Witt, Alicia, 31
Wooden, John, 261–262, 330

Woods, Tiger, C-12
Wozniak, Steve, C-18
Wright, Jennnifer, 424
Wright, Ryan, 76
WuDunn, Sheryl, 396

Y

Yanofsky, Neal, C-27
Youn, Andrew, 214–215
Yunus, Muhammad, 78

Z

Zennstrom, Niklas, 151
Ziemer, Jim, C-35
Zollinger, Cindy, 7–8
Zuckerberg, Mark, 283, 376, C-24

Subject Index

A

Absenteeism, 299
Accommodation, 352, 353
Accountability, 6
Achievement, as need, 310, 428
Acquired needs, 310
Active listening, 371–372
Affiliation, as need, 310, 311
Affirmative action, 234, 388–389
After-action review, 135
Age discrimination, 235
Age Discrimination in Employment Act, 235
Agenda setting, 14
Agreeableness, as Big Five personality trait, 290, 291
Ambition, 283, 301
Americans with Disabilities Act, 235
Amoral managers, 69
Analytics, 45
Anchoring and adjustment heuristic, 103
Angel investors, 440
Antitrust laws, 409
Armed conflicts, 415
ASP (application service provisioning), 164
Assertiveness, as project GLOBE cultural dimension, 397
Assessment centers, 240
Asset management, 149, 150
Attitudes, 297–298
Attribution, 287
Authoritarianism, 292
Authority decisions, 269
Autocratic leaders, 263
Automakers, 158, 161, 163, 187–188, 407
Autonomous work groups, 337
Availability heuristic, 103
Avoidance, 352, 353. See also Withdrawal behaviors

B

B2B business strategies, 164
B2C business strategies, 164
Baby Boomers, 35, 209, 241, 242, 375
Balanced scorecard, 150
Bankruptcy, 161
Bay of Pigs invasion, 351
BCG Matrix, 171
Behavioral decision model, 95
Behavioral management, 38–43
Behaviorally anchored rating scale (BARS), 243
Benchmarking, 125–126
Benefit corporations, 431
Benefits. See Fringe benefits
Best practices, 126
Biculturalism, 388
Big Five personality traits, 290–291
Big Mac index, 412
Black Enterprise magazine, 426
The Blind Side (movie), 55
Boards of directors, 6, 321
Boards of trustees, 6

Bona fide occupational qualifications, 234
Bonus pay, 250
Bossnapping, 294
The Bourne Ultimatum (movie), 423
Breakeven analysis, 149
Breakeven point, 149
Bribery, 415
Budgets, 121
Bureaucracies, 34–35, 198, 199, 216
Bureaucratic control, 142–143
Business incubators, 437
Business model innovation, 213
Business plans, 438
Business strategy, 159–160
Business-to-business (B2B) strategies, 164
Business-to-customer (B2C) strategies, 164
Bus-stop analogy, 158

C

Cake Boss (TV series), 422
Career development, 244–245
Career planning, 245
Cash cows, in BCG Matrix, 171
Centralization, 195
Centralized communication networks, 346
Certain environments, 90–91
Change, planned
    common managerial strategies, 222–224
    resistance to, 224–225
    three phases, 220–221
    transformational vs. incremental, 219–220
Change leaders, 219, 224–225
Changing phase, planned change, 221
Channel richness, 367
Chapter 11 bankruptcy, 161
Character, individual, 55, 63, 65
Charismatic leaders, 272
Chief executive officers (CEOs)
    pay issues, 173
    as top managers, 5
    what they do, 10
Chief financial officers (CFOs),
    as top managers, 5
Chief information officers (CIOs),
    as top managers, 5
Chief operating officers (COOs),
    as top managers, 5
Child labor, 402, 414
Chilean mine collapse, 84, 86
Chimneys (or silos) problem, 186
China
    as car market, 123
    and globalization, 19–20
    Haier factories, 393
    and Internet censorship, 151
    and job migration, 20
    manufacturing statistics, 407
    Nike in, 404
    nonverbal communication, 377
    as outsourcing destination, 156, 162, 407, 414
    PetroChina, 412

CitiVille game, 119
Civil wars, 415
Clan control, 143
Classical decision model, 95
Classical management approaches, 32–36
Classical view of corporate social responsibility, 74
Cloud computing, 164
Coaching, 241
Code of ethics, 69–70
Coercive power, 259
Coffee growers, 406
Cognitive dissonance, 298
Cognitive styles, 90
Cohesiveness, 344
Collaboration, 353, 374. See also Problem solving
Collective bargaining, 252
Collaboration (Hansen), 374
Commercializing innovation, 215–216
Committees, 335
Communication. See also Networking
    credible, 364
    cross-cultural, 375–377, 391
    defined, 361
    effective, 362, 366–369
    efficient, 362–363
    generational, 375
    introduction, 360–364
    key elements in process, 361
    as "must have" managerial skill, 17
    nonverbal, 368, 377
    openness in, 374
    persuasive, 363–364
    role of proxemics, 373
    sender vs. receiver, 361–362
    skills quick-check, 360
    team networks, 346
    transparency, 374
    ways to improve, 371–377
Communication channels, 367
Commutative justice, 59
Competition, 352–353
Competitive advantage, 159, 170
Competitive strategies model, 169–171
Complacency trap, 114
Compressed workweek, 199–200
Compromise, 352–353
Concentration, 160
Conceptual skills, 16
Concurrent controls, 141
Confirmation error, 104
Conflict resolution, 353
Conflicts
    defined, 352
    emotional, 352
    managing in teams, 352–353
    resolving, 353
    substantive, 352
Conflicts of interest, 62
Conscientiousness, as Big Five personality trait, 290, 291
Consensus, 349, 350

Constructive feedback, 372
Constructive stress, 294
Consultative decisions, 269
Contingency leadership perspective, 265–266
Contingency planning, 124
Contingency thinking, 48
Contingency workers, 249
Continuous improvement, 49, 146
Contractors. *See* Independent contractors
Control charts, 146–147
Controlling. *See also* Leading; Locus of control;
    Organizing; Planning; Span of control
  defined, 13, 134
  as function in management process, 11, 13,
    134–135
  in global corporations, 414–415
  steps in process, 135–138
  types of controls, 140–143
Cooperative strategies, 163
Co-opetition, 163
Copyrights. *See* Intellectual property
Core characteristics model, 313–314
Core competencies, 168
Core culture, 209
Core values, 209–210
Corporate culture. *See* Organizational culture
Corporate governance, 20–21
Corporate social responsibility
  cases for and against, 74
  classical view, 74
  defined, 73
  discretionary responsibility, 76
  ethical responsibility, 76
  global issues, 413
  legal responsibility, 76
  social performance audits, 75–76
  socioeconomic view, 74
  sustainability as goal, 76–79
Corporate strategy, 159
Corporate thieves, 136
Corporations, as form of small business ownership,
  439. *See also* Global corporations
Corruption, 414, 415
Cost leadership strategies, 169–170
Cost-benefit analysis, 95
CPM/PERT, 147–148
Cradle-to-grave manufacturing, 75
Creativity, 100–101
Credible communication, 364
Crime, corporate, 136
Crisis, 104–105
Critical incident technique, 243
Critical path, 148
Critical thinking, 17, 157, 161
Cross-cultural communication, 375–377, 391
Cross-functional teams, 188, 335–336
Crowdsourcing, 164, 351
Cultural awareness, 403, 407
Cultural etiquette, 377
Cultural intelligence, 392–393
Cultural relativism, 61
Culture. *See* National cultures, Hofstede's five
  dimensions; Organizational culture
Culture shock, 391
Currency risk, 415
Customer confidence, violating, as unethical
  behavior, 62
Customer structures, 188

D
Debt financing, 440
Decentralization, 195
Decentralized communication networks, 346
Decision making
  behavioral model, 95
  causes of errors in, 103–104
  classical model, 95
  in crisis, 104–105
  environments for, 90–91
  in groups, 102
  role of creativity, 100–101
  steps in process, 93–98
  team methods, 349–350
Decisional roles, managerial, 13
Decision-making process
  identifying problem, 94
  evaluating alternative courses of action,
    94–95
  decide on preferred course of action, 95–96
  implementing decision, 96–97
  evaluating results, 97–98
  case of Ajax Company, 93–98
  defined, 93
  steps in, 93–98
Decisions
  defined, 88
  optimizing, 95
  programmed *vs.* nonprogrammed, 88
  satisficing, 96
Decoded (Jay-Z), 364
Deepwater Horizon oil spill, 76, 124
Deficit principle, 42, 308
Delegation, 196–197
Democratic leaders, 263
Department heads. *See* First-line managers
Departmentalization, 185
Dependency, 6
Design thinkers, 217
Destructive stress, 294
The Devil Wears Prada (movie), 359
Differentiation strategies, 169, 170
Digital natives, 351
Discrimination, 23, 62, 234–235, 236
Disruptive behaviors, 345
Distributed leadership, 345
Distribution alliances, 163
Distributive justice, 59
Diversification, 160
Diversity
  among global cultures, 391–397
  business case, 384
  defined, 384
  managing, 389
  valuing, 382, 389
  in workplace, 384–389
Diversity maturity, 383, 388
Divestiture, 161
Division of labor, 181
Divisional structures, 187, 188
Dogs, in BCG Matrix, 171
Downsizing, 161
Drive (Pink), 326

E
E-business strategies, 163–164
Ecological fallacies, 396
E-commerce. *See* E-business strategies

Economic development, and international
  business, 406
Economic order quantity, 148
Effective communication, 362, 366–369
Effective managers, 6–7
Effective teams, 339–340
Efficient communication, 362–363
Electronic grapevine, 375
Electronic privacy, 376
Electronic waste, 125
E-mail, 375, 376
Emotional conflict, 352
Emotional intelligence, 16, 273, 300–301
Emotional stability, as Big Five personality trait,
  290, 291
Emotions, 300–301
Empathy, as foundation for emotional
  intelligence, 16
Employee assistance programs, 251
Employee engagement, 299
Employee involvement teams, 336
Employees. *See* Workforce
Employment agreements, 36
Employment tests, 240
Empowerment, 179, 197, 277
Engagement, 307, 314
Entrepreneurs
  characteristics, 426–427, 428
  common myths, 425
  defined, 424
  examples, 425–426
  minorities as, 428–429
  moms as, 424
  as risk takers, 425
  similarities, 426–427, 428
  women as, 428–429
Entrepreneurship, 424, 428–429. *See also* Small
  businesses
Environmental capital, 77
Equal employment opportunity (EEO), 234
Equal Pay Act, 235
Equity financing, 440
Equity theory, 316–318
ERG theory, 309–310
Escalating commitment, 104
Ethical behavior
  defined, 56
  levels of moral development, 66
  maintaining high standards of conduct, 65–70
  moral leadership, 275–276
  as values driven, 57–58
  variations across cultures, 60–61
  and views of moral reasoning, 58–60
  in workplace, 56–63
Ethical dilemmas, 61–62
Ethical frameworks, 65–66
Ethical imperialism, 61
Ethics
  and China's outsourcing factories, 156, 162
  defined, 20–21, 56
  formal codes, 69–70
  global challenges, 414
  rationalizing unethical behavior, 63
Ethics training, 67
Ethnic subcultures, 386
Ethnocentrism, 377, 385
Evidence-based management, 50
E-waste, 125

Existence needs, 309
Expectancy theory, 318–320
Expert power, 260
Exporting, 407
External control, 142
Extinction, 324
Extraversion, as Big Five personality trait, 290, 291

F

Fair Pay Act, 236
Fair trade, 394
Family and Medical Leave Act, 235
Family business feuds, 436
Family-friendly benefits, 251
Family-owned businesses, 435–436
FarmVille game, 119
Feedback, 243–244, 361, 372
Feedback controls, 141
Feedforward controls, 140
Filtering, 369
Financial budgets, 121
Finding Forrester (movie), 383
First-line managers, 4–5
First-mover advantage, 425
Fixed budgets, 121
Flexibility, 247–248, 428
Flexible benefits, 251
Flexible budgets, 121
Flexible working hours, 200
Focused cost leadership strategy, 170
Focused differentiation strategy, 170
Force-coercion strategy, 222–223
Forecasting, 123
Foreign Corrupt Practices Act (FCPA), 414
Foreign subsidiaries, 408
Formal structures, 181
Formal teams, 334–335
Forrest Gump (movie), 133
Framing error, 104
Franchising, 407, 426, 427
Free-agent economy, 23–24
Freelancers, 248
Fringe benefits, 250–251
Frustration-regression principle, 310
Functional chimneys (or silos) problem, 186
Functional plans, 119
Functional strategy, 160
Functional structures, 185–186
Fundamental attribution error, 287
Future orientation, as project GLOBE cultural dimension, 397

G

Gain sharing, 250
Gantt charts, 46, 147
Gender, and leadership, 274–275
Gender egalitarianism, as project GLOBE cultural dimension, 397
Gender similarities hypothesis, 274
Gender subcultures, 386
General partnerships, 439
Generation X, 35, 209, 242
Generational subcultures, 35, 209, 241–242, 375, 386–387
Geographical structures, 188
Glass ceiling, 387, 429
Glass-ceiling effect, 22

Global corporations. *See also* International business
controversial actions, 413–414
defined, 412
ethical challenges, 413
leadership in, 416–417
organizing in, 416
planning and controlling, 414–415
Global economy, 405
Global managers, 216–217
Global sourcing, 20, 406–407
Global strategic alliances, 408
Globalization
defined, 19, 405
impact on international business, 404–410
impact on workplace, 19–20
T-shirt example, 404–405
Globalization gap, 413
Globalization strategies, 162
GLOBE. *See* Project GLOBE
Goal setting, 127
Goal-setting theory, 320–321
Governance, 6
Graphic rating scales, 243
Green innovation, 214
Greenfield ventures, 408
Greenhouse gases, 103
Group decision making, 102, 269
Groupthink, 350–351
Growth needs, 309
Growth strategies, 160

H

Half the Sky (Kristof and WuDunn), 396
Halo effect, 285
Harry Potter books, 306, 308
Hawthorne effect, defined, 40
Hawthorne studies, 38, 40
Hersey-Blanchard situational leadership model, 267
Heuristics, 103
Hierarchy of human needs, 41–42, 308–309
Hierarchy of objectives, 115
High-context cultures, 393
Higher-order needs, 308, 309
High-performance organizations, 50
Hiring employees, 238–240
Hot, Flat, and Crowded 2.0 (Friedman), 417
Human capital, 233
Human relations leaders, 263
Human resource management (HRM)
careers in, 233
compensation issues, 249–251
current issues, 247–252
defined, 232–233
employee retention, 244–245
major responsibilities, 233
performance management, 242–244, 249
recruitment practices, 238–239
role of government legislation, 234–236
selecting whom to hire, 240
strategic, 233
Human skills, 15–16
Humane orientation, as project GLOBE cultural dimension, 397
Hygiene factor, 312

I

Immoral managers, 69
Importing, 407

Impression management, 287–288
Improvement objectives, 144
Inclusivity, 385
The Incredibles (movie), 307
Incremental change, 220
Independent contractors, 248
India
and globalization, 19–20
Slumdog Millionaire, 3
Tata Group, 404, 412
Individual character, 55, 63, 65
Individualism view of ethical behavior, 58, 59
Individualism-collectivism, cultural value differences, 395
Informal groups, 335
Informal structures
defined, 182
pros and cons, 183
social network analysis, 182
Information competency, 87
Informational roles, managerial, 13
In-group collectivism, as project GLOBE cultural dimension, 397
Initial public offerings (IPOs), 440
Innovation
commercializing, 215–216
defined, 213
green, 214
organizational characteristics, 216–217
reverse, 215–216
types, 213–215
Input standards, 136
Insourcing, 405
Institutional collectivism, as project GLOBE cultural dimension, 397
Instrumental values, 57–58
Instrumentality, 318, 319
Integrity, 276, 277
Intellectual capital, 24
Intellectual property, 409–410
Interactional justice, 59
Interactive leadership, 275
Internal control, 142
International business. *See also* Global corporations
defined, 405
direct investments in foreign operations, 408
and economic development, 406
impact of globalization, 404–410
legal problems, 409–410
political complications, 409–410
reasons for going global, 406
Internet
impact of Web on human mind, 96
online privacy issues, 142, 376
small business on, 433–434
Web-based business models, 163
Interpersonal roles, managerial, 13
Intrapreneurs, 427
Intuitive feelers, 90
Intuitive thinking, 89, 90
Inventory analysis, 46
Inventory controls, 148–149
Iron Man 2 (movie), 231
ISO 14001 standard, 78

J

Japan
  earthquake and tsunami, 76, 91, 110, 149, 191
  and just-in-time scheduling, 148
  as power distance culture, 395
  professional women in workplace, 395–396
  proxemics in, 394
  and total quality management, 49
Jay-Z, 364
Job burnout, 294
Job design, 313
Job discrimination, 234–235
Job enrichment, 313
Job migration, 20
Job satisfaction. *See also* Quality of work life (QWL)
  defined, 298–299
  relationship to job performance, 300
  and work behavior, 299
Job seekers
  career development and planning, 244–245
  getting hired, 238–240
  handling telephone interviews, 239
  obtaining realistic job preview, 239–240
Job sharing, 200
Joint ventures, 408
Justice view of ethical behavior, 58, 59
Just-in-time scheduling (JIT), 148–149

K

Kawamata-cho, Japan, 110
Knowledge workers, 25, 87

L

Labor contracts, 252
Labor relations, 251–252
Labor unions, 251–252
Lack-of-participation error, 96–97
Laissez faire leaders, 263
Law of contingent reinforcement, 325
Law of effect, 323
Law of immediate reinforcement, 325
Leader-member exchange theory (LMX), 268–269
Leaders
  autocratic, 263
  and change, 219–225
  charismatic, 272
  effective, 262
  interactive, 275
  symbolic, 210–211
Leadership
  defined, 258
  Fiedler's contingency model, 265–266
  and gender, 274–275
  Hersey-Blanchard situational model, 267
  moral, 275–276
  as "must have" managerial skill, 17
  and path-goal theory, 267–268
  relationship to power, 259
  substitutes for, 268
  visionary, 262
Leadership styles, 262–263
Leading. *See also* Controlling; Organizing;
    Planning
  defined, 12
  as function in management process, 11, 12,
    258–259
  in global corporations, 416–417
Learning, lifelong, 16–17

Learning styles, 31, 43
Legitimate power, 259
Leverage, 149, 150
Licensing, 407
Lifelong learning, 16–17
Lilly Ledbetter Fair Pay Act, 236
Limited liability corporations (LLCs), 439
Limited liability partnerships (LLPs), 439
Limited partnerships, 439
Linear programming, 46
Liquidation, 161
Liquidity, 149, 150
LMX (leader-member exchange) theory, 268–269
Locus of control, 292, 428
Long-range plans, 118
Lose-lose conflicts, 352
Lost (TV series), 331
Love Happens (movie), 257
Low-context cultures, 393
Lower-order needs, 308, 309

M

Machiavellianism, 292
Maintenance activities, 345
Management
  behavioral, 38–43
  classical approaches, 32–36
  evidence-based, 50
  functions in process, 11–13, 112, 134–135, 180,
    258–259
  value-based, 210–211
Management by exception, 138
Management process, 11, 12–13, 112, 134–135,
    180, 258–259
Management science, 45–46
Managers
  accountability, 6
  background, 4–8
  as change leaders, 219–225
  characteristics of best, 8
  as coaches, 8
  common change strategies, 222–224
  defined, 4
  effective, 6–7
  essential skills, 15–16, 17
  first-line, 4–5
  functions in management process, 11–13, 112,
    134–135, 180, 258–259
  middle, 5
  moral, 69
  as problem solvers, 86–88
  role in ethical workplace, 57
  role of agenda setting, 14
  role of networking, 14
  sets of roles, 13
  skills survey, 199
  span of control, 181, 194, 195
  top, 5
  types, 4–6
  what they do, 10–17
Managing by objectives (MBO), 143–144, 321
Managing diversity, 389
Market control, 143
Masculinity-femininity, cultural value
    differences, 395–396
Mathematical forecasting, 46
Matrix structures, 188–189
Mechanistic designs, 198, 199

Membership composition, 340–341
Mentoring, 241–242
Merit pay, 249
Microcredit, 424
Middle managers, 5, 192
Millennials, 35, 242, 375
Minorities. *See also* Workforce diversity
  and diversity bias, 387–388
  as entrepreneurs, 428–429
Mission, 167
Mixed messages, 368
MNCs (multinational corporations). *See* Global
    corporations
Mompreneurs, 424
Monochronic cultures, 393
Mood contagion, 301
Moods, 301
Moral absolutism, 61
Moral leadership, 275–276
Moral managers, 69
Moral rights view of ethical behavior, 58, 60
Most favored nation status, 410
Motion study, 33
Motivation. *See also* Needs
  acquired needs, 310–311
  defined, 308
  equity theory, 316–318
  and ERG theory, 309–310
  expectancy theory, 318–320
  as foundation for emotional intelligence, 16
  needs hierarchy, 308–309
  two-factor theory, 312
Movies. *See also* Television shows
  The Blind Side, 55
  The Bourne Ultimatum, 423
  The Devil Wears Prada, 359
  Finding Forrester, 383
  Forrest Gump, 133
  The Incredibles, 307
  Iron Man 2, 231
  Love Happens, 257
  Mr. Holland's Opus, 31
  Patch Adams, 179
  Red Eye, 85
  Slumdog Millionaire, 3
  The Social Network, 283
  The Terminal, 205
  Tron: Legacy, 157
  27 Dresses, 111
Mr. Holland's Opus (movie), 31
Mt. Everest, 98
Multicultural organization, 385
Multinational corporations (MNCs). *See* Global
    corporations
Multiperson comparisons, 244
Myers-Briggs Type Indicator, 291–292

N

National cultures, Hofstede's five dimensions
  individualism collectivism, 395
  masculinity-femininity, 395–396
  power distance, 395
  time orientation, 396
  uncertainty avoidance, 395
National subcultures, 386
Nationalization, 410, 415
Natural capital, 77
Necessity-based entrepreneurship, 428–429

Needs
    achievement-based, 310
    acquired, 310
    affiliation-based, 310, 311
    defined, 41, 308
    existence-type, 309
    growth-type, 309
    hierarchy, 41–42, 308–309
    higher-order, 308, 309
    lower-order, 308, 309
    power-based, 310, 311
    relatedness-type, 309
Negative reinforcement, 324
Network models, 46
Network structures, 190–192
Networking, 14, 359, 363. *See also* Social
    networking
No-compete clauses, 36
Noise, 366
Nondisclosure agreements, 36
Nonmonetary budgets, 121
Nonprofit organizations, 4, 6
Nonprogrammed decisions, 88
Nontariff barriers, 410
Nonverbal communication, 368, 377
Norms, 344

O

Objectives. *See also* Managing by
        objectives (MBO)
    defined, 113
    improvement type, 144
    operating, 167, 168
    personal development type, 144
Observable culture, 208–209
Occupational subcultures, 386
Office romances, 121
Open systems, 46–47
Open-book management, 374
Openness, in communication, 374
Openness to experience, as Big Five personality
        trait, 290, 291
Operant conditioning, 323
Operating budgets, 121
Operating objectives, 167, 168
Operational plans, 119
Operations management, 46
Operations research, 45–46
Opportunities and threats. *See* SWOT analysis
Optimizing decision, 95
Organic designs, 198
Organization charts, 181
Organization structures
    defined, 181
    formal *vs.* informal, 182–183
    types, 185–192
Organizational citizenship behaviors, 299
Organizational culture, 206–211
Organizational design
    defined, 194
    trends, 194–200
Organizational subcultures, 385–387
Organizations
    benefits of teams, 332–333
    describing structure, 181–183
    design trends, 194–200
    formal teams in, 334–335
    informal groups in, 335

information flows in, 87–88
mechanistic *vs.* organic design, 198–199
as open systems, 46–47
and social responsibility, 73–79
stakeholders, 72
types of managers, 4–6
types of strategies, 159–160
types of structures, 185–192
Organizing. *See also* Controlling; Leading;
        Planning
    defined, 11, 180
    as function in management process,
        11–12, 180
    in global corporations, 416
Orientation, employee, 241
Outliers (Gladwell), 49
Output standards, 136
Outsourcing
    Chinese factories, 156, 162
    defined, 405
    role of China, 407, 414
    and social responsibility, 413
    strategic alliances for, 163
Overworked employees, 195

P

Participatory planning, 126–127
Partnerships, 439
Patch Adams (movie), 179
Patents. *See* Intellectual property
Path-goal theory, 267–268
Pay discrimination, 235, 236
Pearl Harbor, 351
Perceived negative inequity, 317
Perceived positive inequity, 317
Perception
    as cause of attribution errors, 287
    defined, 284
    distortions, 285–286
    selective, 285
Performance appraisal, 242–243, 249
Performance norms, 344
Performance objectives, writing, 144
Performance opportunities, 87
Performance orientation, as project GLOBE
        cultural dimension, 397
Performance threats, 87
Personal development objectives, 144
Personal power, 260–261
Personal wellness, 295
Personality
    Big Five traits, 290–291
    defined, 290
Personality testing, 295
Persuasive communication, 363–364
Pittsburgh Pirates mascot, 211
Person-job fit, 238
Person-organization fit, 238
Planned change
    common managerial strategies, 222–224
    resistance to, 224–225
    three phases, 220–221
    transformational *vs.* incremental,
        219–220
Planning. *See also* Controlling; Leading;
        Organizing
    alternative future conditions, 124–125
    benefits, 113, 114–116

for contingencies, 124
defined, 11, 112
as function in management process,
    11, 112
in global corporations, 414–415
participatory, 126–127
steps in process, 113
tools and techniques, 123–127
Plans
    budgets as, 121
    defined, 113
    organizational policies and procedures,
        119–120
    short-range *vs.* long-range, 118
    for small businesses, 438
    strategic *vs.* operational, 118–119
    types, 118–121
Policies, 119
Political risk, 415
Political-risk analysis, 415
Polychronic cultures, 393
Portfolio planning, 171
Positive reinforcement, 324, 325
Power
    defined, 259
    as need, 310, 311
    personal *vs.* social, 311
Power (Pfeffer), 260
Power distance, 395, 397
Pregnancy discrimination, 235, 236
Prejudice, 23
Presentation skills, 366, 367
Presidents, as top managers, 5
Privacy, 142, 236, 376
Problem solving, 86–87. *See also* Collaboration
Procedural justice, 59
Procedures, 120
Process innovation, 213
Product innovation, 213
Product structures, 187–188
Professionalism, 17, 231
Profit sharing, 250
Profitability, 149, 150
Programmed decisions, 88
Progression principle, 308
Progressive principle, 41
Project GLOBE, 397
Project management, 147–148
Project teams, 335
Projection, 286
Projects, 147
Protectionism, 410, 413
Proxemics, 373, 393–394
3 Ps of organizational performance, 73
Punishment, 324, 325–326
Pyramid, upside-down, 8

Q

Quality circles, 336
Quality control, 146–147
Quality of work life (QWL), 7
Quantitative analysis, 45–46
Question marks, in BCG Matrix, 171
Queuing theory, 46

R

Rational persuasion strategy, 223–224
Realistic job previews, 239–240

Recruitment, employee, 238–239
Red Eye (movie), 85
Referent power, 261
Refreezing, 221
Reinforcement theory, 323–326
Relatedness needs, 309
Reliability, in employment test results, 240
Representativeness heuristic, 103
Resiliency, 133, 138
Restricted communication networks, 346
Restructuring, 161
Retrenchment strategy, 161
Reverse innovation, 215–216
Reverse mentoring, 242
Reward power, 259
Risk environments, 91
Risk taking, 423, 425, 427

S

Saas (software as a service) business
   model, 164
Satisficing decisions, 96
Satisfier factor, 312
Saudi Arabia, 392
Scalar chain principle, 36
Scenario planning, 124–125
Scientific management, 32–33
Scientific method, 50
Selection, employee, 240
Selective perception, 285
Self-awareness, as foundation for emotional
   intelligence, 16
Self-confidence, 85, 101, 428
Self-control, 142
Self-efficacy, 319
Self-fulfilling prophecies, 42
Self-management, 3, 17, 25
Self-managing teams, 337–338
Self-monitoring, 292–293
Self-regulation, as foundation for emotional
   intelligence, 16
Self-reliance, 428
Self-serving bias, 287
Sensation feelers, 90
Sensation thinkers, 90
Servant leadership, 277
Sexual harassment, 62
The Shallows (Carr), 96
Shamrock organizations, 23–24
Shaping, 325
Shared power strategy, 224
Short-range plans, 118
Silos (or chimneys) problem, 186
Six sigma, 147
Skills
   continually developing, 241–242
   technical *vs.* human, 15–16
   writing and communication, 17, 360, 366
Skunkworks, 216
Slumdog Millionaire (movie), 3
Small businesses
   business plans for, 438
   defined, 433
   economic advantages, 433–434
   failure, 436–437
   family-owned, 435–436
   forms of ownership, 439
   Internet-based, 433–434

   life-cycle stages, 434–435
   start-up assistance, 437–438
   statistics, 433
   ways of financing, 440
Smartphones, 10, 282
Smoothing. *See* Accommodation
Social businesses, 79
Social capital, 14, 360
Social entrepreneurs, 79, 430
Social entrepreneurship, 214–215
Social innovation, 214–215
Social loafing, 333, 334
Social media strategies, 164
The Social Network (movie), 283
Social network analysis, 182
Social networking, 305, 375
Social responsibility. *See* Corporate social
   responsibility
Social responsibility audits, 75–76
Social skills, as foundation for emotional
   intelligence, 16
Socialization, 207–208, 241
Socioeconomic view of corporate social
   responsibility, 74
Sole proprietorships, 439
Span of control, 181, 194, 195
Spirituality, workplace, 211
Spotlight questions, 67, 98
Stakeholders, 72
Stereotypes, 285
Stock options, 250
Strategic alliances, 163, 408
Strategic control, 174
Strategic human resource management, 233
Strategic intent, 158
Strategic leadership, 172–173
Strategic management, 166–167
Strategic plans, 118–119
Strategies
   business, 159–160
   for consolidation, 161
   cooperative, 163
   corporate, 159
   defined, 158–159
   e-business, 163–164
   formulating, 166–168
   functional, 160
   global, 162
   for growth, 160
   implementing, 166–172
   Porter's five forces model, 168–169
   types, 158–164
Strategy formulation, 166–168
Strategy implementation, 168
Strengths and weaknesses. *See* SWOT
   analysis
Stress
   constructive *vs.* destructive, 294
   defined, 293–294
   managing, 295
Stretch goals, 127
Strong cultures, 207
Subcultures, organizational, 385–387
Subscription Web sites, 163
Subsidiaries, foreign, 408
Substantive conflict, 352
Substitutes for leadership, 268
Subsystems, 47

Succession plans, family-owned businesses, 436
Succession problems, family-owned
   businesses, 436
Supervisors. *See* First-line managers
Supplier alliances, 163
Supply chain
   green example, 75
   strategic alliances, 163
Sustainability
   cradle-to-grave manufacturing example, 75
   defined, 77
   as social responsibility goal, 76–79
   UN role, 76, 77
Sustainable businesses, 77
Sustainable competitive advantage, 159
Sustainable development, 77
Sustainable innovation, 214
Sweatshops, 414
SWOT analysis, 167–168
Symbolic leaders, 210–211
Synergy, 332
Systematic thinking, 89

T

Tactical plans, 119
Tariffs, 410
Task activities, 345
Task forces, 335
Team building, 348–349
Team contributions, 331, 343
Team leaders. *See* First-line managers
Team process, 342
Team structures, 189–190
Teams and teamwork
   background, 332–337
   benefits to organizations, 332–333
   building blocks, 339–353
   cohesiveness, 344
   communication networks, 346
   decision-making methods, 349–350
   defined, 332
   effective, 339–340
   impact of social loafing on performance, 333
   Lost as example, 331
   membership composition, 340–341
   as "must have" managerial skill, 17
   stages of development, 342–343
   task and maintenance roles, 345
Technical skills, 15
Telecommuting, 200
Television shows. *See also* Movies
   The Amazing Race, 403
   Cake Boss, 422
   Lost, 331
The Terminal (movie), 205
Terminal values, 57–58
Terrorism, 415
Text messages, 358, 375
The Amazing Race (TV series), 403
Thematic Apperception Test (TAT), 310
Theory X, 38, 42
Theory Y, 38, 42, 142
Threats. *See* SWOT analysis
360-degree feedback, 243–244
Time management, 111, 115–116
Time orientation, cultural value
   differences, 396
Tolerance for ambiguity, 205, 225, 428

Top managers, 5
Total quality management (TQM), 49, 146
TQM. *See* Total quality management (TQM)
Trade barriers, 410
Trademarks. *See* Intellectual property
Training,
   on ethics, 67
   workforce, 241–242
Transactional leadership, 272
Transformational change, 219–220
Transformational leadership, 272–273
Transnational corporations, 412
Transnational firms, 162
Transparency, in communication, 374
Triple bottom line, 73
Tron: Legacy (movie), 157
T-shirts, 404–405
Turnover, 299
27 Dresses (movie), 111
Two-tier wage systems, 252
Type A personality, 293–294

U

Uncertain environments, 91
Uncertainty, 205
Uncertainty avoidance, 395, 397
Underground bosses, 375
Unfreezing, 220–221
Unit managers. *See* First-line managers
Unity of command principle, 36
Universal Declaration of Human Rights, United
   Nations, 60
Upside-down pyramid, 8
US Airways Flight 1549, 89–90
Utilitarian view of ethical behavior, 58–59

V

Valence, 318, 319
Validity, in employment test results, 240
Value-based management, 210–211
Values, 57–58, 209–210
Venture capital, 429
Venture capitalists, 440
Vertical integration, 160
Vice presidents, as top managers, 5
Virtual organizations, 191–192
Virtual teams, 336–337
Virtuous circle, 74
Vision, 118, 261
Visionary leadership, 262
Vroom-Jago model, 269–270

W

Weaknesses. *See* SWOT analysis
Web-based business models, 163
Wellness, personal, 295
Whistleblowers, 68
Win-lose conflicts, 352–353
Win-win conflicts, 353
Withdrawal behaviors, 299. *See also*
   Avoidance
Women. *See also* Workforce diversity
   as board members, 321
   and diversity bias, 387–388
   as entrepreneurs, 424, 428–429
   and leadership, 274–275
   leadership statistics, 286
   as mompreneurs, 424
   multicultural, 7
   Working Mother magazine, 7
Women Count (Butler), 286

Work sampling, 240
Workforce
   alternative work schedules, 199–200
   career development and planning, 244–245
   compensation issues, 249–251
   employee morale worldwide, 392
   hiring, 238–240
   job satisfaction, 298–299
   Mommy drain, 200
   overworking, 195
   retention, 244–245
   survey of leaders and top managers, 275
   training, 241–242
   work-life issues, 209, 247–248
Workforce diversity, 22–23, 384–389
Working Mother magazine, 7, 200
Work-life balance, 209, 247–248
Workplace
   China's outsourcing factories, 156, 162
   Chinese factories, 414
   diversity in, 22–23, 384–389
   ethics and ethical behavior in, 56–63
   impact of globalization, 19–20
   impact of job migration, 19–20
   in information age, 25, 376
   in shamrock organizations, 23–25
Workplace privacy, 236
Workplace rage, 294
Workplace spirituality, 211
Writing skills, 366

Z

Zero-based budgets, 121
Zone of indifference, 276

Organization Index

A

Abbott Labs, 247
Abercrombie & Fitch, 206
Activision, C-12, C-13
adidas, C-17
Aldi Group, C-3
Allstate, 7, 136
Amazon.com, 89, 109, 163, 206, 209, 213, 217, 341,
   C-8–C-9, C-20, C-21
American Express, 7, 126
American Machine and Foundry Co.
   (AMF), C-34
Amnesty International, 151
Anheuser-Busch, 404
Anthropologie, 206
AOL, 373
Apple Inc., 159, 160, 162, 163, 209, 213, 216,
   229, 414, C-8, C-9, C-13, C-17, C-18–C-19,
   C-20, C-21
Applebee's, 250
Armour, 209
AutoNation, 425
Avon, 23

B

Bailard Inc., 374
Barnes and Noble, C-9
Baskin-Robbins, C-15
Bath & Body Works, 409
Bellisio Foods, 76
Ben & Jerry's, 404, 431
Blockbuster Video, 425, C-21
BMW, 163, 412
Bob Evans Farms, 320
Body Shop, 425, 429
Boeing, 121, 149, 196, 404
Border Green Energy Team (BGET), 214
Boston Consulting Group, 171, 295
BP, 76, 124, 412
Brickhouse, 216
Bristol Myers, 162
British Airways, 219, 287
Build-A-Bear Workshop, 182
Burger King, C-36

C

C. O. Bigelow, 409
Cadbury, 274
Careerbuilder.com, 239
Catalyst, 22, 384, 385
Caterpillar, 412
Center for Creative Leadership, 371
Chemical Bank, 67
Chick-fil-A, 141
Chrysler, 123, 161, 187
Cisco Systems, 241–242, 376, 405
Civco Medical Instruments, 150
Cleaning for a Reason, 430
Cleveland Orchestra, 135
Coca-Cola, 21, 158, 160, 170
Cognos, C-23

Coinstar, C-21
Colgate Palmolive, 21, 162
Cornerstone Research, 7–8
Count-Me-In, 424
Cummins Engine Company, 134
Cypress Semiconductor Corp., 127

D

Daimler, 163
Danone. See Grameen Danone
DataDyne, 431
Dell, 149, 162
Deloitte, 7
Delta Air, 191
Desso, 75
Development Dimensions International, 199
Devine Foods, 424
Dial Corporation, 21
Disney, 208, 211, 241, C-28, C-29
Domino's Pizza, 375
Dow Corning, 7
DreamWorks, C-28, C-29
Dunkin' Donuts, 177, C-14–C-15

E

Eastman Kodak, 389
eBay, 161, 163, 213
EDS, 163
eHarmony.com, 163
Electronic Arts, 155, C-12–C-13
Epinions, 163
Equal Employment Opportunity Commission
   (EEOC), 236, 387
Ernst & Young, 7, 11–12, 13
European Union, 409
Exxon/Mobil, 160, 413

F

Facebook, 119, 142, 163, 164, 211, 213, 233, 236,
   283, 288, 305, 336, 376, C-13, C-24–C-25
Fair Indigo, 394
Fedex, 209
Fiat, 123, 187
Flickr, 426
Ford Motor Co., 126, 196, 223–224, 300, 386,
   405, C-33
Foxconn Technology Group, 156, 162
Frederick Douglass Academy, 261, 277

G

Gap Inc., 69–70, C-4
Gazprom, 412
General Electric, 127, 136, 159, 171, 220, 222–223
General Mills, 7
General Motors, 93, 94–95, 123, 161, 187–188
   C-32, C-33
Gillette, 162
Girl Scouts, 206
Goodyear, 236, 252
Google, 151, 163, 209, 213, 216, 217, 233, 240
Grameen Danone, 78

Green Mountain Coffee Roasters, 406
GreenBox, 424
Groupon, 192, 207, 213

H

Häagen-Dazs, 412
Haier, 393
Hallmark, C-29
Harley-Davidson, 421, C-34–C-35
Harris Interactive, 275, 276
HCL Industries, 373–374
Henri Bendel, 409
Herman Miller, 25, 277
Hewlett-Packard, 19, 162, 209, 412
Hitachi, 412
H&M, C-5
Hollister, 206
Home Depot, 233
Honda, 404
HopeLab, 311
HP. See Hewlett-Packard
Human Rights Campaign, 389
Hunch.com, 426
Husk Power Systems, 431

I

IBM, 7, 135, 158, 159, 163, 412, C-18
IDEO, 216, 232
IKEA, 213, 405
InBev, 404
Inditex, C-4–C-5
Infosys, 163
In-N-Out Burger, 430, 443, C-36–C-37
Intel, 162, 409
International Labour Organization, 402
International Standards Organization, 78
International Trade Commission, C-34–C-35
ITunes Store, 163
Izod, 160

J

Jaguar, 404
Johnson & Johnson, 217

K

Kenexa, 35
KFC, 377
KPMG, 248
Kraft Foods, 374

L

La Sanza, 409
Land Rover, 404
Life Is Good Company, 39
The Limited, 362, 409
LinkedIn, 238, C-25
LiveOps, 249
L.L. Bean, 126
Long John Silver's, 320
Lufthansa, 163

M

Macy's, C-10, C-11
Mad Gab's Inc., 68–69
Mail Boxes Etc., 427
Marriott, 336
Mars Inc., 186
Massmart, 389
Mazda Corporation, 366
McDonald's, 120, 140, 141, 160, 162, 412, 415,
     430, C-14, C-36
Medtronic, 4
Mercedes-Benz, 404
Merck, 209
Miami Dolphins, 425
Microsoft, 151, 198–199, 216, 248, 414, C-19, C-29
Minority Business Development
     Agency, 429
Monster.com, 238
Mozilla, 209

N

NASCAR, 349
National Foundation for Women Business
     Owners (NFWBO), 429
NBA (National Basketball Association),
     332–333
Nestlé, 412
Netflix, 163, 207, 213, 255, C-20–C-21
New Profit Inc., 79
NFL Properties Inc., 274
Nike, 203, 213, 404, 406, C-16–C-17
Nintendo, C-12
Nissan, 404, 412
Nokia, 413
Nordstrom, 131, C-10–C-11

O

Obvious Corporation, C-30
Odeo, C-30
Ogilvy Public Relations, 360
One Acre Fund, 215
Oracle, C-23, C-29

P

Palmolive, 431
Panera Bread, 329, C-26–C-27
Patagonia Inc., 83, 172, 214, C-6–C-7
Pear Analytics, C-30
Peet's Coffee & Tea, 406
PepsiCo, 21, 97, 159, 160, 170, 377
Petrobas, 412
PetroChina, 412
Pixar, 357, C-19, C-28–C-29

PixArts, 427
Polaroid Corporation, 189
Polo Ralph Lauren, 169
PriceGrabber, 163
Priceline, 163
Procter & Gamble, 5, 12, 162, 164, 241, 245, 412

R

Redbox, C-21
RetiredBrains.com, 424
Rockport Company, 219
Rocky Brands, 20, 36
Royal Dutch/Shell, 124–125

S

Saks, C-10, C-11
Salesforce.com, 164, 213
Samsung, 412
Sandleman & Associates, C-27
SAP, C-23
SAS Institute, 248, 281, C-22–C-23
Schwab Corporation, 247
7-Eleven, 126
Shell. *See* Royal Dutch/Shell
Shopzilla, 163
Sierra Nevada Brewing Company, 214
SiteQuest Technologies, C-23
Skype, 151, 336
Small Business Development Centers, 438
Society for Human Resource Management, 244,
     247, 295, 389
Sony, 405, 412
Southwest Airlines, 213, 276
Spanx, 293
Sprinkles, C-37
S&S Sports Cards, 434
Star Alliance, 163
Starbucks, 406, C-14, C-15, C-27
State Farm, 16
Stonyfield Farm, 73
Sungard, C-23

T

Tata Group, 404, 412
TerraCycle, 223
Tetley Tea, 404
Third Sun Solar Wind and Power, Ltd., 434
Threadless.com, 164
3M Corporation, 188, 215, 216
TIAA-CREF, 159
Tiny Speck (gaming studio), 426
Tom's of Maine, 210, 336, 431
TOMS Shoes, 431, C-27

Total (French oil and gas producer), 412
Toyota, 105, 132, 134, 401, 404, 412, C-32–C-33
Trader Joe's, 29, C-2–C-3
Transparency International, 415
Tropicana, 160
Twitter, 164, 211, 213, 288, 375, 381, C-30–C-31

U

Unilever, 77, 162, 404, 431
United Airlines, 163
United Nations, 60, 76, 413
United Way, 309–310
UPS (United Parcel Service), 138, 188
U.S. Army, 135
U.S. Cellular, 238
U.S. Equal Employment Opportunity
     Commission (EEOC), 236, 387

V

Verizon, C-19
Victoria's Secret, 409
Virgin Group, 287, 288, 325
VisionIT Inc., 386
Vodafone, 214

W

Walmart, 103, 143, 160, 164, 169–170, 223, 364,
     389, 412, C-3, C-6, C-15, C-16, C-21
Wendy's, 426
Western Electric Company, 40
White Barn Candle Co., 409
Whole Foods, 70, 209
Wieden & Kennedy, C-16
Wii, C-12, C-13
Wolters Kluwer, 376
Women for Hire Inc., 375
World Trade Organization (WTO), 410

X

Xerox, 12, 126, 248, 385

Y

Yahoo!, 48, 151, 163, 178, 186, 216, 426, C-24
Yammer, C-31
Yelp, 163
YouTube, 375
Yum! Brands, 320, 325

Z

Zappos, 2, 24, 206, 207, 209, 238, C-9, C-11
Zara International, 53, 126, C-4–C-5
Zynga, 119, 209, C-13

{ SPECIAL CHAPTER FEATURES

MANAGER'S LIBRARY

Delivering Happiness by Tony Hsieh
The Outliers by Malcolm Gladwell
Creating a World Without Poverty
   by Muhammad Yunus
The Shallows by Nicholas Carr
Analytics at Work by
   Thomas Davenport, et al.
The Facebook Effect by David Kirkpatrick
Behind the Cloud by Marc Benioff and
   Carlye Adler
The Truth About Middle Managers by
   Paul Osterman

Change by Design by Tim Brown
The Trophy Kids Grow Up by Ron Alsop
Power by Jeffrey Pfeffer
Women Count by Susan Bukeley Butler
Drive by Daniel Pink
Crowdsourcing by Jeff Howe
Collaboration by Morten Hansen
Half the Sky by Nicolas Kristof and
   Sheryl WuDunn
Hot, Flat and Crowded 2.0 by
   Thomas Friedman
In-N-Out Burger by Stacy Perman

ETHICS CHECK

Coke's secret formula a tempting target
Employment agreements can be tricky
Committing to a green supply chain
Left to die on Mt. Everest
E-waste graveyards as easy way out
Privacy and censorship worries
Life and death at an outsourcing factory
Flattened into exhaustion
Facebook follies

Help wanted: saleswomen
When the boss asks too much
Personality test required
Information goldmine is equity dilemma
Social loafing is closer than you think
In France, bloggers beware
Fair trade fashion
Nationalism and protectionism
Entrepreneurship and philanthropy

ROLE MODELS

Ursula Burns—Xerox
Carol Bartz—Yahoo!
Gary Hirshberg—Stonyfield Farms
Indra Nooyi—Pepsi
Don Thompson—McDonald's
Patricia Karter—Dancing Deer Baking
Roger W. Ferguson Jr.—TIAA/CREF
Alan Mulally—Ford
Tom Szaky—TerraCycle

Jim Goodnight—SAS
Lorraine Monroe—Leadership Academy
Richard Branson—Virgin Group
Charlie Butcher—Butcher Company
Jeff Bezos—Amazon
Linda Heasley—The Limited
David Segura—VisionIt
Les Wexner—Limited Brands
Michelle Greenfield—Third Sun

FACTS TO CONSIDER

Employment contradictions in workforce
   diversity
Generations differ when rating their bosses
Behavior of managers key to ethical
   workplace
Greenhouse gas emissions as executive
   priorities
Policies on office romances vary widely
Beware of corporate thieves
CEO pay is heading high again
Bosses overestimate their management skills
Organization cultures face up to work-life
   trends

HRM executives worry about performance
   measurement
Workers report shortcomings of leaders
Trends show job satisfaction drifting lower
Unproductive meetings are major time
   wasters
Europe turning to quotas to increase
   female board members
Employees should worry about electronic
   monitoring
Employee morale varies around the world
Corruption and bribes haunt global business
Minority entrepreneurs are on the move

{ ACTIVE LEARNING RESOURCES

CASES FOR CRITICAL THINKING

- 1 Trader Joe's
- 2 Zara International
- 3 Patagonia
- 4 Amazon/Barnes & Noble
- 5 Nordstrom/Zappos
- 6 Electronic Arts/Zynga
- 7 Dunkin' Donuts
- 8 Nike
- 9 Apple
- 10 Netflix/Redbox
- 11 SAS/Sungard
- 12 Facebook/LinkedIn
- 13 Panera/TOMS
- 14 Pixar/DreamWorks
- 15 Twitter/Yammer
- 16 Toyota/Ford
- 17 Harley Davidson
- 18 In-N-Out Burger/Sprinkles

SELF-ASSESSMENTS

Personal Career Readiness
Managerial Assumptions
Terminal Values Survey
Intuitive Ability
Time Management Profile
Internal/External Control
Handling Facts and Inferences
Empowering Others
Tolerance for Ambiguity

Performance Appraisal Assumptions
Least Preferred Co-Worker Scale
Feedback and Assertiveness
Stress Test
Two-Factor Profile
Team Leader Skills
Diversity Awareness
Global Intelligence
Entrepreneurship Orientation

CLASS EXERCISES

My Best Manager
Evidence-Based Management Quiz
Confronting Ethical Dilemmas
Lost at Sea
The Future Workplace
Stakeholder Maps
Strategic Scenarios
Organizational Metaphors
Force-Field Analysis
Upward Appraisal

Leading by Participation
Job Satisfaction Preferences
Why We Work
Understanding Team Dynamics
Communication and Teamwork
    Dilemmas
Alligator River Story
American Football
Entrepreneurs Among Us

TEAM PROJECTS

Managing Millennials
Management in Popular Culture
Organizational Commitment to
    Sustainability
Crisis Management Realities
Personal Career Planning
After Meeting/Project Review
Contrasting Strategies
Network "U"

Organizational Culture Walk
The Future of Labor Unions
Difficult Personalities
CEO Pay
Superstars on the Team
How Words Count
Job Satisfaction Around the World
Globalization Pros and Cons
Community Entrepreneurs

{ BRIEF CONTENTS

Chapter 1   Managers and the Management Process

Chapter 2   Management Learning

Chapter 3   Ethics and Social Responsibility

Chapter 4   Managers as Decision Makers

Chapter 5   Plans and Planning Techniques

Chapter 6   Controls and Control Systems

Chapter 7   Strategy and Strategic Management

Chapter 8   Organization Structure and Design

Chapter 9   Organizational Cultures, Innovation, and Change

Chapter 10   Human Resource Management

Chapter 11   Leadership

Chapter 12   Individual Behavior

Chapter 13   Motivation

Chapter 14   Teams and Teamwork

Chapter 15   Communication

Chapter 16   Diversity and Global Cultures

Chapter 17   Globalization and International Business

Chapter 18   Entrepreneurship and Small Business

Managers and Management

Planning and Controlling

Organizing

Leading

Environment